W9-BND-617

EGYPT

Burdens of the Past / Options for the Future

JOHN WATERBURY

EGYPT

EGYPT

Burdens of the Past,
Options for the Future

JOHN WATERBURY

Published in Association with the
American Universities Field Staff
Indiana University Press   Bloomington & London

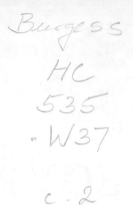

Manufactured in the United States of America

Library of Congress Cataloging in Publication Data

Waterbury, John.
Egypt.

1. Egypt—Economic conditions—1952-
—Addresses, essays, lectures.
2. Egypt—Politics and government—1970-
—Addresses, essays, lectures. I. Title.
HC535.W37 330.9′62′05 78-3248
ISBN 0-253-31943-9
ISBN 0-253-28092-3 pbk.   2 3 4 5 82 81 80 79

CONTENTS

INTRODUCTION

Any period in the life of a Third World country is crucial for its development prospects, but some periods are more crucial than others. As Egypt enters the last quarter of the twentieth century, it is burdened with the cumulative weight of all the decisions that have been made in previous years, the roads not taken as well as those that were. Its present range of options—for growth strategies, internal politics, and regional influence—has narrowed over the years, representing polar alternatives less and less susceptible to compromise or reconciliation. Yet choices cannot be avoided much longer without risk of aggravating a whole range of problems that are already attaining crisis proportions. Seizing issues by the horns has become imperative; the manner in which this is done within the next five years will determine Egypt's fate for at least a generation.

Politics, in its essence, consists of choice, not always willed and as often as not avoided. Developing polities and their policy-makers in particular are unceasingly called upon to make choices committing meager resources to policies that may do no more than maintain low standards of living and at best hold out the prospect of prosperity for generations yet unborn. These are not marginal issues; there are none of the options available to developed nations which may choose either to reinforce prosperity and high standards of living or to mitigate the effects of recession. Frequently policy-makers in developing countries do not control the basic elements that govern the decision-making process and hence the charting of their own development strategies. They are at the mercy of international commodity pricing, external markets for agricultural produce and raw materials, sources of technology and expertise, suppliers of heavy capital goods, and the providers of foreign exchange, investment, and development assistance. Each of these factors furnishes interests and forces outside the developing nation a means to impinge, sometimes decisively, upon its decision-making process.

For most well-informed readers the image of Egypt is associated first with conflict with Israel, then with crusades for Arab unity and clashes with the West over issues of imperialism and Great Power alignment. Many Egyptians at the highest government levels also share the sense that these are the priority issues. Yet these are, in fact, the surface manifestations of far more profound crises in the country's approach to development. It has always been the gift of politicians in all countries to redefine issues in such a way that the real choices and options are obscured. There is nothing so distasteful to a politician as making choices, especially when the adoption of option A cannot be reconciled with option B. In Egypt, choices about growth strategies and derivative policies have increasingly become mutually exclusive. These are the fundamental political options in the Lasswellian sense of who gets what, when, and how. Because Egypt is a poor country, this means not the sharing of abundance but the distribution of the burdens of poverty and sacrifice. In some ways coping with the Israelis is easier than coping with these issues, and the one tends to become a surrogate for the other. The point is, however, that the trees of the Arab-Israeli conflict must not be allowed to obscure the forest of Egypt's fundamental Third Worldliness, and it is upon this that I have attempted to focus in the Reports in this collection.

What then are Egypt's basic options? Threaded through these 16 essays are seven inter-related policy themes, decisions (or their absence) about which have ramifications in all other domains:

Guns and/or Butter
Coping with Population Growth and Fertility Control
Agricultural versus Industrial Development
Socialism or State Capitalism versus Private Enterprise
Authoritarianism versus Controlled Liberalism
Arabism versus Egypt-Firstism
Positive Neutrality versus Alignment with the West

The first, because it is the most salient and the most familiar, is that of war and peace, or, in more economic terms, guns and butter. Military preparedness, heavy defense outlays, and outright combat are impediments to growth in poor economies. Egypt has no military-industrial complex that could profit from the Arab-Israeli dispute, although it does have a large professional military constituency which is understandably reluctant to face the Israelis on less than an equal footing. It has been the practice since 1952, under both Presidents Nasser and Sadat, to strive simultaneously for economic growth and military credibility. The quest for guns *and* butter has placed well-nigh intolerable strains upon the Egyptian economy, and President Sadat has demonstrated his will to seek a settlement, if not formal peace, with Israel. But this option is complicated by the fact that a settlement will depend upon a general Arab consensus as to its desirability. Certain of the wealthy Arab states may be in no rush for a settlement and, as providers of foreign exchange for Egypt's investment programs and military acquisitions, they are in a position to perpetuate the notion that it is feasible to reconcile the imperatives of growth with those of military preparedness. Some of the elements of this fundamental choice were highlighted during the period of no-war, no-peace in 1971-72 and the October War of 1973, and they are explored in Part I of this collection.

Leaving aside external pressures and forces, the parameters of national decision-making and decision-avoidance are set within the context of available resources, and these are in short supply, save in the all-important realm of population. Egypt is population-rich which is simply a euphemistic way of saying that its human resources have outstripped its natural and financial resources. Agricultural land is scarce, and the land base can be expanded only at great cost. Existing acreage is intensively farmed and per unit yields cannot be expected to increase dramatically. A set of choices derives from this situation, bearing upon direct intervention to lower fertility, and policies to educate, train, and redeploy existing Egyptians. Coping with an outsized population is the central theme of the first two Reports in Part II.

It has been a given of Egyptian growth strategy since 1952 that the only solution to overpopulation is education and industrialization. Egypt opted for mass education and heavy industrialization without, however, abandoning the rural world to its fate, and it has been in the domain of the trade-off between industrial and agricultural growth that the basic question of opportunity costs has been most starkly posed. Not only is Egypt a food-deficit country, but it has relatively little industrial experience and hardly any foreign buyers of its manufactured goods. With the pressing needs for foreign exchange to import food, raw materials, and capital goods, what is the optimal mix in investment outlays in agriculture and industry? The options involved under this rubric are presented in the third and fourth essays in Part II and throughout Part III. A concomitant phenomenon of incalculable significance is that of rapid urbanization, a reflection of dwindling per capita land resources. It is a process that has not been accompanied by a proportionate increase in industrial work opportunities. The results of these imbalances in employment and population distribution have been most graphically manifested in the Cairo megalopolis which gives us, I believe, some glimpse of the Egypt of the future. The most urgent problems in containing the Cairo "primate," as well as the policy responses to them, are delineated in the last four Reports of Part II.

It was a premise of Egypt's growth strategy in the late 1950s and throughout the 1960s that the state must undertake far more than infrastructural investment and the mobilization of development capital and, through public enterprises, nationalized banks, and state-controlled foreign trade, must dominate and lead the entire economy. With this self-proclaimed socialist philosophy, undergirded in a practical sense by increasingly strong military, aid, and trade links with the U.S.S.R. and Eastern Europe, the more conventional economic wisdom of Western banking and business institutions was rejected. Welfare social-ism without class conflict, without anyone but the very rich compelled to crimp their style of life, became the goal. It proved unattainable because of the burden of military expenditures and the inefficiencies in the approach itself. Since 1965 the Egyptian regime has had to wrestle with increasingly dichotomized options—socialist intensification (i.e., more revolu-tion) or a capitalist revival relying upon foreign exchange support and technology from the West. Sadat has reluctantly grasped the nettle and moved in the latter direction. His and Egypt's journey "westward" is treated throughout Part III.

A reorientation in growth strategy of this nature entails a rethinking of the domestic con-stituencies to whom the regime will appeal and upon whom it will rely. The socialist phase, at least rhetorically, was launched in the name of the peasants and workers while the growing middle classes were contained in their material aspirations. The new economic look since 1971 has been implicitly pitched to cater to the interests of the middle classes. The result has been not only economic liberalization to provide greater scope for the entrepreneur, but also political liberalization to provide a forum for middle-class liberals. On both counts an in-creasingly direct assault has been mounted on Nasser's political and economic formulas. The question is whether or not limited and orchestrated democracy can be made compatible with poverty and the likely accentuation of skewed income distribution within the country.

A developing country cannot, with rare exceptions, remake its internal economic and polit-ical policies without concomitant shifts in alignments with its neighbors and the Great Powers. Indeed, in the case of Egypt, conservative neighbors among the Arab oil-exporting states, frequently speaking in the name of long-term Western, not to say United States' goals, have persistently urged Egyptian policy-makers to move in the new directions mentioned above. One result has been a redefinition of Egypt's place in Arab affairs (an abandonment of militant Arabism), but a tentative reaffirmation of Egypt's need to be Arab. Yet a spin-off of internal liberalization and de-Nasserization has been the re-emergence of strong sentiments of Egypt-firstism. How can these be balanced against Egypt's needs for foreign exchange support, food supply, outlets for surplus labor, and regional markets? Decisions along this dimension have been avoided with rare but understandable obstinacy. Egypt would like to have it both ways.

The adumbration of new approaches to growth has had far-reaching consequences for Egypt's relations with the Great Powers. The considerable erosion of Nasserist socialism has placed in jeopardy ongoing programs of military and economic assistance from socialist countries, especially the U.S.S.R., leaving Egypt with the as yet unfulfilled hope and promise of Western arms, aid, investment, and markets. The immediate consequence of this shift has been and remains a dangerous interregnum generally referred to as changing horses in mid stream. This may be impossible, for the internal will to do so, as well as any long-term Western commitment, may be lacking.

What one must draw from all the above is the notion of a policy package the contents of which are inseparable. To devise strategy with respect to one facet of this package, let us say in the sphere of industrial development, sooner or later entails adjustments and revisions in all others. Egypt, as a prototypical Third World state, demonstrates not only the interrelatedness of all aspects of development strategy, but, equally significantly, the exposure and vulnerability of developing economies to a broad array of external forces and interests. Ultimately the basic option governing the fate of Egypt will be taken or rejected in Cairo, but to no small extent they will have been predetermined by countries and institutions willing to invest in Egypt's growth for a variety of political and economic reasons. Egyptian leaders cannot openly admit to this far-reaching dependency, and external interests are not always aware of the nature and extent of their influence nor the full consequences of their acts. This is a serious, potentially tragic situation for the stakes, in terms of Egypt's viability as a nation and an economy, are very high.

Part I: The Domestic and Regional Setting

Of all the options taken in Egypt in recent years, none was so dramatic as that to launch a frontal assault on Israeli positions across the Suez Canal. The October War of 1973 (commonly referred to by the Israelis as the Yom Kippur War and by the Arabs as the Ramadan War) symbolically and practically shattered a stalemate in diplomacy and internal policy that had plagued Egypt since 1967. The crossing of the Suez Canal was a necessary although not sufficient condition for moving ahead on issues of economic liberalization, foreign investment, and political reform. It established Sadat as a national hero, and having acquired his own image and stature, independent of his association with Gamal Abdul Nasser, he could afford to advocate and implement new policy initiatives. Of equal importance was the fact that the October War restored the Egyptian army to the role of a conventional military force rather than the collection of officer-led cliques that had involved themselves so intimately in domestic politics under Nasser. With a satisfactory military performance under their belts, the armed forces could finally (although assuredly not definitively) return to their barracks for the first time since 1952. Egypt under Sadat is no more a military regime than France under de Gaulle or Israel under Rabin.

Whatever the real extent of Egyptian military success in 1973, it was proclaimed in Cairo as quasi-total, and on the strength of that claim it then became politically feasible to move on to questions of a settlement with Israel and a *rapprochement* with the United States. Since his accession to the presidency, Sadat has time and again demonstrated his overwhelming preoccupation with moving toward a *modus vivendi* with Israel. In his view, only the United States, because it has consistently underwritten Israel's military superiority and economic viability, could cajole or push the Israelis toward compromise. This view remains the fundamental hypothesis of Egyptian foreign policy, but the Egyptians knew well that the United States would do nothing to break a regional stalemate that in no way threatened United States and/or Israeli interests unless Egypt were to offer some incentives.

Egypt did. Some were negative incentives; the very war itself with the threat of a total conflagration involving the Great Powers, accompanied by the oil embargo and petroleum price increases threatening oil-dependent Western economies. These incentives drove home the message that the old stalemate was no longer tolerable. In the aftermath of the war came more positive incentives, including Egypt's growing distance from the U.S.S.R., a whittling away at some of the socialist legislation of the 1960s, the issuance of a new code to encourage foreign investment, and the triumphant visit in June 1974 of Richard Nixon, a president already fatally crippled at home.

The October War also placed Egypt in a strong position to solicit massive financial support from the Arab oil-rich to help bail out Egypt's economy. In short the 1973 war created options, it made possible movement and new initiatives after years of decision-making paralysis and diplomatic stalemate. The following two Reports, the first written a few months before the war and the second just after it, amplify upon these propositions.

Egypt in 1973

Egypt is, in all things, betwixt and between. It is between war and peace, Nasserism and Sadatism, Egypt firstism and Arab unity, economic liberalization and socialist intensification. The options are great and the risks of opting for any one of them even greater. It is not merely a characteristic of the Sadat era, but of all the years since 1967—and thus of Nasser's era as well—that Egyptian leaders have steadfastly attempted to give the impression of movement while carefully avoiding the agonizing choices inherent in the current situation of no war, no peace.

Numerous of Sadat's critics in and outside Egypt, and on both the left and the right, charge that Sadat has moved away from Nasserism and is watering down the "Revolution of July 23 [1952]." While Sadat surely wants to be his own man, and while it can hardly be reassuring to live in the shadow of the great leader, the President cannot fail to acknowledge that his legitimacy is derived almost solely from his role in the free officers movement and the Revolutionary Command Council, a group that Nasser built, occasionally purged, and which he directed at will. Given the origins of Sadat's claims to leadership, I was momentarily struck by his speech May 1, 1973 at Mehalla al-Kubra in which his only mention of Nasser was to note that it was he who accepted the Rogers Plan and the cease-fire with Israel in June and July 1970, and then to continue by asserting that the cease-fire served no one's interests but those of the Americans and the Israelis. Sadat had come a long way in setting himself apart from the Nasserist legacy, but that legacy is too massive and, in a sense, too autonomous for Sadat to escape except in the most superficial manner. The fundamental problems remain the same, changing only in emphasis and stress, except perhaps as regards relations with the U.S.S.R., a question to which we shall return. On the whole, then, continuity rather than innovation characterizes Egypt since Nasser.

For example, Sadat appears to have adhered faithfully to policies towards the United States, Western Europe, Israel, and the Palestinian resistance that Nasser himself had initiated. The United States is still seen as holding the key to peace in the Middle East, first because Russia has made it clear that it will not risk confrontation with the United States for the sake of the Arab cause, and second, because of the great financial and military leverage the United States could bring to bear upon Israel to pressure it into a more "reasonable" position. Nasser's acceptance, after consultation with the Soviet Union, of the Rogers Plan and the cease-fire in the summer of 1970 set the tone of an appeal for American, specifically Nixonian, even-handedness which, in the event, was not forthcoming.

The cease-fire and the acceptance of a direct American role in seeking a lasting peace would seem to have been premised on the hope that the United States would work towards implementation of United Nations' Resolution 242 of November 1967. This resolution, presented by Great Britain's Representative to the United Nations and supported by most Western European nations (and ambivalently by the United States) also had the support of several Arab governments, the most prominent among them being Egypt. Both Israel and the Palestinians perceived the resolution as inimical to their interests—although Israel eventually voted in its favor—for it would compel the Israelis to relinquish territories won in 1967 in exchange for what Tel Aviv regards as flimsy and insincere Arab declarations of peaceful relations, and it would offer the Palestinians nothing more than a pious and nonoperational statement of the relevance of their "legitimate rights" and the need for a "just and lasting solution" to their plight.

The Palestinian ox would have to be gored one way or another if the political settlement was to be pursued, and the massacres of "black September"

1970, triggered by the resistance itself but turned to the advantage of King Hussein's army, could have surprised Nasser only by their magnitude and the ferocity of the fighting.

The Israeli ox would have to be gored as well, and that was to have been the task of the United States. Nasser's death intervened, however, and Sadat, having subsequently been elected President in November 1970, had to face general international skepticism as to his power to survive. To revive interest in the Nasser formula, and to establish his own ability to shape policy, Sadat announced in February 1971 that an accord for the reopening of the Suez Canal, the crossing over of Egyptian troops to the east bank, and the partial withdrawal of Israeli troops from western Sinai would be the first step toward a general settlement. In subsequent interviews he stated his willingness to allow Israeli shipping through the canal and to sign a peace treaty with Israel.

The initiative achieved its objective, and Secretary of State Rogers paid an official visit to Cairo in May 1971, despite the fact that Egypt and the United States did not and do not maintain diplomatic relations. To demonstrate his capacity to make a political solution stick, Sadat had implemented two other policies consisting of further steps toward union with Libya and the simultaneous elimination of elements of the Egyptian elite considered to be close to Moscow. It is important to note that neither was designed primarily to impress Secretary of State Rogers. Sadat first announced Egypt's intention to pursue union with Libya and Syria within the context of a Federation of Arab Republics. On the one hand, Colonel Mu'ammar Kaddafi, who had come to power in September 1969, well after the Six Day War, was known to be staunchly anticommunist and thus a credible counterweight to the general Soviet presence in Egypt. On the other hand, Syria had never accepted Resolution 242, and its association with the Federation, in which Egypt would inevitably be the senior partner, signaled Syria's readiness to relax its stance.

The issue of the Federation itself provided a major pretext for the confrontation between Sadat and several of those leaders who had been close to Nasser and were still in power. The principal figures were Ali Sabry, Vice-Premier; Sami Sharaf, who had been Nasser's number one aide; Muhammed Fayek, the Minister of Information; Muhsin Abu al-Nur, First Secretary of the Central Committee of the Arab Socialist Union; Labib Shuqair, speaker of the National Assembly (Maglis al-Umma); General Muhammed Fawzi, Minister of Defense; and Sharawi Goma'a, Minister of Interior. In the Egyptian political lexicon, these men had constituted a "power center" that was inherently subversive. Even the term is Nasserian, used before his death to refer primarily to Field Marshal Hakim Amer and his entourage. (Amer, it will be recalled, committed suicide in the late summer of 1967.)

The accusation of subversion that was eventually leveled at the Sabry group resulted from a stormy meeting of the Executive Committee of the Arab Socialist Union (ASU), Egypt's only political organization. The meeting was held on April 23, 1971 and was attended by seven people. The committee discussed President Sadat's publicly proposed Federation with Syria and Libya. Although Nasser himself had initiated steps in this direction with Libya and the Sudan, Sabry, Abu al-Nur, and Shuqair, three of the seven attending, were highly critical of Sadat's plan. In the meeting Sadat could count on his own vote, of course, those of Mahmud Fawzi and Hussein Shafa'i, and in absentia Kemal Ramzi as-Stino. But the latter's absence produced a 3-3 deadlock. Sadat then called upon Interior Minister Sharawi Goma'a, who attended these meetings ex-officio, to voice his opinion. He sided with Sabry et al.

It was clear from this meeting that either Sadat or Sabry would have to go. In his May Day speech of that year, Sadat referred ominously to the formation of dangerous "centers of power" (marakiz al-quwwa), and Sabry and his colleagues knew beyond doubt that the message was intended for them. What subsequently happened is somewhat obscure, except that in the days following the speech Sabry and his companions all resigned their posts, perhaps hoping thereby to embarrass and isolate Sadat while at the same time utilizing the ASU and police apparatus to organize "mass" demonstrations in their support. Sadat never gave them a chance. All of the members of the group plus a great many others were arrested on May 14. Later tried for subversion and treason, they were all sentenced to varying terms of prison. None were executed.

Within the context of Egyptian-American relations, the removal of Sabry, often referred to as Moscow's man in Cairo, seemed, whatever its basic causes, a gift to the United States and another impressive indication of Sadat's ability to develop his own policies and to make them stick.

No matter how impressive, the United States did not respond. Yet Sadat had at least one more card to play, and it turned out to be the expulsion of most of the 15,000 Soviet military advisors in Egypt in July 1972. Once again the move does not seem to have been designed primarily to arouse American interest, but it was obviously taken into consideration that it could not fail to do so. Indeed, publicly at any rate, relations between Egypt and the United States were at a very low ebb as neither William Rogers nor other government representatives had indicated a positive response to Sadat's initiatives of the winter and spring of 1971. At the same time, the Brezhnev-Nixon meetings of spring 1972 were taken in Egypt as near certain evidence that the Big Two had privately agreed to leave the Arab-Israeli crisis in suspended animation, a situation that Egypt found increasingly intolerable.

Sadat had proclaimed 1971 the decisive year in Egypt's confrontation with Israel. It ended most indecisively, and in early 1972 Sadat explained, somewhat lamely, that the Indo-Pakistani crisis had distracted world attention from the Middle East just at the critical moment that Sadat had planned to confront Israel militarily. The President's domestic and external prestige sank precipitously and he clearly needed to demonstrate that he was master of the situation. This need, combined with the nature of Soviet aid (nonoffensive weapons) and their coolness to the Egyptian regime since Nasser's death,[1] set the stage for a spectacular move. Some suggest that in Sadat's mind it was to have the symbolic impact of Nasser's nationalization of the Suez Canal in 1956, another daring move to protect Egypt's sovereignty and dignity. Thus, in July 1972, 16 years after the canal nationalization, President Sadat announced that all Soviet training missions in Egypt were henceforth terminated and that all military installations

Salah Jahin, *Al-Ahram*, December 12, 1972, caricaturing the assault on Aziz Sidqi's government and its accomplishments in one year. The figure on the pedestal is the Peoples Assembly conducting a group of problems entitled from left to right: bilharzia, administrative deficiency, illiteracy, population growth, press censorship, and negligence. Overhead is a rain cloud symbolizing the rain storms that paralyzed Cairo in the midst of the debates and were cause for acerbic attacks on the efficacy of the government's efforts to prepare the country for war.

on Egyptian soil were from that moment under the complete control of Egypt and Egyptian personnel. The Israeli argument that Egypt was virtually under Soviet military control, a judgment that highly placed Americans such as Henry Kissinger seemed to share after the winter of 1970, was suddenly deprived of nearly all its substance.

Again, this was not the primary motive of Sadat's decision, but he surely must have hoped that it would draw a favorable reaction from the United States. Other than Melvin Laird's* public skepticism that the withdrawal was real, it drew little response at all. Some Egyptians wondered why Sadat made his move before the American elections instead of after when a President with a fresh mandate could make policy departures. Moreover,

1. Part of the coolness resulted from Sadat's direct action to effect a countercoup in the Sudan in July 1971 that toppled a three-day old Marxist military regime that had come to power there.

*then Secretary of Defense.

while the expulsion of the missions was generally popular in Egypt, it led ultimately to the weakening of Egypt's military credibility and hence its bargaining position vis-à-vis Israel. In short, this act represents Sadat's major policy innovation since Nasser's demise, and it certainly cannot be judged an unqualified success.

In domestic as well as foreign affairs those changes which have occurred have been changes of emphasis. The regime has moved to the right in the Sadat era, although the terms right and left have peculiarly slippery connotations in the Egyptian context. (All Egyptians, at least for public purposes, are socialists, but some are Marxist or scientific socialist, others Islamic socialist, some enlightened bourgeoisie, and some I have heard Marxists describe as "reactionary socialists.") The drift to the right has been unmistakable if not precisely definable and has revealed itself in on-going ideological and intellectual debates and in the reappraisal of the organization of the economy.

Since 1965-66, when Egypt faced a severe balance of payments problem that disrupted its second five year plan, a policy of economic retrenchment has been sporadically pursued. The military defeat and enormous losses resulting from the Six Day War necessarily reinforced this trend. Huge outlays on defense, averaging at least LE 700,000,000 per annum since 1967 (National Income in 1970, for instance, stood at LE 2,508,000,000) absorbed so much public capital that the civilian sector had funding adequate only for the maintenance of existing operations, or, as in the exceptional cases of the High Dam and the Helwan Iron and Steel complex, for cautious expansion. The move away from the expansionist period of 1960-1965 has been given further impetus by the fact that Egypt is so heavily dependent on the hard currency payments of Saudi Arabia, Kuwait, and Libya. These payments, agreed upon at the Arab summit at Khartoum in August 1967, are intended to compensate Egypt for the loss of revenues from the Suez Canal, the decline in tourism, the oil industry in Sinai, and other war-related causes. None of the three major suppliers are friendly to socialist experiments in economic planning and their hold on Egypt's hard currency purse strings must surely have promoted the trend toward economic orthodoxy. It is an eloquent comment on Egypt's persistent problems of economic growth that President Sadat, in July 1971, announced a new ten year plan that would double national income in that period. Ten years earlier Nasser had announced the same goal which was never achieved.

Akhbar al-Yom, February 3, 1973, in light of Sadat's speech on the student plot. The caption reads "ONE WAY!" "Neither toward the right...nor toward the left...toward Egypt..! The one way street with left and right blocked off leads to Egypt emblazoned in the heavens.

اتجـــاه واحـــد !
– لا الى اليمين .. ولا الى اليســــار .. الى مصر .. !

Salah Jahin, *Al-Ahram*, June 23, 1973. The UN
Security Council is presenting Nixon and Brezhnev
with a dossier marked "The Middle East Case"
which they are emphatically refusing to consider.
The old Egyptian proverb is quoted below: "I come
to you, oh Abd al-Mu'ain, looking for help; I find
you, oh Abd al Mu'uin helping yourself."

There has not been and probably will not be any
dramatic departures from the heavy reliance upon
the state sector and upon public capital in all
aspects of economic planning. Recent discussions
of the next five year plan have assumed a private investment rate of only ca. 10 per cent of all investments. There has been, nevertheless, a growing
recognition of the need to attract foreign private
capital to Egypt and to open new opportunities for
domestic private capital. An intensive effort has
been under way for the last two years to attract
Arab capital to Egypt, mainly from the oil-rich
states. It is hoped that this will be channelled
through the Egyptian International Bank, under
the direction of former Minister of Economy, Dr.
Abdelmoneim al-Qaissuni. A new foreign investment code has been established simultaneously,
and it has been made clear that foreign investment
of all kinds and sources, including the United
States, would be welcome. These attempts have not
as yet been notably successful. Even the
Suez-Mediterranean Pipeline (SUMED) project to
build an oil pipeline from the Red Sea to the Mediterranean has run into funding snags, although
several international oil companies have made
formal pledges—now totaling some 60 million tons
annually—to use the pipeline once completed.

Efforts to stimulate foreign investment have not
been without their critics in Egypt. Some feel that it
is illusory to hope that the Arab oil sheikhdoms will
ever do more than pay Egypt conscience money,
putting the bulk of their massive oil earnings into
European banks or investment markets where the
rate of return is higher than in Egypt. The same
argument would hold for European investors
although some heavily guaranteed investments,
motivated by political considerations, may be forthcoming. The critics leave unanswered the fundamental question of where and how is investment
capital and hard currency to be found given the
present and absolute priority of defense outlays.

The new liberal emphasis was given an added
fillip in April 1973 when Aziz Sidqi, who had been
Prime Minister for about 13 months, was relieved
of his position. Sidqi had been closely associated
with the development of Egypt's industrial sector
since 1956, having been Minister of Industry for
much of the intervening 16 years. He was known to
have an overriding concern with industrial expansion in the public sector, frequently without due
attention to cost and feasibility.

In the new government, in which Sadat is his own
Prime Minister, Abdelaziz Higazi, the Minister of
Treasury since 1968, became Deputy Prime Minister with most of the economy under his purview.
Higazi is concerned with financial solvency and
thorough cost-benefit analysis. It is expected that
he will give a very hard look at all enterprises in the
public sector to seek out, case by case, the causes of
idle capacity, inadequate or mistrained personnel,
poor marketing, outmoded machinery, and other
ills that have plagued the public sector in past
years. Concurrently, Higazi would like to see a
greater role for local and foreign private investment.

In economic and in foreign policy, therefore,
with the exception of the expulsion of the Soviet
missions, Sadat has not made any sharp breaks
with the preceding era. On the other hand, he has,

Ruz al-Yussif, May 22, 1972, two months before the expulsion of the Soviet missions. The cover shows Sadat and presumably Marshall Gretchko watching an advanced MIG swooping by trailing Egyptian Soviet Friendship in its wake. It was rumored at that time that the U.S.S.R. was to deliver some of its most advanced attack aircraft to Egypt. The delivery was never made.

Cover of *Ruz al-Yussif* September 28, 1971 on the first anniversary of Nasser's death. President Sadat presents his condolences by a weeping Egypt: "Your life goes on, oh Egypt."

willingly or not, abandoned to some extent a style and tactic of rule that Nasser had always used to good effect. It consisted of a careful balancing of interests and pressure groups—such as elements of the officers corps, civilian technocrats, left and right wing ideologues, etc.—so that all had a share in power and Nasser could arbitrate among them.

Sadat's confrontation with Sabry and company had the important consequence of weakening the whole left-technocratic wing of the elite while at the same time forcing Sadat into an ostensible overreliance upon the senior officers corps, which stood by him in the crisis despite the fact that General Fawzi, the Minister of Defense, sided with Sabry. It may be that Sadat's dependence on the army is more apparent than real, for, in the fall of 1972, he calmly eliminated Minister of Defense Mohammed Ahmad Sadiq who had been the principal officer (Chief of Staff) to have supported the President in May 1971. While there is good evidence that certain elements of the army were very unhappy with the firing of Sadiq, their inability to act decisively would seem to indicate that the Egyptian army has simply become too big and too internally complex to sustain a collective mentality or even collective grievances. Nor, for the same reason, can any one group within it permit itself the assurance of acting independently without fear of being countered or betrayed by other military groups.

Sadat has also abandoned the middle position in ideological affairs and has come to rely increasingly on a mixture of elements from the liberal, bourgeois, and the Islamic right. A number of factors have contributed to their re-emergence (their other period of prominence having been 1952-1960). The elimination of Sabry, Goma'a, Sami Sharaf, and others was officially interpreted as the first step in the dismantling of a vast and unaccountable intelligence and police network that had come to poison Egyptian life. From May 15, 1971 on, in what became known as the Revolution of Rectification (thawrat at-tashih), President Sadat proclaimed that true democracy would emerge under the umbrella of the sovereignty of law and due process. A permanent constitution, approved by referendum in the fall of 1971, was to institutionalize these concepts. There followed the election of a People's Assembly (Maglis as-Sha'ab) which, in keeping with the new look, occasionally showed its teeth in

vigorous parliamentary assaults upon various government policies. In the winter of 1972, the Arab Socialist Union, Ali Sabry's former fief, was placed under the tutelage of Sayyid Marei, long-time Minister of Agrarian Reform and a civilian known for his conservative tendencies. The ASU was no longer to be both an instrument and a forum for mass politicization. (Marei himself has subsequently been replaced by the even less salient figure of Hafiz Ghanem, a professor of international law.)

Instead the People's Assembly emerged as a forum for the bourgeois right. Some voices spoke from the liberal tradition of the old Wafd Party, others from a purely technocratic point of view, and yet others from that of Islamic revivalism or, what one Egyptian described to me as the Neo-Ikhwan (a nonorganized variant of the banned Muslim Brethren, al-Ikhwan al-Muslimin). Colonel Kaddafi's growing influence in Egyptian affairs, itself tied directly to the masses of hard currency he is able to manipulate, has encouraged this latter current, sometimes, it is said, through direct support and subsidies. Sadat's own chief counsellors and ministers seem to reflect this alliance of technocracy, Islamic revival, and bourgeois liberalism. The principal figures have been Mahmud Fawzi, civilian, a vice-president and counsellor for foreign affairs who was also Sadat's first Prime Minister; Aziz Sidqi, civilian, former Minister of Industry and Sadat's second Prime Minister; Mamduh Salem, the Minister of Interior after May 15, 1971; Hafiz Ismail, military, presidential advisor on security affairs; Hussein Shafa'i, Vice-President and, other than Sadat himself, the only original member of the RCC left in the regime; Abdelqader Hatem, also a former army officer, and now Deputy Prime Minister for Information and Culture; Deputy Prime Minister Abdelaziz Kamil, former member of the Muslim Brethren and now Minister of Religious Affairs; Deputy Prime Minister Abdelaziz Higazi, civilian and the Minister of Treasury since 1968. The only voice of the left in the entire Council of Ministers is Ismail Sabry Abdullah, Minister of State for Planning.

President Sadat's initial political and economic liberalization after May 15, 1971 was on the whole well received throughout Egyptian society, and his popularity was probably never higher. But in a wartime situation in which consumer desires simply cannot be satisfied, and the free expression of

Salah Jahin, *Al-Ahram*, June 18, 1973: Brezhnev meets Nixon in Washington. Brezhnev: "The peace upon you" Nixon: "And upon you the Soviet Jews and the mercy of God and his blessings."

political opinions may be quickly interpreted by some as treasonous, liberalism is costly and difficult to sustain. Added to this was the unhappy fact, mentioned above, that 1971, the year that President Sadat had proclaimed as "decisive" in Egypt's struggle with Israel, was anything but that. The President's growing credibility gap was first exploited by university students in the winter of 1972 through strikes, leafletting, and some demonstrations. The Egyptian authorities and police reacted with restraint and the heat eventually died down. However, the People's Assembly took up the slack and subjected the SUMED project, and indirectly Prime Minister Aziz Sidqi, to heavy criticism during the spring session. Sadat took back the initiative with the expulsion of the Soviet missions in the summer. But then came the fall of 1972 during which there were a number of clashes between Coptic and Muslim Egyptians which may have resulted from the growing Islamic fervor in the country, particularly noticeable in the content of the mass media, as well as from Coptic resentment that their place in the national struggle was not receiving equal time. In November, to cap it all, the People's Assembly unmercifully roasted Aziz Sidqi's government for its lethargic performance in the preceding ten months. The following month, clashes between groups of left- and right-wing students at the universities led to widespread arrests in early January. President Sadat announced subsequently that the arrests were made in order to head off a plot by the "adventurist left" which had been inadvertently abetted by the "reactionary right," and that sought to undermine the foundations of the state and to attack the principles of the July 23 Revolution. Most of the arrests were on the left, however, and when, in June 1973, over 100 of those arrested were finally charged and referred to a military tribunal, virtually all the accused were from the left.

The crackdown on the students was followed by a crackdown on the intellectuals and journalists, again mostly of the left. Some had signed petitions in favor of the students, some had criticized Egypt abroad, others argued vociferously for the lifting of press censorship in a meeting of the press syndicate, still others were purged as unauthorized intruders on university campuses, and some were surely victims of personal grudges. All these writers and journalists (well over 100 of them) were dropped as members of the ASU, which automatically entailed the loss of their right to work. One can only guess at the criteria applied in any given case for terminating ASU membership as no public, substantive explanation was ever provided.

When all is said and done, the move to the right and the skirmishes with the left are in essence marginal to the more fundamental questions of economic policy, investment programs, supplying needed public services, and, even more important, essential consumer goods to a growing population buffeted by price inflation and relatively fixed wages. Economic policy itself is overwhelmingly a function of the state of no war, no peace and the vast sums of money paid into military preparedness. Everything else Sadat does depends on this question, exactly in the same manner that all that Nasser undertook after 1967 was a function of the same situation. This kind of continuity Egypt could do without, and Sadat's options in breaking it are extremely limited, ranging from capitulation to military suicide. He must attract international attention to the crisis without exploding it, but it may be impossible to set only little fires. The middle course that has been Egypt's for the last six years may be the only one possible in the next few: hang on dexterously and grimly in the face of growing internal malaise and external indifference.

The Crossing
From the Bar Lev Line to Geneva

I would prefer the respect of the world without its sympathy, to the sympathy of the world without its respect.

Anwar Sadat
October 1973

History has granted Israel superiority over some of the Arabs some of the time; but history will not grant Israel superiority over all of the Arabs all of the time.

Mohammed Hassanein Heikal
December 1973

At 2 P.M. October 6, 1973, Egyptian forces crossed the Suez Canal and assaulted the Bar Lev Line that ran a hundred miles along the canal's eastern bank. Within a few days Egypt had put the better part of two armies across the canal accompanied by hundreds of tanks and a forward air defense screen of SAM-6 surface-to-air missiles. The Bar Lev Line was seized and then systematically destroyed by the Egyptians.

Eight days later, on October 14, the Israelis began the operation that turned the course of the war on the Egyptian front. An armored task force slipped between the Egyptian Second and Third Armies at the northern end of the Great Bitter Lake and began to destroy missile sites and disrupt supplies to the Third Army. What had been a limited but undeniable Egyptian victory was transformed into an indecisive stalemate. The state of "no war, no peace" that had prevailed from June 1967 to October 1973 was replaced, in the words of Mohammed Hassanein Heikal, editor of *al-Ahram*, by a state of "no victory, no defeat."

The military facts of the situation, however, pale beside the symbolism of what had transpired. Egypt's President Sadat, a man derided both inside and outside Egypt, went ahead and did what he

had always said he would do, but which few ever believed. For three years he had cried wolf about the inevitability of the battle to the extent that Egyptian students and intellectuals questioned his credibility and the international press delighted in calling his bluff. David Hirst wrote an article for the *New York Times Sunday Magazine* in July 1973, entitled "Sadat Goes to War...Again," and the editors obligingly accompanied the piece with a cartoon showing Sadat riding backwards on a camel. His own people were hardly more generous. One joke making the Cairo rounds had two ignorant peasants visiting the city for the first time. They repair to a type of popular beer joint known as a "*booza*," and there on the wall are pictures of Nasser and Sadat side by side. One peasant asks the other, "Ahmad, who are those fellows?" Pointing to Nasser, Ahmad says, "That is Gamal Abd al-Nasser, leader of the revolution, builder of socialism, may God rest his soul." "Well then, who's the other one?", to which a puzzled Ahmad replies, "I don't know...he must be the owner of the *booza*."

October 6 conferred upon Sadat something short of charisma but nonetheless the hero's mantle. Not untypical was the postcrossing reassessment of the President written by Yussef Idris, one of Egypt's leading writers. He was among a group of over one hundred journalists and intellectuals who had been suspended from membership in the Arab Socialist Union, the country's only legal political organization, in February 1973. Suspension meant they lost their right to work and to be published. It was charged that those suspended had abetted "leftist adventurism" of certain student groups as well as having criticized the regime in public. It is a fact that Idris had strongly criticized Sadat's decision to expel the Soviet military missions in the summer of 1972. A week before the October War, Sadat reinstated in ASU membership all those who had been suspended eight months earlier. After the crossing of the canal, Yussef Idris wrote a panegyric to Sadat entitled "Deliverance":[1]

.   .   .

I had never before believed in the role of the
individual in history
I did not know that one person alone, in
setting his own will, set that of a Nation, and
the history of a people, and the strength of a
civilization
But the hero, Anwar Sadat, is beyond my
ken
He crushed the defeat lying deep within us
all when he resolved upon the crossing
And by his decision not only the army
crossed the canal
But the people crossed with it and trans-
cended their submissiveness and misery
Left behind their humiliation and shame

.   .   .

The crossing is deliverance

No Egyptian, it seems, has failed to understand that The Crossing has ushered in a new era. Heikal compared it to Egypt's crossing a sea of fear and self-doubt, while Musa Sabry, fired with the euphoria of the first week's fighting, wrote in his happily unique style: "Our fighters have raised the Egyptian flag; the flags of Egypt; Sinai has been re-gained!...God is Great! God is Great!...Forgive me...my pen has stopped...I am weeping."[2] The dean of Egyptian letters, Tawfiq al-Hakim, made his own appraisal well after the fighting had stopped and the indecisive results were in: "The profound meaning of October 6 is not merely a military victory or a material crossing, as much as it

Territory held by Israel on October 22, when cease-fire was called, is indicated by dots. Vertical lines mark area Egypt charges Israel seized after truce. Israel says Arabs blockaded Bab el Mandeb (inset).

is a spiritual crossing to a new stage in our history...and that stage is the reconstruction of [our] civilization."[3]

By comparison to the epic content of the crossing indicated in these statements, October 6 had a more prosaic but nonetheless momentous meaning: Egypt (and Syria, with manifest reluctance) could now negotiate. After the war, Ahmad Baha al-Din recalled that Lord Caradon, author of United Nations Resolution 242 in 1967, had proposed that Geneva be the site of talks between Arabs and Israelis under United Nations auspices. But, Baha al-Din notes,

> Arab participation in such a conference was not possible at that time nor at any time prior to the October War. Before that war the Arabs had no cards to play in negotiations....They had only their memoranda, and talk of legitimate rights, things that have no weight in international life. They were not fighting; moreover it had become fixed in the world's mind that they would never fight. They talked of using oil as a weapon, but it was unconvincing. And their differences seemed more important than their shared interests. After the October War all that changed....4

From the physical recapture of the east bank of the canal, occupied by Israel since 1967, Egypt derived the dignity and self-esteem to enable her representatives to enter into peace talks with the Israelis at Geneva.

Sadat's Legacy

Since acceding to the presidency in late 1970, following the death of Nasser, Sadat had appeared to be a more-or-less skilled improviser, manipulating international and internal situations on a month-to-month basis. He seemingly painted himself into a corner by claiming that 1971 was "the decisive year" in confrontation with Israel, and then attributed the lack of military action at year's end to fog over the front. Finding the fog insubstantial, thousands of students demonstrated in Egypt's universities and in the streets. He then threw out the Soviet military missions in July 1972 but without having obtained any prior assurances from the United States that such an act would bring a favorable response. The major elements of the overall situation were obvious, but that he had a plan or strategy to deal with them appeared unlikely. It was expected that he would simply spin out his improvisations until there were no more.

Even those who thought the President had a strategy misread its objectives. This was so primarily because it was widely assumed, on the basis of reliable analyses, that Egypt had no credible military option. The expulsion of the 25,000 Soviet military advisors was believed to have reduced the effectiveness of Egypt's air and missile defenses by at least 50 per cent. It was said that Egypt's senior officers, rather than urging a hawkish policy on Sadat, warned him of the risks of any military action. Fu'ad Matar, one of the most astute analysts of Egyptian affairs, summed up the prevailing

Egyptian soldiers on captured Israeli tank on exhibit in Cairo.   This soldier's face tells the mood of Egypt after the crossing.

view: "The battle without Soviet support is impossible. Sadat himself knows this. The generals of the Egyptian Army, who were vexed by the Soviet military advisors, know this. The United States knows this. And Israel knows it too."[5] Paul Martin, writing in *The Times*, concurred:

A recent survey which has gone the rounds of the Egyptian commanders has shown that of the equipment in the Army's possession 40 per cent is virtually unusable, 20 per cent is suspect, and the decision of the Russians to withhold vital spares has placed the rest in jeopardy.

The same survey, which appears to have been a deliberate effort to make the situation clear to hotheads and others within the ranks, shows that the airforce is, if anything, in worse shape than before.[6]

If it were true that Egypt had no military option then it followed that Egypt had no diplomatic option short of capitulating to Israeli terms whatever they might be. Was there any middle ground? Yes, the prolongation of the increasingly intolerable situation of no war, no peace that was draining the country economically (LE700 million or $1.5 billion in defense expenditures each year) and was not advancing Egypt one step toward recovering the territories occupied by Israel after 1967. There was another option, cautiously advocated by the left, consisting in the intensification of the socioeconomic revolution in order to mobilize all potential savings in the country, and the mobilization of workers, peasants, and students for a long people's war. It was pointed out that the Egyptian masses went spontaneously into the streets to protest Nasser's resignation after the June War and to demand that he refuse to capitulate to the Israelis and the Americans. Nineteen hundred sixty-seven, in the eyes of many, had demonstrated the inadequacy of conventional warfare and the need to turn to the masses who were manifestly eager to respond.

Such a view, if it had been widely broadcast, would undoubtedly have struck a responsive chord among broad sectors of the population. However, it was inimical to Sadat and the large middle class that had emerged from the Army and the administration after 15 years of "statist" development. Going to the masses, even if it could be construed to make military sense, would necessitate a leveling process and a sharing of the burden of sacrifice that might have undone the very alliance of forces upon which Sadat founded his legitimacy. Consequently, the theme of the revolutionary option, no matter how discreetly phrased, was confined to student groups, a handful of intellectuals, and oblique references in one or two leftist journals.[7]

It distorts reality to attribute to the Egyptian middle classes a single set of goals and motives, but it may not be unfair to say that—as patriots—they have wanted to maintain their nation's honor and independence, and—as relatively privileged citizens—their way of life. If a compromise could be found that would honor both these objectives, they would accept it.

Nasser had clearly begun to work toward such a compromise before his death, and Sadat continued his effort. Indeed compromise was inherent in the situation resulting from the June War. Although militarily crippled, Egypt, it was felt, had lost a battle but not the war. For Israel to impose its terms (it will be recalled that Moshe Dayan expected a phone call from Nasser after the war asking for Israel's terms) would have required the occupation of the Egyptian heartland and the creation of a new regime willing to bow to a *diktat*. Prolonged occupation and administration of a country the size of Egypt was simply out of the question. Israel could not force upon Egypt an unconditional surrender, but Egypt could not bargain effectively with Israel until it had restored its military potential. In order to rebuild Egypt militarily, Nasser had to give up much of his international and regional leverage. First he had to plunge deep into moral and material debt to the Soviet Union, which immediately after the war had agreed to rebuild and retrain the Egyptian Armed Forces. Such dependency was probably distasteful to Nasser but was all the more necessary in view of the fact that the United States had openly become Israel's major arms supplier. With the first deliveries of Phantoms and other sophisticated offensive weaponry the United States began to define what it means by "the military balance in the Middle East." In the last months of the Johnson administration, and throughout Nixon's tenure, "balance" meant providing Israel with the military wherewithal to engage simultaneously and destroy within a few days the armed forces of the three states most likely to enter into hostilities with her: Syria, Jordan, and Egypt.

Only the U.S.S.R. could have corrected the fundamental military imbalance wrought by the United States, but the Russians refrained from doing so out of fear of great power confrontation and an informed estimate that Egyptian forces were not yet competent to use more advanced weaponry. The Soviet Union, like most Arabs, probably believed that another round with Israel was not only inevitable but necessary in order to move toward an acceptable solution. However, they would not condone any military initiative on the part of the Egyptians before they were judged to be ready. The crux of the falling-out between Egypt and the Russians lay in their conflicting appraisals of the competence and level of preparedness of the Egyptian Armed Forces, and this appraisal was the controlling factor in the level and type of arms delivered.[8]

As a result, Nasser had to resign himself to a state of no war, no negotiations, no settlement, and very little economic development. Simply to meet current expenses Nasser was beholden to the conservative, oil-rich states of Kuwait, Saudi Arabia, and Libya. At the Khartoum conference of August 1967, they agreed to compensate Egypt for hard currency losses incurred by the June War at a rate of over $350 million annually. The leaders of all three countries (the monarchy in Libya was not overthrown until September 1969) had been the object of Egyptian invective throughout the sixties, depicted as "feudal reactionaries" and "imperialist stooges." Egypt and Saudi Arabia had even fought an indirect war in the Yemen between 1962 and 1967. Nasser could not accept their postwar handouts without eating crow. [9]

Nasser had come to power in the name of the Egyptian Army and in order to restore its and the nation's dignity. Yet the June War led to the disgrace of the Egyptian Army, the suicide of its leader, Field Marshal Hakim Amer, and treason trials for its senior officers. Student-worker riots in the winter of 1968, protesting the lenient sentences meted out to Egypt's generals, were graphic evidence of the depths to which the Army's reputation had fallen.[10] Not only was the Egyptian Army discredited after the June War, but so too the belief in the efficacy of conventional warfare. The growing activity and prestige of the Palestinian guerrilla organizations were founded on the notion that the time had come for unconventional tactics, people's wars, and the sapping of Israeli society from within.

All these factors shifted attention away from Egypt, and despite the fact that it remained the biggest economic and military power in the area, left it on the sidelines, dependent on Soviet arms and Arab subsidies.

Nasser did not remain passive. With the benefit of hindsight, we can see that the basic steps toward a way out were being considered by the beginning of 1969. It was clear by then to the Egyptians, as it has been ever since, that the United States held the key to an acceptable negotiated settlement. The Americans had supported United Nations Resolution 242 (see appendix), voted by the Security Council in 1967, which called for Israeli withdrawal "from territories" occupied as a result of the war. Yet as the months went by, it became obvious that Israel preferred territory and "military security" to "flimsy" declarations of Arab willingness to live in peace with Israel were she to withdraw to the pre-1967 lines, and were some sort of settlement to be worked out for the Palestinians. Resolution 242 was thus viewed by the Israelis as threatening, and as long as Israel held a clear military edge in the area and enjoyed United States backing there was little hope that the resolution would be applied.

With the inauguration of the Nixon administration and the new President's proclaimed intentions to develop a more "even-handed" policy in the Middle East, Nasser may have seen a chance for a breakthrough. The Israelis had to be made to pay a high price in men, equipment, and economic mobilization for continued occupation of Sinai. In addition, the situation in the area had to be "heated up" sufficiently to alarm the United States and, in order to avoid great power confrontation, to bring its full weight to bear on Israel to seek a rapid political solution. The result was the "War of Attrition" launched in March 1969.

On balance the War of Attrition was not a success for the Egyptians. It did not bleed the Israelis militarily. The heavy artillery barrages across the canal (in one exchange the Egyptian Chief of Staff was killed) simply caused the Israelis to dig in and complete the Bar Lev Line, begun in October 1968. They responded to the Egyptian action with intense artillery barrages and air raids all along the west bank of the canal. One result was that the on-going process of evacuating the civilian populations of the canal cities of Suez, Port Tawfiq, Ismailia, and Port

Said was completed, while the cities themselves, and their industrial dependencies, took a terrible beating.

Summit of Arab heads of state in December 1969 the Rogers Plan was discussed, but no formal position was adopted. At the same time the Egyptian

Suez city 1972.

The clashes did attract the attention of the United States and may have prompted, in December 1969, the first articulation by the American Secretary of State of what became known as the Rogers Plan. This was essentially a modified version of United Nations Resolution 242, with the difference that it was directly sponsored by the United States, made no mention of Syrian-occupied territories, and would have probably involved direct talks between Arabs and Israelis. The War of Attrition also served to refocus the Arab world's attention on Egypt and on conventional military operations, and to steal a little of the guerrillas' thunder. But neither process went far enough to extricate Nasser from his dilemma. At the Rabat

Minister of War, Mohammed Fawzi,[11] explained his country's military situation and, along with Nasser, argued that Egypt needed more time and substantial additional subsidies from the oil-rich states in order to build a real war machine. No additional subsidies were forthcoming. His failure at the conference prompted Nasser to give serious thought to the two-month-old republican regime in Libya and its ardently Nasserist leader, Colonel Mu'ammar Qaddafi. On December 24, 1969 Nasser met at Tripoli with Qaddafi and General Ga'afar Numeiri of the Sudan, and a federation of the Sudan, Libya, and Egypt was announced.[12] Perhaps oil-rich, and now republican Libya would foot the bill of attrition.

Soviet presence in Egypt, and Israel stressed in Washington that the best way to avoid confrontation in the area was to assure Israel's military preparedness and the armed forces would take care of the rest. Time was on their side, they argued, and eventually the Arabs would have to come to terms for they could neither close the military gap nor sustain the immense costs of their own war effort. Short of bringing Soviet troops into the field, there was no military threat to the stabilized situation in the area, and because there was no real "crisis," there was no need for American intervention to bring about a settlement. Moshe Dayan, reflecting this mood, began to state in public that Israel might have to hang on to the occupied territories for 25 years before a settlement could be reached.

Sadat's Strategy

Nasser said that the Rogers Plan had about one chance in a hundred of succeeding, and Sadat inherited those odds. With Nasser's death the odds became even longer. Sadat had none of Nasser's cumulative prestige, and it may be that he succeeded so easily to the presidency because he was not taken seriously by other rival leaders (Ali Sabry and Zacharia Muhy al-Din) and was thus tepidly acceptable to all.

Under those circumstances, what Sadat had to demonstrate was his mastery of the domestic arena so that the Israelis, or anyone else, could not question his ability to make decisions affecting the course of war and peace and to make them stick. At the same time he sought to refine and perfect the Nasserist strategy of pulling the United States into the process of a political settlement by maintaining a crisis situation founded on the threat of or direct resort to military action. The irreproachable legality of the Egyptian case had to be demonstrated by "exhausting every possible means to a peaceful settlement." This consisted in underscoring in Africa, Europe, and the United Nations that Israel was responsible for blocking the application of Resolution 242, and that its ability to do so was founded upon the one-sided military support she received from the United States. The "exhausting" strategy served both to justify Egypt's oft-repeated conclusion that she had no alternative but to resort to combat in order to take back the occupied territories, as well as isolating the United States and Israel together in several diplomatic situations in which the rest of the world, including the United States' NATO allies, stood by neutrally or hostilely.

Diplomatic isolation of the United States would serve no practical purpose unless a suitable combination of rewards and punishments could be devised to compel the Americans to change their position. The rewards could be a diminution of the Soviet presence in Egypt, the possibility of the restoration of normal economic and diplomatic relations with Arab countries, and the lessening of the threat of great power confrontation. The punishments would be a semiconstant crisis situation in which all the above rewards would be denied, and would entail the utilization of Arab oil supplies as a means of leverage on the oil-consuming industrial Goliaths of Western Europe and the United States. The only problem is that Egypt does not control much oil. So the final facet of the strategy became the rebuilding of Arab unity, the "mobilization of Arab resources," and the establishment of "unity in the struggle" regardless of the political regime. The Soviet Union would not be happy. But then they too wanted to avoid confrontation with the United States, and their economic and military investment in the Arab world was of an order such that writing it off was unthinkable. Moreover, in the Third World political arena the Soviet Union could not afford not to come to Egypt's aid in the event that hostilities were renewed. China would have reminded the developing world in such an event that Russia was an ideological paper tiger and a fair weather friend. Just as Nasser knew that the Soviet Union could not effectively block his acceptance of the Rogers Plan, so Sadat knew that he could manipulate the Soviet military presence in Egypt as an enticement to the United States without fear that the Soviets would abandon him in a crisis.

Sadat's strategy was not developed as an integrated whole at a fixed moment in time. In retrospect we can see how the various pieces must have come together in his and his advisors' minds. Some aspects were emphasized more than others according to the international situation; certain possibilities, such as new United States involvement, a new type of Soviet military aid, or the primacy of oil, would momentarily loom large in Egyptian thinking and then, perhaps, fade away. To see how the pieces fell into place, we must look at the process over time.

In February 1971 the first six–month period of the cease-fire was nearing its end. It is widely asserted that Sadat wanted to let it lapse and renew

Soviet presence in Egypt, and Israel stressed in Washington that the best way to avoid confrontation in the area was to assure Israel's military preparedness and the armed forces would take care of the rest. Time was on their side, they argued, and eventually the Arabs would have to come to terms for they could neither close the military gap nor sustain the immense costs of their own war effort. Short of bringing Soviet troops into the field, there was no military threat to the stabilized situation in the area, and because there was no real "crisis," there was no need for American intervention to bring about a settlement. Moshe Dayan, reflecting this mood, began to state in public that Israel might have to hang on to the occupied territories for 25 years before a settlement could be reached.

Sadat's Strategy

Nasser said that the Rogers Plan had about one chance in a hundred of succeeding, and Sadat inherited those odds. With Nasser's death the odds became even longer. Sadat had none of Nasser's cumulative prestige, and it may be that he succeeded so easily to the presidency because he was not taken seriously by other rival leaders (Ali Sabry and Zacharia Muhy al-Din) and was thus tepidly acceptable to all.

Under those circumstances, what Sadat had to demonstrate was his mastery of the domestic arena so that the Israelis, or anyone else, could not question his ability to make decisions affecting the course of war and peace and to make them stick. At the same time he sought to refine and perfect the Nasserist strategy of pulling the United States into the process of a political settlement by maintaining a crisis situation founded on the threat of or direct resort to military action. The irreproachable legality of the Egyptian case had to be demonstrated by "exhausting every possible means to a peaceful settlement." This consisted in underscoring in Africa, Europe, and the United Nations that Israel was responsible for blocking the application of Resolution 242, and that its ability to do so was founded upon the one-sided military support she received from the United States. The "exhausting" strategy served both to justify Egypt's oft-repeated conclusion that she had no alternative but to resort to combat in order to take back the occupied territories, as well as isolating the United States and Israel together in several diplomatic situations in which the rest of the world, including the United States' NATO allies, stood by neutrally or hostilely.

Diplomatic isolation of the United States would serve no practical purpose unless a suitable combination of rewards and punishments could be devised to compel the Americans to change their position. The rewards could be a diminution of the Soviet presence in Egypt, the possibility of the restoration of normal economic and diplomatic relations with Arab countries, and the lessening of the threat of great power confrontation. The punishments would be a semiconstant crisis situation in which all the above rewards would be denied, and would entail the utilization of Arab oil supplies as a means of leverage on the oil-consuming industrial Goliaths of Western Europe and the United States. The only problem is that Egypt does not control much oil. So the final facet of the strategy became the rebuilding of Arab unity, the "mobilization of Arab resources," and the establishment of "unity in the struggle" regardless of the political regime. The Soviet Union would not be happy. But then they too wanted to avoid confrontation with the United States, and their economic and military investment in the Arab world was of an order such that writing it off was unthinkable. Moreover, in the Third World political arena the Soviet Union could not afford not to come to Egypt's aid in the event that hostilities were renewed. China would have reminded the developing world in such an event that Russia was an ideological paper tiger and a fair weather friend. Just as Nasser knew that the Soviet Union could not effectively block his acceptance of the Rogers Plan, so Sadat knew that he could manipulate the Soviet military presence in Egypt as an enticement to the United States without fear that the Soviets would abandon him in a crisis.

Sadat's strategy was not developed as an integrated whole at a fixed moment in time. In retrospect we can see how the various pieces must have come together in his and his advisors' minds. Some aspects were emphasized more than others according to the international situation; certain possibilities, such as new United States involvement, a new type of Soviet military aid, or the primacy of oil, would momentarily loom large in Egyptian thinking and then, perhaps, fade away. To see how the pieces fell into place, we must look at the process over time.

In February 1971 the first six–month period of the cease-fire was nearing its end. It is widely asserted that Sadat wanted to let it lapse and renew hostilities at an undetermined level. He was dissuaded from doing so—some say by the United States, others the Soviet Union, others his Minister of War Mohammed Fawzi; perhaps a combination of all three. But what is so easily forgotten about Sadat after that time was that from the outset he felt that military action was crucial to bring about any progress.

One cause of the world's forgetfulness was that Sadat quickly reversed ground in February 1971 and extended the cease-fire. At the same time he proposed that, as a first step toward comprehensive negotiations, Israel withdraw well back from the Suez Canal and that Egypt undertake the re-opening of the waterway. Sadat intimated that at the end of the process peaceful relations with and de facto recognition of Israel would be perfectly possible. Sadat followed this initiative by signing, on April 3, the declaration of the Federation of Arab Republics with Syria and Libya (but without the Sudan).[13] On the one hand Libya, under the militantly anticommunist leadership of Colonel Qaddafi, could be seen as a counterweight to the Soviet presence in Egypt (and in Syria). On the other, Syria had never formally accepted Resolution 242, but its inclusion in the Federation could be interpreted as de facto recognition.

Sadat's initiatives brought back into the picture William Rogers who visited Cairo in mid-May in an effort to resuscitate his peace plan. Accompanied by Assistant Secretary Joseph Sisco, the Secretary of State's talks with the Egyptians went well, and it is said that Rogers told Sadat, "You have done all that we could possibly ask of you." Rogers and Sisco then tried to convince the Israelis that Egypt was serious. Golda Meir, however, viewed Sadat's proposals as a gimmick to put Egyptian troops across the canal and offered an obviously unacceptable counterproposal that Egypt pull back from the *west* bank of the canal in return for partial Israeli withdrawal. A similar notion had last been advanced in the form of an ultimatum in November 1956 by Britain and France prior to their armed invasion of Egypt. At one point Rogers' talks with Meir degenerated into a shouting match and the upshot was that Rogers went away empty-handed and Sadat had nothing to show for his initiative. Would it have been different had Kissinger come at that time rather than two-and-a-half years later?

As this little drama was playing itself out, Sadat was bringing the domestic arena under control by confronting and eventually purging the mildly left-wing Nasserists grouped around Ali Sabry, Interior Minister Sharawi Goma'a, Presidential Advisor Sami Sharaf, and War Minister Mohammed Fawzi. The confrontation occurred nominally over the terms of the accord setting up the federation with Libya and Syria, but the main issue was that it had become obvious that Sadat was not about to be the Naguib of a post-Nasserist regime. However, having lopped off the "left-wing" of the Nasserist alliance at almost the same time Rogers was in Cairo, it was believed that he may have timed the purge as an offering to the United States.[14] To put to rest such suspicions and allay the fears of the Soviet Union, on May 27 Sadat signed, along with Nikolai Podgorny, a Soviet-Egyptian Solidarity Pact that ultimately had little operational significance. Sadat was understandably bitter about the course of events, and in July he made his famous pledge that 1971 would be the "decisive year." It wasn't, and because it wasn't Sadat began to suffer from a chronic domestic and international credibility gap. "Sadat is going to submit legislation to Parliament to extend 1971 by several months," it was said in Cairo as December began indecisively. In the new year, Sadat explained that conditions on the front (the famous fog problem), and the distraction of world attention from the Middle East to the war in Bangladesh forced him to call off the military offensive he had planned. Few believed he had planned anything, and when he appointed a new government under Aziz Sidqi "to prepare the nation for war," one easily concluded that it was a charade. We now know that Sadat did intend to "heat it up" in the canal zone, although the kind of operation contemplated was probably on a far more modest scale than that undertaken in October 1973. Nonetheless, from that time on experienced observers and, presumably, the international intelligence community began consistently to misread Sadat's objectives thus setting themselves up for the big surprise he held in store for them.

December 1971 conveyed a message to Sadat that he was to act upon six months later. In India's hour of need the Soviets set up an airlift of military equipment to the subcontinent and used Egyptian airfields and airspace to transit some of the material. Were Egypt's needs not equally pressing? Was the Soviet Union encouraging and exploiting a situation of no war, no peace in the Middle East in order to maintain its position in the Arab world and gain certain tactical military advantages? Was the Soviet Union systematically denying Egypt advanced offensive weapons to preclude the possibility that Egypt would launch hostilities? Sadat's tentative answer to all these questions must have been yes, but he wanted to put the Russians to the test. The formation of the government headed by Sidqi (January 18, 1972), a man who as Minister of Industry had had long and cordial dealings with the Soviets, was a sign of Egyptian good will. On February 3, Sadat flew secretly to Moscow to discuss the resumption of hostilities, but his Soviet counterparts talked only of applying Resolution 242 and promised no new arms.

It may be that at this juncture Sadat began to think seriously of requesting the repatriation of the Soviet missions in Egypt. On his return to Cairo, he stopped off in Belgrade and Tripoli where we may assume that Tito and Qaddafi, for differing reasons, encouraged him along these lines. Elements of the Egyptian Army, led by Minister of War Ahmad Sadoq, were outspokenly unhappy with the Soviet advisors, and prominent civilians (Abdellatif Baghdadi, Kemal al-Din Hussein, Hassan Ibrahim, et cetera) even petitioned the President in April to reduce the Soviet presence in the country, following which *al-Ahram* organized an Egypto-Soviet colloquium to discuss relations between the two countries. Ismail Fahmy, an Under Secretary in the Ministry of Foreign Affairs, had some particularly trenchant remarks to make about the Soviet Union which resulted in a brief "vacation" from his post. But after his momentary disgrace, Fahmy became Egypt's Foreign Minister after the cease-fire of October 22, 1973.

The Soviets hastened to do a little fence-mending in May 1972 when Marshal Gretchko visited Egypt and put on display the performance capacity of the MIG-25. It was briefly thought that the Russians might be ready to deliver this very advanced aircraft to Egypt. Such was not the case; the show was no more than that, and the situation remained unchanged. Adding to Egyptian suspicions about Soviet intentions was the first Nixon-Brezhnev meeting in Moscow and the commitment of the powers to pursue détente. Détente seemed to mean that neither superpower would allow itself to be drawn into a regional dispute that might entail confrontation with the other. For Egypt the message was that the Soviet Union would never arm Egypt to a level that would give the Egyptians the ability to hold their own against the Israelis. They would

accept the arms imbalance in the area and the state of no war, no peace in the interests of détente. The "Russians" would have to go if Egypt were to play for American support, go to war, or both.

On July 23, 1972, the twentieth anniversary of the revolution, Sadat announced that the Soviet military missions would be repatriated and all military facilities within the country brought under direct Egyptian control. The move was initially popular in both the army and the civilian population. Egypt had regained her sovereignty. Besides, surely Sadat had made a deal with the United States that they would push Israel toward compromise if the Soviet missions left Egypt. After all, had not the Saudi Minister of Defense, Sultan Ibn Abd al-Aziz, visited Sadat on July 6, after his meeting with Nixon, and informed the Egyptians of the American terms? Perhaps, but the United States must then have frustrated Egyptian hopes once again for no new initiative was forthcoming. Why, it was asked, did not Sadat wait until *after* Nixon's re-election when he could respond on the strength of a new mandate? The answer may be that Sadat expected no deal and was already working toward the military venture that came 14 months later.

Egypt's military posture, however, had clearly been weakened, and its crucial air defense system called into question. Sadat may have overplayed his hand. Such considerations could have prompted him, in August, to announce, along with Qaddafi, that "integral union" with Libya—just as rich and anti-Soviet as ever—would be established by September 1, 1973. Integral union was not to be, but its threat stimulated Saudi concern lest Egypt become once again the militantly antimonarchical force it had been under Nasser. Did Sadat foresee that Saudi Arabia would make it worth Egypt's while not to pursue integral union to its end? That is yet another question that defies a firm answer, but throughout the year before the Ramadan War the Saudi counterweight was increasingly felt in Egypt.

Sadat gave some evidence that he had miscalculated the effects of the Soviet expulsion from Egypt. On October 16 He dispatched Prime Minister Aziz Sidqi to Moscow to see if a new modus vivendi in arms supplies could be established. The mission was not judged a success but it may have promoted the first deliveries of the mobile SAM-6 missiles that were to play such an illustrious role a year later. About a week after the Sidqi mission (October 26) Sadat dismissed General Ahmad Sadoq as Minister of War. It was alleged that he had failed to obey orders the previous August to carry out limited operations against the Israelis in the canal zone. At the time, however, it was believed that the staunchly anti-Soviet Sadoq was offering to assuage the hurt feelings of the U.S.S.R. Hindsight once again tells us that Sadat may have indeed intended to fight in August 1972. Before the chiefs of staff General Sadoq argued that any attack would bring in the United States on the side of Israel and leave Egypt at the mercy of Soviet support. "At this point Sadat exploded in one of his famous rages. He shouted, "'I asked you to beat Israel...as for America and Russia, this is the responsibility of political leadership.'" [15]

Compounding Sadoq's sins was the fact that he had been telling the rank and file of the Egyptian Army that the equipment they had received from the Soviet Union was inferior to that received by Israel from the United States. Such remarks could only have had negative effects upon military morale, and some Egyptians opined that Sadoq should have suffered more than disgrace for his "treasonous" behavior. But it is only fair to note that Mohammed Hassanein Heikal must logically be charged with the same sins. In *al-Ahram* of August 2, 1972 Heikal claimed that five MIGs, piloted by Russians, were shot down by Israeli Phantoms at the end of June 1970. Heikal emphasized that Nasser's conclusion was that this constituted proof that Egypt's problem lay in equipment and not, as the Soviets claimed, in the quality of her pilots.

Whatever the inner workings of the Sadoq affair, he was retired and Sadat's former classmate, General Ahmad Ismail, once head of military intelligence, was brought in as Minister of War. [16] It may well have been at this time that the final plans for a large-scale crossing of the canal were first developed. What Sadat was about was overlooked or ignored by most of the foreign press. Only *al-Anwar* of Beirut, to my knowledge, picked up any of Cairo's signals, predicting that Sadat would form a war cabinet. *Al-Anwar* claimed that Sadat "is now convinced of the need to bring about a change of such an order as to upset all the calculations of the enemy and to transform the defensive position of Egypt into an offensive position." [17]

One last attempt was made to see if the United States, in light of Nixon's landslide electoral victory in November, would be prepared to turn its attention to the Middle East. Hafiz Ismail, another of Sadat's classmates, also a former Director of Military Intelligence, and at the time Presidential Advisor on Security Affairs, was sent to Washington in February. The talks did not go badly, and Nixon and Kissinger were sympathetic to the Egyptian case but made no promises. Just a few days after the talks, Congress was asked to approve the sale to Israel of an additional 50 Phantoms. We know that Sadat was incensed by what he regarded as the two-faced behavior of the United States. After October 6 it was posited that this sequence of events forced Egyptian leaders to the conclusion that more than ever Egypt's only remaining option was to go to war. Recently, however, Arab sources have confirmed that the decision to launch a major invasion across the canal had been taken by January, before Ismail's trip to the United States. [18]

At roughly the same time Sadat was sounding out Washington his Minister of War, Ahmad Ismail, had gone to Moscow and, as a result of his trip, concluded what one reliable source termed the single largest arms agreement ever negotiated between Egypt and the Soviets. On the strength of these two missions Sadat dissolved the Sidqi-government, March 26, took over the Prime Ministership himself, announced a government of "total confrontation," and proclaimed himself "military governor of Egypt" with emergency powers.

Despite Arnaud de Borchgrave's now famous *Newsweek* interview with Sadat at the end of March, in which the President said he was totally determined to resume hostilities, most observers saw the government change and the interview as bluff and bravado. *Newsweek* itself qualified the remarks as a ploy to stifle domestic criticism of a do-nothing regime. *The International Herald Tribune* (April 2, 1973) reported:

In Washington and Jerusalem, Mr. Sadat's latest moves were received with studied calm, since Israel has made it clear that its air force will not hesitate to devastate the Egyptians in the event of even a limited war. The Israelis should have little trouble doing just that.

The Israelis do not believe that Mr. Sadat's Arab allies would be of much help in the event of renewed fighting.

No one prior to October 6 would have dissented from this appraisal. Sadat had just weathered another round of student demonstrations and had suspended over 100 journalists and writers from the Arab Socialist Union. It appeared that he was muzzling the so-called "adventurous left" who would be most likely to criticize his inaction—or, if it came to that, his diplomatic sellout. His own cabinet, which was informed by the President on April 25 that he had taken the decision to go to war, did not know whether to take him seriously or not.[19]

Lending substance to such interpretations were the two major policy developments of the late spring. First, pursuing the "exhausting" approach, Egypt labored to bring up the Middle East crisis for debate in the Security Council on the occasion of the sixth anniversary of the June War. Brezhnev was to be in the United States at that time for a second round of talks with Nixon on détente. It was believed that if Egypt had any bellicose intentions, they would become manifest at this time, probably involving some very limited action along the canal to attract the concern of the Security Council in the midst of its debates. Nothing happened militarily, but on July 26 the United States was forced to use its veto to block an otherwise unanimous Security Council motion calling for Israeli withdrawal from the occupied territories. Sadat had what he wanted: Egypt had exhausted all possible means to a political settlement, and it was the United States and Israel, ostentatiously isolated together in the world community, that were blocking the road to peace.

The second policy development consisted of talk of "economic *ouverture*," and a "democratic dialogue" (*al-hiwar ad-dimuqrati*) on the implications of détente for Egypt. The conclusions seemed foregone. Détente, in the light of the second round of Nixon-Brezhnev talks, meant that more than ever the Russians would do nothing to unfreeze the situation in the Middle East. The wheat deal and the promise of massive United States investment in the Soviet Union left Moscow with little leverage in the dispute.   The leverage of the United States grew proportionately, however. The stalemate could go on indefinitely, with a consequent continuation of enormous defense outlays and growing discontent among the Egyptian masses.

Economic *ouverture* could be the way out. The immense hard currency reserves of the Arab oil-producing states could be channeled into the Egyptian economy, and, perhaps, western capital as well. This would get Egypt past a chronic hard currency shortage and contribute to economic growth. To succeed the policy would need to include the establishment of "free industrial zones," a parallel money market for the free conversion of the Egyptian pound, the stimulation of the Egyptian private sector, and, most important, convincingly stable conditions to attract investors. Because no war, no peace was the very opposite of reassuring stability, it was easy to conclude that Sadat would put war on the back burner and talk about a long-range plan to build the country economically for the battle of destiny sometime in the future. The unsigned assessment in *Le Figaro* (August 30, 1973) was typical of this analysis:

> ...the stabilization of relations among Near Eastern states will not promote a solution to the Arab-Israeli dispute. Strengthened by the friendship of Saudi Arabia and Libya, among the most affluent Arab states, President Sadat can afford the luxury...of prolonging the situation of no war, no peace indefinitely.

The "democratic dialogue" launched in the late spring under the auspices of the Arab Socialist Union seemed to be an elaborate staging to bring about ratification by the "masses" of decisions already made. The outcome was to have been the amending of the 1962 Charter, to rid it, in Sadat's words, of certain Marxist interpretations and to issue a document that would be valid until the end of the century.

During the summer overall impressions were reinforced by the deteriorating relations between Egypt and Libya and the increasingly cordial relations between Egypt and Saudi Arabia. Qaddafi was openly calling for a cultural revolution in Egypt and frequently talked of its incompetent leadership. Suspicious of a sellout, he tried to push Egypt to a more radical international stand by appealing to the Egyptian masses within the country, but his advocacy of a cultural revolution alienated the very right-wing, petit bourgeois elements that had been his most ardent supporters. Saudi Arabia meanwhile let it be known that they would like to invest in Egypt, perhaps in direct proportion to the distance Egypt put between herself and antimonarchical Libya. Sadat's secret trip to Saudi Arabia at the end of August resulted in the announcement of

Saudi credits of up to one billion dollars. The integral union between Libya and Egypt that was to have been announced September 1 turned out to be a looser affair in which integration was to be carried out "gradually." Qaddafi swallowed this arrangement bitterly and reluctantly. In all this not much attention was paid to the fact that Sadat also secretly visited Syria at the end of August.

The next hypothesis emanating from "experts" in Cairo was that Saudi Arabia was now in the driver's seat. It had oil and capital which permitted it to bargain with the United States from a position of strength. It could put pressure upon all the "front line" and occasionally radical forces of Egypt, the *fidayin* of al-Fatah, Jordan, and Syria. Saudi Arabia was to play the lead role in moving the United States toward a political solution, and Egypt would follow the Saudi scenario in exchange for hard currency. The first act had to be the rehabilitation of King Hussein of Jordan. Egypt and Syria had broken relations with him when he announced his plan for what amounted to a separate peace with Israel and the establishment of a Jordanian-Israeli condominium over the West Bank. Once Syria, Egypt, and the guerrillas had been assured that the Hussein Plan would be dropped, then relations could be restored with Jordan. With something resembling harmony among the front-line states, Henry Kissinger, the recently appointed Secretary of State (and in King Faysal's eyes, "Super Jew") could perform the arm-twisting on Israel that no other American would have dared.

On September 10, and in seeming conformity with this analysis, Sadat, Hafiz Assad, and Hussein all met in Cairo and announced that the eastern front joint command had been reactivated. A week later King Hussein released several hundred Palestinian guerrillas from Jordanian jails, including al-Fatah's number two, Abu Da'ud, and announced that the Hussein Plan had been allowed to lapse. Now all that remained was for Henry Kissinger to perform his magic. A settlement would represent not only a great personal achievement for Kissinger but would also help protect a conservative pro-western regime in Saudi Arabia whose legitimacy would be more and more profoundly questioned as the stalemated conflict dragged on.

None of these speculations about economic liberalism and the ascendancy of Faysal were wrong,

but they overlooked the fact that Sadat refused to surrender Egypt's capacity for initiative, and that he was determined to demonstrate that ultimately Egypt held the best cards. Moreover, we now know that Sadat told just about everybody in the spring and summer of 1973 that he would undertake major action soon. He had probably talked to several leaders at the Conference of Non-Aligned Nations held at Algiers, September 8-9, which was, incidentally, another diplomatic success for Egypt in isolating the United States and Israel. Hussein, Faysal, Yassir Arafat of al-Fatah, Qaddafi, Tito, and the Soviet were also warned, but they may have discounted the warning or assumed that whatever action took place would be of very limited scope. Indeed, Qaddafi was later to claim that he was told nothing of the war plans whatsoever.[20] Sadat's very lack of credibility turned out to be an asset, for he could get commitments from allies to give support in a hypothetical situation they thought unlikely to occur, without abandoning the element of surprise that would be crucial to the success of the operation. Only Hafiz Assad and General Mustapha Tlas of Syria were in on the detailed planning.

Ihsan Abd al-Quddus (*Akhbar al-Yom*, August 25, 1973) analyzed the situation in a manner that must have been close to Sadat's thinking. He felt that Israel was telling the world that Israel alone could solve the two principal problems of the area. First, Israel could simply occupy the west bank of the Suez Canal and reopen it to shipping and, second, by permitting the fall of King Hussein allow the Palestinians to establish their state in Jordan. He also felt that the Arab oil arm could not be brought into play because of the cautiousness of those who controlled it and the amount of time that would be needed for it to have any effect, and concluded that whether Egypt or Israel began the fighting, an early resumption of hostilities was inevitable. On September 15, again in *Akhbar al-Yom*, he argued that in order to avoid a repetition of June 1967, Egypt had better strike first.

In the meantime Israel had greeted, most probably with malice aforethought, the revivification of the eastern command by provoking, on September 13, an air engagement with the Syrians in which several MIGs were shot down. Palestinian guerrillas added to the growing tension with yet another hijacking; in this instance the guerrillas were able to extract terms from Austria that led to renunciation of official policy allowing Soviet Jews to transit to Israel via Vienna. Israeli reprisals were inevitable. On September 19 Sadat suspended the "democratic dialogue" until after the month of Ramadan (in which Muslims fast from sunrise to sunset), and on September 23, at a meeting of Arab intellectuals, Sadat broadly hinted at what was coming. Six days later, on the third anniversary of Nasser's death, Sadat reinstated all the journalists who had been suspended from the ASU the previous winter. Shortly after that Egypt announced that it had accepted the bid of the American construction firm, Bechtel, to build the Suez-Mediterranean Pipeline. The acceptance of the first major United States-Egyptian deal in several years was real enough, but the timing was deliberately diversionary. The signals of the month's events were mixed, but war was only a few days away. On September 29 Sadat addressed the nation. At the end of his speech he said:

> There is one subject that you have perhaps noticed I have not mentioned, the subject of the battle. I did this on purpose. We have had enough words. I want to tell you just one thing. We know our goal and we are determined to reach it; there is no effort, no sacrifice that we will not accept in order to attain this goal. I will add nothing to this nor enter into any details, but I will simply say that the liberation of our territory is the fundamental task before us. With God's help we will carry it out, we will succeed, we will regain what is ours. That is the will of our people, the will of our nation; it is God's will.

There was no talk here of decisive years, timetables for the battle of destiny or threats of imminent action. Sadat knew the details he refused to discuss for they had been set, according to General Ismail, around September 3.[21] The countdown was on to the most frequently announced and least expected war in the twentieth century.

The Course of Battle

The official code name of the canal crossing was "Badr," the name of the first great battle undertaken by the Prophet Mohammed in 624 A.D.

President Sadat addresses the People's Assembly, October 16, 1973.

an attack was planned for 5 or 6 P.M.—i.e., at sundown—on October 6, but should the information be taken seriously? The day before the attack it is said that General Sharon was allowed to look at some aerial reconnaissance shots which seemed to show camouflaged sections of the bridges Egypt was to use in the crossing. The Israeli cabinet met on the 5th and entrusted General Dayan with mounting a counteroperation. It was at once clear, however, that there was little time to bring it off and that, in any case, it would make Israel look like the aggressor. Despite a flurry of phone calls early in the morning of the 6th (New York time) among Meir, Kissinger, Egypt's Foreign Minister Hassan al-Zayyat who was in New York at the time, and Nixon, the crossing, Cairo time, was only an hour away. Israel with some mild misgivings had decided to accept the first blow. It came three hours earlier than had been expected.[22]

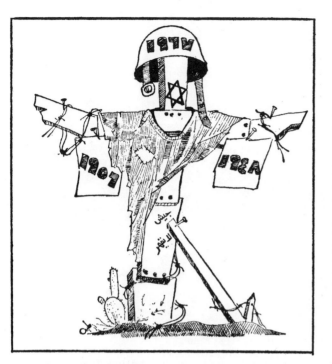

Mohammed Salima, *al-Ahram*, October 12, 1973. "Scarecrow": on the centerstrut of the figure is written "The Army that can't be beaten"; on the arms and helmet are the dates, 1948, 1956, 1967.

during the month of Ramadan. The Egyptian attack—and in Cairo there is no longer any effort made to obfuscate the fact that Egypt attacked first—came during the month of Ramadan. Egyptian troops were not told of the attack until they had begun it, and the morning of the attack, at sunrise, they began their fast as usual. Normally during times of combat a Muslim soldier may break the fast, but Egyptian officers wanted to avoid giving any signal to the Israelis or to their own men that anything unusual was under way. The officers themselves, according to their rank, were informed of the attack in a few rare cases 48 hours in advance, others 24, and the rest on the morning of the attack itself. Commandos were loaded on planes to be parachuted behind Israeli lines; once they were airborne they were told that this trip was for real.

The Israelis knew and did not know. There had been obvious Egyptian troop movements and concentrations but they looked like Egypt's normal pattern of fall maneuvers. Israeli intelligence had picked up information several days in advance that

"The New Wailing Wall"
Ruz al-Yussef n. 2366, October 15, 1973.

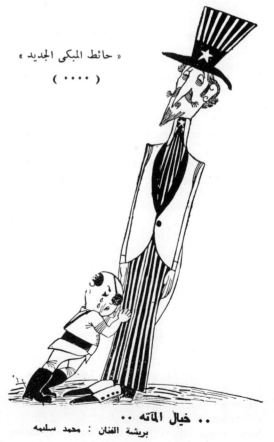

« حائط المبكى الجديد »

(••••)

.. خيال المآته ..

بريشة الفنان : محمد سلمه

One of Egypt's pontoon bridges across the Suez Canal.

President Sadat had his own code word for the crossing, "spark" (*sharara*), but the analogy seems to be more that of setting in motion a catalytic process under relatively controlled conditions than that of igniting an uncontrollable blaze. From a military point of view, Sadat and his general staff had succeeded in devising a plan that drew maximum offensive advantage from arms designed largely for defense. One of the lessons drawn from the War of Attrition was, according to General Hassan al-Gridly, that the Bar Lev Line could not be pounded into disuse but would have to be directly assaulted and taken in hand-to-hand fighting.[23] A plan for crossing the canal, seizing the line and digging in under missile cover probably emerged in mid-1970 as the War of Attrition ended, and came to dominate any other plans in the summer of 1972, after the expulsion of the Soviet missions. The decision to go to war was taken around January 1973, and the launching of hostilities was set, it is reliably reported, for the following May. For unknown reasons the operation was postponed and then reactivated at the beginning of September.

Throughout Sadat took an enormous personal gamble. He may have known that the Egyptian Army was a far better fighting force than any outsiders would have deemed possible, but surely even Sadat must have realized that there was no way to guarantee the success of the crossing. It is said that he relies heavily on the judgment of his senior officers as to the readiness of the troops, but he decided on the scope and timing of the operation. Various Soviet advisors had warned the Egyptians that while the crossing could be made, it would probably take four days and any attacking force could expect at least 50 per cent casualties. Those are sobering prognostications, yet Sadat accepted the risk. Failure would have meant, at the very least, the end of his presidency. In the first 24 hours Egypt put 80,000 men across the canal and lost about 200. But no one except the actual participants could believe what had happened.

After one day of fighting Yves Cuau of the normally cautious *Le Figaro* (October 8, 1973) said there was no analogy between this war and that of 1967 because the Israelis were fighting from advanced positions on only two fronts with much improved training and equipment, whereas the Arabs were more deficient than ever in all these categories. "Even supposing that King Hussein decides to join his Arab allies, the war will certainly not last six days." So obvious did that appear that Cuau concluded that the Israelis must have started it. The Israelis knew who started it, but Chief of Staff Lieutenant-General David Elazar, in a press conference October 8, was excessively optimistic (*New York Times*, October 9, 1973): "On the

The Egyptian flag flies over the wreckage of the Bar Lev Line.

Egyptian front, the general said that most of the Egyptian armor and infantry that had crossed the Suez Canal in the first 30 hours of fighting had been destroyed or driven back. He said the remaining Egyptian units had been cut off and surrounded by Israeli tanks. Slipping into Hebrew, he said, 'We will break their bones.'"

As Egyptian Chief of Staff Saad al-Din Chazli was later to remark (*al-Ahram*, December 9, 1973), the armed forces "used the most sophisticated techniques and the simplest tactics." After a massive air and artillery pounding of the Bar Lev Line, assault teams moved across the canal to establish bridgeheads on the other side. They took with them the deadly hand-held SAM-7 antitank missiles to thwart the inevitable Israeli armored counterattack. Air strikes were made on Israeli air bases in the Sinai, and commandos were parachuted in behind the Line to disrupt Israeli efforts to bring up support. Within 40 minutes of the attack, however, the Israelis had mounted their first air strike and continued the strikes in the remaining three hours of daylight. At that time they lost, according to General Mohammed Ali Fahmy, Chief of Air Defense, 15 planes. [24] In the space of a few hours the Egyptians thus confirmed that they had a good chance of neutralizing the two basic elements of Israeli offensive capacity: armor and aircraft. Key to their success were the mobile SAM-6 missiles, already seen in action in Vietnam, and the SAGGER 3 and 5 antitank missiles. It was well known that Egypt had them, but no one seemed to realize just what they could do.

Meanwhile the army engineers worked feverishly to push floating bridges across the canal. A major technical problem was to open breaches in the 40 to 80-foot high earthwork embankments on the east bank of the canal so that access roads for equipment could be established. The engineers borrowed a technique employed in the construction of the High Aswan Dam, the use of high-power hoses to sluice the earth and sand away.

At the end of the first day, Egyptian troops had established several bridgeheads, seized a number of strongholds on the Line, repulsed the first Israeli armor and air counterattacks and flung pontoon bridges across the canal. During the night the assault on the Line continued and, in the dark, masses of equipment and men were rushed across the canal. Under the highly effective screen provided by their mobile missile batteries, now on the east bank, the Egyptians were prepared at dawn on the 7th to meet the first organized Israeli counterattacks and to extend their grip over the entire length of the Bar Lev Line.

Egyptians take umbrage at the notion that their success was purely a function of good equipment. It is an incontrovertible fact that the Egyptians fought with great tenacity and bravery, and as the initial success became apparent, with overwhelming enthusiasm. An Egyptian Army Captain put it this way: "Personally, I think raising the flag [over the Bar Lev Line] was as decisive a factor as the SAM-6. As soon as the troops saw their flag floating over the east bank, they surged forward sweeping all obstacles in their paths...The cry 'God is Great' [Allah akbar] had a magical effect." "Did you know," said another officer, "that in the 1967 war the battle cry God is Great was abolished and was replaced by 'Land, Sea, Air [barr, bahr, gaw]?'"[25] General Sa'ad Ma'mun, who commanded the Second Army during the attack, had a similar explanation: "We had been six years in the trenches, and there is a war illness known as trench sickness from which people become very weary and lethargic. What can one do?...Training, talks, morale boosting, everything imaginable, but, thanks to God, when we undertook this operation the phrase

God is Great almost was enough to make our people walk on water, and not in the dust."[26]

Once across the Egyptians were victims of their own success. While the Israelis initially turned their attention to the equally impressive Syrian thrust on the Golan Heights, launched at the same time as the Egyptian attack, Egypt completed in three days what they thought would take nine. The Second and Third Armies held the entire east bank of the canal to a depth of up to 15 kilometers. It is important to note, however, that they deployed their forces in five large blocs and not in a continuous line. This, and the fact that the Egyptians put too much of their best armor across the canal, helped prepare the way for the Israeli "infiltration" to the west bank after October 14. But in those first days the question the Egyptians debated was how far to press their advantage. Should they try to seize the three major Sinai passes lying some 40 kilometers away from the canal? Or perhaps strike even farther into Sinai toward Al-Arish, Elath, or even Sharm al-Sheikh? General Chazli may have advocated more daring initiatives, but it was decided instead to consolidate Egyptian positions on the east bank. When, around the 16th and 17th, the Egyptians did try to break out toward the passes, the Israelis were prepared to stop them. Whatever course Egypt might have followed, it is unlikely that they would have thrust deeply into Sinai for fear of losing their missile umbrella and thereby exposing their own lengthy supply lines.[27]

While the Egyptians consolidated, the Syrians bore the brunt of the Israeli counterattack on the Golan front as well as heavy air raids on Syria's ports and interior that destroyed the country's industrial infrastructure. Between October 12 and 16, two Iraqi divisions and a Jordanian brigade entered Syria to help contain the Israeli counterattack, and by October 17 the northern front had begun to stabilize.[28]

It was at this point that Sadat permitted himself the luxury of basking in his new found glory. On October 16 he went through wildly cheering crowds in Cairo's streets to address an equally enthusiastic gathering of the People's Assembly. His speech was moderate but firm in its insistence upon the return of all occupied territories and a just settlement of the Palestinian problem. More than anything, Sadat's speech was the occasion for Egyptians to

Minister of War Ahmad Ismail surrounded, left, by Vice President Mahmoud Fawzy and, right, Presidential Advisor Aziz Sidqi. In the background are members of the People's Assembly. The occasion is President Sadat's October 16 speech.

feel happy with themselves for the first time in years, a time for jubilant but not excessively unrealistic self-congratulation.

Within two days of Sadat's speech, on October 18, the representatives of the Arab oil-producing states took their historic decision in Kuwait to begin monthly 5 per cent cutbacks in production until such time as the oil-importing states of Japan, Europe, and North America forced Israel to withdraw from the occupied territories. Thus Operation Badr had not only elicited an unusual degree of solidarity among Arab states but had also "sparked" the process by which oil was to be used, for the first time, as a political weapon. Better was yet to come. After the decision in Kuwait, Kissinger met in Washington with the foreign ministers of Saudi Arabia, Kuwait, Algeria, and Morocco. The Saudi minister, Omar Saqqaf, came away from the talks confident that the United States would press for a just settlement. He so reported to King Faysal, but the next day Nixon sent a request to Congress for $2.2 billion in emergency military aid for Israel. Faysal was outraged and unilaterally declared a total embargo on Saudi oil exports to the United States, effective November 1. Faysal promised that the embargo would not be lifted until Israel had begun to evacuate, and that they should begin with East Jerusalem, in which he hoped to pray before he died.

Sadat had succeeded, through Badr, in forcing the mobilization of Arab economic and military resources, but the tide of battle had begun to turn. The Israelis were unable to roll up to the gates of Damascus, but they had pushed the Syrians back beyond the 1967 lines in several places. The massive United States airlift of planes, equipment, and ammunition to Israel was under way, and the "infiltration" to the west bank of the canal had begun. Even as Sadat spoke on October 16 an Israeli task force had broken through the Second and Third Armies at the northern end of the Great Bitter Lake at a place known as Deverswar. In the following days, during Alexei Kosygin's visit to Cairo, the task force was heavily reinforced and began to make forays from its bridgehead to destroy missile sites and thus free some Egyptian airspace for the unimpeded use of Israeli attack planes. The Egyptians, having no single commander for the Second and Third Armies, reacted sluggishly to the incursion, regarding it at first as a diversionary action. When it became clear how big the operation was, the Egyptians found that they had insufficient armor on the west bank to meet it, and that without the missile screen Israeli aircraft were able to wreak havoc with Egyptian counterattacks on the ground and in the air. While the Egyptians have only recently begun to publish any details of the infiltration and the establishment of the Israeli "pocket" on the west bank, its importance must have been clear by the last day of Kosygin's visit, October 19. His return to Moscow probably put in motion the precipitous rush towards a cease-fire. On the 19th, upon a Soviet request, Kissinger flew to Moscow for consultations, and then to Israel. Shortly after his return to the United States, on October 22, the Security Council voted the jointly sponsored United States-Soviet Resolution 338 (see appendix) calling for a cease-fire "in place," to be followed by steps toward the implementation of Resolution 242. Egypt and Israel accepted the cease-fire. Syria, which had been planning a large counteroffensive for October 23, did not. But neither did they launch the counteroffensive.

The cease-fire came as a shock to most Egyptians and put the first smudges on Sadat's shining new image. Ihsan Abd al-Quddus had announced categorically at the beginning of the war: "...we refuse any discussion of a cease-fire until the reasons for opening fire have been eliminated...I do not set this down as an expression of personal opinion, or merely as a nationalist *cri de coeur*, but rather because I know that this is what has been decided with regard to the battle." (*Akhbar al-Yom*, October 8, 1973). Sadat, in his October 16 speech, had himself been equally forthright: "We are prepared to accept a cease-fire on the basis of the immediate withdrawal of Israeli forces from all occupied territories...We are prepared immediately upon the completion of this withdrawal to attend an international peace conference at the United Nations...." (*al-Ahram*, October 17, 1973).

The Israeli pocket, and perhaps the reasoning of Alexei Kosygin, changed these stipulations considerably, and we may reasonably suppose that Egypt accepted the Big Power resolution of October 22 on much less favorable terms than those set out above in order to prevent any further expansion of the pocket. Sadat's explanation was that in the first ten days Egypt had been fighting Israel and that, according to Dayan's own admission, Israel was running short of equipment and ammunition. At that point, the United States came to Israel's rescue, and Egypt was, in effect, engaging the mightiest nation on earth, an engagement for which Sadat admittedly had little appetite. Heikal, who published the first detailed and reasonably accurate account of the Israeli infiltration (*al-Ahram*, October 28, 1973), said that the operation had been made possible by detailed

aerial reconnaissance photographs of the positions of the Second and Third Armies taken by United States planes on October 13 and immediately handed over to the Israelis.

General Ariel Sharon, reactivated for the occasion, planned the infiltration against the better judgment of Generals Gonein, Israeli commander in Sinai, and Bar Lev, responsible for planning the war on the Suez front. Heikal, in an article entitled "General Sharon's Adventure," argued that Sharon knew that the Israeli position on the west bank could not be reinforced except by "cheating" (*al-Ahram*, December 21, 1973). Thus Heikal believes the rumor that the Israeli military were opposed to accepting the cease-fire October 22 was merely posturing, at any rate as far as Sharon was concerned, for he was determined to use the cease-fire to bring more equipment across the canal and to expand the pocket.

On October 22 the bulk of the Israeli forces on the west bank had proceeded no farther than the southern end of the Great Bitter Lake, well to the north of the city of Suez. The supply routes of the Egyptian Third Army were thus still intact. After the "cease-fire" the fighting became, if anything, more intense as the Israelis raced southwards to complete the encirclement of the Third Army and to lay siege to the city of Suez.[29] At that point it looked as though Israel was determined to force the surrender of the entire Third Army, a potential humiliation that would have annulled Sadat's gains (it is said he was contemplating resigning at this point), and which would have been unacceptable to the Soviet Union and perhaps even to the United States.

In the same article, Heikal summed up his view of Sharon's adventure:

> It will be shown in the days to come that Israel was on the verge of facing the realities of history, but the adventure of General Sharon delayed this process for some time; and many in Israel will pay the price of this delay many times over. This is the tragedy that General Sharon has brought about, a man who thinks himself a hero while in fact he is an adventurer against [the course] of history.

It was at this juncture that Sadat called upon the two sponsors of United Nations Resolution 338 to put troops in the area to apply the cease-fire, and that the Soviets, on the heels of the American rejection of Sadat's appeal, sent a tough letter to Nixon apparently telling him they were prepared to send in personnel unilaterally. The Soviet threat was no bluff, and it is perfectly possible that they would have put troops into the Suez area in order to prevent the surrender of the Third Army and further violations of the cease-fire. The Americans responded with the now-famous worldwide alert of United States bases, but, more important, joined once again with the Soviets to sponsor Security Council Resolution 339 (see appendix), providing for the immediate dispatch of an international peace-keeping force (United Nations Emergency Force) to implement the cease-fire. With that act the heavy fighting was over and neither side could claim victory.

Enter Kissinger

President Sadat and Egypt now entered a phase in which the basic levers of control over the military situation began to slip away into the hands of others. Once the fighting tapered off, the oil-rich states, led by Saudi Arabia, became the principal Arab actors in confrontation with Israel. Egypt's threat of the resumption of hostilities was certainly credible, but it was a question of oil supplies that was leading western Europe and Japan to adopt stances favorable to the Arabs. Japan condemned continued Israeli retention of the occupied territories and high-level missions were sent out to the Arab world to talk of investment and peacetime reconstruction in the area (such as $150 million to help rebuild the canal zone cities). On November 6, the nine nations of the European Common Market called on Israel to relinquish the occupied territories and emphasized that the rights of the Palestinians must be respected. All these developments were, of course, welcomed by Egypt and might never have occurred had Egypt not gone to war, but Egypt's very success in this respect meant a diminution in her role in guiding the crisis towards a final settlement.

Henry Kissinger and Anwar Sadat; the November 9 meeting.

The levers of control also began to slip away into the hands of the two superpowers, particularly those of the United States, and even more particularly, those of Secretary of State Henry Kissinger. In the space of a few weeks the Kissinger mystique began to spread its effect through Egypt. At the beginning of November Egypt's new Foreign Minister, Ismail Fahmy, spent four days in Washington, D.C. along with Golda Meir as Kissinger conducted what must have been the equivalent of proximity talks. Shortly after these talks Kissinger flew to Cairo, November 8, and within 24 hours had reached agreement with President Sadat on (1) the resumption, in principal, of diplomatic relations with the United States at the ambassadorial level (Hermann Eilts, former United States Ambassador in Saudi Arabia was immediately sent to Cairo with the rank of Ambassador); and (2) a six-point proposition for the exchange of prisoners, resupplying the Third Army with food and medicine, the beginning of direct Egyptian-Israeli talks at Kilometer 101 on the Cairo-Suez road to effect an Israeli pullback to the positions of October 22 (those positions were left unspecified), and to disengage the entangled lines of the two armies (see appendix).

Coming after the harsh words that Sadat and other Egyptians had reserved for the United States following Israel's violation of the cease-fire, the turnabout shocked and surprised most Egyptians. What magic had this man performed?

To some it was perfectly obvious that Kissinger had virtually written a scenario for the war of October 6, encouraging the Egyptians to heat up the stalemate so that he could act in the midst of crisis. The acquiesence of the Soviets to the American scenario was assured, so this theory would have it, as a result of its need for United States wheat and investments. The advocates of this view do not specify how Kissinger could arrange for the Israelis to allow themselves to be pushed out of the Bar Lev Line, but this particular conspiracy theory (matched by the Israelis in a theory advanced by Haim Herzog that the Russians masterminded the whole thing) was given some sustenance by outside observers.[30]

Variants of a more nuanced view were presented by Heikal and Abd al-Quddus. Heikal spoke for many when he intimated that Egypt had undergone an unavoidable "examination" (*imtihan*) to demonstrate its will to fight and die for Sinai and the other occupied territories (*al-Ahram*, November 9, 1973). Until that time the world, and even Arabs such as Faysal, may have thought that Egypt was trying to achieve a cheap victory by brandishing verbal threats to regain some territory about which it cared very little. Egypt demonstrated to all skeptics that it was willing to pay for Sinai. Moreover, it is during a "hot" crisis, another Egyptian remarked, that Kissinger can assess the weights of the protagonists and move toward a resolution of the conflict. In this indirect sense, then, Kissinger may have inadvertently encouraged a new round of fighting.[31]

Abd al-Quddus, in his editorial of December 8, observed that Kissinger's style was to act neither before nor after but during a crisis. That being the case, the best course for Egypt to follow would be to fight and negotiate simultaneously just as the North Vietnamese had done. Abd al-Quddus also implied that this tactic would encourage Saudi Arabia to hold firm in its decision to limit oil production and to ban all sales of oil to the United States.

There emerged in Cairo in those weeks a sort of fascination with Kissinger the man and Kissinger the Jew. For Heikal, and perhaps Sadat, it was a meeting of minds, the establishment of a certain level of trust between single-minded power politicians sincerely interested in a settlement. Heikal managed a two-hour interview with Kissinger which he published in *al-Ahram* on November 16. The picture we have of him is that of a reasonable man explaining his viewpoint with considerable openness: "I find myself in the midst of a crisis, representing the concern of the United States in it. But all that I can rely upon is my own reputation...my own personal balance [of success *rasidi ash-shakhsy*].... I had imagined that [the Middle East] would wait its turn, but the crisis imposed itself upon us all, and I was among those who did not expect it." And he added, smiling: "In that respect you succeeded, and I will not be the last to recognize this success." Heikal argued that there had been a great difference in the quality of the arms the United States sent to Israel during the war as opposed to those received by Egypt from the Soviet Union. Kissinger countered by saying: "There is one thing you must take into consideration. The United States cannot today, nor in the future, allow Soviet arms to achieve a major victory, even if it is not a decisive victory, against American arms."[32]

الاهرام - ٨/١١/٧٣

كيسنجر والسلام

السلام

ـ طب أنا اديتك جايزة نوبل ٠٠ انت ح تديني ايه ؟

Salah Jahin, *al-Ahram*, November 8, 1973. Kissinger and Peace: "O.K., I gave you the Nobel Prize. What are you going to give me?"

Abd al-Quddus, who sometimes comes close to charging the Jews with congenital perfidy, was no less fascinated by the man. "Perhaps the strongest force aiding Nixon in bringing about a solution... is Kissinger. And he is a Jew. No one can accuse him of anti-Semitism or hostility to Israel. He is, however, a Jew concerned about the future of the Jews and their protection from the avidity (*iṭmā'*) of the Zionist order."[33]

Kissinger's small triumph in Cairo triggered some of the city's caustic tongues. Had Egypt crossed the canal simply to sign a piece of paper agreeing to start talks leading to an Israeli pullback to the lines of October 22 on the *west* bank of the canal? "We used Egyptian lives and Soviet arms to renew relations with the United States...." As the Egyptians in turn encircled the Israeli encirclement of the Third Army, elements of the armed forces were allegedly eager to take a crack at the Israeli pocket. The Israelis, however, began to dig in, and once they had received their prisoners back from Egypt, the talks at Kilometer 101 went nowhere at the same time that the violations of the cease-fire grew daily.

As one pundit remarked, the talks at 101 were only a sandwich, and the main course, if there was to be one, would be at Geneva. To go to Geneva Egypt and Syria needed a mandate from their fellow Arab states to sit down with the Israelis (or at least be in the same room with them) and negotiate

a settlement. President Boumedienne of Algeria, who is now emerging as one of the most prominent Arab statesmen, hosted with the Arab League a summit meeting of Arab heads of state that began on November 26 in Algiers. Before it began, Heikal characterized it (*al-Ahram*, November 23, 1973) "The most important Arab summit meeting in all our history. For the first time it will be a conference for action, held in an atmosphere of action, faced with the necessity of action." But already the fragile unity that the war had forged began to fissure. King Hussein, foreseeing the recognition that the conference would confer on the guerrilla groups, refused to attend and sent his foreign minister instead. Presidents Bakr of Iraq and Qaddafi of Libya also refused to attend what they predicted would be a sellout. Abd al-Quddus accused the Libyans and Iraqis of opening new "pockets" in the ranks of the Arabs (*Akhbar al-Yom*, November 24, 1973). Yet the conference went well (it was the first since the ill-fated conference of December 1969 in Rabat), and the Palestinian Liberation Organization (PLO) was recognized as the legitimate representative of the Palestinian people. Egypt and Syria were given the green light to go to Geneva, "at their own risk," to meet the Israelis. Meanwhile Faysal, despite Kissinger's personal blandishments, kept the tap turned firmly off.

فى الطريق الى مؤتمر جنيف

بدون تعليق !

Salah Jahin, *al-Ahram*, December 17, 1973 "On the Way to the Geneva Conference." The tank is entitled "Military Solution," the man leaping out of it "Political Solution." His attaché case is marked "Egypt."

Geneva
1973 conference

For a brief time after Algiers it appeared that Egypt's methodical march toward Geneva had broken down. After several meetings between Generals Ya'ariv (Israel) and al-Gamassi (Egypt) no progress had been made toward the disengagement of forces nor towards Israeli pullback to the October 22 lines. On November 30, Egypt announced that the talks were suspended. It was thought that Egypt might refuse to go to Geneva unless Israel honored the six-point Kissinger plan as a prior condition. It could be, although it is not known for certain, that General Chazli was a proponent of a hard line on this issue and perhaps even of an attack on the Israeli pocket. At any rate he was removed without explanation on December 13 and replaced as Chief of Staff by General Mohammed Abd al-Ghana Gamassi, former Chief of Operations.

It seems probable that the suspension of the talks at Kilometer 101 was yet another Kissinger strategem, or at least was so reported in Cairo's newspapers. It is believed that Kissinger, in light of the Israelis' insistence that nothing of substance could be debated at Geneva until after their elections, December 31, suggested that the questions of disengagement and pullback be carried over to the opening of the Geneva conference, and that the Israelis be prepared to make concessions to get the conference off on a positive note.[34]

Kissinger came back to Cairo one more time, December 13, and then flew on to Syria, Lebanon, Jordan, and Israel to iron out details of the opening of the conference on December 18. The question of a prisoner exchange between the Syrians and the Israelis became a major stumbling block, with the Syrians refusing to turn over any prisoners, or even their names, until some later phase of negotiations. The Israelis threatened not to go to Geneva on that basis, and the opening was postponed until December 21. Then the Syrians announced that they would not attend the conference, but, like the Palestinians, would wait and see if the conference showed that the Israelis were seriously interested in a settlement. To compound the situation, the Israelis, sounding reminiscent of a couple of generations of Arab refusal to deal with Zionism, declared they would never negotiate with Palestinian "murderers," even if others thought the PLO should attend the conference.

The Sadat strategy was looking a little frayed about the edges—but it was still flying. Ismail Fahmy led the Egyptian delegation off to Geneva. The only other Arabs there were the members of King Hussein's Jordanian delegation. On December 21, Secretary General of the United Nations, Kurt Waldheim, opened the conference. No one any longer expected magic results or quick solutions; some even wondered if anything had really changed since October 6. The doubters should make no mistake; something close to a miracle had occurred in the Middle East in the fall of 1973. Operation Badr could have been more successful

Israeli prisoner of war in an Egyptian hospital.

Israeli prisoners of war in Egypt.

militarily, but it also could have been a disaster. The fact that it was not changed everything; a bridgehead on a new era had been established.

Conclusions and Consequences

What is truly remarkable in this unfinished tale is the undeniable success that President Sadat has achieved in coping with the same economic and military constraints as Nasser. Through trial and error, Sadat—a great conspirator but a lousy planner as one Egyptian put it to me—artfully stumbled his way to the catalytic event that made the Middle East conflict ripe for settling. Let us look at some of those achievements.

First, Sadat brought to the Arab world a level of unity of purpose it had seldom achieved before. The President had systematically followed a policy of conciliation since 1971, demonstrably proving his willingness to cooperate with all Arabs regardless of political regime. Symbolic of this was one of Sadat's meetings with King Faysal. He kissed the King's shoulders and beard and said "Ya Amir al-mu'minin (O Commander of the Faithful) all the Arab world looks to you." Nasser, it has been said, once vowed to pluck out Faysal's whiskers one by one.

The unity Sadat had brought about is fragile. Unity with Libya is, for the time being, a dead letter.[35] Iraq is pursuing its typically maverick path,[36] and keeping Jordan, Syria, and the Palestinians together on any kind of common ground will require something close to legerdemain. But the onus is now upon those who break rank with Egypt, and also Syria, for it was those two countries that took the fundamental step of going to war.

The second major Egyptian success was to bring the oil weapon into full play and to tie oil supplies directly to the question of the evacuation of occupied territories. The exchange was and is simple: oil for territory, and it is up to the oil-importing nations to promote the deal by putting pressure on Israel and/or the United States. This is the message that the doubly symbolic team of oil ministers— Sheikh Yamani, Arab and representative of conservative, monarchical Saudi Arabia, and Abdesslam Belaid, Berber and representative of radical, republican Algeria—delivered over several weeks of travel through western Europe and the United States.

There is a general awareness that this gambit can be overplayed, and that a worldwide economic recession, from which no country would be sheltered, could ensue. The decision of the Arab oil-exporting countries, taken fittingly on Christmas Day 1973, to begin to raise production once again was evidence that they had a good sense of tolerable limits. Moreover, they were aware that if the posted price of oil were forced up to the $17 per barrel that Iran attained in an auction of crude, the poorer developing nations would have to close shop. The new posted price suggested by the Arabs in December was still a stunning $11 per barrel.

On a separate issue Egypt also appears to have made remarkable gains. Economic "ouverture" rather than being paralyzed by the October War was given a real boost. In their new found confidence and solidarity and in hope that peace may be at hand, there is talk of the oil-rich funding the rebuilding and development of the front-line states of Egypt, Syria, and Jordan.[37] Noteworthy is the fact that the Kuwaitis have formally agreed to put up the foreign currency component of the Suez-Mediterranean Pipeline. European states and Japan, eager for Arab good will, have announced their willingness to help in several projects. Sadat may have planned it all that way.

The war increased Israel's diplomatic isolation. Europe took a stand following the war that Israel rightly regarded as inimical. Virtually all African states, with the exception of South Africa, had broken off relations with Israel by war's end. At one point there were as many states in the world prepared to recognize a provisional Palestinian government as there were states having diplomatic relations with Israel.

As much as anything, the war called into question the whole concept of Israel's "security borders." Fighting from advanced positions and on only two fronts, Israel suffered casualties vastly superior (at least 3,000 dead) to those sustained in 1967. It turned out that if the Arabs could strike first, Israel was unable to administer a lightning blow to two, not to mention three, of the neighboring states' armed forces. Even Sharm al-Sheikh, whose seizure by the Egyptians in 1967 was regarded by the Israelis as *casus belli*, was reduced in significance by the blockade imposed at the entrance to the Red Sea, at Bab al-Mandeb Straits. The blockade was made possible by the fact that

Ethiopia, long one of Israel's firmest friends in Africa, broke relations with Tel Aviv during the war. In the past Ethiopia might have allowed the Israelis to use its own Red Sea facilities to break an Arab blockade, but that possibility as well as Ethiopian objections to the blockade have now been removed. Heikal summed it up in the middle of the war (*al-Ahram*, October 19, 1973): "We wish to prove that the Israeli's theory of security is mistaken, and Israel wishes to prove that it is sound. And that is the heart of the armed struggle at this point in time."

In this vein, once hostilities had gone beyond a week, it became clear that Israel was far from attaining the self-sufficiency in equipment and ammunition that had been her goal since 1967. Indeed Israel was highly dependent upon the United States, and so obvious was that fact that it would be impossible in the future for the United States to deny that it had major means of leverage over Israeli behavior. That dependency was, moreover, compounded by the enormous monetary debt incurred by Israel as a result of the war. In a general sense the war showed that the Arabs could fight, that Israel could not destroy them, and that if there were no change in the situation Israel could expect repetitions of the October War every few years.

All European nations (plus Turkey), with the exception of Portugal, refused to allow the United States to transit war material to Israel through their air bases. As the oil cuts intensified, Japan and NATO nations took stances on the war that were at variance with United States positions, and the likelihood was that these small cleavages in the European alliance would only be exacerbated by continuation of the crisis. Here again Sadat could claim success, for the war had begun to force the United States to realize that its national security interests were in some very fundamental respects not compatible with Israel's maximum military and territorial goals. Through oil shortages and the specter of big power confrontation, Sadat was trying to push the United States toward the "even-handedness" it had so proclaimed as its policy.

Finally, at least as far as this Report is concerned, the war demonstrated the limits of détente. Before the war it had been pointed out in Egypt that the Middle East had not been an area in which Nixon and Brezhnev had reached agreement.[38] The war confirmed the point. One Egyptian told me the problem was that the Americans have always tried to predict Soviet moves in simple gaming terms, as a function of the manipulation of power factors, threats and rewards. But while the Soviet Union does wish to avoid confrontation, it cannot afford to abandon a just cause, a revolution, or a movement of national liberation in the Third World without losing much of its credibility. The downfall of Allende in Chile may have had immediate relevance to Soviet actions in the Middle East. More than confrontation, the Soviet Union fears being associated with an unjust settlement. Its major ideological and power interests lie in the independence and economic development of the Third World— not in wheat deals. The West consistently loses sight of these priorities. October 6 put things back in their proper perspective.

* * * * *

The war led Egypt out of years of deepening despondency; the entire nation has given the impression of suffering from trench sickness. It gave an immeasurable boost to the Egyptians sense of honor and self-respect. It is, however, too facile to depict this war as a latter-day manifestation of the quaint, old obsession of the Arabs with their honor and image. The war was fought for real things, such as Sinai, and not to salve a wounded sense of machismo. As several Egyptians pointed out to me, the war was yet another phase of a century-old struggle against foreign occupation that had fired the Egyptian nationalist movement and for which Egyptians had been dying ever since 1882 when the British invaded their country. Sadat managed to tap this current of nationalist legitimacy and to become, at least for awhile, its major figure. After October 6 Sadat, for the first time, became his own man—and Egypt was once again a force to be reckoned with.

NOTES

1. Dr. Yussef Idris, "al-Khallas," *al-Ahram*, October 12, 1973; see also Galal Kishk, "Crisis of Egyptian Thought in the Ramadan War," *al-Sayyad*, no. 1526, December 13-20, 1973, pp. 68-71.

2. Musa Sabry, "God is Great," *al-Akhbar*, October 15, 1973.

3. *Al-Ahram*, December 7, 1973. The following day, the newspaper announced the formation of a preparatory committee to arrange for a conference to be held in 1974, the paper's centennial year, to discuss the reconstruction of Arab civilization with other Arab intellectuals.

4. Ahmad Baha al-Din, "Geneva: Israel's likely behavior," *al-Ahram*, December 17, 1973.

5. Fu'ad Matar, *Rusia al-Nasiria was Masr al-Masria*, Dar al-Nahar, Beirut 1972, p. 68.

6. *The Times*, London, December 13, 1973. Martin was writing at the moment Sadat may have decided on resuming fighting on a large scale; in any event war was only ten months away.

7. Primarily the monthly *al-Talia* (L'Avant-Garde) and *al-Katib* (The Scribe). Another Egyptian Marxist, Mahmoud Hussein, has succinctly presented the fundamental and irreconcilable options that have faced Egyptian leaders since 1967. See his *La lutte des classes en Egypte*, Maspéro 1971, p. 338.

8. It is of interest to note one version of the method by which Egypt pays for Soviet arms. An initial accord stipulated that payments would be 75 per cent in Egyptian and 25 per cent in hard currency. After Nasser's death that was changed to 50-50 and then again to 25-75. See Fu'ad Matar, *op. cit.*, p. 70.

9. It is widely believed among many Egyptians, and has been explicitly stated by Heikal, that since Johnson's accession to the presidency in 1963, United States policy in the Arab world was predicated on the downfall of Nasser. This was so because Johnson and the oil lobby saw Nasser's involvement in the Yemen as representing his determination to take over all the Arabian peninsula and the Gulf thus controlling the world's major oil reserves. The United States and Israel worked out a secret pact to dump Nasser; the means was to be a military operation that would so humiliate Egypt that Nasser would be forced to resign or be overthrown, and Egypt's military capacity neutralized for years

to come. The result of the pact was the June War. It was recently recalled in *Akhbar al-Yom* (October 11, 1973) that Secretary of State Dean Rusk told a group of Congressmen on June 7, 1967, "This is a great day for the West."

10. In an interview in *al-Hawades* (Beirut) Egyptian Vice President Hussein Shafai said that Nasser had in essence died in 1967 (no. 872, July 27, 1973).

11. Mohammed Fawzi was arrested and tried after the May 15, 1971 showdown between President Anwar Sadat and Ali Sabry.

12. In November 1970 Hafiz Assad brought Syria into the Federation and about a year later, as he moved toward a settlement of the civil war in the south, Numeiry took the Sudan out.

13. Hafiz Assad, former Syrian Minister of Defense, took power in the fall of 1970, deposing the more radical wing of the Ba'ath party that had ruled Syria since February 1966.

14. For a fascinating account of this confrontation see Fu'ad Matar, *Ayn asbaha abd al-nasr fi gumhuria as-sadat?* (What has become of Nasser in the republic of Sadat?) Dar al-Nahar, Beirut, 1972.

15. See *as-Sayyad*, n.1521, November 8-15, p. 13.

16. General Ismail had been dismissed as Chief of Staff by Nasser following the brief Israeli occupation of the Red Sea island of Shadwan on January 23, 1970. He was replaced at that time by General Sadoq.

17. Cited in *Le Monde*, November 23, 1972.

18. See Ihsan Abd al-Quddus, "We learned from their experiences; they fell into our errors," *Akhbar al-Yom*, November 3, 1973; also Heikal's long interview with General Ismail, *al-Ahram*, November 18, 1973; and *al-Sayyad*, no. 1521, November 8-15, 1973. General Sa'ad al-Din Chazli, Chief of Staff, claimed the battle plan had been drawn up nine months before the crossing, *al-Ahram*, December 6, 1973.

19. See Eric Rouleau, "La chance de ne pas être cru...," *Le Monde*, November 24, 1973.

20. See Qaddafi's interview with Eric Rouleau, *Le Monde*, October 23, 1973.

21. Eric Rouleau claims that "D-Day" had probably been set in August and the military preparations for October 6 begun

on September 3, *Le Monde*, November 24, 1973. Cf. General Ahmad Ismail, *al-Ahram*, November 18, 1973.

22. Heikal paid this backhanded compliment to Israeli intelligence in a long and fascinating article in *al-Ahram*, December 7, 1973.

23. *Al-Ahram*, December 12, 1973. Al-Gridly is the Secretary General of the Ministry of War. General Gamal Mohammed Ali, head of the Army Corps of Engineers gave the following details on the Bar Lev Line. It was 163 kilometers long and cost $238 million. It had 27 strong points at four-kilometer intervals. It was protected by earthworks whose height varied between 12 and 20 meters. At most points it was separated from the canal by 200 to 300 meters of barbed wire and mine fields. Below ground level it housed multistoried, air-conditioned rooms, was armed with artillery, mortars, machine guns, et cetera, and was built to withstand direct hits of bombs up to 1,000 pounds. *Al-Ahram*, December 11, 1973.

24. Egyptian generals reported to the People's Assembly on December 10 and 11 about the military details of the crossing. Verbatim reports were published in *al-Ahram* of December 11 and 12. It is striking that in none of the six reports was any mention made of the role of the Soviet Union.

25. Galal Kishk, *al-Sayyad*, no. 1523, November 22-29, 1973, p. 29.

26. *Al-Ahram*, December 11, 1973, General Ma'mun suffered a heart attack after eight days of fighting and was subsequently appointed Assistant Minister of War.

27. See General André Beaufre, *Le Figaro*, November 28, 1973. General Beaufre commanded the French paratroopers in the Suez invasion of November 1956. See also Eric Rouleau, "Les dédales de l'operation Badr," *Le Monde*, November 25-26, 1973.

28. King Hussein had nominally told Assad and Sadat on September 10 that Jordan could not play an important role in any future war given its inadequate air force. The venerable old Palestinian nationalist, Suleiman Nabulsi, claims that Hussein purposely kept Jordan underarmed and even refused Soviet offers to beef up his armed forces. See Eric Rouleau, *Le Monde*, October 21-22, 1973.

29. See J.C. Guillebaud, "Retour au Goshen," *Le Monde*, November 2, 1973 and Drew Middleton, "Israelis make big gains between cease-fires," *New York Times*, October 25, 1973.

30. See, for instance, Bernard Margueritte, "Les Americains ont-ils encouragé les Egyptiens á reprendre le combat?" *Le Monde*, October 16, 1973.

31. Abd al-Quddus wrote explicitly on September 1, 1973 in *Akhbar al-Yom* that "Kissinger is convinced that a political solution—any political solution—can be achieved only by intensifying the crisis that needs settlement...." The title of the article was "The American Jew who is solving the matter."

32. Kissinger's caveat was confirmed in reports from Washington. See, for instance, Anthony Thomas, "U.S. Officials say Israel was losing war when Europe blocked airlift," *The Times*, October 31, 1973.

33. The occasionally tortured ambivalence of many Egyptians about Judaism and Zionism was never more graphically depicted than during this crisis. In the same issue of *Akhir Sa'a*, November 14, 1973, a mass circulation illustrated weekly, two articles appeared back to back. The first was by M. Shahin and entitled "This Man was a Professor." In it Shahin told of a visit to Harvard in 1957 to attend a conference organized by Kissinger. The article lauded Kissinger's courtesy, hospitality, intellect, and organizational sense. It recalled approvingly that Kissinger had even worked in his own tiny kitchen to serve his guests in his modest Cambridge apartment. Following this article was a short story by Mustafa Sa'adni, "A Bloody Tragedy." It starts off as follows: "This happened in the city of Damascus...around 1840, and it was not the first occurrence of its kind. It has happened frequently and will happen again in other countries: i.e., that a Jew slaughters a Christian or Muslim child or man in order to use his blood in making the bread they use on their feast days!"

34. See "Dr. K's Mideast Gamble," *Newsweek*, December 17, 1973.

35. Qaddafi sent a highly critical open letter to Sadat concerning the talks at Kilometer 101 and subsequently withdrew his ambassador from Cairo. See *Le Monde*, November 17, 1973.

36. Not only did Iraq not go to Algiers but in mid-December announced that it would unilaterally increase its oil production because it felt that cutbacks were not hurting the United States. Only nationalization of the big oil companies and withdrawal of Arab assets from western banks would do that.

37. Almost a blueprint for postwar reconstruction is the excellent article of Abdullah Tariqi, "In Order to Sharpen the Oil Weapon," *al-Ahram*, November 5, 1973.

38. See for instance Gamal Uteifi, "International Changes and their Effects," *al-Talia*, Vol. 9, no. 10, October 1973.

APPENDIX I

TEXTS OF RESOLUTIONS ON THE MIDDLE EAST

October 21—Following are the Texts of the joint United States-Soviet resolution on the Middle East and of United Nations Security Council Resolution 242, adopted November 22, 1967

Joint Resolution

The Security Council

1. Calls upon all parties to the present fighting to cease all firing and terminate all military activity immediately not later than 12 hours after the moment of the adoption of this decision in the positions they now occupy.

2. Calls upon the parties concerned to start immediately after the cease-fire the implementation of Security Council Resolution 242 in all of its parts.

3. Decides that immediately and concurrently with the cease-fire negotiations start between the parties concerned under appropriate auspices aimed at establishing a just and durable peace in the Middle East.

1967 Resolution

The Security Council,
Expressing its continuing concern with the grave situation in the Middle East.

Emphasizing the inadmissibility of the acquisition of territory by war and the need to work for a just and lasting peace in which every state in the area can live in security.

Emphasizing further that all Member States in their acceptance of the Charter of the United Nations have undertaken a commitment to act in accordance with Article 2 of the Charter.

1. Affirms that the fulfillment of Charter principles requires the establishment of just and lasting peace in the Middle East which should include the application of both the following principles:

i) Withdrawal of Israeli armed forces from territories occupied in the recent conflict;

ii) Termination of all claims or states of belligerency and respect for and acknowledgement of the sovereignty, territorial integrity and political independence of every State in the Area and their right to live in peace within secure and recognized boundaries free from threats or acts of force;

2. Affirms further the necessity:

a) For guaranteeing freedom of navigation through international waterways in the area;

b) For achieving a just settlement of the refugee problem.

c) For guaranteeing the territorial inviolability and political independence of every State in the area, through measures including the establishment of demilitarized zones;

3. Requests the Secretary General to designate a Special Representative to proceed to the Middle East to establish and maintain contacts with the States concerned in order to promote agreement and assist efforts to achieve peaceful and accepted settlement in accordance with the provisions and principles in this resolution;

4. Requests the Security General to report to the Security Council on the progress of the efforts of the Special Representative as soon as possible.

APPENDIX II

TEXT OF UNITED NATIONS RESOLUTION 339

Adopted by the Security Council October 25, 1973.

The Security Council,

Recalling its Resolutions 338 (1973) of 22 October, 1973, and 339 (1973) of 23 October, 1973,

Noting with regret the reported repeated violations of the cease-fire in noncompliance with Resolutions 338 (1973) and 339 (1973),

Noting with concern from the Secretary General's report that the United Nations military observers have not yet been enabled to place themselves on both sides of the cease-fire line,

1. Demands that immediate and complete cease-fire be observed and that the parties return to the positions occupied by them at 16:50 hours G.M.T. on 22 October, 1973;

2. Requests the Secretary General, as an immidiate step, to increase the number of United Nations military observers on both sides;

3. Decides to set up immediately under its authority a United Nations emergency force to be composed of personnel drawn from states members of the United Nations except permanent members of the Security Council, and requests the Secretary General to report within 24 hours on the steps taken to this effect;

4. Requests the Secretary General to report to the Council on an urgent and continuing basis on the state of implementation of this resolution as well as Resolutions 338 (1973) and 339 (1973);

5. Requests all member states to extend their full cooperation to the United Nations in the implementation of this resolution as well as Resolutions 338 (1973) and 339 (1973).

APPENDIX III

Text of Secretary of State Henry A. Kissinger's letter to United Nations Secretary-General Kurt Waldheim disclosing the Israeli-Egyptian agreement on the Middle East (November 9, 1973).

Dear Mr. Secretary General:

I have the honor to inform you that the governments of Egypt and Israel are prepared to accept the following agreement which implements Article 1 of the United Nations Security Council Resolution 338 and Article 1 of the United Nations Security Council Resolution 339.

The text of this agreement is as follows:

1. Egypt and Israel agree to observe scrupulously the cease-fire called for by the UN Security Council.

2. Both sides agree that discussions between them will begin immediately to settle the question of the return to the October 22 positions in the framework of agreement on the disengagement and separation of forces under the auspices of the UN.

3. The town of Suez will receive daily supplies of food, water and medicine. All wounded civilians in the town of Suez will be evacuated.

4. There shall be no impediment to the movement of nonmilitary supplies to the east bank.

5. The Israeli checkpoints on the Cairo-Suez road will be replaced by UN checkpoints. At the Suez end of the road, Israeli officers can participate with the UN to supervise the nonmilitary nature of the cargo at the bank of the canal.

6. As soon as the UN checkpoints are established on the Cairo-Suez road, there will be an exchange of all POWs, including wounded.

It has been agreed by the two parties that they will hold a meeting under the auspices of the United Nations commander at the usual place [Kilometer 101 on the Suez-Cairo road] to sign this agreement and to provide for its implementation. I would be most grateful if you would take appropriate steps to insure that a meeting is held on Saturday, November 10, 1973, or at such other time as may be mutually convenient for representatives of the parties to take the appropriate steps.

We intend to announce publicly the agreement at noon New York time, on Friday, November 9, 1973.

Best regards,
Henry A. Kissinger.

Part II: Population and Resources

One often hears from indignant Western observers the accusing question "why don't they [the Egyptians, the Indians, the Indonesians, etc.] do something about their population?" The presumption, one-sided and based on a blatant double standard, is that the Egyptian and other elites *can* curb population growth *and* do so immediately. There seems also to be the presumption that whatever they do will be without political cost.

It would be profitable, it seems to me, to reverse this question and ask the West why it does nothing about its waste, its enormous consumption of resources, for this is our counterpart of the population problem. If there were unlimited resources in the world, and unlimited space, it would not matter how many people there are nor how much they consume. But natural resources are not unlimited, and while the Third World strains them by the weight of numbers, the West (including the Soviet Union) strains them through rampant consumerism. Yet efforts to conserve resources in the West have consistently fallen victim to short-term political expediency. Our recent but as yet futile gestures at curbing petroleum consumption are a case in point. There are always good but short-sighted arguments to show that any change in our lifestyle will hurt our industries and cause recession, and what politician or head of state is willing to take responsibility for that in the name of a future he may never live to see?

So much more so, then, for the Third World head of state. Political survival in Egypt depends on fragile political institutions and a fragile economy. The short view is about the only view the head of state can afford. Nowhere in the world has it proved easy to legislate fertility behavior, and in Egypt and other developing societies there is an instinctive and widespread pronatalist sentiment. It is based on millenia of high mortality, especially among infants, and *under*population, reinforced by decades of confrontation with the imperialist West and a religious view that procreation is in some ways an act of God. In short, anti-natalist interests run up against a bedrock of forces that see fertility control as sacrilegious and possibly part of a Western plot to emasculate the ex-colonial world. Moreover, in many instances, an additional mouth to feed also represents an additional labor increment and is not an economic liability to the family unit. In the midst of the abortion controversy in the United States, in which both 1976 presidential candidates have pander to the most conservative sentiments, is it difficult to understand the constraints under which President Sadat must labor?

Throughout Part II an attempt is made to examine the various facets of population growth in quantitative and perceptual terms. Beyond the sheer size of the population, present and future, there are more important questions of age structure. Rapid population growth constantly replenishes and expands the younger age cohorts that constitute a direct burden on the modern sectors of the economy and upon the educational and social welfare budgets of the state. By diverting investment, they contribute to low economic growth rates and consequently to the inability of the economy to generate the jobs they need when they formally enter the work force.

It is one of the peculiarities of the present situation that although Egypt in the last 60 years has reduced the rate of adult illiteracy from 95 to 70 per cent, the absolute number of illiterates in Egypt has increased substantially over the same period. This is a direct result of rapid population growth. Similarly, rapid population growth has made itself felt in terms of the extension of public education. The present Egyptian regime has consistently declared its intention to provide equal educational opportunities for all Egyptian children of primary school age (6-12 years). Yet confronted with the ever-growing ranks of these age cohorts, the primary school system has gradually fallen behind in keeping up with potential enrollment (see Table 1). It will take the reallocation of major resources to reverse the projections for the period 1975-1985.

Millions of young Egyptians may never receive the rudiments of an education nor perhaps even of literacy. But even those who do may not find job opportunities in the economy at its current fairly low rates of growth. It should be noted that we are talking in this respect almost exclusively of the male half of society. Female employment is a question that sends shivers down the spines of all but a few Egyptian policy-makers. Tables 2 and 3 present projections that indicate some improvement in the rate of female participation in the work force, but by the most optimistic estimate for 1985, that of Dr. Hamdy, there would still be five males for every female, while the more conservative ILO projection shows a ratio in the same year of about 12 to one. Thus, both by sex and level of education, the work force so vital for a shift from agricultural to nonagricultural pursuits, has been handicapped by accelerated population growth. For women in particular the situation is particularly bleak for they are the victims of combined sexual and educational biases. At the same time ever larger cohorts of Egyptian women enter childbearing age (roughly ages 15-44), and unless their fertility is checked, they will contribute further to the exponential growth of the Egyptian population.

This immense problem is acutely felt in Egypt, at least at the elite level, and there is concern that something must be done. What that something is has been the subject of wide-ranging debate, and, in the second Report in Part II, the issues in this debate are delineated. But when hard-pressed policy-makers are told that *whatever measures are taken* Egypt will have at least 60 million inhabitants by the year 2000, there is a comprehensible tendency to write off fertility control and family planning as a waste of time and money. Rapid economic growth, perhaps accompanied by regional integration and population redistribution, are seen as the only viable approaches to "solving" the population problem.

The interplay of growing population and the mobilization of resources for economic growth dominate all aspects of the Egyptian economy. The roots of the problem lie in diminishing land resources and dwindling per capita agricultural production which has left Egypt a chronic food deficit country, saddled with growing food import bills. Precious foreign exchange is, more than figuratively, cannibalized to feed the population but without stimulating economic growth. The way out is not clearly perceived. What is optimal agricultural growth strategy? Is it horizontal expansion through land reclamation? Intensification with an export orientation on existing acreage? Reliance on state farms or private agro-businesses? Bolstering the role of the peasant cultivator? And what, in all this, becomes of the growing millions of landless peasants and migrant laborers?

In theory, the migrant laborers and landless peasants were to have been absorbed into a dynamic industrial sector which, in the event, has not materialized to the extent originally forecast. Here again optimal strategies are still debated: heavy vs. light industry; public vs. private enterprise; foreign vs. purely domestic investments; import-substituting vs. export-oriented industries. It is the same long list of options that bedevil most developing countries. At their heart is the nearly insoluble dilemma of selling enough things abroad to earn the foreign exchange to pay for the imports that will be necessary for further growth. An oil bonanza would come in handy, but until some way out is found, industry will not provide a final answer to the population problem. Instead, the overburdened countryside exports its human resources (often the best) to the cities where, if they find work, they swell the ranks of the service and governmental sectors (the fastest growing of all employment sectors), or somehow make do in the urban environment. Egypt will soon have more people living in urban areas than in the countryside, and what their life may be like is depicted in the Reports that deal with Cairo, the final four in Part II.

Table 1:Actual and Projected Deficits in Primary School Enrollment

Year	Enrollment	Those Eligible	Deficit
1952-53	1,540,202	n.a.	n.a.
1960-61	2,610,169	4,414,000	1,804,000
1964-65	3,294,832	4,863,000	1,568,000
1969-70	3,618,000	5,686,000	2,068,000
1974-75	3,980,000 (est.)	6,509,000 (est.)	2,529,000 (est.)
1979-80	4,478,000 (est.)	8,036,000 (est.)	3,558,000 (est.
1984-85	5,148,000 (est.)	9,500,000 (est.)	4,352,000 (est.)

Table 2: Population Trends, Total Labor Supply and Participation Ratios by Sex to 1985 (in '000)

	1960	1965	1970	1975	1980	1985
Pop. Size	25,054	29,806	34,026	38,548	43,288	48,282
Per cent of Males in Labor Force to Total Males	49.1	49.5	49.9	50.3	50.7	51
Male/Female Ratio in Labor Force	17.2/1	13.1/1	9.4/1	7.3/1	6.0/1	5.0/1
Total Supply	6,780	8,107	9,663	11,410	13,330	14,450

Source: Dr. Mostafa Hamdy (ed.). *Manpower Requirements for the UAR for the Period 1960-1985.* Institute of National Planning, Memo No. 431, May 1964, p. 16.

Table 3

Labor Force Projection for Egypt to
1985 by Sex

Year	Total Population (in millions)	Labor Force		
		Male	Female	Total
1960	26.1	6.9	.5	7.4
1965	29.8	8.0	.6	8.6
1970	34.2	8.8	.8	9.6
1975	39.1	10.4	1.0	11.4
1980	44.4	11.8	1.2	13.0
1985	50.2	13.4	1.6	15.0

Source: ILO, *Rural Employment Problems in the United Arab Republic*, Geneva, 1969, p. 27.

Elite Perceptions of the Population Problem

In a country where virtually the entire elite recognizes that there is a population problem of some gravity, how do those who have to deal with this problem perceive it and analyze it? Most educated Egyptians are openly worried about present trends in population growth. One is liable to hear frequently in Cairo vague pronouncements of the genre, "This thing is really getting out of hand," or, "Well, we just can't go on growing like this." At this level of awareness we seem to be dealing with perceptions no more sophisticated than mutterings in the United States and elsewhere about the lamentable state of the younger generation. Granted, in some countries coping with rapid population growth whole sectors of the elite may refuse to recognize it as a problem or may not be aware of it at all. On this score Egypt is certainly at a more advanced stage. But the simple perception of a problem's existence, or even of its gravity, may be a relatively insignificant step unless followed by a phase of analysis in which policy-makers, planners, and opinion leaders break the problem down into its component parts and advance some hypotheses about the causal relations involved. For only after notions of causality have been developed can priorities be established and rational policy decisions taken.

To gain some appreciation of these perceptions, I interviewed 23 Egyptians who are either directly involved in the family planning program, or in socio-economic fields directly affected by population growth, or in the press which frequently comments upon demographic questions (see Appendix I). Because the interviews in the spring and fall of 1972 came after a considerable amount of less focused discussion with a broader range of Egyptians, I feel confident that the respondents are representative of Egyptian elite thinking on the general question of population growth.

In Appendix II the reader will find a "guide to the discussion," a series of propositions designed to elicit hypotheses and counterpropositions. I will use some of these propositions as subject headings to organize the responses and I will add my own references and comments to place the discussion in context. Also, occasional reference will be made to Egyptian published sources.

Options of Problem Analysis

Analysis of a recognized problem may be broken down into the following processes: (1) defining its dimensions; (2) determining relations of causality (that is, conceiving of the problem in processual terms defined by predictable relations of cause and effect. Obviously, if causal relations can be determined, then one will know, at least in theory, where to enter the process in order to alter and diminish the problem); (3) estimating the consequences of the problem and its impact. (In population matters, frequently the definition of dimensions leads to a definition of consequences [e.g., *if* because of the age structure of the country X thousands of 15-year-olds enter the work force each year, then we will have to create Y number of jobs and reallocate Z number of dollars]); (4) defining solutions and goals vis-à-vis the problem (This flows naturally from hypotheses about causality and leads to the establishment of priorities); (5) anticipating unintended consequences (such as, in Western Europe, dealing with aging populations at levels of ZPG).

It was hoped that these dimensions of analysis might be drawn out in discussion of two options. Put briefly, is high fertility a function of certain kinds of social structures associated with traditional agriculture, illiteracy, and patriarchal families and thus subject to change only through the spread of education, industrialization and urbanization, and equal status for women? Or, is it possible, within the existing socioeconomic framework, to lower fertility through the dynamic implementation of a nationwide, competently staffed, well-financed family planning program? These either-or terms forced the respondent to try to think in causal terms.

The options as presented, it seems to me, are at the very heart of both theoretical and practical efforts to understand and influence population dynamics.[1]

We can classify answers to this question along a spectrum of analytic positions running from right to left ideologically as well as on paper. I hasten to point out that a judgment classified as right or left on this spectrum does not mean that the person who made the judgment maintains a consistently rightist or leftist ideological position.

Let us take the "technicists" first. Their outlook is that there is a large, latent clientele for family planning in most developing countries. The problem is to stimulate awareness among that clientele (mass media propaganda), develop a market, and deliver the goods through good clinics and readily-available, cheap contraceptive materials. In my own mind, I associate this outlook with the climate of opinion among the family planning establishment of a decade ago. The latent clientele was identified by KAP surveys, and the pill was happily there to meet anticipated market demand. It all seemed to be a technical question involving administrative procedures and staffing. Povey and Brown, for instance, predicted for Tunisia that "if a more nearly perfect contraceptive method were available, general family limitation would soon be practised widely throughout the country."[2] Or one may cite Janet Abou-Lughod, an experienced analyst of Egyptian urbanization. In 1964 she wrote:

A third epoch in the history of fertility control, one that may revolutionize birthrates as dramatically as the advances of the 1940s revolutionized death rates throughout the world, appears to be imminent. A technological breakthrough in the provision of a simple, nonrepetitive, inexpensive, and highly effective method of birth control will make it possible for societies now entering the second stage of the demographic transition to transform their fertility rates within a considerably briefer period of time than has ever before been recorded. Again, although motivation must be present, this writer believes that the latent demand for effective birth control is so great that all our current projections will prove to have been overly pessimistic. . . .[3]

The reader will note that Abou-Lughod does not see the technical breakthrough *in vacuo* but rather as part of a specific stage in the demographic transition with its inherent repercussions on several other facets of social change. Thus I would place her, at least as regards this particular judgment, about midway between technicist and ecumenist.

At the other end of the spectrum we find the "determinists," who are liable to argue that family planning programs can only respond to and service clientele created by various processes of social change, without which they would contend, there is no need for technical programs. For the French sociologist and demographer, Alfred Sauvy, the key variable is rising per capita income and by implication whatever socioeconomic changes necessary to bring about a rise in income. Algeria has explicitly adopted this position.[4] Aziz Bindary, Chairman of the Executive Board for Family Planning in Egypt, sees the problem as one of accelerating the processes of social change initiated during the last 20

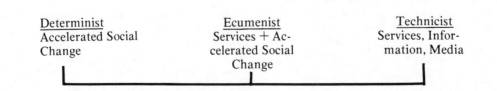

Approaches to Lowering Fertility

Determinist	Ecumenist	Technicist
Accelerated Social Change	Services + Accelerated Social Change	Services, Information, Media

years so as to weaken pervasive patterns of male dominance. Promoting the entry of women, particularly rural women, into remunerative, nondomestic employment is crucial. According to Bindary, "The real solution, in my view, is the liberation of rural women and their entry into the work force. This *alone* is what will lead to a lowering of the birthrate and to the solution of population growth in Egypt."[5] Dr. Bindary finds himself at the head of a conventional family planning program whose scope he feels must be broadened to act as a catalyst to policy decisions affecting existing trends of social change. In the meantime, he seems to be upgrading and perfecting the tools of the conventional program so as to maximize the eventual impact. Bindary would come to rest on the spectrum somewhere between determinist and ecumenist.[6]

The middle position can only be defined in relation to the two extremes. The "ecumenist," broadly speaking, does not wish to waste time over distinguishing factors of causality. The point is to move ahead on all fronts and hope that something gives. This may be the most intelligent position; it is certainly the safest. It was, moreover, this position that attracted the greatest number of my Egyptian respondents. In recent years technicists have had to temper their initial optimism about the efficacy of their programs, retreating into ecumenism where they can at least blame lack of progress on social processes well beyond their control. It is no coincidence that Egypt began its public program in 1966 in a technicist vein and has evolved, like the international establishment, toward the global approach.[7] One respondent, who replied to my phrasing of the options in writing, stated:

Regarding the first question, I agree to a great extent with the first hypothesis set forward by Mr. Waterbury, which is to say that social and economic changes will definitely push the birthrate into a downward trend. All factors mentioned (see Appendix II)—with some reservations on my part—will contribute to the lowering of the birthrate. This was the European pattern and would occur whether there is a national, governmentally operated family planning program or not. Here the second question of willingness to wait prevails. I do not think Egypt is

willing to wait for the demographic transition to occur smoothly. Besides, population growth greatly hinders efforts for social and economic development.

The second hypothesis suggests, alternatively, to *accelerate* [emphasis in the original] the eventual reduction in birthrate. It is my opinion that a well-organized family planning programme will help create receptive audiences and recruit *significant* [emphasis in the original] numbers of users to clinics who would otherwise never have been users. The risk here is that at some time the programme may reach a stagnation level or slow progress if not paralleled by social and economic development.

We may compare this statement with a similar, albeit less specific, appraisal set down by a specialist of the Population Council:

Family planning as an agent of social change: It seems reasonable to assume that any innovation that creates a profound change in the way things have happened for centuries is going to influence people's social attitudes and particularly the ones most closely related to the change. I am fond of this point since it follows my feeling that the abstract argument between the advocates of social change on the one hand and plain family planning on the other is, in my view, rather sterile and not helpful since for the most part what you have is complicated interactions of various factors leading to the desired results, not one factor versus another.[8]

Because a preponderance of those I talked with clustered around the ecumenist position, I will offer one more statement of the position, again from an Egyptian:

The either-or situation of economic growth versus family planning is untenable. If there is economic growth there will be no need for a formal program at all. If there isn't growth, a family planning program won't be of much use. There must be both, and the approach must be global.[9]

General Observations

In terms of the spectrum, it turned out that all respondents clustered center-left, a fitting nesting place for an elite in a center-left regime. No one seemed to buy the technicist argument. That does not mean that technicism did not manifest itself in other respects, especially with regard to modernizing agriculture, coping with emigration, or promoting industrialization. Indeed, ecumenists and determinists alike translated their conceptions of the processes of social change into programmatic, administrative, and technological terms. For instance, someone might bring up peasant mentality as an impediment to lowering fertility and then equate the transformation of that mentality to a simple expansion of the school system. This sort of response is likewise to be expected, for not only is Egypt a center-left regime but one that is sustained to a large degree by a state technocracy.

No one had any difficulty in discussing the dimensions of population growth. Determining relations of causality proved to be far more difficult. Many respondents escaped into an "everything's important" analysis which gave the overall impression of ecumenism. Only about six ecumenists were clearly so out of conviction and knowledge of the basic facts. Only those who had considerable confidence in their knowledge, experience, or ideology risked taking a determinist stance. Predicting the consequences of population growth turned up fairly concrete responses, although there were some impressive gaps in the respondents' perceptions in this respect. Again, because causality proved to be an elusive or perhaps threatening concept, the proposition of solutions and the assigning of priorities were phrased in only the most general terms. Rare were the respondents who, like the Minister of Health, unhesitatingly listed priorities. For Dr. Mahfuz, the greatest effects on lowering fertility would be brought about by education, industrialization, preventive medicine and improved health services, and family planning in that order. Dr. Mahfuz ventured that if a choice had to be made between building a hospital or a school, the school should be built. The terms of his response, incidentally, indicate what I mean by the strand of technicism in ecumenist analysis: education = schools and improved health = more hospitals.

Unintended consequences warrant separate mention.[10] One factor here is lag time. Let us say that respondents believe industrialization, urbanization, education, or lowering the infant mortality rate may all tend to lower the fertility rate. In some instances these processes may cause an upsurge in the birthrate before having a depressing effect. These problems of things getting worse before they get better, as well as questions of how long does it take before process X influences fertility, were treated only by family planning experts. Moreover, there was little specific discussion of opportunity costs in emphasizing one approach over another, not to mention fiscal costs. Perhaps literacy and mass education is the answer, but can Egypt pay for it? Another example can be found in the consensus among Egyptian demographers that the June War and its aftermath has been the major element in lowering the fertility rate since 1967. A majority of the respondents were unaware of this analysis.

There was frequent mention of what I will call the "mentality factor," a congeries of practices, psychological predispositions, and biases generally attributed to the peasant world. At the same time, no respondents suggested that political mobilization might be an appropriate means to change mentality. While many respondents saw the problem in global terms, they drew back from suggesting truly global solutions. Pushing ahead on all fronts meant pushing ahead on all *existing* fronts. Only one respondent, a journalist, alluded to the kind of mobilization that I have in mind: "Even if we had a Chinese-style revolution in this country, it ultimately won't make any difference. Egypt will not be able to support its future population." Implicit in a political approach would be stress on the change in status that family planning symbolizes for women. Yet only female respondents voluntarily mentioned this factor and argued for its propagation.

Pushing ahead on all fronts apparently means pushing ahead at existing rates of speed. Bindary's advocacy of accelerating the creation of jobs for women was the major exception, although a few others mentioned some increase in pace of mechanization in agriculture. The bulk of the respondents clearly felt most comfortable with doing more of the same but only better. One journalist whom I interviewed, Ahmad Baha al-Din, later wrote an article about the government's project to rebuild the Egyptian village that nicely summarizes, while gently chiding, that kind of thinking:

Perhaps the reader will think that the reconstruction of the village…is the substitution of brick houses for mud houses…. But that is not at all what is sought by the reconstruction of the Egyptian village; nor is it even the simple addition of running water and electricity. The goal that we must keep in view is changing people, not walls. In our country there are numerous examples of villages consisting of dwellings of good brick and cement, but these changed not a thing in the life of the *fellah*; not in his customs, nor his level of awareness, nor in his manner of living, nor in his degree of belonging to the surrounding national environment. This is evident when, for instance, we decide on family planning but are incapable of getting the message to the *fellah*….

Thus [the reconstruction of the village] is a project that must have as its goal the transformation and evolution of village life. A project in which education, social awareness, construction, and the furnishing of utilities all enter. But first and foremost there must be the creation of the will to change among the inhabitants of the villages themselves and the transfer to them of a greater degree of responsibility for this change.[11]

Finally, not one respondent recommended legal constraint.

To sum up my impressions of the sample, the respondents are by any standards members of an elite. All combine to some degree education, intellectual status, social standing, political influence, and income far and above the average for the population. They are, then, privileged, and at least some part of their concern about and perceptions of the population problem are shaped by their privileged position. Because they are all dependent to some degree on the state apparatus, the kinds of solutions they propose tend toward the reinforcement of existing state programs. There is a resulting reluctance to see the implications of family planning in its broadest and most significant sense, the acquisition of a sense of individual responsibility and an outlook that certain of the givens of one's existence may be subject to individual control.

The masses can be manipulated, but the motives for their action cannot be imposed upon them. Only individuals are capable of taking decisions, and the more often they do it, the less they can be manipulated. People who freely decide to be masters of their own fecundity thereby acquire new reasons to aspire for political power. Responsible child-rearing cannot be separated from the quest for political power.[12]

Proposition #1: The Effect of Raising Per Capita Income and Standard of Living

The logic of this proposition has already been alluded to with reference to Alfred Sauvy's postulates. It is suggested that the very poor have no incentive to plan their offspring. What will bring about voluntary fertility control is when a significant segment of the population has attained a high enough standard of living to worry about losing what it has. Couples will develop a sense of opportunity costs: if public education becomes a desirable good, for example, rural couples may have to choose between several children who can work in the fields from an early age, or a few children to be supported in dependent status throughout their schooling on the basis of a long-term calculation as to their future earning power. The fundamental assumption is that rising income will lead to mental change: from the passivity, pessimism, and short-term "hedonism" of the poor to the forward-looking, inherently optimistic, rationalistic outlook of the bourgeoisie.

This proposition elicited more support among the Egyptian respondents than any of the others. One respondent cited as proof that family planning had been successful only in the cities where there is a disproportionate concentration of the middle classes. He also noted that among the less well-off, family planning was practiced above all by urban workers who have a steady income. Another respondent explicitly mentioned industrialization and education as being the keys to rising standards of living which he emphatically agreed was the determining factor in lowering fertility. Egypt, he stated, had moved from the equilibrium of poverty in which a relatively stable population had been achieved through high natality and mortality rates, to a state of pronounced disequilibrium in the last

40 years in which the natality of impoverished societies is accompanied by the mortality of advanced societies. He concluded that either Egypt will undergo significant economic development and an "appreciable" rise in the standard of living after which an "equilibrium of prosperity" will be attained, or the economy will regress once again to an equilibrium of poverty. He judged that the next decade would be crucial, determining whether the processes of education and industrialization could produce in Egypt an equilibrium of prosperity. This respondent, like many of the others, essentially begged the questions of what *level* of income or standard of living must be achieved in order to influence fertility, and *how long* (lag time) does it take before the new mentality is developed.

A few dissenters and skeptics did not dispute the outcome of rising standards of living so much as the implications of how the process would work itself out. Bindary, referring to the high levels of income, education, and fertility in Trinidad, concludes that as important as the level of income is the question of *who* earns it; i.e., in his view women must be earners and female and male mentalities must change in tandem. Two others accepted the argument but did not believe that Egypt could in fact raise incomes "appreciably." One called attention to the fact that the highest legal individual income in the country is LE5,000 (roughly $12,000) which is still 75 times as high as the lowest incomes in the countryside. One of these two and one other detractor argued that a higher standard of living would come about only through regional economic unity and emigration of surplus labor.

A family planning expert warned that in the initial stages of rising standards of living the fertility rate might go up. At the same time he hypothesized that there might be an inverse phenomenon that we could call poverty *and* voluntary fertility control. What is at question here is, perhaps, the effect of poverty not in a traditional, pre-industrial society but in one that is undergoing rapid urbanization, industrialization, and the spread of literacy. In coping with the new environment, making ends meet or educating one's children, and caring for one's health, stable or deteriorating standards of living may impel couples to limit the number of births. Since the June War, as this respondent emphasized, there is evidence of deteriorating conditions of life throughout the Nile Valley and it has been accompanied by significant fertility decline,[13] despite the fact that formal family services have scarcely penetrated these areas. In other words, the equilibrium of poverty that could emerge in Egypt would not be one of high mortality and natality but one of low mortality and natality. Only one other respondent, an agricultural expert, took this line, contending that conditions in the Egyptian countryside had reached such a pass that the peasants are aware of the diminishing returns in producing more children. Both these gentlemen, it seems to me, have called our attention to a very important phenomenon which, to my limited knowledge, has not been adequately reflected in demographic research. Economies in the developing countries may regress—that much at least has been postulated by neo-Malthusian analysis—but they will probably seek a new kind of equilibrium within the constraints of their poverty. Certain features of the period of disequilibrium will not disappear, such as systems of mass education and public health, and the existence of large, semi-industrialized urban centers. Their continued existence will obviously have a major influence upon fertility at levels of poverty as well as prosperity.

#2 Industrialization

There is hardly any need to consider this factor in isolation from the above discussion. Efforts to industrialize have been one of the givens of the revolutionary regime since 1952. Respondents seemed to find no reason to believe that industrialization would not have the same impact upon fertility as it is alleged to have had in the West. The question is how rapidly and in what proportions can the population become involved in the industrial process. I would add that an unstated but underlying assumption of many respondents was that if Egypt could not make it industrially, it simply could not make it at all. Again the factor of lag time was ignored. One family planning program professional did refer to studies carried out in the industrial suburb of Shubra al-Kheima that revealed that the average family size there was well above the national average.

Several made specific mention of agro-industries and the need to bring industry to the countryside. One agricultural expert took some care in debunking the widely held notion that land reclamation would absorb significant amounts of rural manpower, concluding that agro-industries were the only solution. Another advocate of industrialization pointed out the Nile Valley is ideally suited for the rapid transmission of new habits and modes, and once the *idea* becomes current that there is an association between education, industrial employment, and income level, the rural population will seek out its own opportunities. The implication is that it may be cheaper for the state to allow individuals to migrate to a few industrial centers (Cairo-Alexandria, Aswan, some day the Canal Zone) undertaking the necessary investments to equip these centers with the basic social and economic infrastructure, than to scatter industry locally with inevitable and perhaps more costly problems of administration, supply, and marketing arrangements carried out by a heavy and slow-moving public bureaucracy.[14]

#3 Women's Employment

There was a handful of strong proponents of this factor, with Dr. Bindary at their head, but the modal response was of the order, "Oh yes, that's very important too." Several respondents were quick to argue that in the rural areas female employment is already very high—they take care of the animals, make butter and cheese which they sell along with eggs, do some farming and weeding, and occasionally engage in handicrafts. The qualifying observation that they work under the supervision of someone else (their husband or father) and without remuneration (although most may salt away part of their butter and egg money) was apparently not relevant to these respondents. Dr. Bindary's contention that women must be employed outside the house on a regular basis so that repeated pregnancies would conflict with maintaining income was not readily recognized except by those already familiar with the argument. One person who supported the proposition informed me that the Arab Socialist Union (Egypt's only political party) is making a considerable effort in this direction by organizing home handicrafts, purchasing the products from the women, and then marketing them. On the whole the idea of women's employment was warmly received, and a number of respondents judged that the Egyptian economy could generate the necessary number of jobs.[15] One minister summed up his views: "We are in a period of transition, a period of war. Once that problem is resolved, we won't be faced with problems of surplus labor. We have many, many projects that will need all the hands we have."

A male planner and a female "manpower" expert both were skeptical about the possible consequences of female employment. The planner wondered what period of time would be necessary before fertility was affected. The woman asked: "How does Dr. Bindary know what choice a woman will make faced with another pregnancy or loss of income?"

Finally, a labor expert mused about the proposition in these terms: "Of course woman's employment is a logical step, but how long will it take and what kind of jobs will they hold? Most are illiterate. Beyond that, should Egyptian society be a society of employees? Self-employment should be preserved. Employment accentuates hierarchies. Put the rural population on a salary and production may fall—it may make better economic sense for the women to stay home. Employees lose their sense of competition and their concern for production."

I am obliged to step outside the universe of my respondents to find someone who has a keen sense of the political and psychological implications of female employment. Dr. Nuwwal Saadawi, in her recent book, *Woman and Sex*,[16] has this to say:

> Work is a human necessity whereas conception is nothing but a biological function in which all living things engage, from amoebae to apes.... (p. 147)

> Unquestionably the emergence of the woman from between the walls of the house to outside employment is the foundation stone upon which is built the return to woman of her natural rights as a human.... (p. 129)

> For this reason, if one day a woman were forced to choose between work outside the house and her work inside the house, it would be better for her as a human being to choose her work outside the house. Any sacrifices a woman makes for the sake of continuing outside employment are, in my opinion, less than the sacrifices she would have to make in remaining in the house and submitting to the same fate as her mother and grandmother before her. These sacrifices might include the arousing of the anger of

the husband thereby leading to the failure of their marriage. But failure in married life is of less damage to a woman than failure in her entire life, and in losing herself between the walls of the house. (pp. 156/57)

This kind of overview brings us directly into the realm of unintended consequences, or perhaps even unrecognized prerequisites, for Dr. Saadawi sees this problem as the catalyst to the entire reordering of a male-dominant society with all its ramifications in the organization of economic life and the exercise of political power. *All* female respondents either pointed out or readily admitted that male policy-makers were nearly blind to the implications of both family planning and female employment with regard to women's rights. They saw the policy-makers as being concerned almost exclusively by the rate of economic growth in the country, and whatever concern they manifest about women has come as a result of that concern.[17]

#4 Education and/or Female Education

There have been enough studies in Egypt and other countries to suggest that there is a strong inverse relationship between levels of female education specifically, or society-wide levels in general, and levels of fertility.[18] On the whole, the respondents seemed prepared to attribute greater significance to this factor than to industrialization, female employment, or urbanization. One journalist specified that if he had to select any single factor that would most influence fertility, he would choose female literacy. Another respondent suggested that assuring that girls made it through the preparatory school level (*i'adadi*, between primary and secondary; would be as important as female employment. Rudimentary literacy is clearly insufficient to give them the option of altering their roles, or even to *think* about altering their roles. Both a feminist leader and a person who has made a career in education concurred that progress in this domain is crucial.

#5 Islam

The religious factor is, of course, but a different optic for returning to the question of mentality. With two or three exceptions, the respondents took the quasi-determinist position that Islam as manifested in Egyptian culture is a function of certain socioeconomic circumstances and not the other way around. As a result most believe that Islam, as a corpus of beliefs, has very little to do with fertility.[19]

What seems to be the consensus is that the religious establishment, from the *shaykh-s* of Al-Azhar to the various dignitaries of Egypt's 22,000 mosques have been something less than enthusiastic supporters of family planning. This despite the fact that the official Islamic position in Egypt is that family planning is a Good Thing. If all members of the establishment were sincerely for family planning they could have considerable impact in spreading its practice, but they can do little to deter determined couples from adopting measures to limit their offspring. One respondent presented the problem in terms of bilharzia, a parasitic worm that develops in a cycle between humans and snails in irrigation canals. The worm lodges in the urinary tract of humans, returns its eggs to the canals when people urinate in them, lodge in the snails along the canal sides, and return through the skin when people enter the canal. This disease has debilitated generations of Egyptian *fellahin*. The cycle could be broken "if people would only turn 180 degrees to urinate or defecate. Surely religious leaders could convince people to take those revolutionary steps."

The second level is the sociocultural one; the fatalism of the poor generally expressed in their submission to the will of God (which is, after all, the literal meaning of the word Islam). The bulk of the respondents saw fatalism as reflecting the material reality of peasant life: subsistence economy, natural disasters (floods, cotton worm), disease (trachoma, bilharzia), high infant mortality, and early death. Islam is excuse, rationalization, and a post facto explanation for a situation that requires fatalism. As Leila Hamamsy succinctly put it: "Surely life would be insupportable were the peasant to believe himself responsible, by his own deeds and efforts, for all that befalls him. It is, therefore, understandable that the Egyptian peasants should select from their Moslem traditions those injunctions that emphasize man's subordination to God and stress that all human successes can be achieved only if God wills it so."[20] It flows logically from this view that what needs changing is the socioeconomic situation in which the religion is practiced. A planner scoffed at the notion of the primacy of Islam in explaining social behavior. He believed this kind of attention to Islam to be diversionary, and that religion is merely symptomatic of other underlying factors. A medical doctor went through the following chain of thought: "Most people believe that children are the gift of God, and that it is against religion to use contraceptives. Religion is both an excuse and a cause. People really do believe—but they also need sons to work and daughters to help out. At night there is nothing to do but sex. Perhaps rural electrification, movies, and that sort of thing will help."

#6 The Socioeconomic Situation

If religion is seen largely as a mediating variable, what are the causal variables bound up in the term "socioeconomic situation"? First of all, as used in the interviews, this term refers primarily to the rural world. With few exceptions the respondents did not believe that the urban areas would be particularly resistant to voluntary fertility control. The mentality problem lies among the peasantry.

In the countryside, the economic structures and status system are closely intertwined. Control of wealth, no matter how limited, is the overriding concern of families and whatever broader political alliances they may enter. Political sovereignty at all levels is, among other criteria, defined by sex: only males are responsible. This is meant quite literally, and Islam has merely confirmed in some instances, and watered down in some others, existing patriarchal authority patterns. In the past, only males exercised political rights, and they reached political and social "maturity" only after having undertaken the responsibility of a family and having produced sons. Only males bore arms, and that is still the case today. Men thus exercise the right of defense whereas women are granted the right to be defended. Males reach adulthood and mental maturity at the age of 40; women never do. Men are enjoined by the Koran to provide and women to be provided for. It is dishonorable, even sacriligious, for a man to allow his wife to share in providing for the family except if she works under his direct supervision (i.e., weeding crops, or minding the shop, etc.) Children are needed to supply labor for the family patrimony; sons are needed to defend it. They will inherit the patrimony in shares twice as large as those of the daughters. Consolidating the patrimony is a prime objective of arranged marriages, the preferred partner being a

cousin in the male line. The virginity of the bride is symbolic of her loyalty to family and elders. Her brothers are responsible for her virginity, but to minimize the risk, marrying her as soon as she reaches puberty is the wisest course. Schooling is irrelevant for a daughter. Her status as wife depends initially on the children she may bear; she must support the constant pressure of her mother-in-law who runs the extended household, and is hyperconscious of the status and honor of her son upon which her own status is built. The rural bride may rest easy as it were and achieve some sort of power only when she in turn becomes a mother-in-law. Her new power will be exercised primarily in socializing the brides of her sons to their maternal roles.[21]

This sketch admittedly depicts a sort of ideal type but many of the themes touched upon above are still of considerable importance in understanding rural behavior. Children may be the gift of God, but they serve an easily discerned socioeconomic function to which husbands and wives caught up in the system must resign themselves. Their fatalism is all the more understandable when one adds to the above, factors of high infant mortality, widespread physical debilitation among the labor force, the continued need for large per-acre labor inputs, and the instinctive equation of family size with family strength, and male status with paternity. One male respondent reflects some of these elements and is all the more significant because he comes from the rural middle class of a Delta village. Four of his ten siblings died during childhood. He himself contracted bilharzia as a youth. He was the only child to be sent to the city—first to Mansura for secondary schooling and then to Cairo for university studies. Most of his brothers and sisters have remained in the village. "The *fellah* understands his difficulties but takes them for granted. They have seen relatively little change. Things appear natural; it's not so much Islam as a sense of continuity."

When this respondent married in 1952, he and his wife agreed to have only two children in order "to give them the best chance in life given our income." By contrast, he has a brother in the village who is responsible for the family property and looks after the sisters. All the sisters are married and living in the village. His brother married his uncle's daughter, and she, perhaps unconsciously, wants more children. She has several sisters-in-law who are known as *wallāda*, or "bearers," with five or six children each, and she must be envious. "Most of this is unconscious and not really thought out. Each time I see her she says, 'You are lucky, you have only two children.' I ask her, 'Why do you want so many?' No answer…no answer…just like that."

To break out of this situation, alternatives in *wealth, status,* and *power* must be offered to those operating within it. The respondents, from their various viewpoints, did not believe that the pill or any other contraceptive represented a real alternative. To limit the number of children leaves no provision for new status systems whereby the female enjoys an active, responsible role while at the same time salvaging the male from individual and social ignominy. All respondents seemed to believe that this process is working itself out in the cities. Several emphasized that in Cairo the desirable bride is no longer the well-off but the educated, who can hold or is holding down a job. But universally it was judged that in the countryside "children are cheap."

Is there some causal chain one of whose links could be altered thereby leading to an overall change in existing status systems? Dr. Bindary believes there is such a chain and sees the linkage in terms of the sequence of women's work→ women's self-identity and responsibility→ responsible maternity. Two respondents took a different tack. Mechanization of rural agriculture (no mention of lag time) would force males to make decisions about limiting family size when less labor is needed, or to go to the cities where, presumably, urbanization would impel them to exercise voluntary fertility control. Two others rejected this argument, opting instead for agricultural intensification to make maximum use of labor, while at the same time promoting industrially valuable crops and the establishment of agro-industries. There was one, nearly classic, technicist response: "Egypt has three natural resources, in vast quantities— sand, sea-water, and sun. Surely modern technology will provide an answer to putting these to use for the benefit of our human resources."

#7 Old-Age Security, Infant Mortality, and Legal Changes

I lump all these together because they touch upon specific aspects of the "socioeconomic situa-

tion" sketched out above. In the traditional society, rural and urban, one's offspring are the only safeguard against enfeeblement, abandonment, or destitution for the aged. The extended family in this sense serves the function of taking care of dependents be they young or old. The shift to nuclear family units in the cities has not really obviated the need for a family-based system to provide security for dependents. Only wage earners are entitled to pensions and social security and they are a distinct minority among the working population. At the other age extreme, there is no state system of day-care centers that would permit the mother to work outside the home. Ironically, women in extended families may more easily enter the work force than women in nuclear families. Thus, a few respondents recommended that the state undertake programs for the establishment of a national system of day-care centers as well as for comprehensive old-age security.[22] When I brought up this problem with others, the reaction was, "all well and good, but won't the cost be prohibitive?"

The infant mortality rate in Egypt is ca. 119/1,000 and may have gone up since 1967. It is frequently argued that Egyptian couples accept a maximum number of pregnancies on the assumption that about 40 per cent of these pregnancies will never result in a child that will live beyond the age of two or three. The argument then runs that if infant mortality rates were drastically lowered, the perception of the new situation would result in couples planning fewer pregnancies.[23] Most respondents agreed but, as usual, there was no discussion of lag time nor of the probable initial upsurge in the crude birthrate. One medical doctor did allude to this factor: "I believe that in the countryside the infant mortality rate is closer to 140. I do not believe that Egyptian couples calculate the survival rate of their children; they take whatever they get. Lowering the infant mortality rate will lead to population increase, that's all."

Some of the patterns of the socioeconomic situation have been codified in law, particularly as regards personal status law dealing with marriage, divorce, and inheritance. Consequently it is not unreasonable to suppose that changing laws may lead to changes in the institutions they regulate, and then to changes in fertility behavior. Several respondents mentioned this in respect to raising the minimum marriage age for girls, at the same time citing the difficulties of enforcing the law. No one mentioned what a public health statistician had pointed out to me last year, that only about 3 per cent of all births occurred to Egyptian women under the age of 20. One female and one male respondent, however, minimized the importance of marriage age, suggesting instead substantial changes in divorce law. On the one hand, divorce is procedurally simple for the husband. On the other, women may want to proliferate children, not only to gain a psychological hold on the husband but also to make divorce financially devastating for the husband who would still have to provide for his dependents. Divorce laws and procedures could be made far more rigorous and difficult. Only one respondent raised the question of revising existing law and enforcement procedures as regards child labor, which is, of course, a phenomenon seminal to the traditional pattern in the countryside.

Reference to an instance of unintended consequences came from one respondent with regard to legal changes. In July 1961 a series of laws known as the "Socialist Decrees" were issued in Egypt, and they marked Egypt's entry into a phase of self-conscious and self-proclaimed socialism. The respondent felt that the psychological atmosphere created by these decrees and the propaganda surrounding them may have contributed to the rise in the crude birthrate in the period 1960-1966. "I have a hunch that people began to think that there would be free everything for everybody and that children would no longer be a liability—but it's just a hunch."

#8 Family Planning Program Changes

Other than Doctors Bindary and Mahfuz, none of the respondents had any specific suggestions to make as to what could be done to improve existing family planning services. The major innovation outlined by the Executive Board (Bindary) and the Ministry of Health (Mahfuz) is to integrate into combined units all family planning and maternal-child health services. But inasmuch as the respondents were for the most part center-left in their analysis (with Dr. Bindary himself close to determinist) there is no reason to expect their responses to reflect much depth of concern over the internal workings of a conventional family planning program.

#9 Emigration

I purposely introduced this question in order to give the respondents a chance to discuss the conse-

quences of population growth and to propose solutions that I would place closer to the technicist than the ecumenist position. In essence, the respondent could beg the question of the necessity of socio-economic change, or even of upgrading family planning services, by advocating the exportation of surplus labor. The responses I received to this question overwhelmingly treated emigration as an interesting idea, but one that is politically unfeasible and not liable ever to involve significant numbers of people.

"Oh, we've heard a lot about that one over the years, exporting the *fellahin* to the Sudan and so forth. How many people know the problem is the other way round? There are something like 500,000 Sudanese living in Egypt!" An agricultural expert stated that *any* agricultural country would be lucky to have the *fellahin*, but politically it is unwise for large scale emigration would only arouse the fears of Egypt's neighbors. Several others added that emigration is too costly. "How many might migrate? A million? There are a million Egyptians born every year." Others noted that the most qualified and skilled would be those most likely to emigrate. The old stereotypic image of the *fellah's* emotional attachment to the Nile Valley was rejected out of hand. "This has not been a question of attachment but of opportunity. Either people want the Egyptian to live in the desert or travel to distant countries at his own expense. But if he is paid well, he will go, and he is going—to Libya, Lebanon, Kuwait, and Europe." Three respondents revealed what may be a pervasive misperception of the population problem in other Arab countries. All judged that Egypt is the only overpopulated country in the region and that the others, with the exception of Lebanon, are positively underpopulated.

The advocates of emigration had some interesting ideas. "We must resort to emigration. Egypt is the only overpopulated Arab country and with the most skillful peasantry. They will emigrate if poverty is their only alternative. In 1958, President Kuwatly [of Syria] wanted three million Egyptians to farm the Jazira [the northeastern panhandle of Syria]. Nasser found the idea bizarre and refused. Now I wonder if the new federation [Egypt, Libya, and Syria] may not be for that.* Egypt gets rid of excess population and the rest of the Arab world develops." A labor expert commented: "A big population is not a liability if it is prosperous, educated, and trained." I asked him, "But at some level

---

*This Federation has never been formally established.

doesn't Egypt's population exceed its resources regardless of its quality?" "We shouldn't think in terms of Egypt alone," he replied, "but in terms of all the neighboring countries, particularly Sudan and Iraq. We must plan emigration rationally. It should be no different from an American going from Michigan to Nevada. We must...encourage an even distribution of population. Then Israel would not just face one population center of 35 million to the south, but an evenly distributed mass on all frontiers—there would be no vacuum in Jordan, Syria, and Iraq."

Two political commentators—distant from one another in left-right terms on most issues—were at least of one mind on the issue of emigration. Both contended that migration and regional unity may be the key to Egypt's problems. Their position is, I believe, neither opportunistic nor escapist but a reflection of their fear that any other solutions may be doomed to failure. One of the commentators, Boutros-Ghali, has set down his own acerbic views in print, so I may cite him directly:[24]

One must never consider Egypt as an independent entity. It must be seen in the context of the Arab world, for Egypt has no hope to make it alone....(p. 35)

There is strong external opposition to an Arab Federation. As for myself, it is essential to have this *ensemble*. I attach very little importance to the formula by which this Federation is established, whether it is of a capitalist type like the Common Market, seems to me secondary. I upset some young people in Rabat two years ago when I gave some lectures telling them that a railroad between Cairo and Rabat and Cairo-Khartoum seemed to me more important at this point in time than a revolution. (p. 36)

Ideological Resistance

Do Egyptian elite members believe that in their concern over the country's population they are playing the imperialists' game in developing a family planning program? This judgment of family planning and birth control is shared by the radical left in the West with many regimes in the Third World. The crux of the argument is that the fat, prosperous industrial societies absorb disproportionate amounts of the world's natural resources and brain power to sustain their way of life. They promote family planning as a means, or, more crudely, as a gimmick by which the poor can contain their poverty without contemplating violent conflict with the industrial countries and the redistribution of world resources. In short, family planning is a device to keep down the hordes at the gates of the industrial world. Malthusian catastrophes may have as their consequence the radicalization of the Third World and its adoption of "unfriendly" ideologies. In this event family planning may serve as a palliative to some of these forces.[25] There is evidence that this view is not without foundation. In an earlier era, when the "Free World" was more confident of its righteousness, none other than Kingsley Davis put the question of population control (no euphemistic use of family planning in 1958) in this context:

If it be granted that the demographic problems of the underdeveloped countries, especially in the areas of non-Western culture, make these nations more vulnerable to communism, the question arises: what population policies can the free world pursue? It would appear that an appropriate policy would be the control of birthrates, the lowering of death rates, the provision of technical assistance and economic aid, and the formation of military alliances. Such a combination of policies, if carried through effectively, would strengthen the free world in its constant fight against encroachment....

If the free nations go their own individual way and fail to unite on a population policy, it means that they are giving up one possible means of strengthening their cause.[26]

While Egyptians have every reason to suspect Western motives, none of the respondents thought that constituted grounds for rejecting family planning. Moreover, most respondents, including one Marxist, claimed never to have heard before this portrayal of Western interest in family planning. One respondent, who was familiar with the argument, said it was one in whose validity President Nasser believed from 1952 until around 1960, after which point, one would gather, he either ceased to believe it or, in the face of Egypt's population, ceased to care.

The respondents believed that even if they played the imperialists' game, the magnitude of Egypt's population problem left them no choice. One planner stated: "I believe that in a major way family planning can be seen as an imperialist tactic to focus our gaze on false problems. World population is growing on an average of 2 per cent a year and aggregate GNP by 4 per cent. The question is how that surplus is being distributed and used. But that doesn't mean that certain Third World countries, like India, Egypt, and China, don't have real population problems about which they must take action. I can reconcile both views as far as Egypt is concerned." Another remarked ruefully: "We must deal with this problem at all costs, but it is aggravating at the same time to hear Michel Debré declare 'We need 80 million Frenchmen.'" One respondent, the same who mentioned the effects of the 1961 decrees, would not at all buy the notion of Western ulterior motives: "The number of millionaires in the U.S. has declined in recent years. The people of the West invested individually and collectively for 250 years before they achieved high standards of living. Some sector of the population must always pay. Russia paid between 1918 and the present time—54 years equivalent to 200 years of U.S. sacrifice. The developing countries want to have their cake and eat it too. But its still the rule of the survival of the fittest that counts."

Backdrop to Perceptions: the War

I cannot lay too much stress on the fact that all elite thinking about population is tempered by the state of war and tension with Israel. All priorities in policy-making are determined in light of Egypt's strategic position. As a result many respondents implied that population could be overdiscussed when the government's money and time are tied up in other areas.[27] Any thought about population inherently requires a long-term view, but Egyptian policy-makers are overwhelmingly caught up in short-term contingency planning for the state of "no peace—no war." As one education expert put it: "The war holds us in thrall. We are self-sufficient, we can support many more people, but the real problem is to mobilize world public opinion and put an end to Israeli aggression." Or an agronomist: "We've had...a whole generation in this terrible situation. We think only of that, we cannot really be constructive. Seven thousand years ago we were constructing on the highest scientific level—that is our

heritage. Egypt could be a lighthouse to this entire part of the world."

Thralldom and the belief that something must be done go hand in hand. President Sadat has established family planning as a national priority. At National Family Planning Week in May 1972, Presidential Advisor Abdesslam al-Zayyat declared that the threat of population growth to Egypt is as great as that posed by the country's Zionist enemies. Finally, Egypt's most famous political commentator, Mohammed Hassanein Heikal,* related population growth to the war in this manner:

> We shall reach the 1990s—after only 20 years—with 72 million people.
> Our hope for the future is the mobilization of all resources for development and growth.
> But if Egypt continues to be drained in this fashion, and if the population continues its extraordinary growth as expected, then the simple meaning of this is that the state of no peace and no war is not only damaging to Egypt's present, but also a barrier to her entire future.[28]

No matter how sincere, one suspects that these declarations of concern are not much more than invocations and determined reaffirmation of the need to do something. Everything hangs in abeyance until the issue of the war is resolved. Yet all but two of the respondents declared themselves to be optimists: "I have to be optimistic, otherwise I don't see how I could keep going." was a typical observation. The two mavericks were the respondents who felt that the next decade will be crucial for Egypt and then left open the possibility that Egypt might not meet the test; the other is Boutros-Ghali who remarked to another interviewer, "I'd be curious to know if among all the people you have met you have found anyone as pessimistic as me. If I am the only one, it's another reason for me to be even more pessimistic."[29]

Conclusion

In this atmosphere, and despite their chins-up attitude, it must be hard for the ecumenist core of respondents to push ahead on all fronts with enthusiasm, knowing that priorities lie elsewhere. They do not accept the notion that there is a cheap way

*Heikal was relieved of his position as editor of *al-Ahram* in February 1974.

out through a technical solution. Nor do they believe for the most part that there is some key social variable that can be turned to set various other parts of the social system in motion. Global change is what is needed, they say, and it will inevitably come one way or another. As members of the state apparatus as well as of the socioeconomic elite, the respondents can only hope that they can guide, control, and accelerate given processes within the framework of existing policies and programs.

NOTES

1. Something of a classic now is the article of Kingsley Davis and Judith Blake, "Social Structure and Fertility, an Analytic Framework," *Economic Development and Cultural Change*, Vol. 4, No. 3 (April 1956), pp. 211-35. The authors inventory the social structural variables involved in the reproductive process but do not pretend to present hypotheses of causality nor to assign weights to variables. A later, and in my view unsatisfactory attempt to do just that is: Irma Adelman and Cynthia Morris, "A Quantitative Study of Social and Political Determinants of Fertility," *Economic Development and Cultural Change*, Vol. 14, No. 2 (January 1966), pp. 129-57. The range of issues involved is well represented in Harrison Brown and Ed. Hutchings (eds.) *Are Our Descendants Doomed?*, Viking, New York City, 1972, especially chapters by Kingsley Davis, Donald Heisel, Bernard Berrelson and R.T. Ravenholt.

2. W.G. Povey and G.F. Brown, "Tunisia's Experience in Family Planning," *Demography*, Vol. 5, No. 2 (1968), pp. 620-26, citation from p. 626. Cf. R.T. Ravenholt, *"Are Our Descendants Doomed?" op. cit.*, p. 241.

3. Janet Abou-Lughod, "Urban-Rural Differences as a Function of the Demographic Transition: Egyptian Data and an Analytic Model," *American Journal of Sociology*, Vol. 69, 1963/64, pp. 476-490, citation from p. 487.

4. See my *Land, Man and Development in Algeria: Part II: Population, Employment, and Emigration* [JW-2-'73], Fieldstaff Reports, North Africa Series, Vol. XVII, No. 2, 1973.

5. Cited in *Al-Ahram*, January 15, 1972. Emphasis added. His ideas are summarized in *The Economist* ("Jobs for the Girls") April 8, 1972. Fuller treatments are to be found in Aziz Bindary, C.B. Baxter, and T.H. Hollingsworth, "Urban-Rural Differences in the Relationship between Women's Employment and Fertility—a Preliminary Study,"

unpub. Cairo, Spring 1972; and Aziz Bindary, "Social Structure Change and Specific Women's Employment: a New Theory of Family Planning," unpub. Cairo, January 1972.

6. Long and short term program goals are set forth in, Executive Board for Family Planning, *Report on Family Planning*, Cairo. June 1972 (in Arabic).

7. Dr. Khalil Mazhar, the first Chairman of the Executive Board, launched the public program almost solely on the basis of the sale of pills and the distribution of incentives. After the initial and spectacular expansion of the program, it quickly plateaued. Mazhar left the Executive Board after the June War. His training to that point had been in medicine, specifically gynecology, but his experience in the program was such a revelation to him that he returned to the university to study sociology and anthropology to gain a better grasp of social processes in Egypt. He is now one of Egypt's most fervent advocates of the global approach and detractor of the technico-medical approach.

8. The author of that judgment will go unnamed because the passage cited is from private correspondence.

9. The respondent is referring here to a notion put most emphatically by Alfred Sauvy: "Lorsqu'une personne ou un ménage est 'sorti du trou,' est parvenu à un certain niveau économique et culturel, l'idée lui vient presque spontanément de lutter contre une prolificité dégradante." *Malthus et les Deux Marx*, p. 138, cited by Gérard Viratelle, *l'Algerié algeriènne*, editions ouvrieres, Paris, 1970, p. 209.

10. See David Sills, "Unanticipated Consequences of Population Policies," *Concerned Demography*, Vol. 2, No. 4 (March 1971), pp. 61-68, for a general discussion of this concept.

11. Ahmad Baha al-Din, "Hadith al-Had," *Al-Ahram*, November 5, 1972.

12. Ivan Illich, "Birth Control et conscience politique," *Esprit*, vol. 37, February 1969, pp. 1056-69; citation p. 1060. Pierre Pradervand argues that the overhaul of corrupt or feudal political institutions in many developing countries may be crucial to the success of family planning. See his "The Ideological Premises of Western Research in the Field of Population Study," paper presented at the African Population Conference, Accra, Ghana, December 9-13, 1971. From a different ideological perspective similar conclusions emerge: see Adelman and Morris, *op. cit.*, esp. p. 142 where they argue that a factor called "Westernization of political institutions" explains 47 per cent of the inter-country variations in fertility among 55 developing countries.

13. See "Report on Family Planning," *op. cit.*, p. 6. The Central Agency for Public Mobilization and Statistics has released survey results that reveal that the crude birthrate has fallen off in all but two of Egypt's 25 governorates, despite the fact that the family planning program has relatively few rural users. See *Al-Ahram*, September 24, 1972.

14. *Al-Ahram* recently published a revealing article about precisely these problems. One example cited was the establishment of a factory utilizing costly imported machinery to manufacture butter and cheese at Nag Hammadi. Once the factory was completed it was discovered that all local milk supplies were consumed at home. Milk was brought in from distant areas but always arrived in a state unfit for use in the factory—which had to be closed.

15. The Algerians, on the other hand, have taken care of this problem, at least definitionally, by not considering women as part of the work force. See my AUFS Report, *Land, Man, and Development in Algeria: Part II, op.cit.* Egyptian planners may profess to be sex-blind in the creation of jobs, but their projected rates for female participation in the work force indicates only minor improvement over the next 20 years. See my *Manpower and Population Planning in the Arab Republic of Egypt, Part II: The Burden of Dependency* [JW-3-'72], Fieldstaff Reports, Northeast Africa Series, Vol. XVII, No. 3, 1972, p.8.

16. Dr. Nuwwal Saadawi, *Women and Sex*, Dar ash-Sha'ab, Cairo, 1972 (in Arabic).

17. *Ibid.*, p. 67; also Aziza Hussein, "Status of Women and Family Planning in a Developing Country: Egypt," mimeo, n.d., pp. 2-3; Dr. Zaynab Subki, "Status of Women and Family Planning in Egypt," Working Paper 19, presented at the UN Seminar on the Status of Women and Family Planning, Istanbul, July 11-24, 1972. A paper that is well-intentioned but might raise the hackles of concerned women is that of Dr. Abdelmaguid al-Abd, "Women power for Economic Development: Analysis for Employment Promotion," presented at the regional conference on educational and vocational training and work opportunities for girls and women of African countries, Rabat, May 20-29, 1971.

18. See T. Paul Schultz, *Fertility Patterns and their Determinants in the Arab Middle East*, Rand Corp. RM-5978-FF, May 1970, p. 19.

19. The basic lines of this debate can be found in Dudley Kirk (pro) "Factors Affecting Moslem Natality," *World Population Conference: Belgrade 1965*, United Nations, Vol.

II, New York City, 1965, pp. 149-55; and Leila Shukry al-Hamamsy (con) "Belief Systems and Family Planning in Peasant Societies" in Harrison Brown and Ed. Hutchings (eds.), *Are Our Descendants Doomed?*, *op. cit.*, pp. 335-57.

20. *Ibid.*, p. 346.

21. Many of these phenomena are familiar to those knowledgeable of non-Islamic peasant societies, but the nonspecialist may find useful the following four basic studies: Hamid Ammar, *Growing Up in an Egyptian Village*, London, 1954; Henry Ayrout, *The Egyptian Peasant*, Beacon Press, 1963; Jacques Berque, *Histoire Sociale d'un Village Egyptien au XXeme Siècle*, Mouton, The Hague, 1957; and Winifred Blackman, *The Fellahin of Upper Egypt*, Frank Cass, London, 1968. See also Dr. Said Awais, "The Most Important Social, Cultural, and Economic Factors that Family Planning Operations Face in Modern Egyptian Society," memo of the National Center for Sociological and Criminological Research, June 1971, 17 pp. (in Arabic).

22. See "Report of Family Planning," *op. cit.*

23. See T. Paul Schultz, *op. cit.*, p. 31.

24. Boutros Boutros-Ghali, "Monde Arabe et Tiers Monde," *Eléments*, (La Nouvelle Réflexion arabe) nos. 8 + 9, 1971/72, pp. 33-42.

25. This argument has been brilliantly presented by Pierre Praderand, "Les pays nantis et la limitation des naissances dans le Tiers Monde" *Developpement et Civilisations*, March-June 1970, pp. 4-39.

26. Kingsley Davis, "Population and Power in the Free World", in Philip Hauser (ed.) *Population and World Politics*, Glencoe, The Free Press, 1958, pp. 193-213, citation p. 213.

27. President Sadat announced in May 1972 that in the five years since the June War, Egyptian defense outlays had totalled four billion pounds or around ten billion dollars. At about the same time (*Al-Ahram*, May 20, 1972), it was announced that total industrial investments for the decade 1972-1982 would reach three billion pounds.

28. Mohammed Hassanein Heikal, "America's Role and Responsibility: No Peace, No War: Part II," *Al-Ahram*, June 23, 1972.

29. Boutros-Ghali, *op. cit.* p. 42.

APPENDIX I

The following persons, listed in alphabetical order, all graciously consented to answer my questions drawn from the general definition of the problem presented in Appendix II. I hereby offer my thanks to my interlocutors who found time to receive me. I would also like to thank Chafiq al-Barr and the staff of the press center of the Ministry of Information for their help in arranging the interviews.

Abdelmaguid al-Abd	former Director, Central Training Organization
Ali Abderrazzak	Minister of Primary and Secondary Education
Hoda Badran	Program specialist, UNICEF, Cairo
Ahmad Baha al-Din	columnist for *Al-Ahram*
Aziz Bindary	Chairman of the Executive Board for Family Planning
Boutros Boutros-Ghali	Professor of International Relations, editor of *Al-Ahram al-Iqtisadi*
Salah Galal	science editor, *Al-Ahram*
Riad Ghoneimy	program specialist, FAO, Cairo
Saad Hagras	Chairman Agrarian Reform Organization, Ministry of Agriculture
Sherif Hattata	Director Planning and Evaluation, Executive Board for Family Planning
Ahmad Khalifa	former Minister of Social Affairs; Director of the Center for Criminological and Sociological Studies
Fathallah Khatib	Professor of Sociology, former Presidential Advisor on Internal Affairs, currently a member of the Council of Ministers of the Federation of Arab Republics
Lutfi al-Kholi	Editor-in-chief of *Al-Tali'a*
El-Zeer al-Maadawi	Director of the Institute of Workers' Culture, Arab Socialist Union
Mahmud Mohammed Mahfuz	Minister of Health
Khalil Mazhar	former chairman of the Executive Board for Family Planning
Ahmad Morshidi	Under-secretary of State for Planning, Ministry of Planning
Latifa Hamdawi (fictitious name)	elected member of an Arab Socialist Union section Cairo
Aisha Rateb	Minister of Social Affairs
Ismail Sabry-Abdullah	Minister of State for Planning
Karima Said	Head of Feminist Organization, Arab Socialist Union
Zaynab Subki	Head of Family Planning Programs, Arab Socialist Union
Nur al-Din Tarraf	Former Minister of Health

Appendix II: A Guide to the Discussion*

Both President Nasser in 1962 and President Sadat in 1971 called attention to the negative effects of rapid population growth upon the process of economic development in Egypt. The following questions are designed to elicit discussion of the interrelation of population and economic growth on the part of Egyptians closely involved in planning and policy formulation for various economic sectors as well as for officials involved in the administration of family planning programs. In no case will specific remarks be attributed to specific people. The object is to gain an overview of varying analytic responses to the questions below which would then be written up in the form of a 15-20 page report.

* * * * *

The relation of population growth to economic growth

1. An hypothesis for discussion: before the family planning program can gain real momentum there must be substantial social and economic changes that *precede* the expansion of the program. This hypothesis suggests that the family planning program *cannot create* the desire for contraceptive devices on the part of individuals, but can only *respond* to needs stimulated or created by the following factors:

   a. greater participation of women in the work force
   b. higher educational levels for all sectors of the population but especially women
   c. changes more favorable to women in divorce and inheritance laws
   d. a general rise in per capita income for all sectors of society
   e. fundamental changes in labor intensive agricultural methods
   f. drastic lowering of infant mortality rates
   g. provision of old-age security for most of the population
   h. raising the minimum marriage age for men and women

There are of course other factors, and I would be interested to learn what others may be considered relevant. In essence this hypothesis implies that Egypt would have to guarantee a high enough rate of economic growth for perhaps a generation to outstrip population growth; economic growth would in turn raise per capita income substantially at which point the population would be responsive to the notion of family planning.

2. The counter-hypothesis would suggest that well-organized family planning programs can *create* receptive audiences and recruit significant numbers of users to the clinics, thereby reducing fertility and population growth, and in turn increasing the per capita rate of economic growth. This hypothesis assumes:

   a. the availability of competent staff and contraceptive materials
   b. a complete network of smoothly functioning clinics and hospitals
   c. easy access of all sectors of the population to family planning services
   d. intensive mass media and education programs

In essence this argument supposes that fertility can be lowered substantially here and now, without major socioeconomic changes coming first; it supposes that there is a large adult population ready, willing, and able to adopt family planning techniques if only they could be made readily available.

I would like to discuss the merits of these two hypotheses.

3. Even assuming a moderate rate of population growth, can Egypt assure its own economic growth and prosperity relying primarily on its own resource base? Or, would increased worker emigration and inter-Arab development schemes be necessary to assure continued growth?

John Waterbury
American Universities Field Staff

*a copy of this was presented to any respondent who requested it. Whether or not requested, I used it to organize the questions and guide the discussion.

Chickens and Eggs:
Egypt's Population Explosion Revisited

In an earlier article dealing with demographic change in Egypt[1] I have attempted to coax from a group of prominent Egyptian policy-makers and opinion leaders their opinions on what are the most important variables affecting fertility behavior in their society. In effect, what was being asked of them was to take a stab at causal analysis or, in more mundane terms, to choose between chickens and eggs. The analytic problem—by what policy measures can fertility be lowered—is bifurcate. The two (mutually compatible) alternatives generally mentioned are conventional family planning programs and concerted programs of economic development in order to raise standards of living, educational levels, etc., and thereby put people into a "planning" mood. If one decides that the *sine qua non* of fertility reduction is economic development and increased individual prosperity one reaches the second part of the conundrum, to wit, how can one achieve rapid economic growth in the face of a population explosion? The circle is closed if the answer comes back that we must push ahead at all costs with the conventional family planning program, for, presumably, such programs will not have a broad impact in the absence of economic growth. Which should come first? Increasingly, Egyptians concerned with this question have decided that both must come first. In terms of time, effort, and money, however, there is a growing consensus that economic development must remain the overriding concern of the central authorities.

The Climate at the Top

This outlook was made abundantly clear at the World Population Conference in Bucharest in August 1974. The Egyptian delegation was led by

Ismail Sabry Abdullah, the Minister for Plan, a Marxist, and at present the man responsible for Egypt's long-range growth strategy.[2] Along with many other developing countries, Egypt declared support for international measures between rich and poor nations to further the development of the latter and to seek a more equitable distribution of world resources. Within Egypt the same tone has been set in several quarters. The Prime Minister, Dr. Abdelaziz Higazi, has long advocated a holistic approach to population growth, subsuming the family planning program within the general framework of human resource planning. The population challenge, in Dr. Higazi's view, does not consist simply in avoiding future births but rather in planning for the productive employment of those already living. His views in this respect overlap with those of Dr. Aziz Bindary, the director of the Population and Family Planning Board. Since his accession to this post five years ago, he has been urging a redefinition of the role of his agency so that it may increasingly sensitize other sectors of the government to the necessity to develop policies that will take into account their ultimate impact upon fertility.[3] The fact that the former Executive Board for Family Planning[4] is now called The Population and Family Planning Board is indicative of the shift in emphasis. While the board continues to administer incentive payments to the public health staff involved in the distribution of pills and the insertion of IUDs, it is placing great stress upon original field research and the use of causal models for influencing fertility behavior. An official brochure issued by the Board sums up their view:

>...the basic assumption is that overall socio-economic development, together with a

Five children and still smiling.

communication program and the provision of family planning services, will lead to a reduction in population growth as changing primary motivation and remedying underlying causes is a sound starting point for curbing high birthrates.[5]

The matter was put even more succinctly by the Board's Director of Planning:

> We believe that the logical approach to significantly reducing high birthrates lies in affecting structural changes in the socioeconomic system to transform it to a state consistent with low birthrates.[6]

The proto-consensus embodied in the above statements can and does lead to several, not always compatible, conclusions. It is still the case, for instance, that just about anyone in Egypt who cares to talk about it is concerned about population growth. The fact that the conventional family planning has not made any spectacular breakthrough in lowering fertility, however, has led to a certain indifference toward efforts to make existing programs work better. In some instances, although none of major importance, resources have actually been diverted from family planning efforts. The Governor of Fayyum Province expressed a mood that many others share. In an interview with a reporter from *Ruz al-Yussef*, the following exchange took place:

Governor: The only thing that has really stymied me [as Governor] is the insane increase in the number of births. Fayyum's population now is one and a quarter million.

Reporter: Will you start a campaign for family planning?

Governor: Family planning? You make me laugh! Family planning, my friend, is tied up with knowledge and learning, with the mentality and culture of people. No one practices planning other than those who understand the necessity of planning. And people who don't read or write don't understand. In my view family planning begins with the eradication of illiteracy. Any effort that does not start from this is useless. For that reason I have decided to transfer a large part of the [provincial] family planning budget to literacy programs.[7]

At a different level a similar atmosphere of indifference to the conventional program prevails. Dr. Hilmy Abd al-Rahman, adviser to the Prime Minister on Technology presented a view that I have found echoed in both the Ministry of Plan and the Population Board:

> The development of the population for the next 25 years has already been determined and can only be changed slightly through family planning efforts. Our population will double in the next 25 years with only a 20 per cent possibility of variation. Family planning policy, whether by political or voluntary action will only show results after being applied for 20-25 years, the normal length of a woman's fertility. Therefore for the next 20 or 25 years the problem in Egypt is mainly to meet the requirements of an increasing population, and if industry and technology develop quickly this will help reduce the population as happened in all advanced societies...industrialization is said to be the best contraceptive. Of course a proper [family planning] policy should be begun, although its action and effectiveness may be delayed.[8]

The view that over the next couple of decades nothing much can be done to affect the contours of Egypt's population growth is of enormous importance. First, it is probably not true, unless we agree that variations of 20 per cent are insignificant. Second, even if it were largely accurate, its acceptance could lead to a great deal of *non*-analysis, *non*-decision-making, and *non*-experimentation in those policy areas that relate most directly to fertility behavior. The Population Board has set itself the task of preventing such a state of lassitude from emerging but it faces monumental bureaucratic inertia, sustained by administrators comforted by the knowledge that no matter how innovative they might be, their efforts would lead to no noticeable change in the general picture.

There is yet another factor, in many ways one of the most profound, relegating concern over rapid population growth and conventional means for dealing with it to a position of secondary importance. It is the fact that population growth and its ramifications are seen as long-term problems, undeniably important but neither pressing nor urgent. What is urgent, and has been in the most acute fashion since 1967, is the economic state of a poor society on a continuous war footing. The question has literally been one of guns and bread. As President Sadat himself said, prior to the war of October 1973, Egypt did not have the wherewithal to pay for the next few months' wheat imports. Since October 1973, the situation has eased slightly, but only slightly, as some hard currency has been credited to the Egyptian treasury from the revenues of the Arab oil-producing states. The fact remains that Egypt must import this year something on the order of four million tons of grains and flour, not to mention edible oils, meat, beans, and sugar.[9] These import needs will inevitably grow in lock step with the population. There are only modest prospects for major increases in agricultural production, which is limited by relatively fixed amounts of agricultural land and already high yields per acre. In short, the two overriding concerns of the government are (1) to seek a stable peace in the area in order to move away from an economy dominated by the necessities of military preparedness; and (2) to generate steady sources of hard currency to meet the growing import bill. As long as the first goal proves elusive, the second will as well, for the proper climate for peace time growth and international investment will be lacking. In the interim,

it is an open secret that economic planning boils down to the short-term management of the hard currency budget. In view of the urgent nature of these twin concerns, population growth has been lost in the shuffle. But it is in large measure a result of rapid population growth that the necessity to deal with the problems is so acute. Back to chickens and eggs.

The Dimensions of Population Growth

Let us take the future first, because it relates directly to the view that little can be done over the next quarter century to change the magnitude of the problem that Egypt faces. This is true only in a general sense, for while the Egyptian population will grow prodigiously, the range between maximal and minimal growth projections is hardly negligible. When one says that by the year 2000 the Egyptian population will be around 60 million, give or take 10 million, the range of 20 million is not to be sniffed at. Assuming for the moment that over the next 25 years there is no diminution in the population growth rate, one can calculate in *current* prices what this will mean to the economy in all but a few sectors. A single low-cost housing unit serving five persons costs *at least* LE 1,000 ($2,200). Thus housing for the 20 million additional Egyptians that would be born according to the maximal hypothesis would alone cost on the order of LE 4 billion. In the first five year plan, it was estimated that to create one new job cost LE 1,300. To absorb simply the male portion of the 20 million additional Egyptians would cost, in 1960-1965 prices, LE 13 billion. One could go on with costs in education, public health, transportation, and so forth.[10] It is perfectly understandable that for those who have to cope with living Egyptians the significant fact is that by the year 2000 there will be at least 50 million Egyptians instead of the 37 million of today; it is equally significant, however, that without commensurate concern, Egypt could be faced with 70 million. The 20 million gap by the end of this century represents, after all, two-thirds of Egypt's present population. Figure 1 presents graphically the significance of the gap between minimal and maximal projections over time.

Long-range projections on Egyptian population growth are nothing more than mathematical exercises, and one can have one's pick of prognosticators.[11] The exercise in Table 1 is based on the

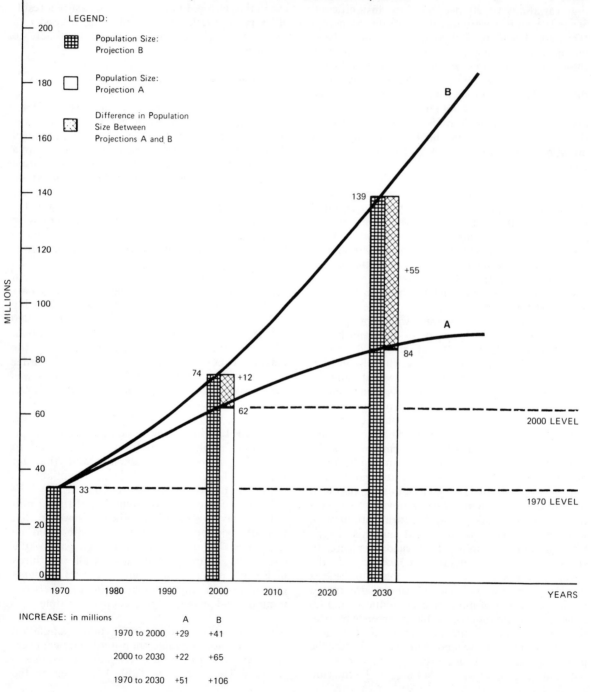

FIGURE 1

THE PROBABLE RANGE OF EGYPT'S POPULATION OVER THE NEXT TWO GENERATIONS

(rounded to nearest million)

Projection A: At Probable Maximum Fertility Decline

Projection B: At Present Trend in Fertility Decline

LEGEND:

Population Size: Projection B

Population Size: Projection A

Difference in Population Size Between Projections A and B

MILLIONS

200

180

160

140

120

100

80

60

40

20

0

B

139

+55

A

84

74

+12

62

2000 LEVEL

33

1970 LEVEL

1970   1980   1990   2000   2010   2020   2030

YEARS

INCREASE: in millions	A	B
1970 to 2000	+29	+41
2000 to 2030	+22	+65
1970 to 2030	+51	+106

assumption that if the net reproduction rate (the number of daughters born to Egyptian mothers who survive the childbearing age, NRR), estimated to be 2.2 for the period 1965-1970, could be reduced to one, then a stable population would be achieved. The table, which sets forth the variations in vital rates according to when this stable state is reached, supports the view that, whatever the efforts devoted to family planning, Egypt's population is going to grow impressively before the turn of the century. Even if the NRR is reduced to one by 1980 there will still be over 50 million Egyptians in the year 2000. It is easy to understand, therefore, why Egyptian policy-makers take the attitude that if it proves possible to attain an economic growth rate sufficient to meet the needs of this population, that in itself will already be a remarkable achievement. If, however, economic growth is insufficient to meet this challenge then worrying about 70 million in the next 25 years would constitute wasted effort. The question is, I suppose, what is the difference between 50 and 70 million when you are at 37 million and not breaking even.

More than intelligent planning, a miracle is needed. In 1973 the density of inhabitants per square kilometer of agricultural and urban land (only about 3.5 per cent of Egypt's total land surface of one million square kilometers) reached 1,012 persons, a density rivaled by few other areas in the world. It is sobering to note that in 1928 density per square kilometer in Egypt was 406 persons. It is, of course, possible and likely that Egypt will add substantially to its cultivated acreage in the coming decades through desert reclamation projects, perhaps an addition of as much as 20 per cent to existing cultivated areas. The new lands, however, are of much poorer quality than the rich alluvial soils of the Nile Valley proper and thus will not sustain the same high population densities as the older areas. It is also true that urban development can take place just about anywhere and totally new urban centers will probably develop over the next quarter century. Cairo itself is now choked with over seven million inhabitants and an overall density per square kilometer of 26,000 persons. In some quarters that

Table 1

Four Hypotheses Concerning the Attainment of a Stable Population in Egypt (NRR = 1)*

CBR = Crude Birthrate   CDR = Crude Death Rate   GR = Growth Rate

Period	Hypothesis I NRR=1 1980			Hypothesis 2 NR=1 2000			Hypothesis 3 (NRR=1 2020			Hypothesis 4 NRR=1 2040		
	CBR	CDR	GR	CBR	CDR	GR	CBR	CDR	GR	CBR	CDR	GR
1965-70	43.4	15.9	2.7	43.4	15.9	2.7	43.4	15.9	2.7	43.4	15.9	2.7
1970-75	35.0	13.6	2.1	39.3	13.9	2.5	40.5	14.0	2.7	41.1	14.0	2.7
1975-80	27.4	11.6	1.6	35.8	12.1	2.4	38.1	12.3	2.6	39.2	12.3	2.7
1980-85	20.0	10.0	1.0	32.9	10.6	2.2	36.6	10.8	2.5	37.8	10.8	2.7
1985-90	21.3	9.7	1.2	30.3	9.6	2.1	34.7	9.7	2.5	36.7	9.7	2.7
1990-95	21.8	9.3	1.2	27.2	8.8	1.8	32.9	8.8	2.4	35.5	8.8	2.7
1995-2000	20.8	9.0	1.2	23.4	8.1	1.5	30.7	7.9	2.3	33.9	7.8	2.6
Total Pop. Year 2000 in millions	50.6			62.4			70.1			74.0		

*Extracted from Population Council, *Arab Republic of Egypt: Country Prospects*, New York City, 1974. It is important to note that the Population Council assumed a growth rate of 2.7 per cent per annum for the period 1965-1970, which is well in excess of official figures. The growth rate for the period 1960-1966 has been calculated at 2.58 per cent, falling off rather markedly thereafter to about 2 per cent by the year 1971. This should be kept in mind, for all four hypotheses are based on the estimates presented in the table for the period 1965-1970.

ratio has risen to 145,000 per square kilometer,[12] and there has been constant, if ineffectual, talk of establishing satellite cities around Cairo, utilizing desert land for the purpose. The costs are so enormous that this must remain a distant dream. Of more immediate import is the gradual reopening of the three cities—Port Said, Ismailia, Suez—of the Suez Canal Zone, a process dependent upon progress toward a settlement of the Arab-Israeli dispute. The million or more persons that inhabited these cities before 1967 have gradually begun to return home. With the reopening of the Canal, the establishment of an international free zone at Port Said, and the relocation and initiation of industries in the area (cement, petrochemicals, fertilizers, refineries), the Canal Zone should become a major pole of attraction, drawing population from Cairo and Alexandria as well as from the Egyptian countryside. Another area that appears destined for urban growth is Mersa Matrouh, lying well to the west of Alexandria along the Mediterranean coast. But even if new lands and new cities are able to absorb some of the population increase, they will have only a marginal impact on reducing the pressure upon habitable land. Under the very best of circumstances, assuming that the population will be no more than 50 million in the year 2000 and that new lands and cities will accommodate five million inhabitants, density per square kilometer in the year 2000 will be 1,265. Assuming a population of 70 million by the turn of the century would give a density ratio of 1,822 per square kilometer.

The miracle that is needed, then, would be a package of peace, rapid industrialization, firm foreign markets and hard currency earnings, bold efforts not so much to make the desert bloom as to populate it, a rapidly declining population growth rate, and prosperity.

Of the contents of that package, two already appear to be present in embryo. Some stabilization of the Arab-Israeli conflict is a distinct possibility, though not yet a likelihood. At the same time, as noted in earlier reports on the subject,[13] there has been a steady decline in fertility rates since 1966-67. It is to this latter trend that we shall now turn in considering the current demographic picture in Egypt.

The fertility decline that manifested itself after 1966 was cause for very cautious hope that Egypt

Salah Jahin, *al-Ahram*, April 24, 1973. The cartoon is entitled "Family Planning Week." In the psychiatrist's office, the man on the couch is saying, "The strange thing is that I hate children...but despite that I'm all messed up if a year goes by without producing one."

had rounded the bend and that the crude birthrate was finally moving towards equilibrium with the crude death rate which had dropped substantially in the 1930s and 1940s. At the same time, it was widely feared that the decline might be no more than a short-term phenomenon resulting from the defeat of 1967 and a kind of psychic depression that inhibited conception. There is surely something to these fears, but those who follow demographic change closely are now convinced that the decline is real and will continue. Following the war of October 1973, and its relatively positive results from the Egyptian point of view, there has been, provisionally, a small-scale baby boom, leading to an increase in the crude birthrate of one per 1,000; it is expected, however, that the rate will once again begin to decline. This prediction seems the more reasonable for the simple fact that there has been no breakthrough in family planning services or, as happened in Japan and Eastern Europe, drastic changes in legislation affecting abortion. Fertility decline in Egypt has been most rapid in the cities (with a CBR of 30/'000 today) where family planning services are concentrated. Although

Table 2   Crude Birth, Crude Death, and Population
Growth Rates, 1952 - 1972*

Year	No. of Births '000	CBR	No. of Deaths '000	CDR	Increase '000	Rate
1952	969	45.2	381	17.8	598	2.74
1960	1,114	42.1	438	16.9	676	2.62
1965	1,221	41.7	412	14.1	809	1.76
1967	1,210	39.2	440	14.2	770	2.50
1968	1,207	38.2	509	16.1	698	2.21
1969	1,197	37.0	468	14.5	729	2.25
1970	1,162	35.1	501	15.1	661	2.00
1971	1,186	35.1	445	13.2	741	2.19
1972	1,118**	34.1**	501**	14.4**	687**	1.97**
1973	----	35.3**	----	14-15**	----	2-2.1**

*Source: Central Agency for Public Mobilization and Statistics, *1973 Year Book*, Cairo 1974.
**represents provisional figures.

less rapid, the decline has also been uniformly registered in the countryside where resort to official family planning services is relatively minor. In other words, a good deal of the decline must be attributed to spontaneous, voluntary, and "home" methods (coitus interruptus, rhythm, condoms, illegal abortions) that indicate a common desire to limit the number of births.

Data pertaining to these methods are understandably scarce. Very few surveys have been conducted that would produce evidence of what goes on outside the framework of the family planning program. This is especially true of induced abortion which is illegal unless a doctor is willing to certify that the mother's life is in danger. Many doctors are prepared to interpret this condition broadly and will take into consideration the existence of lung or heart problems, anemia, or cumulative fatigue resulting from previous births. Beyond this, several doctors guarantee women who have had loops inserted (there is a failure rate of 1.5-2.0 pregnancies per 100 woman years of use) that if they become pregnant they will receive a free abortion. Nonetheless the whole question of induced abortion is cloaked in socio-cultural taboos and thus both difficult to measure or to discuss. Some years back the head of the Obstetrics and Gynecology section of the Qasr al-Aini General

Hospital in Cairo carried out a study of all cases of "complicated" abortion handled by the section over several years. It was found that about a third of all such cases could be unambiguously identified as induced. Other hospitals reported similar ratios. More recently, a village survey of all women between the ages of 15 and 49 was carried out over an entire year. The women were given regular medical checkups, including a urinalysis by which the investigating team could determine the incidence of pregnancy. If in the next periodic exam the urinalysis revealed that the woman was no longer pregnant, she was asked whether she had aborted. If she said yes, then she was asked if it had been spontaneous or induced; if no, it was assumed that she had induced abortion. About 55 per cent of the women of childbearing age were married, not sterile, not already pregnant, not widowed, and not divorced. Of these about one-quarter became pregnant in the course of the study. About one-quarter of all pregnancies resulted in abortion, and about 20 per cent of these were clearly induced. It would of course be unwarranted to extrapolate a national pattern from these limited results, but there are good reasons to believe that the study actually underestimated the number of induced abortions in the village. As a very rough guesstimate, it may be that nationwide something like 5 per cent of all pregnancies result in induced

General Askar, Director of the Central Agency for Public Mobilization and Statistics announced to the local press that on March 18, 1975, the population of Egypt reached 37 million. The figures published by the local press did not include estimates of crude birth and death rates. They did, however, indicate that the net growth of the population over the preceding 12 months had been 812,000 souls. If we compare this net gain with that indicated in Table 2, it becomes clear that 1974-75 represents a bumper crop and can only be explained by a sharp increase in the crude birthrate (a sharp decrease in the crude death rate hardly seems likely). If this is the case, and if it continues, what has been presented as a secular trend in declining fertility could be called into question.

Whatever the case may be, the figures released by General Askar prompted one writer for *al-Ahram*, Salama Ahmad Salama, to register the following opinion (*al-Ahram*, March 26, 1975):

The figures recently released concerning Egypt's population are disturbing, not to say ominous. They confirm for anyone who wishes to listen or to see the future of life on Egyptian soil in the year 2000 is no future at all, especially in view of the fact that in the coming decades the population may grow to 80 million.

The time has come to call things by their right name; we need birth control not family planning. The programs of family planning which have been applied to date have affirmed their deficiencies and their lack of seriousness, and the need for more comprehensive and dynamic approaches is inescapable. The sterilization of men is not an innovation [i.e., something that is contrary to the fundamental tenets of Islam: author's note]. It places the responsibility for limiting fertility upon the male just as contraceptive pills placed the responsibility upon the females. It is a practice that is applied in India and other countries concerned by the population explosion, or even in countries that are not at all worried by population growth, such as Sweden. In this vein, there is no alternative to offering material incentives to anyone who accepts sterilization, although it is a simple operation that does not affect the virility of the male anymore than the pills affect the femininity of the female.

We are, indeed, in need of a new and serious look at what we call the family planning board. We must resuscitate it, reawaken it, and appropriate it for the necessary credits. But above all else those who rely upon it must be convinced that the first and predominant goal to their efforts is birth control, and nothing else.

abortion. In 1972 that would have worked out to be about 70,000 induced abortions, as compared with 360,000 women who had had recourse to the family planning program. The ratio is all the more significant in that abortion is illegal while the family planning program is supported by official propaganda and by a comprehensive medical and paramedical infrastructure.[14]

The family planning program, both governmental and semiprivate, can claim only a modest part in bringing about the decline of fertility. The goal of the Family Planning Board is to reduce the crude birthrate by one per 1,000 annually over the next decade so that it will be no higher than 24/1,000 by 1984. It is conceivable that this decline will come about without the assistance of the official program, as has been the case in the past seven years, but if the program is to contribute significantly to this process, its scope and intensity will

have to be greatly expanded. With something like 5.2 million married women of childbearing age (15-44) in 1974, the government program was reaching less than 10 per cent of them (or ca. 450,000 women).[15] If one takes into account some 150,000 women who buy pills from private pharmacies, another 70-80,000 who have continued use of IUDs and 35,000 utilizing foams, jellies, diaphragms, etc., the percentage of married women of childbearing age following conventional family planning techniques would be 14 per cent. Of greater import is the fact that the number of initiates to family planning is lagging behind the number of women that enter childbearing age each year. This latter figure can be estimated at about 90-95,000 per annum. When the government program was first started in 1966, repetitive pill users ran at about 160,000 per month. The rate by 1973 was 436,000 per month, but the number of new users in the past four years has plateaued. For

بدون تعليق !

This cartoon is based on the old Egyptian proverb that a hopeless cause is like a call to prayer in Malta. The muezzin in the minaret is calling "The pill, O Peasants!"

instance between 1972 and 1973 the net gain in recruits to the program was only 21,000, from 415,634 to 436,616. In other words, the absolute number of married couples not practicing family planning may have been increasing. If that were true the number of live births each year would also be on the increase. The figures in Table 2, however, indicate that the number of births has been declining. The inevitable conclusion is, once again, that voluntary fertility control on an important scale is being practiced outside the framework of the conventional programs.

This is in a sense good news, for it constitutes evidence of growing motivation on the part of Egyptian couples to control the number of their offspring. But before the government program can exploit and reinforce the trend certain questions will have to be answered regarding the factors that have brought about this voluntary change. To put the matter as simply as possible, there is good cause to speculate that the fertility decline is due to economic privation of various sorts rather than to the formula offered by Alfred Sauvy of rising prosperity and the emergence of a planning mentality. Per capita income has, in all likelihood, declined

over the last seven or eight years.* Pressure upon relatively fixed land resources has grown only slightly less rapidly than the population, but the tendency toward fragmentation through inheritance and the formation of dwarf holdings has been intensified. In the cities soaring inflation in food-stuffs and rents has placed major contraints on the millions on fixed industrial and civil service wages. It has been frequently, and accurately, argued that rural families can add additional children to their midst without significant additional cost and that their offspring can, within a few years of birth, begin to contribute to the family's income. In many areas of the Egyptian countryside that probably is no longer the case. So much more so, then, for city inhabitants who must participate in the money economy, find shelter that others have built, and send their children to school, there being *relatively* few opportunities for child employment in urban areas. The message here is not altogether palatable. If the public authorities wish to reinforce the decline in fertility, must they reinforce the trend in declining standards of living? If the state is able to turn the economy around and begin to generate higher per capita incomes, can it be expected that the crude birthrate will initially start to climb? Neither question need be answered

The man marching in place is entitled "Family Planning."

خطوة تنظيم ((محلك سر سابقا))

*Since 1974 there has been a slight increase in per capita income.

in the affirmative for fertility may vary significantly from one sector of the population to another and there may be several intervening layers of causation between the socio-economic environment and fertility behavior. Given the dearth of survey date, the most one can say is that the motives that impel one toward or inhibit one from family planning remain mixed.

The following case material is taken from the monitoring of ten family planning clinics within the semiprivate services offered by the Cairo Family Planning Association.[16] All ten occurred within the crowded, lower-middle-class district of Sayyida Zeinab. The Cairo Family Planning Association, in conjunction with the Social Research Center of the American University in Cairo, has been carrying out a study of means to improve and to extend family planning services in this district with a view to developing guidelines for other areas as well. Some of the material generated by the study consists in recording dialogues, such as the following, between social workers and would-be utilizers of contraceptives.

Woman: I want to tell you about my case.

Social
Worker: I am listening.

Woman: I had 18 births out of which six are now living, two boys and four girls; and this girl sitting opposite you is one of them.

Social
Worker: I was just saying, who is this young lady who is coming for family planning?

Woman: She is 19 years old. When I was her age I was married and had children. As soon as I got married my mother-in-law told me "come on, we want children; this is our primary desire." I was still a child and knew nothing. I kept having children, one after another, until I lost my health. My dear, if I had known about birth control, I would have controlled from the beginning [a long sigh]. I have been using the pills for five years, but I stopped awhile and had a loop. Then I

removed the loop and used the pills. Now my period has stopped coming since a month, but this has happened to me before. For five months, then I remained tired, pale, dizzy, and unable to lift my body from the ground. Anyhow! What is the right thing to do?

Social
Worker: You are supposed to keep one kind of contraceptive, because inserting the loop, removing it, and inserting again affects the uterus and fatigues you. Every time the loop is inserted it causes some bleeding and colics like the period. Therefore every time you come for a new loop you will feel those things, but once the body adjusts you will not feel anything. The same thing for the pills. You must keep up so that the body adjusts to them.

(Another woman enters with her daughter who is to be married in a week. One of the other women present says "What is this, my sister! You should let her bear a child at first to test herself. She shouldn't prevent from the beginning like this."

The
Mother: Never; is it possible that I let her go through what I have gone through? It is enough that we were very young and had our children and our troubles. Let her have her fun with her husband first.

Daughter: Of course! Who would like to have children immediately. It is important that I get my home organized first, then I'll bring one or two children, and that would be enough.

The second dialogue goes as follows:

Social
Worker: Are you coming for an examination or do you want a loop?

Woman: No, I have been taking the pills for eight years and for the last three months the period has stopped. I am afraid that their pills may have made me pregnant.

Social
Worker: You didn't miss taking your pills for even one day, did you?

Woman: Never! I didn't forget one day.

Social
Worker: Alright, you will not be pregnant, especially if you have been taking the pills for eight years and nothing happened to you.

Woman's
Neighbor: Why are you hiding the truth from the lady? Aren't you the one who wants to be pregnant?

The truth is that the husband of this woman, who is 50 years old, married another young woman, 25 years old. This new wife made fun of our friend and told her you are too old now to have children.

Woman: Although I already have five children, and the oldest is 19 years old, this woman calls me barren. Do you think if I were barren I would have had children! I told her that I have controlled by my free will. I am the one taking the pills. She ridiculed me and said pills and birth control, what nonsense! Consequently, I made a vow and promised myself that if my husband divorces this woman I shall show all my neighbors and friends who have been told that I am incapable of bearing children; I shall show them that I am still able to have children. Therefore, I vowed that if my man divorces this woman, I shall become pregnant. My vow was fulfilled sooner than I expected. As soon as I stopped taking the pills, my period stopped.

Social
Worker: Did your husband divorce his new wife?

Woman: Yes, he divorced her six months after they were married, but he left her with a little girl.

Social
Worker: And you, will you be happy once you make sure you are pregnant in spite of the fact that you have grown up children?

"Egypt's population reaches 36 million and Cairo's 7 million" (top). The caption below the cartoon reads "What to do in cases of Population Explosion: head calmly to the [nearest] Family Planning Shelter." Salah Jahin, January 22, 1974, in *al-Ahram*.

Woman: What shall I do, I must fulfill my vow.

Woman's
Neighbor: She's very happy with her pregnancy.

Another
Woman: Isn't it a shame for an older person with a daughter ready for marriage to put herself in that position? How can she bear going again through the trouble of having children after eight years of rest?

(The woman eventually came out of the doctor's clinic full of joy, because the doctor informed her that she was four months pregnant.)

Two examples do not a national profile make. Yet it should be abundantly clear from this case material the variegated and sometimes contradictory pressures that bear upon Egyptian women—and this in an urban setting. Holding the attention of one's husband, affirming one's image in the eyes of one's female peers, asserting one's "feminismo" even when the physical toll will be heavy—all these factors of pride and image intervene between economic constraints and fertility behavior. Such constraints will not disappear. Supporters of family planning must hope that more women will assume the outlook of the uninvited commentator in the last exchange and will come forward to say, "How can she bear going again through the trouble of having children after eight years of rest?"

Too much worrying about the complexities of motivation, however, may well serve as nothing more than an excuse to carry out more studies and to postpone action. Even if the consensus is that Egypt's population problem will be solved to the extent that the country is able to propel its economy forward, there are many changes and improvements in the delivery system of the conventional family planning program that could be initiated without further delay. Some of the more obvious improvements would consist in extending the network of rural clinics so that there would be one for each of Egypt's 4,000 villages (at present there are 2,081 clinics serving the rural areas); specialized training for doctors, midwives, and other paramedical personnel in problems related to the use of pills and IUDs; regularized supply of pills without interruptions and changes in color and format; extension of clinics equipped and staffed for IUD insertions; closer direct supervision of incentive systems to prevent staff exploitation of would-be recruits or the falsification of sales records; greater emphasis on adult education and "consciousness-raising" efforts; more materials dealing with the consequences of rapid population growth incorporated into educational curriculum at all levels, and so forth. These improvements do not appear overly ambitious. They demand some additional investment, greater administrative coordination, and more selfless devotion to the cause. Yet there is scarcely any sector of the Egyptian government and public sector that has not set similar goals for itself and found them extremely hard to achieve. Seemingly simple reforms in priority areas have been lost somewhere in the bureaucratic morass. Efforts to clear Alexandria port of masses of imported goods, equipment, and foodstuffs were stymied for months until the army was called in to take over the clearing operation. Family planning cannot claim such draconian measures. Low priority, low budget, and bureaucratic indifference may paralyze the conventional program at a moment in time when mass feelings, no matter how diffuse and inchoate, indicate a general willingness to control fertility.

The National Census of November 1976

Sixteen years had elapsed since Egypt's last comprehensive national census, but with the return to some sort of normalcy in the Canal Zone, it became possible in the fall of 1976 to take the populations measure. At the time of writing the detailed results of this census have not yet been released. Still, it seems important to present the aggregate data that has been published (CAPMAS, *The Population of Egypt*, published as a special supplement to *al-Ahram al-Iqtisadi*, May 1, 1977) so as to update the material presented in the preceding pages. In addition I shall try to provide a few indicators that, coming from the statistical records of the past few years, may signal the trends of the short and medium range.

Table 3

Egypt's Population 1976

Resident in Egypt Nov. 1976	36,656,180
Resident Abroad Nov. 1976	1,425,000
Pop. of "unliberated" Sinai	147,000
Total	38,228,180

The most salient fact to be drawn from the figures in Table 3 is the significant increase in migration abroad, mainly to surrounding Arab countries. There may be 500,000 Egyptians, including dependents, in Libya alone, with lesser but still substantial migrant communities in Saudi Arabia and throughout the Gulf. This migratory trend has actually led to acute labor shortages in some domains, but as a counterpart, has stimulated worker remittances which in 1977 may have reached about $500 million.

Table 4

Rates of Population Growth

Census Year	Total Population	Absolute Increase	Rate of Growth
1960	26,085,326		
		3,990,532	2.54%
1966	30,075,858		
		8,152,322	2.31%
1976	38,228,180		

As noted earlier, there has been a modest fall-off in the population growth rate since 1966 (Table 4).

One of the major factors adduced by CAPMAS to explain this phenomenon is postponed or late marriage. CAPMAS notes that according to the 1976 figures the proportion of the population never married was 24.9 percent as compared with 17.9 percent in 1960. It is believed that postponement is particularly pronounced in the cities due to the unavailability of housing.

On the other hand, other observers are now convinced of some countertrends. The baby boom following the October 1973 War has apparently not proved itself as short-lived as one might have hoped. Recent birth and death statistics for 1976 reveal growth rates approximating those of the early 1960s.

Estimates of Supreme Council on Family Planning

Fertility	39	births per '000
Mortality	13	deaths per '000
Rate of Natural Inc.	26	per '000

Estimates of CAPMAS

37.7 births per '000
12.2 deaths per '000
25.5   per ,000

It is not clear if we are dealing with a "baby-boom" or a "death-bust," for to some degree it appears to be the reduction in the death rate that explains most of the increase in the rate of natural increase. Nonetheless, if the fertility rate of 34.4 per '000 for 1972 is accurate, there has been a marked increase in fertility as well.

Table 5

Rural-Urban Population Distribution

Census Year	Urban %	Rural %
1960	37.4	62.6
1966	40.5	59.5
1976	43.9	56.1

There are no surprises in the trends represented in Table 5. However, the relative slowness in the rate of growth of greater Cairo's population is surprising. It had reached by November 1976 just slightly over eight million which is less than one would have expected on the basis of growth rates in the 1960s. For instance CAPMAS found that the population of Cairo proper grew from 4,219,853 in 1966 to 5,084,463 in 1976, at an annual rate of 1.8 percent. The number of Cairenes resident abroad in 1976 was judged to be 320,000, and if they are included in the global figure, then the growth rate becomes 2.4 percent. However, even this rate is greatly inferior to the 4.1 percent established between 1960 and 1966.

As Table 6 indicates, some significant inroads would appear to have been made in the battle against illiteracy, but the overall growth of the population means that in absolute numbers the improvement has been considerably less. Moreover, it is still the case that in 1976 only 18 percent of all Egyptians 10 years old or older had actually completed one or more of the cycles of the public education system.

Table 6
Literacy Rates and Educational Levels
(for those 10 years old and older)

Educational Level	1960 Census			1976 Census		
	M	F	Total	M	F	Total
Illiterate	56.9	84	70.5	43.2	71	56.5
Read & Write	32.6	12.4	22.5	33.2	16.2	25.1
Below Hi-Education	9.0	3.4	6.2	20.4	11.6	16.2
Higher Education	1.5	.2	.8	3.2	1.2	2.2
Total	100.0	100.0	100.0	100.0	100.0	100.0

SUPPLEMENTARY STATISTICS AND TABLES

The Family Planning Program

In 1973 the total budget of the Family Planning Board was about LE 6,000,000 or ca. $12 million. $1,722,500 was contributed by the United Nations Family Planning Agency. The rest was supplied by the Egyptian government to cover the cost of contraceptives, incentives, and Board personnel. These figures do not include the indirect contribution of the Ministry of Health whose personnel in the clinics run by the Ministry are made available for family planning consultation an additional nine hours a week.

There are currently 1,107 clinics in urban areas and 2,081 in rural areas for a total of 3,188. This means that each clinic must serve, on the average, over 10,000 inhabitants. It is hoped that this ratio will be reduced to 5,000 by 1982.

Demographic Variables

While vital statistics are recorded at clinics run by the Ministry of Health, the raw data are sent not to the Ministry but to the Central Agency for Public Mobilization and Statistics, the sole authority controlling their analysis and release.

Until 1962, when the expansion of the network of clinics was begun, only about 55 per cent of the population was monitored through the clinics. For the rest vital statistics were provided by village *umda*, or local mayors.

For further information, see Dr. Malek Nomrossy, "The Order of New-Born in Fertility Measurement" in Cairo Demographic Center, *Fertility Trends and Differentials in Arab Countries*, Cairo 1971, pp. 117-131.

TOTAL POPULATION 1/7/1974 (Estimate)

Total Population	36.1 Millions
Male (50.8%)	18.3 Millions
Female (49.2%)	17.8 ''

URBAN and RURAL Distribution

Urban (128 Cities) 42.6%	15.4 Millions
Rural (4100 Villages) 57.4%	20.7 Millions
-- villages less than 2,000	29.0%
-- villages 2,000- 5,000	43.7%
-- villages 5,000- 10,000	22.5%
- villages more than 10,000	4.8%

AGE Distribution:

0 - (15.4%)	5.6 Millions
5 - (13.6%)	4.9 Millions
10 - (11.0%)	4.0 Millions
15 - (11.3%)	4.1 Millions
20 - (48.7%)	17.5 Millions

VITAL RATES (Per thousand) 1972

Birth rate	34.4
Death rate	14.5
Natural Increase rate	19.9
Infant Mortality rate	116.0
Neonatal Mortality rate	21.0
Maternal Mortality rate	0.9
Marriage rate	10.3
Divorce rate	2.2

LIFE EXPECTANCY AT BIRTH (1970)

Males	53.5 Years
Females	55.6 Years

TABLE 7

**Proportion of Married Women of Child-Bearing Age
Utilizing Pills by Geographic Area, 1966-1973**

AREAS	1966			1972			1973		
	No. of Women of Child-bearing Age	No. of Cycles	% of Women Attained	No. of Women of Child-bearing Age	No. of Cycles	% of Women Attained	No. of Women of Child-bearing Age	No. of Cycles	% of Women Attained
Urban Governorates	941,889	642,517	5.3	1,081,625	1,871,306	13.3	1,105,269	1,980,943	13.8
Delta Governorates	1,808,223	762,189	3.2	2,076,490	2,186,750	8.1	2,121,881	2,216,449	8.0
Upper Egypt Governorates	1,508,084	315,593	1.6	1,731,821	898,962	4.0	1,769,679	1,006,387	4.4
Frontier Governorates	29,881	15,745	4.1	34,314	30,588	6.9	35,065	35,617	7.8
TOTAL	4,288,577	1,736,044	3.1	4,924,250	4,987,606	7.8	5,031,894	5,239,396	8.0

TABLE 8

**Proportional Distribution of Family Planning
Recruits and Clinics in Urban and Rural Areas**

	1966			1972			1973		
	Urban	Rural	Total	Urban	Rural	Total	Urban	Rural	Total
No. of Clinics	30.1%	69.9%	100%	34.8%	65.2%	100%	34.7%	65.3%	100%
No. of Recruits	70.4	29.6	100	74.9	25.1	100	74.5	25.5	100
No. of Renewals	68.4	31.6	100	76.4	23.6	100	75.0	25.0	100
No. of Loop insertions	93.4	6.6	100	63.6	36.4	100	63.6	36.4	100
No. of Loop utilizers	98.3	1.7	100	95.9	4.1	100	96.0	4.0	100

TABLE 9

Utilizers of Pills and Loops, Renewals and Monthly Averages of Health Clinics

	1966	1972	1973
No. of Clinics	2,135	3,067	3,188
Married, 15-44	4,288,077	4,924,250	5,031,894
Share of each clinic of Married Women	2,008	1,606	1,578
Recruits (cumulative)	1,736,044	4,987,606	5,239,394
Monthly Average	157,822	415,634	436,616
Stable Users	133,532	383,662	403,030
Stable Users as % of Women of Child-bearing Age	3.1	7.8	8.0
No. of Loop Inserts	41,138	66,963	71,752
Monthly Average	3,428	5,580	5,979

TABLE 10

Inhabitants of School Age, 6-17 1970-2015 in Thousands

	Hypothesis I Minimalist			Hypothesis II Maximalist		
	6-11	12-17	Total	6-11	12-17	Total
1970	5,247.4	4,326.5	9,573.9	5,247.4	4,326.5	9,573.9
1985	7,277.1	6,782.6	14,059.7	8,019.5	6,927.7	14,947.2
2000	8,170.1	8,921.1	16,091.2	11,409.0	9,795.8	21,203.8
2015	7,160.6	7,276.1	14.436.7	14,436.7	13,550.7	28,472.4

TABLE 11

New Entries in the Work Force

(15 Years Old +, in '000)

Year	Hypothesis I Minimalist	Hypothesis II Maximalist
1970	708.6	708.6
1985	1,127.3	1,140.2
2000	1,230.3	1,608.6
2015	1,230.6	2,242.1

TABLE 12

Women of Child Bearing Age
15-44; in '000

Year	Hypothesis I Minimalist	Hypothesis II Maximalist
1970	7,132	7,132
1985	10,845	10,864
2000	15,639	16,673
2015	18,624	24,532

TABLE 13

Absolute Numbers and Rates per '000
Inhabitants of Marriage and Divorce

Year	No. of Marriages	Rate per '000 Inhabitants	No. of Divorces	Rate per '000 Inhabitants
1952	232,000	10.8	70,000	3.2
1960	282,000	10.9	65,000	2.5
1966	295,000	9.8	63,000	2.1
1970	326,000	9.7	69,000	2.0
1971	347,000	10.2	71,000	2.1
1972	359,000	10.3	76,000	2.2

In 1971 the marriage rate in Egypt was 10.6 and the divorce rate was 3.7, but this is misleading in that the structure of Egypt's age pyramid is such that about half the male and female population is under sixteen, the legal minimum age for marriage for girls. In 1971 it was estimated that the average age of marriage for women was 19 years, 10 months, and for men, 26 years, 11 months. See Gamal Askar, "Marriage and Divorce in Egypt," supplement to *al-Ahram al-Iqtisadi*, November 1, 1974. The figure for marriage age of women seems too high and must surely reflect substantial false declaration of age.

NOTES

1. John Waterbury, *Egyptian Elite Perceptions of the Population Problem* [JW-6-'73], Fieldstaff Reports, Northeast Africa Series, Vol. XVIII, No. 3, 1973.

2. Mr. Sabry Abdullah was one of the interviewees in the Report on *Egyptian Elite Perceptions of the Population Problem*. He told me in 1973 that he felt that the next decade would be crucial in determining whether Egypt turned the corner economically or lapsed back into preindustrial patterns. Over the next decade, he pointed out, lowered fertility could have at best only a marginal impact upon the development effort.

3. See, for instance, Aziz Bindary, "Toward Population Planning and Family Planning," *al-Ahram*, June 27, 1973.

4. For a description of the Executive Board see my *Manpower and Population Planning in the Arab Republic of Egypt, Part IV: Egypt's Government Program for Family Planning* [JW-5-'72], Fieldstaff Reports, Northeast Africa Series, Vol. XVII, No. 5, 1972.

5. Supreme Council for Population and Family Planning, *The National Population and Family Planning Policy for the Ten Year Plan* (1973-1982), October 1973, p. 3. The economic plan itself was stillborn and replaced by a transitional plan, 1974-1976, to be followed by a five year plan, 1977-1982.

6. Nader Fargany, "The Development of National Population and Family Planning Policy in Egypt," presented at the First Regional Population Conference of the Economic Commission for West Asia, Beirut, Lebanon, February 18-March 1, 1974. For evidence from Egypt that would support this outlook see Atef M. Khalifa, "A Proposed Explanation of the Fertility Gap Differentials by Socio-Economic Status and Modernity: the Case of Egypt," *Population Studies*, Vol. 27, No. 3 (November 1973), pp. 431-442.

7. Interview with Governor Hussein Dabbus 'Fayyum Province' in *Ruz al-Yussef*, n. 2433, January 27, 1975.

8. Interview with Dr. Hilmy Abd al-Rahman in the *Egyptian Gazette*, February 9, 1975. Dr. Abd al-Rahman is the former Executive Director of the United Nations Industrial Development Organization (UNIDO).

9. I have dealt in detail with Egypt's food crisis in *'Aish: Egypt's Growing Food Crisis* [JW-3-'74], Fieldstaff Reports, Northeast Africa Series, Vol XIX, No. 3, 1974.

10. For an earlier detailed attempt to estimate the costs of rapid population growth, see "The Long-term Burden of the Population Explosion, *al-Ahram al-Iqtisadi*, March 15, 1968.

11. In the past I have used Nabil Azzat Kharzati, "Population Trends in the United Arab Republic by Age Groups and Sex to the Year 2000," Memo No. 642, series 26, Institute of National Planning, October 1968; but see also Executive Board for Family Planning, *Report on Family Planning*, June 1972.

12. Figures from the Central Agency for Public Mobilization and Statistics as reported in *al-Ahram*, January 21, 1974.

13. See my *Manpower and Population Planning in the Arab Republic of Egypt, Part I: Population Review 1971* [JW-2-'72], Fieldstaff Reports, Northeast Africa Series, Vol. XVII, No. 2, 1972.

14. Results of the village study have not yet been released, and thus the data can be presented in only cursory fashion. It was found in the course of the study that while government family planning services are offered in the village, 30 per cent of the women did not know of their existence. For further information on abortion, see Dr. Ibrahim Kamal et al., "A Study of Abortion at Cairo University Hospital," in Abdel R. Omran (ed.) *Egypt: Population Problems and Prospects*, University of North Carolina Press, Chapel Hill, 1973, pp. 387-402; and H.K. and M.K. Toppozada, "Experience with Abortion in a Private Practice," *ibid.*, pp. 403-410.

15. It should be noted that over the period 1956-1967, it is estimated that 21.6 per cent of all women married for the first time were divorced, 17.5 per cent of all married women divorced within the first five years of marriage, and 83 per cent of this latter group were childless at the time of divorce. See Badr Hanna, "The Effect of Divorce on the Level of Fertility in Egypt" in Cairo Demographic Center, *Fertility Trends and Differentials in Arab Countries*, Cairo, 1971, pp. 133-40. See also Gamal Askar, "Marriage and Divorce in Egypt," supplement to *al-Ahram al-Iqtisadi*, November 1, 1974.

16. See Waterbury, *Manpower and Population in the Arab Republic of Egypt, Part III: The Egyptian Family Planning Association* [JW-4-'72], Fieldstaff Reports, Northeast Africa Series, Vol. XVII, No. 4, 1972.

The Balance of People, Land, and Water

Egypt enjoys the dubious distinction of demonstrating basic resource ratios in stark simplicity. Until the post-World War II era Egypt was an overwhelmingly agricultural country. The limiting factors of the economy were the waters of the Nile, the land along its banks and in the Delta, and the people who lived upon the land. The Nile Valley was one of the world's first centrally managed hydraulic systems, a characteristic that has persisted throughout most of the Valley's history. The Nile Valley was always a prosperous gem in an otherwise forbidding region, one that was coveted by others in search of a stable resource base, and one that many Egyptians believe is still so coveted. When the first Muslim general, Amr ibn al-As, established his control over Egypt, he was so impressed by what he saw that he ordered, "Use a third of the revenues to increase and maintain canals, dikes and bridges...."[1]

With Egypt's population closing in rapidly in sheer quantity with those of France or Italy, it is difficult to imagine the country as it was a century and a half ago, or even 50 years ago. When Napoleon invaded Egypt, the country contained perhaps 2.5 million inhabitants. The same number could be easily absorbed today in Cairo's northern sector alone. The population has grown 14 times over in the ensuing years. By contrast the amount of cultivated land has not quite doubled, rising from something like 3.5 million *feddans* (one *feddan* equals 1.038 acres) to 5.9 million feddans in 1973. The intensification of agricultural production has made this shift in the land-man ratio somewhat less unfavorable, but we should not allow Egypt's present land hunger to obscure the fact that until 1900 or so the major limiting factor of Egypt's agricultural development was lack of manpower.

Mohammed Ali, the Ottoman Governor of Egypt, spent the first decades of the nineteenth century trying to put Egypt's economy on a modern footing after centuries of neglect by previous Ottoman administrators. While industrialization may have been his ultimate goal, his point of attack was the reorganization of Egyptian agriculture. It was Mohammed Ali who encouraged the cultivation of cotton to supply his own factories and to sell in international markets. Towards this end, enormous efforts were made to repair and extend the canal system. Canals along both the Damietta and Rosetta branches of the Nile mobilized hundreds of thousands of laborers annually. The Mahmudia Canal begun in 1817 initially mobilized a *corvée* of 60,000, rising to 300,000 in 1819, conceivably 10 per cent of the entire population. Estimates of deaths among the laborers range from 12,000 to 100,000 for the ten-month period of labor in 1819.[2] It is small wonder that Mohammed Ali's major concern was to find manpower for his public works projects all the while expanding agricultural production and finding recruits for his peasant army. Despite severe labor shortages Mohammed Ali regulated the flow of both major branches of the Nile and, in 1833, started work on the Nile barrages north of Cairo which would eventually maximize the availability of summer water for the cultivation of cotton. It is really in these early decades of the nineteenth century that one must look for the sources of the ecological degradation of the Nile Valley and the Delta coastlines rather than in the much later but better publicized era of the Aswan High Dam.

Although it is difficult to measure with precision, it was during these years that several hundred thousand feddans in the Delta were converted from flood (basin) irrigation to perennial irrigation. The extent of such intensification can be measured by the surfaces given over each summer to the cultivation of cotton and rice. Reliable figures are not available until the end of the century, but production figures show enormous gains in cotton particularly during the period corresponding to the

American Civil War. From a level of 147,000 *cantars* (1 *cantar* equals 99.05 pounds) in 1830-1834, cotton production jumped to 515,000 cantars in 1855-1859, 944,000 in 1860-1864, reaching 2,700,000 cantars at the time of the British occupation in 1882. At about the same time the cultivated area for all Egypt stood at 4,758 feddans and the cropped area at 5,754. The difference was presumably accounted for by summer cotton cultivation.[3] Indeed Egypt had reached one of the highest levels of cotton feddanage ever attained by 1910 when 1,711,241 feddans were so planted.[4]

Agricultural expansion in the period 1820-1880 was impressive and in many ways has been unequalled since. While the population may have doubled in that period, cultivated land grew by about a third and cropped feddanage by somewhat more. Nonetheless, per capita agricultural production nearly sextupled.

O'Brien sums up the period: "If the term 'revolution' in economic history is defined as a positive and sustained acceleration in the rate of growth, then during this half century Egypt seems to have passed through an agrarian revolution."[5] He also advances figures that demonstrate a slightly less spectacular revolution for the period 1872-1899. He assumes a more rapid rate of population growth and thus finds that per capita agricultural production grew by less than one per cent a year. In addition, while per feddan production rose by nearly 3 per cent a year, this rate is substantially below that of the earlier period.[6]

There is then good evidence that the revolution had begun to slow sometime after the British occupation. Britain's determined policy over the next half century was to shackle Egypt to its agricultural "vocation" while systematically hindering local efforts at industrialization. This may have cost the country its best opportunity to allow the economy to walk on two legs. In the nineteenth century the agricultural sector conceivably could have been sweated for the investments necessary to revive or continue Mohammed Ali's industrialization projects which had ground to a halt through Big Power pressure in 1844. No one was to try again for over a century. By the time Gamal Abdul Nasser attempted to launch another industrialization drive, population growth had determined that there would be little surplus that could be skimmed off the agricultural sector. Egypt nonetheless was still shackled to an agricultural base suffering from

Table 1

A. Indices of Agricultural Production
1821 - 1878

Year	Agric. Output	Population	Rural Population	Cultivated Area	Cropped Area
1821	100	100	100	100	100
1830-35	164	119	118	109	--
1872-78	1,208	209	206	156	178

B. Indices of Agricultural Production

Year	Per Cap. Output	Output Per Cap. Rural Pop.	Output Per Unit Cult. Land	Output Per Unit Cropped Land
1821	100	100	100	100
1830-35	138	139	150	--
1872-78	578	586	774	679

Source: Patrick O'Brien, "The Long-Term Growth of Agricultural Production in Egypt," in P.M. Holt (ed.) *Political and Social Change in Modern Egypt,* Oxford University Press, 1968, p. 180.

Table 2

Growth of Population, Cultivated and Cropped Land,
Egypt, 1821 - 1970*

Year	Population**	Cultivated Area '000 Feddans	Per Capita Cult. Area	Cropped Area '000 Feddans	Per Capita Cropped Area
1821	4,230,000	3,053	.73	3,053	.73
1846	5,290,000	3,764	.71	--	--
1882	7,930,000	4,758	.60	5,754	.72
1897	9,717,000	4,943	.53	6,725	.71
1907	11,190,000	5,374	.48	7,595	.67
1917	12,718,000	5,309	.41	7,729	.60
1927	14,178,000	5,544	.39	8,522	.61
1937	15,921,000	5,312	.33	8,302	.53
1947	18,967,000	5,761	.31	9,133	.48
1960	26,085,000	5,900	.23	10,200	.39
1966	30,075,000	6,000	.20	10,400	.34
1970	33,200,000	5,900	.18	10,900	.33
1975	37,000,000	5,700	.15	10,700	.29

*The cropped area of Egypt measures that surface that is cultivated more than once each year. As a rule of thumb, for every feddan (1.038 acres) of cultivated land under perennial irrigation there are 1.6-1.7 feddans of cropped land. The sources for this table are varied and not always in total accord. See Gabriel Baer, "The Beginnings of Urbanization," in his *Studies in the Social History of Modern Egypt*, Chicago University Press, 1969, pp. 133-148. The population *estimates* 1821-1882 are drawn from his table, p. 136. They do not correspond to a more prevalent estimate for 1821 of between 2,158,580 (For. Ex. Helen Rivlin, *The Agricultural Policy of Mohammed Ali in Egypt*, Harvard University Press, 1961, p. 256) and 2,536,400 which Baer himself advances in order to refute it. He sets forth his reasons, which I will not reproduce here, for assuming that the 1821 population was grossly underestimated. The cultivated and cropped surface figures were taken from Patrick O'Brien, *The Revolution in Egypt's Economic System*, Oxford University Press 1966, p. 5 up to 1947. O'Brien, like Rivlin, uses a population figure of 2,514,000 for 1821. However, in another article, he rejects Rivlin's estimates of cultivated acreage for the same period. She uses tax records to suggest that the land under cultivation at the time of the French Occupation ca. 1800 may have been as much as 4,038,177 feddans and that by the end of the reign of Mohammed Ali it had decreased to 3,890,423 feddans in 1844 (pp. 265-70). O'Brien argues that Rivlin's sources are inadequate to sustain her argument, "The Long-Term Growth of Agricultural Production in Egypt: 1821-1962," in P.M. Holt (ed.) *Political and Social Change in Modern Egypt*, Oxford University Press, pp. 162-95, especially p. 173. More recent figures on land and population have been taken from Central Agency for Public Mobilization and Statistics (CAPMAS), *Population and Development*, Cairo, 1973, p. 172, and CAPMAS, *Statistical Yearbook* (1952-1971), July 1972.

**It is worth noting that as regards both land and population there is general consensus on the figures presented for the period 1897-1966. Thereafter population estimates frequently follow growth rates established in the period 1960-1966 rather than vital statistics registries, and the rate of loss of agricultural land due to expansion of built-up areas as well as the rate of effective land reclamation are subject to varying interpretations.

diminishing returns on labor and land, and incapable of generating the savings and buying power for a nascent industrial sector. In launching her five year plan in 1960, Egypt found herself between two stools. The Aswan High Dam was seen as the solution to the dilemma by which Egyptian agriculture could be revitalized through land reclamation and Egyptian industry promoted through the generation of cheap hydroelectric power. Neither dream has been fulfilled. While we are not here concerned with the progress in Egyptian industry, we may obtain some grasp of the agricultural side of the equation by close examination of changes in land tenure, the productivity of the land, and the productivity of labor.

Land Tenure

Until 1855 only about one-seventh of Egypt's cultivated land was under private ownership. The bulk was owned by the government (*kharijia*) and each village, according to the directives of a government official, periodically redistributed the land around the village. This system of periodic redistribution caused little friction among the *fellahin* inasmuch as "the number of cultivators [was] almost always too small for the quantity of cultivable land...."[7] In addition, each village was collectively responsible for meeting tax levies and supplying the annual quota of men for the work corvées. With manpower so scarce, collective responsibility for taxes, debts, and work amounted to a system of indentured labor tying the peasant to the land.

Between 1855-1858, new laws were enacted that introduced the principles of private property and Muslim inheritance to the Egyptian countryside. Any peasant who could demonstrate that he had continuously tilled a plot of land for five years and had paid taxes on it could gain title to it and cede it to his heirs. Periodic redistribution came to an end, but village responsibility for the corvée was maintained until 1882. By 1896 the great bulk of Egyptian agricultural land was privately owned.

From then on we find two trends occurring simultaneously. The conjunction of the expansion of cotton cultivation with the extension of perennial irrigation as a result of the construction of the first Aswan Dam in 1902 led to a concentration of landholdings among wealthy commercial farmers. Many of the latter were foreigners, and by 1920 about 10 per cent of all Egypt's cultivated land was foreign-owned. Land values, rents, and taxes rose precipitously. At the same time population growth combined with the effects of Muslim inheritance, prescribing equal shares of property for all male heirs and half-shares for female heirs, led to severe fragmentation of holdings among peasant cultivators. Throughout the twentieth century and even with the land reform measures enacted after 1952, there has been a constant process of peasant proprietors selling off their dwarf-holdings to wealthy owners and then regaining access to the land through tenancy or as hired labor. The only other alternative has been migration to the cities.

By the time of the revolutionary take over in 1952 a small minority of 2,136 owners were in possession of 1.2 million feddans, 20 per cent of all cultivated land at an average of 560 feddans per person. Conversely, 2.6 million owners, 94 per cent of all freeholders, possessed only 2.1 million feddans, 35 per cent of the total for an average of .8 feddans per owner. Three land reform measures in 1952, 1961, and 1969 dealt first with the small band of big landowners and then lowered the maximum holding per family to 100 feddans and individual ownership to 50 feddans. Given the quality of Egypt's land, 50 feddans is a substantial holding, and the general effect of land reform has been the destruction of a landed aristocracy, the swelling of the ranks of those with less than five feddans, and the maintenance of the class of middle-range landowners of 10-50 feddans. By 1971, 850,000 feddans had been redistributed to 410,000 families owning less than two feddans. The successive reforms have done little to discourage absentee ownership. It is estimated that despite fairly strict rent controls, 50 per cent of all cultivated land is still rented. Owners of 10-50 feddans or of 1-5 tend to rent their land because on the one hand they have too much and on the other too little to warrant their direct cultivation.[8]

Recent statistics on land tenure are deficient in at least three respects. First, I have been unable to find any hard information regarding distribution according to size of holding since the reform of 1969. Second, the lowest level of holding generally reported is "five feddans or less." However, a substantial part of this group may be in the "two feddans or less" category, which is probably the minimal holding sufficient for family subsistence. For instance, in 1961, the time of the last agricultural census, it was calculated that there were

Table 3

Indices of Agricultural Growth, 1895-1962

Years	Output	Population	Rural Population	Agric. Labor Force	Cropped Area	Cult. Area	Chem. Fertilizer Inputs
1895-99	100	100	100	100	100	100	
1900-04	110	108	108	108	109	108	
1905-09	116	116	117	118	113	109	
1910-14	121	124	125	126	114	107	
1915-19	103	132	131	136	115	107	100
1920-24	113	140	138	153	120	107	144
1925-29	133	147	143	169	127	113	387
1930-34	135	156	150	186	126	111	474
1935-39	153	166	156	207	123	107	910
1940-44	131	177	162	205	133	108	397
1945-49	140	197	173	204	136	116	600
1950-54	150	222	188	206	140	115	1,246
1955-59	184	250	208	209	151	118	1,528
1960-62	204	271	213	212	152	119	

Source: Patrick O'Brien, "The Long-Term Growth of Agricultural Production in Egypt: 1821-1962," in P.M. Holt (ed.), *Political and Social Change in Modern Egypt*, Oxford University Press, 1968, p. 188. Total output is the weighted index of eight major crops. The data in this table are also presented in Figure 1. Note the dramatic drops in production during the two World Wars.

Table 4

Active Male Population in Rural
Areas and Per Capita Land Resources
1937 - 1970

Year	Active Male Population Rural Areas	Cult. Area '000 feddans	Per Capita	Crop Area '000 Feddans	Per Capita
1937	2,976,000	5,312	1.8	8,302	2.8
1947	3,139,000	5,761	1.8	9,133	2.9
1960	3,560,000	5,900	1.6	10,200	2.8
1966	3,815,000	6,000	1.57	10,400	2.7
1970	4,048,300 (est.)	5,900	1.4	10,700	2.6

Source: This table has been pieced together from the following sources: Donald Mead, *Growth and Structural Change in the Egyptian Economy*, Homewood, Ill., 1967, p. 33; CAPMAS "Population and Development," *op. cit.*, p. 200; ILO, *Rural Employment Problems in the United Arab Republic*, Geneva 1969, p. 29. It would have been preferable to use other statistics such as total active population or total rural workforce, but these statistics are not available to me in sources at my disposal over a sufficiently long time period to measure any trends.

Table 5

Land Tenure in Egypt, 1894 and 1964

Size of Holding	1894				1964			
	Owners in '000	%	Area '000 fds.	%	Owners in '000	%	Area '000 fds.	%
- 5 feddans	512	77.5	930	19.8	2,965	94.4	3,353	54.8
5-10	75	11.4	550	11.7	78	2.5	614	10.0
10-20	40	6.1	555	11.8	61	1.9	527	8.6
20-50	22	3.3	667	14.2	29	.9	815	13.3
50+	11	1.7	1,998	42.5	10	.3	813	13.3
TOTAL	660	100.0	4,700	100.0	3,143	100.0	6,122	100.0

Source: ILO, *Rural Employment Problems in the United Arab Republic*, Geneva, 1969, p. 35.

911,703 peasants (59 per cent of all owners) owning less than two feddans for a total of 741,635 feddans (roughly 8 per cent of the total).[9] Finally, we can only guess at the number of landless peasants. Assuming a rural population of 20.3 millions in 1973 (58 per cent of the total population), 3.3 million landowners supporting 12.7 million dependents, we may estimate the number of rural landless families at 760,000, or 3.8 million people.

Land Productivity and Crops

Until the 1960s, the growth of agricultural production was brought about almost exclusively by the more intense use of existing lands. Between 1882 and 1960 the cultivated area was expanded by only 20 per cent while the cropped area more than doubled. By the 1950s, with six million feddans under cultivation, we find that 3.5 million feddans in the Delta and 1.8 million feddans in the valley south of Cairo had been brought under perennial irrigation. The availability of summer water allowed the emergence, at least on medium- and large-scale holdings, of a complicated seasonal and bi- or tri-annual crop rotation system. This was dictated by the varying lengths of time a given crop stays in the field (sugar cane twelve months, cotton nine, rice six, wheat 7.5), its growing season (wheat and clover [berseem], onions, beans in the winter, rice and cotton in the summer, maize in the fall) and the need for fallow periods or the planting of soil-enrichers such as *berseem* and alfalfa (see

Table 6 for current seasonal land usage). In short, the combination of regular water supplies and a rationalized rotation system led to significant gains in per feddan production. This was true especially of cotton aided by constant experimentation in the development of varieties of improved seed.

In the 1870s and 1880s the average cotton yield per feddan was 3-3.5 cantars. The completion of the Delta barrages caused a jump to 5.2 cantars per feddan by 1894. Yields then began to decline, and the reasons why presage to some extent the problems that have become more acute in the 1960s and 1970s. First, the water table in the Delta gradually rose, particularly after the completion of the first Aswan Dam in 1902. Overwatering of summer crops, inadequate drainage, and seepage from irrigation canals may have been the principal causes. The cumulative effect became alarmingly clear with the high flood of 1908. It was also found that longer summer fallows were needed to allow the soil to heat sufficiently to kill protozoa that inhibited the development of nitrifying bacteria. A third factor was the spread of the boll and cotton-leaf worm, present since the 1860s. Pest destruction in 1905 may have accounted for 600-800,000 cantars of cotton. Finally, and in sharp contrast with the situation today, standards of cultivation deteriorated as acreage expanded, and as late as 1911 experienced observers attributed this deterioration to labor and animal shortages.[10]

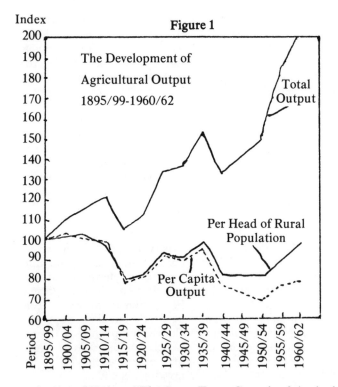

Figure 1

Index

The Development of
Agricultural Output
1895/99-1960/62

Total Output

Per Head of Rural Population

Per Capita Output

Source: From Patrick O'Brien, "The Long-Term Growth of Agricultural Production in Egypt," in P.M. Holt (ed.), *Political and Social Change in Modern Egypt*, Oxford University Press, 1968, p. 189.

Table 6

Aggregate Cropped Surface ('000 Feddans)

Agric. Season	1952	1966	1967	1968	1969	1970	1971 (est.)
Winter	4,364	4,739	4,776	4,929	4,849	4,835	4,871
Summer	3,026	4,794	4,857	4,945	5,050	5,053	5,012
Autumn	1,824	760	622	646	601	618	610
"Garden"	94	195	207	225	232	244	249
TOTAL	9,308	10,488	10,462	10,745	10,732	10,750	10,742

Source: CAPMAS, *Statistical Yearbook* (1952-1971), Cairo, July 1972, p. 27. The impressive shift to summer crops, relying heavily on the waters provided by the High Dam, has involved a spectacular increase in rice cultivation and both a shift from fall to summer, and an expansion of maize cultivation. Modern waterworks have made the old autumn season (nili) following the flood, a pale reflection of its former importance.

Generally speaking, from 1900 on to the present time agricultural production has shown a steady increase in terms of quantity, value, and production per feddan. As Patrick O'Brien has pointed out (see Table 3 and Figure 1) despite the severe production losses during the two World Wars, Egypt still managed to achieve a compound growth rate of 1.2 per cent per annum for the entire period 1895-1962. Output per unit of land grew more slowly, and with reference to the base period of 1895-1899 the index stood at only 107 in 1950-1954. It rose rapidly, however, to 134 by 1962.

Looking at individual crops, there has been a steady rise in practically all of them in absolute quantities and in per feddan output (with the possible exception of sugar cane). Despite a reduction in the cultivated area of cotton from 1,986,252 feddans in 1961 to 1,525,000 feddans in 1971, total production rose from roughly 9.5 million cantars in 1960 to 10.2 million cantars in 1971. Yields per feddan increased from 4.8 to 6.2 cantars per feddan in the period 1966-1970.[11] Rice cultivation has been the real star of agricultural development in modern Egypt. The area given over to rice rose from 362,000 feddans in 1952 to 1,149,000 feddans in 1971. Take-off in conversion to rice occurred in 1966 with the provision of more summer water as a result of the completion of the first stage of the High Dam. Total production rose from 1,776,000 *daribas* (one *dariba* equals 995 kilos) in 1966 to 2,681,000 daribas in 1971. Over those same five years rice production per feddan has remained fairly stable, varying between 2.1 and 2.3 daribas per feddan. In sum, the rice revolution has been one of the most indisputable benefits rendered Egypt by the High Dam. It would be tedious to proceed through all Egypt's field crops in this manner, and to round out this picture we may look at wheat and sugar cane production. Wheat production rose from 7,206,000 *ardebs* in 1952 (one *ardeb* equals 5.4 bushels) to 11,529,000 in 1971. The feddanage under wheat varied little over that period, hovering between 1,240,000 and 1,400,000 feddans. Per feddan production, however, rose from 5.2 to 8.5 ardebs; mainly due to the introduction of improved seeds. Sugar cane feddanage was expanded from 92,000 in 1952 to 193,000 in 1971. Production rose from 3,258,000 metric tons in 1952 to 6,930,000 metric tons in 1970. However, the highest production level of 1,069 cantars per feddan was achieved in 1967 and has subsequently

dropped off to 829 in 1970. The long period the crop stays in the ground, high production costs and fertilizer shortages, drainage problems in Upper Egypt where the crop is grown, have provoked a flight from sugar cane, and, apparently, a drop in the cane's sugar content. Egypt currently is meeting its local needs of 550,000 tons of refined sugar annually and is exporting about 40,000 tons each year. According to one source, however, acreage and production are falling so rapidly that the slight surplus may soon be a deficit. It suggests that the cultivation of sugar beets on reclaimed land may be the only solution.[12]

Given Egypt's century-old reliance upon cotton exports as a foreign currency earner, the country's basic strategy in meeting domestic food needs has long been determined. It may have been hoped at one time that wheat and maize production might be sufficient to meet local demand, but the country's out-sized population has probably precluded that possibility forever. The export of commercial crops, cotton, rice, citrus fruits, onions, and other vegetables is designed to offset the growing dependence on imports of food grains and vegetable oils. In 1969 agricultural exports accounted for 67 per cent of all Egypt's exports in value (cotton 44.4 per cent, rice 16.5 per cent, fruits and vegetables 5.5 per cent) while manufactured goods, exclusive of yarns and fabrics, accounted for only 5.5 per cent.[13] At the same time, Egypt annually consumes 3.5 million metric tons of wheat while only producing 1.5 million tons. Grain imports between 1969 and 1971 required annual hard currency outlays of LE60 million or the equivalent in value of one-sixth of all imports and one-fifth of all exports. In 1973 Egypt was faced with importing two million tons of wheat and 300,000 tons of corn. For the wheat alone the cost in that year would be, including shipping, about $135 a ton, nearly double 1972 prices. The rise in world prices may tax the Egyptians an additional $120,000,000 in hard currency. Because the country suffers from chronic hard currency shortages, it must maintain current levels of wheat production and acreage, although, in the best of all possible worlds that acreage might be better used for winter vegetable production for European markets. To alleviate the immediate problem of wheat imports, the surface given over to Mexican wheat is to be raised in 1973-74 from about 60,000 to 800,000 feddans.[14]

Figure 2

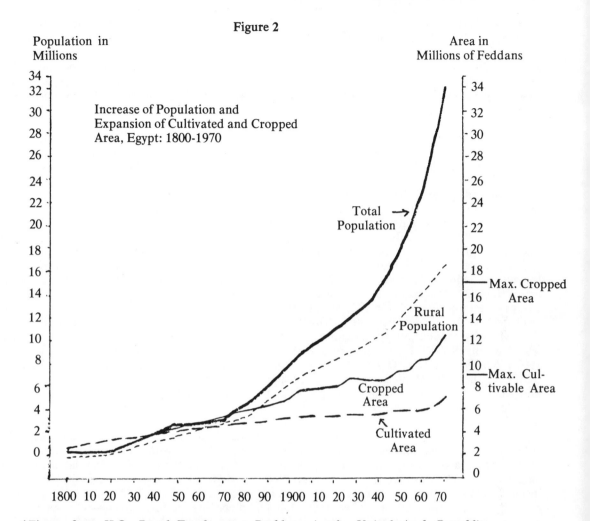

Population in
Millions

Area in
Millions of Feddans

Increase of Population and
Expansion of Cultivated and Cropped
Area, Egypt: 1800-1970

Total
Population →

Max. Cropped
Area

Rural
Population

Cropped
Area

Max. Cul-
tivable Area

Cultivated
Area

1800 10 20 30 40 50 60 70 80 90 1900 10 20 30 40 50 60 70

*Figure from ILO, *Rural Employment Problems in the United Arab Republic,* Geneva, 1969, p. 24. While the lines representing population are accurate, those representing cultivated and cropped areas for 1970 are overestimates, representing what Egyptian planners would have liked to have achieved. Actual expansion fell short of these levels as is set forth in the section on vertical and horizontal expansion.

Labor Productivity

It is difficult to find any qualified economic analysts who fail to assert that the marginal productivity of labor in Egyptian agriculture is falling rapidly, and some, like Issawi, feel that it has probably reached zero. However, there are exceptions to this chorus, Bent Hansen being the leading figure and, to a lesser extent, Donald Mead. Somewhere between Issawi and Hansen, but firmly on the side of conventional wisdom are Patrick O'Brien, Yussef Shibl, and the first Egyptian Five-Year

Plan, to mention only a few. Issawi defines his position thus:

A survey of the last fifty years shows that the Ricardian analysis of rents and wages applies remarkably well to Egypt. An increase in population and wealth was accompanied by a considerable remuneration of the scarce factor, land, and by a fall in that of the abundant factor, labour. Indeed, wages seem to have reached the minimum level described by early nineteenth-century economists, below which

they can hardly descend. (i.e., 10 piastres—
22¢ a day for 150 days a year).[15]

Yussef Shibl, referring to the same period, points
out that between 1913 and 1954, the cultivated area
grew by 8 per cent, the cropped area by 25 per cent,
the average yield per feddan by 10 per cent, and the
population by 70 per cent. Consequently, it is
logical to assume that marginal productivity was
approaching zero on the eve of the Free Officers'
take over in 1952.[16]

It seems indisputable that until the last 15 years
or so agricultural labor productivity was indeed
falling, as a glance at Patrick O'Brien's Figure 1
and Table 3 will confirm. By 1905 the race between
output and the growth of the agricultural labor
force was on, and by 1950 the output index stood at
150 and the labor force index at 206. At the same
time, after 1930 the agricultural labor force grew at
a very modest rate. From 207 in 1930-1934 to 212 in
1960-1962. O'Brien calculates using 1895-1899 as
the base period that output per agricultural worker
fell to 69 in 1950-1954 and then rose to 95 in
1960-1962. On that basis O'Brien cautiously concludes "...the tasks of producing a given output
were shared among a greater number of people and
some labour could have been removed without any
loss of production."[17]

Mead is even more cautious, stating that available trend data on rural wages, nonremunerated
employment, and seasonal fluctuations are too
incomplete, not to mention contradictory, to warrant firm conclusions about labor redundancy
although he feels that such redundancy existed in
1955 and only a massive shift of about 5 per cent a
year to other employment sectors could overcome
the accumulation of surplus labor in the countryside.[18]

Hansen, by contrast, is categoric in his rejection
of the conventional argument and refers to the
analysis of "disguised unemployment" as a "red
herring."[19] He dismisses the assumption of the
authors of Egypt's First Five-Year Plan that 23 per
cent of the rural labor force was redundant. His
reasons for doing so are based largely on the
findings of the ILO rural labor survey carried out in
the early 1960s which measured the available
man-hours in the countryside and the number of
man-hours required for production. The study
concludes, "As for men, the degree of overall

underemployment for the whole sample is very
small, amounting to 7 per cent for the whole year.
Underemployment during the off-season from
October till February seems to be almost balanced
by overemployment during the peak season from
March till September."[20] Hansen's principal argument is that agricultural work has hitherto been
poorly defined. It turns out that rural males spent
only 53 per cent of their labor time in actual field
work and that on the average male laborers devoted
14 per cent of their time to work outside their own
land. Plots of anything over two feddans require
seasonal hired labor and the Egyptian countryside
experiences seasonal labor shortages. The fact that
wage levels for the sample averaged about 18
piastres a day, well above the legal minimum,
would indicate that the marginal productivity of
labor was above zero. Moreover, for the males in
the survey, employment ranged from 2062 to 2420
hours a year, the equivalent of full employment.[21]

Can we draw any conclusions from this debate?
Foolishly, perhaps, I am prepared to argue that
Hansen's analysis is valid as far as it goes, but it
does not go very far and hence is fundamentally
misleading. Hansen is concerned with employed
time, not with production per hour or per worker.
He leaves the question of per capita production
pretty much open. Nor does he address himself to a
standard question regarding marginality: to wit,
can labor be withdrawn without lowering production? If so, there is redundant labor within a given
system of farming techniques and practices.
Between 1947 and 1960—that is, in the period just
preceding the ILO survey—over one million Egyptians left the land. They had been doing so in
increasing numbers since 1940 and up to the
present time. Yet as we have seen agricultural production has steadily risen in the last 30 years. Perhaps it could be countered that techniques have
been improved through mechanization, fertilizers,
and improved seeds so that the argument is not
valid. But precisely the same argument applies to
Hansen when he warns that Egypt should plan for a
tight rural labor supply as if the cultivation techniques of 1964 were to remain unchanged and that
no technological displacement of labor would
occur.

In addition Hansen deals only with the level of
employment of those actually employed while
glossing over the possibility of redundancy rede-
fined as "non-active." The ILO itself notes a 7 per

cent unemployment rate among active males which is not to be sniffed at, while Hansen, by contrast, emphasizes that in the ILO sample 45 per cent of all women over 15 years old and 72 per cent of men over 15 were active. This is an impressive activity rate but it still leaves us with 55 and 28 per cent of this eligible population inactive.

The major problem with Hansen's presentation is that it is static, a snapshot of rural employment taken at a moment in recent Egyptian agricultural development that has been uncharacteristically bullish. The period of the First Five-Year Plan saw an annual growth rate in the value of agricultural productivity of 3.6 per cent. After 1965 a downturn occurred, corresponding to a generalized economic slump, producing a rate of 1.5 per cent that has been the norm ever since.

I have tried my own crude hand at measuring agricultural labor productivity for the period 1965/66-1969/70. In that period agricultural employment grew from 3,877,000 to 4,048,000 or just under one per cent a year. The value of agricultural production in current prices rose from LE884 million to 1,075 million or over 4 per cent per annum. Allowing for a general rate of inflation of 2.5 per cent a year, the real growth rate in labor productivity would be about 1.5 per cent per annum. Thus it would seem that per capita labor productivity in the rural areas may be growing at about half a per cent a year. In the absence of recent combined quantity indices it is impossible to know if per capita quantitative production is increasing at the same, or any other rate. The picture then is not as happy as Hansen would have us believe nor, at least perhaps for a decade, as despairing as depicted by Issawi. There is still considerable scope for intensification through improved drainage and seeds, and horizontal expansion through land reclamation. But in the happiest circumstances there are outer limits to Egyptian agricultural expansion, at least at a cost that Egypt is likely to be able to bear in the foreseeable future. One may fantasize about desalinating the waters of the Mediterranean, but that is technologically and financially beyond Egypt's means. Intermediate technologies of water management, agricultural intensification, land reclamation, and industrialization have appeared to Egyptian leaders as the only way out for at least 15 years. The Aswan High Dam was to be the key to the raising of agricultural productivity and the redistribution of the active population from agricultural to industrial pursuits.

Water Management, Reclamation, Intensification

Until 1929 the major concern of Egyptian and British authorities in Egypt was to better the management and regulation of the annual flow of the Nile rather than to increase the supply of water available annually. As early as 1886, the natural flow of the Nile was being used to its fullest in the summer with hardly any water escaping into the Mediterranean. Principally to guarantee adequate summer water, a number of important waterworks were undertaken the length of the Nile, supplementing and completing the installations begun b, Mohammed Ali. Two more Delta barrages were constructed at Zifta (1903) and Idfina (1951) while in Upper Egypt three barrages were built at Assiut (1902), Esna (1908), and Nag Hammadi (1908). By far the most important effort in this respect was the completion of the Aswan Dam in 1902. This dam had an annual storage capacity of 1 billion cubic meters (M^3). It was raised in 1912 and again in 1933, increasing its capacity to 5 billion M^3. Along with the barrage at Assiut, the Aswan Dam was the key to the conversion of most of Egypt's cultivated acreage to perennial irrigation, spawning in the process a network of 23,000 kilometers of irrigation canals.

It was only after the First World War that serious attention was given to the possibility that over the long haul Egypt might not have sufficient water to maintain, not to mention expand, its existing agricultural base. There had of course always been years in the past when the discharge of the Nile was particularly low. At such times those areas depending on summer water, in particular areas given over to the major money crop of cotton, were especially vulnerable. But the real problem emerging after the Great War was that the Sudan was giving every indication of being a major competitor for the use of the Nile's annual discharge. The development of the Gezira Scheme for irrigated cotton cultivation beginning in 1911 and the construction of the Sennar Dam (storage capacity 930 million M^3) on the Blue Nile in 1925 were clear signals that the Nile would have to be carefully apportioned in the future. The upshot of this realization was the first Nile Water Agreement of 1929 apportioning the natural flow of the river on the basis of existing storage facilities and the assumption of a large annual run-off into the Mediterranean. Thus, assuming an average annual discharge at Aswan of 84 billion M^3, it was agreed that Egypt would be

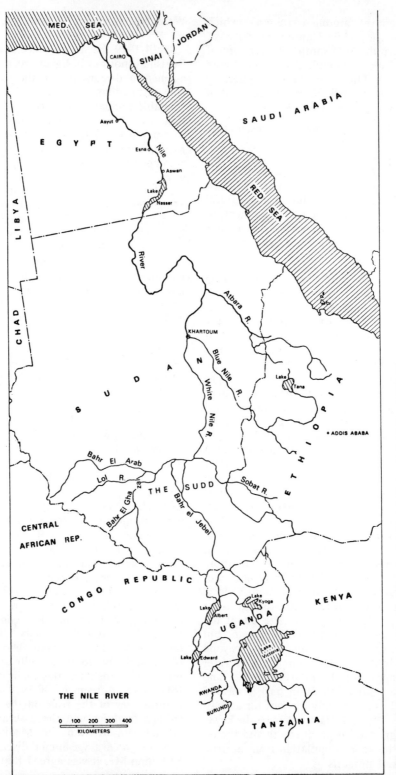

THE NILE RIVER

0   100 200 300 400
KILOMETERS

From Marion Clawson, et al., *The Agricultural Potential of the Middle East*, Elsevier, New York, 1971.

guaranteed a minimum of 48 billion M^3 and the Sudan four billion M^3. The entire flow of the Nile from January through July was assigned to Egypt.

Egyptian and Sudanese authorities had only a decade before the Second World War to contemplate the prospect that growing population and the concomitant need to expand cultivated areas would place real constraints upon the availability of water. The unwanted hiatus of the War years was followed by serious consideration of the Century Storage scheme proposed by Dr. H.E. Hurst, an outstanding irrigation expert in the Egyptian Ministry of Irrigation. In essence, this project would have used long-term storage in Lakes Albert and Victoria at the headwaters of the Nile combined with the cutting of a channel through the vast Sudd swamps in the southern Sudan that would diminish the annual loss of about 12 billion M^3 through evaporation. Another step would have been in developing Lake Tana in Ethiopia for long-term storage of waters of the Blue Nile.

At the heart of the proposal is the same argument that inspired the High Dam: long-term storage. Annual storage facilities such as the Aswan or Sennar Dams could not meet the Valley's future needs. This was so for the simple reason that the annual discharge of the Nile varies so widely (and almost entirely as a function of variations in the discharge of the Blue Nile) that in any given year such annual storage dams could neither store enough water to prevent devastating floods by the high Nile nor severe summer droughts following a low Nile. In recent times, it has been noted, the flood of 1887 literally swamped Egypt with 150 billion M^3 while the flood of 1912 brought the country only 42 billion M^3. With a mean discharge of 84 billion M^3, it is instructive to note that the annual standard deviation is 20 billion M^3. The Century Storage scheme was designed to iron out these "wrinkles" which had become intolerable.

Although given serious consideration that plan was never given any practical effect. Instead, a coup d'état occurred in Egypt in July 1952 and a team of young officers came to power. They were naturally skeptical about a scheme that would involve cooperation among at least four countries, two of which, the Sudan and Uganda, were under colonial control, a third, Egypt, only partially liberated, and the fourth, Ethiopia, an unknown quantity. There was, of course, a fifth partner to any multinational scheme, Great Britain, the very power whose influence the Free Officers were set on undermining. More pleasing to their conceptions of Egyptian sovereignty was the proposal of an Egypto-Greek engineer Adrien Daninos who for years had been promoting the idea of a single great dam in the Aswan region, totally within Egyptian territory. No sooner had the Free Officers taken control than Daninos, with a crusader's zeal, made contact with the two officers most intimately involved in technological projects, army engineers, Colonels Samir Hilmy and Mahmud Younes. By October 8, 1952, the Revolutionary Command Council had approved the project in principle and a feasibility study was undertaken by the West German firm of Hochtief and Dortmund Union.[22]

The basic rationale for the project was to furnish Egypt with long-term storage and an even supply of water year in and year out, regardless of the level of the annual discharge of the Nile. The Century Storage scheme could have provided this also, but the new regime preferred the single dam approach on three counts: (1) it would be Egypt's sole responsibility and not dependent upon the cooperation of several foreign, possibly hostile states; (2) it could be completed more quickly than the multidam scheme bringing thereby a quicker return on the initial investment; (3) the High Dam would be cheaper, estimates of construction costs including power plant ran at about LE110 million (ca. $250 million).

In the final analysis, the Egyptian officers were right only on the first count. For reasons not entirely under their control the whole project took

Table 7

Annual Discharge of the Nile

No. of Years	Period	Mean billion M^3	Std. Deviation billion M^3
30	1870-1899	110	17.1
60	1900-1959	84.5	13.5
90	1870-1950	92.6	19.8

Source: From Harold Hurst, Robert Black, and Yusuf Samaika, *Nile Basin*, Vol. X, Cairo, Ministry of Public Works, 1965, p. 81, reproduced in Yussef Shibl, *The Aswan High Dam*, Arab Institute for Research and Publishing, Beirut, 1971, p. 22.

THE HIGH DAM IN FIGURES

MEASUREMENTS OF THE DAM:

Length at crest	3,600 m.
Length of part in river	520 m.
Length of right wing	2,325 m.
Length of left wing	755 m.
Maximum height above bed level	111 m.
Width at crest	40 m.
Width at base	980 m.
Volume of materials of construction	42.7 million m^3
River bed level	85 m.
Crest level	196 m.

HYDROLOGY AND RESERVOIR:

Maximum recorded flow of the Nile at Aswan	13,500 m^3/sec.
Minimum recorded flow of the Nile at Aswan	275 m.
Maximum water level of reservoir	182 m.
Total capacity	162 billion m^3
Dead storage capacity	30,000 million m^3
Operational storage capacity	90,000 million m^3
Flood operation storage capacity	37,000 million m^3
Length of the reservoir	500 kilometers
Average width	10 kilometers
Surface area	5,000 sq. kilometers
Possible constant annual draft of water from reservoir	84,000 million m^3
Average annual evaporation and seepage losses	10,000 million m^3
Present annual amounts of water used for irrigation in both U.A.R. and the Sudan	52,000 million m^3
Net annual benefit	22,000 million m^3

DIVERSION CHANNEL:

Length of upstream canal	1,150m.
Length of spillway structure and power house	315 m.
Length of downstream canal	485 m.
Total length of diversion canal	1,950 m.
Total rock excavation	9,000,000 m
Minimum bed width	40 m.
Maximum possible flow	11,000 m^3/sec.
Number of control tunnels	6
Diameter of each tunnel	15 m.
Total length of tunnels	2,030 m.
Corresponding total excavation	590,000 m
Weight of gates and erected equipment	20,000 tons

TURBINES:

Type	Francis
Number of Turbines	12
Capacity of each turbine at design head	180,000 kw.
Discharge at design head (57.5 m)	346 m^3/sec.
Diameter of turbine runner	6.3 m.
Rated speed	100 r.p.m.
Head	77 to 35 m.
Weight of turbine including runner	765 tons
Weight of runner	150 tons

GENERATORS:

Capacity	175,000 kW
Voltage	15.75 kv
Rated speed	100 r.p.m.
Total weight of generator including rotor	1,600 tons
Weight of rotor	800 tons
Total installed capacity	2,100,000 kW
Maximum available annual energy	10,000,000 kWh
Total weight of hydropower equipment	30,000 tons

TRANSMISSION NETWORKS:

Voltage of main transmission lines to Cairo	500 kv
Number of main transmission lines	2
Length of main transmission lines	2 x 900 kilometers
Number of 500 kv substations	3
Voltage of branch transmission lines	220/132 kv
Length of branch transmission lines	1,000 kilometers
Number of 220 kv and 132 kv substations	12

twice as long as had been hoped, and as a direct consequence total costs were drastically revised as the years trickled by, and the projected benefits of early returns on the investment lost to the economy. This is not the place to go into the international imbroglio affecting the funding of the Dam. Suffice it to note that the IBRD, England, and the United States withdrew their offer to fund the first stage of the project in 1956, although the Bank as well as an array of international experts had pronounced favorably on the feasibility of the Dam and upon its likely positive influence upon the Egyptian economy. Still the project remained in limbo for over two years. The grandiose package that the Free Officers had vividly depicted included the reclamation of nearly two million feddans of new land, the development of a new fertile belt around the lake behind the Dam, and the launching of Egypt into the industrial age on the strength of the electrical power to be generated at the Dam. Indeed, the electrification of the old Aswan Dam after 1957 and the construction of the Kima Fertilizer plant to use its energy was the first step on this path. But lack of funding led to the erosion of the original image. During 1958 other projects were given more emphasis: drainage water could be recuperated in the Delta to reclaim desert land; union with Syria would provide space for Egyptian peasants; the New Valley in the Western Desert could become a new agricultural Eden drawing on its vast stores of subterranean water; new oil discoveries opened up the possibility of generating cheap thermal power. Then, suddenly, in October 1958 the Soviet Union announced its willingness to finance the construction of the first phase of the Dam. The U.S.S.R. eventually participated financially in all phases of

House and private garden typical of those provided technicians and workers at the 10,000 feddan mechanized farm.

Sorting potatoes at reclamation area, Northwest Tahrir—even here child labor is in use.

"Before"—Preparing land for irrigation and drainage: Northwest Tahrir.

"After"—Vineyards in an older sector of Northwest Tahrir.

the Dam's construction. The Russians did not tamper substantially with the original plans calling for a rock-fill, clay core dam with a grout curtain sunk deep into the bed of the Nile.

In the second phase of preparing for the Dam, cost estimates were revised upwards to LE404 millions including construction of the Dam, the power plant and grid, and land reclamation. We might note now that final costs (and they are final only in a relative sense) were closer to LE600 million. In addition a new agreement for the division of the waters of the Nile had to be reached with the Sudan. On November 8, 1959 the second Nile Waters agreement was signed. It is significant to note that the whole question of water availability had been tied to the question of population growth from 1929 onwards. The Egyptians justified their claim to the lion's share on the basis of their large and growing population while the Sudan countered with their projected and much more rapid rate of population growth. The heart of the agreement that emerged was that the annual average discharge of 84 billion M^3 would be divided as follows:[23]

Evaporation and Seepage	10 billion M^3
Egypt's Old Share (1929)	48 billion M^3
Sudan's Old Share (1929)	4 billion M^3
Sudan's Additional Share 1959	14.5 billion M^3
Egypt's Additional Share 1959	7.5 billion M^3
Total	84 billion M^3

The characteristics of the Dam itself go a good way toward explaining what it may do for the Egyptian economy. The Dam has caused the formation of a lake (Lake Nasser) some 500 kilometers long and with a surface area of 5000 kilometers^2. If the lake were to rise to its maximum level of 182M—a phenomenon the planners would like to avoid because of the enormous evaporation losses at this level—its capacity would be 157 billion M^3. The reservoir provides 30 billion M^3 for dead storage, that is the deposit of silt, and at current rates of deposit it would take 500 years to fill that volume. In addition, the lake provides 90 billion M^3 of live storage, the heart of the long-term storage system. The remaining capacity up to 157 billion M^3 can be used to absorb the excess waters of high floods.

With these characteristics in mind we can now consider the benefits the Dam was to render Egypt.

1. One million feddans of reclaimed land. The calculation here is of considerable importance. It is estimated that on the average each feddan of cultivated land requires 7,400 M^3 per annum. With an additional 7.5 billion M^3 provided by the 1959 agreement, the amount of new water would cover the needs of one million feddans. The new land could accommodate two million settlers.

2. The conversion of 700,000 feddans of basin-irrigated land in Upper Egypt to perennial irrigation.

3. The provision of water adequate to bring one million feddans under rice cultivation (one of the few underestimates, other than cost, associated with the project). Through its over-year storage capacity, the Dam minimizes wastage of water, even that allotted to Egypt by the 1929 agreement. The Dam regulates the flow and supply so that more water is available on a regular basis for summer cultivation, hence permitting the conversion of other crops and fallows to rice cultivation.

4. The generation of ten billion kWh annually through the Dam's power plant.

5. Improvement of drainage, particularly in the Delta, through lowering the water table.

6. Improvement of navigation through the regularization of the river's flow.

7. Vastly improved flood control.

8. The eventual provision of 50,000 tons of fish annually from Lake Nasser.

Most if not all these objectives have been achieved or are likely to be in the near future. Where plans went seriously awry was on cost and time estimates. The project itself, as well as derivative programs for electrification and land reclamation, lagged somewhat behind schedule for numerous reasons, not least among which was the Six Day War of 1967. The internal rate of return (IRR) on the project was initially predicted to be on the order of 40-50 per cent per annum, that is the Dam would pay for itself within three years of completion. That has proved illusory because derivative projects have not been completed, but even at its real IRR of perhaps 8 or 9 per cent per annum, the High Dam would seem to have justified itself. With the benefit of hindsight, Egyptian experts are likely today to place less stress on land reclamation and the resettlement of Egyptians or upon overall agricultural growth. On the other hand, they will cite the income generated by increased rice production. In 1963, the last year before the diversion of the Nile, the rice harvest was valued at LE6.7 million. By 1969 it had risen to LE55 million. Over the period 1964 to 1971, the total value of rice production was LE258,961,000, an impressive figure.

Another benefit, indeed the Dam's original *raison d'être*, has been given particular emphasis in the last year. The flood of 1972-73 proved to be one of the lowest in this century, perhaps only 47 billion M^3, that is slightly above the record low flood of 1912-13. But because the Dam had stored sufficient water, the summer cotton and rice crops did not suffer. Had there been no dam both crops would have been lost and agricultural income reduced by at least 40 per cent. Such an occurrence would have plunged Egypt even deeper into economic crisis, depriving the state of hard currency it desperately needs to cover food and capital goods imports, as well as depriving domestic markets of rural buying power. But lo! the Dam was there and Egypt could struggle on.

Still, as Yussef Shibl has pointed out, the Dam can be judged a success only if the basic assumptions concerning evaporation and seepage prove correct, and there more time is needed.[24] In addition there have been other side effects that have drawn a good deal of attention from foreign and Egyptian observers and that we shall treat briefly here.

Seepage and Evaporation

Combined seepage and evaporation losses at the lake site were not to exceed, according to the 1959 agreement, ten billion M^3 a year. If initial estimates of seepage and evaporation proved conservative, Egypt would find that much of the 7.5 billion M^3 of additional Nile waters won through construction of the Dam would be lost to the country; worse yet, some analysts suggested that evaporation and seepage would be so high in the arid Aswan area that Egypt might wind up with a *net water loss* as a result of building the Dam. Such was the conclusion of one Egyptian irrigation engineer (whose specialty was not evaporation or seepage) Abdelaziz Ahmad, who thought that seepage losses alone might reach nine billion M^3 a year.[25] While his dire predictions have so far not been confirmed, it is true that major testing of seepage and evaporation rates at the lake site did not get under way until after 1960.

Definitive answers to these highly complex questions are not yet in nor may they ever be. The rates depend on constantly changing variables such as wind, temperature, rock porosity and saturation at different parts of the lake and different lake levels, and subterranean water pressure. Still it would seem that to date seepage and evaporation rates have been within the limits originally laid down in 1959. Egypt's two leading experts in the field, engineers Taher Abu Wafa and Aziz Labib, assert that, given the porosity of the sandstone bordering 300 kilometers of the lake shore, seepage would range from none at all if the level of the lake were only 120 meters, to 838 million M^3 at 160 meters (in 1971 the lake level stood at 164 meters), to 1.1 billion M^3 at 180 meters. Over a long period of time "vertical" seepage leading to rock saturation, may absorb 48 billion M^3. "Horizontal" seepage, dependent on the changing level of the Dam, is less than one billion M^3 a year. The same authors advance evidence that evaporation losses have likewise been well within the outer limit of nine billion M^3 per annum. In 1971, the Minister of Irrigation stated that total losses due to evaporation, absorption, and seepage amounted to 11.4 billion M^3.

Silt Loss

There has been considerable outcry about the rich, chocolate waters of the Nile in flood becoming as translucent as a mountain freshet. Claire Sterling, the High Dam's self-appointed Cassandra, balefully reported that from her balcony at the Semiramis Hotel overlooking the Nile, she could see the river's bottom.[27] There is no doubt that most of the Nile's silt discharge is being precipitated well to the south of the Dam, and very little is reaching Egypt's fields. The fact that is persistently overlooked is that relatively little of this silt ever reached the fields even before the Dam was built. Prior to 1964, 88 per cent of the Nile's annual load of 90 million tons of silt was deposited in the Mediterranean. Of the remaining 12 per cent, two-thirds was deposited in the basin-irrigated areas of upper Egypt (8.7 million tons), 2.82 million upon reclaimed areas, and 1.49 million in the Nile Delta. The precipitation of most of the silt behind the Dam has not directly affected agricultural production, although adverse effects may have been masked by the conversion from basin to perennial irrigation, larger inputs of fertilizers, and improved drainage.[28] Three negative consequences of the reduced load of silt have been a growing market for

Table 8

High Dam Reservoir Losses
(billion m³)

Period	Max. Reservoir Level Meters	1. Inflow	2. Outflow + water accumulation	Actual Losses 1-2	Theoretically Calculated Losses		
					4. Absorption	5. Evaporation	6. Total 4+5
1964/65	127.60	119.430	119.082	.348	.091	.942	1.033
1965/66	132.70	79.550	78.497	1.053	.295	1.552	1.847
1966/67	142.45	69,120	67.760	1.360	1.190	2.679	3.869
1967/68	151.25	93.370	87.290	5.080	2.427	4.485	6.912
1968/69	156.55	71.102	62.740	8.362	4.034	5,773	9.807
TOTAL		431.572	415.369	16.203	8.037	15.431	23.468

Source: Tahar Abu-Wafa and Aziz Hanna Labib, "Investigations and Observations of Seepage Losses from the Aswan High Dam Reservoir," Dixième Congrès des Grands Barrages, Montreal, 1970, p. 1066.

top soil, several manifestations of scouring of the river bed, and an increased rate of coastal erosion. The first is potentially of least consequence. The sprawling, quasi-artisanal, Egyptian red brick industry with its kilns scattered the length of the Nile Valley, mixes silt or top soil in the preparation of the bricks. The red bricks are Egypt's traditional building material, and brick manufacturers have been offering peasants attractive sums for the sale of their top soil. The problem had become sufficiently serious by the winter of 1973 that a decree was prepared to do away with the red brick industry entirely. Implementation of the decree is another matter.

Scouring

With less silt content, the Nile now flows more swiftly, causing in the process some erosion or "scouring" of the river's bed. This is particularly serious on the downstream sides of the various barrages as well as around the foundations of bridges and embankments. It was contemplated before construction of the High Dam that three to six additional barrages might be built between Aswan and Cairo in order to slow the river's velocity and in effect transform that sector of the Nile into a series of steps and cascades which could promote lateral irrigation and the generation of additional hydroelectric power. Negotiations with the U.S.S.R. regarding a feasibility study have been under way for some time, but the project may be in some disfavor

as one of its likely consequences would be to raise the water table in Upper Egypt, thereby increasing soil salinity. As a result, another approach is being considered. It is based on the construction of weirs to the immediate north of each of the existing barrages where scouring is most serious. Another barrage might be built between Aswan and Esna with a seven meter drop, to provide additional water and power for the Kom Ombo region. Whether or not any of these projects are implemented, it is believed that because the river has established a steady velocity (ca. 250 million M³ a day) since 1964, the river bed has begun to stabilize.

Coastal Erosion

This is potentially the most serious problem that Egypt faces as a result of the loss of silt in the Nile's flow. It should be pointed out that the Dam did not create this problem but rather aggravated a process that has been going on for at least a century as the management of the river became increasingly sophisticated. There is some dispute as to the rate of coastal erosion due to lack of silt. Recent estimates are that the problem is severe only at the mouths of the two branches of the Nile at Rosetta and Damietta, particularly the latter. In these spots, because the discharge of the Nile is so weak, wave action has caused considerable damage. However, it is believed that a series of jetties at both mouths of the river can check this wave action.[29]

There is still the undeniable possibility that coastal erosion may lead to breaches in the narrow land spits separating the Mediterranean from the five brackish lakes at the northern tip of the Delta. Were the salinity of these lakes to increase, seepage from them into the underground water table could have incalculable harmful effects upon agriculture in the northern delta. Some preliminary experiments would indicate, however, that salt water seepage occurs at about 20 meters below the surface of the land while the water table is at one to three meters. Thus salt water seepage does not appear to be a major threat.

Land Reclamation

With the revival of the High Dam project in 1958, agricultural development was founded on the credo of horizontal expansion at the expense of vertical expansion through more intense cultivation of existing acreage. In Egypt's First Five-Year Plan, 61 per cent of all planned agricultural investment went into horizontal expansion. A project launched in 1956 that would have extended tile or covered drains to most of the Delta over a 20-year period was temporarily shelved. Over 14 per cent of Egypt's cultivated acreage is taken up by open field drains, and this land could be recuperated through the introduction of covered drains. As the euphoria associated with massive land reclamation waned, Egypt, in association with the IBRD, began in 1970 to introduce tile drainage to one million feddans in the Nile Delta and will move on to Upper Egypt in Phase II of this project.

During the 1960s, however, Egypt rushed headlong into reclamation, and one of the ironies of the effort was that more land was reclaimed before the construction of the High Dam than after it. By 1973 reclamation had been begun, and occasionally completed, on over 902,000 feddans, but the bulk of that land, 624,000 feddans, was first improved in the period 1960-1965.

In terms of initial expectations, land reclamation has not been a success. A soil survey that was not completed until 1964 showed that most of the areas subject to reclamation, except for drained lake bottoms, were distinctly inferior to the marine alluvial soils of the Delta (classes I and II). The survey revealed that of about two million potentially recuperable feddans, the distribution by class was as follows:

Grade I	8,328 feddans
II	217,000 feddans
III	604,542 feddans
IV	1,391,682 feddans

In the new lands the soil is mostly sandy or calcareous and in either case unsuited to the traditional crops of the valley. When such crops have been planted, their yields have seldom exceeded a third of the yields in the old lands. As a result, new crops such as grapes, citrus, sugar beets and soya beans have been introduced. In addition, the drainage systems of the new lands have not always been well-planned, and salinity has become a serious problem.

The costs of reclamation were clearly greatly underestimated. It was initially thought that on the average each reclamation site would cost LE165 per feddan, including irrigation, roads, housing, and social infrastructure. That figure was attained probably only at the thoroughly atypical Abis project started on a drained portion of Lake Maryout. Otherwise, current estimates range from LE300 to LE600 per feddan. Total investments over the period 1960-1971 skyrocketed to LE429 million. Some projects proved hopeless such as Wadi Natrun which, after an investment of LE8 million, is still costing the state LE500,000 a year and producing only LE200,000.[30]

The long time between the initiation of the reclamation process and bringing the land to its marginal level of productivity has proved a particular headache. Perhaps only half the land subject to reclamation is actually being cultivated. Even then, we do not know its level of productivity.[31] Official estimates are that calcareous soil demands four years of preparation and sandy soil seven. In 1971, the Minister of State for Reclamation, Osman Badran, stated that of the 912,000 feddans undergoing reclamation, the net cultivable area was 770,000 feddans, of which 518,000 feddans were actually being cultivated and 189,000 undergoing preparation.[32] The long period before the land reaches a marginal level of productivity has prevented any widescale distribution or renting of the new lands to peasants, and, indeed, there are many experts who would prefer to see the reclaimed areas run as state farms. Although it may be a temporary phenomenon, they have in any case been state farms up to the present time.

Table 9

Land Reclamations Sites
Nature of Holdings

Project	Feddans	Rented	Distributed
San El-Hagger	68,000	24,500	---
Hamoul	69,700	35,000	---
Mansour	83,500	20,100	---
N.W. Delta	71,800	25,900	7,300
Mariut	52,100	2,900	---
N. Tahrir	40,000	1,100	---
W. Nobania	13,200	---	---
Tahadi, S.W. Tahrir	37,200	844	---
S. Tahrir	57,100	1,100	---
Mid Egypt	58,200	4,800	---
Upper Egypt	65,100	7,800	(19,500)
			(New Nubia)

Source: Egyptian Organization for Cultivation and Land Development, *Egypt: The New Land*, Cairo, 1973, the figures do not include desert reclamation sites in the New Valley, Mersa Matrah, Sinai, nor, apparently, Abis.

In the wake of the June War, particularly after 1968, land reclamation nearly ground to a halt. In 1972, the new Minister of Agriculture, Mustapha Gabali, proclaimed a moratorium on the opening of new reclamation sites and the cessation of further efforts at Wadi Natrun, the New Valley, and South Tahrir.[33] A year later Gabali delivered startling testimony before the Egyptian parliament (Maglis as-Shaab):

> The agricultural area of Egypt is limited, and it is decreasing and not increasing despite the fact that we added 912,000 feddans of new land. The cropped area, from 1963 to 1973, despite this addition, lost 200,000 feddans (net). During the same period the population grew by about eight millions.[34]

The stagnation of the reclamation effort on the one hand and the constant nibbling away of existing cultivated acreage by such things as urban expansion, roads, factories, and military installations absorbing over 600,000 feddans or 10 per cent of the cultivated area, have led to the net loss pointed out by Gabali.

It is likely that during Egypt's current Ten-Year Plan period, 1972-1982, a more even balance between horizontal and vertical expansion will be pursued.[35] On the other hand, reclamation projects will be gradually expanded; beginning with the North Tahrir and West Nobaria projects and then the Port Said Valley and reclamation of lakeland. Only 74,000 feddans will be treated before 1972, but then 600,000 will be added in the next ten years. Areas reclaimed by underground water and that have experienced severe salinization problems—the New Valley, Wadi Natrun, South Tahrir—are not likely to be salvaged. The net cultivated area of all reclamation projects in 1982 should be 1.3 million feddans. Thirty years after its espousal by the Revolutionary Command Council, the High Dam project will have achieved one of its principal goals. The effect upon population growth will have been negligible, however, as the reclamation sites have not and probably will not absorb much labor or settlers. Consequently, they will be oriented more towards the production of crops that can act as hard currency earners on foreign markets (fruits and vegetables) and sugar, poultry, beef, and dairy products for local consumption. The state farm principle will probably be maintained in most instances.

At the same time greater investments in drainage, fertilizers, improved seeds, herbicides, and pesticides should lead to substantial production gains in land already under cultivation. Farming techniques could stand substantial change as well. Water, for example, is supplied by the state to all cultivators at no cost. This has persistently led to the overuse of irrigation water and in some instances the lowering of productivity or crop quality. Some observers believe that in this fashion as much as nine billion M^3 of water is wasted annually—somewhat more than the additional water provided by the Aswan Dam.[36]

Conclusion

In the face of its mounting population Egypt has undertaken ambitious programs of land and water management to make maximum use of the country's agricultural resources. Many specific policy decisions have been criticized and others suggested as more viable or economic. What is most striking about the developments of recent years is that Egypt is clearly on the path to implementing *all* the policy options that have been bruited about over the last 25 years. Due concern for vertical expansion, although delayed, has finally manifested itself. Moreover, the old Century Storage scheme has re-emerged as the Sudan and Egypt face growing demands for additional water. In 1955, Colonel Samir Hilmy wrote, "No doubt the Upper Nile projects combined with the High Aswan project will secure the maximum utilization of the water of the Nile."[37] Both countries could gain as much as another seven billion M^3 apiece by channeling through the Sudd swamp. As negotiations quietly proceed along these lines, one hears of plans such as digging a canal from Lake Nasser to the New Valley so that one million feddans may some day be cultivated there.

Another project that has resurfaced is the filling of the Qattara depression with sea water from the Mediterranean. Interest in this project, and the awarding of a feasibility study to West Germany, has revived because Egypt is anticipating electrical power shortages in the next decade despite the ten billion kWh to be generated at the High Dam. The plan is to generate electricity by the gravity flow of sea water into the depression. The rate of flow will be regulated so as to be exactly matched by the rate of evaporation from the lake that will form. While the generation of power is the basic objective, it is expected that the formation of this coastal lake may cause a major climate change and stimulate rainfall along the western coastline.

Still further in the future is the desalinization of sea water using nuclear or solar energy. The fact is that the triangular relationship between land, man, and water in Egypt has become so strained that any and all solutions must be considered regardless of their cost. Ultimately, the final solution may be the relegation of the agricultural sector to a role of minimal significance in Egypt's economy, and that in turn will depend on the success of the industrialization effort. But the conundrum remains: the agricultural sector must carry the economy by providing surplus value, domestic buying power, and foreign-export earnings at the same time that its masters plan its demise. It is a moot question whether or not Egypt will be able to make the transition without trials even more severe than those of the last 20 years.

NOTES

1. Helen Rivlin, *The Agricultural Policy of Muhammed Ali in Egypt* (Harvard University Press, 1961), Chapter 12.

2. *Ibid.*

3. Figures from Patrick O'Brien, *The Revolution in Egypt's Economic System* (Oxford University Press, 1966), p. 5. O'Brien is reluctant to make any estimates of cropped acreage until the period 1870-1874.

4. E.R.J. Owen, *Cotton and the Egyptian Economy 1820-1914* (Oxford University Press, 1969), p. 186.

5. O'Brien, "The Long-term Growth of Agricultural Production in Egypt," in P.M. Holt (ed.) *Political and Social Change in Modern Egypt* (Oxford University Press, 1968), p. 18-181.

6. O'Brien assumes the standard population estimate of ca. 2.5 million inhabitants in 1821, a figure which Gabriel Baer feels is much too low, offering instead a figure of 4.2 million (see Table 2). If Baer is correct then the rises in per capita production for 1821-1878 would be less spectacular than O'Brien suggests and the drop-off after 1872 less severe.

7. M.A. Lancet, "Mémoire sur le système d'Imposition territoriale et sur l'administration des provinces de l'Egypte," *Description de l'Egypte état moderne*, I, Paris, 1809, pp. 246-47, cited by Gabriel Baer, *Studies in the Social History of Modern Egypt* (Chicago University Press, 1969), p. 18.

8. See Saad Hagras, *The Implementation and Appraisal of Results of Land Reform Programme after Twenty Years* (Agrarian Reform Organization, Cairo 1972?). His figures are somewhat contradicted by the Central Agency for Public Mobilization and Statistics (CAPMAS), *Statistical Yearbook* (Cairo) 1972. CAPMAS stresses that through 1971, 822,923 feddans have been distributed (p. 59). On direct cultivation see *Al-Talia*, special study on land use, Vol. 8, No. 10, October 1972, pp. 22-26.

9. Price Planning Agency, *The Distribution of Personal Income*, January 1973. See also *Al-Talia*, pp. 70-71. It is not possible to reconcile these figures with that of 2,058,000 holdings of one feddan or less in 1957 offered by Charles Issawi, *Egypt in Revolution, An Economic Analysis* (Oxford University Press, 1963), pp. 155-161.

10. See E.R.J. Owen, *Cotton and the Egyptian Economy 1820-1914* (Oxford University Press, 1969), p. 194, and the article he cites; J.J. Craig, "Notes on Cotton Statistics in Egypt," *l'Egypte Contemporaine*, No. 6, March 1911, pp. 180-1.

11. Figures from CAPMAS, *The Evolution of Agricultural Production 1920-1969*, Ref. #50-003, June 1972, p. 93 and CAPMAS, *Statistical Yearbook*, 1972, pp. 37 and 41.

12. An article in *Akhbar al-Yom* of April 14, 1973 claims that the area under cane has fallen from 197,000 to 150,000 feddans and that cultivators are not meeting state contracts for supplying sugar refineries. Ahmad Hassan Ibrahim in *Al-Talia*, special study on land use, Vol. 8, No. 10, October 1972, p. 35, purports to show production declines for the period 1960-1970 but does not specify the unit of analysis or his sources.

13. K. Nasheshibi, "Foreign Trade and Economic Development in the UAR: A Case Study," in Lee Preston, *Trade Patterns in the Middle East*, American Enterprise, October 1970, p. 79.

14. See the testimony of former Minister of Agriculture, Mustapha Gabali, before the parliament, reported in *Al-Ahram*, February 7, 1973, and Abdelaziz Sabrut, "The Trade Balance and the Growing Burden of Wheat," *al-Ahram al-Iqtisadi*, No. 424, April 15, 1973, pp. 14-15. On Mexican wheat, *Al-Ahram*, August 16, 1973. For a solid presentation of these problems see Galal Amin, *Food Supply and Economic Development with Special Reference to Egypt*, (Frank Cass, London: 1966), throughout.

15. Charles Issawi, *Egypt in Revolution, an Economic Analysis* (Oxford University Press, 1963), p. 155; see also on marginal productivity, pp. 298-299.

16. See Yussef Shibl, *The Aswan High Dam*, (Arab Institute for Research and Publishing, Beirut, 1971), pp. 24-25, and Robert Mabro, "Industrial Growth; Agricultural Under-Employment and the Lewis Model: the Egyptian Case 1937-65," *Journal of Development Studies*, Vol. 3, No. 4, 1967, pp. 322-351.

17. Patrick O'Brien, "The Long-Term Growth of Agricultural Production in Egypt" in P.M. Holt (ed.), *Political and Social Change in Modern Egypt* (Oxford University Press, 1968), p. 191.

18. Donald Mead, *Growth and Structural Change in the Egyptian Economy* (Homewood, Illinois, 1967), pp.. 82-98.

19. Bent Hansen, "Economic Development of Egypt" in Charles Cooper and Sidney Alexander (eds.), *Economic Development and Population Growth in the Middle East* (American Elsevier Publishing Company, New York City, 1972), p. 27.

20. ILO, *Rural Employment Problems in the United Arab Republic* (Geneva, 1969), p. 61.

21. Bent Hansen, "Employment and Wages in Rural Egypt," *The American Economic Review*, Vol. LIX, No. 3, June 1969, pp. 298-313.

22. Two readable accounts of this period are to be found in Tom Little, *High Dam at Aswan*, (Methuen, London, 1965), especially pp. 36-45; and Keith Wheelock, *Nasser's New Egypt* (London, 1960), pp. 173-205.

23. See I.H. Abdalla, "The 1959 Nile Waters Agreement in Sudanese-Egyptian Relations," *Middle Eastern Studies*, October 1971, Vol. 7, No. 3, pp. 329-41; and Sudan, Ministry of Irrigation, *The Nile Waters Question: the Case for the Sudan* (Khartoum, 1955).

24. The most serious cost-benefit analysis of the High Dam has been carried out by Yussef Shibl, *The Aswan High Dam*, Arab Institute for Research and Publishing, Beirut 1971. See also Mohammed Abdel Rakeeb, *The High Dam Project; Its Benefits Far Outweigh Adverse Doubts of Side Effects*, General Authority for High Dam, 1971, throughout. On the ninth anniversary of the diversion of the Nile, May 16, 1973, it was declared that income generated by the Dam had covered the cost of the construction of the Dam and the power station, i.e., LE320 million—see *Al-Ahram*, May 17, 1973.

25. See Abdelaziz Ahmad, "Recent Developments in Nile Water Control," *Proceedings*, Institute of Civil Engineers (London, October 1960), pp. 137-80. The counter argument is presented in Tahar Abu Wafa and Aziz Hanna Labib, "Investigations and Observations of Seepage Losses from the Aswan High Dam Reservoir," *10th Great Dams Congress*, (Montreal, 1970), (Q. 38, R. 55), pp. 1047-69).

26. Mohammed Abdel Rakeeb, *The High Dam Project: Its Benefits Far Outweigh Adverse Doubts of Side Effects*, General Authority for High Dam, 1971.

27. Claire Sterling, "The Aswan High Dam: A Mixed Blessing," *International Herald Tribune*, February 18, 1971.

28. Mohammed Abdel Rakeeb, *The High Dam Project: Its Benefits Far Outweigh Adverse Doubts of Side Effects*,

General Authority for High Dam, 1971, and Yussef Shibl, *The Aswan High Dam* (Arab Institute for Research and Publishing, Beirut, 1971), p. 65.

29. M. Kassas, "Impact of River Control Schemes on the Shoreline of the Nile Delta" in H.T. Farvar and J. Milton (eds.), *The Careless Technology* (Natural History Press, 1972), pp. 179-188; and Ibrahim Kinawy and Osman al-Ghamry, "Some Effects of the High Dam on Environment," a paper prepared for the 13th Congress of Great Dams, throughout.

30. See interview of the Minister of Land Reclamation, Dr. Osman Badran, *Al-Ahram*, June 10, 1972; also Wyn Owen, "Land and Water Use in the Egyptian High Dam Era," *Land Economics*, Vol. XL, No. 3, August 1964, pp. 277-294; John Waterbury, *The Cairo Workshop on Land Reclamation and Resettlement in the Arab World* [JW-1-'72], Fieldstaff Reports, Northeast Africa Series, Vol. XVII, No. 1, 1971; Ministry of Agrarian Reform and Land Reclamation, *Agrarian Reform and Land Reclamation in Ten Years* (Cairo, 1962?), especially p. 73; and *Al-Talia*, special study on land use, Vol. 8, No. 10, October 1972, pp. 37-53.

31. Central Bank of Egypt, *Report*, Vol. 9, Nos. 1 and 2, 1969, pp. 26-27 and *Report of the Board of Directors*, January 11, 1973, p. 20.

32. *Al-Ahram*, June 20, 1972.

33. *Al-Ahram*, March 6, 1972.

34. *Al-Ahram*, February 7, 1973.

35. See Central Bank, *Report of the Board of Directors*, January 11, 1973, and *Akhir Sa'a*, No. 2020, July 11, 1973.

36. See Yussef Shibl, *The Aswan High Dam* (Arab Institute for Research and Publishing, Beirut, 1971), p. 47.

37. See Sudan, Ministry of Irrigation, *The Nile Waters Question: The Case for the Sudan* (Khartoum, 1955), p. 36.

BIBLIOGRAPHY ON
The Balance of People, Land, and Water

Abdalla, I.H., "The 1959 Nile Waters Agreement in Sudanese-Egyptian Relations," *Middle Eastern Studies*, October 1971, Vol. 7, No. 3, pp. 329-41.

Abdel Rakeeb, Mohammed, *The High Dam Project: Its Benefits Far Outweigh Adverse Doubts of Side Effects*, General Authority for High Dam, 1971.

Abu Wafa, Tahar and Labib, Aziz Hanna, "Investigations and Observations of Seepage Losses from the Aswan High Dam Reservoir," *10th Great Dams Congress*, Montreal, 1970 (Q. 38, R. 55), pp. 1047-69.

Ahmad, Abdelaziz, "Recent Developments in Nile Water Control," *Proceedings*: Institute of Civil Engineers (London), October 1960, pp. 137-80.

Amin, Galal. *Food Supply and Economic Development with Special Reference to Egypt*, Frank Cass, London, 1966.

Baer, Gabriel. *Studies in the Social History of Modern Egypt*, Chicago University Press, 1969.

Central Agency for Public Mobilization and Statistics (CAPMAS), *Statistical Yearbook*, Cairo, 1972.

———. *The Evolution of Agricultural Production 1920-1969*, Ref. #50-003, June 1972.

———. *Population and Development*, Cairo, 1973.

Central Bank of Egypt. *Report*, Vol. 9, Nos. 1 and 2, 1969.

———. *Report of the Board of Directors*, January 11, 1973.

Clawson, Marion, et al. *The Agricultural Potential of the Middle East*, American Elsevie Publishing Company, New York City, 1971.

Feiner, Leon. "The Aswan Dam Development Project," *Middle East Journal*, Vol 6, No. 4, 1952, pp. 464-467.

Hagras, Saad. *The Implementation and Appraisal of Results of Land Reform Programme after 20 Years*, Agrarian Reform Organization, Cairo, 1972?.

Hansen, Bent, "Employment and Wages in Rural Egypt," *The American Economic Review*, Vol. LIX, No. 3, June 1969, pp. 298-313.

———. "Economic Development of Egypt," in Charles Cooper and Sidney Alexander (eds.), *Economic Development and Population Growth in the Middle East*, American Elsevier Publishing Company, New York 1972.

ILO. *Rural Employment Problems in the United Arab Republic*, Geneva, 1969, p. 61.

Issawi, Charles. *Egypt in Revolution, an Economic Analysis*, Oxford University Press, 1963.

Kassas, M. "Impact of River Control Schemes on the Shoreline of the Nile Delta," in H.T. Farvar and J. Milton (eds.), *The Careless Technology*, Natural History Press, 1972, pp. 179-88.

Kinawy, Ibrahim and al-Ghamry, Osman. "Some Effects of the High Dam on Environment," a paper prepared for the 13th Congress of Great Dams.

Little, Tom. *High Dam at Aswan*, Methuen, London, 1965.

Mabro, Robert. "Industrial Growth; Agricultural Under-Employment and the Lewis Model: the Egyptian Case 1937-65," *Journal of Development Studies*, Vol. 3, No. 4, 1967, pp. 322-51.

Mead, Donald. *Growth and Structural Change in the Egyptian Economy*, Homewood, Illinois, 1967.

Ministry of Agrarian Reform and Land Reclamation, *Agrarian Reform and Land Reclamation in Ten Years*, Cairo, 1962?.

Nasheshibi, K. "Foreign Trade and Economic Development in the UAR: A Case Study," in Lee Preston, *Trade Patterns in the Middle East*, American Enterprise, October 1970.

O'Brien, Patrick. *The Revolution in Egypt's Economic System*, Oxford University Press, 1966.

————. "The Long-Term Growth of Agricultural Production in Egypt," in P.M. Holt (ed.), *Political and Social Change in Modern Egypt*, Oxford University Press, 1968.

Owen, E.R.J. *Cotton and the Egyptian Economy 1820-1914*, Oxford University Press, 1969.

Owen, Wyn. "Land and Water Use in the Egyptian High Dam Era," *Land Economics*, Vol. XL, No. 3, August 1964, pp. 277-294.

Price Planning Agency. *The Distribution of Personal Income*, January 1973.

Rivlin, Helen. *The Agricultural Policy of Muhammed Ali in Egypt*, Harvard University Press, 1961.

Sabrut, Abdelaziz, "The Trade Balance and the Growing Burden of Wheat," *al-Ahram al-Iqtisadi*, No. 424, April 15, 1973, pp. 14-15.
Shibl, Yussef. *The Aswan High Dam*, Arab Institute for Research and Publishing, Beirut, 1971.

Sterling, Claire. "The Aswan High Dam: A Mixed Blessing," *International Herald Tribune*, February 18, 1971.

Sudan, Ministry of Irrigation. *The Nile Waters Question: the Case for the Sudan*, Khartoum, 1955.

Al-Talia. Special study on land use, Vol. 8, No. 10, October 1972.

Waterbury, John, *The Cairo Workshop on Land Reclamation and Resettlement in the Arab World* [JW-1-'72], Fieldstaff Reports, Northeast Africa Series, Vol. XVII, No. 1, 1971.

Wheelock, Keith. *Nasser's New Egypt*, London, 1960.

'Aish: The Growing Food Crisis

Egyptian society represents one of the oldest peasant-based communities in the world. It is a society that has traditionally relied upon grain as its major food source and, on that basis, can be compared to other peasant economies founded on river systems, such as portions of China and India, as well as with the paddy rice areas of Southeast Asia. By the same token Egypt is somewhat unique within the context of the Middle East. *Grosso modo*, the rural economies of this area have been founded on animal husbandry as the principal source of food and revenues. Agriculture was a supplementary activity, practiced in the poorly watered rain-fed areas, and employing extremely primitive agricultural techniques. Until the last few decades countries like Morocco, Algeria, Tunisia, parts of the Sudan, Iraq, Syria, Somalia, Iran, and Afghanistan were characterized by dualistic rural economies consisting of small islands of modern, commercial agriculture, surrounded by vast steppe lands and low rainfall zones where sheep, goats, and cattle were supreme. For these societies, bread was simply bread, a necessary but not particularly cherished food item.

For the Egyptians, bread is *'aish*, life, the gift of Egypt's enduring fertility symbol, the Nile River. In the Nile Valley, grain is king, and, whether watered by flood or perennial irrigation, there has not been sufficient land within the narrow confines of the valley to permit the development of extensive grazing areas. The only part of Egypt that could conceivably maintain rainfed pasturage is along the northwest Mediterranean coast. Otherwise Egypt is dry and unsuited for grazing. Nonetheless, as we shall see in greater detail below, the country does maintain a large animal population. But it is fed largely on agricultural remains and fodder crops and does not graze. Indeed the major justification for the existence of this population is that it consists to a significant degree of draft animals that contribute directly to the production of grain.

Egyptian agricultural technology is traditional, even ancient, without being primitive. It is man- and animal-intensive, based for the most part on small holdings that require constant and meticulous care in the processes of planting, fertilization, weeding, de-pesting (frequently carried out by hand) and harvesting. With the generalization of perennial irrigation there is never really a dead season for the peasant. Complex two- and three-year rotation schedules keep the peasant in the fields all year round. Because of the intense use of the land, and the massive inputs of human and animal power, Egypt has achieved fairly high levels of per acre production in several crops, particularly cotton, rice, and corn.

Despite the industry of the Egyptian peasantry, agricultural productivity and levels of available per capita foodstuffs have tended to stagnate over the last 15 to 20 years. As with all data dealing with Egypt's economy and demographic structure, it is very difficult to reconstruct long-term trends in agricultural productivity. Some trend data come in the form of indexes whose components and internal weighting are not made explicit. Second, the plethora of weights and measures used in reporting data range from conventional kilograms and metric tons, to pounds and bushels, to *ardebs*, *daribas*, quintals, and *qantars*. To confuse matters further, some measures are of volume and some of weight. Translating one set of figures into the weights and measures of another becomes a hazardous task. Finally, total production figures of a given crop are sometimes reported without any mention of the total acreage given over to them. Thus, the crucial questions of yields per acre is sometimes obscured. The upshot is that any judgments based on these data must be of the "more-or-less" variety. Per capita grain consumption or per feddan (the standard land measure in Egypt, equalling 1.038 acres) yields in any one year should not be taken too literally.

Egypt's principal grain crops are maize and millet, wheat, barley, and rice. Maize, or corn, and wheat, but especially corn, has long been the staple food item in the Egyptian diet and the major ingredient in the making of bread. If we take first the example of wheat, we find some increase in production per feddan since World War I, but the gains have been very uneven. During the 1920s the average per feddan yield of wheat was 735 kilos (assuming 150 kilos to one *ardeb* of wheat) and in the 1960s that average had risen to 1,080 (i.e., 1.08 metric tons). Despite these gains, the per capita share of locally produced wheat declined from 72 kilos per year in the 1920s to 51 kilos per year in 1971. The population of Egypt during these same 50 years had grown from about 13.5 million to 34 million. A similar overall decline in per capita grain resources is reflected in the production of maize and millet. In the middle 1920s there were 163 kilos of these two corns available for each Egyptian. In

1971 that figure had declined to 83 kilos. In contrast, the gains in rice production have been spectacular. Yields per feddan have nearly doubled since the 1920s while the area put under rice each year has gone up nearly tenfold (from 137,000 feddans in 1925-26 to 1,157,000 in 1971). Per capita shares in locally grown rice have risen commensurately, from 12.5 kilos per year in 1925 to 72.5 kilos in 1971.

Since World War II total production of food grains has continued to grow. Table 1 gives the basic picture for the period 1950-1972. The major increases in grain production in the last two decades have come in corn and rice production; wheat has failed to show any major increase. The expansion of rice and corn production has resulted principally from the increased amounts of summer water stored, since 1964, behind the High Dam at Aswan. The availability of this water led to a

TABLE 1

Production of Food Grains in Egypt
Thousands of Tons
Millions of Inhabitants

	Wheat	Maize	Rice	Millet	Barley	Total	Pop.	Per Cap. Kg.
1950-1954	1318	1568	830	519	105	4340	21.4	202
1955-1957	1489	1620	1454	566	161	5290	23.4	226
1958	1412	1759	1024	543	135	4876	24.6	198
1959	1442	1500	1535	630	142	5249	25.2	208
1960	1498	1692	1486	602	156	5434	25.8	211
1961	1435	1618	1142	630	133	4958	26.5	187
1962	1592	2004	2039	658	146	6439	27.2	237
1963	1492	1868	2219	728	134	6441	28.0	230
1964	1500	1935	2036	740	142	6353	28.7	221
1965	1273	2142	1788	806	131	6140	29.4	209
1966	1467	2388	1679	859	102	6495	30.1	216
1967	1299	2167	2283	882	114	6745	30.9	218
1968	1526	2300	2591	907	126	7450	31.7	235
1969	1277	2368	2961	814	117	7537	32.5	232
1970	1519	2397	2605	874	84	7479	33.3	225
1971	1729	2342	2534	854	76	7535	34.1	221
1972	1616	2439	2505	890	133	7583	35.0	217

Source: All but the last row of entries in this table have been taken from Central Agency for Public Mobilization and Statistics, *Population and Development,* Cairo, June 1973, p. 245. The last entry has been taken from data presented in *ardebs* and *daribas* (rice) and converted into tons and kg.s at 150 kg.s to one *ardeb,* and 945 kg.s to one *dariba.* The data is in Egyptian Federation of Industries, *Yearbook: 1973,* p. 5 of the statistical section.

TABLE 2

Production of Main Crops in Metric Tons

Year/Crop	Wheat surface	Wheat Prod.	Wheat YPF	Maize Corn (Shami) surface	Maize Corn (Shami) Prod.	Maize Corn (Shami) YPF	Millet Corn (Rafia) surface	Millet Corn (Rafia) Prod.	Millet Corn (Rafia) YPF	Barley surface	Barley Prod.	Barley YPF
1960	1,456	1,499	1.03	1,821	1,691	.93	404	603	1.33	148	156	1.05
1961	1,384	1,436	1.04	1,603	1,617	1.01	458	631	1.34	121	133	1.1
1962	1,455	1,593	1.09	1,832	2,004	1.09	454	659	1.45	131	146	1.12
1963	1,345	1,493	1.11	1,721	1,867	1.08	484	729	1.51	121	134	1.11
1964	1,295	1,499	1.16	1,660	1,934	1.17	494	740	1.50	121	141	1.17
1965	1,145	1,272	1.11	1,451	2,141	1.48	500	806	1.61	125	130	1.04
1966	1,291	1,465	1.13	1,575	2,376	1.51	518	859	1.66	98	102	1.04
1967	1,245	1,291	1.04	1,485	2,163	1.46	522	881	1.69	107	100	.93
1968	1,413	1,518	1.07	1,554	2,297	1.48	532	906	1.70	117	121	1.03
1969	1,246	1,269	1.02	1,484	2,366	1.59	470	813	1.72	103	105	1.02
1970	1,304	1,516	1.16	1,503	2,393	1.59	501	874	1.74	83	83	1.0
1971	1,349	1,729	1.28	1,522	2,343	1.54	494	854	1.73	70	76	1.08

Year/Crop	Rice surface	Rice Prod.	Rice YPF	Berseem (clover) surface	Berseem (clover) Prod.	Berseem (clover) YPF	Ful (beans) surface	Ful (beans) Prod.	Ful (beans) YPF	Lentils surface	Lentils Prod.	Lentils YPF
1960	706	1,486	2.1	2,414	41	.18	377	290	.77	85	50	.59
1961	537	1,142	2.13	2,448	39	.17	361	161	.45	63	34	.54
1962	830	2,038	2.46	2,442	33	.18	383	328	.86	79	56	.71
1963	959	2,219	2.31	2,434	27	.19	382	263	.69	78	47	.60
1964	962	2,036	2.12	2,480	27	.18	428	366	.86	79	52	.66
1965	848	1,788	2.11	2,493	28	.19	433	344	.79	89	61	.69
1966	844	1,679	1.99	2,532	34	.19	418	381	.91	75	44	.59
1967	1,075	2,279	2.12	2,716	31	.19	336	188	.56	66	34	.52
1968	1,204	2,586	2.15	2,679	37	.20	335	283	.92	51	35	.69
1969	1,192	2,556	2.14	2,726	37	.20	362	297	.88	45	24	.53
1970	1,143	2,604	2.28	2,748	38	.21	330	277	.92	47	33	.70
1971	1,157	2,534	2.23	2,770	40	.22	289	256	.98	65	50	.77

Year/Crop	Sugar Cane surface	Sugar Cane Prod.	Sugar Cane YPF
1960	111	4,545	40.9
1961	112	4,186	37.38
1962	121	4,080	39.73
1963	133	5,153	38.74
1964	134	4,890	36.49
1965	129	4,739	37.74
1966	133	5,189	39.02
1967	137	5,257	38.37
1968	155	6,083	39.2
1969	170	6,878	40.5
1970	186	—	—
1971	193	—	—

Source: National Bank of Egypt, Economic Report, Vol. 17, no. 1 (1974). Surface area is presented in thousands of feddans; production is in thousands of metric tons. YPF = yield per feddan. For longer trend data, but that do not go beyond the year 1966, see Marion Clawson, et al., *The Agricultural Potential of the Middle East*, American Elsevier Publishing Company, New York (1971), pp. 236-37.

It will be noted that there are certain discrepancies between production entries in this table and those of Table 1. While they do not seem to be significant, their existence is indicative of the problems one faces when two official sources report different statistics for basic production sectors.

marked increase in the acreage given over to rice (from 706,000 feddans in 1960 to 1,157,000 in 1971) and has allowed Egyptian peasants to plant corn in May and June. In the past much of the corn crop was planted in July, at the beginning of the flood season, and harvested in the fall. This was the so-called "Nili" season. The greatly expanded supply of summer water has made feasible the earlier planting and has led to increases of 20-50 per cent in yields.

Maize and rice, then, have been the only grain crops to show substantial increases in yields, in large measure due to the Aswan High Dam, and secondarily to improved seeds and fertilizer inputs. For other crops, including cotton, there has been less growth and occasionally stagnation in yields. Barley, lentils, berseem (clover), and sugar cane have plateaued over the last three or four decades, and yields for Egyptian broad beans (*ful*) have recently begun to decline. Some of these trends are reflected in the data presented in Table 2, covering the period 1960-1971, but the data for lentils, berseem, and sugar cane do not go back far enough in time adequately to represent the stagnation in yields, and for beans the data are not recent enough.

While it is not within the scope of this paper nor within the competence of its author to discuss the intricacies of crop productivity, some general observations are in order to better understand what the future may bear. In the last century a series of state-guided innovations led to the complete overhaul of Egypt's agricultural infrastructure and some modernization in farming techniques. The primary innovation has been the conversion of virtually all Egypt's 5.9 million cultivable feddans to perennial irrigation. The last 700,000 basin irrigated (flood) feddans in Upper Egypt were so converted after 1964. The result has been a more intense use of the land, with extensive double-cropping and shorter or less frequent fallows. This has meant that Egypt's cultivated area has been effectively inflated to encompass a "cropped area" of some ten million feddans. The second innovation of significance has been the spectacular expansion in the use of chemical fertilizers to maintain the productivity of the overworked soil. By 1929, Egyptian peasants were already using, on the average, 39 kilograms of chemical fertilizers per feddan. After World War II total annual consumption of fertilizers averaged

804,000 tons per year (1948-1953), rising to 2,322,000 tons per year, 1961-1966, and reaching three million tons in 1971. Finally, there were innovations in the use of improved seeds, particularly in wheat, corn, and cotton. All these factors led to a great surge in agricultural production at the end of the nineteenth century and the beginning of the twentieth, concomitant with an equally pronounced growth in Egypt's human population. It is hard to know if one can find support in this process for Esther Boserup's thesis that increased density among rural populations leads to major technological breakthroughs in agriculture and hence increased production.[1] It is not clear that population growth preceded the above-mentioned technological innovations or whether they themselves contributed to population growth. Two facts are clear: it was the government that initiated and managed these changes, and that, in the presence of continued rapid population growth, a new set of innovations is called for if per capita, per feddan, and perhaps even total production are not to fall. The major benefits of the first phase of technological innovation have already been exhausted and diminishing returns on labor and fertilizer inputs have been evident for some time.[2]

Since the middle 50s the backlash from the intensification of agricultural practices has become pronounced, but the only response to it has so far been more intensification. Soil depletion, increasing soil salinity, water-logging through over-irrigation, new generations of pests and weeds have been confronted with more massive doses of chemical fertilizers, belated efforts to improve drainage, and increased doses of pesticides and herbicides. It is at the price of the long-term degradation of the soil that levels of production have been maintained or marginally increased over the last 15 years.

Egyptian planners are well aware that Egyptian agriculture is at a crossroads and that a new set of innovations, equal to those of the last century, is called for if Egypt is merely to hold steady at current per capita yields. Some measures have already been taken, but their execution must be extended and accelerated. The first of these, chronologically, has been land reclamation. In the last 20 years Egypt has started the reclamation process on some 900,000 feddans. Probably only about a third of those have reached marginal levels of productivity, and only about 50,000 feddans of the Abis project on Lake Maryout can be said to be profitable. The poor quality of the soils, the enormous costs of infrastructure in the form of roads, housing, schools, irrigation, and drainage, and limits in the amount of water available for further reclamation cast in doubt the notion that reclamation can offer Egypt a way out of its present agricultural crisis. It seems reasonable to suppose that in the next ten years Egypt may be able to add about 1,200,000 feddans to the cultivable area, but the levels of production of this land will be for the most part distinctly inferior to the feddanage of the Nile Valley proper. At the same time an ominous counterprocess is at work. Egyptian agricultural experts estimate that something like 60,000 feddans per year of Egypt's best lands are being lost to cultivation as cities and villages encroach upon them and as they are covered in roads, factories, and military installations.* Despite the efforts at land reclamation Egypt may have registered a net loss in its cultivable surface of 20,000 feddans since 1964. The director of the Arab Organization for Agricultural Development, Dr. Kemal Ramzi Stino, has warned that by the year 2000 Egypt may have only four million feddans of cultivable land.[3]

A second set of innovations, involving new and old lands alike, are centered on the transformation and extension of the irrigation and drainage facilities. Work has been under way for over a decade on the introduction of covered field drains in various parts of Egypt. The new, tile drains are not only more efficient but will conserve land for cultivation that might otherwise be taken up with open drains, taking out of production about 12 per cent of the cultivable surface. Covered drains have been installed in only about 20 per cent of the cultivated area. On the irrigation side of the equation, it may become necessary to line and cover the main network and the feeder canals in order to minimize the loss of water through seepage and evaporation. At the same time, an efficient, nonwasteful utilization of irrigation water would indicate a move toward sprinkler and trickle irrigation.

All these innovations would entail enormous investments in rehabilitating millions of feddans and tens of thousands of kilometers of irrigation and drainage canals, blanketing Egypt in a dense network of pipes, pumps, gauges, and sprinklers. Perhaps most formidably, it requires the emergence of a peasantry and extension service capable of understanding, using, maintaining, and monitor-

ing what would, and what must, become one of the most sophisticated and integrated agricultural systems in the world. We may leave aside questions of land tenure, the growing need for obligatory crop rotation schedules, and the reinforcement of the role of agricultural cooperatives in coordinating local agricultural activities. These are, of course, questions of basic importance, but they should not obscure the point that *a technological revolution is required in Egypt for the country simply to hold even.*

The final, and perhaps least important set of innovations will come in the form of improved seeds, the so-called high-yield varieties (HYV). The technology involved in their development has evolved so rapidly that it is foolish to make any predictions even about the near future. But with 1974's technology, high-yield varieties may have a significant impact in raising Egyptian wheat yields, a somewhat lesser impact in raising maize production, and only a marginal impact on rice yields.[4] In contrast, it should be possible through the introduction of HYV wheat strains to raise yields by as much as 30 per cent. Egypt is moving in precisely this direction. In the winter of 1974, 700,000 of a possible 1,400,000 feddans were planted with several high-yield wheat varieties, including Mexipak, Super X, and Shenab. The results of the experiment were not conclusive. In test areas some of the improved seeds resulted in harvests of 15 *ardebs* per feddan as opposed to the best local strains (Giza 155) which reached 8-9 *ardebs*. However, the high yield varieties averaged out to 10.2 *ardebs* per feddan while Giza 155 averaged 8.5 *ardebs*. The additional cost in seed and fertilizers wiped out any gain for the individual peasant. The less than spectacular performance of the new seeds was to be expected. They were overpublicized and the peasants expected a miracle. They required different watering schedules than familiar wheat varieties and heavier doses of fertilizers (70 as opposed to 30 kilograms of nitrate fertilizers per feddan). Most had to be harvested while the plant was still green, yet Egyptian peasants are accustomed to harvesting their wheat when the plant is brown. Traditional harvesting methods and transportation of the wheat to the mills by animals resulted in extensive losses of wheat kernels from the over-ripe plants. But all these problems can and should be avoided in the future.[5]

What sort of balance sheet can be drawn from all these considerations? Egypt has exhausted the

---

*The Ministry of Agriculture admits officially to an annual net loss of 20,000 feddans.

benefits of an earlier period of agricultural expansion and is awaiting the fruits of another which will not really change anything but at best keep things as they are. In the interim, Egyptian agriculture is in crisis. Yields of all major crops have stagnated since the middle 60s as have available per capita resources in food grains. With the population growing inexorably by a million or more each year and with good land going out of production, it is impossible to avoid the judgment that all these ratios will get worse before they get better, if they ever do.

So far the growing crisis has not had any noticeable impact upon the nutritional level of Egyptians because the government has been willing to meet emerging deficits in foodstuffs through massive importations. From the point of view of both calorie and protein intake, the diet of the mythical average Egyptian is adequate. The supply per capita of cereals increased from 182 kilograms in the period 1934-1939 to 217 kilograms in 1972 (see Tables 1, 3, and 4). Total proteins in grams per day rose from 73 in the middle 30s to 83.5 in 1968.

Total calories per day discreetly increased from 2,450 to 2,891 in the same period. Grain provided from 72-77 per cent of all calories throughout these decades and 68 to 72 per cent of all protein. Only about 6 per cent of daily protein intake is derived from meat and poultry in contrast with the United States where 39 per cent of all protein consumed is so derived. Nonetheless Egypt's average per capita consumption of 2,500 calories and 75 grams of protein daily would suggest that Egyptians, by FAO standards, are adequately fed.

The problem is, of course, that actual consumption of food supplies is not evenly distributed, nor do we know what the exact level of actual supplies really is. Exports of foodstuffs, autoconsumption, animal consumption, and rural-urban differences in both consumption and political clout make hash of the mythical average Egyptian and average per capita consumption.

A major problem in agricultural reporting derives from the fact that a good deal of the maize and millet crops are consumed at the source and

TABLE 3

Net Available Supply of Cereals, Protein and Calories, (1934/35 - 1960/61)

Year	Net Supply of Cereals, Kg. per annum	Total Protein, Grams per day	Animal Protein, Grams per day*	Total Calories per day	% of Calories derived from cereals, sugar, starchy roots
1934/5-38/9	182	73	9	2450	77
1947/8	178	68	9	2364	--
1948/9-50/1	174	70	12	2370	78
1951/2	172	70	11	2360	79
1952/3	167	67	11	2315	78
1953/4	176	73	10	2520	80
1954/5-56/7	188	75	13	2570	78
1957/8-59/60	184	73	12	2530	78
1960/61	182	75	12	2530	77

Source: Galal Amin, *Food Supply and Economic Development with Special Reference to Egypt*, Frank Cass, London (1966), p. 56. There are some discrepancies between various entries in this table and those in Table 1. Dr. Amin's data come from FAO, WHO, and Egyptian Ministry of Agriculture sources.

*With reference to meat consumption, it was estimated in 1974 that average per capita consumption in absolute terms was 12 Kg.s per year, as opposed to 16 Kg.s in Turkey, 45 in England, 70 Kg.s in the United States. See Gihane Mikawi, "The Gap Between Production and Consumption of Meat," *al-Ahram al-Iqtisadi*, No. 418, January 15, 1974, pp. 16-18.

TABLE 4

Consumption of Foodstuffs in Egypt: 1968/1969
A. Per Capita Share of Calories Per Day

Foodstuff	1951/52	1962	1965	1967	1968
Grains	1,643	2,098	2,127	2,091	2,108
Tubers and Starches	20	24	29	22	30
Sugar and Derivatives	165	173	188	166	175
Legumes, Beans	107	115	129	76	89
Fresh Vegetables	31	61	59	71	74
Fruits	103	108	104	106	97
Meat and Poultry	53	55	48	53	48
Fresh Fish	8	18	12	11	10
Milk + Milk Products	119	109	112	120	118
Eggs	3	5	6	7	6
Vegetable Oils	72	163	208	128	136
Total	2,324	2,929	3,021	2,851	2,891

B. Per Capita Share of Proteins Per Day in Grams

Foodstuff	1951/52	1962	1965	1967	1968
Grains	47.0	58.3	59.7	60.1	60.5
Tubers and Starches	.3	.5	1.0	.3	.6
Sugar and Derivatives	--	--	--	--	--
Legumes, Beans	6.7	7.1	8.0	4.8	5.5
Fresh Vegetables	1.8	3.7	9	4.5	4.8
Fruit	1.4	1.9	1.8	1.8	1.7
Meat and Poulty	4.8	4.8	4.8	4.5	4.1
Fresh Fish	1.2	2.5	1.8	1.6	1.4
Milk	5.1	4.8	4.9	5.1	5.0
Eggs	.2	.4	.5	.5	.4
Vegetable Oils	--	--	--	--	--
Total	68.5	84.0	86.0	83.2	83.5

Source: Central Agency for Public Mobilization and Statistics, *Consumption of Food-stuffs in the UAR* (1968/69), memo 22/01; cited by Farruq Shalaby and Mohammed Farag Mustapha, *Nutritional Levels from the Point of View of Prices*, Price Planning Agency, Memo #12, June 1972.

never marketed. Thus production figures for these two crops have inherent in them a large margin of error. The same holds true, but to a much lesser degree for wheat. A certain quantity of grain, particularly corn and barley, may be utilized as animal feed, and another portion of any year's harvest held for the next planting. Further, about 200,000 tons of rice are exported annually. Then, finally, there is the annual loss of about 7 per cent (500,000 tons) of all grain production due to poor storage, humidity, birds and rodents, and the post-harvest effects of pesticides.[6] What all this means is that per capita consumption in grains cited in Table 1 and the per capita intake of calories and proteins cited in Tables 3 and 4 most probably represent theoretical maximums computed by dividing the total number of inhabitants into the total locally available supply of foodstuffs.

The two most important factors in determining the actual level of food consumption in Egypt are rural/urban residence and income level. About 40 per cent of Egypt's population is urban and its average per capita income is higher than that of the peasantry. It is clear for the lower-middle, middle, and upper-middle classes of the urban areas that their consumption of meat, poultry, eggs, milk, and wheat flour are well above the national averages indicated in the preceding tables. Rural populations seldom see meat, although they do have on big occasions locally raised pigeons, ducks, or chickens (plus an occasional fish out of the Nile). Their bread is made of home-grown, home-ground corn flour. Onions, broad beans, and goat's cheese round out their diet. Urbanites eat more food, in greater varieties, with a higher protein content and with greater reliance on wheat flour. In surveys of family budgets it has been shown that even at relatively high incomes the propensity to spend on food is very high.[7]

Many of the government's food policies are determined by the masses and elites of Cairo, and secondarily of Alexandria, at the expense of the rural masses. It is in the urban centers that rising expectations can be most dramatically and visibly frustrated among the urban poor, many of whom came, after all, from the countryside to gain a more dignified standard of living. The lower-middle classes, mostly educated, literate, and salaried have only their education, their clothes, perhaps a TV, and a varied diet to set them apart from street vendors and peasants. The well-off consume food on the same scale as they buy clothes, appliances, and apartment houses. Any or all of these groups, were they to be frustrated in their consumerist ways, could pose serious political problems for Egypt. It may be stretching the point a bit to note that bread was one of the causes of the October War of 1973. On several occasions after that encounter, President Sadat mentioned that six days before the war, he called a meeting of the Egyptian National Security Council to inform its members of his decision to fight. One of the reasons he advanced for the need to launch hostilities was that Egypt had reached "the zero point," ostensibly in terms of hard currency, and had the country not gone to war and rallied the financial support of oil-rich Arabs, there would not have been the wherewithal to buy for the Egyptian masses its "loaf of bread" (*raghif*).

Catering essentially to the urbanites has had two momentous consequences for Egyptian investment policies and allocation of hard currency. On the one hand the state has shouldered the burden of subsidizing the prices of basic food and clothing items. For 1975 total price subsidies have been estimated at LE 600 million (ca. $1.5 billion) or around 16 per cent of GDP. Of these subsidies LE 463 million will be accounted for by food items alone. It has become a matter of great symbolic and practical importance, in the urban areas, that as the cost of living rises vertiginously (20+ per cent per year since 1973), a loaf of bread still sells for one-half or one piastre (US$.01 or .02) according to the quality of the wheat flour. In addition, oil, sugar, flour, rice, tea, clarified butter (*semna*), and other food items are sold at subsidized prices. Let us note once again that these subsidies have meaning mainly for urban populations. Other than for sugar and tea, the rural masses "bake their own" and "make their own."

The second consequence of the politics of food has been the growing imports of foodstuffs, especially wheat and wheat flour. One may surmise that these imports serve mainly to sustain the levels of consumption of the urban areas that are already well above national averages. The estimates of food imports for 1975 are impressive:[8]

Wheat	2.8 million tons
Wheat Flour	750 thousand tons
Corn	750 thousand tons
Broad beans (ful)	75 thousand tons
Lentils	20 thousand tons
Sesame	40 thousand tons
Animal Fats	190 thousand tons
Vegetable Fats	112 thousand tons
Frozen Meat	24 thousand tons
Fresh Meat	12 thousand tons
Tea	31 thousand tons
Coffee	6 thousand tons
Sugar	172 thousand tons
Fish	50 thousand tons

These estimates are all the more interesting when we cast them in the framework of Egypt's investment priorities. Total investments in 1975 are expected to be an all-time record of LE 1185 million. This, relative to previous investment levels, is a mind-boggling figure. But then one takes note of estimated imports for 1975, set at LE 2174 million of which food imports will account for LE 689 million. In other words the cost of food imports is over one-half the value of all scheduled investments for 1975 and well in excess of the investment levels of all preceding years.[9]

The internal subsidies have obviously oriented large sums of capital away from productive investment, and the rising imports, in a time of rising international prices for agricultural produce, have cannibalized large amounts of precious foreign currency. Since the Soviet-American wheat deal of 1972, world market prices for wheat have more than trebled (from ca. $60 per ton according to the variety to $200-250 per ton in 1974-75). With the added impact of the energy crisis after 1973, and rising fertilizer, processing, and transportation costs, there is little reason to expect these prices to decline. The result for Egypt has been the aggravation of an already serious balance of payments problem. Egypt produces between 1.6 and 1.7 million tons of wheat a year and has been importing growing amounts, now reaching 2.8 million tons per year. Five years ago, when imports were at a level of about two million tons, hard currency outlays did not exceed $120 million. Today with import needs of 2.8 million tons (not including wheat flour) the bill may run between $600 and $700 million.

Over the short and medium haul, these import needs are not going to go away, and consequently some hard strategic choices are posed. The basic strategy followed in the past has been to maximize cotton exports in order to pay for grain imports (and it should not be forgotten that there were no major grain imports until after World War II). The strategy worked reasonably well until the last two or three years. The following figures, in millions of dollars, present the picture graphically:

	1971	1972	1973
Total Exports	$850	$813	$1,014
(of which cotton)	404	373	438
Total Imports	$1,244	$1,286	$1,593
(of which wheat)	144	147	400

By 1973 the value of cotton exports and wheat imports were nearly in balance and since then the balance has surely turned in favor of wheat. Other

exports have mitigated this new imbalance. The world market price of rice has risen even more dramatically than that of wheat, and Egypt has been exporting about 200,000 tons annually. Citrus fruits have also risen in value. Egypt expects to export 250,000 tons of oranges in 1975, at $250 a ton, up from $87 a ton in recent years. Thus one strategic choice involves export orientation and the thrust toward offsetting import expenditures by increased production and exportation of crops better suited to Egypt's intensive irrigation system and planting seasons: rice, citrus fruits, vegetables, and cotton. But this is no more than an exchange of goods that Egyptians increasingly desire for goods that they must have. Other choices must be made.

To grasp these choices some long-term projections must be made. My estimates are admittedly and necessarily arbitrary. They cannot take into consideration possible, if not likely, technological breakthroughs in seed development and soil management. On the basis of current knowledge, however, we may take Egypt's total production of grains in 1972, 7,583,000 tons, and assume a 30 per cent increase in wheat production, a 10 per cent increase in maize, a 5 per cent increase in rice, and slight increases in millet and barley, and come out with an optimal figure of 8,250,000 tons. Part of the assumption is that Egypt will not add to its cultivable surface more than what is annually removed through the expansion of built-up areas. Now, turning to the population growth, it is virtually certain that Egypt's population by the year 2000 will range between 55 million and 70+ million. Let us take a conservative 60 million as our estimate. Assuming that, on the basis of current trends, the average per capita consumption of grains is 190 kilograms of locally produced and 60 kilograms of imported grains per annum, then total demand in the year 2000 will be 15 million tons of grain, while local production may be no more than 8.2 million tons.[10] Meeting that gargantuan deficit, even if it can be paid for, is, and will be, problematic as long as countries like Japan and the Soviet Union import well over 10 million tons a year apiece and when the surplus of the United States, Canada, and Australia are being sucked into home consumption. How can Egypt feed itself?

First, it can juggle with crop allocation. Two principal avenues present themselves. Traditionally Egypt has tried to cover the hard currency costs of food imports, and, for that matter, nonfood imports, by earnings from the export of agricultural goods: cotton and secondarily rice and onions. This strategy as mentioned appears to be losing its efficacy. While the demand for imports will grow with the population, the amounts of agricultural produce available for export will tend to stagnate as a result of both growing internal demand and stable or diminishing feddanage upon which to grow them. A deficit in Egypt's agricultural trade abroad should become a fact of life for the rest of the century. It might make sense to scrap the old policy altogether and put Egypt's cotton feddanage, planted in the summer, over to rice and corn. That would serve to increase the local supply of food grains and perhaps reduce the import burden. However, the hard fact is that only about 1.7 million feddans are given over to cotton each year. If, for the sake of argument, we assume that half that surface would be put under rice and the rest under corn, and that present yields per feddan are maintained, then the increase in grain production would consist of 1.8 million tons of rice and 1.9 million tons of corn per year. Egypt's total grain production might then be on the order of 12 million tons per year, reducing its end-of-the-century deficit to three million tons. But Egypt would have lost cotton export earnings as well as cotton produced for local industries. Moreover, rice requires heavy doses of irrigation water which probably would not be available in sufficient quantities to meet the needs of increased acreage.

The second avenue would consist in the systematic mechanization of Egyptian agriculture in order to do away with draft animals and thus free feddanage normally utilized for fodder crops for grain cultivation. The major crop in this respect is berseem, Egyptian clover, annually absorbing about three million feddans in the winter months and thus in direct competition with wheat. Were anything like three million additional feddans to be sown with wheat, Egypt might be able to attain an annual production level of about five million tons. In combination with shifts in the summer crops it would be theoretically possible to meet the nation's grain needs at current per capita levels of consumption. Yet the disadvantages are numerous. To mechanize will require tremendous hard currency outlays in imported equipment, farm machinery assemblies, spare parts, and perhaps fuel imports. To succeed, mechanization, like the modernization of the irrigation system mentioned

above, would require the transformation of the Egyptian peasant, the obligatory consolidation of minifundia, and the strengthening of the cooperatives in mandatory crop rotations. Second, Egypt would and should continue to have major requirements in fodder crops. Less than half the country's total animal population is used for field work. The rest, consisting of sheep, goats, pigs, and cattle would presumably be maintained. Some of the draft animals, such as buffalo, might be kept for their milk. Moreover, it is the government's intention, especially in the reclamation areas, to expand grazing herds for meat and milk. Thus it is highly unlikely that all three million feddans of the winter berseem crop could be converted to other purposes.

The essential conclusion that one must draw from the foregoing analyses, and one that several Egyptian experts have already drawn, is that there is no optimization plan for land use and crop allocation that will in any way "solve" Egypt's production problems nor meet the country's food needs. The strategy for the future will be threefold. Ismail Sabry Abdullah, the Minister of Planning, phrased the major element of the strategy succinctly: "Egypt's future lies in the export of manufactured goods and the import of foodstuffs. The worldwide rise in the price of food must act as an incentive to increase the rates of growth [of the economy] so that from the earnings on our industrial exports we can pay for our food." [11] How realistic this goal may be is beyond the scope of this Report, but it surely represents Egypt's best, if not last, hope.

The second element of the strategy for the future will entail holding the line in domestic production, resorting to some combination of the measures discussed in the preceding pages. Rationalization of land use and crop patterns, land reclamation, partial mechanization, up-grading of animal populations, the introduction of more efficient irrigation and drainage systems—all may serve to maintain existing soil quality, the number of feddans available for cultivation, and current per capita levels of production. [12]

The third element is that of regional agricultural integration. Unlike the late '40s and early '50s, it is no longer the politicians who are the major advocates of Arab unity but rather the technocrats. To establish markets for industrial exports and to stabilize sources of agricultural imports Egypt must irrevocably tie its fate to the rest of the Arab world. It has become a matter of sheer economic necessity and not one of political choice. But it will be years, if not decades, before economic integration can begin to pay off, assuming that it gets started. In terms of agriculture, Egyptian experts look to the Sudan, Iraq, and Syria as areas of great promise that are presently underexploited. The Sudan actually cultivates only about 15 million out of 100 million acres of good cultivable land. Only 10 per cent of what is cultivated is irrigated despite the availability of water from the Nile, and there is a great deal that can be done with the southern, rainfed areas without borrowing from Nile waters. On the whole, Sudan's crop yields per acre are quite low, frequently only half those of Egypt. The Sudan also has great potential in animal raising with vast savannah lands that could furnish adequate pasturage. It is the intention of the Sudanese government to become self-sufficient in wheat and perhaps to generate an exportable surplus. Most knowledgeable observers concur that due to the high temperatures year round in the Sudan, the country is not well suited to wheat production and should concentrate on oleaginous plants such as peanuts and sesame as well as maize, sorghum, and safflower. It might also have a good future in rice and sugar cane. In short, the Sudan could become a major exporter of a whole range of foodstuffs not only to Egypt but to all the Arab world. The Egyptians hope that with a combination of Egyptian, Sudanese and foreign know-how and capital from the Arab oil-rich states, the Sudan's unused land can rapidly be brought into production.

A certain number of projects are already under study and execution may begin within the coming months. Three separate projects have the highest priority. The first will be the digging of the Jongeli Canal[13] in the southern Sudan in order to make a passage for the White Nile through the Sudd swamps. This will reduce water loss due to evaporation in the swamps and save about 4 billion m^3 of Nile water annually that will be used to reclaim or irrigate 500,000 feddans in the Sudan and an equal amount in Egypt. A second project will consist in regrouping and improving cattle herds in the region of Damazin with the hope of eventually producing 24,000 tons of slaughtered beef each year. Finally, one million feddans of clay soils in the central Sudan, along the Blue Nile (Damazin and Rosseires regions) will be planted with corn,

safflower, sunflower, sesame, and fodder crops. While these are modest beginnings, it is hoped that the Sudan will rapidly develop exportable surplus.

Egypt and the Sudan enjoy good political relations. For other Arab countries with considerable agricultural potential operational economic integration is a more distant prospect. Nonetheless the factors necessary for rapid development are there: land and peasant labor, abundant capital, and considerable reserves of technical know-how. Overall it is estimated that the Arab world has about 300,000 million feddans suitable for cultivation (by this measure one-third of them would be in the Sudan alone) of which only about a quarter are presently cultivated. Even these are poorly exploited so that the Arab nations produce in aggregate only 10 million tons of grain each year while consumption in aggregate is 15 million tons. With the introduction of mechanization, improved irrigation, soil improvement techniques, high yield variety seeds, it is estimated that the Arab world could produce 46 million tons of grain per year by the end of the century, at a time when local consumption may not be more than 33 million tons.[14] While the projects are as yet but a gleam in certain planners' eyes, there are great hopes that the vast acreage of Iraq in the Tigris-Euphrates valley, of which as much as 13 million acres have been salted out due to improper irrigation and drainage, can be recuperated. In addition, probably pending a settlement of Baghdad's war with the Kurds, the steppe and mountain pasturage land of northern Iraq could become the base for a modern animal-raising industry. Similar, although more modest prospects hold for Syria as well, especially now that the giant Tabaqa dam on the Euphrates will permit the irrigation of large parts of the eastern Gazira area of Syria.

It is thus only through increased Arab economic integration that Egypt will be able to feed its population in the future. It cannot become self-sufficient except at the cost of distorting its comparative advantage in the kind of crops suitable for intensive irrigation systems and at the cost of reduced hard currency earnings. It probably should not expect to be able to draw upon the United States, Canada, and Australia for its growing annual import needs for grain, for in some years it seems highly probable that these countries will not be able to deliver large enough exportable surplus to world markets to meet the aggregate demands of the food-deficit nations.

In short, the question of the modernization and intensification of agriculture in the Arab world has become a matter of survival for Egypt. Egypt is faced *now* with a food crisis that must be remedied in the next few years. Other Arab countries may face the same problem in the next 15 to 20 years unless they undertake a concerted effort to develop their considerable agricultural potential now. Egypt *needs* to have them start as soon as possible so that an exportable surplus may become available soon. Thumb-twiddling on the part of Iraq, Syria, and the Sudan would ultimately cost them dearly, but for Egypt it would be disastrous. While it is simple to talk of bringing the factors of production together rapidly and coherently, that would presuppose a level of political trust that past rivalries among the Arabs tends to inhibit and which is all the more difficult to attain when attention is focused primarily upon the conflict with Israel.

A Key to Weights and Measures for Egyptian Data

1 Feddan = 1.038 acres = 4,200.8$_M$²
1 Qirat = 1/24 of a feddan
1 metric ton = 1,000 kilograms (kgs) = 10 quintals
=2,200 pounds
1 quintal = 100 kgs
1 qantar = 44.9 kgs

1 ardeb (metric) = 120 kgs
1 ardeb wheat = 150 kgs = 5.44 bushels = 198 litres
1 ardeb beans = 155 kgs
1 ardeb corn = 140 kgs
1 dariba = 945 kgs

NOTES

1. See Esther Boserup, *The Conditions of Agricultural Growth*, London, 1965, especially Chapter 4.

2. See Patrick O'Brien, "The Long-term Growth of Agricultural Production in Egypt," in P.M. Hold (ed.) *Political and Social Change in Modern Egypt*, Oxford University Press, 1968, pp. 162-195; especially p. 191.

3. See the debates on land reclamation of the Agricultural Committee of the Egyptian Parliament, reproduced in "This New Land: for Whom?", *al-Tali'a*, Vol. 10, no. 8 (August 1974), pp. 11-61. Dr. Stino's remarks were reported in *al-Ahram*, September 4, 1974. On several occasions Dr. Mustapha al-Gabali, former Minister of Agriculture and one of Egypt's leading soil experts, has presented evidence of net land loss. See for instance his article in *al-Ahram*, July 7, 1974.

4. G.W. McLean and K.Toriyama, *First Comprehensive Rice Research and Production Discussion Paper for Egypt*, Ford Foundation, Cairo (April 1973), p. 29.

5. See "Mexican Wheat—What's its Problem and What Must it Do?", *al-Ahram al-Iqtisadi*, #457, September 1, 1974, pp. 14-16. It is at least theoretically possible that were all production factors brought together in the proper mix, wheat yields could be doubled to over two tons per feddan, or even higher. My more conservative estimate of a 30 per cent increase is based on the judgment that it will be extremely difficult to achieve that "proper mix." For a counterview, see Mustapha Gabali, "The Mexican Wheat Case," *al-Ahram*, November 26, 1974.

6. *al-Ahram*, June 18, 1974.

7. Azzat Sa'dni, "In Every Home a Supply Crisis," *al-Ahram al-Iqtisadi*, #456, August 15, 1974, pp. 32-33.

8. Figures supplied by Abderrahman Shazli, Minister of Supply, to parliament, and reported in *al-Ahram*, November 17, 1974.

9. Note also that Egypt is importing items that it has previously produced in relative abundance: beans, sesame, corn, oils. Moreover, Egypt is now a net importer of refined sugar after years in which it was a net exporter. This is the more ironic in that Egypt's refining capacity is 750,000 tons annually but actual produce does not exceed 545,000 tons. This is due to lowered cane production in Upper Egypt, lower sugar content of the cane, and a flight of the peasants to other crops whose purchase prices are not fixed by the State.

10. These estimates correspond roughly to those presented by Dr. Mustapha al-Gabali, "The Necessity of Integrated Growth for the Countryside...," *al-Ahram*, May 5, 1974.

11. From an interview in *al-Ahram*, November 19, 1974.

12. New crops might offer some chance of quick breakthroughs. One option is soy beans with their high protein content and suitability for poultry feed. Yet soy beans are sensitive to salt and need good soil. Egypt's reclaimed areas would not be suitable for soy cultivation. The plants also need long daylight hours but not excessive heat, a combination difficult to attain in Egypt's torrid springs. Finally, if planted in the older soils of the valley proper, soy would compete with corn, cotton, and rice.

13. The "first stage" of the Jongeli canal (whatever that means) will cost LE 70 million, and the land reclamation project will cost LE 36 million, and employ 1.9 million workers five months a year over a five-year period. Very conceivably many of these workers would be Egyptian.

14. See Mustapha al-Gabali, *al-Ahram*, January 17, 1974; Dr. Abderrazaq Sidqi, "The Arab Base for Agricultural Crops," *al-Ahram*, January 10, 1974; Dr. Kemal Ramzi Stino, "The World Food Crisis and its Impact upon the Arab States," *al-Katib*, Pt. I, Vol. 14, No. 163 (October 1974), pp. 83-88 and Pt. II, No. 164 (November 1974), pp. 53-58.

Cairo: Third World Metropolis
Growth, Administration, and Planning

The importance of Cairo to the student of urbanization and economic development is commensurate with its size. Cairo is big and getting bigger: some would say monstrous. In this and the following two Reports there will be no attempt to cover all the relevant aspects of Cairo's growth and internal restructuring. Rather, a limited number of subjects have been selected that either have received little attention in published sources or have not been brought up to date.[1] Thus this article will examine certain facets of demographic change in Cairo, the administrative apparatus charged with the task of coping with the city's growth, and the efforts to devise a master plan for the city's future. Detailed consideration will then be given to the two policy areas upon which rapid urbanization has had its most telling effects: housing (shelter of any kind) and transportation (the movement by whatever means of goods and people within the city limits).

The fundamental premise underlying this very partial view of contemporary Cairo is that this metropolis embodies or holds nascent urban forms and patterns of growth that are not only common to the Third World giants such as Calcutta, Djakarta, or Lima, but for whose understanding we have no valid precedents. No one, I am convinced, really knows where these cities are going or what kind of urban phenomenon they will represent 20 years from now. A United Nations study has summed up the rather awesome unpredictability of it all: "The process of urbanization may come to surpass itself and give rise to geographic and social forms of human settlement to which current vocabulary can no longer be validly applied."[2] One can be sure, perhaps, of only two things: most Third World cities will be of unprecedented size by the year 2000, and, in the aggregate, of an unprecedentedly low urban standard of living. Their sprawl and style of life will probably not be that of Los Angeles or even

Tokyo but, at best, that of Shanghai, or at worst, no one knows. Our ignorance of the future is understandable. Less understandable and less excusable is our ignorance of the present which is our only possible baseline to looking ahead.

* * * * *

Soon after its founding some one thousand years ago, Cairo became one of the world's major cities. At certain points in time it may have been the largest city in the world. Gamal Hamdan adventurously claims that it had reached one million inhabitants under the Fatamids in the eleventh century.[3] In the fourteenth century its population stood at 500,090.[4] It has been only in the nineteenth and early twentieth century that Cairo declined in status, as the urban centers of industrializing Europe and North America mushroomed.[5] In 1800, after Napoleon's invasion of Egypt, Cairo may have had 250,000 inhabitants.[6] Even that may be something of an overestimation. Gabriel Baer advances a figure of 218,000 for 1821-1826, rising to 256,679 in 1846, 374,838 in 1882, and 570,062 in 1897 (see Table 1). The potential for major fluctuations in Cairo's "premodern" population can be grasped when it is noted that the plague of 1835 probably killed 50-80,000 of the city's inhabitants, or about a third of the total.[7] By the beginning of the twentieth century Cairo had once again attained the half-million mark but at that level was only one of a myriad of medium-size cities in a rapidly urbanizing world. Seventy years later, Cairo would again claim the dubious privilege of being one of the world's major urban centers—perhaps ninth or tenth—with a population of nearly six million for greater Cairo. Therein lies Cairo's drama, and its dimensions can only grow. Depending on crude birth and death rates and rates of migration into the city, Cairo will

Table 1: Comparative Growth Rates: Cairo vs. Egypt*
1897-1972

Year	Cairo Pop.	Growth Rate %	Egypt Pop.	Growth Rate %
1897	590,000		9,591,000	
1907	678,011	1.4	11,136,000	1.5
1917	791,000	1.6	12,670,000	1.3
1927	1,071,000	3.0	14,083,000	1.1
1937	1,312,000	2.1	15,811,000	1.2
1947	2,091,000	4.8	18,806,000	1.8
1960	3,353,000	3.6	26,085,326	2.38
1966	4,964,004	4.13	30,075,858	2.54
1970	5,900,000 (est.)	4.1	33,329,000 (est.)	2.54
1972	6,170,000 (est.)	4.0	35,000,000 (est.)	2.24

*This table has been reassembled from several sources and requires extensive commentary. The principal sources are 1897-1960, Alphonse M. Said, "The Growth and Development of Urbanization in Egypt" Social Research Center, American University in Cairo, 1960 (typescript); Janet Abu-Lughod, "Urbanization in Egypt: Present State and Future Prospects," *Economic Development and Cultural Change*, Vol. 13 (April 1965), pp. 313-343; Gamal Hamdan, *Studies in Egyptian Urbanism*, Cairo, 1959; Central Agency for Public Mobilization and Statistics (CAPMAS), *Cairo: 1970*, Reference #200/01, January 1971; Gamal Askar (Director CAPMAS), "The Population Explosion in Cairo" (in Arabic) *al-Ahram al-Iqtisadi*, supplement to issue of December 1972.

As with virtually all Egyptian demographic statistics, there are significant variations from one source to another for reasons that can seldom be determined. The method of calculating a given statistic is almost never explained. For instance, one often finds a population total for "Cairo." Is it Greater Cairo, or the center city proper? Only Abu-Lughod has consistently controlled for Cairo's changing boundaries but her data do not run beyond 1960. In essence Greater Cairo would include on the west bank of the Nile all of Giza, Dokki, and Imbaba, and to the north Shubra 'al-Kheima. The actual districting of Cairo has been quite complicated since the Second World War, particularly as regards Giza, but until 1960 the units had such low populations that the total city figures were not much distorted by inclusion or exclusion of these areas. In the period 1947-1960, however, all those districts mentioned grew enormously and the ostensible slowing of the growth rate in the period 1947-1960 may be accounted for by the exclusion of Giza and Shubra al-Kheima from the Cairo total in 1960. The figures for 1966 and 1970 were drawn from the study by Gamal Askar and both refer to Greater Cairo. In 1970 CAPMAS estimates that Cairo proper had a total population of 5,220,000. In *al-Ahram* of September 18, 1972, General Askar cited the 1972 figure for Greater Cairo and estimated that Cairo proper (including Helwan) totaled 5,384,000. The west bank plus Shubra al-Kheima would thus account over the last decade for some 700-900,000 of Cairo's total population.

Finally to further confuse matters, there has been evidence since 1967 of a general fertility decline throughout Egypt, but particularly in the cities. The Executive Board for Family Planning has offered a figure for 1970 that estimates that the net reproduction rate had reached 1.93 per cent per annum. CAPMAS, for its part, has noted a similar but less dramatic decline. Its estimates of total population for Egypt are based on a rate of 2.54 per cent for the entire decade 1960-1970 with a slight decline to 2.24 per cent for 1970-1972. See CAPMAS, *Statistical Year Book: 1952-1971*, Cairo, July 1972, p. 11.

Table 2: Net Migration to Cairo, 1907-1970*

Time Period	No. of Migrants for entire Period	Annual Rate of Migration to Cairo (%) **
1907-1917	157,557	2.0
1917-1927	296,851	2.84
1927-1937	358,673	2.62
1937-1947	606,561	2.83
1947-1960	952,663	2.18
1960-1965	274,000	1.6
1965-1970	428,000 (est.)	2.1 (est.)

*The figures for 1907-1960 have been drawn from Muhammed Subhy Abdulkrim "Emigration to Cairo: Report Submitted to the Greater Cairo Planning Commission" (1968: in Arabic) as cited by Ahmad an-Naklawi, *Cairo: a Study in Urban Sociology*, Dar an-Nahda al-Arabia, Cairo (1973: in Arabic), p. 161. The figures for 1960-1970 are from Gamal Askar (Director of CAPMAS) "The Population Explosion in Cairo," supplement to *al-Ahram al-Iqtisadi,*(December 1, 1972:in Arabic).It should be noted that CAPMAS has assumed a lower rate of emigration into Cairo than the Greater Cairo Planning Commission in the period since the last census in 1966; 2.1 per cent as opposed to 2.6 per cent. In the absence of another census, no one can know for sure who is correct.

**The rate of migration is the annually calculated proportion of migrants into the city to the entire population of the city.

Table 3: Comparative Crude Birthrates, Cairo vs. Egypt*

	1960/64	1965	1966	1967	1970
Cairo	44.6	39.3	35.8	33.4	30
Egypt	42.5	41.4	41.0	39.2	35.5

*These figures have been taken from various publications oı the Executive Board for Family Planning, especially *The Report on Family Planning* (June 1972: in Arabic). They correspond to fertility trends expressed in a chart prepared by the Ministry of Health, based on annual figures from the civil registries.

have at a minimum some 12 million inhabitants by 2000 but quite conceivably as many as 16 million (Egypt as a whole will have between 54 and 70 million inhabitants).

The two major components of Cairo's growth are derived from the rate of natural increase of the city's resident population and the rate of net migration into the city (see Tables 2 and 3, and Figure 1). Both in their actual level and in their significance, these rates are the subject of considerable controversy. For educated, urban Egyptians, acutely aware of the crowding of their city, the major concern is the "flood" of migrants into the city. Frequently one hears that Cairo and its facilities are designed to handle a population of about 1.5 million, a level exceeded during the Second World War with a massive influx of migrants (606,561 in the period 1937-1947). Lightly veiled and apprehensive references to the rural hoardes have been

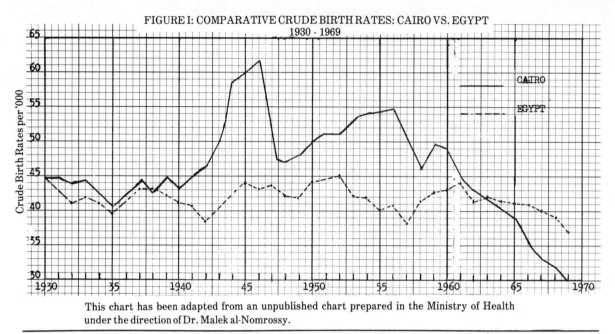

FIGURE I: COMPARATIVE CRUDE BIRTH RATES: CAIRO VS. EGYPT
1930 - 1969

This chart has been adapted from an unpublished chart prepared in the Ministry of Health under the direction of Dr. Malek al-Nomrossy.

commonplace ever since. Cairenes who study their city's problems are only too ready to accept the validity of arguments that instead of Cairo urbanizing the migrant peasantry, the latter are ruralizing the city.[8] Urban sociologists have even invented an Arabic equivalent to "ruralization": *taryif*. A high official in the Greater Cairo Planning Commission (henceforth GCPC) lamented to me that Cairo was becoming an enormous village, with none of the virtues of village life such as solidarity, mutual respect, and self-help, and all the city vices of impersonalism, disregard for others, and lack of civic spirit.

Although it is not directly pertinent to the focus of these articles, it should be stressed that whatever Cairo's shortcomings, the city is probably still a more attractive residence than Egypt's villages. Urban wage levels are higher, housing, no matter how substandard, superior, schools and health facilities better, and amenities such as movies more abundant than in the countryside. For most Cairenes life in the city is monotonous and even grim—but never so monotonous or grim as life in the village. In short urbanites prefer, without necessarily liking, living where they do.

Again, while push-pull factors in the rural exodus lie beyond the scope of this article, the very serious rural crowding in the Nile Valley has surely led to considerable labor redundancy and underemployment. While the city may not abound in employment opportunities, it appears to be a more attractive place in which to eke out one's existence.

Periodically high level commissions meet to consider how to stop migrants from coming into the city. One such has been meeting under the auspices of Hamdy Ashur, the Governor of Cairo since September 1972. Practical measures to stem the tide are elusive. Some of those suggested are to declare Greater Cairo off-limits to any further industrial projects; decentralize governmental and public sector bureaucracies; oblige all entrants into the city to show proof of employment; and limit all rentals only to those who can show proof of local employment.[9] One would anticipate that all these policies would be met with considerable resistance on the part of public and private sector firms that would be reluctant to sacrifice proximity to Cairo's infrastructure and power elites; on the part of bureaucrats who prefer a crowded Cairo to life in a provincial backwater, and on the part of the migrants themselves, over whose entry there is no real means of control. Landlords will rent to whomever can muster the cash, and the need for proof of work will probably generate a lively trade in falsified papers. Muhsin Idriss, Director of the GCPC, summarized the situation accurately:

... in December 1967 we undertook a serious study demonstrating that the rate of migration to Cairo is very high. In the report nine recommendations were made to the Cairo Governorate, all of which were designed for immediate application. However, to apply them would have required a force greater than the Egyptian army....[10]

"CAIRO ESTABLISHES A CONFERENCE TO LIMIT MIGRATION TO IT"

The Egyptian people offers a machine gun to Hamdy Ashur, the new governor of Cairo. He is musing over the best way to end migration to the city. The "people," says: "Do you want me to tell you the best way of all?..Liberate the canal!" Salah Jahin in *al-Ahram*, October 4, 1972.

Precisely because there is no systematic registry for or means of control over the migrant influx, it is almost impossible to make anything more than an intelligent guess as to the annual rate of in-migration. It is currently estimated at 2.1 per cent per annum for the period 1965-1970. That is a slightly higher rate than the 1.5 per cent of the preceding half-decade. At least that figure has some "hardness" to it for it was computed from census data for the years 1960 and 1966. Since then there has been no census. The estimated rise in the rate is probably due to the influx of evacuees from the Suez Canal Zone following the Six-Day War of 1967. One would probably not be far off in assuming that, as of 1972, 100,000 migrants a year are arriving in Cairo. It is likewise not unreasonable to assume that with a 2 per cent in-migration rate and a 2 per cent natural increase rate Greater Cairo crossed the six million mark sometime in 1972.

Some demographers, such as Kingsley Davis, have decried what they view as an overconcern with cityward migration at the expense of attention to high urban birthrates.[11] A glance at Cairo's crude birthrates over the last decades (see Figure 1 and Table 3) would seem to confirm that judgment to some extent. Since 1947 the city's total growth rate has hovered around the 4 per cent mark with migration and natural reproduction each accounting for about half the total growth. It is also significant that throughout the period 1938-1963 Cairo's crude birthrate was generally higher than that of Egypt as a whole. It has been only in the last decade, and especially since 1967, that the urban environment has produced its depressing effects upon the crude birthrate. It may well be that today migration accounts for more of Cairo's growth than natural increase. But even with regard to the situation of ten years ago, Davis' point may not be as true to the mark as it seems. Between 1947 and 1965, at least 1.2 million migrants poured into Cairo. Surely these migrants must account in some measure for the high crude birthrates of the same period. Of course many migrants were unaccompanied males, but the majority brought their wives and probably their rural sexual habits. It would seem, therefore, at least worth considering that migration rates and urban crude birthrates are not separate phenomena but closely linked, and that it would be misleading to develop policies that deal with one to the exclusion of the other.

A city suited for a million and a half people is obviously crowded with six million residents. Indeed, to the extent that population densities are a major indicator of urbanization, Cairo is very urban. In the future we may have to rephrase this indicator totally, however, as much of the Nile Valley will have achieved densities of an urban level. Will all of settled Egypt have become an agro-city or the Nile Valley a linear village? That is another of those questions that defies answering at present. Let us concentrate on Cairo today, deferring close attention to the various facets of density levels within Cairo to the Report on housing. At present a few global figures should suffice (see Table 4).

The overall population density per square kilometer for the city proper in 1966 was 19,594 in an area of about 240 km^2. Some quarters reached truly astounding densities: Bab ash-Sha'ria in the

Table 4: Comparative Densities per Kilometer^2
Cairo, Alexandria, Tanta, Assiut, Egypt*

Year	Cairo	Alexandria	Tanta	Assiut	Egypt
1927	6,584	2,000	7,100	2.500	410
1937	7,957	2,400	7,600	2,600	466
1947	11,704	3,200	11,100	3,900	546
1960	15,634	5,200	14,600	5.600	724
1966	19,594	n.a.	n.a.	n.a.	845
1970	23,204 (est.)	7,000 (est.)	20.000 (est.)	7,400 (est.)	926 (est.)

*Figures drawn from Executive Board, *Report on Family Planning* (Cairo 1972: in Arabic); 'Izzat Higazi, *Cairo: A Study of the Urban Phenomenon*, National Center for Sociological and Criminological Research,(Cairo, 1971: in Arabic); and "Cairo in the Language of Figures," *al-Tali'a*, Vol. 5, No. 2 (February 1969), pp. 68-71. The reader, like the author, may be struck by the very high densities at Tanta, the capital of Gharbia Province and the major city of the Nile Delta. Its population reached 230,000 in 1966. The densities for Egypt as a whole are based on the ratio of population to *inhabited* surface which is only 35.6 thousand km^2 out of the total surface of one million km^2.

oldest part of the city reached 136,000 per km^2; Rod al-Farag in the northern zone of expansion subject to heavy in-migration from the Delta, 105,000; and Bulaq, the original industrial center founded in the early nineteenth century, 75,000; Sayyida Zeinab, a lower-middle class district, 78,000. One district, Gamalia, the heart of medieval Cairo, has stabilized at 53,000 per km^2 over the last two censuses—it may have reached the limit of further absorption. It is estimated that in 1970 the city's overall density was 23,000 per km^2. Cairo, it should be remembered, is a city of relatively low structures. The high-rise apartment building is confined to high income districts of low density. The most crowded districts are those with buildings seldom exceeding three or four stories. Yet Cairo's densities are superior to those of New York (25,000 per square mile ca. 1965) with its high-rise housing and skyscrapers.

Several years ago a French research group offered some fascinating statistics on the occupational composition of Egypt's cities. Out of a total urban population of eight million in 1958, the active population totaled 1.9 million. Their distribution is shown in Table 5.

The authors of this study refer to nearly three million urbanites of working age without declared employment. This category, like all those presented in Table 6, is almost impossible to extrapolate from data as presented in Egyptian census results or manpower surveys. The crucial knowledge of the degree of economic stratification in their urban society is thus denied us, nor do we ever come across occupational breakdowns that would give us an idea of the number of household servants, people engaged in parasite trades, or unemployed in Cairo or other cities. In 1968, for instance, a labor survey estimated that there were only 53,000 men and 8,600 women unemployed in Cairo.[12] For 1970, the figures were even lower: 48,100 men and 10,700 women. The distribution by occupational branch is presented in Table 7. Neither Table 6 nor 7, unfortunately, gives us any idea of level of income.

Service sector, government, and public sector employees dominate the employment structure of Cairo, probably accounting for as much as one million active inhabitants. It would be useful to be able to replicate the income statistics of the I.E.D.E.S. study, but I do not have access to the requisite sources. Still, the same stratification of revenues may prevail today as was the case 15 years ago. Salaried employees, leaving aside doctors, lawyers, engineers, architects with private practices, and high-ranking bureaucrats, are universally remunerated at very low levels—LE30 or $75

Table 5: Occupational and Income Distribution
of Egyptian Urban Population*

Occupational Category	No.	Per Annum Revenues Millions LE	Per Annum Per Cap. Revenue LE
Household servants	400,000	20	50
Sous-proletariat	80,000	5	60
Wage-earners traditional sector	170,000	16	90
Proletariat	341,000	48	140
Employees	480,000	84	175
Traditional self-employed	230,000	69	300
Middle-range employees, low income professions	190,000	58	290
Hi-level employees, wealthy professionals, and capitalist entrepreneurs	46,500	86	1,870
Total	1,939,500	385 mill.	

*I.E.D.E.S. "La Société urbaine égyptienne" *Tiers Monde*, Vol. 2, No. 6, (April-June 1961), pp. 183-210, table p. 203.

Table 6: Number of People in Cairo Work Force 1970
Aged 12 - 65*

Category	Men	Women	Total
Wage earners	994,600	151,400	1,535,900
Self-employed	227,400	9,100	236,500
Employers	50,900	1,500	52,400
Family-work w.o. salary	31,000	3,700	34,700
Works for others w.o. salary	7,100	400	7,500
UNEMPLOYED	48,100	10,700	58,800
Total	1,359,100	176,800	1,535,900

*CAPMAS, *Cairo: 1970*, Source #200/01, January 1971, p. 37.

Table 7

Active Population of Cairo According to
Type of Activity
Aged 12 - 65*

Branch	Men	Women	Total
Agriculture and fishing	49,700	3,800	53,500
Mining and quarrying	4,700	600	5,300
Transformation industries	442,900	29,800	472,700
Building and construction	84,400	700	85,100
Electricity, Gas, and Water	24,100	600	24,700
Commerce, trade	229,300	19,400	248,700
Transport, Communic., Storage	126,300	6,100	132,400
Services	397,700	115,800	513,500
Total	1,359,100	176,800	1,535,900

*CAPMAS, *Cairo: 1970*, p. 39. The term "active population" presumably refers to all those who directly generate some form of personal income whether through formal or informal employment.

per month would be considered a very good salary. How to survive at such income levels in Cairo would warrant at least a Report in itself, but the implications of this phenomenon for the city's ability to provide services and cope with the exigencies of growth should be fairly obvious.

By 1972 Cairo had grown to account for at least 15 per cent of the country's population. Alexandria was second with perhaps 6 or 7 per cent. Cairo is about two and a half times as big as Alexandria. Besides these two cities, Egypt lacked, up until 1966, any middle range city between 250-500,000 inhabitants.[13] Even in 1966 only Giza, part of Greater Cairo, had attained this level with 571,000 inhabitants. Port Said and Suez had crept past the 250,000 level only to be devastated by the June War of 1967. Cairo today is more than ever a "primate" city. This term, first used by Mark Jefferson in 1939, referred to cities whose size was at least twice as large as the second leading city. According to Jefferson, if we treat Cairo's population of 1937 as an index of 100, then Alexandria equals 52 and Port Said equals 9.[14] In the late 1950s, Cairo was

2.4 times as big as Alexandria and was the nineteenth ranking primate city in the world.[15] Mehta, using a different measure, calculated that 62 per cent of the total population of Egypt's four largest cities resided in Cairo alone, and on that basis ranked Cairo thirty-seventh in "primacy" among the world's cities.[16]

A city may manifest its primacy in realms other than population concentration, and Cairo does. There are many indicators that we could examine, but I will cite only a few. While the city contains 15 per cent of the nation's population, it has 66 per cent of all television sets, 52 per cent of all telephones, 33 per cent of all pharmacies, 33 per cent of all medical doctors, 27 per cent of all hospital beds and 62 per cent of all university graduates. Twenty-three per cent of all degrees at all educational levels in Egypt are awarded to Cairo's students. Cairo consumes 27 per cent of the nation's entire electrical output and 40 per cent of its vegetables, fruits, and meat.

Over half the nation's skilled tradesmen reside in Cairo and 36 per cent of its production workers. In

Roofscape - Gamalia

transformation industries alone Cairo houses 42,000 establishments (30 per cent of the nation's total) and 52 per cent of national employment in this sector. One could go on. The point is that despite the immensity of its problems, Cairo is privileged, relative to most of the rest of the nation. For those who govern it, live in it, and plan for it, however, that fact is easily overlooked.

It was not until 1949 that the city of Cairo was granted the juridical status of a municipality. Until that time the city, the nation's capital, had been subject to a fragmented and tenuously coordinated administration based on relevant ministries (for example, Interior and Health, Education, Housing) and private concessions for gas, electricity, tramways, etc. A unit known as the Council of Tanzim, presided over by an official from the Ministry of Public Works (now Housing), afforded the city its only forum for the development of integrated policy. It is thus overly generous to say that Cairo was "designed" for 1.5 million inhabitants; it just happened that way. Perhaps the discovery in 1947 that the city had reached 3.3 million propelled the "authorities" toward the establishment of "home rule" for the city. One of the first tasks assigned to the new municipality in 1949 was to supervise the

design of a Master Plan for Cairo. This was completed in 1956, and we shall return to its contents later.[17]

In 1960 the Local Administration Law merged the administration of the Governorate with that of the municipality to create a single, multipurpose administrative unit. Although the Ministry of Local Affairs, created in 1960 to supervise all provincial and local units of administration, was dissolved in 1971, the combined municipal-governorate unit has been retained. The basic elements of the structure are the Governor, a person with ministerial rank appointed by the President, and the Executive Committee of the Governorate. This committee groups Under-Secretaries from all the Service Ministries (Education, Housing, Health, Social Affairs, Labor, Supply) and the Ministries of Finance and Interior (for police and security). The Under-Secretaries, who remain career functionaries in their mother ministries rather than in the Governorate, work full time with the Governor to achieve coordination between city and ministry objectives. Under their supervision are some 24 "administrations" (*idarāt*) covering everything from bridges and tunnels to civil defense.[18]

In the last few years there has been a well-intentioned, but initially abortive, attempt to decentralize the Governorate's administration. The city is divided into 24 districts (*qism*) which correspond to police precincts. The districts in turn were grouped into seven "quarters" (*Hay, Ahyā*): Masr al-Gedida, East, North, Central, West, South Cairo, and Helwan. Employees of the Governorate were redistributed to the seven new entities where they found there were no offices ready to receive them. At the head of each *Hay* was and is a "chief" (*ra'is*), appointed by the Governor. It turned out that no criteria governing qualifications for appointment had been laid down and some of the first chiefs were clearly unqualified for their jobs. In addition, the chiefs were deprived of the practical means to undertake their new duties, while for its part the Governorate was granted only the right to "advise" the administrations of the quarters. When it is realized that, for instance, the processing and approval of all requests for building permits as well as responsibility for maintenance of all roads and other public facilities falls to the *Hay*, then one can grasp the harmful effects that unplanned decentralization incurred.[19]

For all its initial faults, this arrangement has been retained. Incompetent quarter chiefs have been replaced and presumably adequate office space and support have been found for the now-dispersed bureaucrats. As a check on local abuse, each quarter will have a committee of 20 members, elected from among the members of the Arab Socialist Union (ASU), Egypt's only recognized political organization, to oversee the local administration.

Taken as a whole, the local and central administration of the Governorate, known as the *diwan al-Am*, comprises an impressive total of 30,000 functionaries.[20]

The salaries and expenses of the *diwan al-Am* cannibalize all, and sometimes more than all, the city's locally generated revenues. That is not because these civil servants are handsomely salaried but because the city is able to tap such a low level of urban resources. The city budget in the last 20 years has confirmed three basic characteristics: (1) local revenues account annually for only a quarter to a third of all city resources; (2) the budget as a whole is devoted overwhelmingly to current operational expenses with little left for investment; (3)

the total size of the budget has been growing at best slowly and sometimes not at all.

In 1963 the city's (Cairo proper) approved budget stood at LE29 million (ca. $66 million) and rose gradually over a decade to LE39 million (ca. $90 million) in 1973. That would mean an annual average increase of about 3.4 per cent, significantly behind the city's rate of population growth, but nonetheless a fairly high rate. Still, because budget figures are in current prices we must deflate rates of increase by the generally accepted 2 per cent per annum. Thus the rate of real growth in budgetary outlays is probably closer to 1.4 per cent per annum. Not only is the rate low, but the absolute level of expenditures is as well. Ninety million dollars to provide services, maintenance, and some investment to a city of over five million souls is some indication of how desperate the situation is. That works out to annual outlays of $18 per capita. Low as that may seem, it should be kept in mind that the average per capita income (share of GDP) in Egypt was, in 1970, about $167 (LE76), and, although the incomes of urbanites are probably higher than the national level, per capita city outlays may represent as much as 10 per cent of the average urbanite's annual income.

From 60-75 per cent of all city revenues have been provided over the last decade through subsidies from the Ministry of Local Affairs. In 1971 this Ministry was reabsorbed by the Ministry of Interior, but the system of subsidies will continue as before. In real terms, it has been the case that locally generated income has stagnated at a level of LE12-13 million. The Governorate, in consultation with the city's representative assembly, has then usually requested subsidies of LE40-50 million. Sums of that size are never approved, and actual subsidies are in the range of LE20-25 million. For instance, for 1973 the Governorate estimated local revenues at LE12 million and then requested subsidies of LE51 million for a total budget of LE63 million. LE27 million was eventually approved for a total budget of LE39. In the event, that figure corresponds precisely to the 1972 budget. Cairo in this respect is not privileged relative to the rest of the country, receiving about 17 per cent of all local subsidies which in 1972 totaled about LE160 million. Of course, being the nation's capital, the major industrial area, a pole for tourists, the locus for three of the country's five universities, and the home of a sprawling bureaucracy,

Source of Revenues	CAIRO'S REVENUES (in Egyptian Pounds, LE)		
	1963/64	1966/67	1968/69
Taxes on housing, real estate, and agriculture	1,210,000	1,411,080	1,298,100
Amusements tax	585,000	632,452	571,000
Automobile fees	1,950,000	2,722,668	3,254,900
Share of common revenues*	427,800	821,509	1,302,600
Revenues from city housing demolition, improvement*	922,000	483,364	606,200
Local taxes and fees	2,201,000	1,828,045	1,500,000
Diverse	816,900	3,452,033	1,756,500
Non-repetitive and irregular taxes and fees	4,077,000	1,092,311	1,083,000
Revenues from quarries	126,200	109,516	143,600
Public accommodations	100,000	--	--
Special capital investments	500,000	--	--
Surplus from preceding year	--	--	1,787,800
Total local revenues	12,915,900	12,552,978	13,303,700
Subsidy from Min. of Local Administration	16,258,200	22,347,022	25,149,200
Total	29,174,100	34,900,000	38,452,900

This table has been drawn for the revenues of 1963/64 from Abu-Lughod, "1001 Years," *op. cit.*, p. 225; and from Galal Bakeer, *op. cit.*, for 1966/67 and 1968/69. Some of the revenue categories in Abu-Lughod's tables were rearranged according to my own judgment to correspond to the categories in Bakeer's tables. Given the wide variations in entries from budget to budget, it is remarkable how little the total of local revenues varies.

  * Cairo's share in import and export taxes and on transferable wealth.
 ** In 1968, for instance, the city owned and rented 21,642 units of low-cost housing.

I do not have confirmed figures on Governorate expenditures. However, the proposed budget of 1973 (total LE63 million) was broken down as follows:

LE 6,334,000 housing, roads, lighting, bridges and tunnels
    22,727,000 education (of which LE19,580,000 in wages)
    10,615,352 health
     3,750,940 social affairs
       258,000 supplies
     1,457,975 police and civil defense

    44,543,267 Total

I cannot account for the discrepancy between the above total and the entire request. The Governorate was eventually authorized expenditures of only LE39 million. One can assume that at least 80 percent of this will go to salaries and maintenance of existing facilities. The Diwan al-Am alone will take some LE13 million. The same situation holds for Giza Governorate whose budget in 1971/72 was LE8 million, LE7 million of which went into salaries.

the city receives a relatively high level of public, private, and international investment outside the framework just described. Unfortunately I can make no estimate of the level these other investments might attain.

Cairo's citizenry expresses whatever opinions it has about the running of the city through two channels. One is the Arab Socialist Union, and the other is the nation's parliament, the People's Assembly (Maglis as-Sha'ab). The ASU Secretariate for all Cairo is headed by Sayyid Zaki, a former officer long associated with the Ministry of Social Affairs and especially interested in the problems of the city's craftsmen.* The Secretariate contains subsections that examine the problems of specific policy areas such as education, housing, and sanitation. The Secretariate also supervises the activities of 27 sections of the ASU, 24 of which correspond to the city's police districts, and three of which represent Cairo's universities and higher institutes (ironically, however, Cairo University is not in Cairo but in Giza). Each district is endowed with a committee elected by the local members of the ASU. These in turn elect the Committee of Cairo (lagna-t-il-Qahira) over which Sayyid Zaki presides. The district committees are, in theory, the points of contact with the masses, and they are supposed to study local grievances and problems and bring them to the attention of concerned public bureaucracies. A superficial view would indicate that to some extent they perform their duties, and in the last months the ASU officials have been involved in, among other things, inspecting bakeries that sell loaves below official weights, relocating families expelled from condemned buildings, and remedying the shortages in hides supplied to leather workers.

Since 1960, Cairo has had a representative assembly. This was initially known as the Cairo Governorate Council and, of its 85 members, only 42 were elected, through the Arab Socialist Union, and the rest appointed. In the fall of 1971, this system was considerably altered. A new body, known as the Popular Assembly (al-Maglis as-Sha'abi), consisting of 58 members, was appointed from among the elected ASU officials of the 27 districts and the Cairo Committee. No longer were the Governor and other important administrative officials of the city to be considered ex-officio members. This assembly, presided over by Dr. Galal Bakeer,

*In 1976 he was moved up to Secretary for Discipline for all the ASU, and his Cairo slot was taken over by Dr. Galal Bakeer.

has been meeting monthly and its various committees have undertaken some serious investigations of Cairo's problems, particularly as regards housing and transportation. The Governor and members of the Executive Committee have been attending all meetings. Also attending are officials from the national-level Secretariate of the ASU, and Cairo's elected representatives to the People's Assembly. All have the right to take the floor, but only the 58 official members have the right to vote. Having attended three sessions of the Cairo Popular Assembly, I can attest both to the quality and the occasional heat of the debates.

At a higher representational level Cairo can make its voice heard as well. This level is Egypt's 360-member parliament, the People's Assembly (Maglis-as-Sha'ab: up until 1971 it was known as the Assembly of the Nation: Maglis al-Umma). All members of this parliament are elected by direct universal adult suffrage. All candidates are members of the Arab Socialist Union, but the voters need not be. Cairo has 40 elected representatives in this Assembly, including Sayyid Zaki (from Gamalia) who is, as mentioned, secretary of the ASU for Cairo. Cairo's deputies in this body feel themselves to be the "legitimate" representatives of the city, in contradistinction to the "appointed" members of the city's Popular Assembly. Several of them attend the meetings of the Popular Assembly and speak out frequently on the city's problems. At the parliamentary level, they are very active in committees that affect the city's future, such as housing, communications, industry, finance, etc. The deputy speaker of the parliament, Gamal Uteify, is a Cairene, elected from the central business district of Qasr al-Nil. It is my estimate that both the Popular Assembly and the Cairo delegation of the People's Assembly, to demonstrate their responsiveness to constituency needs, frequently make unrealistic proposals that would cut into the state's basic investment priorities in defense, industry, and rural electrification. If their constituencies can eat symbolism, well and good, but the Council of Ministers inevitably cuts Cairo back to its perennial shoestring budget.

The frustrations of the representative are equalled by those of the planner. His dilemma is simple: the plans he makes to bring some rationality to the city's growth are seldom listened to, and even if they were, they cost too much. One planning official remarked to me, "The political authorities are frightened by our cost estimates. Over the next five years, if we were to develop adequate housing

Gezira Sporting Club and the Cairo Tower

and communications for Cairo alone, it would cost LE800 million. How can anyone pay for it?"

Although the Governorate has its own planning unit, long-term, planning for the city has been entrusted to the Greater Cairo Planning Commission created in July 1965 by Presidential Decree. The commission was given impressive responsibilities, and its decisions were to be final and binding on all ministries. The commission would be responsible to the Prime Minister (from 1967 until his death in September 1970, that was Nasser himself), and would have an independent budget. By 1971 the GCPC had a full-time staff of 500, mostly architects and engineers secured from the Ministry of Housing. Abu-Lughod, who witnessed the commission's impressive birth, soberly and prophetically noted, "If...the committee does not succeed in its mission, this attempt to circumvent rather than strengthen normal administrative channels will have delayed rather than hastened the day of eventual adequate planning for the city.[21]

The GCPC has not succeeded. Like so much else that takes the long-term view, it has been the victim of the June War and Egypt's short-term struggle to survive the consequences of military defeat. The President who was also Prime Minister had his mind elsewhere than on the problems of Cairo. Moreover, three governorates, and hence three governors, fell within the purview of the GCPC as did various ministries with vested interests, established connections, and considerable concern for protecting their turf. Furthermore, the GCPC tended to become an adjunct of the Ministry of Housing which supplied most of its staff. The GCPC has never really become autonomous, and in most respects closely resembles the Executive Board for Family Planning which also was placed under the Prime Minister's jurisdiction, but which entered into a semicolonial relationship with the Ministry of Health.[22]

It is generally conceded that the GCPC has become little more than a technical consulting outfit. It can tell the Ministry of Industry what the establishment of a factory in Shubra al-Kheima will mean to traffic flows in northern Cairo. It helps plan and design bridges and new traffic arteries; it attempts to integrate project proposals, such as the new Opera House, with certain broad concepts of optimal land use.[23] The GCPC seldom proposes and, seemingly, never disposes.

Ataba Square - Victorian Cairo gently decaying.

Yet it has made some proposals, and it has certainly undertaken some long-needed studies on the city's future. Looking to the next 20 years, the Commission predicted a population by 1990 of 16.5 million if the city grew at 4.7 per cent per annum and a minimum of 13 million if both migration and natural reproduction rates dropped. The estimate may have erred on the pessimistic side, thereby compensating for the inverse miscalculation of the city's first master plan in 1956. As a documentary landmark in the course of demographic prediction, it is probably worth paying some attention to that document. The studies on which it was based were begun in 1954. The authors, extrapolating the city's growth rate from rates established in the period 1917-1947, note that by the year 2000 Cairo would have ten million inhabitants, "which is far above a reasonable forecast." They felt that the growth of the city in 1937-1947 was unnatural and that at the worst Cairo would reach seven million by the year 2000. Even this, it was judged, might be too high as the regime planned to develop secondary industrial towns, and the rise in the general standard of living would depress fertility rates. With some artful juggling of fertility projections, the authors found that the population of the city in 2000 would more

likely be 4.2 million. Despite that sanguine conclusion, the authors recommended that the size of the city be limited to 3.5 millions.[24] The 1960 census was to reveal that that number had almost been reached. One suggestion the authors made that has carried over to subsequent planning efforts was to curtail the growth of Cairo proper by the establishment of self-contained satellite cities outside the Cairo limits.

This theme was taken up once again by the GCPC when, in 1969, it proposed the establishment of four satellite cities of one million inhabitants each in the desert land west and east of Cairo. The commission felt that it could thus avoid further encroachment on agricultural land that will be needed to meet the city's growing demand for fresh produce, as well as to provide more open recreational space for Cairo's inhabitants (2.0 *feddans* per 1,000 inhabitants rather than the actual .4 *feddans*). Moreover, the Commission's engineers estimated that the continued physical expansion of the city would cost more in the extension of basic services, public utilities, and housing than to break off and start afresh in a new locale (or locales).[25] It is hoped that, exclusive of housing, the total investment per capita for utilities and other public

GREATER CAIRO

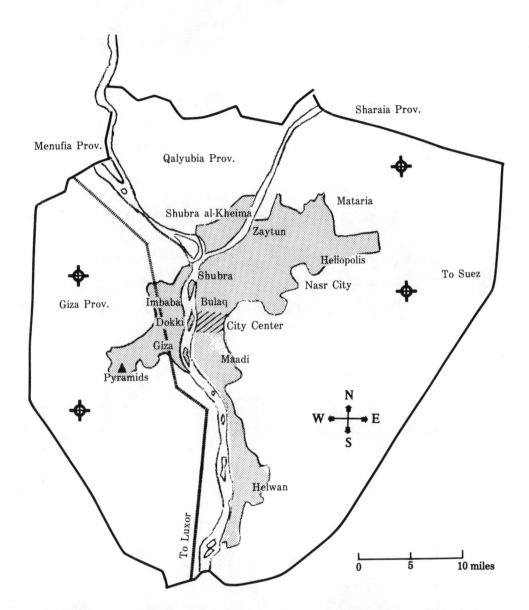

*My apologies to connoisseurs of Cairo and to cartographers for this very imperfect rendering. It has been adapted from a brochure from the Greater Cairo Planning Commission that did not include a scale. I have had to devise my own which is at best approximate. All of Cairo proper lies on the east bank of the Nile except for the two islands of Zamalek and Roda which are part of the city. All the shaded area on the west bank of the Nile is part of Greater Cairo as is Shubra al-Kheima to the north. ▨ represents the city center. The outer line represents the planning area for the Greater Cairo Planning Commission. The crosses (✛) represent tentative sites in desert areas for four proposed satellite cities.

The urban village with cart traffic, Masr al-Qadima.

The Nile looking southwest toward Giza Gold Coast.

Old Cairo of a thousand minarets.

Intersection of Sharia Mu'izz al-Din and Sharia al-Azhar.

Houseboat at Imbaba.

facilities would be LE700. Although it is proposed that the development of the cities would take at least 20 years, the total, minimum outlay would be LE2.8 billion. Each city would be entrusted to a development corporation like those that developed Heliopolis, Maadi, and Nasr City.

Given the price tag, the project has few backers outside the GCPC. Regardless of price, the project has a host of critics who cite, among other things, the example of Nasr City as precisely what should not be done. Do these satellites not run the risk of becoming desolate dormitory cities, or perhaps refuges for the better-off, leaving Cairo to the poor and the migrants?[26] It is judged that if the project is not done properly, it had best not be done at all. However, with the wafting of lucre in the air, potential beneficiaries are not about to let the proposal drop. In October 1972, the Establishment of Housing and Construction, an appendage of the Ministry of Housing, announced that it had decided to "begin work" on the development of five suburban cities, but apparently only the Maadi Company was given rights to develop 400 *feddans* capable of absorbing about 25,000 inhabitants. The matter floated to the surface once again, more significantly but as inconclusively, in the Executive Committee of the Governorate. Muhsin Idriss, Director of the GCPC, was invited in June 1973 to attend a meeting of the Executive Committee in order to discuss the satellite cities. The result was that the Committee resolved that the existing settlements of Nasr City, Misr al-Gidida, Helwan, Maadi, Khanka, and Kirdassa should be developed as self-contained economic units, but nothing was decided regarding the construction of new urban units.* There the matter lies until further notice.

At the time of writing this article, the GCPC appears to have been dissolved. Presidential Decrees in July 1973 resulted in the establishment of a special Agency for Urban Planning to be placed under the direct authority of the Ministry of Housing. It was not stated that the GCPC had ceased to exist, but that would be the logic of the new situation.

The last word in this article on planning the future of Cairo goes to Hassan Fathy, for he is sure not to have the last word where it counts, in the city and in the government. Hassan Fathy, besides being a gifted architect, is an artist, an intellect, and a patrician gadfly inflicting minimal damage on the city's stubborn course toward mediocrity. Fathy wants Cairo to be again what it once was, an

---

*Since 1974 plans have been reformulated and some Arab funding is now available for the satellites. The first may be on the road to Fayyum (lower left on map on page 16) and named after King Khalid of Saudi Arabia.

The heart of Baron Empain's Heliopolis.

organic entity growing through the spontaneous yet harmonized efforts of its citizens and citizen architects. All Cairenes were once involved in the construction and maintenance of their city, and they had a perhaps unarticulated grasp of the implicit principles that gave the city its character. The implicit in medieval Cairo was always honored so that improvisations on the basic theme became masterpieces. Whether one agrees with Fathy or not on his image of medieval Cairo, one cannot help but admire his vision of what the future should be. For without the involvement of Cairenes, without the tapping of the hidden genius of citizen architects, the implicit principles of the city's future harmony will never emerge. Without this, Fathy flatly declares, city planners should stick to cost accounting. The most a planner can do is to help organize the activities and movements of people within the city in such a manner that a maximum sense of community and self-sufficiency is fostered in each sub-center. Planners can encourage but not create communities.

But...if the planners happen to be geniuses, perhaps there is hope. Fathy in an important but little known article has made a fascinating proposal for the future of Cairo.[27] He has noted the two factors that have complicated the city's expansion. First, the original center of the city has continuously moved westward, leaving behind the center of gravity of the city's population in the Azhar, old-Cairo area. Second, the northward and southward elongation of the city forces an inordinately heavy flow through the new throat of the city. Fathy's argument is startlingly simple. The center of the city can be moved eastward again by developing the Muqattem hills and the tomb areas that lie between them and the built-up area of the city. Indeed the hills had always blocked Cairo's eastward expansion, but with the possibility through modern pumping stations of bringing water to the hills and of planting and landscaping them, the whole area would provide an unexcelled palette for artistic architects. The author himself explains his vision far better:

> Some of the hills are rather precipitous, and others are just mounds of debris, but if they were suitably terraced and landscaped, they could provide a very fine site for building; in

Cairo: The view from Giza looking east toward the Citadel and the Muqattem hills.

fact they offer a wonderful opportunity to the architect for sculpturing huge masses of rock (by controlled quarrying) and integrating natural rocky forms with the main buildings of the city in a really dramatic and beautiful composition....

Indeed, one would hesitate to suggest so daring an operation if the case were not so desperate. No one goes lightly to a plastic surgeon to have his face remolded, and those who do, like to be assured of the doctor's taste as well as of his skill. To reshape the Muqattem hills is an undertaking like shaping Hymettus—something never meant to be dreamt of unless to save the city's life. Then, since it is the only solution, it must be entrusted to artists of surpassing genius. Only a person of the widest and most delicate visual sensibility can ensure that the new skyline will be as beautiful as the old.

Cairo can become a triumph of man's artistry, a work of cooperative art worthy to rank with the world's finest examples of town-scape, with Verona, in fact with old Cairo itself, which before 1890 or so was the lovely and dignified City of 1,000 minarets. But such a work as this is not to be undertaken lightly. Building a city for 5,000,000 new inhabitants on a 40-year plan, establishing the character of Egypt's capital for hundreds of years, recreating one of the greatest cities in the world, calls for the most responsible and humble approach.

First made in 1961, Hassan Fathy's call has gone and probably will go unanswered. The vision of breaking Cairo loose from its plight is obscured by the sheer welter of salvage operations needed to meet the short-term crises that are the lot of Cairenes every day. It may be the old conundrum of the forest and the trees, but the overwhelming question for a city of employees is paying for a place to sleep and getting themselves to work. The prosaic will be the subject of the next two Reports, when we look at transportation and housing.

Transportation

Egypt is locked inextricably in the grips of three crises: transportation, housing, and hostilities with Israel, or so one would conclude judging by the amount of newspaper coverage given them. All that the first two share with the last is their seeming insolubility. Both transport and housing are direct reflections of rapid population growth and even more rapid urbanization in conditions of poverty. More specifically, whatever Cairo may be—quasi-urbanized village or ruralized city—it does manifest at least three characteristics of the urban environment: great physical mobility among its inhabitants, relatively vast movements of goods, and extremely high densities of population in residential districts. In this Report we shall deal with the movement of people and things in Cairo.

The city's transportation problem is as much a drama as a crisis, and Cairo's streets are the stage for a daily tragicomedy in which all Cairenes are both actors and spectators. Indeed, it is my hunch that the drama of the streets is willed, consciously or not, by the denizens of Cairo who have little else to disrupt the "grinding monotony" of their lives. In the streets they can display physical prowess—whether at the wheel of a decrepit taxi or on foot dodging it—righteous indignation, studied nonchalance, bargaining skills (particularly in talking policemen out of applying the rules), pathos, desperation, and grace. Getting from here to there is the bane of the Cairenes' existence and the spice of their lives.

Take, for instance, the bus—luckily for you figuratively and not literally. It is rumored that Cairo buses, when new, are taken at night into a huge empty lot and driven into each other until their windows are popped out, their lights smashed, and their chassis have taken on the proper shape, suggestive of a red sack of melons on wheels. New

horns are installed with a husky, slightly prehistoric wheeze, the rear and front doors are wrenched away, and the whole superstructure is tilted about 45° to starboard. With this preparation the fleet is ready to take to the road and face the hordes.*

Some of us a year or so ago had the rare privilege of seeing in Cairo new, two-sectioned buses, 18 meters in length, that served the long commuter lines into and out of downtown Cairo. They arrived bravely, gleaming blue and white, and while it was by no means an overnight affair, within a few months the new arrivals had been reduced to the same level as the rest of the fleet.

It is little wonder that such should be the fate of Cairo's public transport. It is a simple question of supply and demand. The supply includes some 1,300 buses, 140 trolley buses, and 230 trams for a total of about 1,800 units theoretically available to meet daily demands. In fact because of disabled equipment, particularly among buses, only about 1,100-1,200 vehicles may be operative in any one day. There to greet them are over 3.5 million passengers a day, or 1.2 billion per year.[1] Two million of these passengers daily beseige the system during the six rush hours. The most heavily traveled line from Shubra in the northern sector of the city to the heart of town handles 45,000 passengers an hour. In any given day the operative fleet covers about 400,000 kilometers or about 100 million miles a year. Half the bus fleet is over seven years old, when statutory retirement age should be after five years. Age, brutal handling and driving, overloading, inadequate maintenance, and the chronic lack of spare parts account for the rate of disabled vehicles. The only wonder is that it is not higher.[2]

Yussef Saïd, the Director of the Cairo Transport Authority, pointed out to me that while the city's

*These have never materialized.

population grows at 4 per cent per annum, the number of passengers carried by the public system has been growing at 15 per cent per annum. (The size of the fleet seems to have stabilized at about 1,800 units since 1969.) With an annual budget of around LE30 million ($75 million) the Transport Authority has been running growing deficits, now at LE7 million. Fixed fares (3-5^c depending on the line and/or first or second class), rising costs of maintenance and spare parts, and deteriorating equipment have determined this situation.

The analysts who argue that the exodus from the countryside to Cairo has led to the ruralization of the city would do well to keep one factor in mind. Something like half the city's working population is employed in locales outside the police district (*qism*) in which they reside. Unlike the village, work site and household are not in close proximity for a substantial part of Cairo's population. For the city as a whole in 1966, 48.5 per cent of the work force were employed in their district of residence, 37 per cent were employed outside their residential district and presumably might resort to public means of transport, and 15 per cent could not be accounted for. Moreover the *qism* is large enough that some

residents would use public transport to commute to work within it. The great northern belt of the city, the major zone of expansion for rural migrants, is heavily involved in the movement of workers with a number of quarters exporting daily over 40 per cent of their working population to other parts of the city (see Table 1).

The long and short of it is that Cairo is a workers' and employees' city, where hundreds of thousands commute to work each day. Factory workers, mechanics, sales personnel, bureaucrats, school teachers, servants, and so on fight it out daily to leave wherever they live and get to wherever they work. Add to these hundreds of thousands more primary, secondary, and university students, vast arrays of military personnel stationed in and around Cairo, and kids who ride for kicks, and you have the full cast assembled for Cairo's daily theatrics.

A colleague recently arrived to Cairo was immediately transfixed by the marvel of Cairo's public transport and remarked in amazement, "The first free mass transit system I've ever seen." As we shall see, he was wrong, but surely the vision before his eyes warranted his conclusion.

Filling up the bus at an obligatory stop: in front of the Al-Azhar Mosque.

Table 1

Distribution of households according to
place of residence and place of work:
1966. In percentages*

District (qism)	Within District	Outside District	Outside Cairo	Undeter-mined
Shubra al-Kheima	80.3	11.2	1.1	7.4
*Mataria	40.8	35.8	3.1	20.3
*Zaytun	40.6	37.5	2.6	19.3
Nuzha	.4	70.8	3.8	25.0
*Masr al-Gidida	51.1	25.3	3.4	20.2
Wayli	50.8	26.5	2.4	20.4
*Shubra	49.6	35.8	2.0	12.7
*Sahil	36.3	40.8	2.9	20.0
*Rod al-Farag	45.1	44.3	2.6	8.0
Boulaq	63.0	24.3	1.8	10.9
Ezbekia	54.3	36.5	2.3	6.9
Zahir	29.5	49.7	3.0	17.8
Bab as-Sha'ria	52.9	36.0	1.4	9.7
Gamalia	59.8	27.9	.8	11.9
Darb al-Ahmar	52.9	36.0	1.4	9.7
Mouski	63.1	77.0	1.1	8.8
Abdine	49.6	33.7	2.3	14.4
Qasr al-Nil	45.1	15.2	1.8	37.9
Sayyida Zayneb	48.1	37.8	3.1	11.0
Khalifa	48.1	40.3	1.5	10.1
Masr al-Qadima	47.9	39.7	3.5	8.9
Ma'adi	56.9	30.2	2.4	10.5
Helwan	81.0	5.0	1.7	12.3
Giza City	38.0	30.9	8.1	23.0
Total	48.5	33.4	3.0	15.1

*CAPMAS, CAIRO: 1970, Ref. #200/01 (January 1971), p. 60. The principal northern districts have been starred. Boulaq shows a heavy concentration of work and residence befitting the city's original industrial district, as do Shubra al-Kheima and Helwan, which have developed since World War II. The latter two have a very high proportion of workers who enter and exit every day. Qasr al-Nil is Cairo's central business district.

Many Cairo buses, between 8 A.M. and 7 P.M., are full beyond capacity. This does not simply mean that the interior of the vehicles is unbelievably crammed with humans, but the outer surface as well is liberally sprinkled, and frequently submerged with passengers. To facilitate boarding, the two right-hand doors, the right-hand windows, and the rear windows are frequently either jammed open or entirely missing. Into them disappear, and occasionally reappear, baskets, babies, and people who through a miracle of agility and tenacity find accommodation where all logic would tell us there is none. Thus loaded the bus laboriously quits the scene of an obligatory stop and begins its route.

It may not stop again before reaching the other end of its route. It will reduce its speed as it passes bus stops along the way, producing thereby the occasion for the revelation of the average Cairene's extraordinary athletic prowess. The typical civil servant on his way to work is an unprepossessing sort, shortish, plumpish, determinedly dignified as befits an educated person. At his work undue haste or any ruffling of his composure is resolutely avoided. Yet this same creature becomes, when boarding or leaving the bus, an acrobat of great agility.

The bus generally makes no effort to swing in near the curb even when it does not intend to stop. Descending passengers must therefore practice what some of the seasoned spectators among us call the "flying dismount." This consists in our roundish civil servant wriggling his way through the dense mass of fellow passengers until reaching some sort of opening (no matter which) and then launching himself clear of the vehicle, generally spread-eagle with briefcase firmly clutched in hand, until his feet hit the ground, at which point he runs furiously to compensate for his forward momentum. But his feat is not limited to that, for having become airborne in the middle of the road with traffic coming along on the inside of the bus, he must spin, fake, and zig out like a split end, darting between cars, carts, bicycles, and the onslaught of would-be passengers that converge on the moving vehicle he has just abandoned.

They in turn, similarly determined men and occasionally women, charge after the bus, leaping and clutching at whatever they can grasp on the outside of the bus: window and door openings, dents, cracks, rips and bumpers, and other external passengers. It is said with truth that many of Cairo's bus passengers have no physical contact with the bus but only with other passengers. And here one must note the truly admirable spirit of the Cairene who, already crushed and packed in the interior of the bus or clinging precariously with all the dexterity of an alpinist to the vehicle's carapace, will nonetheless extend a hand, not to beat back the aspirant passenger sprinting after the bus, but to help him on board.

The outer cargo accounts, over time, for much of the characteristically lumpish appearance of the average bus as passengers have fashioned the necessary hand and foot holds for survival on the outside. It also accounts for the standard right-hand list of the buses, as well as for the Transport Authority's reluctance to introduce double-decker buses to Cairo for fear they would tip over. The out-riders in general have raised the art of the flying dismount to its highest level, and they will practice their art at fairly high speeds and in the densest

traffic. One civil servant, honoring the canons of Cairo's street theater, dismounted a careening bus after a heavy rainstorm and found himself churning calf-deep through a curbside mud puddle. With a crowd of connoisseurs watching, he refused to acknowledge this little contretemps, and strode sedately and sloshily off to his work place. Another truly astounding dismount was witnessed on Qasr al-Nil Bridge when a brown, disheveled figure cast itself loose from the side of a speeding bus in heavy traffic, dancing his way successfully to the sidewalk. On closer inspection, this apparition turned out to be a stubble-faced, one-legged man in a tattered *galabia* who performed his act with the aid of a stout stick that served as a crutch.

The appearance of out-riders is what gives rise to the notion of a free mass transit system, and, indeed, many passengers, especially fleet-footed urchins, ride for free. But the system has another remarkable acrobat, the fare-collector, known as the *kumsary* (from the French *commissaire*).[3] At moments when no one else on the bus is able to move, this man is capable of swimming like a shark among a school of fish, collecting his tithe. His omnipresent hand will reach out a door or a window to the out-riders who then have the choice to pay up or bail out. He has also been known to refuse to make change for passengers who then may protest or fight their way slowly to the exit in order to be able to get off when they want. The *kumsary's* trade in this manner can be quite lucrative.[4] To round out the picture of inside Houdinis are the pickpockets who are happily at home in the jam. Moreover, because the transit system theoretically has its own police, the Cairo police force does not judge itself responsible for thefts that occur on buses. The pickpocket thrives in the world between conflicting jurisdictions. A favorite gambit is to pick a pocket on the bridge leading from Cairo Governorate to Giza. The theft is performed in Cairo and the criminal flees in Giza. Whose police are responsible for apprehending the felon...?

Lest the reader see in all the above the fantasizing and hyperbole of a foreign observer, let us look at one of several descriptions found in the Egyptian press:

> We cannot tell if this is a transportation crisis or a morals crisis. When the passenger is able to find a place for his feet or for his finger or toenails, he finds a strange world.

A Cairo trolley.

Freebees on the trolley—Ataba Square.

A passenger in first class insists on paying only for a second class ticket. He argues with the *kumsary* and the bus stops. The *kumsary* collars the offender and expels him. Another passenger shows a pass valid for a different line. The bus stops; the *kumsary* collars him and off he goes. A woman complains of the bad manners of a man next to her; the bus stops and another is expelled. Another passenger demands his change, and the *kumsary* claims he has none. A new argument and the bus stops once again....

The passengers are surprised by an unannounced stop of the bus and while pondering its cause they hear the driver call out the door to a cafe waiter, "Two teas, easy on the sugar, and two glasses of water." This is duly delivered and the driver and *kumsary* calmly take tea for five minutes. To the relief of the passengers the needs of the crew are satiated and the bus proceeds on...only to stop in front of a grocery store. The *kumsary* gets out, having been instructed by the driver, "Listen, a couple of fat sandwiches...and don't forget the pickle."[5]

In these circumstances the Cairene commuter has developed a stolid patience in the face of inexplicable delays and the querulous behavior of bus drivers that contrasts markedly with the alacrity displayed in catching the bus. People may be seen chasing a bus for a block just to ride it for three or four more, or going after one as if it were the last that would ever come (a perhaps logical apprehension under the circumstances). Yet many of the same passengers will sit stoically in a disabled bus for as long as it takes for the monster to continue its route.

With fares fixed and unchanged since 1953, the buses are relatively cheap, and for many, such as students or the military, even the base rate is reduced. For most of Cairo's commuters there is no alternative to taking the bus other than walking. Still the resort to other means of transport in the city is growing rapidly. Since 1966 the Transport Authority has operated eight "river buses" with fixed stops along Cairo's Nile front. The number of river buses is to be raised to 20. There is surprisingly little resort to bicycles and motorbikes. Both of these types of locomotion seem to be confined to delivery boys and are really involved in the transportation of goods rather than people. By far the

Delivering bread—Midan Talaat Harb: CBD.

most rapidly expanding means of transportation, with the exception of the private automobile, is Cairo's taxi fleet.

This phenomenon is at least superficially paradoxical in that the *metier* or taxi driver and owner is as deeply immersed in crisis as the public transportation system. In early November 1971, most of Cairo's taxi drivers went on strike, an event of some rarity in any profession in revolutionary Egypt. An alleged minority among their union members had decided upon the strike to protest the arrest of a few drivers who had refused fares. In turn the taxi strike provoked the arrest of some 200 more drivers whom the Minister of Interior depicted as having disrupted crucial communications flows in wartime—the implicit charge was sabotage whether voluntary or involuntary.

The strike, which could in no way be hidden from the populace, brought to light many of the weaknesses and strengths of this growing profession.

The basic plight of the taxi driver is, on the one hand, continually rising operating costs and, on the other, fares that have been unchanged since 1950. The base rate for all those years has been an initial six piastres (ca. 15¢) on the meter, three piastres per kilometer, and 12 piastres for each hour of use. On a typical run of one kilometer, the cabby might make 11-12 piastres (25¢). Over the same 20-year period the cost of gasoline, spare parts, and above all the purchase price of the car itself have soared. A locally manufactured Fiat 1100 carrying three passengers is worth LE2000 with meter (ca. $5000) and a five-passenger Mercedes diesel LE3500 (ca. $8500). Most cabs are driven by hired drivers who take 25 per cent of the daily income while the owner, who may own several cabs and drive occasionally himself, receives the rest and is responsible for the cab's operating expenses. Both owner and driver have a strong interest in maximizing revenues, and one way to do this is to accept only the relatively long-distance passengers and refuse those who wish to go, say, half a kilometer or less. After the strike, taxi owners and drivers were brought together by the Arab Socialist Union and they agreed to a so-called "Charter of Professional Honor" whereby they promised not to refuse fares and to make a special effort to be accommodating during rush hours, which is precisely when many cabbies like to rest their machines. The Charter quickly became and remained a dead letter.[6]

Can money be made operating a taxi in Cairo? There is no lack of passengers, probably over half a million a day for the combined fleet of Giza and Cairo, which has now reached 16,000 units. During rush hours and in the summer when droves of Arab tourists come to Cairo there is a distinct lack of taxis. But that begs the question. Some experts are convinced that owner-driver cabs are on the whole a losing proposition when depreciation of the vehicle is taken into account. For the Fiat 1100, the net annual loss might be as much as LE100.[7] However, one interested party, Adil Gazarin, Director of the Nasser Motor Company which manufactures the Fiats, claims that they should make a net profit of LE221 per year.[8]

The truth of the matter seems to be that under a certain set of conditions the operation of taxicabs becomes a relatively attractive investment, and that set of conditions is becoming applicable to a growing number of Cairenes. First we might note the striking growth in the cab fleet over the last 13 years. In 1960 there were 4,235 taxis in Cairo. That number rose slowly to 4,600 in 1965. But in the ensuing years there was a "cab explosion" so that the fleet reached 7,405 in 1969, 10,000 by 1971, and 11,303 in 1973. In addition, about a quarter of the cabs circulating in Cairo's streets are registered in Giza, and their number in 1973 stood at 4,665, up from 3,500 in 1971. The total fleet, then, is currently about 16,000 strong, and there are at least 18,000 registered drivers. This growth is surely an indication that something is going right with the taxi business.

One thing that is going right is the increased demand, which is not a simple function of the city's population growth. Rather, it reflects the growing proportion of the city's population that must move about daily, and the consequent discomfort and inadequacy of the public system. The cab can even be competitive in cost to the bus. Some commuters must change buses two or three times and pay a new fare for each change. Three people with the same destination might be able to take a cab in relative comfort for no more than their combined bus fares.

Demand is by no means the whole explanation. In 1965, after which year the cab fleet began to grow rapidly, the Egyptian economy entered into a long depression brought on by the Yemeni war, reaffirmed by the Six Day War, and in which Egypt is still plunged. Inflation, fixed wages, and economic stagnation made it increasingly difficult for Cairenes to make ends meet. Even the relatively well-to-do felt the pinch. A common stratagem, for the educated above all, is to hold down two jobs in order to create a second source of income. But the second source might be as "fixed" as the first. In this situation investment in the purchase of a cab became relatively attractive. I met a young intern from Kasr el-Aini Hospital who, with his brothers, owns three Mercedes which they all occasionally drive after their regular working hours, and farm out to hired drivers at other times. All three brothers earn more from their cabs than from their jobs for which a university education was an initial requirement. Bigger cats with more money to invest own small fleets of cabs which are driven exclusively by hired drivers. As long as they keep their equipment new, each unit can make good profits. As a machine wears down, it can still be sold at considerable profit to the substantial number of desperate men who are willing to risk making money off a dying machine.

Good and new equipment is essential to the cost equation. One owner-driver of a Mercedes diesel, four years old, told me that he nets LE100 a month and is on the waiting list for a Fiat 1500. He drives 14 hours daily (7 A.M.-3 P.M. and 6-12 P.M.) and takes Fridays off. A general estimate in which I have some faith is that normally functioning cabs bring in on the average of LE5 per day. An owner may expect to make LE100 a month at a time when a good civil service salary would be LE30. Even hired drivers can do well in the system. If they take in LE4 in fares in one day, LE1 goes into their pocket. Several of these drivers have told me that they earn LE30 per month. The economic pinch of the last eight years has made the taxi business a relatively remunerative affair, and the fleet has consequently nearly trebled. But the new breed of owners, who are not real pros, are precisely those who husband their equipment by keeping their cabs off the streets during rush hours, or by driving them less during the summer when people want them more.

The losers in the system are the owner-drivers or hired drivers stuck with overaged machines. They are ground mercilessly by high maintenance costs, long periods of disability, and a very high initial investment. Until 1960 there was a law applied that forced the retirement of any taxis over ten years old. In that year, importations of foreign cars were severely limited so that the cab fleet could not be renewed. As a result the law was no longer applied. In 1971 Cairo's fleet of 10,000 had 2,500 cabs that were at least ten years old. The fleet included more than 34 different makes with variety and age being closely associated.

The average Cairo cab covers about 300 kilometers a day (250 kilometers a day in the summer) and the entire fleet a total of over three million kilometers a day. Again on the average, the cab is carrying passengers for only about 150 out of those 300 kilometers, cruising the streets empty for the rest of its daily rounds. This exacerbates the traffic congestion in Cairo out of all proportion to the cabs' numbers. The slow meanderings of the cruising cab, the abrupt halt in mid-traffic to pick up or disgorge passengers, and the impromptu rest and repair stops just about anywhere inevitably snarl traffic. The day of the strike in November 1971, traffic experts watched in astonishment at the uncharacteristic order and regularity that were restored to traffic flow in the city.[9]

The Cairo cabby is an understandably ornery sort, behind the wheel 14 hours a day in some of the most chaotic traffic conditions imaginable. That he in the aggregate makes a generous contribution to this chaos is of little comfort to the individual cabby who seeks to protect an enormous personal investment if the cab is his own, or to reach a certain daily revenue if he is a hired driver. In both instances the cabby may find it preferable to avoid rush hour hordes or the hottest hours of the day. With the major advent of very large numbers of Arab tourists to Cairo the problem has been further complicated. Most tourists—Kuwaitis, Saudis, Libyans—come *en famille* and for relatively long stays. Frequently they do not have private automobiles with them but are wealthy enough not to have to resort to public transport. The Arab tourist is a choice target for the taxi driver. With them he can negotiate special fares above the metered rate, or rent his vehicle by the hour. The upshot is that the cabby more than ever may be tempted to shun the local citizenry and to refuse passengers. When he feels he has earned enough or simply wishes to rest his machine he places a yellow bag over the meter on the outside of the cab, indicating that he is off duty. A recent cartoon depicted a cabby in bed, a yellow bag over his head, refusing the attentions of his wife.

Growing just as rapidly as the taxi fleet is the number of private automobiles. In 1962 there were 32,891 private cars registered in Cairo. By 1969 that figure had nearly doubled to 64,836, and in 1973 had shot up to 104,000. In recent years about 10,000 cars have been registered annually. These figures do not include the tens of thousands of private automobiles in Cairo's streets that are registered in Giza, Qalyub, and other provinces. It is safe to assume that during the day there are probably 200,000 private vehicles circulating in Cairo. Some of the growth can be accounted for by sales of locally manufactured Fiats, but untold numbers of automobiles have been brought in from outside through various maneuvers and paid for in hard currency. (It is said the Egyptian pound is the strongest currency in the world: an Egyptian going on a trip abroad is allowed to take with him only LE5, but when he comes back he brings in a Mercedes.) The former Minister of Economy, Abdullah Marzipan, reported that in the period 1968-1972 33,000 foreign automobiles had been brought into the country under "shady circumstances."[10]

The private car is obviously a great prestige item and measure of economic and social standing. The Nasser Motor Company, which in 1969-70 was able to produce only 2,500 automobiles, nonetheless announced plans in 1971 to start production of a

"People's Car" which would cost "only" LE700 (ca. $1800). The average per capita income in Egypt is about LE76. Production was to be set at 25,000 units a year, but so far the plan does not seem to have materialized.[11] It is important to remember that the city itself can hardly help but it does have ambivalent attitudes toward the dilemma of private versus mass transport. Cairo's single largest source of local revenue comes from fees on private automobiles. In 1969 that source brought the city LE3.2 million.

When it is realized that Rome, for instance, contains over 1.5 million registered private automobiles, Cairo's fleet seems positively miniscule in comparison. Indeed, the city's frequent traffic jams and generally slow-moving and haphazard traffic flows are not the result of the number of vehicles in the streets but of their nature and handling, the habits of pedestrians, the ignorance of the police, and the various uses of street space itself.

We have already noted a few things about street use: buses disgorge and load up in the middle of the street as do taxis which also cruise slowly and whimsically in the search for fares. Pedestrians habitually walk in the street itself although there is

A quasi-medieval traffic jam—motorized vehicles are overwhelmed by pedestrian and animal traffic.

Everything in the street: taxis, carts, pedestrians, and the sweet potato vendor.

Midan al-Tahrir with its elevated footbridge.

Street use: cars, etc., on the sidewalk, people in the street.

well, without doing such visual violence to the city's squares. To have dug down, however, would have entailed ripping up large chunks of telephone and electricity cables, water mains, and sewage pipes that converge at these points in a nexus so complex that most municipal agencies are terrified at the thought of touching them. So the pedestrian hordes are herded aloft, frequently against their outspoken will, by determined policemen. As one pedestrian bargains (I've got to catch that bus) with the policeman, ten others slip gleefully out into the traffic. A man with a severe limp appears, his face contorted in pain, the policeman motions him up to the walkway. "Can't do it, my ankle hurts too much." The policeman relents, the man hobbles across the main thoroughfare and sprints like a rabbit after his bus.

Basic driving rules seem to be ignored equally by drivers and policemen. It is virtually impossible to predict what the Cairene behind the wheel is going to do. Making turns, parking, keeping to the right, signaling, and some uncategorizable maneuvers are matters clearly of some mystery. The average policeman, probably not being a driver himself, is not sensitized to obvious abuse of driving rules or even common sense. Moreover, the Cairene is impressed only by de facto situations. The de jure doesn't interest him. The light is red only if there are too many cars coming across with the green to allow a quick crossing of the intersection. A one-way street is one way only if a car is coming from the opposite direction. A stop sign is never a stop sign. Most police acquiesce to the *fait accompli* for they are forced to bargain to apply a rule, exchanging curses and blandishments with possible offenders, while tens of others take the opportunity to violate the rule the good officer was seeking to uphold. The policeman's pragmatic approach to his job is to try to keep traffic moving even if a few rules are violated in the process. Towards this end policemen will even help push stalled or disabled vehicles to get them going or out of the way.

In sum, Cairo's drivers, whether at the helm of a bus, taxi, car, or army truck (with which the city is afflicted in untold numbers) are capricious and unpredictable, creating traffic problems worthy of far greater numbers. One thing is predictable, the use of the horn. Most drivers regard this as the most essential piece of equipment on their cars, and it is clear that as such it does not serve primarily as a warning device but as an identification. The Cairene's absent-minded beep-beeping acts as a

ample sidewalk space in the city. The problem is that sidewalks are used for anything but pedestrians: they serve as convenient car parks, space for sidewalk vendors, barbers, newspaper stalls, vegetable and fruit carts, garbage dumps, auto repair and body workshops, etc. Sidewalks are most definitely not for walking. The street is, thus further slowing the general movement of traffic by a clutter of human bodies. So serious had the problem of the intermixture of pedestrian and motorized traffic become in Cairo's main squares that a series of elevated walkways are being constructed (the first two at Tahrir and Falaki Squares) to get the people up above the traffic flow. The result is an aesthetic disaster but a definite boon to the average driver. It had been contemplated that underground walkways could have served just as

The baker's delivery van.

kind of sonar system indicating his presence and position to other similarly beeping vehicles. If a Cairene doesn't hear you, he cannot see you.

Most of the motorized equipment in Cairo, even when relatively new, functions poorly. The quality of gas, the lack of spare parts, the variety of cars and trucks, the lack of expertise among mechanics, lead to the rapid deterioration of the vehicle. Cairo's traffic moves slowly and smoggily because of low maintenance standards. This is a blessing for the pedestrian in the street who can cope with relatively slow-moving objects and who is likely to inflict as much damage upon the vehicle as himself in the event of a collision. But Cairo's streets are filled with other slow-moving vehicles whose numbers appear to be growing as fast as those of taxis and private cars: these vehicles are animal-drawn carts.

It is one of the ironies of modern, burgeoning Cairo that as this city grows and ostensibly modernizes, its traditional modes of transportation grow apace. Around 1870, a century ago, Cairo's vehicular traffic consisted of 174 water carts, 1,675 carts for goods, 400 privately owned passenger carriages,

and 486 passenger carriages for hire.[12] Today in Cairo one finds 60-80,000 animal-drawn vehicles (*'arabia karo*), using horses, mules, or donkeys, and involved predominantly in the movement of goods.[13] In its various forms—flat-bed carriages, mounted bins, bakery vans, butchers' tumbrels—animal traffic is omnipresent in Cairo's streets, and this fleet probably hauls more goods daily than the 8-9,000 trucks operating in the city. The 5-6,000 tons of household garbage is collected and hauled daily by a fleet of 1,500 donkey carts, whereas the city itself commands only about 300 trucks for hauling refuse. The city's warehouses almost invariably distribute their goods—bricks, paper, cement, plaster, crated goods, beverages—on horse-drawn, flat-bed wagons. The big fruit and vegetable wholesale market at Rod al-Farag calls upon some 20,000 carts a day to haul its produce to various sectors of the city. One may add to this traditional transport the thousands of pushcarts involved in gathering, salvaging, and retailing operations of all kinds, mobile restaurants and soup kitchens, the municipal sweepers' green iron push-bins, and the old-fashioned horse and carriages (*'arabia hantour*) that still ply Cairo's streets.

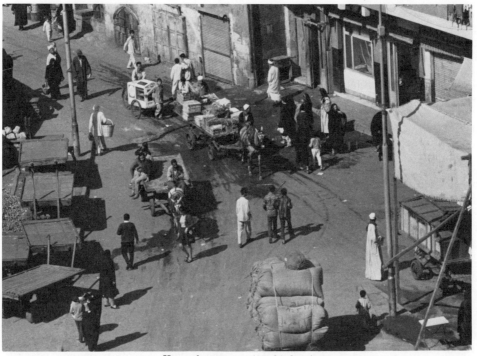

Horse-drawn carts (*'arabia karo*).

Only 20,000 of these vehicles are licensed; the rest simply appear in the streets and no one challenges their right to do so. This expansion may be a reflection of the rural exodus to Cairo, representing an activity into which migrants, who would be otherwise unemployed, can integrate themselves with relative familiarity. In fact, city officials see in the strict licensing of animal-drawn vehicles and pushcarts a means to discourage migration to the city.

In the meantime such traffic, although partially zoned away from some sections of Cairo, is to be found almost everywhere. Carts clutter the streets, slow traffic, are loaded and unloaded wherever the driver judges it to be convenient. There are several proposals before the Governor for stricter zoning regulations and for discouraging the traffic altogether by moving all warehouses and wholesale markets to the outskirts of the city at distances that would make it prohibitive to use animal-drawn vehicles in hauling goods. Still, one wonders if the city can offer any feasible alternative to this crucial element in the movement of things around the city. Animals and carts cost very little in comparison to trucks, motorcycle-carts, and pickup vans that

would be the only practical alternatives to the existing system. Moreover, all the essential elements in the traditional system—drivers, animals, and wagons—can be easily maintained, repaired, or replaced, in sharp contrast with any motorized vehicle.

In sum, one finds in Cairo's streets a hodgepodge of lopsided buses, meandering taxis, streams of pedestrians, over 100,000 private automobiles, plodding donkey– and horse-carts, pushcarts, mobile restaurants, trolleys, trams, garbage carts, and street sweepers. The sidewalk becomes parking lot, recreational facility, dormitory, and workshop. The result is the transportation crisis of a poor city in a poor country, with dung in the gutters and smog in the air.

Naturally, many responsible Cairenes have thought seriously about solutions to these problems, but like solutions to all of Egypt's other problems, the price appears too high. As a consequence, stopgap or utopian measures are sought. One city official pointed out to me that only 12 per cent of Cairo's surface is taken up by street and parking space "whereas it is generally acknowledged that a city must devote at least 25 per cent of its surface to such purposes." That may be true for a country with a high standard of living and a massive private automobile fleet, but will Cairo ever attain the one or sustain the other? Should not the city move toward the development of a rational, pervasive, and dependable mass transit system that would be better suited to the needs and incomes of the city's commuters and that would spare the city the plague of the private automobile?

Some people are only too happy to endorse the mass transit motion, but from where, they rightly query, will the financing come? Once again the war, the really big crisis, overshadows the city's problems and leaves it no alternative but to hang on grimly.

For some optimists final solutions, like the light at the end of the tunnel, are constantly within sight. Five years ago, Minister of Transport Ali Zein al-Abdin announced a three-phase solution to the problem: (1) extend existing means of transport to "lance" the crisis; (2) establish within three years new electrical lines for trolley buses and rapid trams; (3) the final solution would seemingly emerge by itself but would probably include the building of Cairo's first subway.[14]

The only practical step taken at that time was to import the two-section buses for long-distance lines that can haul 200 passengers at a time. The easiest way out has remained the importation of new equipment which, in the end, simply puts more cumbersome vehicles in streets that are already too choked to permit easy passage to the existing fleet. Even extending existing tram lines or building new ones may bear a high opportunity cost for, despite their superior handling capacity (60,000 passengers per hour as opposed to 8,000 for a bus), they are slow, take up a relatively vast area, and are expensive to operate and maintain.[15] As in the past, the official response to the crisis is to import. Three hundred fifty new buses are to be in Cairo's streets by October 1973.

Other perennial solutions involve the reorganization of the movement of people and of traffic flows at the macrolevel. Inasmuch as these solutions usually involve large engineering projects and substantial cost outlays, they tend to be popular with concerned ministries and construction firms. We have mentioned the construction of the steel footbridges at Tahrir and Falaki Squares. At the same

time a major new bridge is being built from Dokki on the west bank to the heart of Cairo on the east. Its terminal points are as yet unclear, but the notion of extending it as a sort of elevated highway to the big square in front of the railroad station is being discussed. If that is what is ultimately done, it will be dumping yet more vehicles into Cairo's most congested square. The bridge will also facilitate westward expansion in Giza, a process that city planners want to discourage rather than encourage.

A third engineering project is to extend the Helwan (southern) metro line to the "Kubry Limun," again adjacent to the main railroad station. At the same time a northern metro line from Shubra al-Kheima to Ain Shams and eventually to Kubry Limun would be developed as well.

The most grandiose engineering scheme is that of the Cairo subway. This plan has been kicking around since 1954 and if it were started today would not be completed before 1980. French consultants first studied this project soon after the Free Officers came to power, but the cost estimates—one million Egyptian pounds per kilometer for simple construction—appeared prohibitive for a project that must have seemed something of a nonessential bagatelle at the time. As the transportation crisis deepened, cost estimates grew proportionally. Another French mission returned in 1963, followed by English consultants in 1964 and then Japanese and Russian. In 1968 minimal cost estimates were LE3.5 million per kilometer.

At present the French are back on the scene through a consulting firm (SOFRETU) which has completed a feasibility study on an initial project for a north-south line, 20 kilometers long, that could be extended to 34 kilometers to cover the entire north-south axis of the city from Shubra al-Kheima to Helwan. Current cost estimates are not being published, but as long ago as 1968 the generally accepted price tag was LE200 million for construction costs and equipment. It was also estimated that the project would take eight years to complete.

Any project that big is sure to whet appetites of interested parties—such as the Ministry of Transport, public sector construction outfits, and foreign consultants—who would be likely to get a piece of the action. Likewise the Cairo Transit Authority would welcome the project because of the

The typical clutter of Cairo street traffic—Ataba Square.

evaluation of London's underground, one of the most developed in the world with 408 kilometers of track serving all parts of the city. Yet it handles only 675,000 passengers [presumably per day] while other means of public transport carry 3,198,000—i.e., the underground handles about 20 per cent of the load. Cairo, with 40 kilometers of subway and assuming London's ratio, would only handle about one-twentieth of the city's daily passenger load.) Given this likelihood, it seems unwarranted to invest LE200 million, much of it in hard currency, in a project that will deal with such a small part of the problem.

Ashmawi, and others, are looking for short-term, less costly alternatives. For instance, for a few million pounds Cairo's existing road system could be substantially upgraded. Sidewalks could be cleared, particularly in downtown Cairo, of auto repair shops and street vendors. No parking zones could be strictly enforced in conjunction with the construction of multitiered parking structures along the city's edges. In fact, Ashmawi was able to incite the city's authorities to enforce no-parking rules the length of Sharia al-Azhar. Thereafter transit time of this major thoroughfare was reduced from over ten minutes to under three. Another practical step would consist in the strict zoning and gradual replacement of animal-drawn vehicles as well as in a moratorium on the licensing of additional vehicles and handcarts. With pedestrians off the streets, carts out of most of them, private cars parked away from the downtown area, and street surfaces upgraded and maintained, there would be vast scope for the expansion of the bus fleet and the creation of conditions for the more efficient use of units in service now.

A factor that Ashmawi believes has greatly complicated Cairo's transportation problems has been the attempt to scatter government ministries and agencies throughout the city and in Giza, and, more important, the establishment of new government cities, especially Medinat al-Nasr. The latter was intended to be a self-contained unit with civil servants living in close proximity to their place of work. But even if the project had been adequately equipped with schools, clinics, shops, and recreational facilities—which it was not—the planners should have realized that civil servants do not select their residence with reference to their place of work. They may rather look for a fairly permanent home in a convivial residential area, or continue residence in rent-controlled apartments, logically

subway's superior hauling capacity, as long as someone else pays for it. It has become commonplace to hear members of the city's Popular Assembly or the national parliament say that the subway is the only possible solution. Yet there may be less costly and less grandiose schemes that would be more effective in meeting the transportation problem.

Dr. Saad al-Din Ashmawi, for one, has tried to put the project into focus. First, he notes that even the project's most enthusiastic supporters do not believe its effects will be felt before 20 years. But Cairo's problems clearly cannot wait that long. Second, on the assumption that the system will include at most 40 kilometers of line, it will handle no more than one-twentieth of Cairo's daily commuter volume. (This estimate is derived from an assuming that their place of work may change periodically during their careers.

Consequently, most of the people who work at Nasr City commute to it, and because it is far from the downtown area, they must commute a long distance. The city is faced with extending more and more public transport lines to this area. Moreover, the governmental units that have been transferred there are inevitably involved in moving personnel and correspondence back and forth between relevant ministries and agencies in the city's heart. On the strength of this experiment, careful thought should be given before any other such projects are launched.

Finally, Ashmawi suggests that if the notion of the subway cannot be done away with entirely, then the best alternative would be to develop existing above-ground metro lines and to link the southern and northern systems. [16] As we have already noted, this is precisely what the Cairo Governorate is proposing to do. In addition, the city's Governor, Hamdy Ashur, is not eager to pursue the subway project. He favors instead the construction of elevated roadways as a substitute. [17] The one factor that has not been the subject for much discussion is that the development of the subway, or of above-ground metros, or of elevated highways *along the city's north-south axis* will tend to confirm the city in its present growth patterns. Like the new bridge from western Giza to downtown Cairo, the reinforcement of transportation in the north and the south will encourage urban expansion into the agricultural zones that lie in both directions. Most everyone is agreed that this is undesirable and that the city should expand in an east-northeasterly direction into desert lands. Developing mass transit systems in that direction could have given a practical incentive to that kind of urban expansion.

Without the financial means to think big, the city ineluctably falls back on stopgap measures and on programs for which it is not likely to be responsible. The Committee for Public Services in the city's Arab Socialist Union secretariat has recommended the formation of a Transport Planning Organization for the city. It suggests that no new industrial projects be established in Cairo and that the public sector reorganize its working day to mitigate rush hour traffic problems. None of these measures, however, even if adopted, could be applied through municipal auspices.

The Governor, likewise, has not been without ideas. After a 13-year absence, Governor Ashur recently visited Beirut for a conference and was struck by the relatively sane movement of traffic in a city that should suffer more than Cairo from congestion. He determined, rightly or wrongly, that one of the keys of Beirut's success is the use of so-called "service" taxis that ply fixed routes at fixed fares filling up and emptying as they move along. Cairo is now to be endowed with a similar system. By the fall of 1973 there are to be 200 "service" cabs following ten routes throughout Cairo. The single fare is to be 12¢. The project is to be financed through private Arab capital and the taxis leased to the city.

Other measures that have been decided upon are the introduction of a single 5¢ bus fare, thereby eliminating first-class tickets. First-class space theoretically takes up a third of bus seating, but on the average the sale of first-class tickets has brought in only 9 per cent of total ticket income. The Cairo Transport Authority itself is to be divided into six units corresponding to the city's major geographical divisions and a special unit for repairs and maintenance. The rationale behind this move is not entirely clear.

Cairo's transportation problems are by no means insoluble and the major stumbling blocks may be people's habits, confused municipal jurisdictions, and the lack of overall planning and policy, rather than lack of money. Any solution that costs a lot is probably doomed to failure, but there are several intermediate measures that can be taken at relatively low cost if the necessary coordination is attained. Yet, as pointed out in Part I of this series, there is no planning agency that has binding authority over all of Greater Cairo (or even over Cairo proper), and the city's transportation crisis, like all its other problems, involves not one but three Governorates (Cairo, Giza, and Qalyub) with their separate administrations and institutional jealousies. For the foreseeable future, therefore, the growing pressure upon all means of transport will continue at a rate sufficient to offset the annual palliatives and emergency measures that the city introduces to meet the situation. Cairo's millions—animal, human, and vehicular—will be on stage, and the show will go on.

Buses and Subways to the Rescue

The streets of Cairo are ready to accommodate new buses. Indeed fifty buses were put on the streets last July.... Next month we will receive another fifty buses from Iran...and our agreement with Iran guarantees two hundred buses arriving at a rate of fifty a month. They will come with spare parts and they will be continuously maintained. We have the requisite workshops and mechanics.... In addition we will repair two hundred of our four hundred disabled vehicles. Every day we have about one disabled vehicle that we can't repair for lack of spares. Also we'll get one hundred and fifty buses from other agreements. That means that in six months there will be five hundred and fifty additional buses in the streets of Cairo; in other words Cairo's transportation crisis will be substantially relieved. Why are you smiling? You talk about a crisis of confidence and lack of credibility?! No, I promise this.

Mahmud abd al-Hafiz
Governor of Cairo, interview
with Mahmud Murad, *al-Ahram*,
September 17, 1974

A decade ago Cairo's total bus fleet was 1,033 units, and we may presume that in any one day 20 to 30 per cent of them were disabled. The effective fleet of 900 or so units handled nearly 600 million passengers a year. Three years later the fleet had grown to 1,375 units, or about 1,000 operative buses, accommodating 775 million passengers. When Cairo's governor, Mahmud Abd al-Hafiz, gave his interview, the bus fleet had stabilized at about 1,200 units, but a few months later the disabled rate was so high that only 600 buses were in the streets (Mohammed Basha, *al-Ahram*, November 7, 1974). Meanwhile the passenger load hovered around the billion per annum mark. Although Iran has been nowhere near as prompt as expected in shipping its 200 Iranian-assembled Mercedes buses to Egypt, a fair number of new units have appeared on the streets since 1974. Gamal al-Din Sidqi, the Minister of Transportation, announced (*al-Ahram*, February 6, 1976) that despite the addition of 460 new buses from various sources to Cairo's fleet during 1975, the net effect had only been to increase available units from 1,200 to 1,262. He noted that for all Egypt, public means of transport had not increased over the last decade while passenger loads had

doubled. The transportation crisis for Cairo's eight millions has therefore not been eased.

Some readers may recall our earlier glimpse into the dramas of physical movement in Cairo.[1] The subject ineluctably draws one back to it for at least three reasons: its undeniable vividness, the fact that any resident of Cairo spends a good deal of time coping with it, and the fact that the transportation system encapsulates a far broader range of elements inherent in large, poor, growing urban agglomerations striving at worst to survive, at best to become modern cities.

That latter term—modern cities—in its very value-ladenness in some ways goes to the roots of Cairo's problems. It is doubtful that 95 per cent of Cairo's inhabitants have any vision of what they would like their city to be in five, ten, or 20 years. Where they may be able to manipulate some small corner of their environment, and perhaps even hope

---

1. John Waterbury, *Cairo: Third World Metropolis, Part II: Transportation* [JW-10-'73], Fieldstaff Reports, Northeast Africa Series, Vol. XVIII, No. 7, 1973.

to improve it, they can scarcely be more than passive in the face of what others do and plan for the city's future. What Cairo *should* be and become is the aggregate brainchild of the city's well-off, the national technocracy, and university and governmental elites. There is of course considerable overlap among these categories. Whether Cairo *can* become what they feel it should become is the fundamental question, for if it cannot, then these elites are tilting at windmills.

More prosaically, upper-class Cairenes in their various occupational and policy-making garbs, cling stubbornly to the aspiration of making Cairo a prosperous replica of Paris or London, mainly, one suspects, because their own tastes and styles of life could be most comfortably accommodated in such a setting. There are voices increasingly heard today harking to the Cairo of the 1930s and 1940s when the streets were clean (at least where the elite moved about), when cinema seats were free from fleas and the floor about them devoid of mounds of expended pumpkin seeds, when one could walk down Suleiman Pasha without being jostled into the street, when there was a far richer cultural life revolving about the opera and ballet, when public parks and avenues were well planted and well-kept. Those days are dead and gone, and Cairo has in most ways become geographically democratic and massively plebeian. There are no restricted zones and the city with all its meager amenities is freely used, and overused, by all (save the myriad of sporting clubs, the last fragile havens of the upper-middle class). The city has taken a frightful battering in the democratization process, one that can only be exacerbated if its population grows to 16 million by the year 2000 as seems all too likely.

What remedies do the city fathers envisage to salvage their realm? If one pieces together various kinds of policy recommendations over recent years, a set of implicit assumptions seems to emerge. Cairo as a whole cannot be saved; there are too many people and too little money. To meet city housing and transportation needs, even at modest levels, not to mention health, education, recreation, entertainment, and work opportunities, could absorb all the nation's resources—at least if present approaches to dealing with these problems are to be maintained, and few seem prepared to question them. This presumably being the case certain segments of the population and areas of the city must be left to their own devices, benign neglect being the watchword unless some really major crisis blows up.

Containment is a parallel strategy but one that raises all sorts of mutually contradictory policies. Cairo must stop growing, it is said. Migration to the city must be checked. This can be done (although no one has tried) by strict control of entry, dependent on proof of work, expulsion of unlicensed tradesmen and other parasitic workers, denial of housing to the unemployed, etc. Simultaneously, one must stop the construction of new industries around Cairo, shift some government services to other areas and, in general, limit economic opportunities in Cairo. Any notions along these lines have already been demolished by the countervailing force of Egypt's economic open-door policy whereby foreign businessmen, bankers, company headquarters, Egyptian staff, consultants, lawyers, partners, and perhaps one day manufacturing concerns all coagulate in and around Cairo for the obvious reason that communications and access to decision-making centers are relatively less difficult here than elsewhere. The reopening of the canal zone cities may ease the pressure on Cairo and has probably already pulled some population away, but Port Said, Ismailia, and Suez City are not likely to have more than a combined population of three million in the year 2000. This would make some, but not much of a dent on Cairo's expected growth. While recognizing the objective need to contemplate them, plans for building new cities and settlements in the desert appear well beyond Egypt's present financial and planning capacities. Put bluntly, this writer believes that Cairo cannot be contained over the next 25 years and suspects that the city fathers recognize that fact as well.

It is not in the cards that Cairo's population, any more than Egypt's, is going to become prosperous in the foreseeable future. The city's average per capita income may be twice the national average of LE 100 (roughly US$200) annually, but then again the actual skew in distribution, because of the heavy concentration of high income earners in the city, is more pronounced than elsewhere. The well-to-do probably constitute no more than 10 per cent of Cairo's total population, yet in many ways the future of the city is being decided in light of their own psychological and material needs. For them, the priority areas concern good housing, good schools, good medical attention, private means of transport, the ability to consume more or less conspicuously, and opportunities for distraction. These priorities are shared for the most part by the important, growing expatriate communities: a large diplomatic corps, the personnel of several regional UN agencies, new foreign banks, business consultants, oil companies, hotels, management consultants—and last but obviously by no means least, the Peninsula and Gulf Arabs.

Since October 1973 and Egypt's self-proclaimed victory in its campaign against Israel, the lid has been taken off the upper-middle classes in Egypt whose appetites had been contained during the preceding 15 years. Some policies were fairly expeditiously implemented. Import-export trade was gradually liberalized so that urban markets became well supplied with foreign luxury items. Effective restrictions on the movement of foreign exchange in and out of Egypt fell into abeyance. Egyptians resident abroad were permitted to bring back, each time they returned, virtually limitless amounts of personal effects, appliances and gifts. The upshot has been a booming market in high-priced consumer goods—symbolized by and concentrated on Cairo's notorious Shawarbi Street—where customers abound for 7-Up at $1.20 a can, Lanvin perfumes, Italian knitwear, and Ronson lighters. Ostentatious consumption is now blatant, but so far, rather than sparking sharp cleavages between haves and have-nots, one encounters instead the upwardly mobile semi-haves. The privately owned, owner-driven taxi cab is a bellwether. The swingers in this profession now increasingly equip their Fiats, Skodas, and Mercedes diesels with cassette tape decks and twin speakers to regale their passengers with Umm Kalthoum and Farid al-Atrash.

Another kind of enclave consists in the development of a private system of quality education, to be capped one day by a university that charges substantial fees. Good (and bad) private primary and secondary schools have long been a feature of Cairo, but as standards have steadily deteriorated in the public system, the pressure to create a "quality" fee-based system has become pronounced. So too the pressures to establish high quality and inevitably high-priced medical facilities and hospitals. Foreign Arab pressure in this latter sphere, combined with the capital this source can provide, may prove determinant.

So far what we have been describing is a tendency toward the development of functionally specific urban enclaves, where the functions, heretofore largely under public supervision, are gradually privatized and priced right out of the general market. Public services, grossly underfinanced, are left for the poor. One senses the development of enclaves in other spheres. As speculative Arab, and some Western, capital comes into Egypt, it moves toward the urban real estate and tourism sectors. If some of all the various projects adumbrated are actually achieved, Cairo will, within ten years, be endowed with several tourist "complexes," replete with shopping centers, theaters, restaurants, auditoriums, conference centers, and probably ice-skating rinks, and business office buildings, centrally air-conditioned, wall-to-wall carpeted and "Musaked" (Umm Kalthoum?). Luxury housing, at prices that New York and Paris struggle to rival, has preceded the tourist-business surge. The Pyramids Road has pioneered in nightclubs but other areas of the city are sure to follow. Ninety per cent of Cairo's population does not participate in any of these enclaves. For the rest that do, the private automobile is the crucial link to get the kids to school, hubby to the office, to the club, the doctor's, the party at the neighbor's, the nightclub near the Pyramids, the beach cabana at Alexandria—and the vehicle itself must conform to certain standards.

The Private Automobile

In 1966-67 only 1,400 private cars were imported into Egypt, rising to 15,000 in the early 1970s with a sharp drop under the Sidqi government in 1972. Since then imports have increased dramatically: over 18,000 in 1974 and probably over 35,000 in 1975. Locally assembled Fiats have hovered between 5,000 and 8,000 each year. These imported vehicles are probably worth on the average LE 3,000 apiece on the local market. If, as seems likely, something like 40,000 vehicles are imported during 1976, their value, modestly estimated at LE 12 million, would represent about a third of the Cairo Transport Authority's annual budget, and a good deal more than that Authority's annual deficit. Yet Cairo's private automobiles haul only about 10 per cent of the city's daily passenger load, while public buses and trams haul about 80 per cent with taxis making up for the rest. Not all the 40,000 private automobiles to be imported into Egypt will wind up in Cairo, but the bulk will.

In October 1975 there were nearly 140,000 private vehicles of various kinds circulating in Cairo's streets, including about 21,000 taxis. Over 4,000 additional taxis started plying Cairo's streets during 1975 alone. These figures do not include private automobiles and taxis registered in Giza, jurisdictionally separate from Cairo Governorate but very much part of Greater Cairo's traffic patterns and problems. In fact Cairo's streets are being ripped apart and its traffic disrupted (temporarily it is said) in the name of the city's western, southern, and northern suburbanites.

A crucial set of options has confronted Cairo's planners for at least 20 years, to wit whether or not to place primary emphasis on designing the city's road system and use of space to cater to the private automobile or to stress the development of a public mass transit system. The latter option has not been ruled out. With the exception of emergency measures, however, most investment has gone into servicing the needs of the private automobile owner, that is a group which, with its dependents, represents no more than 5 per cent of the city's total population.

The most visible sign of this policy has been the construction of the October 6 (formerly Ramses) Bridge across the Nile. The bridge was started six years ago and has not yet been completed. Its major function will be to provide an additional artery for the middle-class residents of Cairo's western suburbs—Giza, Doqqi, and Agouza—many of whom make up to two round trips a day between place of residence and place of work in and around the central business district. The bridge roadway will eventually be extended further west, to the Pyramids, along an axis that is greater Cairo's fastest growing middle-class area. One might note that it is also in these suburbs that Gulf and Peninsula Arabs reside by preference, and their sizable population of temporarily imported vehicles has placed further stress on the west-east route into downtown Cairo. Similar to the October 6 Bridge will be a second one, further south, linking Imbaba and Zamalek to central Cairo. This will be an elevated passenger vehicle bridge, suspended over 26 of July Street, running from Zamalek and across the Nile over the existing bridge. Both the October 6 Bridge and its future cousin will disgorge traffic into central Cairo, but also will probably link up in a single elevated roadway that will run on a northerly axis along Ramses Avenue out to

Heliopolis, another middle-class residential area. Also under construction is a "belt" highway encircling Greater Cairo, the first leg of which will link Heliopolis and Nasser City in the North with the upper-middle-class suburb of Ma'adi in the south.

What can be drawn from all these projects? First that they will serve the essential function of moving about the well-to-do among their places of residence, work, schooling, shopping, and distraction. Second, while public means of transport can use these arteries, they were not devised with any integrated plan for the development of public transport in mind. Third, their initial impact (six years old in the case of the October 6 Bridge) has been to disrupt traffic in central Cairo and Gezira Island because of the construction itself. Fourth, they constitute an added incentive to the proliferation of private vehicles in Cairo.

Another straw in the wind is the growing phenomenon of two-car families. In the past this might occur if the husband were a high-ranking government official with a public sector car at his disposal for public business while the wife and children used the family car (and sometimes the government car as well). Now, regardless of the availability of a public sector vehicle, finding two private cars per upper-middle-class family is not uncommon. It is said that before new residential and business buildings are approved for construction, they must provide for parking for their tenants. The goal, within present thinking, is reasonable but will also entail increasing construction and subsequent rental costs as well as the use of more urban space for the private automobile.

For some time now various of the city's elite have pointed out as a sign of backwardness that Cairo devotes only 12 per cent of its surface to roadways and parking facilities, whereas most "modern" cities average 25 per cent. This alleged paucity of surface space is blamed for Cairo's formidable congestion, but these analysts overlook the fact that Cairo's vehicular fleet, public and private, is only about a tenth of that operating in "modern" cities. Still one hears of plans for multistoried parking garages, central district parking lots, and tourist-office complexes of high rises which will free urban space from existing slums. One such complex is projected for the Bulaq slum area on the fringes of the central business district, and one can

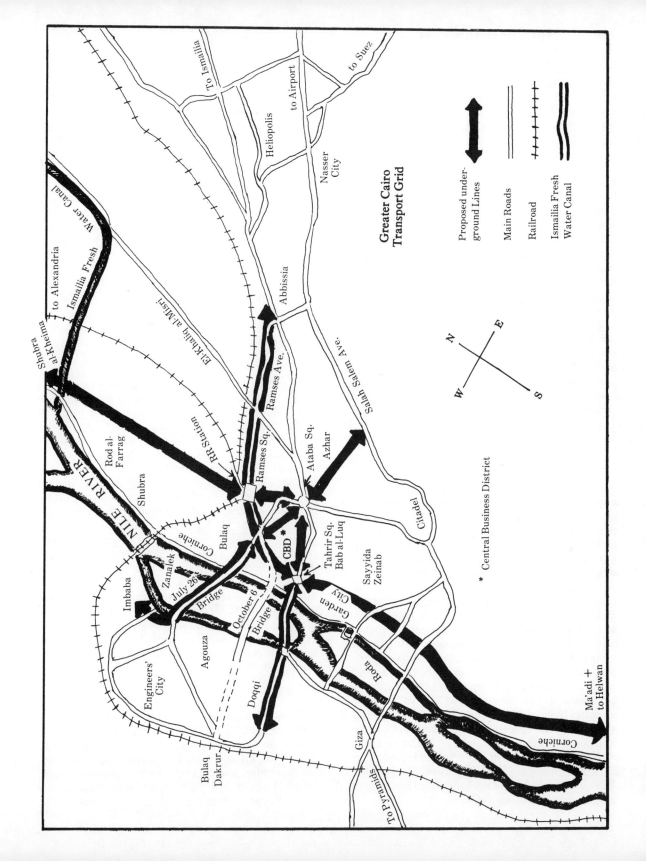

Greater Cairo Transport Grid

Proposed under-
ground Lines

Main Roads

Railroad

Ismailia Fresh
Water Canal

* Central Business District

only suppose that the slum dwellers will be moved out along the city's northeast axis to places like Mataria where they will either be brought back downtown by the already overburdened public transit system or left to their own devices.

A final anomaly in this vein is the price of high octane gasoline. Under International Monetary Fund pressure, and in order to qualify for the Fund's special oil facility, Egypt was obliged, in the name of conservation, to raise the price of a liter of high-octane from 6.8 to 8 piastres, i.e., from about US$.14 to $.16 or the equivalent of 63 and 72 cents a gallon. This is far below prices in most European countries, dependent as is Egypt on gasoline imports. The price rise may do little to curb gas consumption among the well-to-do. Just as stiff import duties have failed to curb the influx of foreign cars, so too increased gas prices will not discourage the private car driver. Those who may be hurt are small businesses, haulers, deliverers, etc., who use high octane because the "regular" gas is so full of impurities that it reduces vehicle life considerably. It may also affect the taxi fleet by eliminating marginal units, especially those that are overaged and driver-operated. It will do nothing to make public modes of transportation more attractive.

Perhaps within a certain set of values this approach to Cairo's transportation problems is realistic. Here, as elsewhere, conventional wisdom tells us that no force can stand between modern man and his compulsive drive to acquire and keep a private set of wheels. Pragmatism dictates that this drive be accommodated, not thwarted. Here, as elsewhere, the possibility that this drive is cultivated if not created by automobile manufacturers, and that individuals might react differently if attractive alternatives were held open to them, is dismissed as naïve and utopian. But in Cairo, unlike elsewhere in the developed world, no one is prepared to spell out how any more than an infinitesimal proportion of the urban population will ever own a car. Even if, as Egypt's national planners hope, per capita income quadruples to LE 400 by the year 2000 (itself a *very* ambitious target), who could afford an automobile? At last reckoning, in 1973, the local Nasr Motorworks talked of producing a "people's car" that would sell for LE 700—and to the best of my knowledge not even that unit is actually being built.

Buses and Subways

It would be inaccurate and unfair to argue that the opinion of the well-off and the experts is homogeneous in respect to these problems. Voices have been raised in several quarters, not least among which is the Ministry of Transport's, calling for the development of the public transit system before all else. Even Ahmad Osman, Minister of Housing and Reconstruction and whose contracting company Ahmad Osman, the Arab Engineers, is building the October 6 Bridge and other roadways, allegedly vetoed a plan put forth by the Japanese to build a suspended monorail through the heart of Cairo. Whatever its benefit to the road construction interests and whatever its prestige, glamor, and positive impact on Nippo-Egyptian relations, there was a general perception that this expensive project would simply compound rather than solve existing problems.

There is, moreover, considerable concern as always over the bus fleet. It was announced in April 1976 that Egypt would import 1,600 buses from the United States, most of which would be destined for Greater Cairo. The deal is worth $50 million and is to be financed by a U.S. loan to be repaid over 30 years at 2 per cent interest with a ten-year grace period. Laudable as this endeavor may be, it does not get round the fundamental problem of putting additional buses into streets that are too congested to handle them. Egyptian traffic experts have pointed this out for years. The most heavily traveled routes along the northeast axis, where demand for public transport is greatest, cannot make sensible use of new units because traffic is already nearly at a standstill during rush hours. The same holds for lines coming from or going to Helwan in the south and anywhere that a line crosses one of the Nile bridges. New buses can pick up additional passengers, but may further reduce the speed at which they are moved.

While frantically and expensively importing new buses, Egypt's domestic bus industry has stagnated. In 1965-66 Nasr Automotive Industries assembled 1,155 buses. Production then dropped off markedly, seldom rising over 400 units a year. In 1974 about 360 buses were assembled locally while Egypt contracted with Iran to import 200.

One of Cairo's 1,000 operating buses, with resourceful passengers.

The dilemma of the local assembly is repeated throughout Egyptian industry. A good proportion of the bus components must be imported and paid for in foreign exchange, and exports of assembled buses have been so low that the company's foreign exchange needs have not been covered. Requests for foreign exchange have not been fully met by the Treasury, which is beseiged by similar requests from all quarters. Production has fallen as the importation of components dropped, and per unit costs rose. Thus Egypt has found itself obliged to contract for a large foreign exchange financing package to import the buses that the local industry could not produce for want of foreign exchange. Any integrated plan to develop Egypt's mass transit facilities should and must depend on local industries—the potential size of the market and scale of the industries would warrant such a policy. Massive importation to meet those needs puts off the day of drafting an integrated approach.

The other major token of concern about the bolstering of the mass transit system is the apparently firm decision to move ahead with the construction of an extensive underground network. Variants of this project have been studied since 1954. In that year a French firm, RATP, carried out a feasibility study, followed by another French group, SOFRETU, in 1964. Sir William Halcrow of the United Kingdom also carried out a feasibility study in 1964. It was followed by Overseas Technical Cooperation Agency of Japan in 1966, a Soviet group in the same year, and the Greater Cairo Planning Commission in 1969. In 1971 SOFRETU was called back on the job. By this time, what had been regarded as an expensive and incidental urban facility had become recognized as vital to the city's survival. As the first step in detailing a plan for a Cairo subway, SOFRETU, a technical consulting and management outfit affiliated with the Paris Metro company, conducted a comprehensive survey of all aspects of Cairo's transport system, including pedestrian movements. This three-volume study is at once the most detailed description of physical movement in Cairo as well as a plan for the rationalization of all modes of urban transport until the year 1990.[2]

This study provided a wealth of material and several important conclusions, some of which, bordering on the obvious, needed stating. The capacity of Cairo's road system, for instance, is adequate; its organization is what leads to congestion. The level of physical mobility in Cairo is relatively low because of the youth of the population (30 per cent under ten years old by their estimates), low mobility of women, insufficient transport, and low incomes. About 30 per cent of the population undertakes at least one trip a day of one kilometer or more. In other words the public transport system is in crisis at relatively low rates of population mobility; if these accelerate toward more "normal" levels, the crisis will get out of hand unless other measures are taken. The basic assumptions of the study are:

(1) the population will reach 13.6 to 14 million by 1990

(2) mobility will increase from 0.8 to 1 "trip" per inhabitant a day

(3) the share of walking in total trips will decrease from 25 to 13.5 per cent

(4) the number of trips handled by public transport will grow from a daily rate of 3.4 million in 1971 to 8.9 million in 1990—or a rise from 60 to 64 per cent of all trips (including walking). The share of private cars will grow from 15 to 22 per cent of all trips.

Not surprisingly, the least costly and most efficient solution to the growing problem is, in SOFRETU's opinion, the construction of an underground grid combined with immediate measures in traffic management. Specifically, the study counsels against the "American solution" whereby the free mix of public and private vehicles is allowed by enlarging road surfaces and reserving special lanes for public transport. This solution is unsuitable for Cairo for it wastes space and would probably require the demolition of substantial areas of the central business district. Nor would a package of traffic-management measures, separating public from private transport, zoning the city for certain types of traffic, implementing one-way street systems and designated parking areas, suffice in and of itself to deal with the situation. Rather, SOFRETU advocates a combination of traffic management, including a gradual restriction of access of private vehicles to the central business district, expansion of existing tram and urban rail lines, and the construction of an underground.

The logic of the underground is compelling. It utilizes little or no surface space, and it can haul far more passengers per hour than any rival mode of transportation. The underground could carry 60,000 passengers per hour in either direction as compared with 20,000 by tram, somewhat less by bus (especially during congested rush hours), and only 2,000-2,500 by private vehicles. If one takes only Cairo's northern district, where the daily flow is 416,000 passengers (in 1971) in both directions, the actual strain on existing mass transit modes and the potential benefits of the proposed underground lines can be readily seen.

Cairo's basically linear physical alignment lends itself to the underground. A major north-south axis, with a minimum of spurs, could put the bulk of Cairo's eight million inhabitants within walking distance of a subway stop. If linked with existing surface urban railroad lines—that running from Bab-al-Luq to Helwan and the northeastern al-Marg line, 30 kilometers of underground tracks could complete the system. This should be compared with Paris' 172 kilometers, New York's 385, London's 387, and Moscow's 412. The 1973 cost estimate was LE 4.5 million per underground kilometer, exclusive of rolling stock. The timetable works out as follows:

(1) 1974-1979—rationalization program of existing facilities.

a. bus priority lanes (none so far established)

b. one-way street systems to hinder cross-artery movements of private vehicles and

---

2. Arab Republic of Egypt, Ministry of Transport, *Greater Cairo Transportation Economic Study* (May 1973) RATP-SOFRETU, Paris: Vols. A, B, C.

to speed up movement of public transport on main arteries (begun in some areas)

c. hierarchical road network for central business district (not yet begun)

d. improvement of traffic termini at Ramses, Tahrir, and Ataba Squares (not yet begun)

e. restriction of private car use in certain zones (not yet begun)

f. make Ramses and Gala' Avenues one-way streets in opposite directions (partially implemented)

(2) By 1980—linkage of Helwan and al-Marg railroad lines by 4 kilometers of underground track from Bab-al-Luq to Ramses Square. The al-Marg line would be electrified. A total of 41 kilometers of surface and underground track would be integrated. Concomitantly 44 kilometers of double tracked train lines would be developed.

(3) By 1985—the northern industrial district of Shabra al-Kheima would be linked underground to Tahrir Square.

(4) By 1990—underground lines across the Nile to Bulaq Dakrur and to Imbaba would be completed.

Altogether there would be three major underground lines meeting in the city center, totaling 62 kilometers, and a tram and railroad network with 110 kilometers of separate track. Costing, in 1973 prices, would be along the following lines:

SOFRETU estimates total outlays at 1.5 per cent of GNP over the 17-year period. If the entire system were not implemented, total investments in public transport would still be on the order of LE 242 million. The additional investment needed would be LE 4.6 million per year with a rate of return of 13.6 per cent per annum. For a number of reasons, some of them political, the underground project has been approved in principle by the Egyptian government, and SOFRETU is undertaking the engineering studies for the first 4.9 kilometers of underground track running from a point south of Bab-al-Luq on the Helwan line to Kubri Limun next to the railroad station. As part of several bilateral deals arranged during reciprocal visits of high-ranking French and Egyptian officials, consummated by state visits of Giscard d'Estaing to Egypt and Sadat to France, it seems certain that France will finance a good part of the foreign exchange component of the project. So Cairo may one day have its underground.

But this system, like all others involving Cairo's transport, will be ineffective if imposed on an unprepared populace. One shudders to think of the legions of Cairo's transport users, the same ingenious and indefatigable hordes that brought us the leaning buses of Cairo, the flying dismounts, the rooftop squat, and other feats of legerdemain and *leger de pied*, coping with the system the Paris Metro people propose. First, they recommend that fares be three-tiered, based on distances of up to five kilometers, between five and 15, and over 15. Also there would be first and second classes so that the well-to-do might take the underground to work rather than their private cars. Passengers will purchase tickets either from a ticket machine, where they put in change and push buttons for distance

	1974-80	1981-85	1986-90	
		Costs in LE 1,000		
Regional Underground	77,038	10,112	16,770	103,920
Urban Underground		54,409	69,927	124,336
SUBTOTAL	77,038	64,521	86,697	**228,256**
Trams	51,150	8,250	5,700	65,100
Buses	1,240	13,136	13,350	27,726
TOTAL	129,428	85,907	105,747	**321,082**
Yearly Average	18,490	17,181	21,150	18,887

and class, or from a ticket window. All tickets must then be validated by a stamp machine that prints the exact time on the ticket. Tickets will be valid after punching for 45 minutes for short trips, an hour for medium, and 90 minutes for long trips. There will be roving inspectors to spot-check tickets and to slap stiff fines on passengers in the wrong class or riding beyond authorized distance or time. Access to platforms will, as in Paris, be controlled by gates that close automatically when a train approaches the station, or when the crowding on the platform becomes excessive.

It may work in Paris, but it will not work in Cairo unless there has been a revolution in mass conduct and civic pride. Most Cairenes are illiterate and, anyway, unused to automation. Those ticket-issuing machines will be battered senseless in short order (like automatic doors on buses which are generally simply ripped off) for how can one expect the harried passenger to fathom class, distance, validation, and to have anything approximating the correct change? The ticket window with a human being of sorts behind it is at least familiar to our underground novices, but if he is not asleep, absent, making tea, or calling his girlfriend, the place will not be Cairo.

But let us assume he is there, alert, responsive, helpful. Is SOFRETU unaware of one of Cairo's (all Egypt's) basic unwritten laws? Any constructed space must be filled to at least double its theoretic capacity. Underground stations will be no exception and they had best be constructed with the onslaught in mind. What will happen to those automatically closing gates as the train approaches the platform? Initially they may mangle a few vanguard elements, but the sheer weight of numbers will neutralize them sooner or later. Could it then be that a kind of Dantean drama will develop in the caverns below Cairo's streets, a faithful replica of the sunlit derring-do above? The mass swarms onto the train, it groans forward, hands grasp open doors, open windows, the roof, other hands, and the overladen reptile slogs forward into the next tunnel come what may. Or, some safety-conscious official may stop the beast and demand that the outriders get off. It wouldn't happen, but even if it did the official's well-being would be up for grabs, and pandemonium, enough to paralyze all the other 40 kilometers of track, would be the result. What does one do, call the cops? They are too humanitarian and have to ride the bus or metro

anyway, and besides their adversaries are, nine times out of ten, likely to be army recruits. And the roving inspectors? Roving is hardly what they will be able to do, but if they are of the breed of *kumsaris* who collect bus fares, they will get their take. But someone will have to pay them more than $30 a month before they slap stiff fines on anyone (short of putting the stiff fine in their pockets) or simply taking a bribe at half the rate.

Even if these problems of local culture, habit, and volume can be ironed out, the underground might still amount to no more than an expensive palliative. If surface traffic and transportation patterns are not drastically reformed, underground transport will merely take some of the edge off above-ground crises. In desultory fashion measures are discussed, and occasionally implemented, to improve traffic flow in Cairo's streets, while other measures are eroded or abandoned. The strictly enforced no-parking regulation along al-Azhar Avenue, about which I wrote in 1973, is a distant memory. The latest of a seemingly interminable series of "crash" programs to ease the traffic problem has been announced, in April 1976, resting squarely on the shoulders of United States traffic experts. With the United States committed to disbursing $750 million in various forms of aid to Egypt in 1976-77, the role of these experts may be no more than to soak up funds that must, in one way or another, be spent. One wishes them luck in all their endeavors.

The Other 90 Per Cent

While plans waft above their heads and, sometime in the future, tunnels burrow below their feet, over seven million Cairenes take their licks on 1,200 buses, 114 electrified trolley buses, and 230 trams. If they feel affluent they can try to beat a Kuwaiti or Western businessman to a cab.

A Cairene has his dignity, and walking is not dignified. Walking, in the author's opinion, is the most efficient means of movement in Cairo, although it does expose one to homicidal bus, taxi, and army truck drivers and, increasingly, the powerful monsters that wealthy Egyptians and Gulf Arabs gun around town. The days when the pedestrian's greatest threat were 15-year-old Austins and Fiats with 200,000 miles on them are gone. But these predictable dangers do not detract from the fact that for anything under four kilometers the rational man or woman should stay on foot. Cairenes are not convinced by this logic. They persist in chasing buses further than they will ride them. To abandon a bus, even when it is on fire, is an act of cowardice and capitulation. Men, women, and children will grunt and sweat to push a stalled bus and then chase it to get on. They will sit or hang stoically through more major breakdowns in hope that some miracle will bring their steed back to life.

One of the most graphic manifestations of the Cairene's dogged persistence in such matters was witnessed on January 1, 1975. The day is memorable on several counts. Matters started early in the morning when the electrified Bab-al-Luq-Helwan train line broke down for the umpteenth time. This is the line that carries thousands of workers daily to and from Helwan's heavy industrial plants. The main cable on the line is 15 years old and allegedly cannot be replaced without paralyzing the whole line, and there are no alternative means to get the workers to Helwan. So, periodically, the old cable gives out. Such was the case on New Year's Day 1975, although the authorities later claimed that the line had been sabotaged by leftists who wished to prevent workers from reaching their factories so that they could claim a general strike had taken place.

Indeed, the next day hundreds of "leftists" were arrested, but to the best of my knowledge none was ever convicted of sabotage or any other of the accusations leveled at them. What did happen is that Bab-al-Luq station and the surrounding streets filled with thousands of workers for whom there were no trains. The crowd grew angry and began chanting slogans about the high cost of living and governmental indifference.[3] Riot police were dispatched to close off the area, but over a thousand workers broke free, soon joined by street ruffians and urchins, and all headed toward nearby Tahrir Square, the heart of the city. Armed with bits of brick and stones they rushed into the square bringing traffic to a halt and pelting any vehicles that failed to stop. From the suspended walkway around

the square civil servants and others on their way to work observed the spectacle and commented variously on the rights and wrongs involved. It was at this point that a standard right-listing Cairo Transport Authority bus came slowly down Qasr al-Aini Avenue toward the square, the driver, bean sandwich in hand, oblivious of what was going on. As he drew within range a barrage of bricks and stones crashed into the bus's windows and body. In what seemed a matter of seconds the bus ground to a halt, the driver vaulted through the left front window, and the rest of the passengers, both in and outside the bus, old women, children, men in suits or gallibias, scrambled, lept, and wriggled through all available apertures, leaving the recently life-laden vehicle an empty, shattered lifeless hulk. The agility of the mass exit was wondrous—even the Egyptians on the walkway were impressed. As wondrous was the fact that after the rioters had been dispersed, what seemed to be the bus's original passengers (minus the driver) began to materialize, sniffing hopefully around the carcass that it might once again breathe.

Since last I wrote about Cairo's street theater, the old bus fleet has been somewhat spruced up, although, as we noted earlier, not expanded. The big Spanish Pegasos buses have been in Cairo's streets for three years now (by standard reckoning they have covered about 270,000 kilometers so far and are already halfway through their theoretic life) joined in the summer of 1974 by Iranian Mercedes buses. For those who can get inside them, the additions may have improved matters, but for the outriders the situation is more hazardous. The new buses seem to have fewer hand holds, bumpers do not protrude sufficiently to get a good foothold, the body is more resistant to the shaping of grips. In short, out-riding has become more of a challenge than ever. *Al-Ahram*'s photographers engaged for a while in a can-you-top-this contest on bus riding. The capper, a photograph that launched a thousand jokes, showed a bus with a not unusual rooftop population, but in their midst was a sweet potato vendor with his big portable oven and chimney.

Even the newer buses have begun to succumb in various ways to the habits of the riders and drivers. Ahmad Bahgat (*al-Ahram*, October 17, 1974) wrote:

---

3. *Ya basha, ya bey, mish 'arifin akl wal-gazm xamsa giney:* O basha, O bey, we don't eat and shoes go for five pounds. *Ya batl al-'ubur, fayn al futur?* O Hero of the Crossing (i.e., Sadat), where's our breakfast?

I want to describe for the Minister of Transport and the Director of the Transit Authority a scene that could have been sold to the Italian or American movies for several million pounds, or enough for the Ministry to import all the buses it needs. Here's the scene: a huge red bus approached the bus station, moving at a strangely slow speed, the driver looking as if he were out for a pleasure or a stroll.... The *kumsari* (commissaire, or ticket men) jumped off the rear with some tile and broken stones in his hands. Just as the bus drew in front of the station, the *kumsari* knelt in front of the wheels. You think he's going to commit suicide. Not at all, my friend. With extraordinary dexterity he put the tiles and stones under the front wheels of the bus and it came to a halt. This was the bus's brakes! This new bus had gone out without any brakes!... Aren't we a people of genius, even if a bit unlucky?

Another observer suggested that the Ministry of Tourism could capitalize on Cairo's buses. After all was not the leaning Tower of Pisa a symbol by which all the world knows Italy and which attracts millions of tourists? Why could not the leaning buses of Cairo serve a similar purpose?

"Don't you know what the building is? That's the Ministry of Transport." (Note sweet potato vendor on roof.) Salah Jahin *al-Ahram*, March 12, 1975.

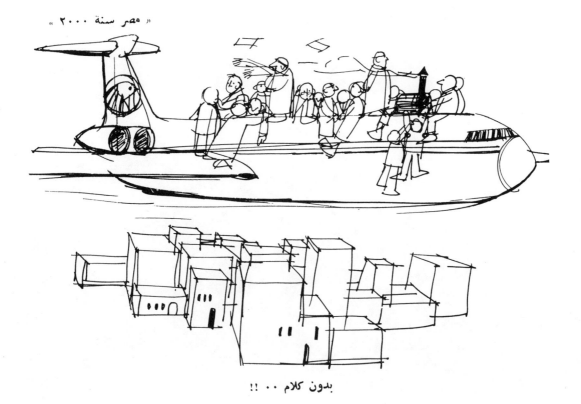

« مصر سنة ٢٠٠٠ »

بدون كلام ٠٠ !!

"Egypt, the year 2000." *Ruz al-Yussef*, n. 2439, March 10, 1975.

Conclusion

Every year that Cairo's authorities spend in trying to deal with the problems of physical movement by conventional means will put effective solutions that much further out of reach. Traffic flows and systems must be designed with the nonaffluent 90 per cent of the city's population in mind. This majority will not be one that will accede to the private automobile. Cairo is not unique among Third World cities in this respect, but the problem is that the experience of cities in developed countries, as well as those countries' experts, do not have much tested advice to offer the poorer cities. I am reasonably convinced that Cairo could offer most of its citizens decent, efficient public transportation and develop traffic patterns that would help those who either must or prefer to walk or ride a bike or motorbike. The Nile, for instance, determines Cairo's linear design, yet it is underutilized as a means of moving people. There are only eight river buses operating now but there could be far more

frequent service utilizing craft with greater capacity all along the north-south axis. During peak hours river buses and the underground could handle a substantial portion of the flow without putting any additional vehicles into the streets, and, indeed, taking a good many people out of them. Other measures would involve a revolution in the application of regulations on no-parking, one-way streets, and the zoning of animal-drawn vehicles to certain streets and certain nonpeak hours of the day. Most of downtown Cairo should be totally denied to private vehicles, or at least parking should be restricted there. This would allow for a freer flow of public transport and the possibility of widening sidewalks to permit more pedestrians.

Sidewalks and road surfaces should be reserved for pedestrians and vehicles. Vendors, sidewalk tradesmen and repairmen, cafes, and so forth should be relocated. This would have the simple effect of allowing pedestrians to walk somewhere other than in the street, and it would permit buses

Why are these people smiling?

to pull alongside the curb to pick up passengers rather than doing it in the middle of the thoroughfare. There should be designated taxi stands throughout the city where passengers queue rather than the random meandering and mid-stream passenger pick-ups that are currently the norm. Freed to some degree of parking (triple-parking in downtown Cairo is a common phenomenon) private vehicles, pushcarts, animal-drawn vehicles, and cruising taxis, the main arteries, streets, and sidewalks of the Cairo business district could revert to the functions for which they were designed. At that point bus and taxi lanes and other traffic manage-

ment measures might have some impact. Simultaneously, the city must recognize that public transport is the top priority and must be prepared to invest large sums in the purchase and upkeep of municipal equipment. The Transit Authority may continue to lose money, but the city, as a result of a far more efficient movement of people and goods, stands to make a considerable net gain.

All these measures presume a marked transformation of citizen behavior and the rigor with which laws and regulations are applied. Bus and taxi drivers (not to mention private citizens and Cairo's number one menace, Army vehicle drivers) must be adequately trained and held accountable for violations of traffic regulations. Traffic police must be sufficiently well-paid and their general working conditions improved enough to have an incentive to apply regulations. They must be instructed in the logic of these regulations so that they know when and where to apply them. This is decidedly not the case now. Moreover, tickets for public and private traffic violations should be issued, and if possible, paid on the spot. As it is, traffic police simply write down a violator's license number and nature of violation and when it comes time to renew the vehicle's registration one pays the cumulative fines without knowing for sure if one actually committed the violation. The policeman gets a percentage of whatever he reports. This system may earn the traffic department some money but it does little else. On-the-spot tickets to violators followed by withdrawal of licenses would be more effective if combined with periodic spot checks on licenses and car registrations. (There are few enough vehicles in Cairo that this would not be difficult, yet in five years of driving here the author has never once been asked to show his license or registration papers.)

The general citizenry might behave more responsibly in their movements if they felt the traffic system was designed for their benefit rather than for that of the well-to-do. A new bus filled to overflowing is no more comfortable than an old one and thus merits no greater respect. A sidewalk covered with private automobiles forces people into the streets where they ignore red lights as blithely as all vehicular traffic. As it now stands civic responsibility has no observable payoff for the average citizen. If Cairo confines its efforts to meeting the traffic crisis by improving conditions for the private automobile, the city risks writing a prescription for future paralysis and intermittent violence.

Housing and Shelter

The most pressing and at the same time the most costly problem facing the city of Cairo is the provision of housing for the city's 5.5 million inhabitants (and over six million in the "Greater Cairo" area). The problem long ago reached crisis proportions, and if, as seems likely, the city's population is somewhere between 12 and 16 million in the year 2000, then the nature of shelter in the Cairo of tomorrow can scarcely be imagined. Vast tracts of Cairo have been for decades, are now, or are becoming slum areas. It is difficult to find a euphemism for this term which I use to encompass extraordinarily high room-densities in substandard, structurally unsound buildings frequently without water, electricity, garbage disposal, and sanitation. Abrams, in his now-classic study, summarized the situation for the developed and the developing worlds: "The slum exists because no nation is able to produce adequate housing at a cost workers can afford. It is the shelter that the industrial age provides for its rank and file. Housing has remained the Cinderella of the Industrial Revolution, and the humble cover to which she has been indefinitely assigned." [1]

One might quibble with Abrams on a few points. In Third World cities like Cairo it is as much the burgeoning ranks of civil servants and service sector personnel as the workers who are unable to afford adequate housing, unless, as in Cairo, there is increasing resort to households in which both husbands and wives work. In Cairo then it is not only the industrial proletariat—a distinct minority of the city's working population (see Part I in this series)—that is relegated to substandard housing. The housing crisis is as serious for educated Cairenes who consider themselves a part of the middle class but are unable to obtain shelter commensurate with their self-image.

Excepting only a handful of people at the top, no one can take for granted access to decent housing. I cannot make an accurate guess as to the number of exceptions, but it is not likely to be more than 200-300,000 Egyptians and foreigners in professions such as law, medicine, and journalism, public and private sector companies, government ministries, embassies, and United Nations agencies. They monopolize the best housing in Cairo and Giza: the island quarters of Zamalek and Roda, parts of Garden City and Qasr al-Nil in the city's center, Heliopolis in the north, the suburb of Ma'adi in the south, the corniche of Giza, the villa cities of Dokki and Agouza, and the Avenue of the Pyramids in the west. These are low-density residential areas of relatively well-kept apartment buildings and villas, dotted with private sporting clubs. In the rest of Cairo quality drops off precipitously. There is still some pretense to former urbanity in the center districts of Abdine and Ezbekia and the slightly more northerly quarters of Sakkakini, Wayli, and parts of Shubra. For the rest, however, the appellation of slum is not inappropriate, and while the quarters vary greatly in age, the style and quality of the residential buildings in them have taken on a certain sameness. The best and the worst among Cairo's buildings fall victim to a democratic patina brought on by dust and overuse that borders on instant decay. Thus the oldest districts, the original Cairo of 1,000 minarets, Darb al-Ahmar, Gamalia, Bab as-Shari'a, Qala'a, Masr al-Qadima ("Old Egypt"), are not, with the exception of the minarets, very different physically from nineteenth century quarters such as Sayyida Zeinab and Bulaq, or from the great northern belt that has been the receptacle for most of the twentieth century rural migrants: Shubra, Sahel, Rod al-Farag, Zeitun, and Mataria.

These latter districts are somewhat more "rural" in appearance than the rest, but the distinction is not of much significance (see map). In all outlying districts and even in some parts of the center city in Bulaq, Sebtia, and Maaruf, there are quasi-villages that have survived the city's advance and have been partially incorporated into it. As the city extends northward into agricultural land, villages and farms around Mataria or Shubra al-Kheima are transformed into dormitories for the city's work force, or way stations for migrants. The same is true for Basatin on the road to Ma'adi, and several villages on the west bank such as Imbaba, Agouza, and Bulaq Dakrur. A third distinct but generally low-quality type housing is to be found in the new industrial suburbs of Helwan (south) and Shubra al-Kheima (north) where the construction of factories and the attraction of labor preceded the construction of low-cost housing which is still grossly inadequate. Finally, one encounters the extensive tomb cities along Cairo's eastern edges which house a considerable squatter population.

It is perhaps one of Cairo's misfortunes that it does not have extensive shantytowns surrounding it like Ankara or Casablanca or Baghdad. Insalubrious as these may be, they offer a solution to their existence through "self-help housing." As John Turner has argued persuasively in several articles, if squatters are given rights to tenancy or occupancy of the shacks and the land upon which they are erected, and if arrangements are made to provide them with low-interest credit and cheap building materials, they generally respond over time by transforming their shacks and huts into solid structures. These in turn are built with labor and "architects" from the squatter settlement itself. The city's overall investment is far less than what would be required for extensive low-cost public housing projects, probably with subsidized rents.[2]

Cairo does not have the luxury of this way out, although the reconstruction of the Egyptian village could be promoted through self-help principles. There are a few shack settlements, particularly in the northern sector of the city, but they provide shelter to a relatively small segment of the city's population. In general, Cairo's ability over the last two decades to absorb a rapidly growing population

Giza and Dokki growing westward into agricultural land.

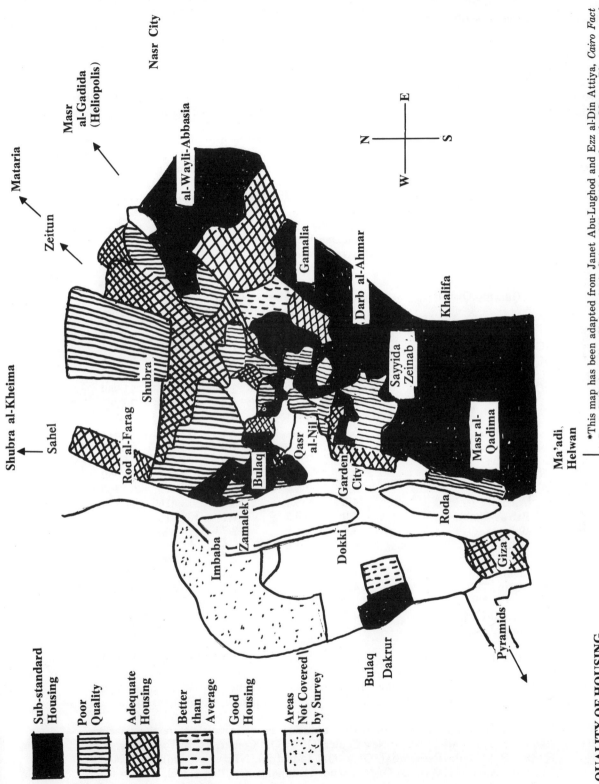

QUALITY OF HOUSING
CAIRO*

Sub-standard
Housing

Poor
Quality

Adequate
Housing

Better
than
Average

Good
Housing

Areas
Not Covered
by Survey

*This map has been adapted from Janet Abu-Lughod and Ezz al-Din Attiya, *Cairo Fact Book*, SRC, American University in Cairo, 1963, p. 262, based on the Master Plan survey of the late 1950s.

into a slowly growing housing infrastructure has been brought about by simply cramming more and more people into or *onto* existing units. This process does, however, reveal some interesting subpatterns.

There are two ways of looking at growing population densities in Cairo, and both speak grimly of the city's present and future. One indicator for which there is relatively ample data is the number of people per square kilometer of municipal space. In 1966 the average city density was 19,953 per kilometer ^{2} and had risen by 1973 to over 23,000. Cairo, by this measure, is more densely inhabited than New York City, despite the fact that the population of the former resides in buildings that seldom exceed five floors. But this indicator does not really give us the full measure of Cairo's density, for much of the city is taken up by streets, parks, nonresidential buildings, factories, shops, schools, cemeteries, and, to no small extent, agricultural land. Looking at Table 1, we find the three

Table 1
Population Densities per Km^2
by Quarter, City of Cairo
1960-1966*

| Quarter (Qism) | Average Family Size | | Qism | No. of Inhabitants per Km² | |
	1960	1966	surface Km²	1960	1966
NC Ezbekia	4.3	4.8	1.8	37,666	37,455
OC Gamalia	4.8	5.1	4.8	29,526	30,419
TC al-Khalifa	4.8	5.0	8.6	18,832	27,403
OC Darb al-Ahmar	5.1	5.3	2.8	53,074	53,989
N Zeitun	4.8	4.9	4.2	23,899	30,987
N Sahel	4.9	5.1	6.2	48,968	60,754
NC Sayyida Zeinab	5.0	5.1	3.5	72,471	78,417
OC Zahir	5.1	5.0	1.9	52,430	54,580
N Mataria	4.9	5.0	67.9	2,368	4,606
SR Ma'adi	4.7	5.0	25.1	2,307	5,589
OC Muski	4.8	5.4	.6	64,115	60,460
N Wayli	4.8	5.1	16.5	18,616	21,774
OC Bab as-Sha'ria	4.9	5.3	1.1	139,210	135,901
OI Bulaq	4.5	4.9	2.7	74,823	74,716
NI Helwan	4.9	4.8	6.4	14,748	31,434
N Rod al-Farag	5.0	5.2	2.7	98,199	104,623
N Shubra	4.7	4.9	7.3	40,549	55,997
NC Abdine	4.6	4.7	1.7	55,864	57,853
NC Qasr al-Nil	3.7	4.1	6.0	7,182	6,764
NR Masr al-Gadida	4.7	4.5	32.3	3,863	5,196
OS Masr al-Qadima	4.9	5.0	10.2	20,807	24,864
CITY TOTAL	4.8	5.0	214.2	15,633	19,592

*From Central Agency for Public Mobilization and Statistics, Director Gamal Askar, "The Population Explosion in Cairo," *al-Ahram al-Iqtisadi*, supplement to issue of December 1, 1972, Table 8. This same source estimates density per km^2 in 1972 to be 23,000 for all of Cairo. The admittedly confusing set of initials before the quarters stands for the following: NC = New Center, OC = Old Center, TC = Tomb City, N = North, SR = South Residential, OI = Old Industrial, NI = New Industrial, NR = North Residential (Masr al-Gadida and Heliopolis are the same), OS = Old South—Masr al-Qadima is the most ancient part of Cairo, its original port and the site of Fustat.

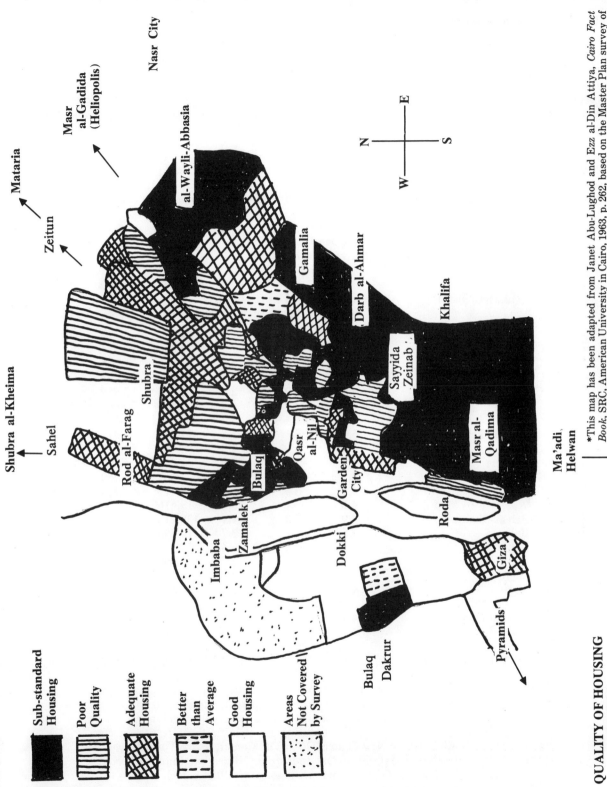

**QUALITY OF HOUSING
CAIRO***

Legend:
- ■ Sub-standard Housing
- ▤ Poor Quality
- ▥ Adequate Housing
- ⊟ Better than Average
- ☐ Good Housing
- ⦂ Areas Not Covered by Survey

N
W — E
S

*This map has been adapted from Janet Abu-Lughod and Ezz al-Din Attiya, *Cairo Fact Book*, SRC, American University in Cairo, 1963, p. 262, based on the Master Plan survey of the late 1950s.

Labels: Shubra al-Kheima, Sahel, Mataria, Zeitun, Masr al-Gadida (Heliopolis), Nasr City, al-Wayli-Abbasia, Gamalia, Darb al-Ahmar, Khalifa, Sayyida Zeinab, Masr al-Qadima, Ma'adi, Helwan, Rod al-Farag, Shubra, Bulaq, Qasr al-Nil, Zamalek, Imbaba, Garden City, Dokki, Roda, Bulaq Dakrur, Giza, Pyramids into a slowly growing housing infrastructure has been brought about by simply cramming more and more people into or *onto* existing units. This process does, however, reveal some interesting subpatterns.

There are two ways of looking at growing population densities in Cairo, and both speak grimly of the city's present and future. One indicator for which there is relatively ample data is the number of people per square kilometer of municipal space. In 1966 the average city density was 19,953 per kilometer ^{2} and had risen by 1973 to over 23,000. Cairo, by this measure, is more densely inhabited than New York City, despite the fact that the population of the former resides in buildings that seldom exceed five floors. But this indicator does not really give us the full measure of Cairo's density, for much of the city is taken up by streets, parks, nonresidential buildings, factories, shops, schools, cemeteries, and, to no small extent, agricultural land. Looking at Table 1, we find the three

Table 1
Population Densities per Km^2
by Quarter, City of Cairo
1960-1966*

Quarter (Qism)	Average Family Size 1960	1966	Qism surface Km^2	No. of Inhabitants per Km^2 1960	1966
NC Ezbekia	4.3	4.8	1.8	37,666	37,455
OC Gamalia	4.8	5.1	4.8	29,526	30,419
TC al-Khalifa	4.8	5.0	8.6	18,832	27,403
OC Darb al-Ahmar	5.1	5.3	2.8	53,074	53,989
N Zeitun	4.8	4.9	4.2	23,899	30,987
N Sahel	4.9	5.1	6.2	48,968	60,754
NC Sayyida Zeinab	5.0	5.1	3.5	72,471	78,417
OC Zahir	5.1	5.0	1.9	52,430	54,580
N Mataria	4.9	5.0	67.9	2,368	4,606
SR Ma'adi	4.7	5.0	25.1	2,307	5,589
OC Muski	4.8	5.4	.6	64,115	60,460
N Wayli	4.8	5.1	16.5	18,616	21,774
OC Bab as-Sha'ria	4.9	5.3	1.1	139,210	135,901
OI Bulaq	4.5	4.9	2.7	74,823	74,716
NI Helwan	4.9	4.8	6.4	14,748	31,434
N Rod al-Farag	5.0	5.2	2.7	98,199	104,623
N Shubra	4.7	4.9	7.3	40,549	55,997
NC Abdine	4.6	4.7	1.7	55,864	57,853
NC Qasr al-Nil	3.7	4.1	6.0	7,182	6,764
NR Masr al-Gadida	4.7	4.5	32.3	3,863	5,196
OS Masr al-Qadima	4.9	5.0	10.2	20,807	24,864
CITY TOTAL	4.8	5.0	214.2	15,633	19,592

*From Central Agency for Public Mobilization and Statistics, Director Gamal Askar, "The Population Explosion in Cairo," *al-Ahram al-Iqtisadi*, supplement to issue of December 1, 1972, Table 8. This same source estimates density per km^2 in 1972 to be 23,000 for all of Cairo. The admittedly confusing set of initials before the quarters stands for the following: NC = New Center, OC = Old Center, TC = Tomb City, N = North, SR = South Residential, OI = Old Industrial, NI = New Industrial, NR = North Residential (Masr al-Gadida and Heliopolis are the same), OS = Old South—Masr al-Qadima is the most ancient part of Cairo, its original port and the site of Fustat.

At home on the roof: Darb al-Ahmar.

biggest districts of Cairo are Mataria (67.9 km²), Ma'adi (25.1 km²), and Masr al-Gadida (32.3 km²). The latter two are upper-class residential areas with a fair amount of unused land still available for expansion. Mataria is a lower-class area extending into the farm land north of the city. Some day it may well reach densities similar to Rod al-Farag and Sahel, taking over the role from these districts of the major zone of absorption of migrants from the Delta. These three districts—Mataria, Ma'adi, Masr al-Gadida—alone account for nearly half of Cairo's total area, and with their low densities depress the average density for the city somewhat artificially.

To avoid distortions of this kind, a far more sensitive measure is that of the number of people per room in residential dwellings. In Table 3 I have tried to construct an up-to-date picture of room densities, although this kind of data is not regularly reported. (I have been obliged to make estimates for 1966 and 1972 on the basis of past ratios. I am reasonably confident that, if anything, my estimates understate the situation.) Over the period 1947-1972 average room densities have risen steadily from 2.0 per room to 3.1. The population of the city in that period more than doubled while

the number of available rooms probably increased by no more than one-third. The gap between habitable rooms and a population growing at 4 per cent per annum is likely only to increase in the future. Cairo, and Egypt in general, can ill afford major outlays on housing as long as the state of hostilities with Israel, and the enormous investments that state entails, remain the dominant feature of Egyptian political and economic life.

Even room densities do not tell the whole tale, and in some ways the housing crisis is marginally less acute than the figures presented so far would indicate. This is because in Cairo there are at least three types of clandestine housing. Because they are clandestine it is hard to know how many housing units are involved. We must simply describe them without measuring them. One form is Cairo's so-called "second city," consisting of roof-dwellers who build huts, shacks, poultry runs, and so forth on the roofs of Cairo's buildings. As long as such structures are not built in brick and mortar, or some other permanent material, they are not illegal and require no building permit. Any attentive visitor to Cairo will notice that they are legion, and in the poor districts of town hardly a

Table 2

Greater Cairo: People and Shelter, 1966*,

Cairo's Parts	Population	Buildings	Housing Units	Families
Cairo Proper	4,232,663	236,362	779,789	847,483
Shubra al-Kheima	172,902	17,437	31,838	32,751
Giza	571,249	38,683	116,235	115,260
Total	4,976,814	292,482	927,862	995,494

*From CAPMAS, *Final Results of the Sample Survey Census*, Vol. II "The Urban Governorates," July 1967.

Table 3

Estimates of Room Densities
for the City of Cairo*
1947 - 1972

Year	City Population	No. of Housing Units	No. of Rooms	People per Room
1947	2,090,064	448,333	1,039,742	2.0
1960	3,348,779	687,858	1,439,158	2.3
1966	4,232,663	779,789	1,559,578 (est.)	2.7
1972	5,200,000 (est.)	860,039 (est.)	1,720,078 (est.)	3.1

*In Egypt a housing unit apparently is any shelter that includes at least one household. Thus there is no fixed number of rooms per unit. A one-room bachelor's flat or a ten-room luxury flat would each be considered a unit. The figures for 1947 and 1960 are fairly reliable and are drawn from the census of those two years. See Janet Abu-Lughod, *Cairo: 1001 Years of the City Victorious*, Princeton University Press (1971) p. 164. For 1966 total population and number of housing units, see Central Agency for Public Mobilization and Statistics, *Final Results of the Sample Survey Census*, Vol. II "The Urban Governorates," July 1967. The number of rooms was derived by multiplying the number of units by two, for in 1960 the average number of rooms per unit was two, down from 2.3 in 1947. Egyptian statistics do not consider the kitchen as a room. For 1972 I calculated the number of housing units on the basis of a report that states since 1960 the public sector has built on the average 3,375 units annually, and the private sector about 10,000, for a rate of 13,375 per year. That may be an overestimate as the public sector has fallen off in the last two years. Once again I multiplied the number of units by two rooms per unit. Note that all these figures pertain only to the city of Cairo proper and not to greater Cairo which includes Giza and Shubra al-Kheima.

roof has escaped their implantation. If there were but one such "housing unit" for half of Cairo's buildings—i.e., about 110,000 units—with five people to a family, well over half a million Cairenes might be living on rooftops. With them is an equally impressive animal population. The combination of the two has led to periodic and futile efforts to clear the roofs of a phenomenon that has pernicious effects upon building safety and sanitation.[3]

Roofscape—Boulaq.

Housing in Bab as Sha'ria.

Another phenomenon of unknown proportions is that of building regular structures without permit, or converting substandard, mainly village housing into urban dwelling units. In Giza to the west and Mataria to the north, for instance, farm land is being built over rapidly, often without permit. For one reason or another such violations go undetected until construction is completed. The city then has the unsavory choice of expelling the tenants, who are thus unjustly penalized, or of acceding to the *fait accompli*. About all the city can do is deny the new premises water and electricity, but that is a hollow gesture if it has been decided to allow the building to remain. A variation on the same theme is the conversion of Cairo's villages into dormitory cities. Bulaq Dakrur lying on the far side of the railroad tracks that constitute Giza's western border is such a village. From a population of 15,000 in 1960, the village now houses 13,000 families or 66,000 people. Almost all of the growth is accounted for by migrants, including some 3,000 who came from other parts of Cairo itself. The village has apparently been partially rebuilt, or simply packed, without much supervision from the Giza authorities. The process has been carried out by the villagers and traditional entrepreneurs and speculators—sometimes the local grocer or scrap metal wholesaler—and despite its dirt roads, rudimentary utilities, and rural appearance, Bulaq Dakrur attracts many because of its relatively low rents and proximity to downtown Cairo only two and a half miles away. The average income per family there is about LE13 ($30) per month which is not dissimilar from levels of lower-middle-class districts such as Sayyida Zeinab.[4]

There are other such dormitory villages in close proximity to downtown Cairo, such as Shirkis and Hakr Abu Duma, or near convenient transportation links, such as Basatin on the Helwan train line or the villages of Mataria on the northern Mataria line. This type of community does share some of the peculiarities of the shantytown. They are integral parts of the city, exporting their working population—mechanics, peddlers, pickpockets, clerks, maids, garbage men, et cetera—to other areas, yet they maintain a distinct insularity vis-à-vis the city. One does not venture into these enclaves with the same assurance as one would in Cairo's older slums. It may be that the villages have attracted somewhat more than their share of the urban underworld of dope, prostitutes, and petty thieves, and, like American ghettos, develop the reputation of a no-man's land. A city committee that visited Shirkis and Hakr Abu Duma in the summer of 1971, as part of a slum clearance project to move their inhabitants elsewhere, got more than they bargained for. The officials found urchins in the dirt streets and alleys, women at the public water pump, men in the street cafes—all sullen, occasionally derisive, and manifestly hostile to the invaders whatever their purpose.

Similar in some ways are the populations of the tomb cities, Cairo's unique contribution to urban housing. The tomb cities lie in a long belt along Cairo's eastern edge, blocked by the Muqattem hills and divided into a southern (Khalifa) and northern section by the westward projection of the Citadel. These areas consist of the mosque-tombs of former royal and princely families, the two- or

The City of the Dead looking north toward new housing at Abbasia.

three-room tomb-houses of the wealthy bourgeois families, and the communal burial houses of certain craft or village migrant associations. Perhaps a mutation of the old Pharaonic notion of making a tomb a home for the dead, the tombs are houses where the relatives of the deceased may come to visit two or three times a year and to live and eat in the company of the deceased. But for most of the year the tombs and adjacent rooms are unused. The cities of the dead had long had a resident population, mostly housed in buildings constructed amongst the tombs. As more migrants have come into the city, and particularly with the influx of evacuees from the Suez Canal Zone as a result of the Six Day War, the tombs themselves have become dwelling places for squatters. In 1960 there were 80,000 people living in the tomb cities, but that number is clearly far greater now. There is no way of knowing exactly how many Cairenes are squatting there, but one authoritative source, Cairo's Governor, Hamdy Ashur, has ventured a figure of one million.[5] It is some indication of the importance of these sectors of Cairo that the Ministry of Education maintains 18 primary schools in and around Khalifa alone.[6]

The organization of economic life in Egypt is officially founded upon socialist principles, and since 1952 the regime has consistently honored in word, and occasionally in deed, an overriding concern for social and economic equity. To promote equity the major capital and productive resources of the nation were placed under state management and ownership in 1961. Egypt's leaders rightly surmised that where resources are scarce and demands

great, equity and efficiency could not be served by leaving the economic sphere to the uncoordinated, profit-oriented concerns of the private sector. The problem is that socialist or state capitalist controls appear to become effective only after some critical level of resource scarcity has been overcome. Conversely, if the state sector is unable to meet a significant proportion of the demands placed upon it, it may in some instances stimulate forms of exploitation that are fully as pernicious as those of the old capitalist sector. Egypt has not been able to overcome the resource scarcity that faced the regime in 1952. Over the last 20 years the regime has fought a holding operation sufficient to maintain but not dramatically raise the standard of living. Rapid population growth and a series of costly external crises have continuously hampered the process of capital formation. Progress has been made in some areas, such as education and heavy industry, but other sectors have necessarily been neglected. Housing is the prime example.

As the density figures already presented would tend to confirm, there is a housing shortage at all income levels in Cairo, but the most blatant deficit occurs with respect to low-cost housing. There are plenty of private contractors who would be more than happy to meet the demand for middle- and high-income groups if only they could obtain the necessary building materials, but under no circumstances would they consider building for the city's poor for they could never hope for a return on their investment. Neither can the state, because of the malfunctioning of the economic system as a whole, contemplate massive involvement in subsidized

Northern sector, City of the Dead.

housing and rents. Consequently most Cairenes are faced with two alternatives: to shoe-horn more people into existing units, or to beg, borrow, and steal their way into housing they cannot really afford. There do appear to be limits to the amount of cramming that can be done, and increasingly Cairenes must surrender themselves to the housing sharks that thrive on the scarcity of housing and the evasion of rent control laws.

The gap between the urgent demands of the city's lower classes and the state's ability to provide housing constitutes Egypt's major urban crisis, far outweighing, in my opinion, the transportation crisis described in Part II of this series. Figures furnished by Muhsin Idris give graphic evidence of the magnitude of the problem (see Table 4). He estimates that housing needs—or, more specifically, the housing deficit—may be on the order of two million units for the entire country by 1975. The state calculates that it costs the public sector on the average LE1,000 (ca. $2,400) to construct a single unit of low-cost housing, so that if all the required housing were of that kind the outlay would be LE2 billion. That would seem a conservative estimate, but even at that level investments in housing would be nearly

the equivalent of all public and private investment in the high-priority industrial sector since 1952.

The Ministry of Housing reports that the 300,000 urban units actually constructed between 1960 and 1970 were distributed in the manner described by Table 5. The private sector is still the nation's major provider of urban housing and its share has been increasing. Another report notes that over the last decade in Cairo, the private sector has been building 10,000 units a year while the public sector provides only 3,375. The same report estimates Cairo's annual housing needs at 62,000 units. This is over twice the rate of 30,000 units per year *for all of Egypt* established in the decade 1960-1970.[7]

Cairo is probably suffering no more from the crisis than any other Egyptian city, but the magnitude of its particular deficit is in keeping with the size of the city. The Cairo Popular Assembly's report on housing cites a cumulative housing deficit of 20,000 units. To overcome this, it is recommended that 2,000 units be built annually. The report also calculates that the city is growing by 200,000 inhabitants a year, and assuming a ratio of five people per unit, *an additional 40,000 new*

New middle income housing—Agouza.

Table 4

An Estimate of Urban Housing Needs in the UAR
to the Year 1975*

Deficit in Urban Housing Units, 1960:	298,000
Needed to meet Crowding (four or more families in a single dwelling):	103,000
Needed to meet the Increase in the Number of Families, 1960-1975:	1,448,000
To meet Relocation Needs:	225,000
To Demolish Unsound Urban Dwellings:	286,000
TOTAL	2,360,000
Units Actually Built 1960-1970	300,000
HOUSING NEEDS	2,060,000

UNITS

*From Engineer Muhsin Idris (Director Greater Cairo Planning Commission) "Problems of Housing and Planning to Meet Them," *14th Annual Conference for Social Affairs*, League of Arab States, Tripoli, Libya (July 3-8, 1971), Vol. II, pp. 77-117 (table from page 117).

Table 5

Distribution of Housing Construction,
1960-1970, by Public and Private Sectors

Period	Public Units	Value	Private Units	Value
1960-64	61,000	LE51,000,000	79,000	LE57,000,000
1965-70	56,000	LE57,000,000	110,000	LE129,000,000
TOTAL	117,000	LE108,000,000	189,000	LE186,000,000

*See *al-Ahram*, July 23, 1972, p. 7.

units each year are required to house them. At least another 20,000 units a year are needed to replace buildings verging on collapse. All in all, the city needs at a minimum 62,000 new units a year. The authors of the report believe that only 16,000 units of the annual total need be in the low-cost category, and hence the responsibility of the public sector. The other 46,000 units of middle- and upper-income housing would be undertaken by the private sector. The annual cost would be LE83 million with a public share of only LE16 million. By contrast we may note that in its budget proposals for 1973, the Ministry of Housing projected public sector outlays of LE30 million and private sector outlays of LE23 million for all of Egypt. As already mentioned, with a rhythm of 10,000 and 3,375 units respectively per annum, the private and public sectors are falling about 48,000 units short of what city leaders feel should be their minimum combined goal.

Unfortunately the crisis does not end there. The Cairo Housing Survey of 1959 (which to my

Table 6

Public and Private Investment in Urban Housing
1970-1971*

Low Cost Housing	No. of Units Planned	Total Investment LE '000
Public Sector	6,270	2,418.1
Private Sector	13,000	13,000.0
Total	19,270	15,418.1
Middle-Income Housing		
Public Sector	2,328	2,769.9
Private Sector	4,064	6,500.0
Total	6,392	9,269.9
Upper-Income Housing		
Public Sector	65	197.5
Private Sector	700	2,000.0
Total	765	2,197.5
Total Public Sector	8,663	5,385.5
Total Private Sector	17,764	21,500.0
Total Projected Urban Housing	26,427	26,885.5

*Egyptian Federation of Industries, *Year Book 1972*, Cairo, 1972, p. 309 (Arabic edition).

knowledge has not been repeated) revealed that there were 130,000 "properties" (*'aqār*) that were structurally unsound and in theory not fit for habitation. The Popular Assembly report, pointing out that the problem has certainly become worse since 1959, estimates that this deficient housing contains at a minimum a half million units, and conceivably 2.5 million inhabitants. The Governor himself has mentioned a figure of 30,000 structurally unsound "buildings," and Mrs. Ulfit Kamil, a member of Parliament, a figure of 127,000 "dwellings." The probable margin of error in measuring this phenomenon does little to diminish its enormity. The city and the government can hardly hope to make a dent in it under present circumstances, and the sense of futility that permeates the housing crisis is reflected eloquently in the fact that the public sector constructed 1,680 units in 1970-71 and only 108 in 1971-72. For 1973, the city requested investments of LE9 million from the Ministry of Housing and received LE3.5 million.

In light of this situation, the Popular Assembly of Cairo made the following recommendations:

(1) Establish a special committee in each major quarter (*hay*) to study its housing problems. It would also supervise the granting of building permits, the allocation of building materials, and the division of plots.

(2) Draw up a master guide to all the city's needs and possibilities for action in the field of housing.

(3) Simplify the building procedures.

(4) Urge the council of ministers to make available sufficient credits to meet the situation.

(5) Deal with the problem of rural migration to the cities.

(6) Encourage the private sector and the cooperative housing societies, making available to the latter state-owned lands. Provide easier loan terms, up to 80 per cent of the value of the property upon which the builder intends to build.

(7) Work to encourage Arab capital from outside Egypt to invest in housing by permitting convertibility of earnings, customs free importation of materials, and a grace period of five years during which no real estate taxes will be charged.

(8) Zone specific areas of Cairo in which furnished apartments can be rented.

(9) Oblige government agencies and departments to give up housing units that are currently used as work space.[8]

As relevant as these suggestions may be, they fail to address themselves to Cairo's most critical problem of substandard, structurally unsound housing and the provision of shelter for the poor. Neither wealthy Arabs nor the Egyptian private sector stand to make money off the poor even if, as some suggest, rent controls are raised and building materials made plentiful. The poor simply cannot pay enough to make an attractive return on a private investment.

The guidelines for low-cost housing in Egypt are premised on two assumptions: (1) that each unit will cost LE1,000 to construct; and (2) that monthly rent for such a unit should not exceed 20 per cent of the monthly income of the household that inhabits it. The Ministry of Housing estimates that it cannot rent well-constructed, low-cost units at less than LE10 (ca. $25) per month with any hope of covering their initial investment. According to these ground rules, the lessee would have to earn LE50 per month in order to pay no more than 20 per cent of his monthly income in rent. The Central Agency for Public Mobilization and Statistics has ascertained that about half Egypt's urban households earn less than LE50 per month.[9] That seems to me a conservative estimate in that I doubt that half of Egypt's urban households earn *more* than LE50 per month, but I am reasonably certain that the poorer half is earning much less than LE50 per month. In a study carried out in Sayyida Zeinab, 75 per cent of a sample of families earned less than LE20 per month and only 4 per cent over LE50. By contrast a similar sample in Masr al-Gadida revealed that 60 per cent of the families earned over LE50 per month, and 27 per cent over LE100.[10] Masr al-Gadida is, however, as atypical of the rest of Cairo in terms of income level and quality of housing as Sayyida Zeinab is typical.

Given this kind of income distribution, private capital will go to Masr al-Gadida and public capital will make a marginal attack on the rest. Even the 16,000 public units recommended in the Popular Assembly's report appear woefully inadequate. Unfortunately I do not have recent, accurate figures on the amount of low-cost housing constructed and managed by the city, but in 1968 the total number of "dwellings" (*masākin*) was 21,642. That number may have crept up slightly. Some of the principal sites are Zeinhum, near Old Egypt, the Workers City at Imbaba, and slum clearance projects in Bulaq (Amiria), Rod al-Farag, and Sahel. Housing is being built at Mataria to absorb people from Shirkis and Hakr Abu Duma. In low-cost housing the minimal rent of one pound per room is charged, and according to former Prime Minister Aziz Sidqi, that ceiling will be maintained over the next five years regardless of the rise in building costs.[11] Until this year there was no provision to set aside a portion of collected rents for maintenance of public housing. In 1973 it was decided to utilize 10 per cent of all rents towards this end. In 1969 rent revenues amounted to only LE606,000, so that the maintenance fund under the new order would not exceed LE70,000 ($180,000). Cairo's public housing projects offer visual testimony to their "benign" neglect.

The public sector has been involved in several other limited housing efforts. One approach that could ease the strain for middle-income Cairenes in their search for housing has been the formation of cooperative housing societies. While Cairo and the Ministry of Housing have experimented with this form since 1953, its impact has been minimal. The coordinating body for cooperative housing is the General Organization for Cooperative Building and Housing under the supervision of the Ministry of Housing. I do not know how many dwelling units may be included in this sector. However, the former Minister of Housing, Ali Said, deploring the lack of activity in this respect, noted by way of example, that the Land Bank had made loans (presumably in 1971) totaling LE13 million, of which the cooperative societies had borrowed only one million.[12] The problem may be that because these societies cater to middle-income groups, they are competing in an area in which the greatest speculative profits can be made. Co-op societies generally do not earn more than 6.5 per cent per annum on their investment (the same rate at which the Land Bank makes building loans) while the return on black market housing can be many times that rate.

Nasr City is an area in which there is a fair amount of cooperative housing. More than that, it is Egypt's first attempt under public auspices to develop a self-contained subcity, although there have been partial precedents. At the turn of the century Heliopolis was planned and developed by Belgian private capital as a totally new residential suburb in the desert land to the northeast of the city. A tram line was built, and the new area fully equipped with shops, schools, theaters and, perhaps most important, an amusement park. Heliopolis has been unquestionably a success, paying back its founders many times over. The more recent residential development of Ma'adi to the south of the city has been equally successful.

Less outstanding has been the Medinat al-Awqaf near Imbaba, built on lands owned by the Ministry of Waqf (religious mortmaine property) and managed by the ministry itself. Other than housing, the project did not take into account necessities such as shops, recreational facilities, and adequate transportation to the downtown area. Within Medinat al-Awqaf is the Engineers City (Medinat al-Muhandissin) which was to be reserved for engineers. Once the housing units in the project had been rented out to engineers, the latter quickly began to sublet or sell their properties at handsome profits as other less conspicuous professionals vied for scarce housing.[13]

Nasr City, under construction for over a decade along the desert fringe east of Wayli-Abbasia, sought to overcome some of these deficiencies by combining residence and place of work in the same area. Various governmental bodies such as the Ministry of Planning, the National Institute of Planning, the Central Accounting Agency, the Central Agency for Public Mobilization and Statistics, were obliged to headquarter themselves in the new city. The objective was to create a truly self-contained unit while at the same time relieving the pressure on downtown transportation, housing, and office space.

It is quite obvious that the project has not been a complete success, even in terms of its own objective of attracting middle-income residents. As noted in Part II of this Report, civil servants probably choose their residence, to the extent they have a choice, on the basis of rent levels, neighbors, recreational facilities, schooling, and likely permanency. A civil servant prepared to overlook the distance from downtown Cairo, and the lack of schools, theaters, and shops, would still seem foolish to have abandoned a rent-controlled apartment or pleasant housing in Dokki to move to Nasr City only to be transferred by his ministry to some other part of the city or the country.[14] Cairenes have simply not shown any great enthusiasm for moving into Nasr City, and this fact bodes ill for the more grandiose schemes of establishing four satellite cities around Cairo. Inasmuch as the government's leverage in relocating people can be brought to bear primarily on public bodies and civil servants, the satellite cities might fall victim to the same fate as Nasr City.

The housing crisis in Cairo's two major industrial suburbs (indeed the major industrial centers of Egypt and probably of the Arab world), Shubra al-Kheima and Helwan, is in many ways more acute than in the rest of the city. The pace of establishing factories and bringing workers into both areas has far outstripped the construction of housing. The blame for the problem at Shubra al-Kheima is shared by the public and private sectors which have built over 346 factories there. Helwan, however, has been developed almost exclusively by public capital concentrated in the iron and steel complex. In 1969 Muhsin Idris estimated that Helwan would be facing a deficit of 130,000 housing units by 1975.[15]

Given all the above, it should come as no surprise that the city and the government have been unable even to begin to attack the problem of structurally unsound housing in Cairo. All parties concerned—the city officials, the building owners, and the lessees—are inclined to say nothing about it. First, there is no regular inspection of residential buildings. Tenants who have reason to believe that the building in which they live may be verging on collapse may contact the city officials directly at the level of the quarter (*hay*), or do it through the Arab Socialist Union. The city then dispatches an engineer for an appraisal. If he decides the building is unsound, he orders the tenants out and closes it. Within 15 days a special technical committee meets to review the engineer's decision. If they confirm it, the building is officially condemned or occasionally the owner is ordered to carry out repairs. The engineers tend to condemn rather than salvage, however, for if the building collapses despite repairs they are legally liable. Moreover, the kind of training these architects and civil engineers receive emphasizes construction at the expense of repairs and salvage. They can see what is wrong with a building but not always what could be done to save it short of tearing it down and beginning again.

The real losers, as usual, are the tenants who receive no compensation except emergency housing in the schools and mosques, and priority on waiting lists for public housing which, besides being scarce, is generally located far from the center of Cairo. Most tenants, one would assume, prefer the risks of bad housing to no housing at all. Building owners obviously feel little incentive to call attention to their own neglect for which in most instances they are not legally liable. Moreover, rent controls combined with the effects of overcrowding make it difficult even for the well-intentioned landlord to invest in upkeep and repairs. Finally, the city does not want to look for trouble unless forced to, for ultimately it cannot make any dent in the problem given current levels of housing subsidies. Consequently only the tenants of a building may be moved to call attention to its structural defects, but even they are not so moved very often for fear of losing what little shelter they have.

A general pattern in Cairo's growth, one that is common to most cities, is the rise and decline of various residential and business districts. As an area becomes overcrowded and deteriorates, the better-off are able to move into new districts. The pattern has been repeating itself continually over the last century. Cairenes began to move westward out of the city's traditional core, toward Ezbekia, Tewfiqia, Kasr al-Aini, and Shubra, as Cairo's center of gravity, under European influence, shifted in that direction. With the tram lines of the 1890s to Heliopolis and the Pyramids, Shubra, Wayli, and Giza began to receive middle-income groups. In the period since the revolution, the northward migration has been intensified (Nasser and many of the officers were residents of Masr al-Gadida) as has the westward shift to Roda Island, Giza, Dokki, and Agouza. The gradual exodus of Europeans and other non-Egyptians has led to a rush on housing in the distinctly upper-income areas of Zamalek, Garden City, Ma'adi, and along the east and west banks of the Nile.

The last phase has corresponded to the effort of the regime to impose strict rent controls on housing in Cairo, but demand is so great and potential profits so appealing that real estate speculation and exploitation is thriving as never before.

Some analysts are prepared to attribute the housing shortage to rent control laws: "If we should wish to present the history of this [housing] crisis, we would have to look back to the Second World War, for in 1942 decrees were promulgated freezing rents of dwellings that had been built before this date. Subsequently, decrees and laws have been issued that lowered rents on housing constructed after 1942." [16] It is indeed true that in 1952 a decree was announced that reduced by 15 per cent rents on buildings erected since 1944. Following that, in June 1958, a new law lowered rents by 20 per cent on all buildings constructed between 1952 and 1958. A law of 1961 reduced rents yet further, affecting units whose rental value did not exceed LE5 per room. Buildings of this kind were relieved of property tax, and the rents of individual tenants were reduced proportionately. [17] Units constructed since the 1958 decree also had their rents reduced by 20 per cent. It was additionally stipulated that while the rents on buildings constructed before 1944 would not be further reduced, they could not be raised. Finally, in 1964 it was decreed that the rental return on investments each year should not exceed the total of 5 per cent of the value of the land and 3 per cent of the cost of the building.

There is no doubt that these laws have inhibited the construction of new housing in Cairo, and the building booms of the early 1900s and the interwar years have never been equalled. Yet secondary booms have occurred in the late 40s and early 50s. In the latter period landlords affected by the land reform measures of 1952 used their negotiable compensatory bonds to invest in urban housing and real estate. Total private investment in housing in Cairo and Alexandria in the period 1949-1956 may have averaged LE20 million each year. [18] One can be reasonably certain that if there is a substantial demand for housing on the part of middle-income groups, ways will be found for private capital to supply it. In Cairo, the ways are numerous and ingenious. All that rent controls have meant is that builders must step outside the law in order to obtain an acceptable return on their investment. Rent controls have not inhibited the construction of low-cost housing which the private sector would

Luxury housing—Zamalak.

The faded glory of old Cairo: Gamalia.

Roofscape—Birkil al-Fil.

have shunned in any case. Land values give some notion of the profits at stake: a *feddan* (1.038 acres) off the road to the Pyramids is now worth about LE8,000 (ca. $20,000). A few years ago, the same *feddan* would have been worth only LE2,000. In the northern agricultural areas around Mataria, a *feddan* may be worth as much as LE10,000. If speculators and developers are ready to pay such prices, the potential return must be equally great.[19]

The developer may make his killing in numerous ways, but once under way his profits are self-perpetuating and substantial. Acquiring the capital to purchase a piece of land may be the most difficult step, perhaps requiring several developers to pool resources to buy a choice plot. With title in hand, they may then approach the licensing authorities in the quarter (*hay*) in which they plan to build. The developer presents blueprints for the structure that have been countersigned by an architect recognized by the municipality. The city's experts, following the rudimentary building code,[20] check the plan according to three criteria:

(1) That the height of the building is no more than one and a half times the width of the road on which it fronts. If it is higher, each additional floor must be terraced inwards by 10 meters. Buildings fronting on the Nile have no height limit, a fact accounting for the deplorable development of highrise buildings along the river's banks, blocking the view for the rest of the city of its major asset.

(2) Use of space so that toilet areas are adequately ventilated.

(3) The use of suitable building materials.

Once approved there is little follow-up to see that the plan is actually executed. Some builders may try to cheat on building materials and height specifications. The architect who countersigns the plans does have some interest in assuring that they are followed, for if the building were to collapse or be condemned, he could be barred from his profession and imprisoned. One suspects, on the other hand, that given the profits involved, there might be fairly extensive collusion between public authorities and private constructors to overlook violations of city codes. The law stipulates, for instance, that if the city experts have not pronounced upon a proposed building one way or another within 40 days of the submission of the plans, the builder may assume

that the plans have been approved. Recently a multistory apartment house on the main thoroughfare of Zamalek went up without formal approval. Once up, with space rented or sold to people in ardent need of housing, the city can do little but recognize the *fait accompli*—and happily in so doing no one is really guilty of malfeasance.

With property title and building permit in hand, the developer may make his way to the bank for a loan. At the Land Credit Bank he may borrow up to 50 per cent of the total value of the land and the estimated building costs. This general arrangement, which has been in practice for several years, was designed to encourage private investment in housing. We may recall, moreover, that the city's Popular Assembly recommended that banks make loans up to 80 per cent of the land and building costs, which leads one to suspect that there may be a few developers in the Assembly's midst.

It has been observed in recent years that the above-mentioned bank was making about 80 loans a month, and that the same applicants were returning regularly. There is no mystery as to what is at work here, for the way to beat the system had been perfected by 1965. With the capital borrowed at 6.5 per cent interest, the developer begins construction of his building. Almost as soon as ground is broken (sometimes sooner) he will begin to contract for the sale of apartments or for the sale of the building itself. Selling apartments, rather than renting them, is the easiest way for a developer to assure a quick return on his money, although there are many ways, as we shall see, in which renting apartments can be made profitable. The standard sales procedure is to take half the agreed-upon price of the apartment as a down payment and the other half in installments until the unit is ready for occupancy. Take an example from 1965. A building of 19 apartments in Zamalek was planned. The developer sold each apartment for LE4,200 (ca. $10,000) and was able to extract a total of LE54,000 in down payments almost as soon as he broke ground, and received the remaining LE25,800 in installments during the construction phase. The cost of the land may have been LE10,000 and building costs (if he received his allotment of rationed building materials) around LE38,000, for a total outlay of LE48,000. Thus he was able to cover that amount and make LE6,000 as soon as construction had begun, and everything that followed was pure profit. Before one building was up, the developer would have the capital to purchase more land, submit new plans, and make a return visit to the bank for a new loan. It is also the custom that once the apartment is sold, part of the developer's debt to the bank is transferred to the new owner at 6.5 per cent interest.

Once having acquired property, it seems impossible for the developer to lose. The sales value of apartments have skyrocketed. Luxury flats near Giza's "Gold Coast" sell for LE8,000-10,000. Three buildings going up near the Gezira Sporting Club in Zamalek were allegedly sold off at ground breaking at LE15,000-18,000 an apartment.* Buying an apartment may be the only way to find acceptable housing for some people, but, like owning taxi cabs, Cairenes on fixed incomes have found that the housing crisis can stimulate a source of additional income. Once purchased an apartment can be resold at handsome profits. Or families may pool resources to construct an apartment house, keep one unit in it for their own use, and sell or rent the rest.[21]

Those who lease apartments have two ways of beating rent control laws. One is to furnish the apartment, more or less scantily, for the laws do not apply to furnished flats. Then the lessor will try to rent to members of the diplomatic community or Arab visitors who cannot afford to furnish their apartments locally. One finds furnished luxury flats renting for LE300 and similar unfurnished flats that may have been built before 1942 renting for LE12.

Egyptians, of course, can provide their own furnishings so that they do not fall victim to the furnished flat racket. But they do fall victim to the "key money" (khalu rigl) racket. The aspirant lessee may pay substantial tribute, perhaps LE200-500, to have the right to rent an unfurnished apartment at a modest monthly fee, say LE30. But the possibilities of key money, which is entirely illegal, pale beside the licit gains to be made from apartment sales. A builder in Agouza in 1968 accepted, in a variant on the key money gambit, LE1,000 in "advance rent" (nominally legal) from would-be tenants in a building under construction. The rent committee of Agouza had determined the legal rents of the apartments in the building to vary between LE55 and LE80 per month. Five years later, as the building neared completion, the owner notified the tenants that he had decided to sell rather than lease the apartments. He offered the tenants first option on purchasing the flats at

*By 1976, with an influx of wealthy Arabs, luxury apartments moved up into the LE 30,000 to LE 100,000 range.

LE12,600 each, failing which he would return their rent advances. After having waited five years, the tenants had the impossible choice of raising over LE12,000 or starting the quest for housing all over again. Their solution was simply to invade the uncompleted building and to squat in it. The prosecutor in the ensuing court case against the owner persuaded the court to uphold the claims of the tenants.[22] Others have not been so fortunate, and owners of occupied buildings have occasionally decided to sell the units in them, obliging the tenants to put up or move out.

One very important factor that drives rents and sales prices even higher is the severe shortage of building materials, such as cement, steel reinforcing bars, window and door frames, and window glass. When a building permit is awarded, the awardee is placed on a waiting list for these rationed materials that are distributed by the state. Public sector enterprises, government agencies, and the armed forces have priority in receiving building materials. Whatever is left over goes to the private sector which, as already noted, builds most of the nation's housing. Builders in Cairo must frequently wait as much as two years to receive their allotments. Back orders for steel in Cairo alone now total 40,000 tons. Moreover, the rental value of a building is determined on the basis of construction costs using these rationed materials at what amount to subsidized prices. The way round the dilemma is for the builder to buy his materials on the black market, into which, one would gather, there is considerable leakage from the public sector. There a ton of steel sells for LE190 while its official price is LE95. Obviously building costs far exceed the rent committees' estimates, and the owner is obliged to pass on the difference to the lessee by extracting "rent advances," or to the purchaser by grossly inflating the price of the apartment.[23]

Everyone but the developer is a loser in this situation. The poor lose because the state cannot and the private developers will not meet their needs. Middle-income groups lose as they tie up their savings in overpriced housing. The city loses as it is unable to tax anything but legally paid rents (netting the city a meager LE1,298,000 in 1969) when most of these transfers are carried out through unorthodox, unmonitored channels. Finally, the state loses through the siphoning-off of scarce materials into the black market and the

diversion of savings and investment into speculative, nonproductive ventures.[24]

No one is offering any partial, not to mention
definitive solutions. There has been talk, as
mentioned, of satellite cities, but the costs are
staggering (see Part I in this series). There has been
some effort to develop a prefabricated housing
industry in Egypt, but it is in its infancy, and there
is no guarantee that the country can produce prefabricated units at low cost. There is some limited
effort at slum clearance but it in no way keeps pace
with the emergence of new slums. For middle-
income groups the present and future are hardly
pleasant, but they will probably be able to find
housing. Lower-income groups cannot pay beyond
a certain level, nor can they continue to pack themselves into existing housing indefinitely. The best
hope for Cairo is that the attractions of the city will
become less as the housing crisis deepens, and that
migrants will head for other centers where, presumably, regional development schemes are being
carried out. It may even be that the village will
become more attractive than the city. Still Cairo
will continue to grow, and the housing crisis will
remain acute. Like the future of the city itself,
housing in Cairo will in all likelihood develop forms
that have few precedents, and about which past
experience and conventional wisdom have little to
tell us.

NOTES

Growth, Administration, and Planning

1. The best scholarly treatment of contemporary Cairo is by Janet L. Abu-Lughod, *Cairo: 1001 Years of the City Victorious*, Princeton University Press, 1971. Elsewhere Abu-Lughod has published several focused sociological studies of the city which are partially reproduced in her book. See, "Urbanization in Egypt: Present Rate and Future Prospects," *Economic Development and Cultural Change*, Vol. 13, 1965, pp. 313-43; "Migrant Adjustment to City Life," *The American Journal of Sociology*, LXVII, July 1961, pp. 22-32; "Urban-Rural Differences as a Function of the Demographic Transition: Egyptian Data and an Analytic Model," *The American Journal of Sociology*, LXIX, March 1964, pp. 476-90; "The Emergence of Differential Fertility in Urban Egypt," *Milbank Memorial Fund Quarterly*, XLIII, pt. 1, April 1965, pp. 235-53; "Tale of Two Cities: the Origins of Modern Cairo," *Comparative Studies in Society and History*, VII, July 1965, pp. 429-60. Now dated, but still excellent, is Marcel Clerget, *Le Caire:Etude de géographie urbaine et d'histoire économique*, Cairo, 2 vols., 1934. Recent but less thorough studies are: Dr. Izzat Higazi, *Cairo: a Study of the Urban Phenomenon*, National Center for Sociological and Criminological Research, Cairo 1971; Dr. Ahmad Neklawi, *Cairo: A Study in Urban Sociology*, Dar al-Nahda al-Arabia, Cairo, 1973; "Cairo 1000: Past, Present, Future," a special section of *al-Talia*, vol. 5, no. 2, February 1969. Finally one must note the monumental study being carried out by the Ministry of Social Affairs since 1957, consisting of a quarter-by-quarter sociological and economic survey of the city. Over twenty such quarter studies have been published to date, but unfortunately their distribution has been restricted. The series has been supervised by Dr. Fahmy Badrawi.

2. United Nations Population Division, "World Urbanization Trends, 1920-1960," in Gerald Breese (ed.) *The City in the Newly Developing Countries*, Prentice-Hall, 1969, p. 45.

3. Gamal Hamdan, "The Pattern of Medieval Urbanism in the Arab World," *Geography*, Vol. 47, no. 215, April 1962, p. 122-34; and "Capitals of the New Africa," *Economic Geography*, Vol. 40, no. 3, July 1964, pp. 239-53; reprinted in Breese, *op. cit.*, pp. 141-161.

4. Janet Abu-Lughod, "Varieties of Urban Experience: Contrast, Coexistence, and Coalescence in Cairo," in Ira Lapidus (ed.), *Middle Eastern Cities*, University of California Press, 1969, p. 162.

5. See Charles Issawi, "Economic Change and Urbanization in the Middle East," in Lapidus, *op. cit.*, p. 104.

6. *Ibid.*, p. 102.

7. Gabriel Baer, "The Beginnings of Urbanization," *Studies in the Social History of Modern Egypt*, Chicago University Press, 1969, pp. 133-148.

8. This phenomenon has been explored at length by Abu-Lughod in "City Victorious," especially Chapter 12. An Egyptian scholar who has taken up the same theme is Ahmad Neklawi, *op. cit.*, pp. 126-32. See also Karen Kay Petersen, "Villagers in Cairo: Hypotheses vs. Data," *The American Journal of Sociology*, Vol. 77, no. 3, November 1971, pp. 56-73.

9. Besides the Governor, on the committee were Dr. Suleiman Huzzayin, Director of the Cairo Demographic Center; General Gamal Askar, Director of CAPMAS; Eng. Muhsin Idriss, Director of the GCPC; Dr. Imam Salim, Under-Secretary for Planning. See *al-Ahram*, November 1, 1972 and January 1, 1973.

10. Muhsin Idriss in a round table discussion, *al-Talia*, Vol. 2, No. 2, February 1969, p. 82.

11. Kingsley Davis, "The Urbanization of the Human Population," *Scientific American*, September 1965, pp. 41-53, reprinted in Sylvia Fleis Fava (ed.), *Urbanism in World Perspective*, New York, 1968, pp. 32-45, especially 40-45.

12. CAPMAS, *Sample Survey of Labor in the UAR: Results of the May 1968 Round*, source #1-222, October 1970.

13. Gamal Hamdan, *Studies in Egyptian Urbanism*, Cairo 1959, p. 19.

14. Mark Jefferson, "The Law of the Primate City," *The Geographical Review*, Vol. 29, 1939, pp. 226-32, especially p. 228.

15. See Arnold Linsky, "Some Generalizations Concerning Primate Cities," in Breese, *op. cit.*, pp. 285-94.

16. S.K. Mehta, "Some Demographic and Economic Correlates of Primate Cities: A Case for Re-Evaluation," in

Breese, *op. cit.*, pp. 295-308. Mehta's cross-sectional data show convincingly that there is no correlation between level of economic development and degree of primacy.

17. For an excellent discussion of city administration see Abu-Lughod, "City Victorious," *op. cit.*, pp. 146-53 and 222-39.

18. Besides Abu-Lughod, I have been able to draw on the very thorough thesis of Dr. Galal Bakeer, *The Practical Application of Financial Administration and Local Government in the UAR*, Faculty of Commerce, Cairo University, 1969.

19. *Akhbar al-Yom* of November 11, 1972 gives the history in all its grisly details, including the story of the previous governor who evidently exploited the decentralisation measures to augment his own patronage system through the appointment of chiefs and the rebudgeting of city revenues.

20. See Governor Hamdy Ashur's interview with *al-Ahram*, March 15, 1973.

21. Abu-Lughod, "City Victorious," p. 228.

22. See my Report, *Manpower and Population Planning in the Arab Republic of Egypt, Part IV: Egypt's Governmental Program for Family Planning* [JW-5-'72], Fieldstaff Reports, Northeast Africa Series, Vol. XVII, No. 5, 1972.

23. It is perhaps indicative of how things move that the project for the new opera house—the old one having burnt in the fall of 1971—was approved by President Sadat upon the recommendation of the Ministry of Culture in consultation with Egypt's major engineering consulting and construction firm, Osman Ahmad Osman: The Arab Contractors Ltd.

24. See Ministry of Municipal and Rural Affairs, Municipality of Cairo, Planning Commission, *Master Plan of Cairo*, S.O.P. Press 1957. In a careful study, Mohammed Ali Hafiz, former Director of Planning for Cairo Governorate noted the instant obsolescence of the Master Plan. However, he himself suggested that densities in Cairo should not anywhere exceed 30,000 per km^2 and that total population should not exceed six million. See his "Current Planning for the City of Cairo and Future Trends," May 1965 (in Arabic).

26. Ahmad Baha al-Din, in an important series of articles in *al-Ahram* from the end of July through October 1971 (on successive Sundays) treated many of these problems. See the various installments of his "Towards a New Map of Egypt," also articles by Abdel-Moneim Heikal and Hussein Shafei in *al-Ahram*, November 17, 1971.

27. Hassan Fathy, "Cairo of the Future," *Architectural Bulletin* (Egyptian Architects Association), January 1969, pp. 4-17 (in Arabic with a résumé in English). The original study was completed by Fathy in 1961. His most famous book is *Gourna, a Tale of Two Villages*, Ministry of Culture, Cairo, 1969.

Transportation

1. In addition to buses, taxis, trams, and trolley buses, there is the Heliopolis Metro which in 1969 carried 83,479,000 passengers, and the Helwan metro which carried 56,357,000, and the Mataria Railroad that carried 35,288,000. See Central Agency for Public Mobilization and Statistics (CAPMAS) *Cairo 1970*, Reference #200/01 (January 1971), p. 58; also the first-rate study of Dr. Sa'ad al-Din Ashmawi, *The Organization of Transportation*, Dar al-Taba'a al-Haditha, Cairo, 1971 (in Arabic), p. 131.

2. Typical is the report that the Cairo Transport Authority had received authorization to utilize LE4 million to import spare parts necessary for the repair of 345 disabled buses. It would be five months before the operation could begin, *al-Ahram*, July 13, 1973. A recent report stated that the Governor of Cairo had decided to retire all those buses whose annual maintenance costs were superior to their market value.

3. As an historical note, Cairo's modern transportation system was begun after 1896 with tramlines established and run by a Belgian company. Until the revolution of 1952, and especially the nationalizations of 1961, much of the public means of transport in the city remained in foreign hands, and much of the terminology, such as *kumsary*, was adapted from foreign languages, mainly French.

4. In theory both the *kumsary* and the driver receive bonus or incentive payments if their bus exceeds a certain level of paid fares each day. However, one driver estimated that even in a new perfectly functioning bus, the most a driver could hope for in a single day would be 30 piastres (ca. 75¢). See *al-Gumhuria*, February 22, 1973, "The Bus Driver Speaks his Mind."

5. "Is there really a Transportation Crisis?" *al-Ahram*, January 8, 1972.

6. "The Taxi between the Native Son and the Tourist," *Ruz al-Yussef*, n.2353, July 16, 1973.

7. See Dr. Mohammed Abdelwahab Ismail, "Taxis," *al-Ahram al-Iqtisadi*, May 1, 1969.

8. Dr. Aadil Gazarin, "Reply," *al-Ahram al-Iqtisadi*, May 15, 1969.

9. *Al-Ahram*, December 20, 1971.

10. Raymond Anderson, *New York Times*, February 10, 1972.

11. See *al-Ahram al-Iqtisadi*, n.390, November 15, 1971.

12. See Janet Abu-Lughod, *Cairo 1001 Years of the City Victorious*, Princeton University Press, 1971, p. 110.

13. See Dr. Sa'ad al-Din Ashmawi "An End to Light Transport in Cairo," *al-Ahram al-Iqtisadi*, December 1, 1972.

14. "When will the Plan to Solve the Transportation Crisis be Completed?" *al-Musawwar*, n.2304, December 6, 1968.

15. One of the most persistent and well-informed critics of existing transportation policies is Dr. Sa'ad al-Din Ashmawi. See his "The Organization of Transportation," *op. cit.*, and "Rational Organization and the Transportation Problem," special supplement to *al-Ahram al-Iqtisadi*, January 15, 1969.

16. Ashmawi, "The Organization of Transportation," *op. cit.*, pp. 123-33.

17. *al-Ahram*, July 18, 1973.

Housing and Shelter

1. Charles Abrams, *Man's Struggle for Shelter in an Urbanizing World*, MIT Press, 1964, p. 5.

2. See John C. Turner, "Housing Priorities, Settlement Patterns, and Urban Development in Modernizing Countries," *American Institute of Planners*, Vol. 34, no. 6 (November 1968), pp. 354-363; and "Uncontrolled Urban Settlement: Problems and Policies," in Gerald Breese (ed.), *The City in the Newly Developing Countries*, Prentice-Hall, 1969, pp. 507-34.

3. On April 5, 1973 the Minister of Interior ordered that all clandestine roof housing must be removed at the expense of the building owners. Failure to do so would entail a week's imprisonment and a fine of LE10 ($25), *al-Ahram*, April 5, 1973.

4. Much of my information on Bulaq Dakrur came through an interview with the former Governor of Giza Province, Dr. Fuad Muhy al-Din. A sample survey in Sayyida Zeinab showed that 75 per cent of the families had monthly incomes of under LE20. See Ahmad Neklawi, *Cairo: A Study in Urban Sociology*, Dar al-Nahda al-Arabia, Cairo 1973, p. 235.

5. See Mohammed Basha's interview with the Governor, *al-Ahram*, March 15, 1973.

6. See *al-Ahram*, November 24, 1971.

7. See Nabil Sabbagh, "Housing—an Aggravated Crisis Awaiting Solutions," *al-Ahram al-Iqtisadi*, no. 429, July 1, 1973, reporting on a study carried out by the Housing Committee of the Popular Assembly of Cairo Governorate, presented by Dr. Gharib al-Gamal.

8. *Ibid.*

9. See Mohammed Kamil Zaytun, "The Situation of Low-Income Populations vis-à-vis Economic Housing," *al-Ahram al-Iqtisadi*, May 15, 1972, p. 12.

10. Neklawi, *loc. cit.*

11. *Al-Ahram*, May 8, 1972.

12. *Al-Ahram*, September 29, 1971.

13. For a trenchant series of articles on urban planning, see Ahmad Baha al-Din, in *al-Ahram*, August-October 1971, especially "From drafting the new map of Egypt to redrafting Liberation Square," October 24, 1971.

14. See the critique of Nasr City by Dr. Sa'ad al-Din al-Ashmawi, "Rational Organization and the Transportation Problem," *al-Ahram al-Iqtisadi*, January 15, 1969 (supplement).

15. See the round table discussion, "The Way to the Cairo of the Future," *al-Talia*, Vol. 5, no. 2, February 1969, p. 82.

16. Nabil Sabbagh, *op. cit.*, p. 36.

17. See Gamal al-Uteifi, *al-Ahram al-Iqtisadi*, November 15, 1961. Uteifi gives the following hypothetical accounting for a four-room apartment renting for LE10 per month (i.e., less than LE3 per month per room).

Rental value per year	LE 120
Standard 20% reduction for operating cost	24
amount subject to 10% tax	96
ACTUAL TAX	9.6
Suppl. taxes at 20% of actual tax	1.92
Municipal fees at 26.6% of actual tax	2.56

Tenants fees at 25% of actual tax	2.40
Defense tax at 25% of actual tax	2.40
TOTAL TAX	18.88

The annual rent on the hypothetical unit would thus be reduced by LE18.88.

18. See Anouar Abdel-Malek, *Egypt: Military Society*, Vintage, New York City, 1968, p. 81.

19. "Egypt: Red Hot Property Climber," *Sketch* (Beirut), vol. 2, no. 8, June 1, 1973, and *Akhbar al-Yom*, April 7, 1973.

20. There are no zoning laws in Cairo. The nearest approximation concerns the old Fatimid city of medieval Cairo comprising Gamalia, Darb al-Ahmar, Ghuria, etc. It was determined that no new construction could be undertaken there that was not in harmony with the older buildings. However, these are some of Cairo's most densely inhabited areas with many structurally unsound buildings. Because of the law, hardly any building permits had been issued over the last eight years. The present Governor, Hamdy Ashur, is trying to reverse this trend by opening up the possibility of construction even if it be at the cost of harmony.

21. See Kemal Sa'ad, "Selling Apartments" *al-Musawar*, no. 2112, April 12, 1965; Nadia Abdelhamid, "Apartments for Sale," *al-Ahram*, August 16, 1972; and Dr. Milad Hanna, "Parasitic Incomes and the Housing Crisis," *al-Talia*, Vol. 9, July 1973, pp. 32-34.

22. *Al-Ahram*, December 20, 1972 and *Akhbar al-Yom*, February 8, 1973.

23. Samir Izzat, "Key Money Reaches LE5,000," *Ruz al-Yussef*, no. 2290, May 1, 1972.

24. Many of these problems are examined in a stimulating article by Dr. Galal Amin, *Urbanization and Economic Development in the Arab World*, Arab University, Beirut, 1972.

Part III: Strategies and Solutions

A synthesis of current thinking and policy recommendations emanating from Egypt's planning community might give the following order of priorities. Over the short haul a stable *modus vivendi* with Israel must be established. Without it, defense expenditures will remain unconscionably high, and the tense atmosphere will drive off potential foreign investment. Over the short and medium term, let us say up to 1985, the goal is to bring Egypt's foreign payments into some sort of manageable balance. This will depend on a much improved export performance, remittances from workers abroad, Suez Canal fees, tourism, and petroleum exports. None of these can be realized with a real threat of war hanging over the region. In a final stage, presuming that Egypt is able to generate a steady flow of foreign exchange earnings, the foundations for self-sustaining growth through industrialization can be laid.

Two of these three goals had been proclaimed as such throughout the Nasserist period. They were self-sustaining growth and foreign-exchange earning capacity ideally seen as emerging together. The third, a *modus vivendi* with Israel, may have been tacitly pursued up to 1967, but the signals were undeniably mixed. It was believed at that time that Egypt could pay for both growth and arms.

The catastrophic results of the 1967 War bore at least two messages. First, the investment in military preparedness had failed, and, second, the war and its aftermath rendered academic all talk of self-sustaining growth. What had gone wrong, and what or who was to blame? These questions have been the very stuff of the political debate that has been waged in Egypt since 1971. There are those who argue that Nasser's approach was sound, but that continuing hostilities with Israel, and the 1967 War itself, had been forced upon Egypt by the blind Western, especially United States, support of Israeli intransigence. Western neo-imperialism was therefore to blame for the "setback" (*al-naksa*).

More sophisticated inheritors of the Nasserist formula were not content with this simplistic explanation. They have argued that as important as neo-imperialist conniving has been the fact that the socialist experiment after 1961 was not applied by socialists but rather by opportunists in the regime who built a grossly inefficient state capitalist system and then milked it for their own private ends. The need therefore is, in their view, to apply faithfully the socialist principles that had never been given a chance.

By contrast, under Sadat the weight of official legitimacy lies with another constituency that contends that the Nasserist experiment failed precisely because of its socialism. Be it the reliance on public enterprise, the close economic links with the U.S.S.R., the hostility to foreign investment, or Nasser's so-called subversive activities against conservative Arab regimes, all are seen as misguided policies that must be overhauled or jettisoned.

What can or should replace them? That is probably the most delicate question that currently faces the Egyptian regime for it must service an array of important domestic and foreign constituencies whose immediate interests are not always compatible and sometimes are diametrically opposed.

For important sectors of the middle classes, the ideal solution would be as follows. The state sector would be maintained insofar as it mobilizes investment for infrastructure and operates a few enterprises too big for private capital to contemplate. Uneconomic enterprises would be sold off or liquidated. The state would also maintain its subsidies of basic consumer goods, agricultural inputs, and building materials. These alleviate the plight of the poor masses and subsidize the production of both poor and wealthy peasants and urban developers. Similarly, the state would be responsible for importing basic foodstuffs that are lacking in Egypt, although it might contract out to private importers to arrange the deals. At the same time, the private sector would be allowed once again to play a big role in import-export trade and in local industry. It could, if it wished, enter into joint ventures with foreign investors without restriction. The free movement of currency in and out of Egypt would be promoted, and corporate and personal income tax would be reduced. It is already the case, as we shall see in the first two Reports in Part III, that major steps toward several of these goals have been taken since June 1974.

Few of the advocates of these policies are so naïve as to think that Egypt could, at present, actually afford them, although some clearly do not care. But for those who care the hope is, or perhaps was, that (1) foreign investment would come into the country in significant amounts, and private entrepreneurial drive, free from state shackles, would turn the economy around; and (2) the conservative oil-rich states of the region would come to Egypt's rescue with massive aid packages. By 1985 or thereabouts it is prophesied that this aid would no longer be needed. Egypt would be self-financing and, having gotten to this happy state, no domestic constituencies would have been unduly hurt in the process.

This package has not been bought by those who count. Foreign investors have hung offshore, frightened by an overpriced Egyptian pound and the specter of a tentacular and inefficient public bureaucracy. The oil-rich are not in a gift-giving mood and insist upon a commercial return on their capital. Moreover, it may be less than reassuring to them to contemplate an economically resurgent Egypt with its 40 millions, earning its own foreign exchange and dropping, if not threatening its former benefactors. Finally, the Arab oil-rich and Western banking institutions are agreed that a costless reform of the Egyptian economy should not be encouraged because it may not amount to anything more than an ever more costly international salvage operation. The watchword today is financial orthodoxy, cost-benefit analysis, an end to subsidies and administered prices, tighter credit and reduced money supply, and full convertibility of the pound. These may not be goals that one would want to see achieved overnight, but it is in their direction that Egypt's creditors are pushing. Inevitably, they say, the masses may experience some discomfiture as prices rise, but the bullet must be bitten and the price paid. If President Sadat acts on this advice, his successor may appreciate his courage, but for the incumbent this option is no less risk-laden than that of hurling the Egyptian army across the Suez Canal in 1973. At least then the issue was settled fairly quickly, but economic reform takes a long time, it hurts a good deal before it produces results, and even then there is no guarantee that it will lead Egypt out of its development problems.

Egypt's Economic New Look

The economic opening merits our attention and concern for it confirms the essential difference between big capital and national capital. While big capital sees in the opening a means to return Egypt to a capitalist framework, locally and internationally, national capital sees in it a way to face the crisis of financing economic growth by attracting foreign and Arab capital, all the while safeguarding Egypt's economic independence.

> Dr. Fu'ad Mursi
> "Meeting the Thrust of Big Capital"
> *al Tali'a*, Vol. 11, No. 3, March 1975

There are some people who try to depict the economic "opening" [*al-infitah al-iqtisadi*] as a basic change in our ideological framework, that is our socialism; but this is a grave error.

So that I can give you an idea of what the opening is all about, I must go back to the 4th of Ramadan of last year [October 1, 1973], six days before the battle. I invited to this same house in which we are now seated the members of the National Security Council consisting of the Vice-President, the presidential assistants, the Prime Minister and Deputy Prime Ministers, the Minister of Defense, the director of Military Intelligence, the National Security advisor, and the Minister of Supply.... and I laid before them the situation and asked them to advance their own opinions...we debated for a long time. There were some who advocated fighting, and others who said we were not ready.... At the end I said that I wanted to tell them one thing only, that as of that day we had reached the "zero stage" economically [*marhalat as-sifr*] in every sense of the term. What this meant in concrete terms was that I could not have paid a penny toward our debt installments falling due on January 1 [1974]; nor could I have bought a grain of wheat in 1974. There wouldn't have been bread for the people, that's the least that one can say.... But as soon as the battle of October 6 was over, our Arab brethren came to our aid with $500 million...and this sum would never have come had we not taken effective action as regards the battle. But despite these dollars, we are now in the same situation we were in a year ago, perhaps worse.

> President Anwar al-Sadat
> Interview with *al-Usbu'a al-Arabi*
> republished in *al-Ahram*, October 9, 1974

President Sadat himself would not accept the notion that he went to war in October 1973 solely because of Egypt's foreign debt and the need to pay for food imports. Many other equally weighty factors entered into his decision and have been discussed in an earlier Report.[1] Still, there is no gainsaying the direct correlation that exists, and perhaps has always existed, between Egypt's economic performance and the conduct of her foreign policy, whether by violent or nonviolent means. Three structural factors combined in such a manner that by mid-1973 the regime had very few feasible options in continuing the confrontation with Israel while providing for the needs of the country's 36 million inhabitants.

The first structural factor was the process of socializing the nation's economy. Through a series of nationalizations in 1961 and 1964, the rationale of which was explained in the 1962 National Charter (see Appendix), the state gained ownership of all major industrial establishments, banks, insurance companies, domestic and maritime transport, and foreign trade. While most agricultural land continued to remain under private ownership, the most advanced sectors of the economy were brought under "socialist" control. Nasser's goal was rapid economic development without undue social pain. His formula was a sort of benevolent *étatisme*, officially described as Egyptian socialism, whereby the assets of "exploiting classes," foreign and domestic, could be used as a form of forced savings and reinvested in a state-dominated development plan. The poor and destitute, and, perhaps more important, the lower-middle and middle classes would not be asked to make any excessive sacrifice in the name of socialism; indeed, they were to be offered unprecedented advantages in free welfare and educational services and in the creation of new, occasionally superfluous jobs.

This formula was at the heart of the strategy of the First Five Year plan, 1960-1965. And it worked satisfactorily in some respects. Egypt achieved a respectable annual GNP growth rate of about 6 per cent (although the population was growing during the same years at 2.58 per cent per annum). In the all-important domain of export capacity, however, execution of the plan was far less satisfactory. It was predicted at the outset that by 1965, the value of imports in 1959 prices would have dropped from LE 229.2 to LE 214.9 million (in 1959 the official exchange was US$2.80 to the Egyptian pound), and that in the last year of the Plan the economy would register a balance of payments surplus of LE 40 million. The failure to curtail imports through import substitution and to generate new exports led to a balance of payments deficit in 1966 of LE 142.2 million. Compounding this situation were the spiraling expenses, most of which had to be paid in hard currency, of Egypt's expeditionary force fighting in the Yemen since 1962. Second, Egypt had to defray the hard currency costs of grain imports after the United States suspended surplus wheat shipments, which had been payable in local currency. As Egypt prepared for its Second Five Year Plan, it was faced with a financing problem that could not be handled within the terms of the old formula. Hard currency had to be found to pay for food grains, capital equipment, foreign expertise, and military hardware. The only alternative would have been almost total reliance on barter deals with the Soviet Union and Eastern Europe, tying Egypt's exports to ruble markets and leaving the country dependent on what is frequently regarded as inferior technology and equipment. Moreover, new sources of domestic savings had to be found, yet further nationalizations or other attempts at forced savings would have seriously affected the middle classes and led, perhaps, to serious internal dissidence.

Nasser never found a way out of this dilemma, and from 1966 onward the economy entered a period of decline. Industries that had been up to date at the beginning of the decade slid inexorably toward obsolescence as there was no money to pay for their renewal. Some industries simply could not be completed, while others experienced serious underutilization as necessary raw materials could not be imported in sufficient quantities. Finally, industries that were to depend upon one another for various kinds of supplies (such as the coking plant for the steel complex, or refinery gas for fertilizer installations) never achieved integration; completed units searched desperately for materials abroad and uncompleted units fought for scarce funds to continue installation.

All this led to the production of overpriced goods of inferior quality with no markets in hard currency areas, and thus, what exportable surpluses there were remained within the confines of foreign trade with the Soviet Union and Eastern Europe. It is one of the ironies of the late 1960s that despite the priority given to investments in industry and manufacturing, by the end of the decade industry contributed no more to national income than it had at the end of the First Five Year Plan (see Table 1). Agricultural products continued to make up the bulk of all Egypt's exports. Raw cotton is still king, and the state cannot take credit for textile exports, for the textile industry first was developed under private auspices and then nationalized.

The second structural factor was the impact of the June 1967 War. Even if there had been no war and no defeat, the Egyptian economy would have had to deal with the situation just outlined. But the defeat—and the subsequent occupation of the Sinai—was of such proportions that it must be considered an independent factor. It had two major consequences. The first was to deprive Egypt of at least two sources of hard currency. With the closing

Table 1

Sectoral Distribution of National Income
1964/65 - 1969/70 in constant prices (1964/65) in millions of LE

	1964/65	1965/66	1966/67	1967/68	1968/69	1969/70
Agriculture	582.1	588.1	572.6	595.2	601.5	640.8
Industry & Mining	423.4	433.8	436.9	416.3	457.2	486.7
Electricity	23.2	24.3	25.2	35.4	36.6	44.3
Construction	92.6	94.9	88.5	76.9	105.0	114.1
Total Production Sector	1,121.3	1,141.1	1,123.2	1,123.8	1,200.3	1,285.9
Transport, Communication, Storage	176.0	194.7	201.3	113.3	115.2	127.8
Trade & Finance	168.0	180.2	190.7	191.5	198.9	209.6
Housing	74.9	76.1	78.8	112.9	115.3	118.0
Public Utilities	8.2	9.1	9.4	10.0	10.8	11.7
Other Services	414.2	447.7	462.4	497.2	522.4	559.1
Total Service Sector	841.3	907.8	942.6	924.9	962.6	1,026.2
Price Adjustment	12.4	14.4				
Grand Total	1,975.0	2,063.3	2,065.8	2,048.7	2,162.9	2,312.1

Source: Bulletin of the National Bank of Egypt, Vol. 27, No. 1, January 1974.

of the Suez Canal, Egypt lost substantial revenues from canal fees. Some observers hypothesize that since 1967 the loss has been on the order of LE 4 billion. In addition Egypt lost her Sinai oil fields at Abu Rudeis to Israel. Production from these wells in the last eight years may have been worth LE 2 billion. Another less significant loss was incurred by the sharp drop in tourism due to the threatening atmosphere in the area. These hard currency losses were only partially offset by the annual subsidies of some LE 210 million paid to Egypt by Saudi Arabia, Kuwait, and Libya on the basis of the Khartoum agreement of August 1967. Vital as these subsidies were, their political price was a certain subordination of Egypt's—and Nasser's—activist role in the Arab world to the conservative interests of the oil-rich. (It should be remembered that the monarchy in Libya was not overthrown until September 1969.) The second major consequence of Egypt's defeat in 1967 was the incursion of military expenses that have seemed to grow exponentially. From outlays of about LE 300 million in 1967-68, military expenditures reached LE one billion in 1973-74 and are projected to go steadily higher unless there is a real breakthrough to peace with Israel.[2] Military procurements have been a constant drain on hard currency reserves and a major factor in Egypt's growing external debt.

The debt is the third structural factor that, in combination with the problem of financing development and paying for military preparedness, led to Egypt's intolerable economic situation. Egypt's nonmilitary external debt at the end of 1974 has been estimated to range between LE 1.7 and 2.2 billion. Even if we accept the lower figure, it represents over one-third of national income. In 1965, the debt stood at LE 600 million—also about one-third of national income—but servicing at that time amounted to only LE 15 million or about 2.5 per cent of the net debt. Today, not only has the debt at least trebled, but the burden of servicing is also falling due in ever larger installments. Theoretically, 55 per cent of the debt incurred in the early and mid-1960s was to have been paid off by 1974 and 87 per cent by 1980. In 1974 servicing amounted to LE 170 million or nearly 45 per cent of the total value of Egypt's exports in the same year.[3] Rescheduling the debt servicing (already agreed upon with Japan and West Germany) is a fundamental objective of Egypt's new economic policies.

Caught within this concatenation of hostile economic forces, Nasser and Sadat strove to work within the credo that combined development, war-footing, and welfare socialism. That this was and is an impossible task is clear to Sadat, and while he has some ideas as to how to remedy the situation, he faces some awesome obstacles. First, the sprawling public sector, with its powerful vested interests, will not lightly cede the protection that it was granted in infancy. It is in turn enmeshed in the labyrinthine Egyptian civil service characterized primarily by red tape, low salaries, and a size too vast to allow for accountability in assessing achievement or attributing blame for any of its frequent failures. Yet it is public sector industry and the Egyptian bureaucracy that has been called upon to lead the way in the country's economic renaissance. Meanwhile, the population grows, per capita income dwindles,[4] agricultural production

Table 2

Egypt's Principal Exports by Kind 1965-1971
(Millions of Egyptian Pounds)

	1965	1967	1969	1971
Agricultural Products, not including Cotton*	34.3	46.0	79.7	48.0
Raw Cotton	146.2	121.6	130.7	175.0
Textiles	47.0	47.6	64.4	68.3
Processed Goods**	7.0	6.6	19.7	22.9
Crude Oil	6.6	2.0	7.4	1.9
Phosphates, Manganese	2.2	2.3	1.7	1.2
Refined Petroleum Products***	10.2	7.1	.8	.3
Cement	2.0	1.9	4.2	5.9
Electrical Appliances	.5	1.5	1.0	2.4
Vehicles	.7	1.7	.2	.3
Iron and Steel	.3	.2	2.4	3.7
Other	3.0	3.0	7.3	7.9
Total	260.0	241.5	319.5	337.8

Table compiled from statistics presented in the Bulletin of the National Bank of Egypt, Vol. 27, No. 1, 1974.

*Agricultural products include onions, potatoes, rice, fruit.
**Processed goods include sugar, alcoholic beverages, animal fodder, paper, leather goods.
***Refined petroleum products consist of gasoline, kerosene, and tar.

fails to keep pace with domestic consumption,[5] and industry, as noted, has drained away rather than provided hard currency.

Two indicators may suffice to demonstrate the rock and the hard place between which Egyptian planners find themselves. On the one hand, the regime's socialist commitment has led it to maintain policies subsidizing prices of basic goods. These have diverted substantial funds from directly productive investment. In 1975, it is estimated that the state will invest about LE 625 million in price subsidies (or about one-seventh of national income in current prices). The breakdown is revealing:

Foodstuffs	LE 464.4 million
Cloth and Clothing	LE 23.0 million
Fertilizer	LE 95.0 million
Pesticides	LE 11.5 million
Agricultural Production	LE 25.5 million
Uncollected interest	LE 5.4 million

To some extent the subsidies sustain a high level of consumerism that has as a direct consequence greater state outlays for food and other commodity imports. The figures in Table 3, representing imports and exports, show how Egypt's commercial balance has deteriorated over the last 25 years. Egypt plans to import about four million tons of grain in 1975, or approximately half the import bill by value.

Further aggravating Egypt's commercial deficit is the pattern of her imports and exports. Over 60 per cent of Egyptian exports go to the Soviet Union and Eastern Europe, but less than half her imports come from the same sources. Conversely less than a third of Egypt's exports go to hard currency markets from which she receives over half her imports. This inversion in the trade pattern must be adjusted if Egypt is to meet the demands of hard currency to pay for grain shipments and for raw materials, capital goods, and technology from the highly developed economies of Western Europe, Japan, Australia, and North America.

Anwar Sadat, soon after his succession to the Presidency in 1970, came to a conclusion regarding this situation that President Nasser artfully strove to avoid: war and development are not compatible. In Sadat's view, prolonging the state of no war/no peace that had prevailed since 1967 would condemn the Egyptian economy to stagnation and retrogression. There was even a strong suspicion in Egypt that Israel and the United States (whether under the Johnson or Nixon administrations) would take a certain satisfaction in seeing Egypt's economy so crippled. Certainly there must have been policy planners in both Israel and the United States

Table 3

Commercial Balance of the Arab Republic of Egypt 1951 - 1975 (LE millions)

Year	Imports	Exports	Commercial Balance
1951	283.2	205.0	−78.2
1952	227.7	150.2	−77.5
1957	182.6	171.6	−11.0
1958	240.2	166.3	−73.9
1959	222.2	170.4	−51.8
1960	232.5	197.8	−34.7
1961	243.8	168.9	−74.9
1962	300.9	158.3	−142.6
1963	398.4	226.8	−171.6
1964	414.4	234.4	−180.0
1965	405.8	263.6	−142.2
1966	465.4	263.1	−202.3
1967	344.3	246.1	−98.2
1968	289.6	270.3	−19.3
1969	277.3	324.0	+46.7
1970	342.1	331.2	−10.9
1971	400.0	343.2	−56.8
1972	390.8	358.8	−32.0
1973	632.3 est.	382.5 est.	−249.8
1974	1,266.0 est.	596.0 est.	−670.0
1975	2,178.0 est.	680.0 est.	−1,498.0

Source: Federation of Egyptian Industries, *YEAR-BOOK, 1973*, Cairo, 1973, p. 42. There are some discrepancies between these figures and those used by Mabro, *op. cit.*, and Nashashibi, *op. cit.*, p. 75, but the margin of error is quite small and the order of magnitude unchanged. These accounts do not include arms purchases. The figures cited are presumably and unfortunately current prices. The estimates for 1973, 1974, and 1975 have been taken from official sources as reported in the local press.

who predicted that Egypt's response to the economic malaise would be capitulation to Israeli terms on the diplomatic front. That was indeed one of the few options open to Egypt. A second option included programs of strict austerity and continued military stalemate combined with an intensification of the domestic revolution to iron out inequities in income distribution. This formula was espoused mainly by leftist elements who fancied Cairo as the Hanoi of the Arab world. The third option was war in some form. Egypt could either have planned on a long, perhaps inconclusive campaign in which the strategy would be to bleed Israel until she capitulated, but with a very high risk of great power intervention, or a short, brutal campaign that would set the stage for renewed diplomatic efforts. Despite his lack of military credibility at the time, Sadat opted for the latter course.

The October War of 1973 had direct and mainly positive implications for the Egyptian economy. By breaking the military stalemate and catalytically provoking the Arab embargo on sales of oil to the United States, Sadat was able to draw Washington directly into the process of looking for a rapid settlement to the Arab-Israeli conflict. To bring about a negotiated settlement in light of Egypt's and Syria's limited but highly significant military success would require the "even-handedness" that the Nixon administration had pledged but never applied in its Middle East policies. Having proved Egypt's willingness and determination to fight for its occupied territories, Sadat felt more secure in suggesting that a logical outcome—given a settlement—would be a rapprochement with the West in general and the United States in particular. Part of that rapprochement would certainly consist in renewed and expanded trade relations and the opening of the Egyptian economy to Western technology and investment. Concomitantly, by choosing war, Sadat forced the Arab oil-rich states to come to the aid of brother Egypt (and Syria) against the number one enemy, Israel. President Boumedienne of Algeria responded in person to Egypt's need during the fighting by flying to Moscow to negotiate and pay for emergency shipments of arms to the Egyptian front. Other states, including Saudi Arabia, came across shortly thereafter with credits, loans, and gifts to help Egypt import necessary foodstuffs and raw materials. Still, the immediate impact of the fighting was to worsen Egypt's internal economic conditions. Raw materials

shortages were intensified as international shipping to Alexandria was disrupted for the same reasons. Severe shortages of basic consumer goods became chronic.

But in the euphoria following the Crossing, these privations could be borne by the populace with relative good will, while Egyptian planners looked to the future for the first time in many years with something resembling optimism. An economic new look, quietly discussed since 1971 and given considerable airing in the spring and summer of 1973, appeared to be feasible after the October War. The new look was referred to in the press as the economic "Opening," or the economic open-door policy. While Part II in this series of Reports will explore its basic elements in much greater detail, in general the Opening sought to bring together Arab (and also Western) capital, Western technology and expertise, and Egyptian skilled manpower and markets to rejuvenate the Egyptian economy. All hinged, however, on creating an atmosphere of political stability within Egypt and one of tranquillity and peace within the area. Neither could be achieved so long as Egyptian and other Arab land remained under Israeli occupation and a peace settlement a remote hope. But the Israeli disengagement along the Suez Canal in the winter of 1974, brought about by the persistent efforts of Henry Kissinger, augured well for a final settlement. A very highly placed Egyptian diplomat did not hesitate to predict that the Israelis would be out of all of Sinai before summer. After all, he remarked, when Eisenhower made up his mind that he wanted them out in 1956, they had left Sinai within three months.

It became clear soon thereafter that this diplomat, at least, would have to revise his timetable, because the Israelis were not amenable to trading territory for what they regarded as flimsy and nonoperational promises of peace. Yet there was no cause for gloom. Diplomatic relations with the United States had been restored at the ambassadorial level. Japanese and West German trade delegations flowed continuously through Cairo. Persian Gulf petrodollars began arriving in dribs and drabs, and even American businessmen began to smell the breeze. David Rockefeller, Chairman of the Chase Manhattan Bank, made a highly publicized trip to various Arab countries in January and February 1974. His remarks were indicative of the new image Egypt was trying to project as well as of what most concerns Western businessmen:

> I think that Egypt has come to realize that socialism and extreme Arab nationalism... have not helped the lot of the 37 million people they have in Egypt. And if President Sadat wants to help them, he has got to look to private enterprise and assistance.... I discussed this to a considerable extent with some of the Israeli leaders and they agree with us. They feel that the position of President Sadat vis-à-vis his own country is a constructive one, and they feel there's a better chance of ending the war if help is given to him to build his own country in a sound economic way.[6]

And there were more hopeful straws in the wind. In the late spring the Shah of Iran, sensing an appropriate moment to increase his leverage within the Arab world and simultaneously to outflank Saudi Arabia and Iraq, committed about $700 million in aid and investment in Egypt. Close on the heels of Iran's unprecedented actions came President Nixon's visit to Egypt. It was his last triumph, though not enough to save his presidency, but at the time, however, Egyptians were unwilling to see themselves as part of the President's last efforts to keep himself in office. The popular welcome for the President of the United States was as genuine as it was overwhelming, and the joint communiqué issued by Sadat and Nixon depicted a future so rosy that the local press could hardly refrain from proclaiming that Egypt's salvation was at hand.

> The United States regards with favor and supports the ventures of American enterprises in Egypt. It is noted that such ventures currently being negotiated are in the fields of petrochemicals, transportation, food and agricultural machinery, land development, power, tourism, banking, and a host of other economic sectors.

> The estimated value of projects under serious consideration exceeds $2 billion. American technology and capital combined with Egypt's absorptive capacity, skilled manpower and productive investment opportunities can contribute effectively to

the strengthening and development of the Egyptian economy.[7]

As the months trickled by, it became clear that the $2 billion tied up in projects under "serious" consideration were at best gloss on an official statement. Their substance, a full year later, came to almost nothing, although some banks, some international hotel chains, and one agricultural machinery firm were slowly working their way toward effective participation in the Egyptian economy. But these remarks are made with the benefit of hindsight, and in the summer of 1974 there were good reasons to think that peace and an influx of capital were fully within Egypt's reach.

The Implications of the Opening

The shift in Egyptian economic policy stems from both the political and economic philosophy of Egypt's leaders and from major changes in the international arena. Briefly put, President Sadat, from 1970 on, gradually revealed his dissatisfaction with several aspects of Egypt's politico-economic structure as it had evolved in the 1960s. Specifically he was unhappy with the growing reliance on Soviet technology and markets—and the concomitant isolation from Western technology and hard currency markets—the paralysis of the Egyptian public sector. Thus it can be said that Sadat was ideologically inclined to respond positively to Western concerns over Egypt's far-reaching integration into Soviet trade and credit relations and over the quasi-monopolistic role of the public sector within the nonagricultural domain of the Egyptian economy. The May 1971 purge of those figures in his regime most closely associated with promoting closer Soviet-Egyptian relations, followed in July 1972 by the expulsion of the Soviet military missions, set the stage for the third phase of an opening up to the West and economic liberalization.

While the shift has clear and perhaps profound ideological and structural implications, it could not be acknowledged or discussed in those terms. Sadat's approach since 1971 has been to insist upon the continuity of his policies with those of Nasser. He has staunchly defended the Egyptian public sector and affirmed its role as the leading force within the economy. At the same time he has backed measures that would help it become more efficient and competitive but necessarily less protected. While Sadat has repeatedly professed his faith in Egyptian socialism, he has also warned that the basic interests of the country and the masses should not be enslaved to a rigid doctrine. Ideology must adjust with the times. In all this Sadat has shown his consummate skills as a politician, for it is practically impossible to know to what extent he is masking a desire to make a major break with the past or sincerely stating his position. The fact that he has permitted a wide-ranging debate about all the ideological issues involved in the Opening has been something of a revelation for most Egyptians. Both left and right, for different reasons, have been severe in their assaults upon the way the economy has been managed in the past, and for the first time in 20 years Egyptians are able to read in the newspapers and journals well-documented exposés of the functioning of a heretofore closed system.

There is good evidence that Sadat has in fact moved in directions that Nasser himself would have taken had he lived. The logical extension of Nasser's acceptance of the Rogers' Plan and a cease-fire with Israel in July 1970 was movement toward a negotiated settlement by pulling the United States directly into the process. Had the negotiations succeeded, one of the inevitable consequences would have been a reassertion of the American presence in Egypt, in all likelihood accompanied by aid and investment. This approach was aborted by the Palestinian uprising in Jordan and the bloody civil war that ensued. Not only did the strain of "Black September" 1970 ultimately take Nasser's life, it so divided the Arab states that no united front could be mustered in negotiations with Israel. Sadat followed roughly the same logic in October 1973, but with greater success. Still, the real question remains: if some sort of peace is achieved with Israel, how far is Sadat prepared to go in remodeling the Egyptian economy?

The remodeling being proposed so far has been justified as a shift in light of changes in the international arena, which does not represent a sharp ideological break. The two basic changes have been détente between the Soviet Union and the United States, and the accumulation of large hard currency reserves by the Arab oil-producing states. If the Soviets, as major spokesmen for orthodox Marxism/Leninism, could find their way clear to

buy large amounts of wheat from the United States and to accept direct investment in the Soviet economy from Western capitalist sources, why should socialist, nonaligned Egypt deprive itself of the same advantage? Closer to home, the Yugoslav experience of economic *"ouverture"*—receptivity to Western capital while maintaining their own market socialism—was frequently evoked by the promoters of the Opening in Egypt.[8] These examples were set before the Egyptian left and vested interests within the public sector as well as the more radical regimes in the Arab world, to assure them that Egypt was not "selling out" its revolutionary principles and socialist ideology.

Following chronologically on the heels of détente came the accumulation of ever larger increments of petrodollars in the Arab world. The first major oil price hike came at the OPEC meeting in Teheran in June 1971, and even before the October War and the spectacular price rises at that time, Egyptians frequently talked of mobilizing these vast resources in the interests of the entire Arab nation and, in particular, those of the front line states.

Détente, petrodollars, and the Opening became the subjects of a national "dialogue" conducted in the summer of 1973, before the outbreak of hostilities. With the fighting seemingly out of the way by late October, the Opening entered its operational phase. President Sadat made known his own thoughts on the matter in a document known as the October Paper, which has now taken its place among the basic documents of the revolution.[9] It is, in the best Sadat tradition, moderate in tone and studiously ambiguous. It seeks to placate both the public and private sectors, and argues that foreign investment has an important role to play in Egypt, although it will have to conform to the objectives of the economic plan. The October Paper does not spell out what direction Sadat wants to take, but it does raise the issues that have become the flashpoints of an ongoing debate which the President has observed with benign neutrality.

The only policy changes being discussed by the President (at this writing) revolve around questions of economic liberalization. At the official level the talk is not of revolutionary intensification (for example, though further land reform or nationalizations) but simply of making the existing public sector work better. Since these are the terms of debate, the free enterprise right wing has the upper hand, while the so-called Nasserites and the more radical left find themselves on the defensive. Essentially, what the right is arguing is that the Nasserist-cum-socialist formula of the 1960s has been tried and it has failed. It needs not perfecting but dismantling.

As the debate goes on, various personalities are prepared to urge differing degrees of dismantlement. Sayyid Marei, President of the People's Assembly (parliament) and for many years the architect of Egypt's agricultural policy under Nasser, has stressed the importance of Cairo and Alexandria once again becoming financial centers for the Middle East. He would like to see a heavy influx of foreign capital into Egypt, combined with a liberalization of foreign trade. Likewise, he has urged that far greater attention be paid to individual private owners among the peasantry (he has remarked that the peasant is Egypt's greatest and most neglected engineer) and that less emphasis be placed on state-guided and state-managed farms and reclamation sites. Marei's object is not to undermine the public sector but rather to make it more competitive.

More daring were the recommendations of the Budget and Plan Committee of the People's Assembly in 1974. The Committee severely criticized public sector performance and noted the Central Auditing Agency's report that the return on capital invested in the public sector was only 2.4 per cent a year. Because of technological backwardness and idle capacities, the Budget and Plan Committee recommended that public sector companies sell up to 49 per cent of their shares to foreign, Arab, and Egyptian private investors in order to finance expansion and updating. Further, companies with chronic deficits should simply be liquidated or sold.[10] Dr. Ahmad Abu Ismail, the Committee's Chairman, argued these findings forcefully before parliament. Although he was rebuked by Dr. Gamal Uteifi, the Deputy Speaker, himself an advocate of the Opening, for having overstepped the legitimate area of investigation of his committee, and was castigated by the other MPs for advocating the sale to private persons of profitable public enterprises built up by the state with the people's earnings, Dr. Abu Ismail went on

to become Minister of Finance in April 1975. His appointment must surely be indicative of the direction in which the regime would like to move.

With varying degrees of fervor the following measures have been put forth by the right in the quest for economic liberalization:

(1) Floating the Egyptian pound, so that foreign investors and importers of Egyptian goods can purchase pounds at their true value.

(2) Opening foreign trade to the private sector and allowing private entrepreneurs to deal freely with foreign suppliers and markets.

(3) Reactivating the Egyptian stock and commodity exchange so that shares in public and private enterprises can be openly traded, and, in light of the liberalization of foreign trade, agricultural commodities brought into the futures market.

(4) Raising the ceiling on personal incomes by rescheduling tax rates. At present any income in excess of LE 10,000 is taxed at 90 per cent.

(5) Easing business and corporate profits tax.

(6) Raising the ceiling on land ownership which currently limits any one proprietor and his immediate family to 50 feddans (1 feddan = 1.038 acres).

(7) Permitting foreign banks to open branches in Egypt to deal not only in hard currency but to accept local deposits and deal in local currency.

(8) Allowing the Egyptian private sector to be the local partner in joint-bank ventures rather than the public sector as the law now stipulates.

(9) Allowing investment of foreign or private capital in any sector of the Egyptian economy as long as the project is not *incompatible* with planning goals. (Use of the word "incompatible" is significantly different from being "subordinate" or "integrated into" the National Plan.)

(10) Allowing foreign firms or joint venture enterprises to lease or own Egyptian agricultural land for commercial purposes.

In the course of the debate over these questions voices from the past were heard again for the first time in over two decades. Almost all were persons who had somehow fallen out with Nasser and opposed his policies of the 1960s. Their commentaries ranged from the ironic to the vitriolic. Saba Habashi, a former Minister of Finance, wrote of Nasser's Socialism:

> In our haste to bring about distributive justice and the "melting" of class differences (*tadhwīb al-fawāriq bayn al-tabaqāt*), we resorted to confiscation and described private capital as despicably feudalistic and a contemptible means of class domination and exploitation, without making any distinction between investment and exploitation. One of the results of this misguided policy was that savings melted away with class differences.[11]

Another voice from the past has been that of Ahmad Abu al-Fath, the old Wafdist and former editor of the now-defunct nationalist newspaper, *al-Misri*. Abu al-Fath had been living in exile since the mid-1950s, but returned to Egypt after the October War. His prescription for the future is to bring parliamentary democracy and the free enterprise system to Egypt. He advocates draconian measures in dealing with the errors of the past:

> All those who committed crimes in the past against the rights of the people must be held accountable for their deeds....We must take a new look at all existing laws that hinder the private sector. We do not need laws to regulate the various activities of this sector, but rather one law, with a single clause, that will stipulate the abolition of all other laws that prevent the private sector from undertaking its leading role [in the economy].[12]

Abu al-Fath's exhortations fly directly in the face of the officially canonical 1962 Charter (see Appendix), and there are myriad figures on the center and left who are more than willing to point this out. In general they have claimed that the public sector's poor performance in the past has resulted from the misapplication of socialist principles and that Egypt's socialist "experiment" has never really been given a fair chance. They argue that Nasser's closest advisers and executors were, for all their professed radicalism, paper socialists who were more committed to consolidating their own power within the regime than to building socialism. And their argument has all the more legitimacy, as the part about power hunger and hypocrisy was borrowed directly from President Sadat's denunciation of these individuals in Nasser's inner circle when he swept them out of power in 1971. What is needed, the leftists argue, is extension of the public sector, effective worker participation in factory management, and political and ideological mobilization to create an atmosphere of discipline and efficiency. With this as foundation there would be no objections to a greater role for foreign investment in Egypt, nor for the resuscitation of the Egyptian private sector. But foreign capital and local private endeavor must be limited to nonstrategic areas of the economy and even then subordinated to the goals of the state's Plan.

The left is probably correct in sensing that the current drift is to grant far more latitude to foreign capital and local private initiative than they consider advisable. They fear that incrementalist policies and a series of *faits accomplis* will allow the public sector to stagnate or decline while a parallel economy, built around foreign capital and banks and the Egyptian private sector, will gradually come to dominate the Egyptian economy. This would have several consequences, all deemed bad by the left. Primarily it is felt that it would give rise to a new middle class which would control the major means of production in Egypt, including most agricultural land. Dr. Fu'ad Mursi, one of the founders of the Egyptian Communist Party in the late 1940s, and the Minister of Supply between 1971 and 1973, has hypothesized that the current open-door policy is a response to the growth of a parasitic bourgeoisie in the early 1960s. After decapitating the old bourgeoisie through the sweeping nationalizations of 1961, the state inadvertently (or perhaps consciously) fostered the creation of a new class that thrived on public funds meted out through the development budget and state-private sector contracts. As much as 40 per cent of all investment under the First Five Year Plan (1960-1965) may have found its way into private hands. Similarly, as the state increased price and rent controls and subsidies of wholesale and retail prices of basic commodities, a new and vast network of black marketeers came into existence to exploit chronic shortages and price distortions. Mursi's thesis is that given the lack of incentives under existing laws, this congeries of parasitic groups (he shies from identifying it as a class) could not invest the capital they accumulated and instead wasted it in ostentatious consumption or smuggled it abroad. The Opening may allow these groups to make an attractive return on their capital legitimately and within Egypt.[13]

Even if they do invest their capital locally, the question remains whether it will favor increased productivity and the interests of the masses. The left thinks not, believing it more likely that private interests, in combination with foreign capital, will gradually move to monopolistic situations in new industries and begin to acquire interests in an underfinanced public sector. At the same time speculation in urban real estate and housing, black market operations, and legal or illegal transfers of capital abroad may well continue unabated. Class differences will be exacerbated and wealth once again concentrated within the hands of a few. Moreover, the left fears that as the new private interests will be dependent on foreign capital, technology, and expertise for the success of their ventures, they will fall ineluctably into the role of *compradors* for "imperialist" interests. In that case, Egypt's relative but nonetheless real independence would be sold to the West in exchange for, at best, growth without development. Some committed Marxists might welcome a situation of intensified class conflict, but most Egyptian leftists would rather that Egypt's transition to socialism remain a peaceful one.

In this light, the left would consider the Opening tolerable, perhaps even desirable, if there were an unequivocal commitment to public sector predominance and an insistence upon the application of a coherent plan and a clearly delineated set of development objectives. But the direction is not so clear. On occasion President Sadat has emphasized that the resurgence of the private sector would only be possible if the public sector were growing as well: "I say that if [annual investments] in the private sector were to reach LE 750 million that would be because the public sector had reached 100,000 million [sic.]. No one should fear for the public sector or the workers, for all of this

Dr. Abd al-Aziz Higazi, former Dean of the Faculty of Commerce at Ain Shams University. In 1968 he was appointed Minister of Finance by the late President Nasser, and under President Sadat became the number one economic strategist. He rose to the position of Deputy Prime Minister for Economy and Finance from which he launched the open-door policy prior to the October War. After the war he became Prime Minister but was relieved of that post in April 1975, presumably because implementation of the open-door policy had proceeded too slowly.

are but seeds of doubt, and I know exactly from where they come. When we wish to change something, we will change it openly and not in secret."[14] Dr. Abd al-Aziz Higazi, his Prime Minister until April 1975 and one of the promoters of the economic open-door policy, eloquently defended the public sector before parliament in the winter of 1974, pointing out that the taxes, royalties, forced savings, social security payments, and profits paid out by public sector companies and employees had sustained the Egyptian economy during the lean years between 1967 and 1973.

Practical policy, however, seems to be pointing in other directions. It was, after all, Prime Minister Higazi who remarked in another parliamentary session:

When we talk of the framework of public ownership, what we mean is that the dominant interest [in any joint venture] is Egyptian.... Consequently, I believe that the principle of public ownership is fully protected ... if 51 per cent [of the venture] is in faithful, nonexploitive hands. [15]

Another dynamic exponent of the Opening, Osman Ahmad Osman, the prototype of the Egyptian state capitalist, president of a giant, semi-public construction firm, and Minister of Housing and Reconstruction, put his philosophy even more simply: "If we do not hold to the complete freedom of the individual in a competitive context, then we cannot bring about any progress."[16] A final straw in the wind for the left—and for the right—was the removal of Ismail Sabry Abdullah, a well-known economist and Marxist, as Minister of Planning in April 1975. The last leftist in the cabinet, Sabry Abdullah was in a position to fight for the principle of subordinating foreign and private investment to the state's Plan, but his removal came before the all-important Five Year Plan, 1976-1980, had been drafted. Because Egypt is now, and has been since 1966, essentially without a Plan, there is no clearly identifiable public strategy to which private interests must adhere.

President Sadat has allowed all parties debating the Opening to batter themselves mercilessly with charges and countercharges. He has accorded legitimacy to all views but endorsed none. The brunt of specific challenges and criticism falls upon his Prime Ministers, first Abd al-Aziz Higazi (1973-1975) and then Mamduh Salem (April 1975-). President Sadat, for his part, is almost exclusively concerned with the conduct of foreign relations, military preparedness, and the pursuit of an acceptable settlement with Israel. What goes on within the Egyptian economy will depend in large measure on what he is able to achieve in promoting peace. The collapse of Kissinger's shuttle diplomacy in early April 1975 meant further hardship for the Egyptian masses and further stagnation for the economy. The open-door policy to date has not provided enough capital to alter these hard facts of economic reality in Egypt, and one may surmise that the imperatives of economic growth

once again may become a partial stimulus to the launching of hostilities as they were in 1973. In the meantime, Sadat has opened the door not only to foreign capital but to a debate on what had heretofore been undebatable. This may prepare the way for more profound structural changes than have been adumbrated so far. One suspects that the more the regime insists upon continuity with past policies, the more it will seek to transform or replace them. How much help Egypt may expect from the outside in promoting this process will be the subject of the next Report.

The new Prime Minister, Mamduh Salem, addresses the People's Assembly (Parliament) in April 1975, presenting his ideas on how to accelerate the open-door policy. Seated behind him, partially obscured by the microphones, is Sayyid Marei, Speaker of the Assembly, former Minister of Agrarian Reform and Agriculture. His son married one of President Sadat's daughters in 1974 and the two families are close. Marei and Salem have both been instrumental in shaping the direction of the Opening.

Photographs courtesy *al-Ahram*

NOTES

1. See John Waterbury, *The Crossing*, [JW-9-'73], Fieldstaff Reports, Northeast Africa Series, Vol. XVIII, No. 6, 1973.

2. The massive increases have come about despite the fact that the Egyptian expeditionary force was withdrawn from the Yemen during and after the June War of 1967.

3. The nonmilitary debt to socialist countries is generally put at LE 1 billion. Another billion or so is owed Western sources, including the IMF and IBRD/IDA, while another LE 200 million is tied up in long-term deposits made by Arab oil-producing states in Egyptian banks (note that Libya withdrew its deposits in the fall of 1974). The military debt to the U.S.S.R. may be on the order of LE 2 billion.

4. Dr. Ahmad Morshidi, formerly Under Secretary in the Ministry of Planning, estimated that in 1959/60 prices, per capita income in Egypt declined from LE 121 in 1965 to LE 112 in 1972. See "Colloquium on Foreign and Arab Investment," *al-Tali'a*, Vol. 10, No. 7, July 1974, p. 24.

5. See John Waterbury, *Aish: Egypt's Growing Food Crisis* [JW-3-'74], Fieldstaff Reports, Northeast Africa Series, Vol. XIX, No. 3, 1974.

6. Remarks made on CBS morning news program and reported in the *New York Times*, February 8, 1974.

7. Text of the Nixon-Sadat Statement published in the *New York Times*, June 15, 1974.

8. The Yugoslav experiment encouraging joint ventures between foreign investors and public sector companies began in 1967. Between 1967 and 1974 some 50 agreements of this kind were signed, and total foreign investment coming within their terms amounted to the rather modest sum of $100 million. The Yugoslav ambassador in Cairo, Mr.

Pavacic, publicly urged caution upon his Egyptian colleagues in their pursuit of foreign capital. His particular concern was the loss of skilled workers in public enterprises as they "internally migrated" to firms financed by foreign investors. See *al-Ahram*, June 14, 1974.

9. The other basic documents are the 1962 Charter, the March 30 Declaration of 1968, the Permanent Constitution and National Action Program of 1971. The October Paper was published, *inter alia*, as a supplement to *al-Ahram al-Iqtisadi*, May 1, 1974. Throughout, two of the most articulate and careful proponents of the Opening have been Faruq Guwaida of *al-Ahram*, and Dr. Gamal al-Uteifi, Deputy Speaker of the Parliament (People's Assembly). See especially his "International Changes and their Impact," *al-Tali'a*, Vol. 9, No. 10, October 1973, pp. 38-50.

10. For the Committee's findings see *al-Tali'a*, Vol. 10, No. 3, March 1974. In May 1975 the government decided to sell some small department stores and to sell shares in some public sector firms to their workers and the public at large.

11. *al-Ahram*, April 28, 1974.

12. *al-Ahram*, April 17, 1975.

13. Dr. Fu'ad Mursi, "The Public Sector and Private Investment," *al-Tali'a*, Vol. 10, No. 2, 1974, pp. 16-23. See also Fawzi Habashi, "The Extent of Parasitic Incomes in the Contracting Sector," *al-Tali'a*, Vol. 9, No. 7, June 1973.

14. President Sadat, October 9, 1974.

15. Cited by Adil Hussein, "Critique of the Plan and the Economic Opening," *al-Tali'a*, Vol. 11, No. 4, April 1975, p. 18.

16. *Ibid.*, p. 12.

APPENDIX

What the 1962 National Charter* Has to Say About
the Organization of the Economy

Chapter 6:   The Socialist Solution

"...The socialist path is the sole approach to economic and social progress, and, in all its political and social forms, it is the democratic way.

The control of the people over the means of production does not entail the nationalization of all means of production, and it does not abolish private property nor does it affect legal inheritance. There are two ways by which it can be achieved.

1. The creation of a public sector capable of promoting progress in all fields and bearing the principal responsibility for the development plan.

2. The presence of a private sector participating in this growth within the comprehensive framework of the plan, and without exploitation....
Competent Socialist planning is the sole means by which to assure the full utilization of all national resources, be they material, natural or human, by scientific, practical, and humanitarian methods so that all people may be served and share in a prosperous life....
Planning in our society is called upon to solve a different equation which contains within it the material and human success of our national effort: how can we increase production and at the same time increase consumption of goods and services; all this accompanied by a continuous rise in savings for the sake of new investments?...

With reference to Production:
The basic structures of productive operations—such as railroads, roads, ports, airports, powerful means of locomotion, dams, means of land, sea, and air transport, and other public utilities—must be under public ownership.
With reference to Industry:
All heavy and intermediate industries and most mining operations must be within the framework of public ownership; and if private ownership is permissible within this sector, it must be under the guidance of the public sector, the property of the people....
Light industries must be impeded from monopolistic practices, and if private ownership is free to operate within this context, the public sector must also maintain its role as well so as to orient (light industry) in the interests of the people.
With reference to Commerce and Trade:
Foreign trade must be under the direct control of the people; the import sector must be within the public sector, although private capital may participate in the export sector. However, the bulk of export trade will be in public sector hands to prevent manipulation. More specifically, the public sector should undertake three-fourths of this trade leaving the rest to the private sector.
The public sector should have a role in domestic trade. Over the next eight years, which is the time remaining in the ten-year comprehensive plan to double national income in a decade, the public sector should become responsible for at least one-quarter of this trade in order to prevent monopolies and to leave open a broad field for the activities of private and cooperative efforts....
With reference to Finance:
Banks must be within public ownership for the use of financial assets is for the nation and is not to be subject to speculation or fraud. Likewise, insurance companies must be within the public sphere to protect a large part of the people's savings and to see to their proper utilization.

With reference to Real Estate:
There must be a clear distinction between two kinds of private property, exploitative and nonexploitative....
Within the rubric of privately-owned agricultural land, the land reform laws have stipulated a ceiling upon individual ownership not to exceed 100 feddans (this was lowered to 50 feddans in 1969), although the spirit of the law indicates that this would be the ceiling for the family as a whole....
Likewise, as regards urban real estate and buildings progressive taxes and regulations to lower and fix rents are applied to avoid all forms of exploitation, although constant surveillance is necessary as well as a continual increase in public and cooperative housing to participate effectively in the struggle against exploitation....

Chapter 7:   Society and Production
"...National evolution is prepared to accept the participation of foreign capital in various national endeavors...although this participation must be within vital operations, especially those requiring modern expertise that is difficult to furnish domestically. However, the acceptance of such investment is concomitantly the acceptance of foreign participation in their administration and the annual repatriation of profits to the investors up to a certain limit.
This is a matter that must be closely regulated.
Thus the basic priority is for aid without strings.
The second priority is for credits without strings.
And this is followed by the acceptance of foreign investment in those instances where there is no alternative and in those domains requiring advanced scientific expertise....   "

---

*President Nasser described the Charter as a document that would be subjected to periodic revision in the light of changing circumstances. President Sadat has alluded directly to that necessity since 1973. In the summer of 1973, he warned that erroneous Marxist interpretations of the Charter were inappropriate and counterproductive, and in the fall of 1974 he suggested that the document should be revised or amended by substantial additions. That suggestion has not yet been acted upon.

Luring Foreign Capital

Arab capital + Western technology + Egyptian labor and markets - the population
explosion = economic growth.

From President of the People's Assembly,
Sayyid Marei's Report assessing the
economic open-door policy,
Akhbar al-Yom, April 19, 1975

The Egyptian economy may be on the threshold of a fundamental restructuring that would comprise far-reaching changes not only in the socialist mechanisms developed since 1960, but in Egypt's relations to the great powers as well. None, or very little of this restructuring will come to pass, however, unless a semblance of peace and stability can be conjured up in the area. Short of that, economic conditions in Egypt are likely to worsen, and that would entail severe social conflict and dislocations, political instability, and Egyptian leaders' perhaps rational temptation to try again to break the vicious circle of economic stagnation and the burdens of military preparedness by resorting to war. Such a scenario is all too possible although still avoidable. It is, moreover, a course to which President Sadat and other Egyptian leaders are constantly seeking alternatives in the form of an "honorable," "just" solution to the Arab-Israeli conflict. Since giving up the Prime Ministership following the October War of 1973, President Sadat has devoted himself almost exclusively to pursuit of a diplomatic settlement, leaving domestic affairs and the economy to his Prime Ministers, first Dr. Abd al-Aziz Higazi, and, since April 1975, Mamduh Salem.

To them has fallen the unenviable task of trying to make Egypt an attractive and secure home for foreign investment when it is openly admitted that war may break out at any time. Regional instability has made the survival capacity of Sadat's regime an open question. Since the Egyptian economy cannot yet be converted from a war-time to a peace-time footing, only marginal measures can be applied to deal with Egypt's massive economic problems. The large, inefficient, expensive, underproducing public sector and the sprawling civil service cannot be dealt with head-on without causing further breakdowns in production and administration at a moment when internal boat-rocking could jeopardize Egypt's regional posture. In fact, one of the main hopes of the Opening is that the (as yet unrealized) influx of foreign capital and expertise will gradually stimulate the public sector and bureaucracy to self-imposed reforms in order to compete with the newcomers. In other words, foreign capital is to be the catalyst in streamlining the public sector, a process that the State has consistently shown itself incapable of undertaking. Meanwhile, foreign capital has been kept away by the combination of continued regional hostilities, remembrance of Egypt's past hostility to foreign investment (especially in sweeping nationalizations between 1961 and 1964), and continued bureaucratic red tape. In short, the solution won't come to bear on the problem until the problem begins to correct itself.

Hopeful of luring foreign capital, the numerous advocates of Egypt's Opening (*al-infitāh al-iqtisādi*) are able to present a glowing picture of the nation's potential. Assuming for the moment that peace will be established in the area within the near future, and that all potential foreign investors can assess the investment climate in Egypt strictly on its local merits, foreign capital might be attracted by the following relative advantages.

First, and perhaps foremost, is Egypt's geographic location. Historically a strategic crossroads, ever since the construction of the Suez Canal a century ago Egypt has been astride the most heavily traveled trade routes between Europe, India, and the Far East. For this very reason Egypt, and more particularly the canal zone, was considered the jugular vein of British imperial trade and military communications. Today, with the reopening of the canal, Egypt can offer unrivaled access to the Indian Ocean or the Mediterranean. Rail and river links are available to carry goods to and from the Sudan. Ports are operative at Alexandria, Port Said, and Mersa Matruh on the Mediterranean, and Suez and Safaga on the Red Sea. Safaga will handle phosphate exports from the Aswan, while phosphate deposits and bauxite imports will pass through Abu Tartur en route from Australia to the aluminum complex at Nag Hammadi. Thus, those investors who envisage establishing themselves in free zones inside Egypt can export their products, at minimum distances to North Africa and southern Europe, India, the Far East, and East Africa.

A second frequently cited advantage is the size of Egypt's domestic market. With 37 million inhabitants Egypt is by far the largest Arab country; the only rivals in size in the near vicinity are Iran and Turkey. In theory this market is sufficiently large to warrant the economies of scale that would justify certain types of investment in Egypt.

Third, Egypt's supply of skilled and semiskilled labor and reserves of managerial personnel are large in comparison to most other developing countries. In certain industrial sectors, such as textiles, the Egyptian work force has generations of experience. Thousands of dockers, stevedores, truck drivers, electricians, mechanics, foremen, engineers, and managers are working on or managing the ports, railroads, irrigation systems, dams, land reclamation sites, and public sector factories. In general they are poorly paid and all too frequently migrate abroad, especially to the Arab oil-producing states, at the first opportunity. Foreign investors could tap these reserves, and even if they had to pay above average wages, labor costs should still be considerably lower than in many other developing countries. The minimum monthly wage in Egypt is LE 12, or about $24 at current rates of exchange. University graduates, however, will earn less than twice that salary when starting their careers. Bilingual typists in Cairo's banks (all publicly owned) earn only a few more pounds than

the minimum wage. Concomitantly, it is pointed out quietly, there is no right to strike in Egypt so the foreign investor can be assured of a fair degree of labor docility. The state's massive subsidization of basic retail goods (running LE 600 million annually), is partially justified as an indirect means of keeping wages low (the cost of subsidization is one and a half times that of public sector wages) and maintaining social peace.

A fourth advantage for foreign investors is the country's relatively sophisticated infrastructure in roads, railroads, port facilities, river transport, and power supply. Further, whatever the failings of the Egyptian economy in recent years, a wide range of agricultural production (cotton, rice, fruits, and vegetables) and raw materials industries (ranging from phosphates and manganese to pig iron and semiprocessed steel products) is open to foreign investment.

Finally, it is pointed out more in hope than in fact that Egypt has established a healthy climate for investment, especially since the 1974 passage of Law 43 which lays down the general terms of Arab and foreign capital (see page 7). And there are other atmospheric elements that some proponents of the Opening have singled out for attention. Gamal Nazir, one of the leading analysts at the Agency for Arab and Foreign Investment, has emphasized four factors that in his view place Egypt in a situation analogous to that of Japan a few decades ago. (That Japan is chosen as a model is indicative of the economic philosophy Egypt may move to adopt.) The first factor is that the Egyptian shares with his Japanese counterpart loyalty and devotion to the unit he works in, and will not change his place of work unless compelled to. Second, most Egyptian industries are of average size; very few industries employ more than ten thousand workers. Moderate size facilitates strong ties between the worker and the enterprise for which he works. The third factor is at the heart of a wide-ranging debate going on inside Egypt today.[1] In Nazir's words, "One of the reasons for the success of the Japanese system is the noninterference of the government in the country's economy except within very narrow limits. There is no doubt that those responsible in Egypt appreciate this, and, further, will strive to see that governmental supervision is within the limits that the situation requires." Fourth, Nazir pointed out that

"Islam is a religion of tolerance and humility and does not call for the formation of classes or the creation of obstacles between classes. The way is thus open for the realization of cohesion and cooperation among all those working in an economic unit regardless of differences in their [social] standing."[2]

Foreign investors, Egyptian specialists, and the President himself have all found counterarguments to one or another of these advantages for would-be investors. Geographic location is about the only advantage that holds under almost any circumstances, and it will be particularly compelling when the canal is function at or near capacity. The size of the domestic market is of limited significance since average per capital income is in the neighborhood of LE 100 ($200) per year, the bulk of which goes into rent, food, and clothing of the most basic kind. The government already fixes rents and subsidizes the retail prices of foodstuffs and cloth, so there would be no financial incentive for foreign investors to move into these areas. About all one can see among possible beneficiaries of Egypt's population size are soft drink and other beverage manufacturers (and in fact, 7-Up is coming back) and those who would produce for the numerous consumers in the middle and upper classes who are willing to pay stiff prices for luxury goods. Egypt's labor is relatively skilled, abundant, and cheap, but there are major questions about its productivity after years of the rather lax standards set in the public sector. Moreover, there are already severe shortages of certain kinds of skilled labor in Egypt—mechanics and truck drivers are among these—because of the steady out-migration to Saudi Arabia, Kuwait, the Gulf emirates, Iraq, Libya, and the Sudan. One finds anomalous situations of seasonal agricultural laborers in Upper Egypt working for 15 piastres ($.30) and stone masons on reconstruction sites in the canal zone earning LE 3 ($6.00) a day.

Nor can one take worker docility for granted. Both public and private sector companies have been plagued constantly by wildcat strikes and worker demonstrations, particularly as inflation took its toll from low wages in 1974 and 1975. The General Confederation of Egyptian Trade Unions has already stated its hostility to the Opening, and one can expect that the government will not allow

itself to become the policeman for a foreign private sector, as did some of the governments before the monarchy was overthrown in 1952. Instead, employers may be given the theoretical right to dismiss workers who behave in an "undisciplined" manner, but if such dismissals take place for political reasons, Egyptian unions will see to it that the matter receives wide publicity.

In practice Egypt's sophisticated infrastructure is already overburdened and malfunctioning. Alexandria Port, until recently, worked only one shift a day, while thousands of tons of merchandise piled up on the docks (including wheat, drugs, delicate machinery, cement, etc.) and ships lay offshore awaiting their turn to unload. Each day of waiting cost Egypt substantial sums in fines (fines may run about $10,000 per day per ship and there have been as many as 40-50 ships waiting more than a month to unload). From January through October 1974 total fines reached 40 million pounds sterling. In late 1974 the army had to be called in to clear the port, but soon thereafter the old routine reasserted itself. One of the major snags is inadequate transportation to move goods inland, and this problem will be equally acute for Port Said once it begins to function at full capacity. Other communications problems that must trouble any potential investor are the glaring inadequacies in telephone and telex communications both inside and outside Egypt. It can take up to two days to place a call to a foreign country—and sometimes almost as long to call Aswan from Cairo. Finally, many of the raw materials theoretically available are either in such short supply that incoming foreign investors will be discouraged from buying them in Egypt (as is the case for building materials in general) or are tied up in barter deals or repayment of loans and credits.

The least satisfactory selling point for the Opening has so far been the climate for investment. This is a question not only of war or peace, but of vested interests in the public sector and the sheer weight and cumbersomeness of one of the oldest bureaucracies in the world. After one year of experimenting with the open-door policy, President Sadat had to dismiss the government under Prime Minister Higazi and replace it with a new one under Mamduh Salem, formerly Minister of the Interior. One of the principal reasons for the change was to install a team that would deal with

Mamduh Salem, Egypt's new Prime Minister as of April 1975. Salem, as Governor of Alexandria, had supported Sadat in his confrontation with the "power centers," May 15, 1971. He became Minister of Interior at that time, then, in 1973, Deputy Prime Minister and Minister of the Interior, and finally Prime Minister with the specific mission of accelerating the open-door policy and slowing the sharp rise in the cost of living.

what President Sadat openly termed bureaucratic obstructionism, the result, in his view, of Egypt's historical tradition and eight years of "defiance" (*sumūd*) following the defeat of June 1967. The bureaucratic entanglements are nicely summed up in the following not atypical case study presented by a leading Egyptian analyst of bureaucratic behavior.

In June 1966, the director of a private textile concern was notified by the Social Security Organization that his firm was LE 452,907 in arrears on social security payments, plus fines of LE 148,500. The missing payments apparently covered the period from January 1, 1964 through

May 1966. The textile firm had two factories in different parts of Cairo and its administrative office in a third locale. Before the nationalization of all insurance companies in 1961, the firm had insured its workers through a private company. After nationalization, it was instructed to pay monthly installments to a designated branch of the General Organization for Social Security in South Cairo. A new social security law was promulgated, effective January 1, 1964, and that was when the trouble began.

The textile firm's director had cancelled checks and stamped receipts for all the payments that allegedly had not been made during the eighteen-month period. He personally took the documentation to the East Cairo social security branch which had issued him the statement of arrears. Having made his case to the head of this office, he was referred to an employee who was responsible for his company's files. The employee was unable to find copies of the receipts that the company director had with him and requested a delay in reviewing his dossier. After some weeks, interspersed with frequent visits to the insurance office, the factory director was able to get a clean bill of health from the employee—although not in writing—except for the matter of the first three payments of 1964. These, it turned out, had been paid to the South Cairo office, for the factory director had not received instructions to pay installments to East Cairo until three months after the 1964 law went into effect. East Cairo wanted those three months before it would clear its books, despite the fact that the factory director had with him stamped receipts from South Cairo.

The director then sent a registered letter to South Cairo, and a copy to East Cairo accompanied by full documentation, requesting that South Cairo transfer to East Cairo the payments for the first three months of 1964. South Cairo never responded to this request in any form.

In mid-August 1966, the director of the textile firm was visited by the administrative seizure officer of East Cairo, who carried out a preliminary evaluation of the firm's assets pending seizure within two weeks. A hasty visit to the head of the East Cairo branch, a re-exposure of the now voluminous documentation, led to the judgment that the officer's visit had been in error. The matter lay dormant until November 23, 1966 when the textile firm received another letter from East Cairo demanding payment for all of 1966. Once again the director was able to produce cancelled checks and stamped receipts and the matter was dropped. But then on March 1, 1967 a written warning of administrative seizure, as of March 15, was delivered to factory headquarters. The director went straight to East Cairo where he found that the former head of the branch had been replaced and that the new one knew nothing of the preceding imbroglio. The whole affair had to be gone over again in detail. When the original employee who had first reviewed the company's files was sent for, it turned out that he too had been replaced, and his successor could not locate the file. Another formal request for review had to be submitted, and by March 14 no results had been produced. East Cairo agreed to postpone seizure pending the conclusion of the review. At the end of March the new employee was transferred elsewhere. A third employee took on the review expeditiously and by the end of May concluded that all was in order, except for that small problem of the first three months of 1964. He asked the director of the textile firm to furnish a certificate from the Bank of Cairo that it had in fact paid out these installments, since the stamped receipts from the South Cairo branch apparently were not sufficient proof of payment. The certificate was produced within three days. Three more weeks passed without a formal clearing of the books. Then it was learned that the third employee had been drafted.

A new seizure warning was sent to the firm at the beginning of September 1968. The affair had now dragged on for over two years. Yet another hasty visit to East Cairo revealed that the branch head had forgotten what the problem was and referred the petitioner to the Head of the Division of Administrative Seizures, a recent appointment who was totally unfamiliar with the case.

The story has no conclusion. When the author compiled the materials for his study in June 1969, the textile firm's case was still in suspense.[3] Its significance does not lie in its resolution but in its typicality. This case does not consist of voluntary impediments that can be circumvented by a bribe, although perhaps the factory director could have tried that. The Kafkaesque quality of this affair

was not willed by anyone. Confused and changing jurisdictions, rapid personnel shifts, poorly trained cadres, lack of accountability and consequent lack of a sense of responsibility toward one's clients are, by now, endemic in the civil and public sector bureaucracy that has proliferated in the last two decades. And yet, despite the dire warnings, the plant was not seized (at least as of June 1969). Some way to keep functioning could always be found. This also is typical. There is always a way to achieve one's objectives, but one must be prepared to live in limbo, never sure that all the angles have been accounted for, all the paper work done, all the authorizations obtained, all the strategic people placated in one manner or another. Any foreign investor would have to keep this well in mind when trying to sense the local climate for his venture.

Legislation Governing Investment in Egypt

Central to Egypt's economic climate is the formal legislation governing foreign investment in the country. For the decade 1961-1971, the halcyon years of Egypt's socialist experiment, legislation was either highly restrictive or totally absent. The Charter of 1962 (see the first Report in this series for relevant clauses) reserved large areas of the non-agricultural economy for the public sector, and excluded foreign capital from any role in strategic industries. At the same time it was (and still is) illegal for foreigners to own agricultural land in Egypt. It is hardly surprising that, with the marginal exception of petroleum exploration, foreign capital has kept its distance from Egypt. But that had been the case even in periods when legislation was much more encouraging.

In the early years of the revolution, in 1953 and 1954, a number of decrees and laws were issued to attract foreign capital and to stimulate the Egyptian private sector. Local industries were given high tariff protection while duties on imported raw materials were lowered. Tax holidays were guaranteed to local and foreign investors setting up new enterprises. A 1947 law stipulating that 51 per cent of the assets of all joint stock companies must be owned by Egyptians was amended to make that percentage 49, and if that was not subscribed within a few months, nonsubscribed shares could be sold to anyone. Despite this legislation, however, in the period 1953-1961 only about LE 8 million in foreign investments came into Egypt with over LE 5 million of that tied up in oil exploration. Both periods, 1953-1961 and 1962-1971, would seem to demonstrate that capital movements are determined by the political atmosphere and not by legislation. In the first period Nasser moved from an unknown quantity, a perhaps fragile inexperienced military ruler to, after 1956, a familiar figure called by the Western world a "regional trouble-maker," the "nationalizer of the Suez Canal," and other opprobrious labels the Western world freely attached to Third World leaders. The socialist decrees of 1961 and the near rupture of relations with the United States in 1965 kept most potential investors away, except for hotel chains and oil prospectors. It has been up to Anwar Sadat, since his accession to the presidency in 1970, to remake Egypt's image. Typically, the first step taken was to formulate new legislation.

The first effort to launch Egypt's economic new look came with Law 65 of 1971 which provided for a more liberal foreign investment code and the establishment of the Egyptian International Bank for Trade and Development, which was to help channel funds into the country. The bank was put under the direction of Dr. Abd al-Moneim al-Qaissuni, a respected economist with rather orthodox views who had frequently managed the economy under Nasser in the late '50s and '60s. Almost simultaneous with the bank's founding, in October 1971, Egypt signed the IBRD international accord for the settlement and arbitration of foreign investment disputes, a token of Egypt's earnest to adhere to Western mechanisms for the transfer of capital. The code provided for a five-year tax grace and the establishment of free zones, and included the provision that joint ventures with the Egyptian public sector would be treated as autonomous units. These first timid steps, however, were taken at a moment when Sadat was predicting that war would break out within months. In brief, the net result of Law 65, in the period between its issuance in 1971 and its replacement in 1974, was that some 250 projects with a total value of LE 171 million were submitted for approval within its terms. Of these some 50 were approved with a paper value of LE 13 million. By 1974 none had actually been started. In the meantime the Egyptian International Bank for Trade and Development confined its activities largely to merchant banking.

Throughout the spring and summer of 1973 a great deal of attention was paid in the press and elsewhere to the problem of attracting investment, and the Opening (*infitāh al-iqtisādi*) became a standard part of Egyptian politico-economic vocabulary.[4] Egyptian leaders had become fully aware of the enormous petrodollar reserves accruing to oil-producing states in the region, and Abd al-Aziz Higazi (Deputy Prime Minister and Minister of Finance in the summer of 1973), one of the principal architects of the Opening, made a concerted effort to assure potential Arab investors that Egypt would provide a stable and rewarding home for their capital. Despite voluminous professions of good will and good intentions, however, petrodollars were not forthcoming. By late 1973 Egypt's foreign currency budget was hopelessly unbalanced. The war that President Sadat launched in October 1973, whatever its other objectives, prodded brethren Arab states to turn over to Egypt close to $400 million for emergency food and arms imports. These were no more than stopgap measures but they did help keep Egypt's head above water. With some sort of peace a distinct possibility after the October War, the moment seemed appropriate to introduce new legislation to attract foreign investment. As a result, Law 43 was passed by the People's Assembly on June 9, 1974. In the text of the law, ambiguities in areas where socialist principles may come to blows with capitalist incentives are blended with explicit assurances to potential investors.[5] In neither the law itself nor in its enabling legislation[6] is their specific mention of those areas in which foreign investment is *not* welcome. By proposing what amounts to a case-by-case procedure for evaluating all prospective investments, Law 43 can effectively skirt the implicit and explicit strictures of the 1962 Charter. The law states (and the enabling legislation gives no further amplification) that:

> Investment of Arab and Foreign funds in the Arab Republic of Egypt shall be for the realization of the economic and social development goals within the frame of the general policy of the State and its national plan, provided that this will be applied to projects which require international experience in the fields of modern development or which require foreign capitals within the limits of the lists prepared by the Organization (for Arab and Foreign Investment) and

approved by the Council of Ministers in the following fields:

(1) Industry, mining, energy, tourism, transportation and others (sic.) within the limits approved by the Council of Ministers.

(2) Reclamation of wasteland and its cultivation, and projects of animal production and water wealth....

(3) Housing projects and urban expansion projects....

(4) Investment companies which aim at the employment of funds in the fields stipulated by this law.

(5) Investment banks, commercial banks, and re-insurance companies whose activities are confined to the operations effected in free currencies....

(6) Banks which carry out operations in local currency when such operations are in the form of joint projects with local capital owned by Egyptians which proportion in all conditions shall not be less than 51 per cent.

There are priority areas with the fields covered by Law 43 (see Appendix A), yet certain industries of the strategic variety are not mentioned explicitly as open to foreign investment. These include, among other things, basic iron and steel products, steel sheets, pipes, textile weaving, looming and dyeing, cement, pesticides, and fertilizers. But as the Agency for Arab and Foreign Investment points out, "[the] list does not exclude the possibility of investing in other projects proposed by foreign investors if such proposal is accepted."[7] In short, the law indicates priorities but signals that nothing is *a priori* off-limits. The door is open to propose, to make one's case, and to bargain with relevant interests. Each proposal will be judged on its merits according to criteria that may change over time.

The approach most enthusiastically advocated by the Egyptians is that of joint ventures between foreign investors and public sector enterprises. This has several attractions, and, in the eyes of some several not-so-hidden dangers. First, say its advocates, such ventures will strengthen the public sector. Expansion and updating public industries

can be achieved through infusion of foreign capital and exposure to the latest technology, management, and marketing techniques. This, for instance, is the ostensible rationale for the several joint ventures being set up between Western and Egyptian banks. Second, because of association with a public sector company, the foreign investor can move into the "strategic" areas of the economy. Plans are already afoot for the establishment of a LE 100 million sponge iron plant, and, in the distant future, a one billion dollar petrochemical complex, both at Alexandria, and, perhaps, the expansion of the Kima fertilizer plant at Aswan. Those who believe that the public sector is Egypt's best hope for resisting foreign economic domination constantly call attention to the danger that any such joint ventures, under the terms of Law 43, are automatically considered part of the private sector.[8] As a result, joint ventures may turn out to be no more than a device to transfer to the private sector the most advanced, dynamic, and best-staffed industrial and commercial firms.

There are great hopes in Egypt that foreign investors will be particularly interested in establishing plants in the free zones that will be set up under Law 43. The free zones will be essentially extraterritorial and geared to export. Firms operating in the free zones may freely import and export building materials, capital goods, and their own manufactures without paying customs or export duties. Free zone projects will be exempt from all Egypt's tax laws, but they will be subject to an annual one per cent duty on the value of all goods entering and leaving the zone within the project's activities. Salaries and wages of those working for free zone firms will not be subject to Egyptian income tax. Capital transfers can be made without restrictions between the free zones and all foreign countries. If a free zone enterprise wishes to sell in the Egyptian domestic market, its products will be subject to normal customs duties. Conversely, should a free zone enterprise wish to buy locally, the Egyptian produce, where appropriate, will be sold according to world market prices rather than at subsidized domestic prices. This latter condition would hold as well for projects in Egypt proper.

The strategy of the Egyptian free zone policy is to capitalize on the country's favorable geographic location and low labor costs. That all of the city of

Port Said is to become a free zone speaks eloquently of how important the Suez Canal is to this strategy. Suez City at the southern end of the Canal may receive the same status. Significantly, that Law 51 was issued in 1966 to establish a free zone at Port Said lends credence to arguments that Nasser, at the end of the First Five Year Plan in 1965 and facing severe financing problems for further growth, was already contemplating remedies that Sadat, eight years later, put into a single package, the economic open-door policy.

There are provisions for other free zones. One hundred eighty acres have been set aside near Nasr City in Cairo and 288 acres on the desert road near Alexandria. Another free zone may be established as part of an entirely new industrial city to be built in desert land along the Cairo-Ismailia road. And beyond these, Law 43 provides for the establishment of "special" free zones that may in fact be set up virtually anywhere if the investor can make a good case. A foreign investor may purchase a factory somewhere in Egypt to produce, for example, ready-made clothing for export. That factory, regardless of its location, could be declared a free zone. The implications of this permissiveness are as far-reaching as they will be administratively complex.

What Egypt stands to gain from the free zones are new jobs for Egyptians at all levels, the training of Egyptian personnel in advanced manufacturing techniques, the possibility of profitable joint ventures that will earn hard currency, as well as some hard currency earnings through annual duties and purchases of local materials. As is the case with the entire open-door policy, however, there are dangers. The free zones may bring about further displacement of weight in the Egyptian economy—in terms of the preponderance of capital investment and the concentration of skilled and trained personnel—away from the public sector to, in this instance, extraterritorial entities. There are fears in some quarters that some of the entities, especially the free-floating special free zones, will gradually integrate themselves into the domestic economy. This might come about through the erosion of restrictions on their ability to sell locally and through the sale of shares in their firms to private Egyptian investors, a process sometimes known as salami-slicing in the United States. These apprehensions have been sharpened by recently released figures on foreign investment projects proposed to Egyptian authorities in the last three years. The capitalization of 33 projects approved for the free zones is LE 934,018,000 (or roughly $2 billion) while the capitalization of the 163 projects approved for domestic investment is LE 166,390,000.[9] Of course the debate about the implications of the free zones is, for the moment, purely hypothetical because their future hinges on the return to normalcy of the Canal Zone and the establishment of a credible peace between Israel and the Arab states.

Whether one invests in the free zones or locally, Law 43 holds out several other enticements, however qualified. There is a flat guarantee that foreign investments will not be subject to nationalization, sequestration, or confiscation "except through lawful process," but this must be taken more as a token of good will than an ironclad guarantee. All incoming projects will automatically be considered part of the private sector, regardless of their funding, and will thus be exempted from most public sector legislation affecting wages, worker representation on the management boards, profit-sharing, and so forth. Moreover, such companies will be exempt from rules determining the size and composition of the board of directors and the number of foreigners that the firm can legally employ. The initial importation of building materials and capital goods will not be subject to duty, and there will be a five to eight year grace period, after the beginning of productive operations, during which the company will not be subject to commercial or industrial profits tax. Foreign personnel (outside the free zones) may repatriate up to 50 per cent of their locally paid salaries in hard currency. Company profits can be repatriated within the limits of its hard currency balance. This balance is distinct from its profits and losses so that if, for example, a company earns profits of three units and has a positive hard currency balance of five units, it may then repatriate all its profits. But should profits exceed hard currency assets, only that proportion of the profits covered by the assets can be repatriated unless the firm is judged to play a major role in import substitution, or to bring to Egypt a name of world renown or a technology that could improve the country's overall export posture.[10]

One of the most controversial sections of Law 43 deals with the establishment of foreign banking institutions in Egypt. Provision is made for two categories of operations. The first covers foreign banks and re-insurance companies engaging in investment and commodity purchase financing which would deal exclusively in hard currencies. The second type would be joint banks dealing in local currencies in which the Egyptian partner would own 51 per cent of the assets.

When Law 43 was debated in the People's Assembly in the spring of 1974, the question of foreign banks generated the most heat and smoke. There is small wonder in this. Until the late 1950s the Egyptian economy had been dominated to a considerable degree by European banks. The first steps in the widespread nationalizations following the Suez War of 1956 began with the French and British banks (including Barclay's, the Ottoman Bank, and Credit Lyonnais). These were followed in early 1960 by the nationalization of the two major private Egyptian banks, Bank Misr and the National Bank of Egypt. Since then, the public sector banks of Egypt have dawdled along with antiquated procedures and limited operations. Because traditionally Egypt has survived and at times thrived on foreign trade, the banking system has always been viewed as the core of economic sovereignty, but by 1974, that sovereignty appeared to be in question. Large Western banks with billions of dollars of assets and worldwide networks and connections could easily swamp the Egyptian banks. The Western banks, allowed to operate in local currencies, would be able to take away most deposits from local banks, begin to attract most local shareholders, gain a stronghold on the orientation of investment capital, and eventually repatriate large hard currency earnings made possible by the mobilization of domestic capital. The alacrity with which Western banks expressed their interest in entering the Egyptian field after October 1973 (including a couple of well-publicized trips by David Rockefeller of Chase Manhattan) led many to question the investors' ultimate intentions.[11]

By the spring of 1975 about 20 foreign banks had requested permission to open branches in Egypt. Five joint ventures have been established so far: among them Chase Manhattan in a 49/51 per cent arrangement with the National Bank of Egypt, First Chicago and Banca di Roma in a similar deal with the Misr Bank, and Barclay's with the Bank of Alexandria. While Egyptian public sector banks control the majority shares in these joint ventures (and none are as yet fully licensed), former Prime

Osman Ahmad Osman (left) Minister for Housing and Reconstruction and President of The Arab Contractors Inc. construction company meets with the Secretary of Treasury, William Simon in the Cairo Hilton, July 1974. Simon came to follow up economic and technical assistance projects discussed by President Nixon in his June 1974 trip to Cairo. Behind Simon and Osman is Hermenn Eilts, U.S. Ambassador in Cairo. Simon told the local press that it was not unusual for Americans to do business in their bathing suits.

Minister Higazi and some of his advisers have suggested that eventually the 51 per cent Egyptian ownership may be within private hands. First National City Bank, rather than entering a joint venture, is waiting for this eventuality. Iran, Saudi Arabia, and other Gulf States have also been pressing for private sector association. A joint Saudi-Cairo Bank venture may be the pioneer in this respect, although final licensing has not been arranged. Many Egyptians would like to see Cairo capture Beirut's role as financial clearing house for the Arab world. Egypt has some undeniable advantages. One is its enormous import bill, which is in all other respects a liability. With imports for 1975 estimated at over LE 2 billion, including over four million tons of grain and food commodities, there is enormous scope for short-term financing. In 1973, short-term borrowing amounted to more than LE 1.1 billion and has risen since, with interest rates as high as 18 or 19 per cent. These import needs are but one facet of Egypt's poverty, and in this instance poverty means big business.

The arrival of the big banks has been greeted with mixed emotions by Egypt's bankers, many of whom are strong backers of the Opening but fear its application to the banking sector. They are seeking time to modernize their own plants and to stake out their own autonomy before confronting and competing with the newcomers. Dr. Kaissouni stated bluntly:

> I am against the criticism directed at Egyptian banks because it is unjust. Egyptian banks are restricted, exactly like tying up someone and throwing him into the sea and asking him to be a good swimmer....On the basis of my experience in Arab banking the principal cause of banking success results from the freedom granted [the banks] by the state, and if Egyptian banks were granted a greater measure of freedom, the results would be good. And that is the basis of the economic opening.[12]

Egyptian banks are facing another problem common to all aspects of the Opening: how can public sector firms, with low and inflexible wage levels, retain or recruit competent personnel in the face of outside capital that is willing to pay for the best? The extent of the challenge is summed up in the question of licensing the joint Chase-National Bank venture. Its president will be an Egyptian and his salary at present cannot legally exceed LE 5,000 ($10,000) per annum. The second in command, appointed by Chase, is allegedly slated to earn $100,000 (all perquisites, allowances, and the like included). No bright ideas about how such discrepancies might be remedied have been offered.

The Potential Miracle

All could yet go well were peace to break out. Were a number of processes to gain momentum simultaneously, the Egyptian economy could begin to move ahead. In several respects these processes go well beyond luring foreign capital but are well within the spirit and practice of the Opening. For any kind of forward movement to begin, steady and substantial sources of hard currency must be found. Until a year ago it was estimated that foreign financing amounting to LE 300 million was needed to meet the gap between Egypt's domestic savings rate and investment requirements. However, the ambitious transitional plan of the last half of 1974 and all of 1975 was to more than double the investment rate to LE 1.1 billion for 1975. Only about LE 400 million of that can be raised through domestic capital formation; the other 700 million will have to come from external sources. Furthermore it is likely that Egypt will run a trade deficit of LE 1.5 billion in 1975. The first component of the miracle, then, is massive doses of capital from the oil-rich Arab states to cover investment needs and commercial deficits. There is no denying that the potential source of funds is there. Saudi Arabia's revenue from oil sales in 1974 alone was on the order of $28 billion.

In addition to the hoped-for foreign investment, the revivification of the banking and private sectors, and the establishment of free zones, at least four other factors could channel substantial amounts of hard currency into Egypt. One, the parallel money market, is already doing so. This market, set up in September 1973, serves two basic purposes. The first is to attract the hard currency savings of Egyptians resident abroad by buying their earnings at an attractive rate of exchange (for the dollar, the pound is valued within this market at half its official rate). From the various estimated earnings of the some 200,000 Egyptians working abroad, it seems likely that the parallel market may attract upwards of LE 50 million annually.[13] In addition, tourist receipts, earnings from "non-traditional exports," and returns on a portion of textile exports are paid into the market. Foreign exchange in the money market will probably maintain or exceed its current level of LE 150-200 million. The second primary function of the market is to sell hard currency at more than the official rate to Egyptian private sector importers who, under more liberal import laws, are able now to import a wide range of goods and equipment. This market in essence represents a partial step toward floating the Egyptian pound, and other steps are likely to follow.

Tourism could become a steady hard currency earner under a calmer atmosphere in the region. In 1974 Egypt hosted 680,000 tourists, about 80 per cent of them from neighboring Arab states, and tourist receipts amounted to LE 70 million. The Minister of Tourism declared that his ministry's goal for 1980 was to bring in LE 250 million. It might just be possible, for Egypt has substantial recreational and historical attractions, and foreign capital has shown a particular interest in hotels and tourist facilities.

The reopening of the Suez Canal is also likely to be a source of important hard currency revenues. In the last year before it closed in 1967, over 20,000 ships passed through the canal, paying LE 93 million in tolls. It is now believed that after the first stage of widening, earnings could rise to LE 600 million, and if the canal is further widened to take supertankers Egypt could earn one billion pounds a year. Similarly, the Suez-Mediterranean Pipeline, now under construction by Italian firms and supervised by Bechtel of the United States,[14] will transport upwards of 80 million tons of crude petroleum annually from Ain Sukhna on the Red Sea to Sidi Krir on the Mediterranean. While rates are still indefinite, total annual revenues might amount to LE 60 million.

The last factor in the potential miracle is oil. Despite the 1967 loss of the fields at Abu Rodeis in the Sinai (which the Israelis have "skimmed" of the most accessible oil), Egypt's potential production could be considerable. The bulk of the proven reserves lies in the Gulf of Suez and Red Sea areas, and finds have been made in the Delta and Western Desert. Egypt has contracted with 24 companies for oil exploration in deals whose total worth amounts to $320 million. Current production is only 8-9 million tons a year and Egypt is a net importer of petroleum products. There are hopes, however, that production will rise to 50 million tons by 1980 and that Egypt will become a net exporter of petroleum. A recent IBRD report on Egypt forecasts that the country could earn as much as one billion dollars a year in petroleum exports beginning in 1980.

If all these factors bear fruit according to these projections; *if* Egypt can obtain a rescheduling of its foreign debts (already the case with West Ger-

many and Japan) or grace periods (a request has been made to the Soviet Union) to get over the hump of the middle seventies; *if* idle capacities can be overcome in public sector industries; *if* foreign markets for Egyptian goods can be found; *if* the private sector begins to invest responsibly in the economy;[15] *if* the economy can be converted from its LE one billion war effort to peace-time growth; and *if* tourism, oil, the earnings of Egyptians abroad , and the Suez Canal can rapidly reach their maximum capacity to generate hard currency; *then* a real economic breakthrough may take place.

The Results to Date

The Opening's 18 months of effective operation have not been particularly rewarding. That was predicted, but some Egyptian officials and a part of the Egyptian press insisted on making pie-in-the-sky statements that could only lead to unreasonable expectations. *Akhbar al-Yom* once headlined an alleged billion dollar Saudi grant to Egypt which turned out to be commitments in principle for specific purposes of about $300 million. Since January 1974, the great bulk of the incoming or promised capital has come in the form of bilateral credits and loans and not in the form of direct investments. While the sums of money available theoretically are impressive, they will result in capital transfers only as rapidly as Egypt develops, contracts for, and begins to execute specific projects.

What has actually happened in foreign investment? By the end of 1974, 552 projects of foreign investment had been submitted to the Agency for Foreign and Arab Investment. Of those the Agency initially approved 196 with a total paper value of LE 1,102 million. Approval by the agency, however, simply gives the investor the green light to seek further authorizations from the ministries responsible for the project's sphere of activity (for instance the Ministries of Tourism, Industry, Plan, Finance) and to seek the necessary building sites, permits, and import licenses. Only ten projects have actually begun to "produce." Three are free zone projects consisting of a navigation company, an automobile storage firm, and an automobile import firm. The seven inside Egypt consist of an electronic calculator assembly, Granada Tourist City, a beauty products concern, a fire extinguisher company, a marble and granite plant, a synthetic fiber concern, and a plywood plant. These are modest starts. As noted above, over 80 per cent of the capital invested in approved projects will go to the free zones. The 163 projects accepted for Egypt proper are capitalized at an average rate of only LE 1 million. Bigger projects, such as the sponge iron plant and the petrochemical complex, have been agreed upon but are years away from implementation.

A glance at Table 1 reveals that less than half the capital to be invested in the 163 internal projects is to be raised locally and will not represent any hard currency transfer. It also shows that about 65 per cent of all the capital in these projects will be invested in tourism, hotels, housing, and construction. Tourism is likely to provide relatively quick returns for Arab and foreign investors and there are already plans to tear down the old Semiramis

and replace it with an enormous tourist complex, and to build a new Marriott Hotel and a second Hilton and Sheraton. The capital will be largely Arab while the international hotel corporations will come in under management contracts. Housing, a sphere in which Law 43 gives special rights to Arab investors,[16] is the second boom area. So far this capital has gone largely to middle- and upper-income apartment houses in Cairo where inflation in real estate values is pricing Egyptian investors out of the market. It is not at all unusual now for luxury flats to sell at upwards of LE 30,000 and one was recently advertised at LE 130,000. In the case of one large project for 10,000 "economy flats," to be financed partly by Saudi Arabia and built by Ahmad Osman's construction company, apartments will cost LE 5,000 and more, with down payments of LE 1,000, and occupancy at least three

Table 1

Approved Foreign Investment Projects
September 1971 - December 1974

Nature of Project	No.	Free Zone Projects Capital '000 LE			No.	Internal Egyptian Projects Capital '000 LE		
		Foreign	Local	Total		Foreign	Local	Total
Building Mat.	1	78,261	--	78,261	13	3,735	3,298	7,033
Chemical Ind.	6	2,125	183	2,308	36	11,874	5,138	17,012
Spinning and Weaving	8	41,840	298	42,138	24	4,732	992	5,724
Petroleum	2	528,262	--	528,262	--	--	--	--
Food Ind.	6	6,338	1,200	7,538	10	5,690	2,487	8,177
Commercial Storage	5	2,779	--	2,779	--	--	--	--
Animal Husb.	1	25	--	25	5	3.700	942	4,642
Services	2	3,962	--	3,962	--	--	--	--
Eng. +Mining	2	270,426	50	270,476	19	7,993	7,950	15,943
Tourism and Hotels	--	--	--	--	24	21,263	13,800	35,063
Housing/Const.	--	--	--	--	12	35,982	36,753	72,735
Mining Ind.	--	--	--	--	1	32	20	52
Banks and Investment Co.s	--	--	--	--	--	--	--	--
Total	33	934,018	1,731	935,749	144	95,001	71,380	166,390

Source: the 1974 Report of the Agency for Arab and Foreign Investments as reprinted in *al-Ahram al-Iqtisadi*, No. 473, May 1, 1975, pp. 29-35.

years away. Such housing is logically destined for Egypt's lower-middle classes whose average per capita income is about LE 300 a year, less than a third of the required down payment.

One element of a basic pattern is clearly emerging. Western private interests are not eager to invest capital in Egypt. Instead, they are eager to sell expertise and equipment and to manage projects that are financed by Arab investors. Arrangements similar to several hotel projects and Bechtel's management contract for the SUMED pipeline are being sought by General Motors Corporation, Leyland motors, Food Machinery Corporation, Lonrho Limited, and Otis Elevators, among others. This highly profitable, low risk approach is all the more attractive because several countries have offered Egypt credits and loans of various sorts to finance specific projects or to buy commodities and capital goods. For many foreign investors the name of the game is not investment but supplies, management contracts, and commissions.[17]

In the wake of the October War, the Opening has enjoyed its greatest success in eliciting a great deal of bilateral credit. The total value of this credit in all its forms was $4.4 billion as of January 1, 1975. Of this, about $1.2 billion could have immediate relevance to Egypt's balance of payments problem. These credits are tied for the most part to commodity and goods imports, such as $500 million in Iranian buses or food imports from the United States. They also include a $70 million loan from the IBRD/IDA, and tied or reactivated credits from France, Japan, Holland, West Germany, the U.S.S.R., Romania and others. And there were two outright gifts totaling $200 million in the form of personal checks[18] from King Faisal to the Egyptian treasury. But it should not be forgotten that these credits can be utilized no faster than the rate at which commodities and goods can be contracted for and made available, and even were these credits immediately accessible, their total is miniscule in comparison to Egypt's staggering commercial deficit. The remaining $3.2 billion in bilateral credits are largely tied to the execution of specific projects and thus will be disbursed over a long time period. Considerable credit has been made available for reconstruction in the Suez Canal Zone, worker housing, the re-

habilitation of the Egyptian railroads, the Talkha fertilizer plant, Suez Canal widening, the expansion of al-Azhar University, a spinning mill, and a number of joint investment and construction companies. Kuwait, with $818 million, Saudi Arabia with $661 million, and Iran with $480 million are the leaders in supplying credit of this variety. The United States has put up $170 million for Suez area reconstruction and canal clearance plus another $157 million in commodity credits.

The results of the Opening have been sufficiently disappointing and the country's balance of payments problem sufficiently alarming to prompt a

Ashraf Marwan, President Sadat's principal trouble-shooter in the Arab world. He is Minister of State for Arab Affairs and has been seminal to virtually all bilateral credit, trade, and investment deals between Egypt and various Arab states. He also has the distinction of being married to one of Nasser's daughters.

President Anwar Sadat, center, with the late King Faisal of Saudi Arabia, visit the city of Suez, in the summer of 1974. The city is to be partially rebuilt with Saudi aid. To Sadat's left is Osman Ahmad Osman, Minister for Housing and Reconstruction, and to King Faisal's right is General Mohammed Abd al-Ghani al-Gamassi, Chief of Staff and subsequently appointed Minister of War.

chorus of demands for greater responsiveness to Egypt's needs on the part of her Arab brethren. Egypt contends that since 1948 it has spent billions of pounds and sacrificed thousands of sons in a selfless effort to uphold the Arab and Palestinian cause in the face of "Israeli aggression." It has done so at great cost to the well-being of Egypt's own people and economy. Some have remarked ruefully in recent years that the Arabs are determined to fight on to the last Egyptian. Now, after the fourth round of fighting between Egypt and Israel, Egyptians of all political hues are saying that if the rich Arab states will not come to Egypt's aid out of enlightened self-interest, then they should do so out of moral obligation. The notion of an Arab Marshall Plan, to rebuild the wartime economies of Syria and Egypt, has been appraised by a number of prominent Egyptians, including Sayyid Marei, the President of the People's Assembly and President Sadat himself. No one put the matter more succinctly or bitterly than the Marxist writer, Lutfi al-Kholi who calculated the

balance of what he calls petrodollars and petro-blood: "Every drop of blood spilt in the Sinai, on the Golan and in Palestine has been translated into an increase in the price of oil." In his accounting, because of Egypt's and Syria's military sacrifices, Arab oil-producing states are earning a million dollars every seven minutes. The petrodollar and petroblood accounts must be brought into balance.[19] So far, however, the Arab Marshall Plan notion has received no operational impetus.

The Opening's Immediate Impact

The Egyptian masses were poorly prepared psychologically for the new economic policies. After years of privation and declining living standards, many believed that the October War had set the stage for a rapid conclusion of an honorable peace, and that the billions spent on the armed forces would then be used to purchase prosperity for the masses. The newspapers were stridently optimistic about both the progress Kissinger was making toward a negotiated settlement and the rate at which foreign and Arab capital would come flooding into the country. Few heeded the cautionary remarks of Prime Minister Higazi who frequently stressed that there would be no overnight miracles and that the masses must be prepared for waiting a long time before capital actually entered the economy and even longer before it would have any tangible impact on their lives.

The pent-up consumer demands of the middle classes in particular could no longer be repressed in the months following the October War. Because of the war itself and a worsening of Egypt's foreign exchange position, however, goods of all kinds—from wheat flour, sugar, and oil to radios and spare parts—were in extremely short supply. Simultaneously, precious foreign currency in the parallel money markets was used by private importers to bring into the urban market a wide range of luxury goods such as cosmetics, electrical appliances, instant coffee, French mustard, and so forth. The arrival of large numbers of foreign businessmen and Arab investors, many of whom resided on a semi-permanent basis in Cairo, was yet another factor leading to an inflationary spiral whose roots lay in the general upward surge of world commodity prices in the same period. While it is very difficult in a system of administered prices to calculate inflation rates, the annual rate had probably reached 8 per cent by the outbreak of war in 1973 and may have risen to 25 per cent since. Giving credence to the latter figure, on May 1, 1975, President Sadat decreed a 30 per cent cost-of-living allowance to all public employees earning LE 50 or less a month.

One facet of these inflationary forces has been the burgeoning of an already dynamic black market. With intense competition for scarce goods, there has been an inevitable tendency for those who administer these goods at subsidized prices to sell them to black marketeers who then retail them at their "true market value." The entire state pricing system, including rent controls, is thus being circumvented, further aggravating the rise in the real cost of living. One item that has caused great popular indignation is the sharp increase in the price of shoes—up to LE 5 per pair. In September 1974, with the new school year beginning and the

month of Ramadan with its costly obligations in food and clothing approaching, workers in several locales demonstrated against intolerable inflation. Shoes, school books, notebooks, and uniforms for their children were at astronomic prices. Salah Jahin, whose cartoons chronicle these sorts of situations, depicted a schoolboy in front of a book store where he wants to buy his notebooks. An enormous merchant looks down at him and says: "If you want paper, you'll have to go next door to the shoeshop—the owner bought all my paper to make shoes."

Since September social agitation has been almost constant, with major outbreaks occurring in Cairo on January 1, 1975 and in the big textile center at Mehalla al-Kubra in early April. Aggravation of social cleavages is unmistakable, as is the growth of what is frequently referred to as the parasitic middle classes. Real estate speculators, black marketeers, and contractors were not only able to stay ahead of the inflationary spiral but make money from it. Added to them has been the growing host of middlemen, fixers, and consultants—all hustling for a fee or commission to help foreign investors through the bureaucratic maze, arrange for grain imports, purchase urban property, import refrigerators or taxi cabs, and the like. This activity contributes nothing to economic growth, but it does make for income concentration in the urban areas, and in the new atmosphere the wealthy no longer appear reluctant to display their wealth. Prime Minister Higazi, when queried about this phenomenon, replied rather lamely with a verse from the Koran: "Some of you We [God] have placed over others in rank."[20] The upshot has been an explosion of automobile showrooms and luxury goods shops alongside deteriorating living conditions for the masses.

In April 1975 Henry Kissinger's latest effort at shuttle diplomacy collapsed, which meant an indefinite period of continued war-footing for the Egyptian economy. At the same time the Mehalla riots (in which one worker was killed according to official count) underlined the continuing social malaise reigning in the country. President Sadat saw the implications of both events and made a thorough overhaul of the government (April 15, 1975), placing great emphasis on the economic problems facing the country. He spoke openly of

أثمان الكتب الجامعية *   * الاهرام – ٧٥/١/٢٦ –ص

ـ تشترى كتاب باربعه جنيه ؛ ٠٠ امال الامتحان تشتريه بكام ؛

When rising expectations meet inflation. The cartoon displays the university student trying to coax LE 4 from his lower-middle class, threadbare family to buy books for his courses. The disillusioned father quips "You're going to buy books for four pounds?...and your final exams, how much will you buy them for?"

illicit profits, corruption, and exorbitant commissions and acknowledged an intolerable rate of inflation and black market practices. Finally he said that the open-door policy had been victimized by bureaucratic red-tape and erroneous ideological resistance. The man he chose to replace Higazi was Mamduh Salem, the former Minister of Interior, whose office symbolized law and order. His task is threefold. First, he must make it clear that while the regime sympathizes with the plight of the masses and will try its best to cope with the most pressing problems, it will not tolerate violence and what it calls "sabotage" in the pursuit of mass demands. President Sadat reinforced this position in his May Day speech, when he also promised public sector workers a 30 per cent cost-of-living allowance. Second, as an experienced administrator and a forceful personality, Salem is to lead a campaign against bureaucratic impediments to growth and investment. The organization of public sector industries is likely to undergo major changes in the direction of greater autonomy and closer attention to profitability. Third, while not an economist, Salem is to produce results for foreign investors who are willing to bring their capital to Egypt. His first address to the Egyptian press indicates the kind of approach he and the President favor:

Every condition is a restriction, and every restriction is incomprehensible. The thing is to let the investor direct himself to his natural place according to his own freedom of action and the dictates of the needs of the Egyptian market....Anything that leads to an increase in production and self-sufficiency—or prosperity—we must accept and not refuse. We must welcome all Arab and foreign capital that finds its way to investment in Egypt.[21]

If these remarks constitute the new guidelines for investment in Egypt, a very major change in official philosophy will have taken place. The leading role of the public sector, the determination and regulation of investment opportunities according to the Plan's objectives, and the practice of sectoral "zoning" between public and private interests, will apparently be stressed less in face of the imperative to increase production. If Salem's new guidelines become operational, Egypt's economic door will be wide open—but will anyone come in? The Egyptian economy is the creature of the continued state of hostilities between Israel and the Arab states, and so too is the Opening. Peace might not assure an influx of foreign capital, but continued war will almost certainly preclude its advent.

[Photographs courtesy *al-Ahram*]

NOTES

1. John Waterbury, *The Opening, Part I: Egypt's Economic New Look* [JW-2-'75], Fieldstaff Reports, Northeast Africa Series, Vol. XX, No. 2, 1975.

2. Gamal Nazir, "Foreign Paths to Growth Relevant to Egypt," *al-Ahram al-Iqtisadi*, No. 471, April 1, 1975, pp. 18-20.

3. Dr. Malak Guirguis, *Egyptian Personal Psychology and Impediments to Economic Growth*, Ruz al-Yussef Press, May 1974 (in Arabic), pp. 209-250. For more recent examples see *al-Ahram*, May 9, 1975.

4. See, for instance, one of the several articles by Gamal al-Uteifi on this subject: "Do Foreign Investments Contradict Socialism?", *al-Ahram*, August 16, 1973.

5. The official Arabic and English versions of the Law were published in a special supplement to *al-Ahram al-Iqtisadi*, September 1, 1974.

6. The enabling legislation pertaining to Law 43 was published in Arabic in a supplement to *al-Ahram al-Iqtisadi*, February 15, 1975.

7. From an advertisement published as part of a special supplement to the *London Times*, March 26, 1975.

8. The explanatory clause reads "Companies enjoying the provisions of this Law [43] shall be deemed to belong to the private sector of the economy, irrespective of the legal nature of the indigenous capital participating therein. Legislation, regulations, and the statutes of the public sector of the economy shall not apply to said companies." *London Times*, March 26, 1975.

9. For the apprehensions, see, *inter alia*, Adil Hussein, "Criticism of the Plan and the Economic Opening," *al-Tali'a*, Vol. 11, No. 4, April 1975, p. 16; and Mahmud Maraghi in *Ruz al-Yussef*, No. 2440, March 17, 1975. For the statistics, extracted from the Agency for Arab and Foreign Investment, see *al-Ahram al-Iqtisadi*, No. 473, May 1, 1975.

10. See the excellent collection of articles, John Stephens and P.F. Hayek (eds.), *Investments in Egypt: Law No. 43 and its Implications for the Transfer of Technology*, Fund for Multinational Management Education, November 1974; especially Ahmad Shalaqany, "Repatriation of Earnings under the Investment Law," pp. 27-38.

11. See the *Egyptian Gazette*, February 27, 1975.

12. Cited in Faruq Guwaida, "The Opening; Oppressor or Oppressed?", *al-Ahram*, April 25, 1975. Perhaps the proposal from the Ministry of Finance to allow Egyptian banks to accept foreign currency deposits at high interest rates will also allow both the banks and the depositors to use these currencies locally. See *al-Ahram*, April 6, 1975.

13. The exchange rate has raised some thorny and as yet unresolved issues. Egyptians can buy pounds through the parallel money market at ca. 58 piastres to the dollar. Foreign investors must convert at the official rate of ca. 40 piastres.

14. Bechtel Corporation (San Francisco) was initially awarded the contract to construct the SUMED line in September 1973. The decline of the dollar on world markets had made Bechtel's offer the most competitive. The resurgence of the dollar in early 1974 and rising construction costs prompted Bechtel to withdraw. Several Italian firms—including Montubi, CIME and two ENI subsidiaries stepped in. The total cost of the pipeline may be $420 million. It will be operated by a joint-venture company, half the capital subscribed by the Egyptian General Petroleum Corporation and the other half divided among Petromin of Saudi Arabia, a number of Kuwaiti companies, the Abu Dhabi National Oil Company, and the Qatar National Oil Company. Chase Manhattan Bank has loaned Egypt $80 million to cover its foreign currency equity in the project.

15. Only 10 per cent of total investment in the economy has been undertaken by the private sector in past years, and the bulk of that has been in upper-class housing and real estate speculation.

16. See Article 4 of Law 43 that reserves all housing projects to Arab investors.

17. For instance, in 1974 the value of United States imports from the Middle East rose from $1.8 billion to $5.9 billion, largely represented by increases in the price of oil. However, United States exports to the Middle East rose from $3.5 billion to $6.3 billion in the same period.

18. Figures taken from an unpublished inventory of foreign credit prepared by the economic section of the United States Embassy, Cairo. An important source of capital that does not fit neatly into this picture are Arab credits for arms purchased. Algeria, Saudi Arabia, and other Arab states have paid out several hundred million dollars to cover Egyptian arms needs. At Rabat, Morocco, in 1974 the Arab League members and heads of state agreed to set up a special $2 billion armaments fund for the front-line states.

19. Lutfil al-Kholi, "Petro-dollars and Petro-blood," *al-Ahram*, January 30, 1975.

20. See Higazi's remarks published in *Ruz al-Yussef*, No. 2420, October 27, 1974.

21. See *al-Ahram*, April 24, 1975.

De-Nasserization?

Forgive me, Ó Gamal, my hand cannot grasp the pen. It is not my habit to write when pain and grief harness my mind and cloud my reason. I shan't be long. Sadness has invaded every home, in grieving for you, because in each home there is part of you... for every individual has placed from his heart a brick in the lofty edifice of your making....

It is not merely [a question] of love of your person, but that of the protection of what the life of this, your country, is all about. In you the people have found the incarnation of the image of their freedom. They have made of you, while you lived, a monument of our freedom, and now that you have left us, permit us to erect a great statue in Liberation Square to look upon the coming generations and to be, forever, the symbol of our hopes. It is not fitting that this statue be undertaken by the state but rather by the people themselves from their own meagre resources; and I am one of them. Today I offer what I can, LE 50, to open the subscription to this endeavor. How cheap it is beside what you have left us, Ó Gamal,...

Tewfiq al-Hakim, October 1, 1970

Little by little, voices that were accustomed to debate became faint, and the beloved ruler himself became accustomed to rule without debate. The iron curtain slowly began to descend between the people and the conduct of the absolute ruler. We loved him, yet we did not know his inner thoughts nor the real motives for his conduct. Our hearts pierced the curtain between us, but our faculties of reason were totally isolated, never grasping what went on behind the veil. We never knew of our own affairs, or of foreign affairs except what he told us from on high, during holidays and on other occasions... and when he said of a great power [the United States in 1965] that had an atomic arsenal, "If our conduct displeases them, let them drink the sea," we were filled with pride.

Tewfiq al-Hakim, July 1972 [1]

Tewfiq al-Hakim is the dean of Egyptian letters. He was also Gamal Abd al-Nasser's favorite author. In 1933 he wrote a book entitled *The Return of the Spirit* (*'Awdat ar-Ruh*) which, among other things, suggested that the Egyptian people have a natural proclivity for leaders that they can venerate or worship. Such leaders, whether one approves of them or not, were conspicuously absent in the years before World War II. Nasser admired Hakim's book a great deal, but, the author now suspects, for the wrong reasons. Forty years after *The Return of the Spirit*, Hakim wrote *The Return of Awareness*. Although it was not published until 1974—and then in Beirut—it was written in 1972 at the time of the twentieth anniversary of the Egyptian revolution, and only two years after Nasser's death. The passages cited above amply demonstrate Hakim's change of mind or heart as Nasser's image receded into history. In this most recent book, Hakim makes no effort to resolve the inconsistencies of his behavior during the Nasser era, and his current, highly critical re-evaluation.

Tewfiq al-Hakim shown on the cover of his book *Return of Awareness*. ('Awdat al-Wa'i), Beirut, 1974.

He admits, in essence, that for 20 years he was duped, and that the fault lies ultimately with himself and with other writers and intellectuals who allowed themselves to go to sleep or be silenced. Consequently, he writes, a revolution in which he believed was so distorted by personal rule that it failed to achieve even 10 per cent of what initially had been expected of it. Hakim notes ruefully that when he suggested that a statue in Nasser's memory be erected in Liberation Square, he received many letters of support. One writer, however, thought the statue should be erected in Tel Aviv since without Nasser the Israelis could never have achieved the cultural and military advantage they held over the Arabs after 1967. A visitor to Cairo will observe that there is no statue of Nasser in Liberation Square nor, presumably, is there one in Tel Aviv.

The storm raised by Hakim's book had been brewing since Nasser's death, if not before. A great leader had fallen after dominating the country for

18 years, having had his share of success and perhaps more than his share of failure. The inevitable storm consists in the opening of a debate about Nasser as a person and leader, and about the final balance sheet of his incumbency. All this can be superficially compared to what transpired in the U.S.S.R. after Stalin's death, but one should keep in mind that Nasser did not indulge in political excesses of Stalinesque proportions, nor did he erect a system that would warrant a totalitarian label. His rule was long, his impact upon his own country and in the international arena was enormous, and his own peers, principally in the person of fellow officer and co-conspirator Anwar al-Sadat, will preside over the remaking or gradual erosion of his legacy. But there the analogy stops.

The crux of the debate in many ways set off by Hakim is that the July Revolution, according to many, failed to achieve its basic objectives in terms of Egypt's economic well-being and international stature and independence. Put crudely, Nasser came to power with the British occupying part of Egypt and he died with the Israelis occupying the Sinai. When he took office the bulk of the population lived at subsistence levels in the countryside and virtually no industrial sector existed. When he died Egypt's population was a third again as big as when he took power, and while the population is much more urban today, average per capita income is still no more than $200. The rudiments of an industrial sector have been put in place, but with just over one million industrial workers Egypt is far from being an industrial society.[2] What went wrong?

There is considerable consensus in Egypt that much did go wrong. The remedies that are proffered, however, vary widely according to their source—left, right, or center. While most suggestions have radical implications for systemic overhaul, many are afraid to open the debate too broadly for fear of polarizing national opinion and provoking widespread conflict. Perhaps more prosaically, many who have benefited from the "Nasserist" system do not want to be the victims of change. Hakim drew the heaviest criticism from defenders of the status quo or those who advocated "more of the same." Despite charges of hypocrisy and opportunism, however, he has not ceded an inch. He wrote in *al-Ahram*, "I am an old man [born in 1899] and a candidate for death; I have no ambitions and no hope for anything.... There i pretext of some seriousness, to wit that to criticize the revolution of 1952 or to question Nasserism poses a threat to the "gains of the revolution" [makāsib al-thawra] and is a step backwards. If this were true, then it would truly be a disaster.... The [Nasserist] dossier must be opened."[3]

The Nasserist Dossier

In the course of the debate, several major questions have been raised, apart from consideration of how various protagonists in the debate have marshaled materials for their arguments. There is an undeniable tendency for opinion to sort itself out along a left-right continuum, although one must be careful to use these terms within their Egyptian context. Briefly, the "left" defends the principles of the July Revolution (a more collective way of speaking of Nasserism) and believes that since they were distorted in application, the proper response is not to abandon but to apply them correctly and reinforce them; the "right" believes that since the operational failings of the revolution stem from faulty principles, the principles themselves must be changed. That the revolution failed to achieve its self-proclaimed goals is agreed. The most significant and potentially explosive disagreement is about how to remedy the situation. President Sadat's implicit role, as the debate has developed, has been to try to find and delineate common ground where it exists, insisting upon certain broad questions of principle but otherwise remaining aloof. Nevertheless the fact that he has so far tolerated the debate, and perhaps even encouraged it, is a solid indication that, over time, he is prepared to accept fairly major changes in the political system. He will not, however, make any speeches like Khrushchev's 1956 address to the 20th Congress of the CPSU which launched the de-Stalinization campaign. To the contrary, Sadat has repeatedly insisted upon his shared responsibility for all that Nasser did and his willingness to accept blame for what went wrong (remarks of that kind already impose certain restraints upon the participants in the debate). At the same time he rejects the use of the term Nasserism, referring instead to the principles of the July Revolution.

The View from the Right

The Egyptian right has trained its fire principally on political abuses under the Nasser regime. This is to some extent a construct of those who manage the right-wing press, for their concerns are largely based on fighting communism and restoring a liberal, parliamentary forum for political discourse. Far more circumspect in enunciating their views on the economy, the right wants to curtail the growth of the public sector and to revitalize the private sector in conjunction with an open-door policy toward foreign capital (see Parts I and II of this series). The major spokesmen for the right have been the Amin brothers, Mustapha and Ali, who have resurfaced after several years of disgrace during the Nasserist regime. Mustapha Amin, jailed from 1965 to 1974, was allowed once again to take over Akhbar al-Yom and al-Akhbar, the newspapers he had founded in 1944 with his twin brother Ali. Given his own experience—he was tried and convicted of espionage for the CIA, hence his long years in prison—Mustapha Amin has used his newspapers to launch a crusade against police rule and the abuses of power exercised by Nasser and his cronies in the 1960s.

One major target of the right has been the so-called power centers (marākiz al-quwwa) that Nasser allowed to emerge under his aegis. The term itself seems to have been coined before 1967 to refer to the top brass of the Egyptian armed forces. The senior officers had formed a sort of clique under the patronage of Field Marshall Abd al-Hakim Amir, Nasser's brother-in-law and a founding member of the Revolutionary Command Council (RCC). In his long tenure as Minister of War and/or Chief of Staff, Amir made the armed forces his constituency—one with which he could, and apparently did, threaten Nasser. His chief henchman and "personnel manager," Shams Badran, was allegedly scrupulous in applying the principle of "loyalty before competence." With the crushing defeat of the armed forces in June 1967, followed by Amir's suicide and the trial and condemnation of Badran, the senior officers corps ceased to be an effective power center. Today, however, considerable fuss is being made about the abuse of power by Amir, Badran, and their cronies and the injustices committed in special military tribunals and military prisons. Without explicit attribution, it is broadly hinted that emergence of such powerful and unaccountable figures was inherent in Nasser's style of rule.[4]

With the armed forces collectively in disgrace and without leaders, other power centers took on increasing importance. These emerged from a combination of elements. One of the most significant was the elaborate police and intelligence networks with which Nasser surrounded himself (after 1967 and the removal of former intelligence "czar" Salah Nasr, the major figures were Sami Sharraf, Minister for Presidential Affairs, and Sha'arawi Guma'a, Minister of Interior with the 20,000 man Republican Guard and internal intelligence at his direct command). A second important source was the Arab Socialist Union (ASU), Egypt's only legal political organization, under the control of Ali Sabry and Abd al-Muhsin Abu Nur. Not all these figures were close friends, nor did they always cooperate with one another. Indeed, part of Nasser's strategy was to encourage rivalries in order to avoid concentrations of power and to maximize his own chances of receiving accurate information on their activities. Vice-President Anwar al-Sadat, who acceded to the presidency after Nasser's death, was definitely not a part of this inner circle, nor could he continue Nasser's strategy of divide and rule. Thus the minimal grounds for establishing an effective alliance existed. This congeries of power centers, with acolytes in the Ministry of Information and at the head of the National Assembly (the Egyptian parliament), had built their power bases during the 1960s, a decade characterized by Egypt's most concerted effort to introduce socialist principles and practices. It was highlighted by the First Five Year Plan, the nationalizations of 1961, the Charter of 1962 (with its endorsement of scientific socialism), the increasingly heavy reliance upon the U.S.S.R. for military and economic assistance, and the establishment of the Arab Socialist Union. On the whole, the leaders of the power centers were "left-leaning." The depth and sincerity of the socialist beliefs of Sabry, et al., is moot, but it was the card they had played in the 1960s and they were pretty much stuck with it. Since Sadat was not, at least not to the same extent, an institutional and ideological clash seemed inevitable.

The clash came in May 1971 and was fought out symbolically over the issue of Egypt's union with Libya and Syria. Sadat approved the union, while Sabry and the Executive Committee of the ASU opposed the specific terms under which it was to be established. On May 1, in an address to the workers, Sadat denounced the new power centers and the following day removed Sabry from the ASU Executive Committee. Sabry's cronies did not take this passively and began to mobilize the ASU and the mass media to discredit Sadat, all the while

Turah Prison, to be torn down July 23, 1975. Sadat is seen wielding the pickax. The three prisoners who are released are "Justice," "Democracy," and "Freedom." *Akhbar al-Yom* ran this cartoon on May 10, 1975 in commemoration of the fourth anniversary of the Corrective Revolution.

holding the police apparatus and Republican Guard in reserve. They were even able to recruit the Minister of War, General Mohammed Fawzi. However, Sadat outflanked them on every point. He went directly to the senior officers corps to appeal for their support and got it; and he put Mamduh Salem, then Governor of Alexandria, at the head of the Ministry of the Interior when Guma'a resigned. With neither police nor armed forces at their disposal, the power centers had to rely on the impact of their control of the media and on the "politicized" masses. It is revealing that neither instrument was effective: the masses were not about to go into the streets in response to orders from the distant summit of the ASU (they probably would not have responded to Sadat either but he was wise enough not to try it); nor could the media, which had given out so much misinformation in the past, influence the actions of the citizenry. Sadat won the encounter hands down and put the antagonists on trial. The bulk of the defendants received stiff jail terms. (With the notable exceptions of Sabry and Guma'a, most have been released.) Ironically, the issue of union with Libya turned out to be little short of a fiasco. What was significant about the confrontation was that Sadat became his own man and began to set his own style. The incidents transpiring on May 15, when he cleaned out his rivals, have now been dubbed the Corrective Revolution (*thawrat as-tashīh*) and each year since the right has celebrated it virtually as a national holiday.

President Sadat has provided and legitimated the symbols now being brandished in the political debate, and they are symbols that no one can really contest. Soon after May 15, Sadat personally presided over the public burning of tapes accumulated from over 22,000 telephone taps maintained by the internal security apparatus. Police surveillance, harassment of innocent citizens, violation of individual and public rights of speech and thought have been targets of the right, although the left, whose members suffered perhaps more than all others from such abuses, have denounced such practices as well.[5]

One of the most sensational exposés is contained in the prison memoirs of right-wing leader Mustapha Amin. In these,[6] Amin recounts in spectacular detail the systematic physical torture to which he and others were submitted in Egypt's prisons. He singles out General Hamza Basyuni,

director of military prisons, called the "King of Torture," for particular attention. This psychopath, many of whose misdeeds have been confirmed by others not wishing publicity, personally attended to the torture of certain prisoners and delighted in unleashing his two police dogs on bound victims. When one of these dogs died, the prisoners were flogged round the clock until they had finished building a magnificent tomb for it.[7] Amin's account also contains a point-blank accusation that Nasser had ordered his arrest (it was carried out by Salah Nasser), had determined his sentence, and was fully aware of the torture to which he was submitted. Amin's exposé had equally harsh words for the Amir-Badran clique and implied that Shams Badran may have been the major CIA man in the Egyptian hierarchy. In the pages of *al-Akhbar* and *Akhbar al-Yom*, Amin has provided a forum for all those who suffered from political trials and tortures in prison. It is now claimed, and has been for some time, that there are no political prisoners in Egyptian jails, only persons arrested, charged, and convicted of specific penal or security offenses.

To dramatize the machinations of the Nasserist power centers the right-wing press has given much attention to specific instances of massive abuse. One of these was the incident of May 1966 in Kamshish, a small village in Menufiyya province. In 1966 a local official of the ASU was assassinated there. Officials claimed that a "feudalist" in the village had eliminated this local representative of

Akhbar al-Yom, May 10, in commemoration of the Corrective Revolution. The caption is "The Revolution of May 15 which smashed the shackles." The hatchet is labeled "May 15."

ثورة ١٥ مايو
الثـــــورة التى حطمت الأغـــلال ٠٠ !

the people and progressive principles. Although many were arrested, the principals were brought to trial nearly two years later, before the High Court for State Security. There, most of the accused were declared innocent of participation in any plot on the grounds that they had been systematically tortured to extract confessions. Despite the judgment of the High Court, however, some were put in military prison without charges. They were simply detained. As Mustapha Amin explained "the basic rule in those days was that if you were found guilty, you went to prison; and if you were found innocent, you went to a concentration camp."

Amin and others claim that the Nasserist regime trumped up the Kamshish incident to mask a sordid vengeance killing arising out of an affair between a local prostitute, the landowner, and the ASU official. The ASU official was a friend of Hakim Amir, of Amir's son-in-law, and of Nasser's brother. The regime seized upon this incident, so the skeptics argue, to settle a personal score beneath a rhetorical cloak—the forces of social justice facing the evils of feudalism. Others are more inclined to believe the official version, yet without denying some of the more mundane details of the affair. Regardless of the merits of either interpretation, the point is that the right is currently exploiting this incident to highlight the absence of an independent judiciary under Nasser, the abuse of socialist principles for personal ends, and heavy-handed police rule.[8]

Related to the Kamshish incident, two other events have now become *causes célèbres*. The first was the institution in 1966 of a Committee to Liquidate Feudalism, presided over by Hakim Amir and charged with the investigation of violations of the ceilings on landholdings set down by the land reform acts of 1952 and 1961. It was no secret that violations, through various legal gimmicks, were fairly widespread. Some speculated that putting Amir in charge of a committee investigating many of the senior officers that had acquired land since the revolution would perhaps cause his own patronage system within the army to come unstuck. In any case, critics now claim that the Committee authorized several property seizures and arrests for purely personal reasons, none of which could even distantly be related to violations of land reform laws. Once again, the right today considers power centers in the army and the ASU, with no popular control or surveillance over their activities, as causes of these "injustices."

The second *cause célèbre* is based on a series of confrontations between the Egyptian judiciary and Nasser's chief lieutenants. Friction had been growing throughout the 1960s as the regime placed more stress on socialist mobilization, occasionally at the expense of an independent judiciary. Moreover, the judiciary had more than its principles and traditions to defend; it undeniably harbored some of the more conservative elements of the civilian elite (including sympathizers of the banned Muslim Brotherhood) who were suspected of wielding their judicial privileges to undermine the regime. The confrontation began to heat up when the judiciary made clear its opinion that it would be nearly impossible to sustain the charges brought against the defendants in the Kamshish trial. In the spring of 1968, Dr. Hilmy Murad, an eminent lawyer and then Minister of Education, pleaded with Nasser to try the case in civilian courts rather than before a military tribunal, which would have been presided over by the now-notorious General Fu'ad Dagawy. Murad's advice contradicted the council of Mohammed Abu Nusseir, the Minister of Justice, who recommended a military tribunal despite the fact that such courts lay outside his purview. Nasser accepted Murad's advice and the trial was held before the High Court for State Security, which eventually cleared the defendants.

The confrontation came rapidly to a head thereafter. In 1968, in light of the approaching Kamshish trial, Nasser's lieutenants thought it urgent to purge the judiciary of reactionary and obstructionist elements. The task fell to Abu Nusseir, allegedly a hatchetman for Sabry, Abd al-Muhsin Abu Nur, and Sami Sharraf. In March, widespread student-worker riots—protesting the light sentences handed out to the senior officers in the wake of Egypt's defeat in June 1967—intensified the sense of urgency. The judiciary, through the Lawyers Union, chose this delicate moment to enunciate its basic principles. On March 28, just a few days before Nasser delivered the March 30 Declaration (now one of the "basic documents of the revolution"), the Lawyers Union issued its own declaration. It insisted upon the need to affirm the sovereignty of law in Egypt and to guarantee the absolute independence of the judiciary. In essence, the judiciary was declaring that it resist all attempts to force its members to join the Arab Socialist Union, a step that Sabry and Abu Nusseir felt would be necessary in transforming the judicial mentality. The gauntlet was down, and was finally taken up in July 1969.

Abu Nusseir and Sabry allegedly infiltrated the judiciary and began compiling dossiers on suspect members. A new law was drawn up that would temporarily suspend judicial immunity. With the stage set, Nasser reshuffled the government, dropping Abu Nusseir and Hilmy Murad from the Cabinet. The new law was immediately applied and all 4,000 members of the judiciary were temporarily suspended pending a reorganization of the association. Eventually, nearly 100 judges and counsellors were fired outright and another 40 or so were transferred to other posts. The purge, currently being recounted in considerable detail in the *Akhbar* press, has been labeled "the Massacre of the Judiciary." Abu Nusseir's dismissal from the Ministry of Justice just prior to the purge is now seen as a subterfuge that allowed him to claim, as he has done, that he had nothing to do with the removals. His critics have refused to accept his excuse and repeatedly called for his trial.[9]

The right-wing press has brought a number of other issues to public attention. For instance, criticism, progressively less circumspect, has been directed at the arrests, trial, and execution of Muslim Brethren charged with plotting against the regime in 1965. In a single day in August 1965, 27,000 Egyptians were arrested on suspicion of complicity. The Muslim Brethren, as an organization, had been banned since 1954 when one of its members tried to assassinate Nasser. Indications are, however, that by 1965 it had rebuilt some sort of clandestine organization which, one would gather from the extent of the arrests, was fairly large. The suspects were tried in General Fu'ad Dagawy's court and eventually three were sentenced to death while hundreds of others were given prison terms at hard labor. Of the three who were executed, one was the old and respected Muslim theologian, Sayyid al-Qutb. The right now claims that this venerable figure was severely tortured prior to his trial. During the trial the prosecution tried to establish that the plotters had been acting on the orders of King Faisal of Saudi Arabia, Egypt's number one enemy at the time. (He and Nasser had become bitter adversaries in the course of the protracted war in the Yemen, the outcome of which held substantial stakes for both Egypt and Saudi Arabia.) Since Faisal has become an official hero in Egypt (and after his death something of a martyr) because of his economic assistance after 1973, *Akhbar al-Yom* has taken perverse delight in pointing out that innocent people were sent to jail merely on the suspicion that they had contacts with this now glorious figure.[10]

بيه ــ مافيش حرارة نسـأل الرأى العـــام عاوز أحزاب والا لأ .. !

To the ASU leader on the phone: "O Bey; the phone's dead so we can't ask the people if they want more than one party or not...!" *Ruz al-Yussef* 2422, November 11, 1974.

The right-wing press (including *al-Akhbar, Akhbar al-Yom, Akhir Sa'a,* and *al-Musawwar*) has selected the Arab Socialist Union as a major target because it monopolizes the Egyptian political arena (technically, it owns all Egypt's newspapers) and because it housed one of the principal power centers of the 1960s. To some extent Nasser saw the ASU as little more than a civilian counterweight to the armed forces. At various points in time, however, he seemed to want to use it as a meaningful political instrument for mobilizing the masses, particularly during the First Five Year Plan. Nasser also knew that the ASU, which encompasses almost all adult Egyptians, was too diffuse and sprawling to mobilize much of anything. Consequently, he experimented with setting up a "vanguard organization" within the ASU, whose members would not be known but who would be recruited for their exemplary behavior and devotion to socialism. With the release of the Marxists from concentration camps in 1964 and the dissolution of the Egyptian Communist Party in 1965, many Egyptian leftists found their way into the ASU and the vanguard. Nasser entrusted several of his colleagues with the recruiting process, and each put together his own network of cronies, so that several, not one, clandestine vanguards emerged. These then vied to control access to Nasser or to manipulate strategic sources of information and intelligence. Such internal maneuverings and rivalries frequently spilled over into the kinds of political abuses outlined above. The left itself was not at the head of any of these ASU networks, but did provide the rhetoric and the personal training that could have made the ASU more profoundly socialist. Nevertheless, the presence of communists in the ASU, coupled with the widespread abuses emanating from the power centers, has allowed the right to associate all these abuses with leftist ideology, leftist personnel, and leftist organizational format. It follows, in this view, that the ideology, the personnel, and the organization should all be jettisoned to avoid such abuses in the future.

One writer for *al-Gumhuria*, Ali al-Daly, went so far as to urge that the names of all members of the vanguard organization be published so that appropriate action could be taken. Salah Hafiz, co-editor of the weekly *Ruz al-Yussef* which has been carrying the cudgels for the left, was quick to point out that Daly's argument was no more than undistilled McCarthyism. Further, if one were to act upon it, the list could include the names of most of the Egyptian Cabinet in 1974, for most of these men had served under Nasser and, with more or less good will had followed Nasser's directive to join the vanguard. It is not inconceivable that President Sadat himself was a member of the vanguard, although it was Sadat who disbanded it after May 15, 1971.

In its critique of political legitimacy in Egypt, the right has also focused attention on the successive waves of property sequestration and deprivation of political rights to which hundreds of Egyptians were subject between 1953 and 1966. The first wave engulfed old regime politicians and hangers-on in the court of King Farouq. Their assets were seized after 1952 and they were forced into political isolation. Another group, in large part prominent members of the Egyptian entrepreneurial bourgeoisie, was the object of a new wave between the issuance of the Socialist Decrees of July 1961 and 1964. The investigations and seizures carried out by the Committee for the Liquidation of Feudalism represented the last installment in this process. Clearly what is at issue here for the right is the absolute inviolability of private property, yet the principle of

private property was never rejected by Nasser's regime. In fact, around 90 per cent of Egypt's agricultural land remained in private hands. Nonetheless, politically motivated property seizure, with or without compensation, was particularly repugnant to the right in principal and in practice, they tended to be the victims. Between 1961 and 1967 the state sequestrated 122,808 feddans (one feddan equals 1.038 acres) from 1,615 families. Sa'ad Hagras, the senior official in the Ministry of Agrarian Reform, added fuel to the rightest fires by his estimate that between 1961 and 1974 the land seized had accumulated unpaid rents amounting to LE 700,000.[11]

These much-criticized practices are now being reversed, as sequestrations are lifted and political rights are restored. Fu'ad Serrag al-Din, former Wafdist Minister of the Interior, has been awarded land he formerly owned within the limits of 10 to 40 feddans for each of the nine members of his family. More than 53,000 feddans valued at LE 60 million have been restituted to others. The process will continue, with the exception of land that had been sequestrated under various laws and definitively redistributed to smallholders.[12] As one would expect, restitution has not always gone smoothly. One owner who was given his land back tried to negotiate new terms with the peasants who had been cultivating it in the intervening 13 years. He wanted to replace the rents that the state had charged (at a rate of seven times the agricultural tax) by his former sharecropping arrangements in which the landlord takes half the produce, *after* the government has bought its share of those crops under obligatory quotas.[13] No doubt in all this, the right is ready to endorse Tewfiq al-Hakim's rhetorical query: "and socialism...how has it been applied? Has it been other than the seizure of assets of a certain social class to the profit of a new class that has become as rich as the former?"[14] Curiously, the left is as prepared as the right to ask this same question.

In sum, the right has called attention to the need to restore freedom of the press and freedom of the judiciary, to revive the Egyptian Parliament, and to resuscitate the Egyptian private sector. They see the need for all these components as checks and balances against potential power centers and against the quasi-monopoly of the state over most spheres of economic activity.

The Leftist Defense

Inevitably in the course of this debate the left has found itself on the defensive, particularly since the President has emphasized issues that play to rightist interests. No one can credibly oppose freedom of the press, greater influence for the directly elected representatives of the people in the People's Assembly, an end to police abuse and arbitrary arrest, or an independent judiciary. Naturally the left suspects that the right is using these rubrics purely as slogans, and that their real intention is to roll back the socialist revolution and reassert the upper bourgeoisies' dominance over Egypt's political and economic life. The left is in the difficult position of having to admit past abuses while staunchly defending the principles for which they were committed.

Throughout Egypt's revolution the nation's Marxists have had an uneasy relationship with the regimes of Nasser and Sadat. The first blood shed after the coup d'état in July 1952 was that of Marxist labor leaders at Kafr al-Dawar who were tried and executed for undermining public order after they had led strikes in some of the textile plants. Many leftists were jailed in 1954 and 1955 (during the same period when hundreds of Muslim Brethren were also arrested) and released only when they announced their support for Nasser in his confrontation with the British, French, and Israelis in the Suez War of November 1956. The new *modus vivendi* was short-lived, and hundreds of leftists were once again rounded up on New Year's Day 1959 and sent to concentration camps. They had severely criticized Egypt's support for an Iraqi insurgent, Colonel Shawwaf, inciter of an uprising against the regime of General Kassim, who had established a ruling coalition in Baghdad that included Iraqi communists. Most of Egypt's Marxists remained in confinement until 1964, when the state released them, partially in response to Soviet pressures, and partially because the left had endorsed the Socialist Decrees of 1961 and the National Charter of 1962. In 1965 the left decided to dissolve the Egyptian Communist Party and individually to join the Arab Socialist Union. A number of Marxists (for example, Lutfi al-Kholi, Mahmud al-Alem, Michel Kamil, and Khalid Muhy al-Din) did rise to second-rank importance either by formulating ideological glosses, training personnel and cadre for the ASU, or working in

various branches of the press under ASU control. Their goal was to promote progressive forces and trends within the Egyptian polity, but their alliance with Nasser, and more particularly his "leftist" associates such as Sabry and Sha'arawi Guma'a, was founded on mutual suspicion. The honeymoon was already over by summer 1968 when elections in the ASU were used to remove most of the organization's leftists. President Sadat has continued the process through both the purge of the ASU's vanguard organizations in 1971 and a gradual house-cleaning of the press. In the end, the left got the worst of both worlds: many of their most effective leaders were killed or shattered by years of confinement, yet their abnegation in absorbing abuse from the power centers did not serve to promote or deepen the socialist revolution.

The left is in a predicament. The new symbols of legitimacy associated with the Corrective Revolution have been brandished by the right to call into question the entire institutional framework of the socialist revolution. Uncertain that in defending this framework it will not cross swords with President Sadat himself, who has kept his views on several issues deliberately obscure, the left had to react defensively instead of developing its own independent and coherent line. The resulting role for the left is that of defender of the status quo, growling and snapping querulously at its foes, an inversion of the position leftists normally want to establish. Conservation is for the right, movement and innovation for the left.

The debate between left and right has been acrimonious, ranging from mudslinging to some fairly thoughtful and constructive exchanges. For sheer verbal vitriol, the right can seldom be outdone. The weekly *al-Musawwar* (now under the editorship of two staunch conservatives, Fikri Abaza and Salah Jawdat) has excelled in issuing dire warnings against nameless and shapeless forces of evil on the left. One of the weekly's journalists, Fumil Labib, lashed out vigorously against "them":

...they who befoul the clean air with their odor; who pollute the pure water with their poison; who seek to ignite class struggle at a time when Sadat has given the people the freedom to discuss their fate...it is they who seek to snuff out the lights and who want to transform the democratic dialogue into a blood bath, for it is always upon a sea of blood that they launch their ships....[15]

In less opulent terms, Salah Hafiz set out his warning to the right in *Ruz al-Yussef:*

> ...democratic adjustment began in the Egyptian streets and was built up by the nationalist left which has born the greatest sacrifices in its path. Then Anwar Sadat came to continue its edification and to assure its triumph and to declare it official policy [the Corrective Revolution]. And this was a victory for the nationalist left and not a reversal as claimed by the right in deceiving both itself and the people.

> It is perfectly legitimate for the right in Egypt, as part of the ruling coalition, to adhere to the slogans of the democratic adjustment, but it is not within its right to steal [these slogans] from their originators and those who have sacrificed themselves for them.... Nor can they demand the exclusion [from politics] of their originators in the name of these same slogans! [16]

A far more interesting exchange took place in the pages of *Ruz al-Yussef* between Tewfiq al-Hakim and Abd al-Sittar Tawila, a journalist whose leftist activities have earned him several periods of detention. Shortly after Hakim's *Return of Awareness* appeared, two book-length attacks on it were published in Cairo.[17] Both ranged over the full panoply of leftist criticism: Hakim's inconsistent and seemingly hypocritical behavior in the Nasserist period; the allegation that he may have received an advance of LE 10,000 ($20,000) from his Beiruti publishers; his superficial attacks on many of Nasser's economic and foreign policy decisions; and the flimsiness of his excuse that he was simply afraid to speak out in the era of power centers. *Ruz al-Yussef* granted Hakim a forum to refute critics. In an open letter to the Egyptian left, he sought to defend himself and his book and at the same time warn the left against the dangers of blindly defending the past. A week later the journal printed Tawila's thoughtful reply. First, he noted that it is anyone's right to be afraid. Nor was Hakim alone in being paralyzed by his fear. Referring obliquely to personal experience, Tawila pointed out that those who were beaten regularly in

the camps, and over several years, know the legitimacy of such fear. He then admitted that in his opinion the Egyptian left had misjudged the Nasserist experiment on at least two occasions. Finally, he advised the left to heed Hakim's warning that it could find itself in a reactionary position if it were to respond dogmatically to all rightist attacks on Nasserist policies.[18]

Despite their predicament, the left has not limited itself to rejoinders to resurgent rightist attacks, but has chosen as a target an entirely different set of issues. As Salah Hafiz indicated, the left is perfectly willing to acknowledge the existence and the abuses of power centers at the height of the socialist experiment. But in their view the aberrations they fostered stemmed from their imperfect, some would say superficial undertaking of what socialism is all about. Nasser and his colleagues had mastered some of the jargon. With perhaps the exception of Nasser himself, however, they had never appreciated its essence. In short, nonsocialists mouthing socialist slogans built a state capitalist system reinforced by arbitrary police and intelligence operations and called it Egyptian socialism. The major distortions of the experiment occurred in the economic sphere where growing state sector dominance in the process of allocating national resources actually contributed to the emergence and expansion of a private, entrepreneurial, "parasitic bourgeoisie" that lived off contracts and brokerage fees farmed out by state enterprises. As much as 40 per cent of all investment in the First Five Year Plan may have been channeled through private hands.[19]

Directly related to this phenomenon, which is no mere figment of leftist imagination, are the thriving black market and growing corruption among public service employees at all levels. Both phenomena have become particularly blatant since 1967. The psychological and economic impact of Egypt's military reverses led to relatively fixed salaries, economic stagnation, heavy military expenditures, and growing state outlays on price subsidies. Both of the latter factors contributed to a high inflation rate. The low morale of Egyptians in those years was mirrored in the regime's reluctance to appeal for revolutionary sacrifice or to apply severe (or any) sanctions to those violating public trust. For several years Egypt has had on its books a "where did you get it?" law to monitor the sometimes spectacular earnings of civil servants. The

● موسم الجرد ●

عيازي

— حريق متعمد ، لأنها فتشت بنطلون بابا وأخدت الفلوس اللى فيه !

Higazi of *Ruz al-Yussef* comments on a spreading form of corruption in Egypt. Fires mysteriously break out in public sector warehouses just before annual inventory and all the contents are declared lost. The suspicion is that the contents have simply been turned over to the black market. The little boy explains to his sister, "Arson; because mama found some money in papa's pants and took it." *Ruz al-Yussef* 2421, November 4, 1974.

law has yet to be applied. The upshot was and is rampant *laisser aller* within the administration and public sector enterprises and in their dealings with the private sector.

Although Egyptian morale and self-esteem mounted noticeably after the October War of 1973, corrupt practices that had been perfected since 1967 were, if anything, accelerated as a result of increased inflation and the more liberal policies applied to importation of luxury and other consumer goods. The middle classes, with at least a decade of pent-up consumer demand under their belts, have gone on a shopping spree that has contributed directly to the price spiral. The arrival of Arab investors, who are now allowed to buy property and to enter the urban housing market, along with the influx of Western businessmen and companies in search of housing and office space, has extended the spiral. Everything from housing to cooking oil, sugar, and vegetables has skyrocketed in cost. Rationed and subsidized goods (flour, tea, sugar, soap, rice, cooking fats, etc.), in great demand among the urban poor and lower middle classes, are in short supply and, with the connivance of public employees, large quantities of these goods find their way into the black market. The same can be said for all building materials, spare parts, fertilizers, pesticides, and the like. Finally, because of Egypt's tremendous import needs (about LE 2 billion in goods will be imported in 1975) and the proliferation of contracts with foreign firms and consultants on various projects, there is a lucrative and expanding domain in which public sector managers who supervise imports and contracts can make their 5 per cent (or more).

The left has fastened upon these practices, exposing them with increasing candor. They cite a figure, allegedly derived from official sources, showing that in the last decade more than 180 millionaires have emerged in Egypt. This might not seem noteworthy were it not for the law that since 1961 has stipulated that no individual may enjoy a total income exceeding LE 10,000. *Ruz al-Yussef*, rediscovering its muckraking traditions, has worked over this issue thoroughly in the past months, demonstrating that Egypt's tax laws have virtually not been applied to private individuals. It published income distribution figures compiled by the Price Planning Agency purportedly showing that in Egypt at least 2,000 families, comprising 15,000 individuals, have an average income of LE 33,000.[20] The article drew a direct refutation from then Prime Minister, Abd al-Aziz Higazi, followed by a tacit retraction on the part of the Ministry of Finance, pointing out that the Price Planning Agency had not carried out its survey in a very rigorous manner and that its results *might* thus be suspect.

"Everyone is Talking about the Evolution of the ASU." The cartoon depicts one of Jahin's stock characters known as Reactionary Pasha (*raga'alishi basha* in Arabic which gives its turkish flavor). In #1 the Basha says, "So that the ASU will work well we have to take a new look at the representation of workers and peasants. In my view 50 per cent representation of workers and peasants is not good, it should be 100 per cent (at all levels of the ASU)— but only after we agree on the definition of a worker and peasant. #2, Of course the worker and peasant is anyone who owned up to five farms each of which contained at least 1,000 acres, and who had been active in politics in a period that ended 22 years ago at least. #3, Likewise it is stipulated that his eyes be blue, or at least light, and that he knows how to play bridge, or at least poker, that he speaks French, or at least Dutch, and that his mother is Turkish, or at least Circassian, and that he has the title of Pasha, or at least Doctor. #4, As for the rest of the definition, we can take it from this book— *Membership Qualifications for the Royal Automobile Club, 1934.*" Salah Jahin in *al-Ahram*, August 24, 1974.

In other issues *Ruz al-Yussef* has published detailed exposés on collusion between officials in the Ministry of Housing and Reconstruction and private contractors for the construction of apartment buildings, under the umbrella of dummy cooperative societies, whose units are then sold at exorbitant prices. It has also probed the seemingly invulnerable rural labor recruiters and brokers who exploit underemployed rural labor by hiring them at rates below minimum wage levels, then provide them to private cultivators and entrepreneurs at a higher price and pocket the difference. As *Ruz al-Yussef* points out, however, one of the major customers, the state itself, has often used such middlemen to obtain cheap labor for land reclamation sites. Other targets have been the pattern of contracting for reconstruction of the canal zone cities, which in an initial phase will absorb the tidy sum of one-half billion pounds, the black market pilfering of government cooperative stores, and price fixing by quasi-monopolistic vegetable wholesalers.[21] This is the science of *kusa*, or squash, the etymologically obscure label that Egyptians attach to corruption. The left has not been alone in denouncing corruption, but while the non-Marxist opinion leaders are liable to see it as a phenomenon susceptible to treatment by purely judicial means, the left sees it as an aspect of an evolving set of class interests.[22]

It is precisely in attempting to place the problem at the systemic level that the left must tread most cautiously. The most effective remedy for corruption is more revolution, not more law. Revolution will get at its cause, the new sprawling parasitic middle classes and *bourgeoisie d'état* who symbiotically have feathered their nests in the shadow of Egypt's socialist legislation. The delicacy of the issue was nicely summed up by the experience of *al-Kātib*, a leftist monthly journal dealing mostly in cultural and historical studies and published under the auspices of the Ministry of Culture. In September 1974 Salah 'Issa, a respected historian, wrote an article entitled "The Future of Democracy in Egypt." He pulled no punches in describing the ideological eclecticism and opportunism of the Nasserist regime and announced his own fears that the new class interests in Egypt would push the country upward toward compromises with American imperialism, beginning with excessive concessions to Zionist Israel, that would bring Egypt back into the imperialist fold.[23] The journal was told by

Yussef Sibai, the Minister of Culture, to drop 'Issa and accept a new editor. The old editorial board refused and resigned en masse. *Al-Kātib* is still being published, but it can no longer be said to reflect leftist views.

The left has other less direct but equally trenchant ways in which to approach class phenomena. In December 1974, a large modern apartment building in Dokki, a residential section of Cairo, collapsed—literally within minutes—leaving behind only a pile of rubble and six victims, all members of the owner's family. The building had been declared structurally unsound some months earlier, and all its occupants had been forced to leave the premises. Only the owner and his family continued to use the building, and they paid dearly for their optimism. Hassan Bayumi, the contractor who had built the structure, has several other buildings to his credit throughout Cairo. The scandal, for this edifice and perhaps hundreds of other buildings in Cairo, was that the Governorate of Giza, under whose jurisdiction the site fell, authorized construction and never checked to see whether specifications had been honored. In fact Bayumi built several stories higher than he had been authorized and utilized cheap and faulty materials. Another reason the building collapsed so easily was that little or no steel reinforcement was used in its construction. A building alongside, which Bayumi had also built, has now been condemned for the same reasons. It was widely suspected that Bayumi had benefited from more than negligence on the part of the authorities and had probably materially obtained their benevolence. Even more disturbing, no legal steps were taken against him. Lutfi al-Kholi, editor of the leftist monthly *al-Tali'a*, made Hassan Bayumi the symbol of the new parasitic class thriving on abuse of the people's money. He called such exploiters a fifth column in Egyptian society that has grown in the wake of the 1967 defeat and that secretly celebrates the defeat as a national holiday. Al-Kholi points out that representatives of this fifth column habitually call for "Egypt first," claiming, "we are all Egyptians, all the sons of Adam, all God's creatures—among us there is no left and no right, we are all just Egyptians." This, al-Kholi protested, is crude sophistry. The fact that members of the Cabinet, including the Prime Minister, had utilized roughly the same line made his attack all the more daring. *Al-Ahram*, which normally publishes al-

Kholi's shorter articles, refused this one. *Al-Tali'a* published it in its public opinion section.[24]

The Relatively Silent Center

Something we could call centrist thought still dominates the political debate, by its weight, numbers, and the fact that President Sadat is *probably* part of it. The problem is that its arguments are far more difficult to summarize because they are diffuse, searching, pragmatic, and above all inconsistent. The center, manifesting neither the strident advocacy of the right nor the ideological defensiveness of the left, is seeking not so much to persuade others as to find itself. In a period of flux it is dangerous to speak of constituencies and interest groups, yet we may hazard estimates of the right, left, and centrist constituencies. The right speaks for remnants of the prerevolutionary political system (Mustapha and Ali Amin, Ahmad Abu al-Fath, Fikri Abaza, Ahmad Hussein, Muhammed Fargnali, and so forth), the new legions of middlemen, brokers, and fixers, the so-called "national bourgeoisie" ranging from shopkeepers to textile manufacturers, sectors of the academic and journalistic world, and to a lesser extent the religious right. The left finds its base among the students (but by no means all of them), the major trade and labor unions, sectors of academia and journalism, and perhaps among parts of the civil service. Predictably the center borrows from all the above. The public sector and civil service elite, built up during the Nasserist period, with its progeny in the policy-making elite, are the center's backbone. The Army and the ASU probably reflect all political tendencies, while, for the outside observer at least, the peasantry remains an unknown quantity.

Dr. Fu'ad Zacharia, Chairman of the Department of Philosophy at Ain Shams University, has put the centrist arguments as cogently as anyone. His position does not differ in content from that of Tewfiq al-Hakim who must also be considered a centrist. Zacharia began with a few disclaimers and some self-definition. He is not, he stated, a member of the dispossessed bourgeoisie, he has never personally suffered from the abuses of the power centers, and he considers himself a non-Marxist progressive and socialist. His concern was not so much with the negative aspects of Nasserism as with the left's dogmatic defense of it. In essence he agreed with Hakim; let the "dossier" be opened. The left may claim that too much attention is being paid to what went wrong; this is only natural, Zacharia feels, since for years Egyptians heard only the putative successes "which we had learned by heart." Further, Zacharia claimed that the right has monopolized the investigation of what went wrong. "The right is an ugly demon (*ghūl*) which seeks to tear this people apart in order to devour its flesh once again. But the left, which imagines itself the guardian of the people, is an ignorant guardian (*ghāfil*); it helps the thief without knowing it and delivers to the thief, out of its shortsightedness, services that it could never have hoped for otherwise."

What the left and center must do is look coldly and analytically at the course of the revolution. To what extent have class differences really been eliminated or mitigated? To what extent has mass education really raised the intellectual level of young Egyptians? To these and other questions Zacharia answers that the revolution fell far short of its goals, and he argues that one of the fundamental reasons was lack of effective popular control over the formulation and application of Nasserist policies. Perspective is needed, and by way of example Zacharia mentioned that he had recently reread Nakram Obeid's Black Book, published at the end of World War II, in which Obeid attacked Nahhas Pasha, head of the Wafd Party, for corruption, or at least for tolerating corruption within his government. The book made a tremendous impact at the time and led to the division of the Wafd Party itself. In Zacharia's view, from today's perspective the whole scandal seems a tempest in a teapot, an affair of a few thousand pounds. Zacharia implies that Egypt would be lucky to have corruption on that limited scale today, and even luckier to have as much public indignation aroused by the exposure of what actually goes on.[25]

Fu'ad Zacharia clearly reflects a large body of centrist opinion that cut its teeth in politics under Nasser and that nurtured great expectations in the context of the 1952 revolution. That few of these hopes have been realized does not mean they were unfounded nor that Nasserism was totally without merit. The question, rather, is to find out what went wrong and then to effect the institutional changes that could lead to the fulfillment of earlier expectations. Within this general trend of opinion, however, there is a substrain whose numbers or commitment are surprisingly hard to size up or grasp. This substrain consists of the Nasserists themselves. For the most part they are more firmly on the defensive than the militant left. Several of the most vocal Nasserists have been reduced to relative silence. After the October War, Mohammed Hassanein Heikal, editor-in-chief of *al-Ahram* and one of the few men who could legitimately claim to have been a confidant of Nasser, was removed from his post by order of President Sadat in his capacity as titular head of the ASU, which controls all newspapers. Heikal had been perhaps too bluntly skeptical in questioning whether Kissinger's shuttle diplomacy would ever lead to a durable settlement, and he implied that Sadat had gone too far in placing his hopes on American intervention for bringing about Israeli concessions. Heikal was silenced in January 1974, with the semi-official explanation that he had built his newspaper and his own position into an independent "power center" that had behaved irresponsibly. Since his dismissal, many of his warnings have turned out to be particularly prescient, but while he is privately consulted by the President, his public voice has been almost stilled. Through Beirut publishers, however, he has been able to make his own comments on the Nasserist era.[26] There is a slightly plaintive tone to his defense, an insistence that the balance sheet lies predominantly in Nasser's favor, and that, in any event, the criticisms being directed at him are all rather worn. Even the accusations of abuse of police power are not new, and, Heikal insists, such practices were as marginal as they were reprehensible.

A few other prominent Nasserists have similarly fallen into relative obscurity. When Heikal was forced out of *al-Ahram*, Hatem Sadoq, head of the newspaper's Institute for Strategic and Political Studies and also married to one of Nasser's daughters, resigned from his job. In a shakeup of the press in March 1975, Mustapha Bahgat Badawi, a staunch Nasserist and editor of the daily *al-Gumhuriyya*, was relieved of his post. The self-appointed defenders of Nasserism today seem to consist of various technocrats and civil servants intimately connected with vast projects such as the Aswan High Dam or the Iron and Steel Complex undertaken during Nasser's tenure, and a broad range of university student groups whose center and rallying point is Ain Shams University with its annual colloquium commemorating Nasser's death, when intellectual batteries are recharged in a week devoted to Nasserist thought.

President Sadat and the Staging of the Political Debate

Floating somewhere above all this soul-searching and settling of accounts has been President Sadat. It is hard to imagine how anyone could be serene given Egypt's external problems and their economic repercussions at home, but Sadat has been just that. Sadat's basic strategy has been to set the rules of debate without predetermining the conclusions that are to be drawn, for the course of the debate itself will inform him what concrete steps are warranted. The President has the institutional power to make his own judgments stick. With the army recast in its traditional role of defender of the nation's integrity and its participation in civilian politics disparaged, and with the ASU dormant since 1971, Sadat is in these respects a greater master of the domestic scene than Nasser ever was. Sadat's position is precarious because of Egypt's momentous economic and international problems, but Egypt's President clearly runs the show.

The true brilliance of Sadat's performance is that he gives the impression of not running the show. This is not to suggest that the "liberalism" he has fostered is totally false, for indeed his espousal of liberal political principles is sincere. But Egypt's liberalism in the post-Nasser era is not yet rooted institutionally; it is so far the creature of President Sadat. He professes to want to change this situation by creating a "state of institutions" (*dawla al-mu'assasāt*), clearly distinguished from a state of power centers by wedding the institutions to the rule and sovereignty of law. Several far more than symbolic steps have been taken in this direction.

Following the purge of Sabry and his colleagues in May 1971, Sadat accelerated a process of releasing all political prisoners and detainees who had been accumulating in Egyptian jails for over a decade. Muslim Brethren, some of the "feudalists" of 1966, and some of the "reactionary bourgeois" of 1961-1964 were given their freedom. Citizens who has been deprived of their political rights (i.e., the all-important right to be a member of the ASU upon which the right to exercise a profession was often dependent) regained them. Hundreds of public officials who had been fired from their jobs by arbitrary measures of administrative discipline returned to their jobs (or at least a job) in the universities, the hospitals, the newspapers, and so

forth. The victims of the 1969 massacre of the judiciary have been reinstated, and one, Adil Yunis, was made Minister of Justice in April 1975. In the fall of 1974 the courts awarded the family of Shuhdi Atiya, a Marxist leader who had been beaten to death in July 1960 in Abu Zaabal prison, an indemnity of LE 12,000 and the first admission of the real cause of death. This was followed in April 1975 by a ruling of the same South Cairo court calling upon the Ministry of War to pay damages of LE 30,000 to Counselor Ali Grisha who had been arrested and tortured in military prison in 1965. Shams Badran (himself in jail until 1974) and Hamza Basyuni (deceased) were the main persons accused in the affair.

Arrests stemming from political activities are not yet a thing of the past. Student demonstrations in the winters of 1972 and 1973 led to the roundup of hundreds, as did an attack by some military cadets and civilians on the military academy in Cairo in the summer of 1974. And the New Year's Day riots of 1975 provoked the detention of hundreds more in connection with the founding of secret leftist organizations. The authorities insist, however, that these arrests have been carried out fully within the terms of Egyptian penal and security law. They are not secret, they are done with authorization of the courts, those arrested are provided counsel, and they must be charged with specific acts or released.

The sanctity of the law and due process has also been reaffirmed with respect to those citizens whose property was confiscated for political reasons, a practice discussed above that began shortly after the coup d'état of 1952 and was particularly frequent from 1961 to 1967.[27] From the time of his accession to the presidency in the fall of 1970, Sadat made clear his objections to the sequestration laws. Several victims appealed their cases to Egyptian courts, while opinion built in the People's Assembly favoring new legislation nullifying the old laws and restitution of sequestered property within the limits set by the land reform acts of 1952, 1961, and 1969. In March 1974 the Court of Administrative Justice of the Council of State ruled that sequestration of individuals' property, as distinguished from that of companies or societies, was legally invalid. In July of the same year the People's Assembly passed a law to nullify acts of sequestration from the period 1961 through 1966.[28]

In building a state of institutions, at present Sadat has four in mind. One is the executive branch of government, ultimately controlled by the President but run on a day-to-day basis by a Prime Minister. The Prime Minister is not responsible to Parliament nor to the ASU in any formal sense. He must, however, heed their criticisms. Abd al-Aziz Higazi and Mamduh Salem were the first two Prime Ministers initiating the process of creating this institution.

A second institution is the parliament, the People's Assembly (*Maglis al-Sha'ab*, before 1971 known as the *Maglis al-Umma*) whose members are elected directly (with the exception of a few appointees) from geographic electoral districts. While all are also members of the ASU, they are elected by all adult Egyptians, not just members of the ASU. Members of the People's Assembly can thus point out that they are the true representatives of "all the people." Throughout Sadat's tenure, the People's Assembly has played an increasingly assertive role in policy scrutiny and criticism. True, there are ground rules for debate, and Sadat occasionally indicates that things are going too far, but the Assembly is far from being the rubber stamp that it was under Nasser. Still, its principal innovation has been exposing to the public much of what has gone on within their government, rather than censuring any particular official or reversing policy. The normal pattern, set when Aziz Sidqi was Prime Minister in 1972, has been to tear a given policy to pieces in committee (this was the fate of the Suez-Mediterranean Pipeline project submitted to parliament in 1972 as well as the government's assessment of its accomplishments after one year), to give ample newspaper coverage to the findings, and then to have the Assembly as a whole approve the policy with marginal modifications.

The People's Assembly may adopt more aggressive stances in the future, for they now have a Speaker (or President) with so much weight within the political elite that he can serve as an umbrella for the body as a whole. Sayyid Marei, Speaker since December 1974, comes from an important family of middle-range landowners in Sharqia Province and his father was an active Wafdist politician in the interwar years. Marei, a member of parliament before the revolution of 1952, then went on to implement Egypt's first land reform law and to head the Ministry of Agrarian Reform and intermittently the Ministry of Agriculture. He is an urbane, polished scion of the rural bourgeoisie, and his style is nicely attuned to Sadat's. Indeed, when Anwar Sadat was Speaker of the Parliament in the early 1960s, Sayyid Marei was his deputy. In 1974 when Sadat's daughter married Marei's son, a family linkage was added to a strong personal and political affinity. Marei is one of the three or four men who must be considered close to the President, and when he encourages the parliamentarians to forge ahead bravely in holding the government to account, he is not going out on a limb. As Speaker Marei has pushed specialized committees into an investigation of the costs and benefits of the semi-sacred Aswan High Dam; he has endorsed the notion that a fact-finding committee should determine the causes for the defeat of 1967; he has defended MPs who have formally interrogated Ministers on such matters as foreign contracts; under his supervision parliament separated the office of the Socialist Prosecutor (nominally intended to serve as a popular ombudsman to act on grievances against the authorities) and the Minister of Justice, which had been joined in one person in 1974. The People's Assembly is not made up of members of political parties, for there are none. Instead, the Assembly consists of individuals, often of the liberal professions and on the whole, such members constitute a relatively conservative weight in the polity, despite, or perhaps because of the fact that 50 per cent of the body is made up of workers and peasants.

A third institution is the press which, since 1960, has been owned by the National Union and then by the ASU. Ownership has not always entailed toeing a particular line; within limits a person such as Mohammed Hassanein Heikal could run his own shop. But the basic notion was that the press should be at the service of the regime and its political extension, the ASU. Policy was to be explained and advocated, but not criticized. Today the ASU still owns the press, although there are now proposals afoot to sell 49 per cent of the assets of the newspapers and magazines in the form of shares to their employees. Further, censorship has been abolished except in military matters. Copy no longer has to be submitted before publication to censors. This has meant, in effect, that editors have had to impose their own standards, knowing full well that there is little to protect them beyond the benevolence of President Sadat. Thus most have chosen a line so prudent that today the censors of the past would have little to keep them busy.

It is abundantly clear that the President has laid certain ground rules for freedom of the press. He wants the press to reflect certain currents of opinion, and the spectrum, weighted to the right, works out as follows. *Akhbar, Akhbar al-Yom, al-Musawwar, Akhir Sa'a* (and of less significance the periodicals *al-Jadid, al-Thaqāfa,* and *al-Kātib*) represent the right of various hues from Muslim Brethren to Europeanized liberal. The center of gravity lies with Musa Sabry and the Amin brothers at *Akhbar/Akhbar al-Yom.* The center is occupied predominantly by *al-Ahram* where one can find a spectrum of opinion under carefully centrist editorship. *Al-Gumhuriyya,* a daily that once had fairly radical pretensions, is perhaps now in the same category as *al-Ahram.* On the left, there is no daily but rather the muckraking weekly *Ruz al-Yussef* and *al-Tali'a,* a Marxist monthly with limited circulation. The President has honored all three camps with personal interviews and encouraged their editors to let all opinions flow within the limits of preserving national unity. Figuring out where to draw the line has been left to individual editors, and their inclination has been to play it safe.

Beyond this, Sadat has created a Supreme Press Council whose membership only partially reflects the working press. In its first meeting at the end of May 1975, the President seemed to be warning against too broad an interpretation of press freedom, insisting on the need for responsible reporting at a time when the enemy was still at Egypt's gates. He took complete responsibility for suspending from ASU membership—and hence from the right to work—over a hundred journalists and intellectuals in the winter of 1973. He felt they had pushed their criticisms of the government so far (although never in print) that national unity was in danger. Summing it all up, Sadat said "The [printed] word is sacred; but Egypt is more sacred, and I cannot allow anyone to tamper with her rights."[29] That it is still the President who decides which Egypt must be safeguarded is implicit in his statement.

Fourth in Sadat's group of state institutions, and the most controversial one, is the Arab Socialist Union itself. In calling for a national debate to discuss its future, Sadat gave the green light to almost everyone to make public his or her view on the proper organization of politics in Egypt. Sadat has thus learned how a broad range of hitherto silent groups feel about the future, all the while reserving

to himself the right to decide how fast and in what direction to reorient the polity.

With the Corrective Revolution, it was inevitable that the ASU would become the subject for debate and the target of considerable animosity. As set forth in the 1962 Charter, the ASU was not a party, but through its internally elected National Congress and Central Committee was the final repository of popular sovereignty. With its five to six million members, the ASU was to embody the "alliance of working forces" (*tahalluf al-quwwa al-āmila*) in Egypt. These were and are the peasantry, the workers, the intellectuals, the national capitalists, and the troops. Originally the parliament was to be clearly subordinate to the ASU, as was the press, in theory. The relationship between the ASU and the executive branch was far more ambiguous, because the President of the Republic is statutorily the supreme chief of the ASU, and in practice the ASU Executive Committee has been packed with ministers and presidential confidants. As we have seen, however, the organization was too large and sprawling to give its members any sense of common identity or purpose. Most ASU members joined either collectively, as members of unions and professional associations, or because it seemed the wise thing to do. The vanguard organization which was to move this inchoate mass, dissipated into a congeries of power-seeking or power-defending cliques. Sadat, who had never really been a part of all this, prompted a gradual reassessment of the ASU that has been going on since 1972.

Most of the issues discussed so far were first broached in the winter of 1972 when Sayyid Marei, whom Sadat had appointed as First Secretary of the Central Committee, initiated several weeks of discussion with ASU leaders to determine the future of the organization.[30] Nothing was left unsaid in these discussions; it was openly admitted that the ASU had failed in its mission and, further that no one was very sure what its mission was. Marei later prepared a report that summarized the debates, but it did not lead to any changes in the ASU. In the winter of 1973, he was replaced in his ASU post by a figure of modest stature, Dr. Hafiz Ghanem, a professor of international law. There was some possibility that the changes the President was seeking would be discussed nationally in the summer of 1973 in a "democratic dialogue" that would also have included an attempt to explain the economic open-door policy in light of détente between the great powers. The dialogue never took place because by July 1973, Sadat's attention was totally monopolized by preparation for war. The matter floated to the surface once again in April 1974 when Sadat delivered his October Paper laying down broad guidelines for Egypt's development over the next 25 years. This in turn was followed on August 9, 1974 by a document known as the Paper on the Evolution of the ASU.

This text demonstrated plainly that Sadat was not interested in sweeping changes. The President stated that the three principal errors committed in the name of the ASU in the past were: (1) its nominally optional membership had been seen by most citizens as compulsory; (2) the power centers had imposed their own notions of single-party organization upon the alliance of working forces; and (3) the ASU was so intimately linked to the executive that it could in no way censure government policy and thus rightly appeared to most Egyptians to be the mouthpiece of the authorities. Ihsan Abd al-Quddus, a close friend of the President, put the matter more bluntly: "In reality the

ASU is an official organization, like any other governmental unit, and it could just as easily have been called The Ministry for Political and Popular Affairs."[31]

Sadat made no specific recommendations in his paper, but he did offer some suggestions as to how the ASU could be made a more effective political organization. It might be advisable to separate the presidency from the ASU. Further, it might be possible to allow for several poles of thought to develop within the ASU,[32] and these in turn might be reflected in the press. Membership should probably become meaningfully optional so that only the motivated would join. Sadat suggested that the whole issue of collective membership needed close examination. Leadership at all levels of the ASU pyramid should be directly elected by their peers and the number of appointments greatly reduced. With these few suggestions, the President turned the whole matter over to a "Listening Committee" (*lagna t-il-Istima'*) under Mahmud Abu Wafie, a member of parliament who is related through marriage to the President.

الاهرام – ٧٤/٨/٢١ – ٥

* مناقشة ورقة تطوير الاتحاد الاشتراكى *

— ومن سلبيات تجربة الاتحاد الاشتراكى .. ان الافكار فيه كانت تاتى من اعلى ..

Salah Jahin, August 21, 1974 "Discussing the President's Paper on the Evolution of the ASU." The speaker proclaims "Among the negative aspects of the experiment with the ASU is that all the ideas come down from the top...."

The Listening Committee hearings, conducted during the last three weeks in September 1974, were fascinating both for the substantive issues debated and for the skillful stage-managing that underlay them. Ahmad Baha al-Din, at that time managing editor of *al-Ahram*, set the tone for the opening of the hearings. He noted that Egypt's long and not inglorious experience under a parliamentary, multiparty system had rendered the nation undeniable services. While the process might work itself out over a long period, Baha al-Din implied that a return to such a regime should be open for consideration.[33] The first meetings of the Listening Committee were devoted to the same themes.

The committee, mostly in the person of Abu Wafia, had defined its task as simply recording the diverse views of the members of various functional groups that were invited to appear before it. The first groups consisted of intellectuals, writers, and the press. Such disparate figures as Mustapha Amin and Fikri Abaza on the right traded ideas with Salah 'Issa and Yussef Idriss on the left. Curiously all were fairly unanimous in their disillusionment with the ASU and, significantly, in their hope that Egypt would once again enjoy a multiparty system. Salah 'Issa declared "I am one of those who believe that the ASU has failed and cannot be saved no matter what we try." At the same time he rejected the notion of an organized two-party system as an arbitrary infringement on the freedom of the people. He urged instead that either parties be allowed to form freely or that the ASU be kept as it is despite its faults. 'Issa may have been articulating a generally held Marxist sentiment that the 1965 dissolution of their party and their integration into the ASU on an individual basis had done considerable damage to their image. A multiparty system could give them the opportunity to reorganize legally, even though it would give the same right to conservative forces such as the Amin brothers.

After the press and urban intellectuals, the Listening Committee heard representatives of various professional unions and associations, such as the engineers and the doctors. They took up where the others had left off and some went so far as to call for the dissolution of the ASU (Mustapha Barad'ay, Head of the Lawyer's Union), open presidential elections, the formation of a legal opposition, and scrupulously free elections to parliament. All the middle classes' pent-up liberalism,

like all their pent-up consumerism, seemed to be released at once. But even as the educated, urban middle classes of Cairo and Alexandria dominated the debate, countertrends began to manifest themselves. Hafiz Badawi, at that time Speaker of the People's Assembly, organized a special meeting of the Listening Committee in Suhag Province. There the rural masses affirmed their support of the ASU, although with some modifications, their conviction that the head of the ASU and the President of the Republic must be one in the same person, and their feeling that any more talk of abolishing the guaranteed 50 per cent or more representation of peasants and workers in all elected positions in the country would be deeply resented. This warning was directed at several urban intellectuals who had contested the utility of the 50 per cent representation clause in effect since 1962. (Mohammed Abd as-Shafa'i, a former member of parliament, asserted that the peasants and workers who had entered parliament under this clause had done nothing to help their brethren.)

The counterthrust developed more momentum after September 15. Successive meetings of peasant groups insisted on the safeguarding of the alliance of working forces, seeing in the appeals for a multiparty system a lightly veiled pretense for counterrevolutionary forces to eat away at the "benefits of the revolution": peasant-worker representation, land reform, growth of the public sector, worker-management councils, profit-sharing, free education, and the like. Up to this point, the staging of the hearings was such that a number of radical departures from the prevailing political formula had been amply aired and thus given some legitimacy. They were out in the open, and without endorsing any of them, Sadat could hold them in reserve and if need be reintroduce them later. At the same time, the masses were brought forth to remind the intellectuals of their isolation and to insist upon the need for continuity with the past. The shift was reflected in the editorials of Baha al-Din. After initially praising Egypt's multiparty past, he came out, on September 24, strongly in favor of maintaining the alliance of working forces and developing a "multiplicity of *minbars*" (forums) within that framework.

Next came the labor unions, and their representatives thundered away on all themes advanced by the peasants, adding some biting attacks on the whole purpose of the debate. They vociferously rejected a multiparty system and accused named forces, in particular the Amin brothers, of wanting to abolish not only guaranteed worker representation but the very principles of the July 23 Revolution. One anonymous voice from the floor demanded to know the significance of the President's brother-in-law directing these hearings, while at various other times unidentified voices attacked their own union leaders as puppets of the regime who had been only too willing in the past to neglect the true interests of the working masses. At this stage it was abundantly clear that the intellectual Marxists, speaking in the name of the proletariat and calling for multipartyism, were overruled by the workers themselves who remained loyal to the ASU. Moreover, the union leadership was reminded of the weakness of its own legitimacy and the fact that they had traditionally been handpicked by the executive branch of government. In short, the liberals on the left and right were held in check, but those who did the checking could not express themselves except through the regime's own men.

The final episode in the hearings came with the university professors, students, and feminist organizations. The professors reflected a variety of positions, but the women and the students were nearly unanimous in their denunciations of all attempts to tamper with the benefits of the revolution. Granted, the students were consulted within the context of Ain Shams University's annual colloquium on Nasserist thought, and there was thus surely a strong element of self-election among committed Nasserists, but no other student bodies tried to refute them afterward. The students were warned by Kemal Abu al-Magd, Minister of Information, that they must distinguish between revolutionary Nasserism and Sufistic Nasserism. He implied by the latter term that Nasserism was becoming a sort of mystic cult for some student groups. The warning was ignored as the students voted a series of resolutions that called for strengthening the ASU, strengthening the public sector, affirming the inviolability of the principle of 50 per cent worker-peasant representation, and accelerating the pace of socialist transformation. With respect to foreign affairs, they recommended closer relations with "progressive" regimes, stronger support for the Palestinians, and affirmation of the principle of nonrecognition of Israel. All this was laced with constant attacks upon

Mustapha and Ali Amin. One student laconically pointed out that Mustapha Amin, who had been pardoned by President Sadat, had never formally been cleared of the charges that he worked for the CIA. By this time in the pages of *al-Ahram* Baha al-Din was inveighing against the forces of counter-revolution.[34]

After the hearings were terminated, the committee disbanded pending submission of a report to President Sadat, who remained inscrutably silent about the future for a number of months. He obviously had more pressing matters, in the form of Kissinger's shuttle diplomacy, with which to contend. The major findings of the Listening Committee were published in December 1974,[35] but were as tentative as the original paper on the evolution of the ASU. Moreover, the report did not make any new suggestions, repeating the recommendations that optional membership be affirmed, several forums for debate opened up, and free elections be allowed at all levels. It did state, somewhat surprisingly, that only a minority of those who authored the report advocated separation of the presidency of the Republic from the presidency of the ASU. In April 1975, Sadat removed Hafiz Ghanem as First Secretary of the Central Committee (he was appointed Minister for Higher Education), replacing him with Dr. Rifa'at Mahgub, another law professor who had been in charge of ideology in the ASU. Mahgub set about preparing for top-to-bottom elections in the ASU, to be held in July 1975. As part of the preparations, all those who wished to remain as members of the ASU would have to re-register. By the end of May about four million had done so, including several unions that had joined en masse. In the future it will no longer be necessary to be a member of the ASU in order to hold certain kinds of jobs or to be a member of parliament. But the question remains: what will those who choose not to join do to exercise their political rights as long as political parties cannot be organized?

Dr. Mahgub's answer is that they can seek a forum in parliament, their own professional associations, and the press. But, despite the possibility that parties may eventually be allowed to form in Egypt, now is not the moment. According to Dr. Mahgub, "The current situation, with the continuation of the cruel battle for liberation and the battle for reconstruction and progress, requires us to safeguard our national unity and to affirm the principle of the alliance of working forces in order to face these tasks."[36] This, in a nutshell, is the President's outlook. The alliance is a useful means to contain political conflict that could today take on serious proportions given the increasing burdens placed upon the average Egyptian by inflation, the black market, and the continued state of no war, no peace. While temporarily safeguarding the integrity of the ASU and the alliance, Sadat has reminded each one of its constituent parts of their vulnerability by allowing them to be subjected to a great amount of well-founded criticism. But the critics themselves have been contained and given only minimal satisfaction. Much the same process has been followed with regard to the public sector

of the economy, as the two previous Reports demonstrated. Just as the debate on the Opening has resulted in the legitimization of a mixed economy without predetermining the relative weights of its public and private sectors, so too the political Opening has moved Egypt inches toward a mixed polity. It resembles Nasser's polity only in that Sadat faces the same political and economic problems as his predecessor and feels comfortable in resorting to the same methods of dealing with them. If Sadat can master the economic problems facing Egypt, which in large measure are a function of the on-going state of hostilities with Israel, then far-reaching de-Nasserization may really begin.

NOTES

1. From Tewfiq al-Hakim, *The Return of Awareness* (*'Awdat al-Wa'i*), (Beirut, June 1974), written at the time of the 20th anniversary of the Revolution, July 1972.

2. See the first two Reports in this series by John Waterbury, *The Opening, Part I: Egypt's Economic New Look* [JW-2-'75], and *The Opening, Part II: Luring Foreign Capital* [JW-3-'75], Fieldstaff Reports, Northeast Africa Series, Vol. XX, No. 2 and No. 3, 1975.

3. *al-Ahram*, September 27, 1974. See the reply of the chief editor, Ahmad Baha al-Din, in the same issue.

4. One of the most revealing accounts and indictments to date has been written by General Salah al-Din al-Hadidi, former Director of Military Intelligence, in *A Witness of the 1967 War* (Dar al-Sharuq, Cairo, 1974), in Arabic.

5. Before this debate became fully public, its themes were being handled satyrically by Ali Salem in his play *The Phantoms of New Egypt*. It was written in 1968 but banned by the censors. It was produced and even televised shortly after the Corrective Revolution. See John Waterbury *The Phantoms of New Egypt* [JW-4-'73], Fieldstaff Reports, Northeast Africa Series, Vol. XVIII, No. 1, 1973. A popular movie in Cairo in the spring of 1975, The Dawn Visitor (*za'ir al-fagr*), handles the same theme more dramatically.

6. Mustapha Amin, *The First Year of Prison* (Cairo, September 1974), in Arabic.

7. Basyuni died in an automobile accident in 1971.

8. *Akhbar al-Yom* has worked over this incident in several issues, but see especially November 9, 1974; also the

remarkable book of former Chief Prosecutor Mohammed Abd al-Salam, *Critical Years* (Cairo, 1975), in Arabic.

9. For Hilmy Murad's account see *Akhbar al-Yom*, October 19, 1974. Abu Nusseir's defense appeared in the issue of October 12, 1974. Most of the relevant documentation is presented in Mumtaz Nasar (former President of the Lawyers Union), *The Battle of Justice in Egypt* (Cairo, 1974), in Arabic. One victim of the incident was the lawyer and former minister, Abd al-Fattah Hassan, who was arrested just prior to the purge and held 14 months without charges. See *Akhbar al-Yom*, November 9, 1974.

10. *Akhbar al-Yom*, March 29, 1975. This article claims that 26 Brethren were tortured to death in connection with these arrests.

11. These figures were revealed in the course of debates in the People's Assembly (*Maglis as-Sha'ab*) of a draft law to abolish all measures of sequestration and return property or pay compensation to former owners. See *Akhbar al-Yom*, July 7, 1974; and "The Draft Law for the Settlement of Cases Arising from Sequestration," supplement to *al-Ahram al-Iqtisadi*, July 15, 1974. The law came into effect, July 25, 1974.

12. *al-Ahram*, June 8, 1974.

13. The cost accounting of restitution is laid out in "After the Disaster of Sequestration, the Disaster of Desequestration," *Ruz al-Yussef*, No. 2439, March 10, 1975.

14. Tewfiq al-Hakim, *The Return of Awareness*, op. cit.

15. Fumil Labib, "Those who seek to snuff out the lights," *al-Musawwar*, No. 2607, September 27, 1974.

16. Salah Hafiz, "A Warning to the Egyptian Right," *Ruz al-Yussef*, No. 2412, September 2, 1974.

17. Mahmud Murad, *Hakim…and his Returning Awareness!*, (Cairo, September 1974); Mohammed 'Awda, *Awareness Lost*, (Cairo, 1974), both in Arabic.

18. Hakim's open letter was published in *Ruz al-Yussef*, No. 2420, October 28, 1974, and Abd al-Sittar Tawila's reply in *Ruz al-Yussef*, No. 2421, November 4, 1974. Over several days in the fall of 1974, a group of Egyptian leftists from the monthly *al-Tali'a* (*Avant Garde*) held a colloquium with Tewfiq al-Hakim. The quality of the debate was of a high order and has been published under the title "The Egyptian Left in Dialogue with Tewfiq al-Yakim," in *al-Tali'a*, Vol. 10, No. 12, 1974 through Vol. 11, No. 5, 1975.

19. See for instance Engineer Fawzi Habashi's "The Extent of Parasitic Incomes in the Contracting Sector," *al-Tali'a*, Vol. 9, No. 7, July 1973, pp. 27-31.

20. See *Ruz al-Yussef*, No. 2420, October 28, 1974, p. 12.

21. Almost every week *Ruz al-Yussef* publishes on this subject. See, *inter alia*, Nos. 2420 (October 28, 1974), 2421 (November 4, 1974), 2423 (November 18, 1974), 2427 (December 12, 1974), and 2428 (December 22, 1974).

22. For two rightist viewpoints on corruption, see Sa'id Sinbal, "The Men are there…but" *Akhbar al-Yom*, October 19, 1974, who argues that the laws protecting public goods must be strengthened; and Dr. Mohammed Hilmi Murad, "I Demand the Death Penalty for Anyone who Steals the People's Goods," *Akhbar al-Yom*, January 25, 1975.

23. Salah 'Issa, "The Future of Democracy in Egypt," *al-Katib*, Vol. 14, No. 162, pp. 9-28.

24. Lutfi al-Kholi, "These are the Bayumiyun," *al-Tali'a*, Vol. 11, No. 1, January 1975, pp. 81-85. See also his article in *al-Tali'a*, April 1974, in which he mentions the 180 millionaires; and Adil Hussein, "Criticism of Government Policy," *al-Tali'a*, Vol. 11, No. 1, January 1975, pp. 73-79.

25. Dr. Fu'ad Zacharia, "Is Nasser above Criticism?", *Ruz al-Yussef*, No. 2444, April 14, 1975; "The leftist defense and a reply to it," *Ruz al-Yussef*, No. 2445, April 21, 1975;

"Nasser bent the left to himself, not vice versa," *Ruz al-Yussef*, No. 2446, April 28, 1975. Naguib Mahfuz, along with Hakim the most famous of Egypt's living authors, took essentially the same line as Zacharia in *Ruz al-Yussef*, No. 2450, May 26, 1975. Critical leftist responses to Zacharia were written by Fathi Khalil, *Ruz al-Yussef*, No. 2447, May 5, 1975, and Phillip Ghallab, *Ruz al-Yussef*, No. 2448, May 22, 1975.

26. Fu'ad Matar, *With All Candor about Abd al-Nasser: a Dialogue with Mohammed Hassanein Heikal*, Beirut, 1975.

27. Fu'ad Serrag al-Din, one of the principal figures of the Wafd Party and former Minister of the Interior, was one of those convicted in 1953. In 1975, the nine members of his family had between ten and 40 acres each of land restituted to them. *al-Ahram*, February 20, 1975.

28. For the court ruling see *al-Ahram*, May 8, 1974, and also the draft law cited in note 11.

29. *al-Ahram*, May 27, 1975. All of those suspended were reinstated on September 23, 1973, on the eve of the October War.

30. Extensive transcripts of these debates were published in *al-Tali'a*, Vol. 9, Nos. 5-7, May-June 1972.

31. Ihsan Abd al-Quddus, "Let us discuss the ruling order first, *al-Ahram*, September 6, 1974.

32. Multipolarity within the alliance became known as "the multiplicity of *minbars*," the *minbar* being that part of the mosque that serves as the *imam's* pulpit. Dr. Gamal al-Uteifi, Deputy Speaker of Parliament, gave the term currency in his article, "Multiplicity of Minbars—the True Way towards the Evolution of the ASU," *al-Ahram*, August 11, 1974.

33. Ahmad Baha al-Din, "Democratic Experience in Egypt," *al-Ahram*, August 23, 1974.

34. Ahmad Baha al-Din, "Between Criticism and the Counter-Revolution," *al-Ahram*, September 28, 1974.

35. *al-Ahram*, December 18, 1974.

36. Dr. Rifa'at Mahgub, *al-Ahram*, May 24, 1975.

Long-Range Planning in the Arab World

The Arabs are the sixth power of the world.

President Anwar Sadat

Without oil, the Arab World is the poorest region of the globe.

An official of the Council
on Arab Economic Unity

President Sadat is not alone in claiming great power status for the Arabs, and it is conceivable that if one were to pool all Arab oil, arms, and population the aggregate would be very impressive indeed. But there is not today, any more than in the past, an operational pooling of Arab resources. The Arab World is no more a global power than sub-Saharan Africa or Latin America. It is in light of this fact that the anonymous expert from the Council on Arab Economic Unity (CAEU) can legitimately claim that all that stands between the Arabs and irremediable poverty is oil. The same official went on to point out that if Arab oil is not treated as a common resource, the Arabs will miss a unique opportunity for regional development and prosperity. Inherently poor and temporarily capital-rich, the Arab world calls out for concerted efforts at long-range planning (LRPing) to make rational use of capital resources to promote long-term economic integration.

But different Arab societies have different resource mixes and capital reserves which in turn determine the degree of alacrity and enthusiasm with which they respond to the call. While several of the Arab oil-producing states may be able to establish a spurious kind of prosperity by casting all cost-benefit considerations to the winds, they may do so at the risk of totally dislocating their small, conservative, patronomical societies. Of the Arab oil

producers probably only Iraq and Algeria can contemplate policies of autonomous national development and the edification of sophisticated industrial economies that will outlive both the energy crisis and their own petroleum and natural gas resources.

Saudi Arabia, Kuwait, Libya, Qatar, the United Arab Emirates, and Oman do not have the population, agricultural base, industrial infrastructure, skilled personnel, or mineral resources to warrant ambitions of autonomous national development. What they do have in abundance is surplus foreign exchange earnings from oil exports with which they can purchase foreign expertise, foreign labor, foreign technology, and foreign raw materials in order to fabricate, in a void, viable, multifaceted economies. All of these states are bent on doing just that. The risk, as mentioned, is twofold. Plumping advanced industries down in the midst of Bedouin societies, whatever the sophistication of their elites, may be more than these social systems can bear. Add to this the massive importation of foreign skilled, unskilled, managerial and technological human resources, and one has at best a hybrid society but more likely a compartmentalized, dualistic arrangement of the native minority and the rest. That is already the case in Kuwait and is rapidly becoming so in the other Emirates of the Gulf. Saudi Arabia, despite its large population, may follow the same route as it pursues its gargantuan five-year plan.

The second element of risk, and by far the weightiest, is that the ministate oil exporters, in pursuing their costly development policies, will deny to the oil-poor among the Arabs (not to mention the rest of the Third World) a chance to promote their own economic growth. The oil-less are not uniform in the dimensions of their economic plight. Syria and the Sudan have great agricultural promise, sufficient domestic markets to justify local industries and more or less adequate human resource pools. Similar in most respects is Morocco with the all-important difference that it is the world's major exporter of phosphates. Foreign exchange earnings from phosphate exports place it in a privileged position among the Arab oil-less. Egypt and Tunisia, but especially Egypt, are both resource-poor and population-rich. Egypt's population is more than twice that of any of its Arab neighbors, its industrial base the region's greatest, and its agricultural system the region's most productive. At the same time Egypt has the region's largest deficit and external debt. What all the oil-less states share is chronic foreign exchange shortages because their export capacity is so inferior to their need to import food, intermediate and capital goods. Rising world prices of food grains and raw materials have exacerbated their external debts. Debt-servicing (even as regards the oil-rich) ranges for the oil-poor from 6 per cent of export earnings to Egypt's 35 per cent. Egypt's total external debt is, as far as is known, in excess of its Gross Domestic Product (GDP).

There is, in the Arab World, another group of countries that are like the Gulf and Arabian Peninsula oil-rich except that they have no oil. North and South Yemen, Somalia, and Mauritania are all heavily rural societies with small populations, limited resources, tiny educated elites and tiny Gross National Products. They constitute the Fourth World of the Arab region and where Egypt and Tunisia are poor, they are destitute.

This distribution of economic fortunes among the Arab states is not new, but its dimensions have become more accentuated since the October War of 1973 and the spectacular increase in oil prices laid down by the Arab members of the Organization of Petroleum Exporting Countries (OPEC) at the same time. Prior to 1973, and particularly during the late 1950s and 1960s when Nasser was the moving force for Arab integration, these disparities in regional resource and income distribution were widely recognized. Nasserites, as well as the adherents of the Ba'ath Party, were wont to speak of regional oil reserves as an "Arab" resource that must be used for the good of all. The emphasis in these years was, however, upon political integration and the major spokesmen were politicians. Compatible ideologies, common stances on major cold war issues, military pacts, liberation movements, conflict with Israel, and neo-imperialism were the themes that dominated discussions of Arab unity.

Although in the 1960s the first steps toward customs unions and free trade areas were discussed, purely economic issues of labor exchange, the development of complementaries in industrial and agricultural production, and regional resource development were given only fleeting attention by political elites. What has happened since 1973 is that economic and technocratic elites have become the most vocal standard bearers of Arab integration while national political elites have paid lip service to integration at the same time that they pursue economic policies rooted in the dream of autonomous national development—at the expense, if need be, of the economic health of other regional neighbors.

The agronomists, economists, geologists, engineers, and planners of the region, faced with growing population, limited resources and a temporary capital surplus that could be used locally, have begun to espouse the theme of integration with varying degrees of enthusiasm. Their recommendations, while by no means coincident, lay stress on rational distribution of financial and natural resources and an efficient division of industrial and agricultural production among Arab states regardless of the nature of the regime, its ideology, or position vis-a-vis the great powers. They stress the fact that Arab states and societies tend to be either rich or poor (Lebanon was about the only moderately prosperous state in the area but one wonders if it can even regain statehood not to speak of prosperity) and in either case careful planning of abundant or scarce resources is essential to regional growth.

The year 1973 marked the beginning of a new era, one in which the redistribution of global resources, or the confrontation between rich and poor, will be the dominant issue. The October War and the subsequent oil price-hike threw into focus a number of issues which had lain about in scholarly papers and the proceedings of various UNCTAD meetings throughout the 1960s. It was only fitting that the global debate on the new world economic order should evoke its regional counterpart in the Arab region. For the simple fact is that all the outstanding questions of planetary redistribution are reflected in the contemporary interplay between the Arab rich and poor. However, despite the fact that concerted Arab action in war and energy policy highlighted the urgency of moving toward accommodation among rich and poor on issues of global redistribution, the concerted action itself was taken in light of totally different considerations, to wit, to bring maximum pressure to bear on Israel and its principal Western supporters. This fact is indicative of a general blurring and immersion of elements of the planetary debates in the more parochial and somewhat "nineteenth century" geopolitical confines of Arab-Israeli confrontation. This is not to say that issues of the new world economic order had been previously ignored, but to the extent they were discussed by Arabs at all, they were so in forums such as the Non-Aligned (the seminal meeting was in Algiers in September 1973 *before* the October War), the Group of 77, the special UN sessions, etc., where the focus extended far beyond the Arab World proper; or in forums such as meetings of petroleum ministers or heads of state from OPEC countries where the debate centered on the consequences of trade in a single commodity.

The Cairo Joint Symposium on Long-Range Planning (LRPing) and Regional Integration Among Arab States

In view of these observations, it was of great significance that in January 1976 a group of Arab planners, economists, systems analysts, and technically competent policymakers, assisted by an impressive array of non-Arab experts (list of participants is appended) met in Cairo to take the first steps toward getting out on the table some of the major problems in north-south relations as they manifest themselves in the Arab region. (I hasten to point out that it is the author of this Report who has placed these issues in the north-south context, and not, necessarily, the organizers of the conference. In the same vein it should be kept in mind that what is presented below is a selective and interpretative summary of certain aspects of the

symposium and by no means a comprehensive *compte rendu*.)

The symposium was sponsored by the Egyptian Institute of National Planning (INP), the Council on Arab Economic Unity (CAEU), and the United Nations Industrial Development Organization (UNIDO). Because it was a first attempt, the results were, to say the least, inconclusive. Several Arab countries were not represented: Jordan, Syria, Somalia, Libya, Algeria, and Morocco. The absence of Syria, Morocco, Algeria, and Libya, all with fairly abundant resources and ambitious national development plans, was particularly unfortunate. So too the fact that although the oil-rich—especially Saudi Arabia, Kuwait, and the United Arab Emirates—were minimally represented, none of their experts participated in the formal debate. Those other Arabs that did, with some notable exceptions, presented papers either describing macro- and micro-national planning policies or technical papers on planning techniques, model-building, statistical methodology, and data analysis. There was clearly a kind of feeling-out process going on, itself considerably stimulated by the often pithy presentations of foreign experts who enjoyed the luxury of being non-Arab and hence not directly concerned. Some of the stickiest issues were not directly debated, and when some hardy souls aired them publicly they drew virtually no direct comment.

A. Strategies, Philosophies, and Caveats

It was to some degree left to the foreign experts to set up various kinds of straw men in the form of advice, planning strategies, and development philosophies to which the rest could react. Inevitably the "big question" was adumbrated from the outset: what is development, what is growth, and, derivatively, what sorts of targets should policymakers and planners set for their societies? There were a number of speakers who emphasized the inadequacy of measuring growth merely in terms of rising GNP, *average* per capita income, export surplus, manufacturing components of GNP, and so forth. For instance the 1975 Lima meeting of ministers of industry of UNIDO member states recommended that the share of the developing countries in total world industrial production be increased from its present level of 7 per cent to 25 per cent by the year 2000. But such a goal is meaningless unless founded upon the attainment, within

Left to right: Mssr.'s Scolnik (Fondacion Bariloche), Hilmi Abderrahman (Egypt's Minister of Planning), Le Guay (UNIDO), and A'al-Sakban (Council on Arab Economic Unity). Second row, right side: Mr. A. Farrag (CAEU) and Ibrahim Saad el-Din (Arab Planning Institute, Kuwait).

and among nations, of certain socioeconomic targets. H. Scolnik of Argentina's Fondacion Bariloche argued for a set of growth targets that are best measured in social rather than production terms. Life expectancy is the single most sensitive indicator of general development in the model Scolnik presented, and attaining a minimum life-expectancy level should be a basic goal of any plan. Closely associated with this target is achieving minimum standards in clothing, housing, and nutritional levels. Such basic needs can be modeled and the pattern of resource mobilization necessary to achieve them measured and projected. Explicit in the model is the need for fundamental income redistribution within and among societies. The Bariloche group suggests that a desirable target would be to plan redistribution so that the poorest 20 per cent in all societies would, by the year 2000, actually receive 20 per cent of national incomes. If this kind of target were set for the Arab region as a whole (leave aside the world) the results

in the redistribution of regional wealth would be dramatic. Needless to say, redistribution is not carried out by computer but by political leaders with the ideology and the will to make it stick. Scolnik diplomatically and obliquely stated this fact when he noted that ultimately the basic constraints on economic planning are sociopolitical.

Joining Scolnik in this approach were two other eminent experts: Mahbub al-Haqq of the International Bank for Reconstruction and Development (IBRD) and J. Pronk, Holland's Minister of Economic Development and Cooperation. Pronk has been instrumental in promoting a dialogue between rich and poor and was an important figure in the organization of the 7th Special Session of the United Nations. The parameters of national planning strategies, Pronk contends, are being determined by international forces, in particular the multinational corporations, international commodity and technology markets, and the international monetary system. The internationalization of national economic decisions has so far led to a deterioration of development prospects among the less-developed countries (LDCs). This has taken the form of growing inequality within and among nations, growing scarcity of basic resources, especially food, and international recession, inflation, and unemployment. Pronk feels the targets of developing countries should be growth in the conventional sense, self-reliance, and social justice. Plans must be people- or need-oriented, seeking to minimize resource wastage, to protect the environment, and to strike a balance between present and future needs. Ostensibly contradicting his emphasis on self-reliance, Pronk urged the abolition of the principle of national sovereignty.

Mahbub al-Haqq likewise played a prominent role in the 7th Special Session and is one of the founders of the Third World Forum. Fifteen years ago he was a member of the Pakistan Planning Commission and has lived to see most of his predictions proven false. His first piece of advice is, then, that all planners should be old so that they will not have to evaluate their own work.

The plan itself, according to al-Haqq, should be set within a ten-year time frame, especially if it is to have any operational impact on policy-makers, and policy parameters must be clearly delineated for they tend to outlive their authors. On this subject Hilmi Abderrahman, Egypt's Minister of Planning, at another point in the discussions, seemed to argue for a longer time frame for planners than ten years. Because of the very nonspecificity of the LRP, the inescapable specialist-generalist gap can be bridged. The object is to establish consensus between the decision-making generalist and planning specialist on certain broad policy objectives and priorities. If such consensus can be established then it may become possible to bridge generalist-specialist gaps on the how-to-get-there aspects of medium- and short-range planning. Contradicting both al-Haqq and Abderrahman was Gustav Ranis of Yale who stated that planning beyond five years was probably unprofitable because possible scenarios will grow exponentially with time: "Like death and taxes, exogenous shocks to national planning models are probably inevitable." (One might note that in Egypt only death and exogenous shocks are inevitable.)

Al-Haqq went on to stress planning for human needs to overcome income disparities. Commenting directly on Egypt's experience, he recommended that the trade-off in agricultural and industrial development be carefully studied, and that industry should be linked to agricultural development. It would have been interesting had there been any Algerians present to have their reaction to this advice, for their strategy has been to stand it on its head. Algeria has leapt over agricultural development into heavy industry to produce the goods and equipment upon which agro-industries and agricultural modernization will depend. This approach has been dubbed "industries industrialisantes" based on an Algerian formula of backward linkages—but, alas, no Algerian was there to argue for it.

On another plane al-Haqq warned the Egyptians against expecting too much from their open-door policy and hopes for foreign investment. Economic liberalization is not an end in itself, but should be clearly subordinated to accepted social and economic targets. Otherwise the planning edifice could be built on sand. Taking exception to Pronk, al-Haqq contended that self-reliance should not be overstressed for it could lead to a confusion of means and ends. What is desirable for Egypt, for instance, is that for an Egyptian problem there be an Egyptian solution—that is the end. The means may not nor need they be Egyptian.

"We of the Third World," al-Haqq went on, "cannot seek an alibi in the new world economic order. Our problems of development or lack thereof, in the final analysis, are our responsibility. We cannot seek equality of opportunity at the international level and not within our own societies. If we begin with the latter, the former will simply be a matter of time."

Although there was not much concurrence on time frames, most participants seemed agreed that LRPing is a very different kind of exercise than short- or medium-range planning. Short-range planning involves attaining sectoral investment and production objectives, employment levels, export targets, etc., while long-range planning, as Henry Bruton put it, may initially consist in estimating the long-term consequences of short-term plans. But others reversed this sequence on the premise that the real utility of LRPing lies in the fact that it

Left to right: Abderrahman, lamentably unidentified person, Pecci, and Walid Shafa'i.

addresses itself to the major structural impediments to shorter-term efforts and sets ideal future targets and projects backwards. In other words it might be that LRPing would prove more or less conclusively that short-term targets conceived within national plan frameworks will constantly recede beyond reach unless operational steps toward regional integration are taken. Similarly, if LRPing involves only long-term extrapolations from existing trends "we will," as one participant warned, "merely project our past and present backwardness into the future."

Of equal interest were the judgments of a number of experts from Eastern Europe and the U.S.S.R. who insisted on the qualitative and interpretative nature of LRPing. Professor Nasilowski of Poland wrote, "An attempt to apprehend these and many other problems [of LRPing] in the form of mathematical models and then charging the models to computers is a dream. A subjective element in planning is inevitable. One of the outstanding co-authors of the Soviet system of planning, S. Strumilin, not without reason, says: 'Planning will forever preserve the character of a sort of art because it includes an active creative factor...and its inseparable part is an ideology of a planning subject.'" Nasilowski's colleague, Dr. Zajda, echoed the same view referring to LRPing as a social process and a philosophical dialogue among planners, politicians, and masses. This rather "soft" Marxo-technocratic view is a far cry from the forecasts of Sovietologists of a decade or

more ago to the effect that centralized Marxist economies were moving toward cybernetic planning models where all socioeconomic variables were to be minutely modeled and entire societies "programmed" to conform to the model's projections.

One may extract from these contextual observations of the nature of LRPing the major issues that pertain to the art in the Arab World:

(1) Is LRPing technically and methodologically feasible?

(2) If so, does one assume increasing regional integration and/or the emergence of a new world economic order (what for instance should a Syrian or Egyptian planner assume about the availability of foreign exchange and export markets?); or should one remain within the autonomous national development framework?

(3) Should plans be production- or need-oriented?

(4) What are acceptable instrumentalities in achieving these goals? Multinational Corporations? International organizations? Self-reliance?

(5) Is there any realistic hope of attaining national economic sovereignty or is partial derogation of sovereignty inevitable if not desirable?

We may now consider how these questions were or were not dealt with by the Arab experts themselves.

MY RAVIN'S "THE PLANNER'S LAMENT"
by
DR. G.C. SCOTT
WITH APOLOGIES
to
EDGAR ALLEN POE
and
W.A. HASSOUNA

Goals and objectives, targets and aims
Social capacity, sampling frames
Resources, consumers, and services
Quoth the planner, "What a mess"

Hassen Effendi and pieces of cake
His parable tells us we must take
Care to ensure survival of man
Quoth the planner, "If I can"

Assimilation and integration
Education innovation
Quoth the planner, "For the nation"

Social, "political" cultural goals
Ore and oil and coking coals
Tools and method, the public role
Quoth the planner, "Save my soul."

Cost effect and knee perception
Beliefs and values, intervention
Priorities and education
Quoth the planner, "devastation"

Time oriented? Plagues and rumour
Crises and community tumours
My mistakes are "super boomers"

A planner needs a sense of humor
Sacrifice and tolerance
From poverty and circumstance
Quoth the planner, "What a dance."

The input-output specialist
Poor benighted generalist
Health sector's analyst
Quoth the planner, "optimist"

Optimize or minimize?
What solution to devise
If living standards are to rise
Quote the planner, "What is my prize?"

Partial scope and shortened span
Restricts a comprehensive plan
Why is there not another man
To suffer the financier's ban?

Annual? or perspective?
Rollins or indicative?
Spatial or corrective?
Hear the planner's fierce invective!

What does the future have in store?
Conquered by political lore,
Dejectedly he shuts the door,
Quoth the planner, "Nevermore."

*Faith and hope to ensure
  Program and planning to mature
  Man as agent man to gain
  From our efforts not in vain.

*Added by Dr. Samuel Street Who
                Ethiopia, September 197.

B. National Plans

Several Arab states (principally Egypt, Syria, Iraq, Morocco, Algeria, Tunisia, and Sudan) have had as much as 20 years' experience in devising, and, less frequently, applying national development plans. At least four of them—Egypt, Iraq, Sudan, and Saudi Arabia—are on the brink of launching, more or less simultaneously, new five-year plans. Yet to date there has been no attempt by any Arab state to set its targets and priorities in light of those of its neighbors. The United Arab Republic's five-year plan of 1960 is a partial exception because Egypt and Syria had formally unified in 1958. But the breakup of the UAR in 1961 left the plan a dead letter as far as the Syrians were concerned. It is certainly the case that none of the middle-range plans presently being launched have done more than pay lip-service to regional integration.

One would have expected that Iraq might have given a more conspicuous place to regional integration in its 1976-1980 Plan. Iraq is governed by a regime dominated by the Ba'ath party, which through a different branch, also rules Syria. This party has had, since its inception a quarter century ago, the fundamental aim of establishing Arab unity within a revolutionary socialist framework. The Ba'ath has been ideologically unrelenting in its criticism of existing state boundaries (established by imperialists and essentially artificial) and bodies such as the Arab League that tend to reinforce rather than erode them. The party's vocabulary is indicative: Iraq does not refer to itself as a nation (*watan*) but as an Arab region or zone (*qutr*). Iraq's representatives at the symposium forcefully reiterated their "zone's" commitment to integration. Dr. Aziz al-Qataifi cited the "fundamental" resolutions of the 8th Regional Meeting of the Arab

Socialist Ba'ath Party (1974) that bind Iraq to expend every effort to coordinate economic planning with all other Arab zones "despite the lack of enthusiasm of others for these measures." Yet one searches in vain in Qataifi's paper and that of his colleagues, Tu'ama Gaber al-Bandar and Abd al-Rasul Gasim, for any operational expression of this principle. The Iraqi plan is presented in all too conventional terms founded on sectoral production goals. The principles underlying plan objectives are listed as follows:

(1) expanding the socialist sector in agriculture

(2) putting foreign trade under state control

(3) strengthening the leading role of the public industrial sector and coordinating the efforts of the private sector so that it can fulfill its role in the plan

(4) coordination and integration among the Arab regions.

Not discussed at the symposium, and for cause, were practical policies that belie Ba'athi regional principles. As *The Economist* wrote (April 25, 1975), "Iraq and Syria are neighborly 'sister' Arab countries divided by a common Ba'athist ideology and a common river, the Euphrates." What would be one of the most prosperous and "logical" Arab subregions, the Fertile Crescent, is one of the most divided because of, to the outsider, imperceptible ideological differences. Whether or not the geopolitics of up and downstream states is the real explanation for the Syro-Iraqi rivalry is for the moment not as significant as its existence. Syria, with its giant, Soviet-built Tabaqa Dam on the Euphrates, is resolutely developing its eastern Jazira region, while downstream Iraq protests that its own agriculture is being denied its rightful share of water. Iraq is by no means helpless, and with oil reserves second in the Arab World only to Saudi Arabia's, has considerable weight to throw around. One of its retaliatory measures has been to build an oil pipeline for its northern fields southeast to Basra and thence on to Persian/Arab Gulf tankers. Previously much of Iraq's oil had gone to the Mediterranean through a pipeline terminating in Banias, Syria, for which the Syrians charged substantial transit fees. These, as well as the discount prices at which Iraq has sold Syria oil in the past, have been put in jeopardy.

The point of this is not sententiously to accuse Arab regimes of hypocrisy or the cynical violation of their own proclaimed principles. The real problem is, everyone wants integration but, like peace, on his own terms. What those terms are, and whether they can be reconciled were subjects the conferees carefully skirted.

Saudi Arabia, with earnings from oil sales in excess of $26 billion a year, is on the threshold of a five-year plan of mind-boggling proportions. If it achieves its investment targets, which, perhaps fortunately, is not at all likely, it will make outlays of $25-30 billion a year over five years. Such investments would, in any one year, be three to four times Egypt's total national income. Yet Saudi Arabia's seven to ten million inhabitants have hardly been prepared to play a meaningful role in this endeavor which will inevitably depend on the massive importation of foreign expertise, managerial personnel, and skilled and unskilled labor. Steel mills, fertilizer plants, petrochemical complexes, gas recovery installations, new cities and ports, desalinization projects, advanced hydrophonic agriculture, air-conditioned feed lots are all part of the gold-plated plan. All of them can be paid for, and some if not most of them can actually be implemented, but the real question is, from a regional point of view, should they? Do they make sense or do they constitute a gross misuse of what some regard as "regional" resources? Unfortunately no one was dispatched from Saudi Arabia to discuss the merits of the plan nor did any of the other participants make the slightest reference to it.

There were only two instances in which the Saudis were indirectly questioned. Mihaljo Mesarovic of Cleveland University (co-author with Pestel of *Mankind at the Turning Point*, 1974) presented the bare bones of his computer model of global and regional interactions, and, by way of example, said that it had been possible to demonstrate that, on the basis of available but possibly faulty data, Saudi development and Saudi financing of Egypt's development *could* be made compatible. The one Saudi participant at the symposium received this news, as he did everything else, inscrutably. The second instance occurred when, by proxy, Sayyid Marei's proposal for an Arab "Marshall Plan" was presented. Sayyid Marei is President of Egypt's Parliament, the head of the UN's World Food Conference of November

Left to right: Mesarovic (Cleveland University), W.G. Vogt (University of Pittsburgh), Hilmi Abderrahman (Minister of Planning), Walid Shafa'i (Institute of National Planning).

1974, and for many years Egypt's Minister of Agriculture and Agrarian Reform. For two years he has been advocating an idea that many Egyptians share. Put simply the argument is that Egypt has sacrificed blood and treasure over 25 years ($30 billion since 1967) in the name of confrontation with Israel and the restoration of Palestinian rights. Its economy in the process has taken an unmerciful pounding. At the same time, and as a direct result of Egypt's military initiative of October 1973, the Arab oil-rich were able to quintuple their earnings without any major sacrifice on the battle front. Marei demands compensation from those who have profited from the hostilities and emerged unscathed to the front-line states—Egypt, Syria, Jordan—whose economies have been dislocated. The model would be similar to the U.S. Marshall Plan that led to European reconstruction after World War II. The Marei proposal drew no more response than had Mesarovic's observations.

The Sudan may be one of the first Arab countries to set its planning priorities with explicit acknowledgement of other Arab regional concerns. The Sudan has a relatively vast, underexploited agricultural sector that could, with investment in modernization of agricultural techniques and in infrastructure, generate substantial exportable surplus of certain kinds of produce. These would consist mainly in sugar, edible oils (from sesame and maize), feed cakes, millet, sorghum, carcasses, and live animals. This potential is of particular interest to two Arab regions both of which have growing food deficits. One is Egypt, which annually imports large quantities of beef, edible oils, animal feed, and sugar (120,000 tons from as far away as the Philippines are being negotiated for 1976), and the Sudan could conceivably meet some of these needs. The other region consists of Saudi Arabia and the Gulf Emirates, none of which has an extensive or easily expandable agricultural base. For the

Arabian Peninsula, Sudan is just a short hop away across the Red Sea, and there may be some tendency for the oil-rich to regard their neighbor as a kind of agricultural hinterland. Moreover, and in marked contrast to Egypt, these states have ample foreign exchange not only to buy Sudan's future surplus but also to invest in its development. The Sudan is as hard-pressed for foreign exchange as Egypt.

In short, the Sudan's long-range planning will concentrate on agriculture and agro-industries (sugar refineries, canneries, oil mills, meat packing, textiles) and the absolutely crucial expansion of road, railroad, and power grids. The Sudan is about a third the size of the United States but has only 4,000 kilometers of railroad and less than 1,000 of paved roads. The problem is financing their plans, especially the foreign exchange components. There is a good chance, however, that substantial foreign exchange infusions may become available through the Arab Fund for Social and Economic Development (AFSED). This Fund, headquartered in Kuwait, was founded in 1972 by 18 members of the Arab League. When it began operations in 1973 it was capitalized (all public funds) at 100 million kuwaiti dinars (1 dinar equals ca. US$3.50), subsequently raised to 400 million. One of the Fund's first and biggest projects is Sudanese agricultural development. After the Fund's experts had surveyed Sudan's agricultural sector, a preliminary ten-year program of comprehensive development was drawn up. Its total cost would be the equivalent of £2.2 billion (over US$5 billion) and the Sudanese would be expected to put up a third of it.

Both the plan and the funding would come under the jurisdiction of a Development and Investment Authority, affiliated to the Fund, which would act as a sort of multinational holding company that could extent its activities to other Arab countries. The Authority would take an equity position in all investments, it would repatriate earnings tax free, and would be guaranteed against nationalization or expropriation. The Sudanese government would in turn have an equity position in the Authority as well as benefit from the Authority's investments. Dr. Hamdi Kana'an of AFSED told the conferees that if the Arab member states provide sufficient funds for the Authority (by purchasing shares in it) and if the Sudanese and the Fund agree on the

modalities of the Authority's operations, in ten years the Sudan could provide the Arab World with 40 per cent of its projected edible oil imports, 20 per cent of sugar imports, and 50 per cent of meat imports.

At least two crucial questions lie submerged in this approach to LRPing. The first is that if the AFSED formula becomes operational, the Sudan will have to surrender some portion of its economic sovereignty to a supraregional, extraterritorial Authority. This is an extremely sensitive question for any recently independent country that has spent years in trying to consolidate its political and economic autonomy. Yet the indications are that if the Fund's members come up with the money, the Sudanese will accept the Authority. Both the formula and the precedent are of immense importance, but despite Kana'an's brief description there was no discussion of what was involved.

The second question bears directly upon Egypt. Egyptians seem to have taken for granted a basic complementarity in Sudano-Egyptian development, perhaps assuming they can barter Egyptian manufactures for Sudanese agricultural surplus. But the AFSED program would necessitate direct sales of exportable surplus for foreign exchange in order to pay the Fund's and Sudan's creditors. Barter deals would be of little interest, and besides the Sudan is bent on self-sufficiency in textiles which is Egypt's principal manufactured export. This is a potential "exogenous shock" but to my knowledge Egyptian planners have not tried to gauge its consequences in terms of regional markets for Egyptian manufactures nor sources of agricultural imports. Again, the matter was not discussed at the symposium.

Egypt itself faces monumental development problems, but the tentative conclusions of one Egyptian planner, 'Issam Muntasser, are that they can be overcome within the framework of autonomous national growth. As Muntasser himself remarked, he was surprised that his policy simulation model permitted such a sanguine conclusion given the somber base years, 1973-74. Some of the elements that keep Egypt in perpetual economic crisis are a trade deficit on the order of LE 2 billion, growing food imports currently worth about LE 700 million a year, external debt, military and civilian but excluding short term commitments, approaching $15 billion, a debt-servicing ratio running at about 35 per cent of export earnings, a domestic system of commodity subsidies that costs the state LE 600 million a year, and a domestic rate of dissavings. Yet despite these obstacles, the model demonstrates that it would be possible to quadruple per capita income in Egypt to roughly LE 400 by the year 2000. Muntasser is adamant, however, in asserting that the principal constraint is and will remain capital. As Table 1 shows there are many holes in the projection, particularly as concerns net factor payments abroad, subsidies, and the savings gap. Not only must domestic savings be dramatically increased (to 15 or 20 per cent of GDP it has been suggested elsewhere) but so must investment (from LE 502 million in 1973 to LE 7.972 billion in 2000 or about 25 per cent of the projected GDP for the same year) and industrial exports from LE 206 million in 1973 to LE 6.027 in the year 2000.

Muntasser claims the domestic savings gap could be overcome "by following appropriate savings policies" and providing "savings incentives and outlets." Public and private consumption will have to be contained, the tax-take increased, and disguised unemployment eliminated. Operational policy recommendations on implementation of these goals were beyond the scope of Muntasser's paper. Similarly, the author stressed that the long-term bottleneck in achieving growth will remain foreign exchange, and that to break through this Egypt must increase its industrial exports—twenty- to thirtyfold over present levels! Even if able to produce them, where will Egypt find markets for this volume of goods? Surely logic and priority would dictate a careful search for outlets among other Arab countries, but the fact of the matter is today that Arab states tend to develop the same sorts of industries (textiles, processed foods, cement, petrochemicals, steel, fertilizers) and to put high protective tariffs around them. Moreover, the richest countries are precisely those that can afford to buy the best the West can provide and are under no constraint to accept what might be inferior Egyptian goods.

The constraints Egypt faces in planning its national development differ in degree but not in kind from those of other Arab states. When Muntasser concludes that the key to the future lies in the nexus of foreign exchange sources and industrial exports, his judgment is regional not national.

This being the case, there are compelling if not imperative reasons for regionwide planning and allocation of industrial and agricultural production.

C. Regional Integration

Since the Second World War the Arabs have talked continuously, even incessantly, of their basic unity, put asunder by history and colonialist maneuvers. Yet they have consecrated "colonialist" boundaries through the Arab League. The Arab League has always presented itself as a force for unity, building on independent nation states and moving toward coordination of foreign and military policies and thence to economic integration. This is the ideal of an Arab world of states gravitating toward more profound forms of integration. The ideal is as distant now as it was at its birth 30 years ago. There is no lack of Arabs to say, "I told you so."

Within the context of economic integration the same debate is crystallizing today. Is there an Adam Smithian "guiding hand" to Arab integration whereby the aggregate of the individual national interests of the Arab states will lead to the amelioration of the conditions of all Arabs? Or must national interests be subordinated to some supraregional arrangement of priorities which will assure that all Arabs get their due slice of the future? It is a knotty question from every point of view. National sovereignty is a sacred issue for which Arab and other Third World states have shed considerable blood. One of the central affirmations of the Group of 77 in recent polemics about the new world economic order has been that each nation exercise total sovereignty over the development and utilization of its own national resources. No more staunch adherent of this principle can be found than Algeria. At the same time Algeria has chided other oil-rich Arab states for the failure to use their national resources for the common good of all the Arabs.

In short there are some voices for a new conceptualization of regionalism, but the burden of conventional wisdom lies with the supporters of an Arab world of Arab states, not of peoples, with unity pursued step by step by incremental national policies. While the issue was given minimal attention, this seemed to represent the sense of the symposium.

TABLE 1: A SCENARIO OF EGYPT'S FUTURE GROWTH
('000 of Egyptian Pounds)

Endogenous and Exogenous Variables	1973	1974	1980	1985	2000
Investment	502	730	1621	2357	7972
Inv. Agric.	58	54	169	248	787
Inv. Ind.	154	234	445	685	2759
Inv. Elect. Power	30	30	85	124	394
Inv. Construction	5	11	34	50	158
Inv. Transport, Communic.	123	187	254	323	866
Inv. Housing	63	80	254	372	1181
Inv. Other Services	32	49	169	248	788
Changes in Stock	40	90	141	205	693
Inv. Other			70	102	346
Savings Gap	224	645			
Val. Ad. Agric.	1062	1225	1436	1641	2613
Val. Ad. Ind.	635	775	1557	2543	6985
Val. Ad. Mining, Other			500	734	2159
Val. Ad. Elect.	45	48	83	127	406
Val. Ad. Construct.	108	135	444	798	2136
Val. Ad. Transp., Commun.	159	167	483	722	1903
Val. Ad. Housing	138	141	172	214	491
Val. Ad. Other Serv.	1071	1153	2048	3490	12231
GDP Factor Cost	3217	3644	7223	11004	31083
Net Fac. Payment Abroad	−70	−188			
Indirect Taxes	525	693			
Subsidies	82	381			
GNP	3590	3768			
Direct Taxes	258	287			
Undist. Prof. Business	507	515			
Disposable House Inc.	2452	2842			
Cotton Exports	192	279	204	91	
Industrial Exports	206	275	561	1355	6007
Oil and Mineral Exp.	38	26	500	1087	2367
Invisibles	166	278	492	793	2057
Suez Canal			500	735	1587
Total Exports	564	832	2257	4061	12027
Food Imports	113	380	879	1255	1750
Ind. Imp. excl. Cap. goods	381	738	1557	2607	6007
Cap. Goods Imports	103	149	343	174	272
Invisibles	164	211	433	770	2828
Total Imports	761	1478	3212	4806	10857
Household Food Cons.	1392	1618	2295	2929	7020
Total Household Cons.	2342	2533	3752	4973	13504
Gov. Consumption	1020	1097	1741	2558	9428
Total Consumption	3362	3630	5493	7531	22932
Gross Domestic Savings	278	216			

Source: Dr. Essam Muntasser, "Egypt's Long-term Growth: 1976-2000 (Preliminary Projections)," pp. 20-21.

But there are countercurrents, not necessarily radical, which reject the formulae of the European Economic Community (EEC) and notions of step by step regionalism as being inappropriate or irrelevant for the Arab World. One of the formulators of these countertrends, Mohammed al-Imam, has, since the symposium, replaced Hilmi Abderrahman as Egypt's Minister of Planning. Imam had formerly been associated with the Council on Arab Economic Unity, one of the three sponsors of the symposium, a body that in the mid-60s launched the Arab "Common Market." Clearly, the CAEU wants to move on to bolder and qualitatively different approaches to Arab integration.

Both Mohammed al-Imam and Ibrahim Sa'ad al-Din of the Arab Planning Institute of Kuwait argued that free trade policies and customs unions might promote integration among advanced economies but not among less-developed countries because of the similarity of their productive mix, limited markets and need for protection. Among Arab states, formulae borrowed from EEC experience will act as impediments rather than catalysts to integration. Concessions made to the regional ensemble will be founded on national interests, hence reinforcing the national economic unit, or they will not be made at all.

The experience of the Arab Common Market, summarized in the paper of Ahmad Faris Murad, would seem to confirm this assessment. Incidentally, Murad's study was the only formal presentation that addressed itself exclusively to problems confronting Arab integration. The market came into being in 1965 grouping a nucleus of Arab states to which others have adhered over time. Efforts at tariff reduction on manufactured goods proved futile because of the similarity of industries among Arab states. Indeed the authors of the Sudanese report (Ahmad Usman al-Hajj and Najwa Ahmad al-Qadi) candidly avowed that "the Sudan, until now, has not been able to apply many of the clauses of the agreement on the Arab Common Market because the Sudan continues to rely heavily on customs receipts in financing the public budget and public investments. There are also many infant industries which those responsible feel must be protected until they can stand on their feet and compete in the world market."

Similar responses from other Arab states emasculated the market. According to Murad, trade among member states increased by only one per cent in the period 1965-1970 and actually declined 10 per cent among nonmembers. Another source, Fa'iq Abd al-Rasul, claims that among the five founding members of the Common Market the value of exports among them rose from $78 million to $175 million between 1964 and 1973 while imports among them grew from $87 million to $204 million. But these figures still represented only 2.6 per cent of the total exports of these states and 4.2 per cent of total imports.[1]

In general, such major actors as Syria, Iraq, and Egypt pursued policies of national self-sufficiency, while the others increased their extraregional trade. In the period 1966-1970, Arab trade with the United States increased 111 per cent, with the Federal Republic of Germany 156 per cent and with the United Kingdom 150 per cent.

Dr. Abd al-Aal al-Sakban, an Iraqi and Secretary-General of the CAEU, signaled the more radical approach advocated by this and other organizations. He cited approvingly in his address to the symposium the recent experience of COMECON and the 1971 Comprehensive Program for Socialist Economic Integration—"This program has clearly shown that the main focus in cooperation among the different countries is not only in trade or loans to avoid a deficit or surplus in the balance of payments, but to specialize in production and to cooperate in the exchange of products. This is in order to achieve socialist economic integration within the framework of a comprehensive plan for long-term joint economic activity. Thus the focus would be on production rather than on trade."

The CAEU, the Arab Fund for Social and Economic Development, and the Organization of Arab Oil Exporting States, while not entirely sharing like philosophies, have been promoting an integrationalist formula founded on publicly funded, multinational Arab companies one variant of which is AFSED's proposed Authority for the

1. Fa'iq abd al-Rasul, "Economic Blocs—A Path to Rapid Growth and Economic Integration." *Petroleum and Development*, (Baghdad) Vol. 1, No. 2 (1975), p. 100.

Sudan. These companies would mobilize and "integrate Arab financial resources, especially from the oil-rich, and channel them into projects that have been studied and evaluated from a regional point of view. The hope is that tanker fleets, fertilizer industries, steel complexes, aluminum smelters, and agricultural production can be rationally and profitably distributed among states. The emphasis is on the development of natural and human resources to overcome the major impediments to increased production and interaction. This approach, its advocates believe, may have more rapid and direct payoffs than concentrating on the north-south issues of international commodity trade, indebtedness, and capital and technology transfers. The CAEU would like, for instance, to help create the conditions in which the Arabs can create their own technology. So far, however, these ideas have yet to move very far toward implementation.

As a kind of postscript, and one that encapsulates many of the national and regional planners' frustrations, it is instructive to consider the sudden but as yet undefined emergence of an Arab Fund to Support the Egyptian Economy. At the time of the symposium Egypt was facing one of its periodic foreign exchange crises as well as the longer-term problem of financing its five year plan. In late February and early March President Sadat toured the Arabian Peninsula and Gulf States to come up with emergency and medium-term aid. Both are or may be forthcoming but with strings. The funds to be provided by Saudi Arabia, Kuwait, the UAE,

and Qatar may be administered by an authority similar in nature to the AFSED model for the Sudan. The return on the capital may be guaranteed out of future earnings from the Suez Canal and oil exports. Moreover, the Egyptians will be obliged to undertake a number of internal control measures to curb government expenditures, erode the subsidy system, cut red tape and graft, and do away with redundant labor. It is too early to know the exact contents of the package, but already Egypt has changed its cabinet and announced a five-year austerity program that has apparently left the recently prepared five-year plan stillborn. Egypt's planners were similarly caught short in the spring of 1973 when an earlier five-year plan foundered on the government's decision to put the country on a war footing. In any event, planning the Egyptian economy has suddenly and in operational terms become a regional rather than a purely national concern.

Whether or not the new Fund is the kind of sharing of regional resources that the Egyptians would prefer, or even whether or not it will save the Egyptian economy, it nonetheless constitutes a step toward integration of sorts. If further steps are to be taken, and on a basis of equality between the region's rich and poor, it may require, as Tunisia's delegate noted, a prophet to sensitize the elites and the masses to the unique opportunities at hand. Egypt's Ismail Sabry Abdullah quipped, "On that score, sir, there should be no problem; we, the Arabs, are the main suppliers of prophets."

APPENDIX I

Joint Symposium on Long-Range Planning and Regional Integration
Cairo, January 14 - 21, 1976

List of Participants

Guest Speakers	Position	Country
Engineer Sayyid Marei	President People's Assembly	Egypt
Dr. Abdelkadr Hatem	President Specialized National Councils	Egypt
Dr. J. Pronk	Minister of Economic Cooperation and Development	Netherlands
Dr. Abd al-Azim Abul Atta	Minister of Irrigation	Egypt

Organizers		
Dr. Ibrahim Hilmi Abderrahman	Minister of Planning	Egypt
Dr. Ismail Sabry Abdullah	Director, Institute of National Planning	Egypt
Dr. Abd al-Aal Sakban	Sec. Gen. Council on Arab Economic Unity	Iraq
Monsieur Le Guay	UNIDO	

Participants		
Abdel-Hakim, Dr. Mohammed Subhy	Faculty of Arts, Cairo Univ.	Egypt
Abdel-Kader, A.	Faculty of Economic and Social Studies, Khartoum Univ.	Sudan
Abd al-Rahman, E.H.	Joint ECA/UNIDO Ind. Division	
Abd al-Wahab, E.S.	CAEU	
Abu Maaty, A.	CAEU	
Abulshamat, A.	CAEU	
Anis, A.A.	Faculty of Science, Ain Shams Univ.	Egypt
Aly, A.M.	Director Arab Planning Institute	Kuwait
Bruton, Henry	Ford Foundation	USA
Cho, Y.R.	UNIDO	
Csete, L.	Institute for World Economics	Hungary
Dobosiewcz, Z.		Poland
El-Bindary, Aziz	Director Population and Family Planning Board, Cairo	Egypt
El-Shafa'i, Walid	INP	Egypt
El-Sawy, I.	INP	Egypt
Fahmy, F.R.	INP	Egypt
Farrag, A.	CAEU	Egypt
Fergany, Nader	Population and Family Planning Board	Egypt
Fheodorovitch, F.	Gosplan	USSR
Fossi	OECD	
Gouda, M.A.	CAEU	
Galachov	Gosplan	USSR
Garhy, M. el-	INP	Egypt
Gassem, A.		Iraq
Ghandour, A. el-	Ministry of Economy	Egypt

Ghanem, F.S.B.	Ministry of Planning	PDR of Yemen
Guernier, M.	Club of Rome	Italy
Hagg, A.O. el-		Sudan
Hakim, Sherif el-	American Univ., Cairo	Egypt
Hanafy, S.E.	Ministry of Planning	Egypt
Hassuna, Wafiq Ashraf	INP	Egypt
Haqq, Mahbub al-	IBRD	Pakistan
Hopkins	ILO	
Hradecky, L.	Prague School of Economics	CSSR
Ibrahim, Saad al-Din	American Univ., Cairo	Egypt
Imam, Mohammed el-	CAEU	Egypt
Jacob, E	Hochschule fur Okonomie, Bruno Leuschner	GDR
Jirowec, J.	Central School of Planning and Statistics, Warsaw	Poland
Kanaan, Hamdi	AFSED	Kuwait
Kolloktos	IBRD	
Kurowski, L.	Central School of Planning and Statistics	Poland
Malham, Y.	Min. of Commerce and Ind.	Jordan
Mandi, P.	Inst. of World Economics	Hungary
Mansour, M.B.	AFSED	Kuwait
Mardinov	Gosplan	USSR
Mason, Edward	Harvard University	USA
Maguid, Abderrazaq al-	Ministry of Planning	Egypt
Manoufi, A el-	Ministry of Planning	Iraq
Mesarovic, Mihaljo	Univ. of Cleveland	USA
Mihalik, J.	Bratislava School of Econ.	CSSR
Muhy al-Din, Amr	Fac. of Economics, Cairo Univ.	Egypt
Mongy, A.E.	INP	Egypt
Muntasser, 'Issam	Ministry of Planning	Egypt
Murad, A.	Arab Planning Institute	Kuwait
Nasilowski, M.	Central School of Planning and Statistics	Poland
Noursi, David	IMF	
Nour, S.	Population and Family Planning Council	Egypt
Odeby, I.A. el-	Ministry of Finance	Saudi Arabia
Omar, H.	CAEU	
Pecci, A.	Club of Rome	Italy
Pietrzkiewics, T.	Institute of Planning	Poland
Polaczek, S.	Institute of Planning	Poland
Pustvalov	Gosplan	USSR
Quinn, J.	U.S. Bureau of the Census	USA
Qutaifi, A.A. el-	Ministry of Planning	Iraq
Raouf, M.M. abd el-	INP	Egypt
Ranis, G.	Yale University	USA
Rassoul, R.A.	INP	Egypt
Redzapagic, F.	Institute for Developing Countries	Yugoslavia
Rodgers	ILO	
Saad al-Din, Ibrahim	Arab Planning Institute	Kuwait
Sabry, T.	UNDP	Egypt

Safty, A el-	Faculty of Econ., Cairo Univ.	Egypt
Safty, R. el-	CAEU	
Salib, Rafael	Arab Planning Inst.	Kuwait
Salim, A.	ILO	
Sayf, A.M. el-	Ministry of Finance	Saudi Arabia
Scolnik, H.	Fondacion Bariloche	Argentina
Selim, H.M.	Abu Dhabi Fund for Arab Econ. Development	UAE
Shawky, A.	CAEU	
Soliman, A.	Unicef, Cairo	Egypt
Soliman, A.A.	Univ. of Khartoum	Sudan
Soliman, H.S.	National Planning Commission	Sudan
Soliman, Selwa	Fac. of Economy and Political Science, Cairo Univ.	Egypt
Tagany, A.H. el-	National Planning Commission	Sudan
Theuring, R.	Hoschule fur Okonomie	GDR
Tolkatchov	Institute of Planning	USSR
Vakil, Feruz	Plan and Budget Org.	Iran
Vogt, W.G.	Univ. of Pittsburgh	USA
Voightsberger, S.	Hoschule fur Okonomie	GDR
Watary, A.A. el-	OAPEC	Kuwait
Younis, M.E.	American Univ., Cairo	Egypt
Yurechenko	Gosplan	USSR
Zaghly, M. el-	CERES	Tunisia
Zaid, S.A.	National Inst. of Pub. Admin.	A.R. of Yemen
Zajda	Central School of Planning	Poland

Papers Presented to the Symposium

A = Arabic   E = English   F = French

Abd al-Hakim, Dr. Mohammed Subhy. "Towards a Strategy for Redistributing Population in Egypt" (A)

Abd al-Rahman, Dr. as-Sayyid Hafiz. "Some Ideas and Experiences of Economic Cooperation and Integration, with Special Reference to the Arab World" (E)

Abu al-Atta, Eng. Abd al-Azim. "Long-Range Planning in Drainage and Irrigation" (A)

Bandar, Dr. Tu'ama Gaber and Gassim, Abd al-Rasul. "Aspects of the Actual Situation of Development Planning in the Arab Nation with Special Reference to Planning Experience in the Iraqi Region" (A)

Cole, Henry E. "Aspects of Economic Demographic Models in Development Planning" (E)

Dobosiewicz, Z. "Economic Integration in Latin America" (E)

Fergany, Nader. "The Relationship Between Level of Development and Fertility Level and its Implications for Planning to Reduce Fertility: An Exercise in Macro-Statistical Modelling" (E)

Fergany, and Nour, Sayyid el-. "A two-Level Regionalized Computer Model for Population Projection by Age and Sex" (E)

Fergany, Nader. "Prospects of Long-Range Population Growth and Some Related Characteristics in Egypt" (E)

Hajj, Ahmad Usman al- and Qadi, Najwa Ahmad al-. "The Sudanese Experience in Planning in the Framework of Arab Integration" (A)

Hakim, Sherif Mahmoud al-. "The Principle and Method of Planning Local Community Power Structures" (E)

Hanafi, Eng. Saad al-Din al-. "Hypotheses on the Egyptian Agricultural Sector until the Year 2000" (A)

Hatem, Dr. Abdelqader. Speech on the Specialized National Councils in the ARE (E)

Hopkins, G., Rodgers, G., Standing, G., and Wery, G. "Bachue—An Economic Demographic Model for Long-term Development Planning" (E)

Hopkins, Rodgers, Wery. "A Structural Overview of Bachue-Philippines" (E)

Ibrahim, Saaid al-Din. "A Doctrine of Urban Dispersal: An Imperative for Developmental Planning in the Arab World" (E)

Jacob, Eleonore. "Basic Questions of Long-Term Planning of Investments under Conditions Obtaining in Developing Countries" (E)

Kurowski, Lech. "Elements of the Long-term Plan" (E)

Muntasser, 'Issam. "Egypt's Long-Term Growth: 1976-2000 (Preliminary Projections)" (E)

Murad, Dr. Ahmad Faris. "The Evolution of the Edification of Economic Growth and Commercial Exchange as Two Approaches to Arab Economic Integration" (A)

Nasilowski, Dr. Hab. M. "Selected Problems of Perspective Development in Developing Countries" (E)

Pletrzkiewicz, T. "La Structure informatique et decisive de la plannification a long terme" (F)

Quinn, Joseph E. "Two Examples of the LRPM Models with Emphasis on the Agricultural Sector" (E)

Qutaifi, Dr. Aziz al-. "Long-Range Planning and the National Plan in Iraq" (A)

Rendos, L., Mihalik, J., Hradecky, S. "Experience in Simulating Long-Range Inter-Disciplinary Approach toward Socio-economic development Planning in Czechoslovakia" (E)

Safty, Dr. Ahmad al-. "Adaptive Behavior, Long-Run Demand and Preferences" (E)

Salib, Dr. Rafael. "On Projections for Development Planning with Illustrations in the Field of Manpower Planning—A Methodological Approach" (E)

Sakban, Dr. Abd al-Aal. "Opening Statement" (E + A)

Sayed, M.L. al-. "A Feedback Control System for Long-Range Socioeconomic Models" (E)

Theuring, Dr. Rolf. "On the Approach and the Demands Made on Long-Term Economic Planning in the Conditions of the Developing Countries" (E)

Voigtsberger, S. "Some Problems of Long-Term Planning under a Spatial Point of View" (E)

——————— "Socialist Economic Integration: the Case of the CMEA Countries" (E)

Zajda, Z. "New Problems in Long-Range Planning in the Light of Polish Experience in the Last Few Years" (E)

Economy: Public Versus Private

After five years in Egypt spent in fairly close scrutiny of the country's economy, I am not at all sure, in analytic terms, where the Nasserist economy has been nor where President Sadat is taking it. One is tempted to say that somewhere around 1956 Egypt began to stumble into socialism and that somewhere around 1970 (or was it 1966?) began to stumble out of it. But it can rightly be pointed out that what had emerged from the very outset was not socialism but rather state capitalism and that this formula was, in any event, hardly an innovation in modern Egypt. Mohammed Ali was, after all, Egypt's first state capitalist 150 years ago. Moreover, Nasser's thrust toward public ownership of certain means of production may not have been as profound as the regime itself claimed and consequently Sadat's implicit move away from the Nasserist model may be more superficial than his critics are prepared to believe. What can be said with some assurance is that major policy shifts in the economy were often taken *primarily* for non-economic reasons and that whatever the motives underlying them, they were, in economic terms, improvised. Programmatic and ideological glosses were supplied after the fact. The "Socialist decrees" of July 1961, for example, waited nearly a year for their ideological rationalization in the National Charter of June 1962.

Another set of questions hinges on the claim that the state alone could undertake the necessary mobilization of capital and resources to achieve rapid rates of economic growth. This claim had been reiterated in nearly all Arab states (save Lebanon), even those, such as Morocco, that want the private sector eventually to carry the burden of development. The necessity of massive state intervention is, on the face of it, undeniable, especially in a country like Egypt where capital and natural resources are in such short supply. Empiric proof to sustain such a claim is lacking, however, for the simple sobering fact that very little real growth in per capita terms has taken place over the last two decades of state intervention. Not all Egyptian analysts would concede this fact, nor would I wish to claim that there is not evidence to the contrary. But virtually all analysts will concede that the economy is in a bad way and that state intervention has failed to attain a great many of the goals it set for itself.

Beyond that, however, there is very little agreement as to what went wrong and consequently as to how to put things right. Seriatim, one may note the following: stifling of the private sector and blocking avenues for productive private investment; closing off Egypt to foreign investment; bureaucratic inefficiency, red tape, overstaffing, and corruption; inadequate public savings; inability to tie public sector wages to production levels; low export capability of public sector enterprises; overreliance on Soviet technology, credits, and markets; heavy defense expenditures; and the financial burden of three wars. From this list the critics of the Nasserist system draw most of their ammunition. Its defenders, on the other hand, while not denying the validity of many of the charges would stress international (read Western, United States, Israeli) efforts to destroy Egypt's socialist experiment; the demonstrated inability of the Egyptian private sector to mobilize high levels of investment; the demonstrated reluctance of foreign private capital to move into the LDCs in general except on terms that would ultimately be detrimental to the Egyptian economy; the superficiality with which some Egyptian policy-makers understood the socialist experiment; insufficient education and preparation of the masses, the workers, and the managerial and technocratic personnel in their responsibilities within the new system. In short the critics want to move away (or back away) from the public enterprise system—but to what? The defenders want to move forward in the sense of intensifying the socialist experiment. But what forms would intensification take? These and practically all the other questions alluded to above remain unanswered. All that I intend to do in what follows is present some of the elements in the debate.

An essential point to keep in mind, and one that Bent Hansen, a leading analyst of the Egyptian economy made some time ago, is that Nasserist economics consisted in a kind of social compromise, the careful treading of "the line of least popular dissatisfaction." The second point is that while the results in aggregate national growth terms were far from satisfactory, social peace was maintained: nearly everyone was able to draw a little something from the system. Free education from primary school through university, guaranteed jobs in the public sector for university graduates, relatively high wages for public sector workers, subsidized agricultural in-puts, subsidized retail prices of basic goods, extensive public works and construction projects, rapid expansion in manufacturing capacity, extensive public efforts in land reclamation—all these were facets of state intervention from 1956 on. The private sector paid a price in all this through various kinds of restrictive legislation, nationalizations, and sequestrations. At the same time, the public sector, because of the scale of its programs and expenditures, fostered the emergence of new, or sometimes simply retreaded, private sector interests that undertook the tasks the public sector farmed out because of bureaucratic lethargy or lack of expertise. The public sector meant big business, and in many ways the private sector thrived in its shadow and lived off its fat. This is the case today, perhaps more so than ever. It is for this reason that there is considerable ambivalence in the attacks of the private sector on the public sector, for one suspects that rather than wanting to kill it off, the private sector would simply like to make it more responsive to their needs.

The upshot is that many of the figures most prominent in the debate over Egypt's economic future have a foot in both camps. Mustapha Kemal Murad, 15 years in the public Cotton Organization and head of the so-called right-wing platform within parliament, staunchly espouses the need to resuscitate the Egyptian private sector. One of the instrumentalities he has recommended is to transform public sector organizations, like the Cotton Organization, into publicly financed holding companies that will enter into joint ventures with Egyptian private interests (and foreign interests too) to establish "conglomerates" in a range of manufacturing, touristic, and banking activities. Sayyid Marei, ex-Minister of Agriculture, parliamentarian, business intermediary, and gentleman farmer, is another whose career has bridged the private-public divide and who would like to make Cairo the financial center of the Arab World. The perfect example of this breed, however, is Ahmad Osman, Minister of Housing and Reconstruction as well as President of the Board of the semi-public or semi-private Arab Contractors Ltd., the largest engineering and construction firm in the Arab World. It grew to that stature in large part because of public business—getting the contract for the construction of the High Aswan Dam was a good start.

President Sadat, whose economic philosophy is more instinctive than studied, summed up what may be a widely held view.

> In my view, in the future, the private sector will have about 30 or 35 per cent [presumably of investment outlays] whereas now the public sector has 90 per cent. So if the private sector takes 30 per cent that will leave 70 per cent for the public sector. And naturally if the private sector expands and grows, the public sector will jump ahead too, from its LE7 billion [in fixed investment] to LE20 billion.... (*al-Ahram*, April 15, 1976).

Thus there are no incompatabilities between the two sectors. The only reservation one might formulate about the President's statement is that he has reversed the direction of the link between private and public—it has been the growth in public sector outlays that has stimulated private sector activity, not the other way around.

The Emergence of the Public Sector

In July 1952, when Gamal Abdel Nasser and his co-officers deposed King Faruq, the state's role in the economy was limited to infrastructural investment, mainly in the agricultural irrigation system, and social services. Agricultural production, manufacturing, internal and foreign trade, banking and insurance, and even some basic utilities in electricity, water, and urban transport were all under private control. Table 1 (p. 4) gives the sectoral distribution of Gross Domestic Product for the period 1945 to 1954. At the time of the revolution in 1952 the government or public sector accounted for less than 13 per cent of GDP, while the private sector was responsible for generating the other 87 per cent. Let us note here, in anticipation of a fuller presentation below, that today the public sector's contribution to GDP is about 55 per cent.

Agriculture, manufacturing, commerce, and services were the dominant spheres of the private sector with the agricultural sector then, as now, constituting the center of gravity of the entire economy. Yet within each of these spheres the range in scale of activities was enormous. In 1952 agriculture covered the four-fifths of the rural population that owned (and still owns today) less than two acres per capita as well as commercial estate owners with two thousand or more irrigated acres under cotton or sugar cane. Likewise in manufacturing. In 1945, according to Mahmoud Anis, paid-up capital in industry amounted to LE70 million (at that time ca. $200 million), but 46 per cent of all manufacturing establishments consisted in mini-operations capitalized at less than LE50 each while only 2.7 per cent were capitalized at more than LE10,000. At the upper end of this scale were some relative giants like the Egyptian Spinning and Weaving Company (part of the Misr Group founded by Talaat Harb) with paid-up capital of LE7 million or the Egyptian Sugar and Refining Company capitalized at LE12 million (one of several Ahmad Abboud Pasha's ventures).[1]

The same picture repeats itself in commerce and services where one finds the big Cairo department stores like Cicurel or Salon Vert alongside the myriad of hole-in-the-wall coffee houses and pushcarts. Even when one is able to find statistics broken down by public and private sector, they nonetheless brutalize reality because of the gaping disparities in scale and income among private sector interests which in turn are only slightly more pronounced than those among today's public sector. These disparities, not incidentally, have made it very difficult to define the good guys and

bad guys in ideological terms. Clearly the bulk of the private sector is not exploitative but exploited, and in recent years, likely as not, it has been the upper strata of the public bureaucracy that has done the exploiting.

A. Public and Private Ownership of Land

The new regime's first act regarding the private sector was the agrarian reform of August 1952 placing a ceiling of 200 feddans (1 feddan equals 1.038 acres) upon individual landowners. This and subsequent measures affected about 2,100 large landholders and led, after several years, to the redistribution of 850,000 feddans or one-seventh of Egypt's cultivated surface. The primary motive of the move was not, however, distributive justice, but the assertion of political control. The "latifundists" that were cut down to 200 feddans apiece had in large measure constituted the political elite of the old regime, and to assure the survival of the new regime their economic leverage within the system had to be severely reduced.

The agrarian reform was in no way intended to be an assault upon the principle and fact of private property ownership. Indeed it reinforced it by distributing the excess lands of the super-rich to landless peasants in two-feddan plots. The reform was very much in keeping with the United States notion of that time (and perhaps of today) of promoting agricultural modernization through small peasant holders, hard-working, profit-oriented, and directly involved in production. Sayyid Marei, mentioned above, was as much as anyone the architect of the reform and his views about the basic merits of the yeoman, land-owning peasant have scarcely changed in the last 25 years.

The most radical departure associated with the agrarian reform was the introduction of supply and marketing cooperatives into the areas taken over so as to maintain scale of production and yields per acre. It was at this time that the state developed policies of indirect control over agricultural production that in the 1960s were extended to the rest of the cultivated areas. The basic principle was and is simple. To have access to the agricultural credit banks (before 1952 agricultural credit was predominantly in private hands), to purchase seed, fertilizers, and pesticides at subsidized prices, and to benefit from mechanized plowing and aerial

Table I

Gross National Product, 1945-1954[15]

(£E Million, Current Prices)

	1945	1946	1947	1948	1949	1950	1951	1952	1953	1954
A. Government[1]	58.5	59.8	58.9	64.0	74.1	90.3	109.9	122.4	123.3	136.2
B. Private sector[2]:										
1. Agriculture[2]	215.6	189.8	203.4	246.9	316.8	361.7	348.3	269.2	272.7	309.6
2. Cotton ginning and pressing[3]	1.4	1.9	1.6	1.7	2.1	2.0	2.0	2.8	2.0	2.1
3. Mining, quarrying, and salines[4]	6.9	6.6	7.0	9.8	11.8	13.7	13.2	14.5	14.7	11.8
4. Manufacturing[5]	33.7	34.5	34.9	46.6	46.7	53.4	65.7	63.6	60.7	63.3
5. Building and construction (private and public)[6]	11.3	14.5	17.4	23.0	30.0	28.6	30.8	29.5	26.8	27.6
6. Electricity, gas, and water[7]	2.0	2.2	2.6	3.1	3.5	4.1	4.4	4.8	5.1	5.5
7. Commerce, storage, and transportation[8]	124.5	135.0	154.6	213.6	235.3	282.2	318.4	289.8	250.0	244.8
8. Banking and real estate[9]	6.4	6.5	6.9	7.4	7.4	8.5	8.9	9.3	9.6	10.5
9. Insurance[9]	1.0	1.0	1.0	1.3	1.7	2.0	1.8	2.0	2.3	2.2
10. Services[10]	49.7	51.7	54.7	61.2	62.9	68.3	73.8	74.3	76.5	79.9
11. Ownership of dwelling[11]	35.9	37.2	38.4	40.8	43.5	45.3	47.7	49.6	53.1	55.8
C. Gross domestic product (at market)	546.9	540.7	581.4	719.4	836.0	960.1	1,024.9	931.8	898.8	949.3
D. Rest of the world[12]	4.9	5.3	3.0	1.1	6.9	8.3	9.0	12.1	11.1	13.1
E. Gross national product (at market)	551.8	535.4	578.4	718.3	829.1	951.8	1,015.9	919.7	887.7	936.2
F. Plus subsidies[13]	2.7	5.5	4.8	8.9	10.5	9.7	15.3	15.9	10.6	4.8
G. Less indirect taxes[14]	37.5	48.2	59.1	66.8	76.7	89.8	115.4	99.9	106.6	108.9
H. Gross national product (at factor)	571.0	492.7	524.1	660.4	762.9	871.7	915.8	835.7	791.7	832.1
I. Gross domestic product (at factor)	512.1	498.0	527.1	661.5	769.8	880.0	924.8	847.8	802.8	845.3

1. From government budgets. It was attempted to make them net of depreciation. Includes value added in enterprises as well as wages and salaries in general government.

2. Official estimates of the Ministry of Agriculture.

3. Value added per cantar times quantity handled.

4. Based on analysis of values, costs, and quantities of major commodities.

5. A quantity index times the wholesale price index gives an idea of the value of gross output; this is multiplied by the value of output in 1950 to give a gross value of output series. Inputs are handled in the same way; the difference between the two series measures value added. The figures are generally gross of depreciation.

6. Rough estimates based on materials used.

7. Value added (from 1954 census of industrial production) times output index; prices have remained constant.

8. Weak figures based on a study of trade margins in internal and external trade. Excise taxes and customs duties are included here.

9. From company reports.

10. Professional and household servants' income from employment, and estimated wage rates assuming that the latter change with the cost-of-living index. Other services: 1954 employment (from census of establishments) times wage rates (200 per cent of that for services in survey of wages and working hours), traced back in proportion to commodity production.

11. Fixed percentage of total rental income (from tax data).

12. From balance-of-payments data.

13. Includes only wheat subsidies.

14. The main items are customs duties and tobacco and cigarette dues.

15. Source: S.H. Abdel Rahman, *A Survey of the Foreign Trade of Egypt in the Post-War Period, with Special Reference to Its impact on the National Economy* (Ph.D. dissertation, Faculty of Commerce, Cairo University, 1959). As in the case of Anis' figures, these data are in between being gross and net of depreciation; once again we have called them gross, since depreciation deductions have been limited.

Source: Donald C. Mead, *Growth and Structural Change in the Egyptian Economy*, Richard D. Irwin, Homewood, Illinois, 1967, pp. 272-73.

spraying, the smallholder had to join a cooperative, frequently accept the crop rotation laid down by the state, and sell his produce, or an agreed-upon portion of it, to the cooperative at prices fixed by the state. While it is still the case that, statistically, the agricultural world is included within the private sector, the regulatory powers of the government are so extensive as to deprive the categorization of much meaning.

Still there are those Egyptians who feel that a unique opportunity was lost, at the time of the agrarian reform, to bring about really radical changes in the Egyptian countryside. Magdi Hassanein, the moving force behind the development of Tahrir Province, Egypt's first big desert reclamation project, has argued that the acreage taken over by the state in 1952 should have remained under public ownership and been developed into model farms, following the most efficient methods of mechanization and crop rotation. Instead of offering the peasantry a new life style in a radically altered system of production and village environment (including universal education, complete participation of women in the work force, and total absence of draught animals), Egypt's leaders chose to add new numbers to the country's stolid cohorts of smallholders who must rely on large families, heavy manual labor, animal traction, and small plots for subsistence. Because the possibility to experiment with property relations and life styles was obviated in the lands of the Nile Valley proper, Magdi Hassanein turned to the desert.[2]

Tahrir Province, on the southwestern fringes of the Nile Delta, was Egypt's first large-scale desert reclamation project. Eventually it came to comprise a surface of 20,000 feddans. Neither as a social nor an agricultural experiment has it been much of a success. Hassanein himself was removed from the project after only two years amidst charges of corruption and mismanagement. But his basic idea, that the desert could become the source and model for the modernization of Egyptian agriculture, lived on. In a more ambiguous way, so did his cardinal principle that at Tahrir there would be no private property.

When it became clear after 1958 that Egypt would have its High Aswan Dam and consequently more irrigation water, it was decided to use all additional water in reclaiming about 1.2 million feddans. That would add about 20 per cent to the country's cultivated acreage. Years before the Nile was first closed off at the dam-site in 1964, land preparation and reclamation was begun on half a million feddans, mostly to the west of the Delta. By 1972 reclamation had been started on over 900,000 feddans (although it is important to keep in mind that these figures include surfaces taken up by roads, villages, irrigation and drainage canals—the net surface may be 30 per cent less).

From 1960 on, a quiet but intense debate developed about how best to manage these lands. The general tenor of the authoritative national Charter of 1962 was to consecrate the principle of private ownershihp of land, and in most official pronouncements it was suggested that once the state had brought reclamation sites up to marginal levels of productivity, the land would be distributed to private smallholders.

> Thus the correct solution to the agricultural problem does not lie in the transfer of the land to public ownership, but rather in the consolidation of private ownership and the expansion of this ownership to the greatest number possible....
>
> The (High) Dam has become the symbol of the people in its determination to build a (new) life, as it is the symbol of their desire to grant the right of ownership to the masses of peasants to whom this right was denied across centuries of feudalism.
>
> The National Charter, May 1962
> (in Arabic), pp. 90-91

Yet despite the public affirmation of this principle, there were misgivings in various quarters. Some were doctrinaire, and in the early 1960s economic policy was in the hands of Egyptians who at least talked of a "scientific" socialist approach to economic problems. Close cooperation with the U.S.S.R. at this time reinforced their position. The mechanized farm on 10,000 feddans of reclaimed land set up by the U.S.S.R. was meant to be a showcase of agro-industrial development without owners. Technocrats were likewise disturbed at the prospects of dividing up the new lands among smallholders. They were the first to become aware of several problems arising from reclamation. The actual process was turning out to take far longer and therefore to be far more costly than had been anticipated. Second, the soils were of poor quality and not suitable for the traditional crops of the Nile Valley proper. This meant that the new lands would never absorb very many peasant proprietors because of low yields and the nature of the crops.

A body of opinion developed urging that the new lands be kept under state ownership and run on a modern mechanized basis. Crops would be fed into new agro-industries or exported. Because the initial stages proved to be so capital-intensive (7-10 years to reach marginal levels of productivity at LE500-600 per feddan), it was felt that the state would only recover its investment by relying in the production phase on capital-intensive techniques— mechanization, aerial spraying, sprinkler irrigation, etc.—and relying upon exportable crops (citrus, grapes, melons, potatoes) or import-substitution crops (sugar beets, soy beans, etc.). Significantly it was the former editor of *al-Ahram*, Mohammad Hassanein Heikal, who gave considerable publicity to these views in his article in *al-Ahram* of January 8, 1965. Heikal was no radical socialist but he was close to Nasser.

The debate was continued right up to the present time, ignoring ideological lines, and complicated by the fact that now, in 1976, it is recognized that the existing reclamation sites have so far proven to be a net economic loss to the economy. This record notwithstanding, population pressure dictates that Egypt move ahead with new schemes. No single formula has been devised to cope with the situation. The bulk of existing reclaimed areas still remains under public ownership, and what distribution has taken place has been to graduates of agricultural technical institutes and not to peasants. At the same time various projects have been discussed for turning the reclamation sites over to independent, public companies which would run them on a commercial basis. Finally, since the issuance of the foreign investment code (Law 43) of 1974, there has been much talk of joint ventures between these companies and foreign agro-investors. Arizona Land and Cattle Company for instance is contemplating an integrated cattle-raising scheme on reclaimed land near Ismailia, where the Austrians, French, and others look into the possibilities for raising tomatoes and sugar beets and refining sugar in the northwest and the canal zone.

The ideological parameters of the debate have been confused throughout. Abu Seif Yussef, member of parliament and one of the old guard of the Egyptian Marxists, was active in the parliamentary debates over Law 43. He was particularly disturbed at the possibility of permitting foreign capital to become involved in the new lands. Citing the 1962 Charter, he emphasized the need to broaden the base of ownership by distributing new lands to the landless. "The formation of companies," he said, "operating on thousands of feddans will violate the rights of poor peasants to the land of their country." Prime Minister Abdel Aziz Higazi, considered by most to be on the right in economic matters, rose to the defense of the provisions of Law 43. He asked Abu Seif Yussef if he would advocate breaking up the orchards of South Tahrir in holdings of three or five feddans. "Is it not more reasonable to keep this land within the framework of public ownership through companies?...in order to promote two goals—industrialization and export."[3]

Some of the inconsistencies in this seeming reversal of ideological positions can be accounted for if one simple but essential fact is kept in mind. Any joint venture set up under the terms of Law 43 is considered to be fully within the private sector even if the Egyptian partner is a public body. As we shall see below, the fuzzing of the line between public and private sectors carries over into other domains.

B. Commerce, Banking, and Industry

The Revolutionary Command Council (RCC) that came to power in 1952 was no more radical in its approach to nonagricultural activities than it was toward land tenure. At least until 1956 the primary concern of the RCC was to consolidate its own position vis-à-vis other internal rivals and to shore up the country's external military defenses. While of secondary concern, questions of economic growth strategies were out in the open from the inception of the new regime. Whereas the political elites and political parties of the *ancien régime* were rejected, the economic and financial counsel of the Egyptian private sector was sought out and accepted. Two chains of thought manifested themselves early on. One recognized the need to promote and encourage the Egyptian private sector, above all in industry and in banking, to play a more dynamic role in investment and industrial expansion. The second assumed that in many instances the private sector would be unable to muster the necessary capital to enter into certain basic spheres (the High Aswan Dam was the prime case under this rubric) or would be discouraged by the long lead time required before there would be any return on their investment. Thus the hoped-for dynamism of the private sector and the capital-mobilizing capabilities of the state were seen as the two legs of economic growth. The forum in which these issues were discussed was the Permanent Council for the Development of National Production (set up in the fall of 1952), heavily larded with civilian figures from private sector industry, banking, and commerce. This council nonetheless propelled Egypt toward public participation in railroad expansion, fertilizers, cement, and the Helwan Iron and Steel complex. The need for state intervention as a supplement to private endeavor was fully recognized.

There was also a recognition that foreign private investment should be welcomed, and in 1952 a fairly liberal foreign investment code was developed (Law 156 for 1953), but without much success—only about LE8 million came in between 1953 and 1961, the bulk tied up in oil exploration. There was no assault upon the private sector in this period. It was hoped that the landowners who had been affected by the 1952 reform, and compensated for their land, would reinvest in industry. Unfortunately, but predictably, they invested in quick-return urban real estate instead. Sooner or later more interventionist thinking would have been forthcoming from the regime, but it came sooner, perhaps, because of the invasion of Egypt by Israel, France, and Britain in November 1956.

As a result of the Suez War all French and British assets in Egypt were seized and placed under state control. The core of the interests taken over consisted in seven major banks (including Barclays and Crédit Foncier) and five insurance companies. A special state holding company, the Economic Organization, was set up in 1957 to manage these and other assets in which the state already had a share. The paid-up capital in these

enterprises in January 1957 amounted to LE17 million but rose to LE58 million by the end of 1958 and two years later to LE80 million distributed among 64 companies employing 80,000 people.[4]

Some have seen this sudden spurt into public ownership as windfall socialism whereby a state sector founded on seizures of enemy property emerged well before any ideological or programmatic framework for it. This is in large measure true, but at the same time it should not be forgotten that even prior to 1956 disparate segments of the new elite had begun to campaign for a more direct public role in production as opposed to infrastructure. Egypt's military leaders, for example, generally accepted that the future health of the economy would have to depend on industrialization, since Egypt could not expect to expand and intensify its agricultural base *ad infinitum* but it could expect the population to continue to grow at a rapid rate. The decision to go ahead with the High Aswan Dam was based on the twin objectives of drawing a maximum return from agriculture and of providing a cheap source of hydroelectric power for industrialization. On both counts, however, the state role was confined to the development of infrastructure, as it was also in the decision to go ahead with electrification of the old Aswan Dam.

As for industrial production, that was initially left pretty much to private initiative. The Kima fertilizer plant set up to benefit from the new energy supply from the electrification of the old Aswan Dam was initially a private company. The Helwan Iron and Steel plant provided for a substantial equity share for the West German Demag firm as well as for private Egyptian investors.

Egypt's first comprehensive legislation governing private sector companies, Law 26 of 1954, emitted mixed signals. In some areas it relaxed provisions of a more "nationalistic" piece of legislation enacted in 1947, but it made authorization of the founding of any new company subject to Presidential decree and hence to governmental review. Moving beyond the strengthening of public regulatory functions, the regime established on July 1, 1956, for the first time, a Ministry of Industry. The first minister was thirty-two-year-old Dr. Aziz Sidqi, a Ph.D. in regional planning from Harvard. If any one personality can be credited with the systematic and *purposeful* development of the public sector it is surely Sidqi. From 1956 through 1971, despite periods of eclipse, he was responsible for Egypt's industrial growth. He accumulated enemies in both the right (as a megalomaniac whose fear of being shown up by the private sector led him to destroy it) and the left (as a man who in the name of socialism built Egypt's state capitalist system). He could afford such enemies because of the special relationship he developed with Nasser.

Sidqi seemed to know from the outset the direction in which he wanted to move—in his view the state must not only found its own industries but there must also be a national plan covering both the private and public sectors. There was no question in his mind that if the goal was industrialization then the public sector must play the leading role in capital formation. (The private sector in the generally unsettled conditions following the collapse of the Korean war boom was investing only about LE3 million in industry and manufacturing each year.) In summer, 1957, Sidqi presented to the Council of Ministers a five-year plan for industrial development which went into effect in 1958. Based on some 150 projects, whose logic and relation to one another were not always apparent, the plan sought to invest about LE50 million a year, 61 per cent to come from public sources. One year into the plan, Nasser announced that it would be telescoped into three years. In fact what transpired was that uncompleted projects from this early plan were carried over into Egypt's first comprehensive five-year plan (1960-1965).

Sidqi was and is proud of the ministry's achievements and in one anecdote revealed a good deal of Nasser's philosophy. He had personally presented Nasser with a report on the ministry's accomplishments in one 12-month period, and the President simply said, "Good; we need more." Sidqi felt a bit hurt and added that by any standards the accomplishments were praiseworthy and that his team was exhausted. Nasser replied, "We will all die soon; the factories will not be torn down. We must leave as much as possible, do all we can. We will not live forever."[5] In subsequent years Sidqi was attacked for what was regarded as an irresponsible proliferation of projects summed up in the phrase "Egypt's industry from the needle to the rocket." There is certainly no doubt that careful pre-planning and cost-benefit analysis were not among

the new ministry's most conspicuous endeavors, but Nasser's instincts fastened on the political implications of developing the public sector, and he was determined to go so far so fast that the process could not be undone once he was gone. If sound economics took something of a beating in the process, *tant pis*. There are some today who would like to undo what Sidqi began nearly 20 years ago, and some undoing will undoubtedly occur, but my strong hunch is that Egypt's socialist or state capitalist sector is here to stay.

Paralleling the industrial plan was the institution in 1957 of the National Planning Committee, replacing the Permanent Council for the Development of National Production. The new committee was entirely public, and the only remaining operational channels for coordination between state and private activities lay in a conglomeration of businesses known as the Misr Group. The notion of a comprehensive national economic plan had not yet been adumbrated, but one can see in retrospect a gathering of forces. The question of whether or not the private sector would respond positively to sectoral priorities determined by the government must have been widely discussed at this time, and in this discussion Aziz Sidqi was one of those most skeptical about the likelihood of private sector cooperation.[6]

The primary private sector contact was Bank Misr, and its extensive array of enterprises in shipping, publishing, hotels, insurance, chemicals, pharmaceuticals, cement, edible oils, and above all textiles. In the latter sphere, the Misr Group accounted for about 60 per cent of Egypt's total spinning and weaving output and employed 53 per cent of all textile workers. In the first industrial plan, the Ministry of Industry expected this group to carry the burden of private sector investment, and to no small extent it did. In sum, the Misr Group had prospered under the military regime. The Misr Bank was the center of a holding operation of 29 companies, and, in turn, nearly half the shares in Bank Misr were owned by 50 persons. Ahmad Abboud Pasha, with an industrial empire of his own, held 14 per cent of the Bank's shares.[7]

The first indication that the public and private sectors might be approaching some sort of confrontation was the move to compel all private companies to contain distribution of earnings to shareholders within an increase of 10 per cent over the previous year's distribution. At the same time 5 per cent of earnings would have to go to the purchase of government bonds. A National Bank (private sector) study showed that throughout the 1950s most private joint-stock companies distributed about two-thirds of their profits to shareholders whereas in the United Kingdom, for instance, it was the practice to reinvest about two-thirds of earnings.[8] Ostensibly the new legislation was designed to encourage a higher rate of investment among private sector companies, but its major effect was to raise havoc in the stock market (it was later said this was contrived by the private sector) and leave the public and private sectors eyeing one another suspiciously.

The next step toward the consolidation of the public sector was the nationalization of the Misr Bank, with its LE100 million in deposits, and the National Bank (Bank Ahli) on February 13, 1960.[9] This gave the state control not only over Egypt's largest commercial bank and another that fulfilled functions of a central bank, but over a considerable range of industries as well.

How far was the state prepared to go in bringing the private sector under its thumb? Perhaps no one really knew for sure, but by the time of the nationalizations of Bank Misr and Bank Ahli, Egypt was already well along the path to applying its first comprehensive plan. Conciliatory remarks toward the private sector were frequently pronounced, even by the President, but Abdel Latif Baghdadi, a free officer and the first Minister of Planning, who has seldom been associated with the ideas of Aziz Sidqi, warned in July 1960 that he had no exaggerated hopes that the private sector would willingly comply with plan directives and that public authorities must be prepared to take strong measures to insure compliance. In May 1961, well into the first five-year plan, Minister of Finance Abdel Moneim al-Qaissuny (then and now the Talleyrand of the Egyptian economy) stated that the government was contemplating no further nationalization measures. "We intend to ensure that capital shall remain free as long as it contributes to the general welfare.... To consolidate the socialist, democratic, and cooperative system, public and private capital combine in the implementation of the investment projects planned for economic development."[10] Two months later the

sweeping nationalizations of Egypt's "socialist revolution" were announced.

These nationalizations were of three sorts. Beginning in June 1961 the Alexandria commodity exchange was closed down and the state Cotton Authority given the exclusive right to purchase cotton. The state took a 50 per cent interest in all cotton import-export firms. Eventually all private sector firms engaged in foreign trade came under state control.

A second series of decrees had social equity as their objective. In addition to the requirement that all companies utilize 5 per cent of their annual earnings to purchase government bonds, new legislation stipulated that 25 per cent of all profits must be paid to the workers in the following mix: 10 per cent cash, 5 per cent toward housing, and 10 per cent toward social security. It may be useful to note here that in succeeding years the 15 per cent of profits not directly distributed to workers has simply gone to shore up the central budget and there has been little noticeable return to the workers themselves. Moreover no worker can receive more than LE50 ($100) in distributed profits in any one year. This set of decrees also applied upper limits to public sector or mixed enterprise salaries, i.e., LE5,000 per year. Confiscatory taxation on gross incomes over LE10,000 was introduced, and members of corporate boards of directors were limited to holding but one position in that capacity.

The third arena of the July decrees consisted in the takeover of remaining banks, insurance, and shipping companies (including Abboud Pasha's Khedivial Mail Line). Some 50 enterprises of this nature and in industry and manufacturing were nationalized. The state expropriated half the capital of another 86 companies mainly in commerce and light manufacturing. Finally, the major shareholders in another 147 firms were dispossessed of the bulk of their assets by Law 119 of July 1961 which limited individual shareholdings in any and all enterprises to a market value of LE10,000. Any shares held in excess of that amount passed into public ownership. The nominal capital of all the companies affected by all this legislation was estimated at LE258 million, or about two-thirds of the total share capital then registered in Egypt.[11]

There is no authoritative explanation of what prompted the regime to take these draconian measures. One year into the first five-year plan it was said that the private sector had failed to respond to the state's hopes for investment. After regulations on dividends distribution and the nationalization of Misr and Ahali banks, it is hardly surprising that the private sector was less than enthusiastic. It is hard to dispel the suspicion that this accusation of the private sector was more a pretext than an actual cause of the socialist decrees. Two major considerations were probably closer to the real motive. First, through the nationalizations the state gained control not only of a substantial portfolio of assets but of their earning and reinvestment potential as well. When coupled with the 1961 land reform act lowering the ceiling on ownership from 200 to 100 feddans, it can be seen that the regime gained direct control over the principal *domestic* sources of development financing. Second, Egypt had entered into its second year of union with Syria, and the weight of Egypt within the Arab region had grown considerably. To maintain and increase this regional leverage it became important to subordinate the major means of production in Egypt to state control and state policy objectives.

The socialist offensive of July 1961 to some extent undermined its regional objectives. The still vigorous capitalist and agrarian interests in Syria were profoundly alarmed at the shift in Egyptian policy (as was Saudi Arabia), and in late September a military *coup d'état* resulted in Syria's exit from the United Arab Republic. This in turn spurred another assault upon the Egyptian private sector, this time not in the form of nationalizations but of sequestrations. First 167, then another 500 or so families had their assets and properties expropriated for purely political reasons, to wit that they were suspected of collaborating with "reactionary" Syrian and Saudi Arabian elements to try to overthrow the Nasserist regime. Abboud Pasha and the other great families of the Egyptian upper bourgeoisie all fell victims to the purge. At the same time, and as a result of the Congolese independence crisis, all Belgian assets in Egypt were nationalized, including Cairo's tramways and the Heliopolis Company.

In the following years more politically motivated sequestrations occurred. The state also began to move into wholesale and retail trade by opening "cooperatives" to sell basic foods at fixed prices, so that by 1965, the public sector had reached its maximum outer limits, beyond which it was not to grow substantially. Through direct means, land reclamation and allocation, and indirect means, cooperative supply and marketing systems, the state had a strong hold on the bulk of the peasantry. Heavy and medium industry, banking, insurance, import-export trade, maritime transport, airlines, and some wholesale and retail trade were all totally or predominantly under state control. An attempt was also made to nationalize the trucking industry, but it was a failure.

Politically motivated sequestrations consummated the destruction of the material base of the old bourgeoisie, a process begun with the land reform of 1952. The regime no longer had any serious civilian rivals. Concomitantly, it thought that it had effectively harnessed the economy so that the objectives of the first five-year plan could be attained. Those objectives boiled down to establishing a 9 per cent annual growth rate in GNP, building the High Aswan Dam, reclaiming 1.3 million feddans of desert, building up Egypt's base in heavy and medium industries, and, by the end of the plan, covering most of the country's foreign exchange needs through exports.

The Public and Private Sectors in the Contemporary Period

It would be beyond the scope of this Report to go into all the reasons why many of these objectives were only partially attained. Some of the causes lie in the fact that several industrial projects did not come on stream as quickly as expected, some nationalized enterprises were mismanaged, export markets did not open up, and the suspension of U.S. wheat shipments plus the costly Egyptian involvement in the Yemeni civil war drained away the country's foreign exchange reserves. At the same time real wages in the public sector were allowed to rise more quickly than production, and this, combined with massive investment projects, caused a sharp inflationary spiral during the plan period. Real growth in GNP over the five years may have been 6 per cent per annum, but a considerable part of that growth is accounted for by the expansion in the public bureaucracy and service sector.

By 1965 it was clear that Egypt would face severe difficulties in financing a second five-year plan. There were no more domestic assets that the regime was prepared to take over. Further land reform measures were rejected (until 1969 when the ceiling was lowered to 50 feddans) as politically dangerous and probably counterproductive in terms of agricultural yields. In the nonagricultural sector only small manufacturing enterprises, wholesale and retail trade, small hotels, restaurants, taxis, etc., remained outside state ownership. Their aggregate worth was far from negligible, but it was judged bureaucratically impossible for the state to manage them efficiently if they were divided into a myriad of mini-operations. Following the line of least popular dissatisfaction, the regime refrained from increasing the tax bite on the middle and lower middle classes. Nor was there any attempt to tie wages to production in the public sector. Only the peasantry was, to some extent, sweated for investable surpluses through state-fixed sale prices of agricultural inputs and purchase prices of major crops.

It was also the case that Egypt could not expect much financial support from the West, especially the United States, because of a general hostility to Nasser's regional adventures, his domestic socialism, and his close relations with the U.S.S.R. The Soviet Union, for its part, had shown itself ready, ever since Aziz Sidqi negotiated the first industrial aid package in 1958, to contribute heavily to Egypt's development. The drawbacks were that Egypt regarded (and still regards) Soviet technology as being inferior and that reliance upon it would forever preclude the possibility of exporting manufactured goods to the West. Yet that was precisely what was called for because Western technology would have to be paid for in foreign exchange as would Egypt's growing annual food grain imports which could only come from Western sources.

In short, the period 1965-66 was a watershed in the evolution of Egypt's development strategy and the expansion of the public sector. The dilemma faced by the country's planners in unearthing new financing sources was not and has not been resolved. The June War of 1967 rendered all thought of long or medium term development strategies relatively meaningless. Nasser found himself at a crossroad in 1965 but did not commit himself in any direction. Sadat found himself at the same crossroad after Nasser's death in 1970, but with the "victory" of October 1973 under his belt, opted for an opening to the West, the wooing of foreign and Arab capital, and the resuscitation of the Egyptian private sector.

A. The Private Sector

There are numerous Egyptians, not all of them on the left, who feel the private sector hardly warrants such solicitousness. In their view a not-altogether-new parasitic middle class has emerged that would die if it were not able to live off state business, to manipulate state pricing systems, or exploit the laxity with which the state manages its economic affairs. It is estimated, for instance, that some 40 per cent of total investments under the first five-year plan were contracted out to private firms. Building and labor contractors have thrived on public business and if minimum wage or building standards are violated in the process, contract kickbacks have assured that violations would not be publicized. With the great increase in state activities in import-export, a host of middlemen arose to help fulfill state needs, for fat commissions. The public sector not only tolerated such figures but fostered them so that public sector officials could also get a piece of the commissions. One former army officer, who worked during the 1960s for a state export company, later went private, acting as middleman between Egypt and the U.S.S.R. in citrus exports and allegedly took a LE100,000 commission on a single deal. Variations on this theme are numberless, and symbiotic relations between public officials on fixed salaries and private entrepreneurs with no legal and profitable investment outlets have proliferated.

Nowhere is this more striking than in the manipulation of the state pricing system. The state has tried to hold down the cost of living and the cost of production by subsidizing basic foods as well as agricultural inputs and building materials. Indicative price controls are maintained on a second list of commodities (for example, meat, fish, and vegetables). Very seldom are any of these commodities in sufficient supply to meet demand, and the tendency has been for those public officials engaged in their distribution to siphon off a portion of them to black market entrepreneurs. As the volume of these commodities has risen, so have profits. They in turn may be smuggled abroad to buy hard currency with which to import, legally or illegally, luxury consumer goods which are sold at enormous markups to the local bourgeoisie. Or, again, profits may be used to acquire urban real estate and, with black market building materials, to construct luxury housing for foreign diplomats, wealthy Arabs, or middle class Egyptians desperate for housing.

There is no question that a growing number of private sector entrepreneurs are making spectacular profits off purely or mainly speculative ventures. So have their public sector accomplices. There has been much public outcry of late about Egypt's "500," or sometimes "5,000," millionaires thriving in a system where taxation is confiscatory on incomes above LE10,000. Members of the establishment have demanded proof of these accusations, a singularly hard request to fulfill inasmuch as several of the prime suspects are very highly placed.

The rapaciousness and profit hunger of the new class have probably been somewhat overdrawn but not much. Mahmoud Maraghi of *Ruz al-Yussef* has been dogged in his generally well-founded exposés of private sector abuse. He notes that all Cairo's wholesale trade in fresh produce is in the hands of about 700 merchants, some of whom make LE1,500 a day in profits. Total earnings for the entire country in this sector amounted to LE 186 million in 1974, the bulk of which, Maraghi estimates, went into the pockets of a few thousand merchants. The same picture repeats itself in fresh fish, paper, scrap metal, manually operated calculators, locally manufactured pipes and cables, gas meters, and so forth. In the contracting sector where there is also a strong concentration of relatively large private enterprises, earnings in 1974 amounted to LE109 million, and in housing to LE119 million.[12] The profits to be made in these sectors pale beside those accruing from the booming import trade in luxury consumer goods, especially automobiles.

In the early 1960s it was said that Egypt's socialism was founded on the alliance of working forces, and this is still the official, if not operative, slogan of the present regime. The alliance consists of peasants, workers, intellectuals, soldiers, and national capitalists. With respect to the latter a distinction was made between exploitative capitalists, presumably eliminated between 1961 and

1964 and excluded from the alliance, and non-exploitative capitalists who worked within the frame of the plan and sought only a reasonable return on their efforts. Maraghi and many others across Egypt's political spectrum have called attention to the re-emergence of exploitative capital, but aggregate figures do not give any real measure of the phenomenon, and tax evasion and black market operations make it exceedingly difficult to measure the distribution of real earnings in the private sector. This sector is characterized by the great number of small establishments, few of which make large profits. After the most recent available census of industrial and commercial establishments in Egypt four years ago, it was found that of the total of 678,000 establishments, 92 per cent were in the private sector. Total employment in both sectors was 2.01 millions, and knowing the much larger scale of public enterprises, it can be safely assumed that the bulk of the private establishments were one- or two-person operations.[13]

In other words it would not be surprising, if figures were available, to find that profit levels for private sector "firms" taken in the aggregate, were and are quite low because of the presence of what must be a majority of marginal operations. For instance, one source estimates that in 1973 the private industrial sector made profits of about LE40 million or about 9 per cent of total fixed private investment in that sector. Yet these profits were distributed among some 155,000 "manufacturing" establishments, and in textiles, shoes, food processing, paper, etc., it is known that there are a few relatively big enterprises that account for a high proportion of sectoral profits.[14]

Thus alongside the contractors, the black marketeers, the overnight millionaires in the import business, the real estate speculators, and the fresh produce wholesalers, there are other private sector "moguls" in manufacturing, commerce, and services whose high profit margins stand out in a sea of subsistence operations.

So too in agriculture, where there are still some 39,000 proprietors (*kulaks*) owning more than 20 feddans apiece. Handsome returns can be earned on holdings between 20 and 50 feddans, but many owners have contrived to consolidate farmlands well in excess of the 50 feddan ceiling. There is a growing class of commercial farmers on the larger holdings, using modern farm techniques and generally achieving above average yields. Like most farmers, these owners may be obliged to deliver to the state a per-feddan quota of basic crops such as rice, cotton, and wheat, and at the generally low purchase price set by the government. But the quotas themselves are determined by *average* yields, and the commercial farmers generally have substantial surpluses they can dispose of on the free market. Depending on the crop rotation followed, they may bring to the free market vegetables, fruits, clover, beans, etc., items whose value is determined by market forces. Owners of mango and citrus orchards stand to make the highest profits of all.

Not all the 39,000 *kulaks* are rich, but because of the polarization in income between themselves and the 90 per cent who own less than two feddans, their local economic and political weight is substantial. At the same time they have their spokesmen and representatives in the national parliament, the Cooperative Union, and the government itself. As a pressure group they will in all likelihood stand as an obstacle to any further state encroachment into the agricultural sector and will advocate the reintroduction of market forces into the production and marketing process. Significant for their very mentioning are suggestions that the ceiling on land ownership be raised, but it is improbable that any such steps will be taken. The direction in which the state is moving in the reclaimed areas seems also to reflect the interests of the commercial farmers—the formula being discussed now is for the state to pay for and develop the land and then sell or auction it off to private Egyptians.

We may get a handle on the relative weight of the Egyptian private sector in the national economy by some statistical comparisons. First, the partial reproduction of one of Patrick O'Brien's tables on p. 14 shows the heavy preponderance of the private share in GDP at the beginning of the revolution.

After 20 years of revolutionary transformation one finds a major shift in the balance between public and private activities. The figures presented in Table 3 pertain to the distribution of national income and are not therefore strictly comparable to the figures in Table 2, although comparison does indicate the order of magnitude in the shift to a direct public sector role in the economy.

The private sector continued up to 1973 to generate more than half of national income, but the two sectors are very nearly in balance. Agriculture, commerce, and housing are the spheres in which the private sector is markedly dominant, while it has been frozen out of heavy industry, finance, and public utilities. Since 1974, as we shall see below, it has become possible for the private sector, in combination with foreign capital, to re-enter these areas.

While generating around 50 per cent of national income, the private sector furnishes less than 10 per cent of the annual investment load. The figures in Table 4 are for 1973, and although the level of investments has doubled in the last two years, the private share has remained around 10 per cent. Note that about a third of national income (over one billion pounds in 1973) is generated by the agricultural sector, all nominally in private hands, while private investment in that sector is only LE2 million. The private sector's major outlays still come in the housing sector, and since the institution of the open door policy in 1974 with the attendant influx of foreign businessmen the level of private investment in urban housing has exceeded LE60 million.

The two statistical snapshots displayed as Tables 5 and 6 give us some indication of recent trends in the private industrial sector. In 1974 private investment in the industrial sector rose to some LE37 million out of total private sector investment of LE98 million, and the value of private sector industrial production was put at LE475 million or about one-sixth of total industrial output. Spinning, weaving (the private sector produced 220 million meters of cloth and the public sector 530 million meters in 1974), and ready-made clothes accounted for 31 per cent in value of private sector production; engineering industries 31 per cent; food, beverages, and tobacco, 26 per cent; chemical products, 9 per cent; and building materials, 3 per cent With LE54 million in industrial exports in 1974, mainly to the Soviet Union and Eastern Europe, the private sector accounted for 24 per cent of Egypt's total industrial exports.

Almost two-thirds of the entire work force of over nine million persons is engaged in the private sector, but this includes around five million peasants. The bulk of the nearly one million

Table 2

Output from Public and Private Sectors 1953*
(LE Million)

	Public	Private	Total
Agriculture		272.8	272.8
Industry, Electricity	1.4	74.3	75.7
Transport & Communications	16.6	55.0	71.6
Financial Services		20.8	20.8
Trade		129.4	129.4
Housing		57.7	57.7
Construction		20.3	20.3
Public Administration	110.0		110.0
Other Services		106.3	106.3
Gross Domestic Product	128.0	736.6	864.6

*Patrick O'Brien, *The Revolution in Egypt's Economic System*, RIIA, OUP, 1966, p. 154.

Table 3

Distribution of National Income 1972-73*
LE Million at Current Factor Cost

	1972			1973		
	Public	Private	Total	Public	Private	Total
Agriculture	19.7	913.5	933.1	22.3	1040.1	1062.4
Strategic Ind.	31.5	1.3	32.8	33.0	1.3	34.3
Transformation Ind.	372.9	183.6	556.5	381.7	219.0	600.7
Construction	110.7	10.5	121.2	98.1	9.4	107.5
Electricity	45.8		45.8	44.8		44.8
Transport, Communication, Storage	128.2	26.3	154.5	132.2	26.4	158.6
Commerce	95.6	143.4	239.0	105.0	157.3	262.3
Finance	41.0		41.0	49.1		49.1
Housing	14.1	107.5	121.6	14.6	109.4	124.0
Utilities	13.4		13.4	13.8		13.8
Services	485.0	222.1	697.6	515.2	244.2	759.4
Nat'l. Inc.	1348.3	1608.2	2956.5	1409.8	1807.1	3216.9

*Economic Bulletin of the Central Bank, Vol. 15, No. 2 (1975), p. 147.

Table 4

Private and Public Investment 1973*
LE Millions

	Public	Private	Total
Agriculture	33.7	1.5	35.2
Irrigation, Drainage	21.8	.6	22.4
Strategic Industry	27.5		27.5
Transformation			
Industry	120.8	6.0	126.8
Construction	5.0		5.0
Electricity	30.3		30.3
Trans. Communic.,			
Storage	116.2	6.8	125.0
Commerce, Finance	1.7	1.0	2.7
Housing	19.7	20.7	40.4
Public Utilities	22.8		22.8
Services	27.7	1.5	29.2
Land	2.8	.5	3.3
Total	424.3	37.6	461.9

*Economic Bulletin of the Central Bank, Vol. 15, No. 2 (1975), p. 141. There is a major discrepancy between the entry for transformation industry investments in this table and the much higher figure for the private sector presented in Table 5: as if Table 4 gave an expected rather than actual figure.

Table 5

Private Industrial Investment by Sectors*
1970-1973 LE '000

	1970/71	1971/72	1972/73
Spinning & Weaving	2,109	2,299	1,271
Engineering	1,608	2,146	9,895
Metals	96	589	935
Chemicals	2,457	434	1,259
Foodstuffs	440	541	836
Electrical	252	221	744
Small Industry	922	683	1,616
Mining		26	129
Total	7,884	6,940	16,685**

* General Organization for Industrialization figures published in Federation of Industries Yearbook for 1974, p. 46.
**See note to Table 4.

Table 6

Private Sector and Total Industrial Exports
1970-1974*
(LE '000)

Year	Private Sector Exports			Total Ind. Exports			Private
	Free	Agree-ment	Total	Free	Agree-ment	Total	Sec. Share-%
1970/71	1493	14,702	16,195	36,768	78,038	114,806	14.1
1971/72	1934	15,693	17,627	41,167	83,617	124,784	14.1
1973	2585	27,617	30,202	46,882	101,393	148,275	20.4
1974	4866	49,445	54,311	64,817	161,313	226,140	24.0

*Dr. Mahmud Ali Salih, "Present Role of the Private Industrial Sector in Egypt's National Plan," Conference on Planning in Mixed Economies, Institute of National Planning and the Ford Foundation, Cairo, May 10-14, 1975. "Free" refers to hard currency transactions while "agreement" refers to trade within frame agreements which are the basic vehicles for trade with Eastern Europe and the U.S.S.R. In 1966-67 total private sector exports were only LE1.9 million.

members of the work force in trade and finance are also of the private sector. About half the entire industrial work force—450,000 of 900,000—is privately employed, but the average yearly industrial wage paid in the private sector was, in 1975, LE107 as opposed to LE397 in the public sector.[15]

At the high tide of Egypt's socialist-cum-state capitalist revolution in the early 1960s, the private sector, anchored in peasant agriculture, managed to avoid being swamped, and those branches that did business with the state prospered and expanded. Other than the land reform act of 1969 lowering the ceiling to 50 feddans, no further measures of "socialist intensification" of any significance have been taken. As Egypt faced growing debt-servicing obligations to the U.S.S.R. after the June War of 1967, the private sector was called upon to help out by increasing exports of leather goods, clothes, perfumes, handicrafts, furniture, etc., to the Soviet Union. This was the first step to its resurgence, and one that was followed by more positive incentives once Anwar Sadat had come to power.

The public sector is still the leading force in the economy. That it must remain so was a cardinal principle of the 1962 Charter. Today, however, references to the leading role of the public sector are simply a statement of fact and, with the exception of defensive leftists, not a source of ideological pride.

B. The Public Sector

The Egyptian public sector is centered on industry. It was recognized as early as 1954 that the country's economic future would hinge on industrialization, and that fundamental truth is no less relevant today. One of Egypt's leading planners, 'Issam Muntasser, has argued that the country's chronic foreign exchange deficits can only be met in the future by increasing industrial exports 30 times over by the year 2000 (i.e., from LE226 million in 1974 to LE6 billion in 2000).[16]   Even if this spectacular increase is within the realm of the possible, Muntasser may believe, although he does not say, that the necessary dynamism will come from the private sector or foreign investors. But one can be reasonably confident that this is not his expectation nor that of any other public officials. If this challenge is to be met it must be met essentially by the public sector, and its past track record does not augur well for the future.

A proper assessment of public sector performance over the last 20 years is well-nigh impossible because of incomplete or inaccurate data and because secondary sources generally have an axe to grind in their presentation of the "facts." Critics of the public sector may be indulging in indirect attacks on Nasser's political style by lashing out at mismanagement (Nasser appointed the managers) in the public sector. Or they may be attempting to discredit socialism and socialist planning by "showing" the mess it has put Egypt in. Again, some critics may be loyal to the public sector in principle but yet wish to destroy some figure within it. Aziz Sidqi was not a man who lent himself to consensus on either a personal or policy level, and both his policies and allies have been embroiled in constant dispute. There are, as well, critics on the left who denounced the whole experiment as inefficient state capitalism, bureaucratic *dirigisme*, and a betrayal of real popular ownership of the means of production. Finally, there is a large body of ambivalent opinion, perhaps reflecting the majority of the elite, whose members built their careers in and around the public sector, but many of whom aspire to more opulent life styles. They accept the charges leveled at the public sector of gross inefficiency, but advocate joint ventures with foreign capital as a way to save it.

It is beyond the scope of this Report, as well as the author's knowledge, to offer any kind of balance sheet of public sector performance. What can be said is that it contains within it no shining examples of successful public management. In brief, its shortcomings are well known, while its successes can only be registered in the future.

For some time the accounts of public sector companies were not made public nor even supplied to appropriate committees in the parliament. All such information was regarded as sensitive and related to military preparedness, security, etc., and hence kept under wraps. After the advent of Sadat to the presidency, and with the backing of Abdelaziz Hegazi, then Minister of Finance, information on certain companies was supplied to the parliament in 1972. The Dean of Cairo University's Faculty of Economics, Dr. Ahmad Abu Ismail, was also at that time chairman of the parliamentary

Budget and Plan Committee, which investigated the performance of some 20 public sector companies, all of which were running at a loss. The two careful reports issued by Abu Ismail's committee read like a litany of the ills afflicting the public sector. One of their findings was that total fixed investment in the public sector in 1973 amounted to LE4.245 billion, and the annual profit rate on this sum was about 2.4 per cent.[17] A year later the treasury had to cover LE92 million in losses incurred by public sector companies.[18] Abu Ismail, who became Minister of Finance in April 1975, represents the cost-accounters who feel public sector enterprises must be judged on strict benefit-cost criteria. Whatever his successors in parliament may think, their task should be made easier by the fact that the Central Accounting and Auditing Agency was, in 1975, put under the direct authority of parliament.

Those who defend the public sector maintain that benefit-cost criteria do not measure its real and varied contributions to national welfare. Perhaps the public sector does not give a good return on capital invested, but would the private sector ever have been able to amass and invest over LE4 billion? Gamal Uteifi, former deputy speaker of the parliament and a studied centrist, put the case for the public sector in these terms. It is responsible for generating 55 per cent of national income and in 1973 turned over budget surpluses of LE84 million to the treasury. It pays out annually to its work force over LE250 million and pays the salaries of university graduates for whom the state has undertaken the obligation of being the employer of last resort. In a single year the public sector opened up 160,000 new jobs. In addition the public sector pays the treasury the lion's share of taxes and duties as well as social security payments, amounting, in 1973, to LE231 million in taxes and LE75 million in social security payments. Moreover, public sector companies maintain salary payments of workers who have been drafted into the armed forces. For these reasons it is unfair to judge public sector companies on a profit and loss basis.[19]

Unfair or not, the cost accounters are gradually gaining ground, and we shall look more closely at their specific charges. The major ills plaguing the public sector are labor redundancy, slipshod and inconsistent accounting techniques, idle capacities, faulty sectoral organization and management techniques.

In 1974 the employment and wage structure in the public sector, as shown in Table 7, was indicative of some of the public sector's problems. The figures represent a 10 per cent increase in employment and a 20 per cent increase in wages over 1973 when the growth in the value of public sector production in real terms did not exceed 5 per cent. These sorts of ratios have been typical of the public sector since its inception. They could be defended if they had led to a real distribution of income and contributed to increasing production, but inflation has nullified the redistributional effects of the wage increases and redundancy the contributions to production. While it is a matter of some controversy, the Ministry of Human Resources estimates redundancy at 20 to 25 per cent of the total government and public sector work force.[20]

Table 7

Public Sector Employment and Wages By Type of Activity: 1974*

Sector	No. Employed	Net Wages
Agric. & Irrig.	18,041	8,673,000
Industry, Petroleum Mineral Wealth	619,452	222,235,600
Electricity	2,413	1,540,000
Transport, Communications	64,523	1,540,000
Supply, Internal Trade	76,581	26,558,000
Finance, Security, For. Trade	54,117	29,959,660
Housing, Construction	41,973	35,026,000
Health Services	19,780	7,940,000
Culture, Information	1,282	703,000
Tourism	7,693	3,198,000
Insurance	7,290	3,946,000
Total	913,145	LE366,680,460

*Figures presented by First Deputy Prime Minister, Abdel-Aziz Hegazi, published in *The Egyptian Gazette*, August 30, 1974. Figures do not include the civil service.

Table 8

Sectoral Distribution of Public Sector Work Force
By Level of Qualification: 1972*

Sector/Level	Superior	University	Above Middle	Middle	Below Middle	No Qualifications
Agriculture	24	2,224	2,231	10,220	901	13,857
Industry	1,332	23,771	8,015	103,792	27,920	407,770
Services	939	20,473	3,922	52,626	10,060	178,196
Total	2,295	46,468	14,168	166,638	38,881	599,823
% of Grand Total	.3	5.4	1.6	19	4.5	69

*Dr. Abdel Fattah Mongi, *Study to Delimit and Estimate Public Sector Manpower Needs*, Institute of National Planning, April 1975.

Table 9

Fixed Capital, Production, Workers, and
Idle Capacity in the Public Industrial Sector*

	Fixed Capital thru 1972 LE Mill.	Value of Production 1973 LE Mill.	No. of Workers 1972	Value of Lost Prod. 1973 LE Mill.
Spinning & Weaving	540	406	267,701	14.2
Food	351	426	76,345	82.2
Chemical	393	111	56,358	29.2
Engineering	263	110	142,853	35.2
Building Materials	116	57	25,147	2.2
Metalurgy	387	103	27,826	26.0
Total	2,050	1,213	396,230	189.0

*This table has been compiled from several sources. Fixed capital figures were provided by Mohammed Abd al-Fattah Ibrahim, Under-Secretary of State for Industry in *The Egyptian Gazette*, July 18, 1973. Column 2 contains official Ministry of Industry figures published in *al-Ahram*, July 18, 1973. The number of workers was provided in Dr. Mongi's study (see Table 8) and idle capacity in Ministry of Industry "Unutilized Productive Capacities," unpublished 1974. The same source estimates idle capacity in the private sector at LE 43 million. A general note: official sources only sporadically provide breakdowns by public and private sectors, hence the absence of data any more recent than 1972-73.

Figures based on a 1972 survey of the public sector labor give us some insights on public employment problems. It was found that 20 per cent of the work force was illiterate, and that 51 per cent had mastered only the rudiments of reading and writing. The rest were functionally literate and included 46,000 university graduates and 177 doctorates. As far as skill levels are concerned, the overall picture can be seen in Table 8. The study from which this table was drawn called attention to the generally low educational and skill qualifications of the public sector work force, the general phenomenon of redundancy, and the fact that many of those with high qualifications considered themselves misemployed (agronimists employed in Air Egypt would be an example of such misuse). The study also found that of the public sector's total of 355 companies (160 in the service sector, 170 in industry, and 25 in agriculture) 78 per cent worked a single shift. In industry the rate was 60.5 per cent of all units, while 8 per cent worked two shifts, 23 per cent three shifts, and 8 per cent four shifts. These figures themselves already give us some clues about the problems of idle capacity.

Idle industrial capacity is only partially explained by underutilization of existing plant. The central problem has been, since 1964, lack of foreign exchange with which to import necessary raw materials, spare parts, and new equipment to ensure peak production levels. By 1973 the problem had become particularly acute with the value of lost production set at LE189 million, distributed as shown in Table 9.

The idle capacity problem exacerbates all others in the public sector. At low levels of production excess labor becomes all the more excessive, and per unit production costs rise, often to the point that any possibility of exportation is obviated. Anomalies of striking proportions arise. Top priority industries find their productive capacity curtailed because of foreign exchange shortages, while the state then spends what little it has to import what local industries should in theory be producing. The Kima Fertilizer Company of Aswan, one of the most successful public sector industries, produced 437,000 tons of fertilizers in 1967-68, after which production steadily dropped off to 152,000 tons in 1973. The problem was importing the necessary machinery and spare parts to renovate a system that

had been installed in 1959. The same sorts of problems have afflicted the Helwan Iron and Steel complex, where the value of lost production due to the inability to import spare parts was estimated at LE50 million in 1973.[21] So too the Nasr Motor Company which assembles Fiats in Egypt, 70 per cent of whose components are imported. Similar situations exist throughout the public sector, and Ibrahim Salim Muhammedein, Minister of Industry in 1973, estimated that LE60 million in foreign exchange could lead to an increase in industrial production of LE242 million.[22]

In April 1975 the union of the workers in the Nasser Automotive Company wrote to *al-Ahram* in the name of its 11,000 members. It said that the plant was working at about 70 per cent of capacity and was producing only two to three buses a day along with cars, tractors, and trucks. At the same time the state was utilizing foreign exchange to import buses at over two times the cost of local units because local production was insufficient.[23]

Foreign exchange, of course, is not the only stumbling block. Poor coordination and integration of projects have also taken their toll. A milk processing plant installed in upper Egypt in the noble pursuit of industrial decentralization, found that local milk supplies were insufficient to supply it and that shipments brought from the north curdled on the way. The plant simply had to be moved. Again, at Helwan, the coking plant attached to the steel complex was to provide coking gas for a fertilizer plant. It was discovered that the gas contained impurities that made it unsuitable for the fertilizer plant, which has been forced to limp along well below capacity.

Even when the problem is predominantly that of foreign exchange, individual companies are constrained from dealing with this on their own. Kima fertilizers or the country's sugar refineries might have taken advantage of rising world market prices for their products to cover their foreign exchange needs through exports, but in such basic or strategic items as fertilizers, sugar, or cement, the state has placed a flat ban on exports. Recent legislation has eased this situation with respect to other industries, allowing them within six months to retain and dispose of any foreign exchange earned over and above their export quotas. But the general principle is that any public sector foreign exchange

Table 10
Egypt: Output of Selected Industrial Products
(In Thousands of Metric Tons unless Otherwise Stated)

Split years ended June 30	Previous peak output (and year)	1969/70	1970/71	1971/72	1972	1973	1974
Spinning and weaving							
Cotton yarn	163 (1968/69)	163	169	175	179	182	179
Cotton textiles	104 (1966/67)	110	112	113	115	118	120
Foodstuffs, etc.							
Sugar	495 (1968/69)	531	581	600	610	633	577
Cheese	125 (1968/69)	132	132	134	135	135	135
Preserved fruits and vegetables	14 (1963/64)	18	20	26	25	24	18
Cottonseed oil	152 (1965/66)	139	150	158	145	160	170
Oilseed cakes	733 (1965/66)	565	643	644	607	600	540
Soft drinks (millions of bottles)	751 (1964/65)	565	614	620	660	600	660
Beer (millions of liters)	26 (1965/66)	23	13	29	30	32	29
Cigarettes	18 (1966/67)	17	19	20	23	23	23
Chemicals, etc.							
Sulphuric acid	227 (1967/68)	23	35	28	28	23	30
Paper	124 (1968/69)	119	131	148	149	146	120
Superphosphate	323 (1968/69)	354	447	522	518	419	465
Ammonium nitrate	438 (1967/68)	377	381	345	392	210	320
Tires (thousands)	813 (1968/69)	711	770	924	927	860	814
Engineering products							
Cars (units)	5,406 (1963/64)	2,800	4,241	5,610	6,130	5,590	8,169
Trucks (units)	1,361 (1963/64)	1,117	1,201	1,679	1,709	1,518	1,082
Tractors (units)	984 (1965/66)	1,071	1,078	937	1,247	1,243	1,260
Buses (units)	1,155 (1965/66)	336	407	305	373	413	360
Refrigerators (thousands)	61 (1965/66)	68	54	52	55	39	55
Televisions (thousands)	84 (1966/67)	54	58	70	76	49	68
Metallurgical products							
Reinforcing iron	205 (1968/69)	251	230	230	239	226	232
Steel sections	135 (1968/69)	126	108	84	81	87	81
Steel sheets	45 (1968/69)	43	40	152	179	167	125
Cast iron products	54 (1962/63)	48	48	49	46	53	55
Building materials							
Cement	3,486 (1968/69)	3,760	3,830	3,642	3,868	3,617	3,264
Building bricks	1,137 (1964/65)	782	782	782	810	797	764
Gypsum and plaster	308 (1966/67)	271	294	260	205	320	305
Mining products							
Phosphate	748 (1967/68)	537	539	561	563	540	499
Iron ore	553 (1965/66)	499		472	427		1,033

1. Preliminary estimates.

Source: Ministry of Industry and Mining.

earner must share the wealth with all the non-earners in its sector.

A final example brings together in one depressing package the interaction of idle capacity and surplus employment. One of the 20-odd public sector firms investigated by Abu Ismail's parliamentary committee in 1973 (see note 17) was the Alexandria Shipbuilding Company. This enterprise was begun with Soviet support in 1955, but it was not until 1969 that it built its first ship. In 1973 it was estimated by Soviet standards that if it were operating at full capacity, the company should employ no more than 3,000 full-time (300 days a year) workers. In fact, in that year the company was operating at about 28 per cent of capacity with 5,100 permanent employees and another 2,500 trainees, drafted workers, and foreign experts on its payroll. The wage bill, in the committee's opinion, was about six times what its level of production would justify.

The idle capacities conundrum, by the reckoning of some analysts, goes far deeper than what has so far been mentioned. Their view is that public sector industries were originally set up on the basis of import substitution and that this approach has not fulfilled its objectives. First, to the extent that any substitution has taken place at all, the local produce was overpriced in domestic markets and overprotected. Hence there was no incentive to develop any real export or foreign exchange earning capacity among public sector enterprises. Monopolistic domestically and noncompetitive internationally, public sector units cannot cover their own foreign exchange financing nor supply quality goods at reasonable prices. As long as the regime and society accepts vague, noneconomic criteria to measure the real contribution of the public sector to national growth, that sector's full potential will never be realized.[24]

Many analysts are convinced that a basic cause of poor public sector performance lies in its internal structuring and organization. When the public sector first began to take shape, its productive units were grouped into three General Organizations. The first, as we have seen, was the Economic Organization set up in 1957 around assets seized in the Suez War. It was followed in 1960 by the Misr Organization, grouping the nationalized assets of the Misr Group, and finally came the Nasr Organization managing the firms set up during the first industrial five-year plan. The organizations were intended to be mutually competitive conglomerates or holding companies with a wide range of activities—from insurance and banking to manufacturing—under their supervision. The socialist decrees of 1961 abolished this troika and in its place regrouped all state enterprises in general organizations by sector—i.e., all insurance companies in one organization, all pharmaceuticals in another, all textiles in a third, and so forth. The general organizations were responsible for personnel policy, promotions, budget estimates and final accounts, production goals, marketing, export programs, and financing. The chairmen of the General Organizations were in turn subject to the supervision of the ministers within whose sphere of activities their companies fell. One of the major problems was that the system discouraged initiative and independent decision-making at the company level while leaving the shaping of and responsibility for sectoral policies floating somewhere between relevant ministers and organization chairmen.

Law 64 of 1971 tried to remedy some of these problems in an attempt to restrain the general organizations from interference in the routine operations of the companies and to oblige company heads to take direct responsibility for their performances, a prospect welcomed by some but by no means all. The new law, however, like so many others in Egypt, was never effectively applied, and in 1974, Mustapha Kemal Murad (who later became Chairman of the General Organization for Cotton) referred to the general organizations as "a state within the state."[25] The next piece of legislation dealing with the general organizations was Law 111 of September 1975 which simply abolished them, effective January 1, 1976.

The new legislation has not been greeted with anything like universal enthusiasm, even by some of the most adamant detractors of the old arrangements. Few contest the goals of handing responsibility back to the managers at the production level, more clearly defining responsibilities in production performance, and administering budgets and production programs. The crux of the debate is, however, that under Law 111, the notion of the holding company or conglomerate has been shunted aside leaving each productive unit, regardless of its scale, to sink or swim on its own.

Many insiders would like to see the re-emergence of holding companies with multiple interests competing among themselves. Others have pointed out that the old general organizations performed a number of vital functions that will now, for a time, be lost. Their chairmen were usually the top specialists in their fields, and their careers depended upon the performance of their organizations and their constituent companies. They exercised a vital overview of sectoral needs and frequently could coordinate among the companies they supervised to overcome foreign exchange or raw materials bottlenecks. The top leadership in the general organizations often assumed an entrepreneurial role within an entire sector which will be hard to replace.

Law 111 affects 35 General Organizations comprising over 300 companies and with its promulgation there was a scramble to negotiate special dispensations. The public sector is not made up only of General Organizations but also of General Authorities which, in theory, undertake public services (such as the Cairo General Transport Authority) and direct economic functions (running buses or selling electricity, etc.). General Authorities, even those with subsidiary companies, fall outside the scope of Law 111, and consequently some organizations argued for and obtained the right to be considered General Authorities—such is the case of the General Organization of Petroleum (13 companies), the General Organization for Electricity, the General Organization for Poultry, the General Organization for Meat, and the General Organization for Tourism. Other interests, such as the Suez Canal Authority with seven companies and the Ministry of Finance with seven banks, will not be affected by this law. At the same time in the industrial sphere six General Organizations comprising 117 companies have been abolished while 11 companies in the building materials sector have been transferred from the supervision of the Ministry of Industry to that of the Ministry of Housing and Reconstruction.

The actual abolition will have substantial impact upon a good number of public employees. In industrial General Organizations some 1,100 employees are to be distributed among various companies, the ministry, or the new sectoral high councils (see below). In the Ministry of Supply the corresponding figure is 1,750. The 35 abolished

organizations are to be replaced in a limited sense by 23 Supreme Sectoral Councils, in the following domains:

1. Foodstuffs
2. Spinning, Weaving, Clothing
3. Chemical Industries
4. Mining
5. Metalurgy
6. Petroleum
7. Electricity
8. Financial Institutions
9. Foreign Trade
10. Cotton
11. Insurance
12. Supply and Int. Dist.
13. Domestic Transport
14. Maritime Transport
15. Housing and Utilities
16. Construction/Building Materials
17. Agriculture and Irrigation
18. Co-ops and Agricultural Credit
19. Animal Production
20. Tourism and Air Transportation
21. Pharamaceuticals
22. Paper, Printing, Publication
23. War Production

Each Sectoral Supreme Council will have a full-time president, in several instances the former chairman of the General Organization for the corresponding sector, a small secretarial and research staff, and several part-time members including parliamentarians, company heads within the sector, university professors, and other experts. It was said that consumer interests would be represented on these councils as well but no such representation has yet materialized.

The Supreme Councils are to review company plans, draw up sectoral strategies, make recommendations to the minister(s), and follow up company performance. It is not said how frequently they will meet but the watchword is that they are to interfere in no way with the operations of the companies.

While it is obviously too early to assess the new law a few preliminary observations may be hazarded. It is unlikely that the companies will now have the right to divest themselves of superfluous labor; indeed, in some instances they will be saddled with new hands as the personnel of the abolished organizations are redistributed, and many are skeptical that the companies will be able to refuse university graduates who are alloted each year to public sector companies. Nor is there likely to be much flexibility in setting wage levels which will be determined at the sectoral or industry-wide level.

Equally problematic is the goal of lessening red tape within the public sector and streamlining administrative procedures. Now the minister is directly concerned with the operation of companies under his jurisdiction—and for the Minister of Industry that means 117 companies—without any permant intermediate bodies. Companies are thus left one on one with the minister who inevitably will require more staff to cope with the load. There is some risk then that the bureaucracy of the General Organizations will simply recreate itself at the ministerial level.

C. Selling Off the Public Sector?

We come back to where we began. Is there a concatenation of forces among the cost-accounters, the new millionaires, a resurgent private sector, disillusioned public sector managers, and counsellors of Western economic wisdom (now that the Egyptians have effectively frozen the U.S.S.R. out of future growth plans) to do in the public sector? Probably not, but there does seem to be a sort of "conspiracy" afoot to make the public sector far more responsive to domestic private interests and international business—all in the name of increasing exports, technology transfer, capital transfusions—without, it is said over and over again, any tampering with the socialist formula nor with the rights and gains of the laboring masses accumulated over the last 15 years. Here briefly is some of the evidence for support of this view.

Law 43 of June 1974 regulating Arab and Foreign Investment in Egypt provided, among many other things, a framework for joint ventures between Egyptian public sector enterprises and foreign investors. Any project approved within the terms of Law 43 is considered to be a private sector company no matter what proportion of its capital is held by the public sector. Such projects benefit from various tax and import duty benefits and may repatriate earnings abroad in foreign exchange

commensurate with their capacity to generate foreign exchange. They are not, at the same time, bound by laws on compulsory purchase of state bonds, worker representation on management boards, nor current formulas for profit sharing.

In other words, the establishment of new joint ventures, including joint venture banks, may entail a gradual slippage of public sector activity beyond the range of socialist legislation. If public sector firms put up their share of the equity in a joint venture in the form of land or existing plant, the whole enterprise may, in a *de facto* sense, slide into the private sector (this may happen to Egypt's small tire plant once it links up with Michelin of France).

The drift in this direction was affirmed during the debates on Law 43 (see note 3). Some members of parliament argued that the 1962 Charter stipulates that in several areas of the economy, especially heavy industry, public ownership must be predominant in *each and every* instance. Deputy Speaker Gamal Uteifi countered, "The text of the Charter states that the majority (of heavy industry) must be within the framework of public ownership for the people. This does not preclude a project, in metalurgy for example, in which private capital is invested along with public. *So long as the majority of all projects remain under public ownership, there is no contradiction with the principles of the Charter.*" (Author's emphasis.) Dr. Sherif Lutfi, chairman at that time of the Foreign Investment Authority, went further. He expressed his confidence in the Egyptian private investor and said that in the question of majority ownership in various enterprises the essential guideline is that 51 per cent of the capital be *Egyptian*, whatever the public-private mix.

Another point of unusual sensitivity has centered on joint venture banks. Through the mobilization of capital, banks can play a crucial role in orienting and channeling investment, but there is fear in some quarters that as Egypt's four banks enter into joint ventures with large multinationals like Chase or American Express, the mobilization of domestic and foreign deposits will fall under the thumb of the policy preferences of international capitalism. These joint venture banks, as mentioned, are legally part of the private sector. The state's major line of defense lies in the stipulation that 51 per cent of the banks' shares be owned by Egyptians, whether public or private. But the defenders of the public sector, led by public sector bankers themselves, have advocated that the law should require that the 51 per cent share be retained by Egyptian banks or at least by public sector organizations. Ahmad Taha, a representative of the workers district of Shubra (Cairo) put the matter bluntly: "It would be possible for 2 per cent of private Egyptian shareholders to combine with 49 per cent of the foreign shareholders to dominate the Egyptian economy."

Although in practice none of the joint venture banks so far established has anything less than 51 per cent public ownership, Law 43 does not preclude that possibility, and some foreign bankers believe that it will become reality within a few years. Dr. Qaissuni, President of the Arab International Bank (set up before Law 43 but enjoying many of the law's privileges) has written, "When, one wonders, will we see once again anything so glorious as the great Bank Misr; when shall we see our Egyptian banks begin to work again, and to invite Egyptian shareholders to join in the execution of projects, ahead of any other investors?"[26]

In April 1975, Law 262 was issued establishing the principle of allowing public sector companies to expand their capital by offering new stock issues to private Egyptians. The move had first been adumbrated by Dr. Abu Ismail in parliament in 1973, and it provoked considerable hue and cry about selling off the public sector.[27] When it became law, with Abu Ismail as Minister of Finance, the reaction was no less vociferous. It died down, however, as no companies made any move to exercise their new rights. The Minister of industry indeed talked (although not until February 1976) of 16 public sector industries issuing LE50 million in stock, but so far nothing has been done. There was some apprehension on the part of the government that there would be little response from private investors to the offer to invest in existing public sector enterprises. Perhaps the trial horse will be the newly formed Suez Cement Company.

The company was formally incorporated in April 1976 under Law 43 and capitalized at LE16 million. What is intriguing about it is that all the founding partners are Egyptian public sector companies. There are no foreign or Arab founders, and the foreign exchange necessary for the execution

will come mainly from a $100 million supply credit from the United States. The new company apparently qualifies under Law 43, because its *intention* is to offer 20 per cent of the share capital (i.e., LE3.2 million) to the Egyptian private sector. Half of this amount will be sold at LE4 per share in local currency, the other half will be offered to Egyptians resident abroad against dollars. Thus a company that is to date entirely publicly financed is legally private with all the tax benefits and rights to "repatriate" earnings in hard currency enjoyed by any other projects under Law 43. Ahmad Osman, the Minister of Housing and Reconstruction who signed the final accord on establishing the company, predicted that shareholders would earn no less than 10 per cent per annum on their investment.[28]

The abolition of the General Organizations may portend changes far more profound than the ostensible goal of improving public sector performance. Casting individual companies loose will have several consequences, two of which are pertinent here. Each company is to be judged on its economic performance, and it is likely that those running chronic losses will be subjected to calls for liquidation or sale to anyone interested. Sometimes this would be a fully warranted outcome, but some companies forced to sell basic goods at subsidized prices regardless of rising production costs (the subsidized price of a kilo of sugar has not changed in 20 years) may be hard put to get out of the red under any circumstances. Companies with idle capacities which are prohibited from exporting their products in order to earn foreign exchange (fertilizers, cement, sugar, etc.), will also come under greater pressure. In other words, some observers feel Law 111 is basically a filtering device through which only the commercially strong will pass. The assets of the weak, built up through public investment, will be sold off to the highest bidders.

To survive, the dynamic company head may be eager to arrange joint ventures with foreign investors or capital expansion with the Egyptian private sector, but decision-making authority is not left entirely to them. Law 111 has instituted the principle of the general assembly of shareholders, even for those firms that are fully under public ownership, to oversee company performance. At the same time, the Supreme Sectoral Councils make no provision for worker representatives from public sector industries. Thus the significance of worker participation in worker-management committees in public sector enterprises could be considerably reduced by the general assembly of shareholders on the one hand, and the sectoral councils on the other. Law 262 (on public sector capital expansion) does stipulate that the workers in public sector industries that issue new stock must have first option in purchasing issue. But if within a month this option has not been exercised, all unsold shares will be offered to the public. Even this provision is under attack by some, like Dr. Qaissuni, who contend that in those public sector establishments where there are still private shareholders (for example Helwan Iron and Steel, Kima Fertilizer, Rakta Paper, United Arab Spinning and Weaving, etc.) these latter should have first options on purchasing new issues.

Nothing in Egypt moves swiftly, and the debates over the direction in which the economy is going will be over long before any perceptible movements take place. In the meantime new legislation will have been issued to provide the stuff of more debates about more hypothetical situations. Foreign banks do not yet run Egypt's economy (some have left for lack of business); foreign investors sniff opportunities at a safe distance but the joint venture has not cannibalized the public sector; the private sector has done little more than talk about investing in urban real estate and foreign trade; no public enterprise has sold new share issues to the private sector; and it is questionable at this point whether or not the General Organizations have really been abolished, leave alone whether or not the sectoral supreme councils actually exist. The reality of the situation is that the public sector still dominates the economy and it has yet to be challenged by foreign competition. The private sector, for its part, seems content to talk of the Japanese model of development, while sharpening its teeth for heftier bites of public slush and largesse.

NOTES

1. Mahmoud Amin Anis, "A Study of the National Income of Egypt," l'Egypte Contemporaine, Nos. 261-62 (November-December 1950), p. 791; K.M. Barbour, The Growth, Location, and Structure of Industry in Egypt, Praeger (1972), pp. 60-69; and Samir Radwan, Capital Formation in Egyptian Industry and Agriculture: 1882-1967, St. Antony's Middle East Monographs No. 2, Ithaca Press (London), 1974, pp. 63 and 99.

2. Magdi Hassanein, a second echelon Free Officer, comes, by his own definition, from a "feudalist" family in the Benha area, that spent most of its time in bitter, occasionally bloody, disputes about land and property. His ambition to move Egyptians beyond private property is founded, he claims, not in any doctrinaire socialist theories but in his own upbringing. His views on this score were expressed to me in a private interview, but in general see his, The Desert: Revolution and Potential, The Story of Tahrir Province, General Organization for Books, Cairo (1975) in Arabic.

3. People's Assembly, Proceedings of the Discussions on Law 43 for Foreign and Arab Investments and Free Zones, (June 1974) in Arabic, pp. 478-79.

4. Anouar Abdel-Malek, Egypt: Military Society, Vintage Books, New York, New York (1968), p. 111; and Robert Mabro, The Egyptian Economy: 1952-1972, Clarendon Press: Oxford (1974), pp. 126-27; Patrick O'Brien, The Revolution in Egypt's Economic System, RIIA, Oxford University Press (1966), pp. 90-91.

5. Recounted by Dr. Sidqi to the author in a personal interview.

6. Patrick O'Brien, op. cit., p. 89.

7. Abdel-Malek, op. cit., p. 114.

8. Mabro, op. cit., p. 140; O'Brien, op. cit., p. 113.

9. See al-Tali'a, Vol. 12, No. 2 (1976), pp. 29-31.

10. Dr. Qaissuni, budget report, 1961-62, cited by O'Brien, op. cit., pp. 127-28.

11. See ibid., pp. 130-31 and p. 153; and Abdel-Malek, op. cit., pp. 152-55.

12. See for instance Mahmud Maraghi, Ruz al-Yussef, No. 2380 (January 21, 1974), No. 2423 (November 18, 1974) and No. 2496 (April 12, 1976).

13. *al-Ahram al-Iqtisadi,* No. 413 (November 1, 1973), pp. 14-17.

14. "The Labor Map of Egypt" *al-'Aml,* No. 133, Vol. 12 (June 1974), p. 21; and Mahmud Ali Salih, "Present Role of the Private Industrial Sector in Egypt's National Plan," unpublished paper presented at the Institute of National Planning-Ford Foundation Conference on Planning in Mixed Economies, May 10-14, 1975.

15. Muhammed Nur al-Din, "The Private Sector and the Transition Plan," *Finance and Trade,* Vol. 7, No. 69 (1975), pp. 20-21 (in Arabic).

16. Dr. Essam Muntasser, "Egypt's Long-Term Growth: 1976-2000," paper presented at the Conference on Long-Range Planning in the Arab World, INP-UNIDO-CAEU, Cairo, January 14-20, 1976.

17. People's Assembly, Budget and Plan Committee, *Reports of Public Sector Performance,* Two Parts, (1973).

18. Bulletin of the Egyptian National Bank, Vol. 28, No. 3 (1975).

19. Dr. Gamal Uteifi, *al-Ahram* (March 21, 1974), and *al-Tali'a,* No. 5 (May 1974), p. 87.

20. *al-Ahram* (September 18, 1975).

21. Lutfi Abd al-Azim, "Industry in Egypt; Facing Realities," *al-Ahram al-Iqtisadi,* No. 462 (November 15, 1974), pp. 6-8.

22. *al-Akhbar al-Yom,* (December 1, 1973); see also, "The Story of the Automobile in Egypt," *al-Ahram al-Iqtisadi,* No. 450 (May 15, 1974).

23. *al-Ahram* (April 28, 1975).

24. This view is put forcefully by 'Issam Rifaat, "Idle Capacity, or a New Strategy for Industrialization," *al-Ahram al-Iqtisadi,* No. 439 (December 1, 1973).

25. "How the Public Sector has been Transformed into a State within the State," *al-Akhbar al-Yom* (April 20, 1974).

26. From a report submitted to the National Council on Production by Dr. Abd al-Moneim al-Qaissuni, excerpts published in *al-Ahram al-Iqtisadi,* No. 494 (March 15, 1976). In the same report Qaissuni advocates a range of measures to encourage the private sector, including lighter corporate taxes, modifications in profit sharing, etc.; i.e., many of the laws enacted in 1961 which he fully backed at the time as Minister of the Economy.

27. In 1973 and since, it has frequently been argued that the state should get out of services for which it has little aptitude, such as department stores, theaters, hotels, retail trade, printing, etc.

28. *al-Ahram* (April 20, 1976). The founding companies are Turah Portland Cement Company; Helwan Portland Cement Company; Alexandria Portland Cement Company; National Bank; Bank Misr; Alexandria Bank; Banque du Caire; Nasser Social Bank; Eastern Insurance Company; Egyptian Re-Insurance Company; National Insurance Company; and the Egyptian Foreign Trade Company. Production is expected to begin in 1979 and will reach one million tons of cement per year with a substantial portion for export. No public sector company is at present allowed to export cement because of the domestic scarcity of this and other building materials.

Egypt in 1976

The internal and now regional strife churning within and around Lebanon has dominated press coverage in the Arab World to the exclusion of virtually all else. The situation is violent, gory, gaudy, and full of colorfully despicable characters along with a few heroes, all of whom make good copy. While it is an insurmountable challenge to anyone, including insiders, to understand the drift and portent of these violent machinations, the stakes are undeniably big: the survival of Lebanon as a state, the survival of the Palestinian guerrilla movement, the formation of a Syrian-dominated confederation of itself with Jordan and whatever remains of Lebanon and of the Palestinians. Some have even suggested that what is at stake in Lebanon is a struggle for leadership in the Arab World between President Sadat of Egypt and President Hafiz al-Assad of Syria. Whatever struggles are involved in the Lebanese crisis, leadership of the Arab World is not among them.

There are no leaders in the Arab World who can hope to rise above the ruck and assert themselves in the region as Nasser did. The few candidates for pre-eminence have in recent months made great strides toward destroying their already limited credibility. King Faisal of Saudi Arabia is dead and his successors are not of his stature. Houari Boumedienne of Algeria who had skillfully built a position of predominance in North Africa and an image of seriousness and purposefulness in the encounters between the developed and developing nations, has isolated himself in his confrontation with Morocco over the Spanish Sahara. Hafiz al-Assad of Syria and Saddam Hussein's Iraqi regime have outdone themselves in mutual denigration. This has taken material forms with Syria allegedly depriving downstream Iraq of Euphrates water while Iraq has ceased to pump oil through the pipeline to Tartus in Syria. One suspects that Assad's involvement in Lebanon was initially motivated by his desire to increase his leverage within the Fertile Crescent at the expense of Iraq but not to claim leadership among the Arabs.

Finally there remains President Sadat of Egypt. His fortunes in the Arab World have traced a parabola since he came to power in 1970. Beginning at zero he achieved his apogee in October 1973 with the qualified success of the October War against Israel. He and Assad were military allies, the oil-rich had fallen into line with the application of an embargo on petroleum sales to the United States, and Sadat could take credit for having restored some measure of unity to Arab ranks. The moment was short-lived for that unity was founded on a general perception that Egypt had stimulated the first moves toward a global solution of the Arab-Israeli conflict. But by early 1974 several Arab leaders became increasingly convinced that, rather than a global solution, Egypt was really interested in a separate deal under United States auspices. Discrete suggestions to this effect became outright accusations when, in September 1975, Egypt, after a long round of Kissingerian shuttle diplomacy, concluded a second Sinai disengagement agreement that, for all intents and purposes, included a non-belligerency pledge.

Regional Trees and the Economic Forest

More than any other Arab country Egypt's regional and international policies have been determined by the state of her economy, and for at least the last 15 years it has been in a continuous state of crisis. Of course, as with any state, foreign policy bears directly upon economic performance and vice versa so that it is difficult if not pointless to ascertain cause and effect. What is reasonably certain is that since about 1960 a quiet economic struggle has been going on, parallel to and interacting with the

Egypto-Israeli confrontation. It is the latter, however, that draws most of the attention of the media and of the statesmen involved. In the case of Egypt, however, it may well be the former that is most significant.

The spring of 1976 marked a turning point in Egypt's internal development and foreign relations as dramatic as any that has occurred since the Free Officers overthrew King Faruq in 1952, although events in Lebanon distracted media attention. It did not come out of the blue but after years of half-steps, rejections, and misgivings. To put the matter bluntly Egypt has cast in its economic, diplomatic, and to some extent military lot with the "West," and, more specifically, with the United States. While it is a momentous turning point for Egypt, it has been only minimally debated within the country, probably because it does not constitute such a sharp break with a recent past that still provides most of the legitimating symbols for Sadat's regime. It is also a fairly momentous turning point for the United States, for in many respects the ability of Sadat's regime to survive will now depend directly on American economic and diplomatic support. This United States "responsibility," it seems to me, has scarcely received the critical attention that it deserves.

Cold War Development Packages for Egypt

Egypt freed itself from British domination following the Second World War and eventually became the target of great power rivalries during the cold war. At first Stalinist Russia was not particularly interested in Egypt regarding it, like other Third World states dominated by nationalist elites, as essentially reactionary and solidly embedded in the capitalist camp. The United States, however, as it built its containment policy, rightly saw the matter in a different light. In the early 1950s American policy toward Egypt was premised on two objectives. The first was to bring Egypt formally or informally within the emerging Western system of military alliances and thus to add another crucial link in the chain of pro-Western regimes encircling the U.S.S.R., and, secondly, to bring Egypt around to settling with Israel. The two instruments that the United States could manipulate in seeking to achieve these goals were arms supplies and economic aid. The problem in the 1950s, in contrast with the 1960s, was not, in American eyes, to keep

Egypt from "going socialist" in its economic strategy, for the Nasserist regime, before 1956, evinced few proclivities in that direction. Rather it was to use economic support to coax Egypt into a Western alliance and concomitantly to attend to its own economic affairs at the expense of a regional role (or regional "trouble-making" as Washington generally described it).

In this light one can understand the efforts in 1955 to lure Egypt into the Central Treaty Organization (more commonly known until 1958 as the Baghdad Pact) by holding out the prospect of substantial arms deliveries, coupled with United States, British, and International Bank for Reconstruction and Development (IBRD) commitments to help fund the construction of the High Aswan Dam. Had Egypt bought the package it would have joined a Western military alliance, removed itself from the confrontation with Israel, and, conceivably, developed its economy on the basis of agricultural development founded on the private peasant smallholder.

But Egypt did not buy the package. It wanted arms without alliances, a fair deal for the Palestinians before reaching a settlement with Israel, and a neutral position in the cold war. None of these desiderata were inherent in the Western package. Conventional Western economic wisdom was not rejected, but entangling alliances were. It was thus for purely military reasons, and not out of any shift toward a more radical ideology, that, in September 1955, Egypt entered into an agreement with Czechoslovakia to purchase $200 million worth of (Soviet) arms. With that, all hopes of Egypt buying the Western package collapsed, and, instead, the countdown to the Suez invasion of 1956 was begun.

After 1956 Egypt, both spontaneously and with some (and often overdramatized) Soviet coaxing, began to adopt a "socialist" package. As a result of the Suez War the state found itself owner of a public economic sector consisting in the assets taken over from the French and British who, along with Israel, had initiated hostilities against Egypt. Soon thereafter a public five-year industrialization plan was launched, and agreements were concluded with the U.S.S.R. in 1958 to help in setting up an iron and steel industry and to begin work on the High Aswan Dam. To help cover the costs of this aid, as well as the military equipment contracted for in 1955 and thereafter, required a major reorientation in Egypt's foreign trade toward "socialist" markets. The process of economic transformation reached its peak during the years of the first five-year plan, 1960-1965. The public sector was officially entrusted with the leading role in development plans, the rapid extension of the cooperative system throughout the countryside led to some regimentation of small-holder agriculture, and the rapid expansion in land reclamation projects held out the prospect of the establishment of state farms.

With these developments, Western preoccupations with Egypt were cast in a new light. The question of bringing Egypt into a Western military alliance, not to mention settlement with Israel, were recognized as wildly remote possibilities. More important was eroding the military and economic links between Egypt and the "socialist bloc" and stopping the internal drift toward socialism. With the exception of a few moments of almost friendly United States-Egyptian relations during the Kennedy administration, most efforts in this vein failed. However, two chinks in Egypt's economic armor became apparent during the early 1960s.

Early in the first five year plan, Egypt began to encounter serious balance of payments and foreign exchange difficulties. Simultaneously, the amounts of basic food grains that Egypt had to import to feed its burgeoning population grew steadily. On the first count Egypt had to begin to heed the counsel of the International Monetary Fund (IMF), in this as in many other instances in full harmony with United States policy objectives, and in 1962 the Egyptian pound was devalued by 20 per cent. On the second count, Egypt had to meet its food deficits from Western sources inasmuch as the U.S.S.R. and Eastern Europe did not have an exportable grain surplus. In the event American surplus wheat was provided Egypt against local currency under the PL480 ("Food for Peace") program. Because of a serious falling-out between Egypt and the United States in 1965 over the latter's role in the Congo, these shipments were suspended, further aggravating the country's balance of payments position.

As I have pointed out in several other articles, Egypt reached a watershed in 1965-66. To launch another five-year plan, and thus begin to honor Nasser's promise to double national income in ten years, would have required massive capital goods

and raw materials imports—not to mention food— which would have had to be paid for in foreign exchange or barter with the U.S.S.R. and Eastern Europe. The latter option, if adopted, would have made Egypt almost totally dependent upon the socialist countries, and, as their technology was viewed as inferior to that of the West, Egypt risked being locked into exclusive trade relations with the socialist economies because her exports would be unacceptable in Western markets. Nasser and several of his advisors balked at this option for nationalistic and ideological reasons. At the same time another option, no more to their liking, was being proffered by the West, mainly through the auspices of the IMF. It was a "stabilization" plan that would have entailed a major retrenchment in investment outlays, the setting of a "realistic" exchange rate for the pound in order to promote exports and to attract foreign investment, and some whittling away at internal price subsidies and public sector inefficiency. If Egypt were to accept the plan, the IMF and other Western sources would presumably have stepped in with the foreign exchange support Egypt would require. Although some retrenchment in investment outlays did take place (indeed the second five-year plan was quietly scrapped), Egypt did not accept all the IMF recommendations. The Minister of Finance, Hassan Abbas Zaki, did recommend acceptance, but Nasser personally and instinctively overruled his recommendations. The internal social costs that would have resulted from an economic slowdown combined with rising prices, coupled with the implicit subordination of Egypt to Western economic objectives, appeared too high a price to pay. What alternatives, if any, Nasser saw to these options are not clear, but the necessity to make some sort of choice became all the more acute and all the more difficult after the defeat of Egyptian forces in the June War of 1967.

On the one hand Egypt became more dependent than ever upon the U.S.S.R. as that country undertook to retrain and re-equip the Egyptian armed forces. While the terms are not fully known, the billions of dollars worth of equipment that flowed into Egypt were not gifts. Counterbalancing the Soviet grip, but in a minor way, were the pro-Western, conservative, oil-rich states of Saudi Arabia, Kuwait, and Libya, which, in the summer of 1967, pledged annual subsidies to help Egypt and other "front-line" states over the foreign-exchange losses incurred by the defeat. Within Egypt, some of Nasser's economic advisers, such as Dr. Abdel-moneim al-Qaissuni, the then-Minister of Planning, argued that Egypt should once again move toward a stabilization plan. Again Nasser rejected it, reshuffled his cabinet in March 1968 and came out, not very realistically, for continued military build-up and economic growth. How he expected to pay for both, even with Soviet help, is a mystery, but any further deepening of his links with the U.S.S.R. would have alienated his conservative Arab providers of foreign exchange.

When Nasser died in September 1970 Egypt was saddled with a growing external debt and a massive foreign trade deficit. His successor, Anwar Sadat, whether he realized it or not when he first became president, has had to make the choices that Nasser so stubbornly and artfully resisted. Sadat has not followed any grand design or master plan in this respect, but has taken basic decisions in light of immediate circumstances and his own ideological proclivities. His general drift has been predictable but specific policy outcomes have not.

The directions that Sadat was expected to and did move in were these: taking his distances from the Soviet Union without, if possible, jeopardizing Egypt's military capabilities; normalizing relations with the United States and the conservative oil-rich states; attracting Western capital and investment; stimulating the Egyptian private sector; and moving as rapidly as possible toward a peace settlement with Israel. But in the pursuit of these objectives Sadat was not about to dismantle the welfare state system that had emerged in the 1960s and which, although reaching only a portion of the population, was some insurance against social unrest. Nor did he wish to destroy the public sector which was and is a relatively malleable instrument for controlling and orienting economic resources and investments. Finally Sadat would not put an end to hostilities with Israel until most Arab lands occupied in 1967 had been restituted and until the Palestinians had achieved some form of statehood. Through all this, economic growth had to be stimulated, and the major question was how to pay for it. Sweating the middle class for domestic resources was rejected for several reasons, foremost among them being that Sadat offered its members a release from the controls on income and consumption that Nasser had unevenly applied, and by that token constituted the new President's major source of support. Second, it

would be difficult to encourage private sector investment while at the same time heavily taxing it. So too foreign funding was not likely to come at once from the socialist countries and the oil-rich. A choice had to be made, and it was in the form of the open door policy in June 1974. But to attract foreign investment would depend, among other things, on achieving a settlement with Israel in order to improve the investment climate.

The Antecedents of the 1976 Stabilization Plan

In every respect, as far as Egyptians were concerned, the United States became the key element in reconciling these somewhat contradictory policy objectives and constraints. Only the United States with its great leverage over the Israeli economy and state of military preparedness could force the Israelis to a settlement acceptable to the Arabs. The Soviet Union, it was suspected, had no interest in helping settle a conflict that had provided it with its first entry into the Arab World and as a result of which it had gained great strategic advantages in Egypt and the eastern Mediterranean as a whole. The removal of the Russian military presence in Egypt was desirable both to give Egypt a freer military hand if hostilities became unavoidable and to remove one of the major causes of concern constantly evoked by Israel and the United States as to Egypt's real intentions. Although he was frequently reminded of the fact by Arab emissaries from some of the oil-rich states, Sadat could hardly have forgotten Henry Kissinger's blunt statement of June 26, 1970 (at San Clemente): "We are trying to get a [Middle East] settlement in such a way that the moderate regimes are strengthened and not the radical regimes. We are trying to expel the Soviet military presence...."

In May 1971, freshly in power, Sadat survived his first internal challenge and rid the regime of Ali Sabry and several others who had been branded in the Western press as Moscow's men. The purge coincided with the visit to Cairo of Secretary of State William Rogers at a time when diplomatic relations between the United States and Egypt were still broken. In the spring of 1971, however, Sadat could not afford such a one-sided gesture to the United States and shortly after the purge he and Nicolas Podgorny signed a Treaty of Friendship and Cooperation with the Soviet Union. It was suspected even at that time that the Treaty was no more than a charade designed to camouflage the troubled relations that would ensue.

One did not have to wait long. In July of 1971 Sadat flew Sudanese troops stationed in Egypt to Khartoum to help overthrow a three-day-old Marxist junta and to restore Major General Jaafar Numeiri to power. A year later, a few months prior to the Presidential elections in the United States, Sadat announced that the Soviet military training missions in Egypt were being repatriated. If after his overwhelming re-election Nixon had taken some initiative to break the Arab-Israeli stalemate, perhaps the war of October 1973 would have been avoided. But no initiative was forthcoming and, indeed, in February 1973 the administration authorized new sales of Phantoms to Israel. In short the stalemate was as solid as ever. Egypt was faced with crippling its economy through continued war preparedness, all the while risking what technological capabilities it had in the absence of Soviet advisers. The October 1973 War was a desperate gamble with limited objectives to break out of this situation. It was to provide a violent, negative inducement to the United States, underwritten by the oil embargo, to bring its weight to bear on the Israelis. It was also aimed at winkling out of the oil-rich in the name of Arab solidarity the funds necessary to help Egypt out of its economic distress.

Initially the October War achieved considerable progress in both directions. Kissinger entered into his now-famous shuttle diplomacy with a vengeance and secured the first disengagement of Egyptian and Israeli forces in Sinai. The Saudis and others came across with emergency aid and with talk of more to follow. The Soviet Union had stood fast throughout the crisis and replaced all equipment lost by the Egyptians during the war.

For a while Egypt's salvation appeared at hand— and the possibility of reconciling all Sadat's objectives within reach. The Israelis would be forced to withdraw and the Americans would keep up the pressure—if for no other reason than to avoid another embargo—until a final settlement was achieved. The fabulous new oil earnings of the Arab oil exporters could be used to bank-roll Egypt's development. The defense burden and the obsession with arms supplies would ease as progress toward a settlement was made, freeing further resources for

development. With the smell of peace in the air the tourists would return, the canal would be reopened to shipping, the oil fields in Sinai restituted, and foreign investment would pour in to take advantage of the Arab World's largest market. In June 1974, a fairly liberal foreign investment code was enacted. President Nixon came to Cairo and talked of the potential of over two billion dollars in United States investments. The World Bank prepared a sanguine report about Egypt's economic prospects, and bank officials freely talked of IBRD loans and credits of up to half a billion dollars a year. In this heady atmosphere it seemed that Egypt might be able to solve its foreign exchange problems, find investments for development, achieve a settlement with Israel, without crimping the style of a high-spending middle class nor that of a wasteful, inefficient, overstaffed public sector.

Biting the Bullet

Such as we know now was not to be the case. The Western international financial analysts were wont to say, the time had come for Egypt "to bite the bullet." Several factors became apparent during 1975 that made it abundantly clear that whatever the long- or medium-term prospects of the Egyptian economy, the short-term held no other promise than a crisis of unprecedented proportions. With rising world prices for practically everything, Egypt's import bill skyrocketed. A good proportion of the imports consisted in foodstuffs which the state still sold internally at the old, pre-energy crisis, subsidy levels. It soon became clear that overcoming idle capacities in public sector industries would be a long affair, and that whatever the outcome the socialist countries remained about the only feasible recipients of Egypt's manufactured exports. What incentives Egypt offered foreign investors were far from sufficient to touch off a rush. While private middle class consumption in Egypt rose dramatically, adding further to the import bill and contributing to an internal rate of dissavings, the private sector confined its efforts to real estate speculation and import-export windfalls. To cover the import bill, Egypt relied increasingly on short-term commercial credits ($1.6 billion in 1975) at interest rates between 16 and 19 per cent. All the while the Israelis were firmly ensconced in most of Sinai, all of the West Bank, and most of Golan. Kissinger's shuttle diplomacy had lost its momentum.

A new Western package began to come together in the spring of 1975 as Kissinger tried for a second disengagement. The basic deal was that in return for the Sinai passes, Egypt would assure Israel of its nonbelligerency contingent on further withdrawals, the Suez Canal would be reopened, and, in return, the United States would seek to bring together a Western consortium (including the pro-Western oil-rich states) to help Egypt out of its economic difficulties. Egypt could not bring itself in the spring of 1975 to make a pledge of nonbelligerency and both Kissinger's shuttle and the notion of a consortium evaporated. But Egypt's economic plight was pressing. President Sadat, after the collapse of the Kissinger effort, made a tour through Saudi Arabia and the Gulf states and was able to raise emergency funds to meet Egypt's massive short-term obligations. Yet it was known at the time that these funds were a stopgap in effect and would have no long-term structural impact. To cover continuing import needs especially in food-stuffs, Egypt would simply have to negotiate new short-term credits at high interest. It was said in the summer of 1975 that Egypt would be in serious payments difficulties again within six months. The estimate proved to be fully accurate.

Kissinger re-entered the negotiations on a second disengagement in August 1975 and by September an accord had been reached. Seemingly the major difference with what had transpired the preceding spring lay in the wording of Egypt's nonbelliger-ency pledge; the amount of aid the United States would extend Israel, the return to Egypt of the Abu Rudeis oil fields, and more technical military questions of force deployment, buffer zones, and the United States-manned early-warning system in the Sinai passes. However, the parallel theme of a Western consortium plus IMF-style stabilization plan had dropped out of the picture, presumably because Egypt thought it could obtain the long-term credits from Saudi Arabia (perhaps under the oft-adumbrated rubric of the "Arab Marshal Plan") that would allow Egypt to fund its next five-year plan without "biting the (IMF) bullet."

Egypt's acceptance of the second disengage-ment—with the tacit understanding that no further diplomatic efforts would be likely until 1977, that is after the American presidential elections *and* assuming that Gerald Ford would be re-elected

(an outcome the Egyptian regime ardently hopes for)—confirmed all the worst fears of other Arab leaders that Egypt had effectively removed it-self from the military front and was seeking a separate deal. The Syrians and Palestinians, who had gotten nothing from the September accord but vague promises that Kissinger would try to promote some movement on the Golan question, attacked Sadat bitterly. Other than the Sudan, no Arab state publicly endorsed the second disengagement. Even Egypt's financial benefactors such as Saudi Arabia, who would likely want an American-sponsored solution to the conflict, remained blandly noncommittal on the issue of the second disen-gagement, seeing no reason at this juncture to diminish Egypt's isolation in the Arab World. For, as has now become fairly evident, Saudi objectives toward Egypt consist in minimizing its role in Arab affairs (Saudis cannot forget their own isolation when Nasser thrust Egypt center stage in radical Arab nationalism), sustaining the moderate regime of President Sadat but not helping Egypt out of its fundamental economic difficulties, and encourag-ing a shift in Egypt's links of dependency from the U.S.S.R. to the United States and to Saudi Arabia itself. These objectives are certainly not incom-patible with United States policy aims.

By the end of 1975 the various forces and pres-sures that Egypt had withstood for so long could no longer be denied. IMF missions had regularly come and gone from Cairo without, however, Egypt accepting their stabilization recommendations. One small concession was made at the end of 1975. Egypt raised the price of a liter of high octane gasoline from 6.8 to 8 piastres (roughly from 13 to 16 cents) in order to qualify for the IMF's special facility to ease the payments crunch felt by devel-oping countries importing petroleum. To qualify for credits (and Egypt stood to gain $50 million in credits) necessitated internal measures to restrain consumption.

The Turning Point

The sequence of events that then followed is somewhat obscure, and, indeed, has not by any means worked itself out. Moreover, what has transpired has not been openly discussed mainly because it is so sensitive. What is known is that Egypt once again fell seriously behind on its short-term payments. On March 1, 1976, *The Financial*

Times reported Egypt was 32 to 45 days late in meeting payments on ca. LE700 million in revolving credits. A few days later the same source stated that formulae for a consortium, based on Arab and Western funds up to $11 billion, were once more being discussed. We also know that in January 1976 Prime Minister Mamduh Salem was to undertake a trip through Saudi Arabia and the Gulf Emirates to "discuss the contribution of the oil-exporting states to the financing of the Five Year Plan." Perhaps at the request of Saudi Arabia and others, President Sadat pre-empted his own Prime Minister and undertook the trip himself in late February. At the same time an IMF team (Managing Director Witteven himself arrived March 9) came to Cairo to draw up a report and to make its now-familiar recommendations. This time, however, on January 28, 1976 to be precise, Mamduh Salem reported to Parliament that the government was prepared to go along with some of the IMF proposals.

It may have been known even before Sadat undertook his tour that Egypt's Arab creditors would insist that Egypt acquiesce to the stabilization plan before extending any further credits. Egypt must have agreed in principle to this stipulation but its operational ramifications have yet to be fully worked out. The reciprocal of this acquiescence in principle were Saudi and Kuwaiti promises of $300 million apiece in emergency aid plus agreement to establish an Arab Fund to support the Egyptian Economy. The President's trip was followed up in late March by a meeting of relevant Ministers of Finance, in Riyadh, to work out the details of the Fund. *Akhbar al-Yom* correspondent Gamil George wrote on April 3, 1976 that the fund would be capitalized at $10 billion to finance new investments and to offer soft loans to help meet debt servicing. He added that the IMF and IBRD would participate in the management of the Fund. It was not mentioned that President Sadat also wanted David Rockefeller and other Western bankers to participate in the management of the Fund. Still, the consortium had been reborn and Egypt appeared on the brink of accepting a Western-inspired salvage operation similar to that of Indonesia in 1965.

If a Fund with $10 billion were put at the disposal of the Egyptian economy for five years, it might just be possible that bullet-biting could once again be avoided. It may have been precisely for

that reason that, at the Rabat meeting of the Arab Fund for Social and Economic Development at the end of April, the Finance Ministers of Saudi Arabia, Kuwait, the United Arab Emirates, and Qatar decided to capitalize the Arab Fund to Support the Egyptian Economy at only $2 billion over five years. To put this level of funding into some kind of perspective, one may note that in 1975 Egypt's trade deficit was LE1.386 billion (or ca. $2.1 billion at the old "incentive" exchange rate) and the balance of payments gap was LE2.451 billion (or about $4 billion at the same rate.)[1] Little wonder then that Egypt's Minister of Finance, Dr. Abou Ismail and others were astonished at such a low level of funding. Abou Ismail set Egypt's foreign exchange needs over the next five years at no less than $12 billion and stressed, like many Egyptians before him, that the wars of 1967 and 1973, waged for the Arab cause, had cost the economy, directly and indirectly, something like LE16 billion. But the Arab oil-rich were not to be tweaked in their consciences, and after the one protest at Rabat, Egypt has remained silent on the issue.

Egypt's disappointment in this respect may have been especially bitter in that after Sadat's trip but before the Rabat meetings. Egypt unilaterally renounced the 1971 Soviet-Egyptian Friendship Treaty. The event was of greater symbolic than substantive importance, but its ultimate ramifications are considerable. The ostensible cause of the unilateral move was that Moscow had failed to deliver Egypt new military equipment since October 1973 and that it had vetoed an Egyptian request to India to purchase MIG engines assembled in that country. The latter claim is evidently accurate but the former is questionable because in replacing equipment lost in the October War, the U.S.S.R. has supplied Egypt with more advanced material such as 1100 T-62 tanks and around 30 MIG-23 fighters that it did not possess before. Coming at the time that it did, the abrogation of the treaty must have had at least three objectives. The first was to help clear the way for favorable United States congressional action on the sale of military equipment (six C-130 transport planes initially) to Egypt. Second, as one official remarked to me, Egypt had given Ford and Kissinger, in the heat of the primary battles, a major diplomatic triumph

---

1. See *al-Ahram*, June 4, 1976.

after the fiasco of Angola. Third, in conformity with Saudi urgings, Egypt had further eroded its dependence upon the U.S.S.R.

Over the short and medium term some important questions need answering. One may expect that military cooperation with the U.S.S.R. will come to a halt and the level of preparedness of the Egyptian armed forces can only suffer. While waiting for the United States and other Western sources of arms to prepare public opinion for deliveries to Egypt, Cairo has had to turn to Peking for MIGs and spares. As in Angola the United States and China find themselves de facto allies against the U.S.S.R. Perhaps only in Cairo could David Rockefeller, King Khalid of Saudi Arabia, H.J. Witteven of IMF, Kim il-Sung of North Korea, and Mao tse-Tung all be hailed simultaneously and effusively as great friends of Egypt. But the fact remains that Egypt now lacks military credibility (just as it did prior to October 1973.) It must rely more than ever upon American leverage on Israel if there are to be any further diplomatic moves. Further, one must ask what will become of the U.S.S.R.-financed economic projects within Egypt. These include the Helwan Iron and Steel Complex, the Nag Hammadi Aluminum smelter, the power station at Aswan, and programs for rural electrification. Finally, the U.S.S.R. remains Egypt's largest trading partner (the 1976 trade protocol calls for exchanges worth $640 million) and the holder of a sizable chunk of Egypt's external debt. Can the West and the oil-rich offer alternatives to or compensation for these multifaceted links? The question has scarcely been aired, no less debated, in Cairo.

The Stabilization Program

While the Egyptian authorities have been somewhat coy about the issue, it was in the *al-Gumhuria* interview (April 25, 1976) given by Minister of Economy Dr. Zaki Shafa'i that it was unambiguously stated that Egypt and the IMF were in accord on a stabilization program. President Sadat, at the end of March, had already announced that, given Egypt's economic difficulties, the country would have to face a certain amount of "belt-tightening" and that an "austerity program" would be applied within the public sector. That this austerity

program was directly related to the IMF recommendations was not then known and may not be generally so perceived even today. In any event Zaki Shafa'i, in his interview, stated that the 1976 budget would be trimmed by LE300 million in such things as representational allowances, the government car pool, and other forms of slush. One may surmise, however, that the IMF, like the IBRD, would like to see austerity measures extended to redundant public sector personnel, that is a gradual layoff of superfluous public sector employees. This is a far more sensitive matter than representational allowances.

In this, as in all other aspects of the stabilization program, neither what Egypt will do nor what it has said it intends to do have been made clear. It is known, although the date is not, that P.M. Mamduh Salem has addressed the required "Letter of Intent" to H.J. Witteven at IMF. This presumably would indicate the longer range measures that Egypt would be willing to carry out, whatever and however superficial the immediate measures undertaken. Zaki Shafa'i indicated that there had been considerable give and take between Egypt and the IMF/IBRD on several issues. The notion of an outright devaluation of the Egyptian pound, for instance, was rejected although a two-rate system (of which more below) was accepted. Similarly, the Egyptian government was not prepared to go as far as IMF/IBRD counsellors would have liked in reducing subsidies of basic goods. Nonetheless, in the words of Zaki Shafa'i, "We have a full understanding with the IMF and IBRD. An IBRD team has participated in the elaboration of our five-year plan.... All that we need is three years of self-discipline. If we increase wages without increasing available goods (i.e., production) prices will continue to rise. What good is it to give a cost of living allowance of 20 per cent one day, only to have prices rise by 20 per cent the next? What we want is price stabilization."

Based on past experience the core of the IMF program revolves about the issue of the convertibility of the Egyptian pound. Here, at least in principle, Egypt has made a major concession by agreeing to a partial float of the pound. A decision was made in May to establish a "commercial market" for the pound, in which its value would be determined daily on the basis of supply and demand. Until the time of this writing Egypt has utilized three exchange rates. The first is the official rate (39 piastres to the dollar) by which essential goods—such as foodstuffs, petroleum, building materials, fertilizers, insecticides, etc.—are imported and by which about two-thirds of Egypt's foreign trade is conducted. The second is the "parallel" or "incentive" rate (68 piastres to the dollar) by which the private sector can purchase foreign exchange to finance its own imports. This occasionally adjusted rate is to be abolished. The major sources of foreign exchange that had sustained it came from purchases of Egyptian pounds by Egyptians resident abroad, receipts from tourism and from the proceeds of so-called nontraditional exports. The decision taken by Egypt was to replace the incentive rate by a commercial rate which would make it equivalent to the third "free" or "black market" rate that had been hovering between 72 and 76 piastres per dollar. To institute this rate would be a partial step toward convertibility, and it may be that Egypt has informed the IMF that it intends to move toward full convertibility as soon as possible. That step would be suicidal unless Egypt's visible (cotton, oil, manufactures) and invisible (Suez Canal, tourism) exports become considerably more desirable abroad than they are at present. Even the partial float now *under consideration* is somewhat ominous for it will require substantial amounts of foreign exchange to protect the pound even at a rate of 75 piastres to the dollar. One analyst has said that the council of Ministers agreed to transfer the foreign exchange equivalent of LE415 million to the commercial market[2] while the Minister of Finance cited a figure of LE320 million.[3] Egyptian experts estimate that the market will require $1.5 to $2 billion to cover its operations. It is at this juncture that the IMF would enter the scene with standby funds, but the amount mentioned so far is $125 million for the rest of 1976 supplemented by $50 million from a consortium of American banks. The unknown element here is not what the demand for Egyptian pounds will be, but what will be the Egyptian demand for foreign exchange. Dr. Waguih Shindi, Deputy Minister of Economy, estimates that in one year something like LE350 million have been sold by private Egyptians in

order to buy foreign exchange at black market rates (*al-Ahram*, June 4, 1976). What the required size of the foreign exchange cover will be to protect the value of the Egyptian pound in the future remains, to say the least, uncertain.

What then is the purpose of a partial float of the pound? I have spoken to no one from the IMF, but those experienced in its ways have said that initially its impact will be largely symbolic. First it would seem that in accepting this and other policy recommendations Egypt has accepted the logic of moving gradually toward Western economic orthodoxy. No one contests the standard Egyptian argument that a partial float or even a full devaluation would have only a marginal effect in promoting Egyptian exports whose volume and composition will be for some time pretty much fixed. By contrast both measures would lead to a sharp rise in the import bill and domestic prices. This, however, is the price that must be paid primarily in order to attract foreign investment which has consistently shied away from the notion of transferring capital in and out of Egypt at a totally unrealistic official rate of exchange. In other words Egypt must bite the bullet in an effort to attract foreign private investment.

The commercial money market will have a significant impact upon the Egyptian private sector. It has been announced that for most goods that had been imported by the private sector through the parallel market customs duties would now be calculated on the basis of the commercial exchange rate. If an Egyptian private sector manufacturer imported $10,000 worth of synthetic leather, for instance, at the official rate of exchange, this would be worth LE3,900; if the commercial rate were 72 piastres to the dollar, the value of the import would be LE7200 and the duties paid there on would nearly double. The Minister of Finance estimates that this measure would increase customs revenues by as much as LE260 million a year but would not have any great impact on domestic prices because it would not apply to "essential" goods. Many observers contest this and already there are moves to remove some goods from the list of "nonessential" items or to reduce the duty rates on others. However, for the private sector, both the new customs policy and the commercial exchange rate (neither of which, it bears repeating, are operative policies as of June 1976) are designed to stimulate export-oriented firms (so that they can

2. Adil Hussein, "Facing the New Rise in the Cost of Living and the Advice of the IMF," *al-Tali'a*, Vol. 12, No. 6, June 1976.

3. *Egyptian Gazette*, May 18, 1976.

finance their own, more expensive, imports) and to encourage the exploitation and utilization of local raw materials which in some instances may become cheaper relative to imported materials.

Convertibility of the pound in order to "rationalize" Egypt's external transactions, and to move toward market-determined pricing internally, is the essence of the stabilization plan and the main criterion for the IMF standby agreement. But other measures will or should follow although the time frame has yet to be set. Some measures based on higher interest rates, tighter credit, and more diligent tax collection will aim at reducing the money supply by LE600-700 million or ca. 13 per cent. Second, as mentioned, much tighter controls over recurrent government expenditures will be exercised and, it is claimed, the practice whereby the state is the employer of last resort for university graduates will be phased out. It has also been stated that the price subsidy system which costs the state LE500-600 million a year will be contracted by removing such items as fine flour, sesame seed oil, some qualities of rice, etc. from the subsidy list. Precisely which items has not yet been resolved but the goal initially is to reduce the subsidy bill by about 20 per cent.

If these various policies were to be applied faithfully, not to mention extended, the consequences could be far-reaching. The partial float of the pound may have a long-term rationalizing effect upon the balance of payments but the only short-term beneficiary will be (perhaps) foreign investors. By contrast the Egyptian masses can expect some further price increases in a number of items (shoes, ready-made clothes, household furnishings, new housing, some food and fuel items) while the private sector will be faced with higher prices for foreign exchange. Firms that do not generate their own foreign exchange may be hard put to finance their own imports and may be faced with going under or seeking joint ventures with foreign partners.

Whittling away at price subsidies and redundant personnel combined with a contraction of the money supply, government austerity, and tight credit may *eventually* curb inflation and promote savings on the part of those who earn enough to save. But for the bulk of the population all these measures add up to an attempt to hold the rate of growth in real income below the rate of growth of national production. Whatever the economic merits of this approach, inherent in it is severe social stress which the Egyptian polity may be ill-equipped to withstand without reverting to the more authoritarian ways of a previous era. There is not much play in the pattern of Egyptian mass consumption when per capita income is about $200 a year.

It is precisely because of the social implications of the stabilization program (let alone the international ones) that many are skeptical that Egypt will apply it faithfully rather than simply using it to buy time and some emergency foreign funding. It is for the same reason that Egyptian policy-makers themselves tend alternately to claim too little and too much for the program. On the one hand it is prophesied that it will, over time, correct the basic faults in the Egyptian economy (i.e., by 1980 the balance of payments deficit should be within fully manageable proportions without resort to transfusions of foreign funding) and help Egypt out of its present "crisis." The very vocabulary of this claim implies far-reaching if not draconian measures. Indeed the figures are big: the public budget can be slashed by a couple of hundred million pounds, subsidies reduced by another hundred million, the money supply contracted by half a billion, and customs receipts doubled *all within one year* with more to follow. Surely this new shoe is going to pinch somewhere, but when that is suggested Egyptian officials protest that the standard of living of the masses will not be altered, only some fat will be trimmed from the public budget, only nonessential items will be effected by the subsidy cuts and increased duties, etc. In other words the stabilization program will be felt only at the margins, and if that is the case then one wonders how it can be reconciled with the claims of structural reform and breaking out of the crisis. The answer is simple, it cannot, but the dialectic between marginal and structural "reform," with all its socioeconomic ramification, will be at the heart of Egyptian politics for the next few years.

During that time, and perhaps beyond, the United States will, without perhaps realizing it, be the ultimate guarantor of the political and economic success or failure of the Egyptian regime. It is of course not true that the IMF and IBRD are appendages of American foreign and trade policy, but the weight of the United States within either body is such that neither could for long be significantly out of step with American goals. In the instance of Egypt there seems to have been few disagreements among the protagonists, and those that surfaced were more of a procedural than substantive kind. The result has been a fairly constant flow of IBRD officials and advising teams, the same from USAID, personal visits by Witteven and Gunther of the IMF, as well as those of Secretary of the Treasury William Simon, and Chase Manhattan Bank President David Rockefeller. In any given week these various visitors and assorted teams seem to be stumbling over one another. Adding considerable weight to United States concerns has been congressional approval of a $750 million aid package supplemented by sales of wheat and other agricultural commodities on very soft terms. The issue of the C-130s and other armaments has yet to be resolved. Other Western nations—France, Germany, Austria, and Japan foremost among them—have extended Egypt substantial credits to finance projects ranging from widening the Suez Canal and building a subway in Cairo to a thermal power plant at Abu Kir and a model farm near Ismailia. The IMF is trying to rally these and other states to the notion of a consortium. [4]

But project loans and credits are disbursed no faster than the rate of progress of the project itself and of course add to Egypt's foreign obligations. In short, all the reforms and aid will have as one of their consequences the maintenance of a high level of foreign indebtedness, although scheduled more comfortably for Egypt and at somewhat lower interest rates, and the economy, especially the export sector, *must* perform much better if a series of future payments crises are to be avoided. Some other countries that have gone through similar crises and stabilization programs have remained on the treadmill of internal inflation, low exports, devaluations, massive foreign borrowing with no end in sight. If Egypt does not break this cycle quickly not only its economy but its regime would be jeopardized. Peace, investment, and growth could lead Egypt out of its plight, but movement toward a settlement and the maintenance of a steady flow of foreign funding is no longer in its hands. With most bridges burned between Moscow and Cairo, the keys to Egypt's economic, military, and diplomatic salvation lie in Washington, D.C.

---

4. See *al-Ahram*, June 11, 1976.

POSTSCRIPT: Egypt in 1977

Once again, as in October 1973, President Sadat has taken a spectacular initiative that neither I nor anyone else would have dared predict. His trip to Jerusalem in quest of a comprehensive peace settlement, some have argued, so fundamentally changed all the givens of the situation that nothing will ever be the same again. Arthur Schlesinger, Jr. (*Wall Street Journal*, December 12, 1977) cited the trip as yet another example of those "momentous events" (Pearl Harbor, Khruschev's 1956 de-Stalinization speech, the Bay of Pigs, etc.) that change the course of world events, and, because they were not part of some inevitable unfolding of the historical process, demonstrate the "futility of futurism." I for one could seek comfort in a respected tradition of historicism that belittles our powers to look ahead. But surely that will not and cannot do.

Thus, to bring this series of essays as up-to-date as possible, I must try to catch Sadat's train as it leaves the station without really knowing where it is going. Still, why it left at all, who is on board, how much fuel it is carrying, what the roadbed is like, and where it *intends* to go are all factors that can be described in some detail. To put the matter simply, Sadat's leap into the unknown of November 1977 is basically similar to his military offensive of October 1973 as well as to his abortive peace initiative of February 1971. Neither of his previous efforts bore the fruit he anticipated. On the other hand, the October War at least did not produce the kind of disaster outside observers logically expected. Sadat, obviously, is prepared to take risks in the Arab-Israeli arena that could easily cause his downfall, but surely that reflects a perception on his part that inaction, diplomatic and military stalemate, and economic stagnation would get him in the end anyway. In several important respects the Egypt of fall 1977, despite the intervening years of domestic fuss and furor, was not very dissimilar from the Egypt of fall 1972. Let us note the principal lines of continuity.

1. Egypt's economic performance had not improved appreciably. Agricultural production barely held its own, the cooperative system of marketing was failing, net land loss continued, and land reclamation, still a planner's dream, was held in abeyance. The public sector continued to limp along, short of foreign exchange and raw materials, overloaded with surplus personnel, and producing well below capacity. The external debt grew substantially during the period, and there was little improvement in the balance of trade as Egypt resorted to ever larger food imports.

2. The October War primarily won the reopening of the Suez Canal and the repopulation of the Canal Zone cities. It did not bring about the evacuation of the Sinai, a comprehensive peace settlement, or the reallocation of military outlays for civilian purposes. Moreover the atmosphere in the region after October 1973 was not sufficiently reassuring to put at ease the Western investors Egypt hoped to attract. By 1977 Egypt was back to a state of no peace, no war from which Sadat evidently saw no exit, at least not by way of Geneva.

3. Unquestionably Egypt had come to pin its hopes for a diplomatic breakthrough on the United States, but the Carter-Vance tandem showed itself no more able to take decisive action than had Nixon-Kissinger. To compound the problem, relations with the U.S.S.R. had deteriorated to such a degree that Egypt had an even less credible military option in 1977 than in 1972, while Israel, as recompense for accepting the second disengagement agreement in September 1975, was armed to the teeth.

4. Having cautiously stimulated a more liberal style of politics in the domestic arena, Sadat was forced, principally as a result of the cost-of-living riots of January 1977, to show how

superficial these changes really were. The only real change, and not a very big one at that, was that the whittling down of the ASU was not complemented by the emergence of credible parties as much as by a patent political vacuum. Sadat filled it, temporarily, by his trip to Jerusalem which focused domestic attention on a policy issue where he was and is the sole, legally recognized national actor.

Looking at some of these policy issues in closer detail, we can mark the most significant developments since mid-1976. In the realm of external financing an unsatisfactory standoff was achieved. The stabilization program Egypt had originally proposed to the IMF in early 1976 was pretty much shelved. There was no float of the Egyptian pound. The level of funding proposed by the Gulf Organization for the Development of Egypt (GODE) was, at $2 billion over three to five years, so inferior to Egypt's proclaimed needs that the country's planners pulled back from those elements of the stabilization program that presupposed massive balance of payments support. Moreover, in summer 1976, Egypt prepared for its first openly contested parliamentary elections in over a quarter century, and several ministers felt it unwise for the government to do anything so unpopular as to tamper with price subsidies. In the new government that was formed after the elections, Minister of Economy, Zaki as-Shafi'i, the staunchest backer of the stabilization program, was dropped (as was an opponent, Minister of Finance Abou Ismail, who was, however, elected to Parliament) and a new economic team, led by Abd al-Moneim al-Qaissuni, was brought in.

With the elections out of the way, the new team was able to move ahead on the question of price subsidies. Western and Arab benefactors had consistently been critical of existing practices and the distortions they introduced into the working of market forces. Perhaps Qaissuni et al. felt that if Egypt could demonstrate its will to attack this problem then it would argue more forcibly for (a) an extended facility credit from the IMF over three years, (b) a sympathetic hearing at the meeting of the Consultative Group of Arab and Western creditors organized by the IBRD which met in Paris in May 1977, and (c) higher levels of funding from the GODE. Thus, on January 18, 1977, Qaissuni went before Parliament to announce the government's resolution to end in whole or in part a number of subsidies, primary among them fine flour, some sugar, rice, and oil, bottled gas, cigarettes, and beer. Undoubtedly the government anticipated some grumbling among the masses, and Qaissuni stressed that the cuts would not affect "essential" goods, and that to make matters more equitable measures would be taken—sometime—to increase the tax bite of the well-off. The lower echelons of the civil service and the public sector work force, moreover, were to benefit from various kinds of bonuses, cost-of-living allowances, and pay increases.

These reassurances went for naught, and on January 19 heavy rioting broke out in Egyptian cities from Aswan to Alexandria. In some instances the rioting was spearheaded by workers, especially at Helwan and Alexandria. In Cairo the streets emptied and filled with bands of ragged adolescents, sometimes several thousand strong, intermixed with children and, more rarely, adult men and women. Onlookers outnumbered rioters, despite flying bricks and tear-gas irresistibly drawn to the pageant of their streets. It was hard to know what they really felt about the violence, but they almost surely did *not* feel, as the government subsequently argued, that *their* property was being destroyed. For the first time since the revolution of 1952, the regime was forced to bring the army into the streets to deal with a civil disturbance. That constitutes an ominous precedent. The police and the Ministry of Interior had clearly been caught napping. A strict curfew was slapped on the cities, and when, in Cairo, various bands attacked police stations after hours, blood was drawn. When it was over Cairo alone officially counted 77 dead. The government immediately rescinded all decrees affecting the price subsidies but resolutely stuck to its promise to pay out bonuses and higher wages. The riots had paid off.

Having thus implicitly acknowledged its own ineptness, the government then explicitly tried to pin the blame for the riots on agents provocateurs from the left. There may well be some truth in such allegations, although left and right both had their reasons to seek a confrontation. Whatever triggered the riots, the bitterness of many Egyptians after January 18 was palpable and astonishingly outspoken. It did not take much provocation to put them in a destructive mood. President Sadat's prestige was at its lowest ebb, and it is absurd, in light of this, to suppose, as some did, that the riots were an elaborate ploy by the regime to wheedle more money out of Saudi Arabia and Kuwait. There was something approaching panic in the Egyptian elite after January 19, best reflected in President Sadat's and Prime Minister Mamduh Salem's hasty and vociferous denunciations of the Egyptian left, Marxists, and their external allies. To the best of my knowledge, among the hundreds of leftists arrested not as direct participants in but as accomplices to the riots, not a single one was subsequently convicted in the Egyptian courts. The independence of the magistracy in this instance, unthinkable under Nasser, is more a sign of the political vacuum alluded to above than of the separation of powers.

In all other respects liberal politics were put on the back burner, although the general framework of multipartyism was maintained. It could hardly have been otherwise, for it was President Sadat himself who steered the *manibir* within the ASU to full-fledged partyhood prior to the November elections. The left, center, and right "platforms" became the Progressive Assembly, the Egypt Party, and the Liberal Socialists within the new Parliament. Unsurprisingly, the Egypt Party, presided over by Prime Minister Mamduh Salem, occupied the majority of seats in the legislature. The Liberal Socialists, led by Mustapha Kemal Murad, became the "opposition," while the Progressives formed a small leftist minority. They were unable to effect an alliance within or without Parliament with the Nasserists who remained wary of Marxists. The real surprise of the elections was the emergency of a varicolored group of "Independents," not formally constituted as a party, but which took the second largest number of seats after the Egypt Party. Among their luminaries were Ahmad Taha from the Marxist left, Mahmud al-Qadi, the Wayne Morse of the Egyptian Parliament, Hilmi Murad, former Minister of Education and ex-member of the Socialist Party of Ahmad Hussein, and Kemal al-Din Hussein, an original member of the Revolutionary Command Council (RCC) and close to the Moslem Brethren.

Hardly had these new entities received some legitimation through the elections than the January riots threatened the entire experiment. The left, including the Progressives, was directly implicated in the disturbances, while the center, the opposition, and most of the independents rallied round the regime, perhaps out of bourgeois fear of the street. After the riots, on February 4, Sadat gave a speech in which he directly accused the left of having fomented the riots and announced that, in conformity with the Constitution, he was proclaiming a state of emergency and calling for a referendum on measures to deal with it. Among these measures were strict prohibition of meetings, gatherings, or other actions aimed at or leading to destructive acts and the troubling of public order. Workers who struck for these purposes could be condemned to hard labor for life. At the same time Egyptians earning taxable incomes would have to present a declaration of all the sources of their wealth and promptly acquit themselves of their obligations to the state. A year later no concrete action had been taken on this measure. The referendum on Safe-Guarding National Unity led predictably to the overwhelming approval of all the measures Sadat proposed. Just prior to it, Kemal al-Din Hussein sent an accusatory telegram to Sadat in which he argued that the situation did not require the proclamation of a state of emergency, that the resort to referendum was demagogic, and that the whole maneuver was aimed at shifting the blame from Sadat's own incompetent ministers. Hussein was censured by Parliament, stripped of membership, and denied the right to run again from his constituency in Benha. From then on all sectors of the Parliament hedged their criticism of government policy.

During spring and summer 1977 the press was brought under tighter control without sacrificing the slogan of freedom of the press. Editorial teams loyal to the President were moved into place: Musa Sabry at *al-Akhbar*, Anis Mansur at the newly created *October*, Yussef al-Siba'i at *al-Ahram*, and Mursi al-Shafa'i at *Ruz al-Yussef*, the last mass circulation publication of a vaguely leftist character. The openly leftist *al-Tali'a* lost its editor, Lutfi al-Kholi, and was taken over and transformed by *al-Ahram*'s science editor, Salah al-Galal. Censorship was henceforth to be carried out at the editor's desk rather than in the censor's office.

Although he would have preferred to avoid it, Sadat had made a point in the Arab World and the West: there were clear limits to the amount of belt-tightening in the name of economic reform that could be imposed upon the Egyptian masses *within the vaunted liberal political and economic system.* That point made, some emergency aid did come Egypt's way. President Carter saw to the immediate disbursement of $500 million following the riots while the GODE began to move its funds to pay off Egypt's short-term debt obligations. By fall 1977 some $1.4 billion had been committed toward this end with another half billion promised mainly for project rather than balance of payments support. Morgan Stanley International of New York was retained by the GODE and Egypt to manage repayment of the short-term debt, owed almost exclusively to Western banks. It did not escape the notice of many Egyptians that there was a disquieting similarity between the GODE's grip upon Egypt's foreign exchange position and the Caisse de la Dette Publique set up a century earlier by Egypt's European creditors to manage the country's finances. Today's arrangement constitutes one of the rare triangular projects so ardently sought by the open-door policy whereby Arab capital and Western banking know-how are brought together to work on one of Egypt's great natural resources, its external debt.

Egypt's public domestic debt has been no less troublesome. Efforts to reduce it aborted when the price subsidies were restored after January 1977. Simultaneously there was an upsurge in nominally unauthorized public sector borrowing from Egyptian banks unaccompanied by any of the austerity measures in public expenditures that Zaki as-Shafi'i had urged in 1976. Thus instead of reducing the deficit in government operations to LE 150 million in 1977 (the Qaissuni team's announced goal), it soared to over LE 1 billion, a good part of it covered by printing money. One wonders how this laxity squares with Egypt's Letter of Intent to the IMF and the conditions attached to the $150 million standby loan advanced to Egypt after the January riots. All that remains of the reform program adumbrated in spring 1976 (see again Egypt 1976) is the application of the "incentive" exchange rate for the pound (70 piastres to the dollar as opposed to the official rate of 39) to the valuation of a large portion of Egypt's imports.*

The results of this measure are not yet clear. It has, as intended, raised the costs of imports but has also contributed to increased production costs for several private sector activities (for example, shoes and furniture) and to a general rise in the cost of living. At the same time, the "own-exchange" system has allowed private importers with foreign exchange at their disposal to bring in LE 300 million in imports, most of them consumer items, in 1977. Local manufacturers, because of their rising costs, find it difficult to compete with these imports. Compounding their woes is the fact that President Sadat in summer 1977 announced that Egypt was suspending servicing on its debt to the "Eastern Bloc" and hence the annual trade agreements by which debt payments were made. Because most Egyptian private sector exports went to the Eastern Bloc, Sadat's move constituted another severe blow to private sector enterprise.

---

*By Law 32 of 1977, amending Law 43 of 1974, foreign investors are now authorized to bring in and repatriate their capital and earnings at the incentive rate rather than the official rate.

Against this somewhat somber background there were brighter areas that sustained hopes for the future of the economy. Oil exports, earnings from the Suez Canal, and remittances of Egyptians residing abroad have grown substantially, thereby easing the foreign exchange crisis to some degree. Nearly half a billion dollars in food aid from the United States has also eased the strain. But these achievements have been won without any far-reaching structural changes in the Egyptian economy. One may legitimately ask if the future can really be built upon them. Nonetheless, for the nth time, a five-year plan (1978-1982) is before Parliament with investment and growth goals so ambitious as to defy credibility. The foreign financed component of the huge investment program is estimated at a minimum of $8 billion over the 5-year period. It is a "soft" plan in the sense that it does not constitute an integrated strategy., nor does it clearly set priorities that would entail sectoral sacrifices or restraint upon profligacy. Each sector is scheduled to receive all the investments it could conceivably absorb.

Whatever the realism of this plan—or any other—little progress was likely to be made with the possibility of war with Israel still at hand and one billion pounds each year poured into defense expenditures. Shades of 1973. Once again a new administration in Washington, this time Carter's, seemed no more able to move all the parties to the Arab-Israeli conflict to negotiations at Geneva than had its predecessor. Yet by this time Egypt was overwhelmingly dependent on U.S. diplomatic support and economic aid. The virtual cessation of deliveries of Soviet arms after 1974 led many observers to believe that the technico-military gap between Israel and Egypt had widened enormously. A military venture like that of the October War was out of the question, yet the U.S. reluctance to bring pressure on Israel, the fact that the U.S.S.R. is co-sponsor of the Geneva Conference, and the Palestinians' inability to develop any consensus as to their political goals rendered it unlikely, at least in Sadat's eyes, that much would come of Geneva. (His Foreign Minister, Ismail Fahmy, who resigned when Sadat decided to go to Jerusalem, had a very different view of the prospects for a settlement at Geneva.)

Sadat had to generate some movement, somewhere, and to recapture the popularity he had lost after the January riots. Already various voices from the past—Muslim Brethren, Wafdists, Misr al-Fatatists, Nasserists—sought an audience in the more liberalized political system. The neo-Wafdists, led by Fu'ad Serrag al-Din, were determined to re-establish their party legally. To do so would require a program distinct from that of any of the existing parties, with the ASU secretariat judging the matter, and the adherence of 20 Members of Parliament. The Wafd had dominated Egyptian politics from 1919 to 1952 and retained a kind of mass legitimacy that the Nasserist regime had only partially eroded. Its re-entry into Egyptian politics symbolizes *civilian* government, liberal politics, and a heavier emphasis on the merits of private enterprise. Indeed the New Wafd, as it is now called, may well appeal to disgruntled elements in the private sector by advocating protective measures against foreign investment and higher tariff walls. The point is, however, that none of the officially recognized parties could fill the political vacuum after January 1977 for they had no mass following, no institutional bases, and no public image—this was particularly true for the Egypt Party. Unable to fill the vacuum himself, Sadat could not risk other forces moving into it. Yet he could not prevent them from doing so without openly violating the liberal rules of the game he himself extolled. Despite his denunciations of the New Wafd as a relic from the past, it gathered the 20 requisite signatures, drew up its program, and requested authorization in January 1978.

The President had to recapture the limelight. The brief frontier war with Libya in July 1977 may have been partially motivated by this consideration. There had been numerous incidents along the frontier for several months, but Egypt, allegedly provoked, penetrated by land and air well into eastern Libya during a 48-hour period and then withdrew. Sadat may have wanted to remind Kaddafi of his vulnerability; he may also have sought the kudos of flexing Egypt's muscles. Whatever the actual domestic gains, they were shortlived. Something far more spectacular *and lasting* was needed. As in 1973, Sadat did not beat around the bush. He went straight to the heart of the problem, or at least to the heart of *his* problem. Instead of a military crossing, he undertook a psychological crossing to destroy the barriers of fear and mistrust among the Israelis, who, he felt, constituted 75 percent of the problem. Thus his trip to Jerusalem. One is tempted to say that he had, like a river boat gambler, played his last card, and stood to gain not a little or lose everything. So far he has gained nothing tangible, but we should know by now that Sadat always has another card up his sleeve.

Undeniably Sadat broke ranks with his fellow Arabs, earning thereby the explicit enmity of Syria, Algeria, Libya, Iraq, and the Palestine Liberation Organization (PLO), and the implicit reprobation of Saudi Arabia, Kuwait, and Jordan. Only the Sudan and Morocco openly supported him. Most important, however, was the fact that the Egyptian people supported him enthusiastically. Not only did he hold out for them the prospect of peace, but he embodied a noble and generous image that most Egyptians like to think is a national trait. The vociferous attacks of the other Arabs served only to kindle the country's Egypt-firstism that has been building over the years. Egyptians were fed up with the wealthy sheikhs who use Cairo as their pleasure palace (mobs in the January riots systematically burned down the nightclubs along the Pyramids Road that were the favorite haunts of wealthy Arabs) as well as with Palestinian revolutionaries who called, from the cafes of Beirut, for yet further sacrifices on the part of the Egyptians for their cause. Still, Mohammed Sid Ahmed (*Le Monde Diplomatique*, V. 25, 286, January 1978) is probably right in his contention that, in promising peace and prosperity, Sadat simply channeled the despair, bitterness, and anger of January 1977 to his own account.But how long can it last if neither peace nor prosperity are for tomorrow?

It would, at this point, be very difficult for Sadat to take his distances from the United States and Saudi Arabia or mend his fences with Moscow. Difficult but not impossible. A contrite Sadat could probably rally Libyan support, and the U.S.S.R. has not hesitated in the past to supply arms to leaders of dubious reliability. If Sadat is unable to contemplate or make this kind of agonizing readjustment, he may well have to accept the separate deal with Israel which appears to be Begin's primary objective. Peace of that kind might not outlive Sadat or his regime, nor would it have much impact upon the improvement of the economic situation. Who among us, however, could offer a feasible counterstrategy or way out? Who could delineate realistic options for the future, or volunteer to relieve President Sadat of his burdens from the past.